Making Movies Black

MAKING MOVIES BLACK

The Hollywood Message Movie from World War II to the Civil Rights Era

THOMAS CRIPPS

New York Oxford
OXFORD UNIVERSITY PRESS
1993

Oxford University Press

Oxford New York Toronto
Delhi Bombay Calcutta Madras Karachi
Kuala Lumpur Singapore Hong Kong Tokyo
Nairobi Dar es Salaam Cape Town
Melbourne Auckland Madrid

and associated companies in
Berlin Ibadan

Published by Oxford University Press, Inc.
200 Madison Avenue, New York, New York 10016

Oxford is a registered trademark of Oxford University Press

Library of Congress Cataloging-in-Publication Data
Cripps, Thomas.
Making movies black : the Hollywood message movie from World War II
to the civil rights era /
Thomas Cripps.
p. cm. Includes bibliographical references and index.
ISBN 0–19–503773–1 (cloth). ISBN 0–19–507669–9 (pbk.)
1. Afro-Americans in the motion picture industry.
I. Title.
PN1995.9.N4C687 1993 791.43'08996073—dc20 93–9491

2 4 6 8 9 7 5 3 1

Printed in the United States of America
on acid-free paper

To absent friends

Walter Fisher
Margaret Holland
Elliott Rudwick
and
William F. Walker

Preface

When you make movies you don't change history;
you participate in it.
—Abraham Polonsky, in conversation

Observers of American life have often asserted that popular culture reflects its values. This book is an attempt to examine this idea as it operated during the era of World War II, when many deeply rooted racial customs were shaken and reformed in ways that were anticipated in popular movies. The reader should know that this work appears at the end of an era when movie history written mainly for fans gave way to a rage for history rigorously grounded in theories borrowed from disciplines that included psychoanalysis, feminism, linguistics, anthropology, and Marxist economics. This academic vein of history was also rooted in heretofore inaccessible studio records and therefore less dependent on the flawed memories of octogenarian eyewitnesses.

Elsewhere I have tried to set forth at length a tentative means of applying some of these theories to an African American historical model.[1] Here, rather than risk offering this book as a sort of test of how black history fits this or that theory, I wish to say only that I hope it is a history informed and even disciplined by theoretical borrowings and fresh sources. But in the end I wish also, old-fashioned as it seems, to get the story straight. "The supreme duty of the historian is to write history," said Steven Runciman, the student of Byzantium, and not to "reduce history to a series of economic or sociological laws."[2]

And yet, racial history and movie history are social. Movies have both makers and audiences who effectively bargain within a massive sociology of culture—fan magazines, word-of-mouth appraisals, reviews, and such that constitute an art world—much as Giotto or Rothko painted within an art world of bishops or patrons. In this setting movies are like tribal art: "not mere entertainment" but, as Peggy Harper has written, "a significant part of the cohesion of [the tribe]."[3]

This is not to argue in tandem with the Marxist critics of the Frankfurt school such as T. W. Adorno, who wrote that the notions in popular culture "are always those of the status quo." Rather I wish to argue a plural, even liberal, politics in which there has been a play that allowed for the "countervailing powers" that Galbraith reported in his *American Capitalism*.[4] Popular culture in this sense has been worn as a loose garment rather than as the traces guiding a mule team. The resulting play in the wheels of Hollywood commerce has allowed bargaining between bosses and workers, ideologues and audiences, left and right, maker and audience, which in turn draws attention to theories such as, say, those of Antonio Gramsci, the Italian Marxist for whom bargaining between class-antagonists remained as much a possibility as the more doctrinaire prediction of class conflict.

Moreover, movies should be seen as a pliant medium emerging from a corporate setting that was itself rent by fissures through which, particularly in times of war and crisis, minorities—"Others," as James Snead called them—have been able to exploit cultural politics at those points where momentarily shared goals invite cooperation rather than conflict. For example, African Americans, if well led by, as Gramsci says, "organic intellectuals," should have enhanced their status during a war in which Unity, Tolerance, and Brotherhood become propaganda catchwords. Let it be granted that movies unreel in a dreamlike state in a darkened room that may enhance receptivity, that the closure of Hollywood movies on happy endings confirms things as they are, and that therefore they contribute to a cultural superstructure that has favored dominant mentalities. But it must also be seen that Hollywood has known well which side its political bread is buttered on and has aimed at a "pluricentered" taste-culture. Even then, its ability to "engineer" a mentality has remained so feckless as to only "half create the environment [it is] half created by" (as Jeffrey Morton Paine put it). Black forces in this looser context may affect movies at their source so effectively as to promote a liberal "theatre of consent," according to the Jamaican Marxist Stuart Hall.[5] Indeed, we already know this from the era when critics wrote slyly of directors as "auteurs" whose talents included little tricks of signature by means of which they inserted personal touches in their movies, often under the noses of hostile studio bosses.[6] In much the same way, African Americans have resisted remaining mere Others or even, as Snead has written, "the structured absence" from American movies.[7] Decades ago James K. Feibleman in his *Theory of Culture* identified the social conditions that rendered such changes likely. Wars, he wrote, "despite all the evil they entail, have the good effect of drawing people together," and particularly World War II had this sanguine effect because "the rise of the Nazis in modern Germany ha[d] placed renewed emphasis upon the racial problem."[8]

World War II thus became the occasion for a freshened liberal culture that restored racial issues to a national prominence they had not held since Reconstruction days. And a liberal-Hollywood-black alliance that arose from these wartime circumstances not only defined a new black presence in the nation's propaganda (if not always its behavior) but extended its ideology into postwar America in ways that anticipated the modern civil rights movement. This is not to argue a programmatic liberalism but rather a "conscience-liberalism," deeply felt and fought for but not coherently organized into a movement.[9] And yet it fed on its own expectations and soared, said one activist, as upon "a rising wind." Obviously, much of this liberal energy was no more than, as Richard Dalfiume labeled it, "necessitarian." Yet it not only survived the war but also became a normative element in postwar politics, because of the way the war reintroduced blacks into national corridors of power.[10]

Baltimore, Maryland T. C.
January 1993

Acknowledgments

Every reader knows that books are the products of collaborations, and this one is no exception. I have been particularly blessed with friends in the libraries that have been home bases for me for the last quarter of a century and then some: Barbara Humphrys, Paul Spehr, Pat Sheehan, David Parker, and their younger colleagues, among them Pat Loughney and Cooper Graham, in the Division of Motion Pictures, Broadcasting, and Recorded Sound of the Library of Congress; Helen Cyr and Marc Sober of the Audiovisual Department of the Enoch Pratt Free Library, Faye Houston of its Humanities Department, and the anonymous voices of the library's telephone reference service; and the staff of the Morris A. Soper Library of Morgan State University, particularly its directors the late Walter Fisher and Karen Robertson and their secretary, Alice Woodson. I am also grateful for assistance from other public archives, particularly from William T. Murphy in the Audiovisual Section of the National Archives; the staff of the National Archives branch in Suitland, Maryland; Richard Richardson in the Hall of Records, Annapolis, Maryland; and the Harry S. Truman and Franklin D. Roosevelt Presidential Libraries.

In recent years university libraries have increasingly become repositories of manuscripts, corporate records, and journalistic ephemera related to motion picture history, and I am much indebted to the results of the trend. The indispensable institutions over many years have been the Theatre and Special Collections of the UCLA Research Library and their staffs, particularly Audree Malkin, Brooke Whiting, Brigitte Kueppers, and Hilda Bohem; the Special Collections of the Doheny Library of the University of Southern California and the staff, Robert Knutson, Anne Schlosser (formerly of the Louis B. Mayer Library of the American Film Institute in Los Angeles), and currently, Leith Adams, and Ned Comstock; the UCLA Film Archive and its staff, particularly its manager, Steven Ricci; the Twentieth Century Collection and its curator, Howard Gotlieb, of the Mugar Library of Boston University; the staff of the American Heritage Center at the University of Wyoming in Laramie, particularly Emmet Chisum; the Humanities Research Center of the University of Texas at Austin, particularly Ray Daum; the Special Collections of the University of Tennessee Library in Knoxville; and Richard Harwell, then curator of the Margaret Mitchell Papers and Thomas E. Camden, Head of the Hargrett Rare Book and Manuscript Library, in the University of Georgia.

In addition to these institutions I am grateful to other archives with identities separate from universities. Over many years Ernest Kaiser of the Schomburg Center for Research in Black Culture located in Harlem has been unceasingly helpful, as was Anne Schlosser when she was librarian at the Louis B. Mayer Library of the American Film Institute in Hollywood. At the Museum of Modern Art in Manhattan, Charles Silver and Ron Magliozzi have been unfailingly helpful and patient with my demanding presence. The late George Pratt, and now Jan-Christopher Horak at the George Eastman House Museum of Photography have been generous with time and information. At the Pacific Film Archive in Berkeley Nancy Goldman and her staff have treated my demands on their ephemera collection with uncommon kindness. The Wisconsin Center for Film and Theatre Research is a major repository of the records of corporate Hollywood as well as of episodes in its history such as the era of the blacklist; Don Crofton, Maxine Fleckner, Susan Dalton, and others on the staff have been open, accessible, and even inviting in the style with which they have administered the collection. The Academy of Motion Picture Arts and Sciences' Margaret Herrick Library is a creature of Hollywood and might be expected to allow preserving images to govern the accessibility to its holdings but the staff—Sam Gill, Kristine Krueger, Howard Prouty, Tony Slide, and others—have treated scholars with commendable openness. Over many years the British Film Institute and the National Film Library, particularly in the persons of Harold Brown, Roger Holman, Michelle Snapes, and most recently Brigid Kinally, have shown many kindnesses that can never be repaid. Also among the BFI staff I should like to single out Frank Holland who for a quarter of a century has stopped at nothing to see that I saw films, stills, documents, anything that served my purposes. We—my entire family at times—lived in his house, borrowed his car, followed his maps to Dean Street and Berkhamsted, dined on his cooking, listened to his legends, and used his telephone to interview the retired movie people of Buckinghamshire.

Hollywood studios have not always opened their lots to researchers. But exceptions to this general rule have been John Dales and John Pavlik, in the guilds and associations and in the studios themselves the late Jon Hall of RKO, Herbert Nusbaum of the Legal Department of Metro-Goldwyn-Mayer, and David Smith and Selby Hall of the Disney Studio. The access to archives and the insights into the industry they gave me could have been had in no other way. And for his own brand of insights as well as telephone numbers from his trove I owe David Robb then of the tradepaper *Variety* a similar debt. Black Hollywood would have remained a closed book to me were it not for a quarter-century of advice, gossip, and tips, not to mention the lending of materials, that Carlton Moss has provided. I owe a similar debt to Bill and Peggy Walker, who for as long a time have allowed me to snoop among their friends and memorabilia. And for the politics of race within the studio craft guilds as well as the local chapters of the NAACP I am indebted to Herbert Hill, former Labor Secretary of the NAACP. For life on the left I owe much to Abe Polonsky and David Platt.

For either access to films and ephemera in their collections or for the loan of priceless materials I am indebted to John H. Baker, Ernie Smith, Nate Zelikow, Ted Toddy, Miles Kreuger, John B. Wiseman, K. R. M. Short, Lee Tsiantis, Douglas Lemza, J. Fred MacDonald, Cecile Starr, Richard Grupenhoff, Dave Dixon, Irwin Markisch, Sam Gertner, David Culbert, David Platt, and Mrs. Philleo Nash.

Colleagues, students, scholars, and Hollywood informants over a period of many years have become friends who taught me things in our conversations that they cannot know they have done. We just talked: above all Walter Fisher, and then Carlton Moss, J. R. Lyston, Jannette Dates, Erik Barnouw, my old students Everett Marshburn and Micheal Pounds. In various scholarly enterprises—sharing papers, debates during annual conferences, opportunities to address bodies of colleagues and students, and on one occasion an adventure in coauthorship—I am indebted to David Culbert, Gregory D. Black and Clayton Koppes, Stephen Vaughan, George Roeder, Arthur Knight and his then colleagues in the University of Chicago Mass Culture Seminar, and Associate Director Randall K. Burkett of the W. E. B. DuBois Institute in Harvard University.

During the lengthy course of this book toward its completion I was supported with enough generosity to allow an occasional year and many summers of freedom to study and write. These benefactions include two American Council of Learned Societies fellowships, a Rockefeller Foundation fellowship, a John Simon Guggenheim Memorial Foundation fellowship, resident fellowships at the Woodrow Wilson International Center for Scholars in Washington and the National Humanities Center in Research Triangle Park, North Carolina, a summer's residency at the Rockefeller Study Center in the Villa Serbelloni, Bellagio, Italy, several Morgan State University Faculty Research Grants, and travel grants from the National Endowment for the Humanities, the American Philosophical Society, and the ACLS. Without such support a great deal from basic research to final writing could not have been accomplished.

Once research has been completed, much of the credibility, reliability, authenticity, voice, and flavor of a book are derived from quoting directly from archival sources. This is particularly so in writing the social history of twentieth century popular culture. For permission to quote brief passages from such materials I am indebted and deeply grateful to: Dr. Howard Gotlieb of the Mugar Library of Boston University (the papers of Robert Ardrey, Robert Hardy Andrews, Nunnally Johnson, and Evan Hunter); John L. Balderston, Jr. (for letters of his father, John L. Balderston, in the Library of Congress); Erik Barnouw (for his own writings in the NUL records, Library of Congress); the following for papers in the NAACP records, Library of Congress: Julia Baxter Bates and Gloster B. Current (their own letters); Susan Gethner and Doris Steedman (letters of their father, Mendel Silberberg); Honor Spingarn Tranum (letters of her father, Joel Spingarn, and her sister, Hope Spingarn); Molly Moon Elliott (letters of her father, Henry Lee Moon); Jane White Viazzi (letters of her father, Walter White); Mrs. Roy Wilkins (letters of her husband, Roy Wilkins).

For permission to quote brief passages from the following material I am equally grateful: Julia Bond (for the papers of her husband, Horace Mann Bond, in the library of the University of Massachusetts at Amherst); Virginia De Rochemont and Shaler McReel (for letters in the papers of their father and grandfather, respectively, Louis De Rochemont, in the American Heritage Center, University of Wyoming); Mary Helen and Peter Douglas (letters in the papers of their father, Melvyn Douglas, in the Wisconsin Center for Film and Theatre Research); Philip Dunne (for his own papers in the Special Collections of Doheny Library of the University of Southern California); Truman Gibson (for his letters in the National Archives and the Motion Picture Association of America records in the Academy of Motion Picture Arts and Sciences); Craig Tenney of Harold Ober Associates, agents for Langston Hughes (for an unfinished scenario in Hughes's papers, Beineke Library, Yale, and a letter in the NAACP records); Julian (Bud) Lesser (for memoranda and script revisions in Hughes papers, Yale); Richard Grupenhoff (for letters in his possession that were cited in his own *The Black Valentino: The Stage and Screen Career of Lorenzo Tucker* [Scarecrow Press, 1988]; Thomas E. Camden (for letters in Margaret Mitchell Marsh papers, Hargrett Rare Book and Manuscript Library, University of Georgia); Carlton Moss (for his own letter in the records of the National Negro Congress); Etta Moten (for a letter of her husband, Claude A. Barnett, in Barnett papers, Chicago Historical Society); Mrs. E. L. Wertman (for letters in the papers of General Lyman Munson, American Heritage Center, University of Wyoming); Abraham Polonsky (for his diaries of 1958 in Wisconsin Center for Film and Theatre Research); Mrs. Nancy Prinzmetal (for one letter in the papers of Dore Schary in Wisconsin Center for Film and Theatre Research); Reginald L. McGhee, UAW Public Relations (for a script fragment in UAW records, Walter P. Reuther Library, Wayne State University); Jill Robinson Shaw (for letters of her father, Dore Schary, in the papers of Clarence Brown in the University of Tennessee Library and in the Wisconsin Center for Film and Theatre Research); Joan Scott (for a letter in the papers of her husband, Adrian Scott, in the American Heritage Center, University of Wyoming); Lewis Jeffrey Selznick (for letters in the records of his father, David O. Selznick, in the Humanities Research Center, University of Texas, Austin); Dimitri T. Skouras (for a letter of his father, Spyros Skouras, in the papers of General Lyman Munson); Ann Tanneyhill (for two letters in the NUL records, Library of Congress); John Hall Trotti (for a letter and diary entry of his father, Lamar Trotti, in MPAA records and in his own possession, respectively); Cleo Trumbo (for a letter in the papers of her husband, Dalton Trumbo, in the Wisconsin Center for Film and Theatre Research); Judith Singer of Warner Bros. (for a fan letter in the Warner Bros. Archive, Doheny Library, USC); Brad J. Waring (for a letter of Judge J. Waties Waring in the Clarence Brown papers, the University of Tennessee); Andy Simons of the Amistad Research Center, Tulane University (for a letter in the papers of Fredi Washington); Robert Wise (for a letter in the Wise papers, in the Wisconsin Center for Film and Theatre Research); Jack Valenti, President, MPAA (for letters in the records of the Production Code Administration of the MPAA, in the Margaret Herrick Library of the Academy of Motion Picture Arts and Sciences); Elizabeth Zutt (for her letter to Warner Bros. in the Warner Archive, Doheny Library, USC); and George E. Stephens, Jr., per the Bank of America, executor of the estate of Darryl F. Zanuck (for letters in the papers of Walter White, Philip Dunne, and General Lyman Munson) and Borden Mace (for letters in the DeRochemont Papers).

The sort of grinding work of which this book is a result has often led to adventures in various parts of the world, which I hope have been partial compensation to my wife, Alma Taliaferro Cripps, for her patience and forebearance during the elephantine gestation period of the book.

Contents

Making Movies Black

1

Antebellum Hollywood

One day in 1940 in a small town in Michigan a black teenager with a vaguely studious manner, which may have set him off from other kids, settled in his seat to watch *Gone with the Wind.* Later he remembered the movie as "one thing that marred this time for me." The boy's name was Malcolm Little, a name he would shed in favor of his *nom de politique,* Malcolm X. "I was the only Negro in the theatre," he recalled, "and when Butterfly McQueen went into her act, I felt like crawling under the rug."[1]

Fully three years before this dark scene, David O. Selznick had sat at his desk in Culver City, California, and dictated a memorandum to Sidney Howard, the Pulitzer Prize–winning dramatist whom he had hired to write a movie from *Gone with the Wind.* He had bought the thick novel from its author, a frail, gentle, fey Atlantan named Margaret Mitchell, who had pecked away at its yellow pages for years, stuffing it under the sofa whenever she entertained guests. Selznick wished to transform her cry of Southern despair and hope into a sort of American *Iliad* of Civil War and Reconstruction that neither slighted Northern victory nor taunted Southern defeat.

Among his first requests to Howard was to gut any references either to the Ku Klux Klan or to overly assertive freedmen. Why cut the core of conflict from Mitchell's book? "I, for one, have no desire to produce an anti-Negro film," Selznick told his writer. "In our picture I think we have to be awfully careful that the Negroes come out on the right side of the ledger." Why break with Hollywood racial convention? The answer, Selznick wrote, was that *Gone with the Wind* must not become "an advertisement for intolerant societies in these fascist ridden times."[2]

The gap between what Selznick produced and what Malcolm X received was, of course, a sign of the gap separating the races on the eve of World War II, as well as an echo of Hollywood's classic treatment of controversy and contradiction—to factor them out of movie formulas, thereby rendering them into James Snead's "structured absence." Selznick was far from alone in this rhetorical strategy. American movies, by a well-meaning leaching out of all but the most benign references to ethnicity, had created an organism of universal entertainment that reached across the world's frontiers of language and culture. Indeed, so successful was the formula in foreign markets that most nations had taken measures to blunt the impact of American movies on their national cultures. Moreover, the Motion Picture Producers and Distributors of America (MPPDA) had created their own internal censor, the Production Code Administration (PCA), the famous "Hays" and later "Breen" offices, with the aim of censoring pejorative references to all national, ethnic, and racial groups. By monitoring every project of the studios several times between first treatment and final cut, the PCA effectively reduced every social group to a bland cipher incapable of genuine dramatic conflict. Domestically the Hollywood system mediated between a national mentality and quirks of localism such as Southern racism, always in search of a harmonious monochrome movie culture that diluted cultural density and muted political debate. Blacks, whenever they appeared, were often conservative memory banks of a painless nostalgia, emerging as more rounded, complex figures only when times of crisis opened fissures in the system through which bolder characters and new meanings slipped.

Of all the movies that called this universalizing apparatus into play, *Gone with the Wind* provided the clearest window on the proceedings. As though in a debate, on one side stood the virtues of regionalism: A popular book by a Southerner unknown in literary circles drew a fresh audience to the lore of the Southern "lost cause." In doing so, it robbed slavery of its horrors, thereby implicitly discrediting black political goals. On the other side stood Selznick, seeking to render Mitchell's book into Hollywood's universal marketing terms by muting the racial issues that still alienated Northern victors from Southern vanquished.[3]

Unavoidably, the unforeseen byproduct of Selznick's liberal, harmonizing intentions modulated the historical conflict between blacks and their enemies and not only reduced the legitimacy of the black grievances but seemed to aim at neutering contemporary black protest. Selznick was trapped by his counterfactual history in that a tale of racial struggle during Reconstruction would have shattered the consensus he needed in order to recover his investment. In other words, antebellum

Hollywood's aversion to the racial contradictions in American life reduced African Americans to absent, alibied for, dependent victims of marketing strategies aimed at a profitable universality. Only the onset of war, with its attendant need for a propaganda of national unity, would provide a ground on which countervailing forces of blacks and liberals versus Southerners and conservatives, the former led by organically grown black activists, might contend for political change in movie culture.

Compare how a Southern novel fared in the universalizing Hollywood system even without the benign intervention of Selznick. Stark Young's popular novel of the Civil War, *So Red the Rose* (1934), from the outset at Paramount was symbolized by Y. Frank Freeman, an "unreconstructed" Southerner—the term is that of Walter White of the NAACP (National Association for the Advancement of Colored People)—and Steve Lynch, a former manager of Southern theatre chains. They chose as their director King Vidor, a white Texan admirer of black folk culture, and as their writer the prizewinning dramatist Maxwell Anderson, who professed an abiding "respect" for the book combined with a wish to get right a sense of intersectional fairness. "I'd like to retain as much as possible," he boldly wrote to Russell Holman of Paramount, "of its politics, especially the liberalism of [slaveholders]—and their doubts about slavery," along with the late-war "unrest of the Negroes." As for the soldiers, he wrote that "the boys of the North were victims as much as the boys of the South." The resulting script not only provided the voice of universality that broadened the marketplace but so fulfilled the PCA's wish to avoid controversy that their man complained only of a single reference to "niggers."

Seemed fair enough. But check the black angle. On its face, *So Red the Rose* seemed so liberal as to be willing to face the hard truth of slavery. Slaves wandered off, black soldiers in Grant's army pillaged as they advanced, there was mutiny afoot in the slave quarter. But black drama was hobbled by the need for restraint, much as Selznick had reined in Sidney Howard. Surviving was a rough scene meant to stand for all that had been cut, an abortive slave revolt led by an old hand (Clarence Muse) who gives a rousing speech calling for a rising on the eve of the arrival of, he says, "Yankee men in blue coats." Yet his big scene was discounted and dampened both by its own rhetoric and by the intervention of a house servant in livery. First, the roaring speech ends not with a cry for freedom but with the promise that "we don't work no mo'." Second, the servant (Daniel Haynes) brings the rebels to frozen silence by improbably handwrestling the hardened field hand to his knees. Together the incidents erased a stiff dose of black abolitionist politics and opened the movie to the charge of merely strumming a liberal tune while ratifying the status quo, much as leftists had charged the New Deal with being a conservative expropriation of their ideas.[4]

No Nat Turner here. A rebellious slave (Clarence Muse) meets his match in the person of his staunch mistress (Margaret Sullavan) in *So Red the Rose* (1935). British Film Institute (BFI).

Race-angled movies were not alone in buttering ideological bread on both sides. In his history of Warner Bros. during the Great Depression, Nick Roddick discerned this as a formula in which, as in *Angels with Dirty Faces* (1938), a social problem (such as urban street gangs) is introduced and subsequently solved by neither structural change nor reform but by the intervention of a stock lonewolf hero. Like the New Deal itself, each movie introduced a "tension . . . between rugged individualism and social stability," he wrote, which in the end was resolved by resort to the familiar legend of the lone hero who rises to the occasion, thereby averting the need for more collective action. In *Angels with Dirty Faces,* for example, Rocky (James Cagney) and Jerry (Pat O'Brien), two slum waifs, begin a life of burgling freightcars, but the former matures into a criminal and the latter into a priest; eventually they become rivals for the hearts of the newest crop of slum kids. In the end, on death row, Jerry turns Rocky into a redemptive hero by persuading him to die appearing to be a coward rather than a cocksure devil who will go to the chair with a wink of his eye. The street kids turn from adoration to contempt, of course, and thereafter away from crime. Entirely, to be sure, without resort to a single community or institutional social change in the conditions without which Rocky would not have become Rocky.[5]

At first glance it might seem that *Angels with Dirty Faces* arrived at its denouement in the writers' bungalows in Burbank. Therefore they should be blamed for reporting in reel one that systemic poverty makes streetgangs and then solving the problem not by having recourse to reform but actually undercutting the urge for reform by invoking improbable heroism. Roddick instead locates guilt both in the studio's assembly line methods that required riskfree endings as a form of cost control and in the PCA's urge for moral certitudes that obliged writers to write happy closures. The Breen office in this instance returned the script with a list of two dozen objections, salient among them Rocky as unpunished gangster. A conference between Breen and Sam Bischoff, one of the writers, safely settled the matter without taking up the touchy matter of social change.[6] Routinely, every Hollywood movie followed this path to the screen, accompanied by yet other guarantors of sameness—advertising that touted some "shocking" problem, reviewers who told ticket buyers what to expect, and other institutional influences upon the expectations of audiences. In this way, conscience-liberalism was warped by forces that had scant links to actual political life.

Gone with the Wind, burdened as it was by a racial theme, received particularly cautious treatment from both Selznick and the PCA, so that no matter how Selznick shaped his movie to the voice of liberal conscience, it was still partly shaped by other forces. It was fated, then, to please audiences in search of universal images and discomfit the Malcolm Littles in the theatres—at least until World War II drove up the political value of including more rounded black figures in the casts of movies. In this sense, *Gone with the Wind* was like all other films in reducing all social data, whether war, crime, or slavery, to social dysfunctions susceptible to resolution by heroic effort alone. Were Indians being bilked by their agent? The fault lay with a single heartless bureaucrat. Did poverty cause crime? If so, a crusading reporter would discover it, assuring that *Angels with Dirty Faces* would be followed by *Angels Wash Their Faces.* Did wardens turn their charges into *Boy Slaves?* Then a kindly judge would save them in the last reel. Indeed, such fabled lone intervention in the movies of Frank Capra became such a politics of Oscar-winning, last-reel good intentions that leftist cynics dubbed the genre "Capra-corn."[7]

African Americans often intruded in this system, but with only limited success in the era before depression and war restored them to national attention. Tactically, they lacked not only a friend at court whom the moguls trusted but also a rhetorical alternative to the studios' playing to universal tastes—at least until the need for wartime unity provided a moment when national, black, and Hollywood goals intersected. Certainly the precedent was there for a black lobby in Hollywood, an agency already enjoyed by various regional, religious, and ethnic taste-cultures. Both the producer Cecil B. deMille and Will Hays of the PCA routinely consulted the Jesuit Daniel J. Lord on matters of historicity and morals, while Southern censors such as Lloyd T. Binford of Memphis and Christine Smith of Atlanta served as gatekeepers for their region, thereby denying Southern viewers access to racial drama and daunting studio sales departments that regarded such censors as a market to be catered to rather than authors of taboos. Blacks, at least up to 1940, had penetrated this circle with minimal success, preferring instead a genre of "race movies"—threadbare, all-black versions of Hollywood genres—or demands upon state-level censors for laws against "slandering" racial groups. The results were uneven. The few slander laws probably helped shape the "structured absence" of blacks from the screen more than they aided the black cause. Save for well-mounted successes like the Colored Players' *The Scar of Shame* (1927) or *causes célèbres* such as *The Birth of a Race,* a proposed antidote to *The Birth of a Nation* (1915) that began in Booker T. Washington's Tuskegee Institute and enjoyed the backing of Julius Rosenwald of Sears, Roebuck and other white "angels," race movies generally remained so poorly distributed that they were always at a loss for capital, a talent pool, and a continuity of mission.[8]

So on the eve of World War II, the Hollywood machine ground onward with only incidental participation by black influences. Even a dense, culturally rich, Pulitzer Prize play such as Marc Connelly's *The Green Pastures* suffered ignominy on its way to the screen. Arriving on Broadway in 1929, at the height of Hollywood's interest in soundfilm, Connelly's fable of black folk religion seemed so risky a project that Warner chose Al Jolson in *The Jazz Singer* for its feature-film essay into sound. Blacks, even giants of their craft such as Bessie Smith, Louis Armstrong, or Cab Calloway, remained exiled to tantalizing two-reelers. Only two black musical features, *Hallelujah!* (1929) and *Hearts in Dixie* (1929), each of them rooted in the most old-fashioned notions of the rural black South, reached the screen—each of them, it must be said, earning a round of black applause for their *presence* if not the timeliness of their material.[9] A Southerner inside the PCA praised *Hallelujah!* as "splendidly done" but warned that it would flop among "anyone who doesn't know negro customs," and besides, he wrote, "white people will object to a strong negro exhibiting passion."[10] A similar caution greeted *The Green Pastures,* the PCA pointing out to Warner that three studios had rejected it for want of an adequate audience. Even Daniel Lord, who praised its religiosity, warned that smalltown audiences "would miss" its point and resent the blacks. Organized blacks themselves, fearing the worst, declined to endorse a movie of Connelly's play.[11]

Thus a prizewinning musical drama that had enjoyed a friendly black and white press and years of success on the road took six full years before it found its way to the screen. Even then, the studio timidly held

Marc Connelly directs his own *The Green Pastures* on a cramped, tightly budgeted set rather than the Southern locations for which he had hoped. BFI. Copyright Warner Bros.

back its resources, declined to shoot on location (as Vidor had done *Hallelujah!*), sidestepped shooting in Technicolor, and ignored the advice of its producer, Henry Blanke, to take advantage of pioneering opportunity to make a benchmark color movie.[12] In the end its budget equaled that of a cheap programmer, somewhere between a half million and $800,000, 35 percent of that in recoverable overhead. Indeed, toward the end of shooting the studio suddenly lopped an additional twenty-three pages from a script already stunted by cuts in livestock and set construction.[13] Despite these strictures Connelly thought it grossed three or four million dollars. But a few months after the premiere, *Variety* reported that "sales departments of the film companies have stymied at least two deals [for prospective black films] that were set to go through."[14] It seemed as though no amount of success could override the reluctance to accept the risk attendant upon black material.

None of the foregoing should suggest an ironfisted racism. Rather, the moguls behaved merely tribally, trusting only black mascots of the tribe such as Bill Robinson; corporately, preferring riskfree enterprises;

and traditionally, defining good "race relations" as an appreciation of only the winsome, pious, or musical traits of black culture. And of course they were reinforced in this by every studio's cadre of Southern white counselors—Lamar Trotti, Nunnally Johnson, Freeman, Lynch, and others—who provided advice on local color and racial etiquette. Moreover, in every sort of routine correspondence and conference, studio personnel displayed casual racial folkways shared with the nation at large. They called for "nigger" extras, auditioned "dinges," and spoke of certain set-lights as "niggers."[15] And in the PCA itself, Breen and his staff let pass all manner of racial slight and wit, stiffening only on black heavies or hints of miscegenation as censorable material.[16] Walter White of the NAACP or Floyd Covington of the National Urban League (NUL) offered occasional measured counsel, but Southern hysteria weighed more in the scales. Should RKO use a flippant black servant described in *The Story of Vernon and Irene Castle?* Better play it safe, thought Breen, and go with white, marketable Walter Brennan, and while they were about it, why not drop a needlessly black orchestra. "It is certain that audiences in the south will not like such scenes," he wrote, "and your studio is likely to be deluged with letters of protest."[17]

On the lots, with one eye on the box office, they had little choice but to follow PCA custom. If the studio wished to expose Southern prisons in *I Was a Fugitive from a Georgia Chain Gang,* then caution obliged them to use blacks only when "necessary," said the PCA man, and to emphasize "entertainment over reportage" or else risk a "headache" in the form of "the South's well-known dislike of criticism." *Imitation of Life* (1934) with its whiff of "miscegenation" recalled painful memories of *The Birth of a Nation.* If ever they balked at change, as in the case of Martha Raye's outré dance with Louis Armstrong in *Artists and Models* (1937), Southern exhibitors sent blunt warnings to the PCA to expect angry demonstrations.[18] On the lots, the interoffice memoranda recorded the endless game of outguessing the PCA man. Go as far as we like in shooting black maid and white mistress embracing in *Nothing Sacred* (1937), wrote Val Lewton to his boss, Selznick, providing we give no implication of equality. At screenings animosity often flashed, as when Lewis Milestone slipped some liberal touch into *Of Mice and Men* (1939), to which a PCA man snapped, "You think you're pretty cute, don't you." Early on, social themes of any sort seemed to promise only trouble and box-office poison. Typically, a story editor at Paramount predicted of the Federal Theatre drama about slums, *One Third of a Nation,* that although compelling on stage [it] stood no more chance as movie material than other failed social films.[19]

The effect of this institutional system was to impose on whites an imagery that was ever more irrelevant to the actual changing status of African Americans. As war and depression and Southern soil exhaustion brought black and white Americans together in cities, whether in breadlines or federal projects gangs, movies persisted in old habits. In 1929 a National Committee on Social Values survey reported that blacks still appeared "only to create a laugh on the screen, excepting for 'Uncle Tom's Cabin,'" while a decade later Selznick with unintentional irony confirmed their finding by filing with the MPPDA yet another proposed version of *Uncle Tom's Cabin*.[20]

Sadly within black circles, not only had no consistent critical voice emerged, but a corps of Hollywood Negroes ranging from actors to gossip columnists served as a conservative brake on activism. As early as 1929 Walter White attacked their work, as did Lester Granger of the NUL in 1937 when he included them among the enemies in his the fight for black integration into American life. As timid producers removed black heavies from the screen, unctuous performers such as Stepin Fetchit, Bill Robinson, Louise Beavers, and their peers easily overcame the few protests of the activists. Defending these actors by celebrating their individual accomplishments as the race's achievements were the journalists Harry Levette, Lawrence LaMar, Ruby Goodwin, and other stringers who filed their stories drawn from studio boilerplate and "exclusive" interviews with the black "stars." Their papers ran their stuff as fodder for both fans and prospective advertisers among the exhibitors. Only Claude A. Barnett and his Chicago-based wire service, the Associated Negro Press, tried to make "a dent in the Hollywood situation" both by challenging the blacks to abstain from demeaning work and by prodding conscience-liberals with "the courage to experiment" to make films of "real Negro life." For a few months in the mid-1930s Barnett assigned Fay M. Jackson, a journalist of striking appearance in a town where looks mattered, to replace Levette as his "man" in Hollywood. Her charge: to upset the cozy arrangement in which a coven of black actors "perpetuated their own kind" in an endless run of "maudlin" tales of "cabins in the cotton." Unfortunately, her idealism turned to such bitter contempt for the West Coast blacks that she was soon all but alienated from her sources.[21]

Partly she flopped because she had miscalculated the depth of adoration in which black actors were held by their fans, as well as the respect for their small successes, which fans took as a respite from their own lot in life. Far from being regarded as traitors to the race who merely served white aims, the black actors were regarded as talented high achievers whose roles provided not only signs that at least some blacks might win the game of life but also incomes that they shared with their pet charities, service clubs, and the servants in their bungalows in midtown Los Angeles, where equally comfortable whites once had lived. At the top of the small heap were featured players such as Clarence Muse of *Hearts in Dixie* and a hundred other films, Hattie McDaniel, who would win the first black Oscar for her Mammy in *Gone with the Wind*, and Stepin Fetchit in a string of bucolic romances ranging from *In Old Kentucky*

(1926) to a trilogy of Will Rogers vehicles in the mid-1930s.[22] Beneath them on the scale were the bit players and extras who measured out their careers in terms of minutes on the screen rather than roles. Martin Wilkins, who carried spears or stood in crowds in *The Real Glory,* Tarzan movies, and *Congo Maisie,* compared black auditions to stevedores' shapeups. In these "cattle calls," as actors called them, "they gathered up in gangs" at Central and Twelfth to meet buses for the lots, where "the dollar" mattered more than racial sensitivity. "They didn't care what it was," Wilkins recalled, "any type of Uncle Tom," at least until the Federal Theatre provided alternative income that allowed them "to buck the stereotype."[23]

Not until the end of the decade and a rush of New Deal gestures—black appointments to federal posts, a crescendo of symbolic deeds by Mrs. Roosevelt—did Hollywood take any liberal cues. Southern genre films like *The Littlest Rebel* and *Steamboat Round the Bend* waned, and the options of their black stars were dropped. At Fox the house Southerners, Lamar Trotti and Nunnally Johnson, wrote strong, if Southern-textured, black roles into *Slave Ship* and *The Prisoner of Shark Island.* Out in "the valley" at Universal, Paul Robeson tested the climate by playing Joe in a new *Show Boat.* Social drama presold from successes in other media, such as Clifford Odets's *Golden Boy* (1938) and John Steinbeck's *Of Mice and Men* (1939), arrived with a bit of political consciousness intact. Dramas of the South, such as Owen Davis's *Jezebel* (1938) and Lillian Hellman's *The Little Foxes* (1941), came from Broadway, more barbed and less chary of offending Southern sensibilities. Even conventional Hollywood fare in odd moments played to black tastes. In Jolson's *Wonderbar* (1935), for example, he sang an homage to *The Green Pastures* entitled "Goin' to Heaven on a Mule," which, though featuring a pork-chop orchard and a watermelon palace, served as a lead-in to a pantheon of actual black heroes drawn from history.[24]

A half-dozen films teased the theme of racial integration, only to retreat from it in the last reel. Two of them, *One Mile from Heaven* (1937) and *Rainbow on the River* (1939), narrowed the social distance between the races to the family circle itself. In both movies white children are adopted by black matriarchs who shape them into decent folk. The heavies are the forces of reaction who find the arrangements appalling. But tantalizing clashes with Hollywood racial convention proved unsupportable. Although both movies point toward an interracial closure in which the families defend their happy circle against official snoops, in both a last-reel court proceeding finds in favor of the heavies, separates black from white, and restores the hegemony of convention.[25]

Three musical films in the same era revealed a similar, growing tension between new racial politics and old formulas. Two of them, *The Birth of the Blues* (1939) and *Syncopation* (1942), open on a reverential treatment of jazz as a rich syncretism of Europe and Africa, but both end

A variation on the theme of adoption as a point of intersection of black and white life was sometimes seen through the eyes of a white pupil at the feet of a black jazz master, as here in *Syncopation* (1942) with Jackie Cooper and Todd Duncan on cornets. Copyright RKO.

in lilywhite stories made obligatory by the requirement of a romantic clinch at the end. Their establishing shots reveal their hopes, much as their closures reveal the constraints of Hollywood formula. Under the main titles of *Syncopation* a montage of a map of Africa, a black king under a parasol dickering for a coffle of slaves, a "blackbirder" under full sail, a sprawling cotton field, and a New Orleans streetscape in 1906 all serve as a prologue to the arrival of jazz in Storyville. Indeed, this is where *The Birth of the Blues* begins, complete with ragamuffins, street "arabs" hawking wares, lowdown dives that introduce the beat of jazz life. Then both movies let slip the mood by shifting to their white heroes, both boys struggling at the piano under stern teachers who wish to hear Beethoven as written. Soon the boys are hanging out at the doors of the jazz clubs. In *The Birth of the Blues* the bandmen in Trixy's hear him. "A white boy!" says one, the first he had ever heard playing lowdown style. But gradually the plots slip away into white circles of romance, good-bad women, booze, and jail, and in the last reel the white rebel heroes fulfill themselves by interpolating black music into their own idiom. So a good story idea clashed with an old formula, thereby ending with the erasure of its black premise.[26]

A third fragment of a jazz idiom appeared in a reel of Paramount's *St. Louis Blues* (1939) and revealed much about the prickly sort of resistance that conscience-liberalism might expect even with the onset of a war against racism. At the center of the conflict was Maxine Sullivan, part of whose charm for her Eastern fans had been her whimsically syncopated version of the Scots folksong "Loch Lomond." In first draft the script had included stock black roles as well as Ah Sin, the Chinese cook on a showboat. But before shooting began, Ah Sin became the black servant Ida, Sullivan's role. As though hinting at the social concerns of the writers, the script also included a rising river that wiped out both shacks and mansions without respect for color or class. In any case, the seemingly fluffy movie outraged one of its own writers, John C. Moffitt, who spat out an angry letter complaining of Sullivan's poaching on "Loch Lomond," and attesting to his deep sense of violation brought on by this touch of liberal whimsy.[27]

So far we have taken up the politics of moviemaking on the eve of World War II without reference to external forces, some of which helped arm liberal advocates against the sort of resistance that Moffitt's note anticipated. At the onset of war the Hollywood left felt the pressure from rightwing newspapers, congressional committees, and even gossip columnists in the Los Angeles press who served as a thought-police. Louella O. Parsons, a would-be screenwriter, and Hedda Hopper, a failed actress, helped reduce politics to a sort of world-cup final between simplistic patriots and blood-red communism.[28] The studios not only tolerated but even fed this meddling in their affairs, because it provided a check rein on prima donna stars. Yet the columnists would have been mere paper dragons had it not been for congressional conservatives, many from one-party Southern Districts, who as early as 1939 under Martin Dies (D–Tex.), chair of the House Un-American Activities Committee (HUAC), investigated the "premature anti-fascism" of the Communist party (CPUSA). From the Senate came other investigators of Hollywood "warmongering" in its movies.

To a point the committees were correct in their inferences. The MPPDA had begun the decade by disavowing politics and portraying their movies as "civilizing" appeals to "average standards" limned by endings with "virtue . . . triumphant." But as Hitler rose and war loomed, Hollywood Jews, liberals, and the CPUSA embraced in a "popular front" against fascism. Now and again their sentiments spilled over from their petitions and "mass meetings" into actual movies. In fact, Arthur Mayer, manager of the Rialto in New York, traced a 1940 slump in rentals to "people throughout the land shaken out of their complacence . . . by Europe's war [who] are much more demanding of pictures" as a result.[29]

But the PCA, and foreign consuls and their lobbyists, sided with the right wing in demanding political neutrality. Sensing the prospect for raising the stakes for African Americans, Walter White of the NAACP began cultivating Hollywood liberals and piling up markers that he might later call in. As early as 1939, in a round of dinners with the producer Walter Wanger and a carefully kept list of other liberals, he sought to cast blacks as one of the countervailing powers in a game that they had rarely played well. Meanwhile George Gyssling, the German consul in Los Angeles, threatened the PCA with "serious difficulties" and even "troubles" if the potboiler *Lancer Spy* (1937) or Charles Chaplin's *The Great Dictator* (1940) were released. Breen took Gyssling's case to the lots, warning them of his threats and asking them to avoid labeling the warring camps in Wanger's Spanish Civil War film, *Blockade*. The state censors joined in when Pennsylvania required the makers of *Beasts of Berlin* (1939) to append a disclaimer that it intended no "prejudice" toward any nation.[30] The race angle here, of course, was that to agree to pussyfoot was to subject Jewish characters to the same otherness, erasure, and absence that blacks historically had faced. Already *Beasts of Berlin* had slyly labeled them an unnamed but courageous minority, and in William Dieterle's *The Life of Emile Zola* (1937) the infamous Dreyfus case had unfolded without a single utterance of the word *Jew*. Only Chaplin, not a member of the PCA, unabashedly located Jews at the core of a film, *The Great Dictator*.[31] After the American entry into the war all of this would change; for example, John Balderston, a screenwriter, Elmer Davis of the Office of War Information (OWI), and the historian Henry Pringle pressed Louis B. Mayer for an early release of *Mrs. Miniver* to head off a rise of Anglophobia after the botched British defense of Singapore against the Japanese. Afterward Balderston praised Pringle for "your initiative [which] has resulted in a serious blow being struck against general anti-British feeling."[32]

Observing how the system worked, Walter White could not help but sense an eventual inclusion of African Americans in it as full partners in a worldwide alliance against fascism. The crisis of war had brought blacks, the democracies, and moviemakers into common cause. Up to then, the only filmmakers who had ever paid attention to blacks had been a circle of New York lefties in Nykino, Frontier, and other cells of Eastern documentarists.[33]

At the same time, African Americans had only just begun to link their goals both to the war and to movies. The NAACP, for instance, quietly kept a file of prospectuses of filmmakers who might help them use film as a weapon, even though early in the Depression some officers remained cool to the medium. In 1932, for example, when Walter Niebuhr of the Peace Films Foundation proposed a film on the cultural evolution of Afro-America Joel Spingarn at the NAACP grumbled, "I don't think pure machine-made propaganda does much good." Months later, the black Rhodes scholar Alain Locke struggled to bring filmmakers and black sponsors together but found "no Negroes . . . who would . . . be interested."[34]

The Eastern radical filmmakers offered scant additional hope for a black presence on their screens, eventually leaving only Hollywood as a prospective ally during the oncoming war. Radical filmmakers, often at great personal sacrifice, had spent their professional lives making grainy, seldom seen, class-based propaganda in which blacks held as marginal a place as they had held in Hollywood—mainly because the filmmakers had no wish to muddle the class conflict by stirring racism into the pot. The two most celebrated documentaries of the era, *Native Land* and Time, Inc.'s *The Ramparts We Watch,* both omitted blacks in their alarmist tales of democracy in a hostile world. *Native Land,* despite the celebrated Paul Robeson as narrator, painted out black proletarians in order not to incite narrow, race-based grievances that might divert the eye from the intended heavies, a cabal of nameless "interests" and "bosses." As Leo Hurwitz recalled, "It is important not to indict the whole white race and [thereby] remove the class character of oppression." Oddly, a friendly New York press hinted at an audience ripe for racial advocacy. "Powerful" and even "superb," they said. "Indicts the spirit of the Klan," said the CPUSA's *Daily Worker.*[35]

More politically centrist documentaries also warned of menaces to the American way, including, as *The Ramparts We Watched* did, the same nameless "powerful corporations" as well as foreign fascists, but again blacks held no stake in the outcome. *Land of Liberty,* a pageant of American history made for the New York World's Fair of 1939, also depicted a lilywhite America save for a shot of a black butler. Despite consultation with the historian James T. Shotwell, its agenda never wavered from a European manifest destiny in the American West.[36]

At least *Land of Liberty* focused black rage upon film as propaganda. A year earlier, Edgar Dale, a pioneer in the study of the sociology of film at Ohio State University, had written in the *Crisis,* an organ of the NAACP, that Pare Lorentz's New Deal-ish plea for intervening in the spoliation of arable land, *The Plow That Broke the Plains,* showed how "a single film . . . can make the American public sensitive to [a] problem." Then in 1939, as though taking Dale to heart, J. Richardson Jones of the black Atlanta Mutual Insurance Company saw *Land of Liberty,* bristled at its lilywhite tenor, and fired off an angry letter to Walter White. Thereafter, organized blacks began to join the ranks of the countervailing powers in the moviemaking system.[37]

Not that sanguine results immediately followed. Up to then, save for a few oddments such as Lorentz's films and those of the Scots filmmaker John Grierson, documentary film was marked by an offputting, gray, neutral texture that was preferred by audiovisual librarians who wished to avoid controversy. Typical was *Parade of Progress,* a black-sponsored film that followed Jones's protest to White, a static parade of "talking heads" belonging to black achievers such as Mary McLeod Bethune, a member of Roosevelt's informal "black cabinet," and an NAACP promotional film done in similar style. Ensuing meetings of a "Greater New York Committee for Better Negro Films" built "around the presence of Paul Robeson" generated no better ideas.[38] The documentary genre simply could not become the broadranging advocate that Edgar Dale had predicted—not until it broke with its somber style, its hat-in-hand dependence on inconstant foundations and parent-teacher groups who sponsored films and donated projectors, and its cautious claims to uncontroversial "objectivity." A 1937 report to the American Council on Education found, for example, only four fields that lent themselves to film: voice, hygiene, grammar, and aesthetics. Even the famous *The Plow That Broke the Plains* was praised for its "rhythmic beauty" rather than its advocacy.[39] Even if an engaging film survived this system, audio-visual libraries were few in number, projectors averaged fewer than one per school, the rental firms had only just formed their guild in 1939, and *all* were beholden to donors. Even the catalogues propped up this daunting system. Typically, when one reviewer reported that *America's Disinherited* included an angry sharecropper's slogan, "Yesterday we asked for pity, today we demand justice," he cautioned that "the teacher should also see that the planter side of the story is told."[40]

In this cinematic mood just before the war, African Americans began to sense the prospects for affecting filmmaking at its source, but in the short term the politics of documentary film were as daunting as those in Hollywood itself. Typically, documentarists chose themes and subjects from a narrow inventory of black fables of "self-help," depicting blacks solving some flaw in Southern geography such as erosion or weevils or celebrating black ideologies like Booker T. Washington's "philanthropic efforts on behalf of the Negro." A faithful viewer could only conclude that a good black future required no more than home-canning of food, new flyscreens and privies, and fresh coats of whitewash, all done in the spirit of Washington, in whose name one film promised that the "race would prosper if" only African Americans took up "the common occupations of life." Two typical films of the day were MGM's biopic of the agronomist George Washington Carver and the National Tuberculosis Association's *Let My People Live* (1938), a tale of how modern medicine intervened to reduce the incidence of disease. In the former film, humility and a sense of place rather than achievement set the tone. Carver appeared "as a black common man, who though offered many positions preferred to devote his life to the study of the peanut, an angle Carver personally agreed to, providing it was shot with dignity. As to the latter film, a reviewer found it a useful tool in promoting racial tolerance as though only suffering African Americans were unthreatening and therefore deserving of philanthropic attention.[41] Even supposed "actuality" footage such as newsreels seemed to consider all but the most benign (or comic) blacks ineligible for inclusion. In *The March of Time*, for example, the cult leader Father Divine appeared not as a social phenomenon but as a comic figure at the head of a gimcrack crusade; the annual black Easter parade became "Negroes Strut in Easter Finery in Harlem"; and a report on an annual ball became a "Dizzying Round of Jitterbug and Jive" with a sidebar interview with the psychiatrist A. A. Brill, who told viewers that jitterbugging was a generic Africanism.[42]

Near the end of this dismaying decade in which radicals, documentarists, and Hollywoodians shared a common vision of African Americans that casually erased them from the daily round of American life, *Gone with the Wind* arrived, effectively straddling the critical moment between the stasis of peacetime and the energizing mood of war. As we have seen, Selznick had not only taken up the cause of nationalizing Mitchell's regional epic, but had done so when Hollywood seemed at the height of its powers, like some ancient capital that successfully exported its ideals to almost every national culture on the planet—cultures, it should be said, in which families habitually attended movies twice a week—and earned $40 million annually from American markets alone.[43]

It would be Selznick, then, who would carry Hollywood's golden age into war, thereby having the last racial word of one era and the first of the next. Indeed, his movie was the first case of extended negotiations between maker and audience that included African Americans at the table. Its resulting inner contradictions helped provide a template against which to test black strength during the wartime rising of a Hollywood conscience-liberalism that would give blacks unprecedented access to the moviemaking process. Consequently, movies grew not only more self-consciously political but also less content with their former self-proclaimed role as mere entertainment. Not that *Gone with the Wind* and its peers became political tracts—far from it—but each slight, negotiated change in it was a transaction that demonstrated black power in a society under the impending stress of war.

Besides Howard, Selznick's team soon included the veteran Hollywood body-and-fender man Ben Hecht, as well as the distant figure of Mitchell herself, an Atlantan of uncommon good sense with a wry image of her South as a region that sometimes took itself too seriously. Abetted by Kay Brown, Selznick's most trusted New York aide, she contributed an urbane Southern sensibility. She had been raised as of two minds, soaking up the lore of the Lost Cause in daytrips to the blackened ruins left by Sherman's army and to the Cyclorama at Stone Mountain, but also being broadened by a life that included attending a Yankee college, serving a turn as a reporter on the *Atlanta Journal*, reading Wilbur Cash's heretical *The Mind of the South*, and writing a novella of "flaming youth" that included an interracial liaison.[44] By 1936 her reading embraced both Henry Steele Commager's biography of Theodore Parker, particularly, she told the author, "the parts about the fugitive slaves," and the Negrophobia of Thomas Dixon, to whom she wrote, "I was practically raised on your books and love them very much." Like many Southerners she felt she loved her black servants and believed the Ku Klux Klan to have been a historical necessity, yet of her book she said, "I sweat blood to keep it from being like Uncle Remus." Indeed, she *liked* standing in the wind between the two cultures, although wishing for acceptance by Southern readers. As one of her characters says: "Miss Scarlett, tain' gwine to do you no good to stan' high wid Yankees ef yo' own folks doan' 'prove of you." In the end she had everything: Southerners stood by her; Yankees accepted her tragedy of the South as their own; the book sold millions; and Selznick hoped to make it the greatest movie ever.[45]

As they grappled with their task they searched for common ground, muting or cutting scenes on which there was no compromise. As conscience-liberals they liked Mitchell's blacks. They were, Howard wrote, the best-written Negroes he had ever read, to which Selznick added his wish that they appear "on the right side of the ledger," even at the expense of historicity. "The picture must not emerge," he told Howard," as anything offensive to negroes" nor cast "too bad a light on even the negroes of the Reconstruction period."[46] He even tried to take on black consultants, including Walter White, Charles Wesley of Howard University, and the black actors on the set—some of whom violated the ancient stricture that actors should be neither seen nor heard between takes—and sampled opinion in black Los Angeles.[47]

For Southern lore he turned to Mitchell's friend Susan Myrick of the *Macon Telegraph* and Wilbur Kurtz, a Northern expatriate and Civil War buff who advised on weaponry and plantation life—sans whips and chains. Mitchell reckoned that Myrick shared her own wryness and, despite a pedigree that included a Confederate general, possessed an "utter lack of sentimentality toward what is tearfully known as 'The Old South,'" coupled with a racial mentality that one black Georgian summed up to Mitchell as: "De race got two friends in dis county, sweet Jesus and de *Macon Telegraph.*" Myrick spent her days screening old movies, conferring on costume and manners, and teaching Southern accents to the English actors, and scouting Los Angeles for black actors—in short, as liaison between Atlanta and Hollywood. Of course, none of this assured authenticity; in fact Selznick regarded Kurtz mainly as an overpaid meddler and soon returned to the South he knew best—Hollywood's own.[48] Mitchell caught the drift and feared the worst as Selznick gradually transformed her rustic Tara into a Georgian mansion. As for the fate of the blacks, she expected only maudlin Hollywood complete with, as she told Kay Brown, "three hundred massed Negro singers . . . standing on Miss Pittypat's lawn waving their arms and singing 'Swing low, sweet chariot, comin' for to carry me home,' while Rhett drives up with the wagon."[49]

In this arrangement the politics of moviemaking fell back into Selznick's lap, particularly as the Southerners supplied rich detail from their own lore while he responded to specifically racial problems by erasing them from the script. This left blacks as a sort of coinage in the politics of the marketplace in which Selznick seemed caught between a possibly hostile black press and his wish for a universally acclaimed movie that would return its investment. Thus Selznick smoothed away offending black parts: The epithet "nigger" all but evaporated, of a proposed rape scene Selznick prescribed that "the negro [be] little more than a spectator," and the tragedy of Reconstruction surfaced only as a series of nameless "political meetings."[50]

The blacks, perhaps still not at home in the unaccustomed role of being asked for advice by powerful white men, requested little that Selznick could not deliver. Charles Wesley apparently never responded. As for Walter White, he asked only for "accuracy," promised no "racial chauvinism," and after lunch with Kay Brown seemed a pussycat. He and I are buddies, Brown told Selznick, and she expected only cooperation from "Brother White." This left only the blacks on the set, one of whom, the choir director Hall Johnson, told Myrick he was unhappy that some blacks had failed so obstinately to appreciate *Gone with the Wind*.[51] As insurance, Selznick took on a black journalist, gave him a tour of the studio, and began planting stories in his column along with "exclusive" interviews. Next he let leak the story that the personal maid of Mrs. Roosevelt (a heroine among black Democrats) was up for the role of Mammy. Finally, in an oddly careless gesture, Roy Wilkins, a major figure in the NAACP, lightened Selznick's task by running in the *Crisis* a snapshot of himself visiting a movielot, an image that could not help but convey to black readers that one of their own seemed on good terms with Hollywood. On the set, the black actors contributed to this era of good feelings by being portrayed in the black press as high achievers who had won "coveted" roles of "dignity and earnestness" that in their skilled hands would become "more than" mere servants. In this way they not only contributed to Selznick's strategy but played to a black political consciousness in which personal attainment was celebrated in the black press as though reflecting a general rise in African American fortunes. In the glow of these coups, Selznick's greatest fear was not of black activism but of various watchdogs of historical trivia such as the United Daughters of the Confederacy and the Society for Correct Civil War Information. The Hollywood veteran actors, beholden to the studio for their income and their stature among black fans, played it cool, perhaps tommed it a bit, and, like Oscar Polk, who played Pork the Geechee butler, fed Myrick unctuous testimony that the project "strikingly demonstrate[d] how far we have come in so few years."[52]

Clearly, Selznick had won the public relations game; black protest fixed only on the easily patched matter of how many times "nigger" was to be heard. Voices on the left damning "the glorification of the old rotten system of slavery" as an "incitement to lynching" were all but lost.[53] As early as 1937, Ruby Berkeley Goodwin of the *Los Angeles Sentinel* and other local blacks feared the word "nigger" might leak from page to screen and called for its erasure. Selznick coolly allowed blacks to believe in their newly asserted powers when in fact the Breen office had already warned him against using the word. As late as 1939, he wavered, thinking to reserve the word for only blacks to utter, but finally relented after his staff surveyed black Los Angeles and ruled it "dangerous." "Okay, forget it," he said in the end.[54]

By the time of its premiere in Atlanta in 1939, *Gone with the Wind* had been oven-fired to a glossy, smooth, universal metaphor that pleased almost everyone in one way or another so that dissenters seemed deviant (even Communist). Oddly, even the *Worker* waffled, its reviewer breaking with the CPUSA line in confessing to being charmed despite its politics. Blacks too came away awestruck at the genius that had managed the tale of Reconstruction without raising the old goblins of freedmen's corruption and Ku Klux nightriding. Never mind the attendant erasure of a chapter of black history or the absenting of its participants; Selznick had made his universal classic from the skeleton of a regional book and turned it into a celebration of an American faith in individual heroism, grit in the face of defeat, romantic love, and even interracial harmony (at the price of the history of black politics and struggle and thus the historical basis of their current plight). The black characters were left only with their roles as slaves for whom heroism was measured out in fealty to their masters. Hattie McDaniel handled her end so well that her Mammy won an Oscar, the first ever for a black performer, an accomplishment that met with genuine black approval. If they winced at all, it was as Malcolm X recalled: at a stridently mindless maid named Prissy (Butterfly McQueen).[55]

Selznick's movie taxed the critical faculties of the reviewers at the political center of the nation's press. Even as they sneered at its shrill advertising, outsized girth, swollen budget, and the glitz with which Russell Birdwell trumpeted it in three years of promotional stunts, they confessed to liking it. So critics either sided with James Agee in the *Nation* in attacking its "aesthetically self-defeating" excesses or with Pare Lorentz in *McCall's* in confessing that "If I go on any longer I might as well go to work for MGM."[56] Few of them took up racial angles, mainly because of Selznick's skill in universalizing Mitchell's blacks into icons of social harmony.

This left the task of attacking Selznick's cinema politics to the CPUSA and the black press, neither one of which presented a coherent aesthetic. A "glorification of the old South," said a Socialist paper; "a foul slander of the Negro people . . . in a slick package of sentimentality," said the CPUSA; "a rabid incitement . . . to provoke race riots," said another leftist. And yet their vehemence masked their failure to find a hook on which to hang a more systematic attack on the movie. Indeed, Howard Rushmore of the *Worker* so struggled for an angle that reflected his ambivalence that he broke Party discipline and in its eyes became a "renegade," an act followed up by the *Worker*'s commissioning a rebuttal by the black writer Carlton Moss and, as the veteran CPUSA movie critic David Platt recalled, "boot[ing Rushmore] out" of the *Worker*. With orthodoxy restored, Platt successfully pressed the New York critics to deny it their "best film" award.[57]

But what of the black public? Apart from the fact that the movie was about slavery, it became clear to many blacks that a Hollywood studio had taken a political step that, even if rooted in a sad past, gave racial material a dimension it had never possessed before. The black figures were of uncommon humanity: a mammy so acerbic as to dominate her scenes, a butler so cool as to seem managerial, slaves dressed in honest "Negro cloth"; only the inane Prissy broke the mood. There had even been a fleeting glimpse of a "darktown," through which Scarlett rode,

Dandy black Republicans and their white bosses were reduced to glimpses in *Gone with the Wind* (1939), in keeping with Selznick's wish to place African Americans on "the right side of the ledger." Nederlands Stichting Filmmuseum (NSF). Copyright Metro-Goldwyn-Mayer.

and a dandified town Negro, probably a Republican, who hinted of the subsurface racial politics struggling to break free from universalism.

Some of this reached black viewers, rousing them to unexpected division ranging from predictable hectoring to acute anticipation of changes to come in the politics of movies. Some took comfort in Selznick as an ally against Mitchell's Southern chauvinism. The *Crisis* itself reported that he had "eliminated practically all of the offensive scenes and dialogue so that there is little . . . to which objection can be entered," an opinion close to that of Edward G. Perry's piece in the *Negro Actor* reporting that he "was not offended or annoyed."[58]

Among the newspapers, some black critics began to see more than mere erasure of the offensive and to examine omens of attainment. Some, of course, beholden as they were to exhibitors' advertising, took a soft line, rehashing apologia and measuring success by the hours or days earned by black extras that had brought "economic joy and artistic aplomb to the local colony of sepia screen players," praising individual performances, and cheering each small breach with racial convention. The *Norfolk Journal and Guide*, for example, admired the modernity of the relationship between Rhett Butler and Mammy, while others at least shared the pleasure of the *Crisis* in the erasures that had left "no reason for Negroes to feel indignant." Indeed, some echoed Pare Lorentz in finding it "magnificently done" and even "truly the greatest picture ever made!" Dissent was scattered among a few papers and irate letter-writers.[59]

The same fissures opened among the moviegoers. At modish benefits in half a dozen cities, exhibitors held dressy premieres that divided blacks into two camps, formally attired firstnighters and the picketers whose lines they guiltily crossed. In Washington, the ticketholders walked under signs proclaiming "You'd Be Sweet Too Under a Whip!" Lillian Johnson gave her story in the *Gary American* a personal spin. "I crossed a picket line," she wrote. "I wasn't sorry."[60]

Two incidents that followed the stunning reception of *Gone with the Wind* called attention to yet another political division that anticipated black action during the coming war, a division that separated black East from West, activists from actors. First, in New York, Walter White, who had temporized over *Gone with the Wind*, assailed a proposed remake of *The Birth of a Nation*, thus introducing the prospect of black action against movies at their source. Meanwhile, out west McDaniel received her Oscar, arriving in true Hollywood fashion—late and in a fur against the rigors of California springtime. She sat at Selznick's table, took her statuette from Fay Bainter, got a kiss from Vivien Leigh and a handshake from Gable. She urged black youth to "aim high and work hard" and, in a phrase that soon would make liberals wince, hoped to "keep on being a credit to my race."[61] For the moment, McDaniel's gesture meant more than White's. Her linking the race's success to her own seemed clear, while his step toward a means of imposing the group's will on white America was lost on everyone. Yet in only two years, the war would be in full cry, McDaniel would be out of work, and White would be addressing moguls at Hollywood lunches, reminding them of a linkage between their work and the highflown anticolonial sentiments of the yet to be written Atlantic Charter. Only a handful of pickets outside McDaniel's Oscar dinner hinted at the eventual shift from accommodationism to direct action.

Poor McDaniel felt the changeover first. After 1940, when a fan praised Selznick for giving "the Negro, individually, a chance to display his or her talent," her career slumped despite Selznick's best efforts. He put her on the road to plug the movie and to give blacks the sort of thrill that white people derived from personal appearance tours denied to blacks. But "where does this Negro artist go from here?" asked the radio gossiper Jimmy Fidler. "Why, back to playing incidental comedy maids," he answered wryly. White's brand of conscience-liberal activism with its stress on collective action rather than individual ambition stood ready to replace her and the entire corps of Hollywood Negroes.[62]

But this was never a mere squabble between two archenemies. Already, other Hollywood filmmakers and other African Americans had caught the same drift toward the creative disequilibrium that the war would bring. To take one instance in detail, Sol Lesser, the maker of Tarzan movies, set out to make his own off-the-rack, B-movie *Gone with the Wind,* hiring as writers the black actor Clarence Muse and the author Langston Hughes. Both had displayed urges to make movies, Muse as a lyricist and director of race movies, Hughes as a participant in 1932 in an ill-fated Soviet attempt to make a movie about racism.[63]

Much as Selznick had reworked *Gone with the Wind* from a regional to a national epic, so Lesser on his own scale wrestled with modernizing antebellum black figures. Yet Hughes's first draft must have seemed like strong medicine. It is set in the New South of Henry Grady and the *Atlanta Constitution* and hydroelectric dams, and its blacks are in a multiethnic workforce bonded by a mutual understanding and the quest for the American dream! A hero modeled on the legend of John Henry helps build a dam that eventually lights the homes of black and white alike, and in death he anticipates the coming of racial integration having taught the white juvenile hero his songs.

Boldly, as though anticipating the rhetoric of the Atlantic Charter, Lesser at first gave his writers a free hand. "Messrs. Muse and Hughes are to be given the utmost liberty in developing the Second Draft Screenplay, so that it will contain every element of their conception of the story," he wrote to his staff. Of course, he must have guessed that Hollywood formulas would intrude and color the project. For example, he accepted a sort of Huck-and-Jim pairing that "gradually" exposed "the slave situation," but suggested casting for "a little pickaninny of the Stymie Beard type." In like manner he placed "the colored man's point of view" in the hands of a stock preacher of "quaint dignity, earnestness, and sincerity," while adopting the well-worn device of blaming slavery on coarse "Yankees" or "London businessmen . . . who know nothing of the fine relations that existed between plantation owners and their slaves." His faith in such Hollywood conventions as vehicles for conveying his fresh black angle extended even to the music, as though sugarcoating the new with a glaze of the old made it go down more easily. He imagined an encounter with either John Brown or Dred Scott with the liberal anthem "John Brown's Body" over it, but for an "auction block episode" he suggested "another spiritual," as though the presumed balance would, he said, "avoid the typical hackneyed Hollywood story."[64]

Throughout the spring of 1939, Muse and Hughes held out against Lesser's fondness for plantation legend. As though sheer density of detail would override slippages in theme, they wrote in outsized heroic women and men among their canecutters, a richly drawn New Orleans streetscape speckled with local color Negroes. But soon they quarreled over "weaknesses in the storyline" and reinsertions into "Lesser's revised continuity." As they lost to Hollywood convention on the big points, they held out for the little ones—cutting an old "Tom" and a driver who says "massa"; clinging to evocative bits of work-chants, a slave who refuses to be whipped, a drum hidden in the slave quarter, an African tale told around the slaves' fire, and populist lines such as that of a woman who says "they" get the hams and blacks get the rest.[65]

In the end, of course, convention won, not so much because black lost to white, but because Hollywoodians—Lesser *and* Muse—spoke the same filmic language. After all, Muse's most famous work had been "Sleepy Time Down South," a sentimental plantation ditty that became Louis Armstrong's theme music. Thus when in March Lesser insisted on keeping in "the happy contentment of the slaves [and] . . . the traditional, honest, literal comedy of the Negro folk," burdening the story with a carpetbagger heavy who "does not understand" the "emotional relationship" between slave and master, and creating a mood "sympathetic to the Southern people," he was choosing Muse's local color as against Hughes's populism. Sure enough, the tradepapers spotted the structural split and praised its freshness, particularly the resistance of the white orphan-hero (Bobby Breen) against a Yankee executor's plot to sell off slaves, and they commended the black writers for "breaking away from the sharper lines of formula" by means of their "colorful material."[66]

If this seems like a small victory compromised by convention, it must be remembered that *Way Down South,* as it was called, pointed more toward future change than toward past convention. Moreover, even with its heart cut out *Way Down South* was remembered for years by its black writers, in Muse's case by flying it at the top of his letterhead till the day he died, and in Hughes's by eternally seeking film projects as though the movie roved the back alleys of his memory as a good experience that promised better. His files bulged with possible black biopics, a film of his poem "The Negro Speaks of Rivers," a wartime musical, a documentary inspired by Jean Cocteau's *L'Amitie Noir*, Paul Robeson vehicles including a war movie in which he foils "a gigantic plot [in which] the fascists enslave and exploit the natives," and a black western about the Kansas "Exodusters."[67]

Taken together, *Gone with the Wind* and *Way Down South*, as Selznick had hoped, offered at least timid challenges to Hollywood's plantation legend, partly as a result of the moviemakers' growing attention to the racial stakes of the impending war. The ensuing decline in the stature of this Southern genre surfaced in a memorandum by Lenore Coffey, a Warner's writer who, not long after the release of these movies, panned a proposed new genre film. She confessed puzzlement at why such a remote, old-fashioned story would interest anyone.[68] Thus a "first" of sorts had happened: A Hollywood writer and a black kid in a Michigan theatre had both sneered at the same genre of no-longer-producible material.

Of course, the contempt for "fascism" that was shared by Selznick and Hughes and governed their attitude toward movies could not of itself foreshadow a shifting American racial arrangement, but it did echo a mentality that had begun to resonate in Hollywood and black circles alike. At first Hollywood merely kept a cautious eye on how war might affect markets, but its gestures soon grew more political. Jack Warner helped form the Hollywood Anti-Nazi League; Walter Wanger struggled to bring the Spanish Civil War to the screen in *Blockade;* and even the Breen office stiffened against German opposition to *The Great Dictator*.[69] Gradually, as vague sentiment grew into firm antifascism, it affected acquisition of properties, editorial department readings, advertising angles—the entire process—redirecting audience expectations toward a new politics of movies to be shaped, eventually, by an organic coalition of moviemen, the NAACP, and the OWI, in a shared hegemony over the formerly lilywhite manufacturing of movies.

Moreover, this shift in mentality extended to the entire raffish, liberal bohemia known as show business. Its polyethnic practitioners even found it easy to shift to a national propaganda bent upon neutralizing racial antipathy, first as mere propaganda, then as eventual public policy. Joining with the entertainers was the OWI, at war's beginning no more than an "office of facts and figures" buried in a larger agency, which despite Southern congressmen eager to slash its budget grew into a home for conscience-liberal allies of blacks who became skilled at expanding upon the narrow necessitarian functions of their agency. Not that creators of popular culture and federal agents conspired to make a new national racial ethic. Rather, unbidden by any agency the personal sentiments, conscience-liberalism, and antifascism of entertainers came together with the government's need for a propaganda of national unity, providing a center to which the nation turned for defining the war and its aims.

In this way, popular culture generated an ideological life of its own that carried Americans toward a collective antifascism and eventually a more liberal turn of mind. Much as Picasso's painting of Guernica, the Basque town bombed by the Luftwaffe in 1937, galvanized the world's intellectuals, so a *Life* cover of a weeping, bourgeois Marseillaise watching the Germans march in was not only a shot of *his* violated town but also the *Paris* of Americans' imaginations.[70] Thus popular culture heightened emotion beyond mere necessitarian goals, popularizing a conscience-liberal ideology that sharpened the meaning of hazy notions like "fair play" by setting off Nazi racism-as-policy from American racism as a flaw correctible through "social engineering." At first popular culture offered mere reactive patriotism in songs like "Der Führer's Face" and "Let's Remember Pearl Harbor," comedians' scatological jokes about the Axis, broadcast pleas to save cooking fat, and comic books featuring antifascist heroes such as *Captain America*. But it quickly moved toward setting specific agendas in such movies as Howard Hawks's *Air Force* and songs like John LaTouche's and Earl Robinson's "Ballad for Americans." In this way, without forethought conscience-liberalism bore deep into popular culture not as mere sentiment but also as a means of winning the war.

For African Americans, then, the war was a moment of high opportunity. In movies particularly, blacks became creatures shaped by the Hollywood-OWI-NAACP axis in search of a propaganda of unity rooted in ideas that arose organically from a nutrient broth of historic black grievances stirred in with goals arising from the culture of a war against fascism. The Hollywood end was perhaps the least coherent and least steadfast. Urbane Jewish liberalism coexisted with a profitmaking system that churned out deeply personal movies alongside cheap sentiment that sold tickets. It both awaited and resented guidance from the outside. Within the OWI, tension mounted between its cell of conscience-liberals and the Southern congressmen who held its budget hostage; nevertheless, it opened an office in the Taft Building on Hollywood's famous corner of Hollywood and Vine, as though establishing a beachhead. Residual black inconstancy derived from a clash over the nature of black achievement: Was it to be defined by Walter White at lunches in the Victor Hugo to which no other blacks had access, or by Hollywood actors who earned their keep playing incidental servants and hoofers?[71]

In any case, the war provided a catalyst. Blacks had gained incrementally during the New Deal as clients of various programs, but not as the pace that a national war footing would provide. In war industries they doubled their hourly earnings and entered trade unions at five times their prewar pace, some of the gains ensuing from their own activism on behalf of a federal Fair Employment Practices Commission (FEPC). Membership in the NAACP increased tenfold. By no means a revolution either in behavior or mentality, the changes nonetheless provided an insistent backbeat to the larger war effort. As the historian Thomas C. Cochran wrote, by war's end "'Democracy' had become the major slogan of the period."[72]

Consider how race had already shifted from being a purely local matter to having a place in national politics. Before the war blacks expected mere gestures: a speech by Mrs. Roosevelt, an appointment to the "black cabinet," and other tokens that some blacks sneered at as they did the National Recovery Administration (NRA)—"Negroes Ruined Again." Even then, advisers counseled restraint for fear of alienating the Southern wing of the party. No less a liberal than Henry A. Wallace warned his president against "too much concern for one 'underprivileged' segment."[73] But with the onset of European war came a mood shift. Roosevelt, only a casual liberal in racial matters, gave in to pressure from his wife, Secretary of Interior Harold L. Ickes, and A. Philip Randolph of the black Brotherhood of Sleeping Car Porters in signing the order creating the FEPC to monitor fair labor practices in war industries. Ickes himself had moved from a generalized liberalism toward the specific "goal of a democratic army where there will be no segregation." Will Alexander, a Southern liberal, resigned from the black-oriented Rosenwald Foundation and reentered government when "World War II produced new challenges in race relations." And Representative Helen Gahagan Douglas, herself a movie actor, spent the war stiffening convictions, seeking to toughen the FEPC, and speaking against charges of black cowardice during the Italian campaign.[74]

Black leaders tried to mesh their own aims with those of the war, the most far-reaching gesture being William G. Nunn's *Pittsburgh Courier* and its "Double V" campaign. The letter *V* had become a multitextual sign embracing Churchill's brave gesture during the London blitz and the opening notes of Beethoven's Fifth Symphony (which coincided with Morse code for *V*), both of which became an aural/visual signoff for every movie shown after 1941. Nunn gave it a black twist by calling for a Double V—a simultaneous victory over foreign fascism and domestic racism—and tubthumping the idea by means of cartoons, beauty contests, and editorials. Activists took up the cry, the NAACP by holding its annual convention on Hollywood's doorstep and the NUL by devoting its annual meeting to "The Problems of Negroes in a World at War."[75] Carlton Moss, a young black radio writer, carried the idea into show business. Sponsored by an ad hoc Fight for Freedom group, he mounted a revue that implored blacks to fight despite "evils which still hinder [the

Negro's] complete integration . . . [so victory could] point the way to a better day." Only days after Pearl Harbor his *Salute to the Negro Troops* played a week at the Apollo in Harlem. In a letter to OWI Moss touted his show as an antidote to low black morale and Japanese propaganda portraying itself as "an inspiration to the darker races."[76] In the same spirit Richard Wright, a lapsed Communist whose novel *Native Son* had been the hot book of 1940, also offered his services to OWI, wishing to "be helpful in winning the war," which he described as "the national democratic cause." Specifically he wished to help in "clarifying and popularizing the administration's war policy among the Negro people."[77]

White people, despite the persistence of racial antipathy, suffered these developments if for no other reason than that, as John M. Blum put it, rising black expectations and consciousness formed a "prerequisite for wartime and postwar progress toward desegregation and a warning to Washington to ameliorate at least some black grievances." Roosevelt himself gave voice to these small goals in his "four freedoms" speech, the highflown anticolonial clause of the Atlantic Charter, and personal letters urging repudiating "at home the very [racist] theories which we are fighting abroad."[78] Gallup polls revealed a white forebearance, if not enthusiasm, for change; respondents narrowly approved changes in Southern racial etiquette, Mrs. Roosevelt's resignation from the Daughters of the American Revolution in protest of its racial policies, and even a federal antilynching law despite fears of extending federal powers into local matters.[79]

Southerners joined in at least marginally, not only in polls but also in raising a few liberal voices in the ranks of agencies such as the Southern Conference for Human Welfare. In Birmingham in 1938 it had a brush with the local cops because it ignored race in its seating arrangements; in 1942 in Nashville it gave its Jefferson Award jointly to white Frank Graham and Mary McLeod Bethune of the National Youth Administration; and in its house organ it called for racial reform "after the defeat of Germany and Japan." The latter device, invoking foreigners as a reason for social change, was taken up also by the liberal novelist Lillian Smith, who thought racist incidents "sounded 'just right'" to Japanese and German ears. And in Raleigh at a biracial "Win the War" rally Graham, by then president of the University of North Carolina, portrayed the war as "a people's war," an idea echoed that day by a string of celebrants of black and white heroes.[80]

Of course, slogans are cheap, and speeches may not always lead to action. Around the country, wherever overtaxed facilities strained racial etiquette as in bus station waiting rooms, or where unaccustomed new social roles such as black officers on Southern posts clashed with custom, violence often resulted. Besides, some blacks also reacted coolly to the war. As Horace Cayton told it, a black sharecropper greeted a white man at his gin with the news: "By the way, Captain, I hear the Japs done declare war on you white folks!" Apart from its sounding more like a 125th Street wisecrack than the greeting of a peon, the story reflected a certain black skepticism, which OWI had found in a sample of black opinion, along with outcroppings of sympathy for the "colored" Japanese.[81]

In the main, however, African Americans as well as whites at least tolerated calls for "national unity." Moreover, the war was accompanied by a boom in radio and in recorded music, two media that, along with theatrically performed music, drew audiences of an urbane, "hep," "otherdirected" (as David Riesman would call them), youthful taste-culture that seemed most open to change. Indeed, a reading of *Variety,* the "house paper" in every theatrical hotel on the circuits, revealed an otherwise hidden watershed in American race relations, one driven by the young and hep of both races. "Colored Bands' Bonanza" was one of hundreds of headlines heralding the penetration of blacks into white show business. Black combos signed with white agents in order to get the newly opened gigs—some of them as sidemen with white bands led by Gene Krupa, Benny Goodman, and Charlie Spivak. Sister Rosetta Tharpe, the Golden Gate Quartet, Lucky Millinder—acts that rarely had played outside of black circuits—joined the Ink Spots as crossovers, and some of them, Jimmie Lunceford for example, played Southern dates that included whites in the audiences. As the lines between the races blurred, the Apollo itself booked "ofay [white] dates" such as Charlie Barnett and Louis Prima (whose driving beat led some fans to think him black). Broadway joined the trend with a rash of black shows such as Mike Todd's *The Hot Mikado,* a roadshow *Porgy and Bess,* and Ed Sullivan's "tab" show, *Harlem Cavalcade.* Elsewhere Duke Ellington filled the cathedral of white culture, Carnegie Hall, and the United Service Organizations (USO) began booking black talent for camp shows. Busy black bands began refusing tough gigs like state fairs, demanding larger fees, and seeking dates in big hotels. *Variety* reported that "the shortage of colored bands is more acute than in the ofay field."[82] Dramatic theatre filled the void left by the old Federal Theatre with revivals of *Porgy,* a stock company *Petrified Forest,* and Canada Lee in *Native Son* and as Caliban in *The Tempest.* The American Negro Theatre did Philip Yordan's Polish melodrama, *Anna Lucasta,* and Abram Hill's *Walk Hard* (with Robert Earl Jones, while also playing New Haven in John Patrick's *The Hasty Heart*).[83]

More than any other performer, Paul Robeson rode the mood. His leftist activism, which had taken him to prewar Russia and Spain and thrust him into any number of picket lines protesting discrimination, merged with his performing career. In concerts, a tour with *Othello,* broadcasts, war bond drives, appeals for a second front in western Europe, and singing on demand the liberal anthem "Ballad for Americans," he combined performance with protest.[84] Other actors grew as bold. Road companies elected to pass up segregated theatres, Ruby Elzy quit a roadshow *Porgy* rather than stay in a Jim Crow hotel, and in 1944 accommodating Bill Robinson spoke from the stage against racism. *Variety* itself was caught up in the rush of events and once played such stories on page one for five straight weeks.[85]

Of all the media, radio leapt into the war with the most fervor, probably with one eye on federal monitors who expected it of them and the other eye on audience ratings. The keynote was sounded by endless plays of "Ballad for Americans." Its sentiments echoed on all sorts of programs: talkshows, black time slots, and primetime variety. Among them were Roi Ottley's *New World A'Comin'* on Harlem's WLIB; *Men o' War*, a black show from Great Lakes Naval Station; KNX's *These Are Americans;* Blue Network's *America's Town Meeting of the Air;* and one-shots like Wendell Willkie's reading of *An Open Letter on Race Hatred* following a racial riot in Detroit. Late in the war, Kate Smith on *We the People* boldly called for an end to racial antipathy, not "at a conference table in Geneva" but "in your own home"; the show drew twenty thousand requests for reprints. Even soap operas joined in: *Our Gal Sunday* and *The Romance of Helen Trent* each introduced a black role, while CBS fished for a black audience with its sitcom *Blueberry Hill.* And in primetime, certified lefties such as Norman Corwin wrote occasional race angled dramas.[86]

The armed forces made a couple of gestures of their own in keeping with a mood they probably preferred to do without. In the first case, an American bomber flown by Colin Kelly, a Southern Presbyterian, in late 1941 attacked a Japanese freighter it had mistaken for *Haruna*, the largest cruiser in the Imperial Navy. His bombardier was a Jew named Meyer Levin. Hungry for news of an American score, someone at the navy's press desk noticed the ethnicity of the crew and played it up. Thereafter, despite the mistaken identity of the ship, the story became a subject of a movie, an issue of *True Comics*, and an inspiration for Howard Hawks's *Air Force* (1943). Days earlier at Pearl Harbor, Dorie Miller, a black messman (the only rating open to blacks), had leapt into a dead gunner's seat on the deck of a bombed and burning battleship and begun firing at the enemy bombers. The incident took weeks to reach the white press, but the black press picked up on it because of its peculiar meaning to African Americans: Miller had been freed from his place in the galley by the opening of the war. Like Hezdrel in *The Green Pastures*, he could no longer wait for divine intercession and had taken up arms without waiting for God.[87]

Hollywood in much the same desperate way bumbled into the war. Even before OWI opened its doors, movies, particularly those with East Coast pedigrees such as Lillian Hellman's *The Little Foxes* (1942), kept their strong black roles. Or sometimes a small gesture revealed some conscience-liberal sensibility behind a decision. Take, for example, a mere blip on the screen in John Huston's *The Maltese Falcon* (1941), a fraction of a second that no viewer at the time ever recorded, but nonetheless an image that required forethought and action, if no more than a telephone call specifically asking for two black extras rather than the whites who routinely would have been cast. Sam Spade has in his hands the black bird on which the plot hangs; to protect it from the heavies, he deposits it in a checkroom. In the blink of an eye a neatly dressed black couple rendezvous at the counter and silently walk out of the frame. The moment added nothing to the story, but *someone* at Warner willfully ordered *black* extras months before the idea occurred to anyone in the NAACP.[88]

In a more substantial case, Warner's flawed but reverent adaptation of Ellen Glasgow's Pulitzer Prize–winning novel, *In This Our Life* (1941), a film by two certified liberals, John Huston and Howard Koch, there was a scene of uncommon boldness—so much so that the actor at the center of the frame, Ernest Anderson, received reports that black soldiers at a Southern post stopped the showing and demanded the rerunning of the key scene. One of its stars, Bette Davis, remembered it for the rest of her life and put it in her memoirs. "There was a first in this film," she wrote. "The Negro boy played by Ernest Anderson was written and performed as an educated person. This caused a great deal of joy among Negroes. They were tired of the Stepin Fetchit version of their people."[89]

In the sequence, a spoiled Southern girl evades a charge of hit-and-run driving by blaming Parry Clay, a black student and handyman. Anderson recalled a messenger delivering freshly revised blue pages in which his studious character was expected to "revert to type" and, while in his cell, whine for mercy. He took up the revisions with Huston, arguing for the integrity of the role, after which the director dismissed the rewrites as "the wrong pages" and allowed his actor to give it a more modern reading.[90] As released, Anderson's scenes held a muted strength and a credible tension that gave Davis a chance to act with her usual authority by giving her a self-possessed character against whom to play. Moreover, a glance at the script and the press books suggests that the final cut of the movie, although solidly in step with the changing times, had been designed as a more conventional vehicle. As though ransacking Hollywood's racial past, the script called for Clay's jailmate to sing the stereotyped "Nobody Knows the Trouble I've Seen" in a circle of shabby "darkies," one of whom squats in the pose of a gorilla.[91] The advertising played Anderson with similar ambiguity. He was credited with graduation from both Dunbar High School in Washington and Northwestern, but as though being cut to fit a Booker T. Washington mold, he was described as a discovery among the studio porters, attending night school to obtain a teacher's certificate so he could raise up his race.[92]

The shot heard round African America. Parry Clay (Ernest Anderson) stands up to a *bête blanc,* thereby earning a flurry of black fan mail in praise of *In This Our Life* (1941).

The point is not to catch Hollywood in a few vestiges of its past, but rather to see what Anderson saw—that black audiences had *noticed. In This Our Life* inspired a batch of letters not only from the race's leaders but from the black middle-class moviegoers, who fairly sang of the new note in Hollywood's treatment of the race as normal and intelligent. A spokeswoman for the oldest of black sororities, Alpha Kappa Alpha, expressed deep gratitude for Anderson's portrayal of Parry as a human being rather than a stock black grotesque, an event she construed as Warner's new policy. The most acute sensor of change was John S. Holley, a black Washingtonian and frequent letterwriter to the studios. With uncommon acuity he praised Anderson while pointing out the jarring old-style figures in the cells. Moreover, he reported that exhibitors had cut Anderson's scenes. Thus, the movie in a way unearthed a sort of organically grown cadre of sensitive viewers where none had stood before, a group the AKA sister regarded as breaking with the habit of indifference with which older fans had greeted movies.[93]

Whites too got the message, not always approvingly. *Daily Variety* praised Anderson as a "standout," particularly in his big scene, but the Atlanta censor promised that if the racial politics were not changed there would be trouble in Southern cities. As though confirming the reportedly heightened black attention to movies that broke with the past, one of Breen's informants attributed the increased impertinence of blacks to Hollywood's constantly promoting the Negro.[94] Together with other signs of the impending war, this ferment must have begun to prepare audiences for a war that would destabilize racial arrangements, set loose forces for change, and provide guidance for the conscience-liberal movies to follow. Unpremeditated, fragile, untested, this linkage between war and social change gave blacks unprecedented access to the medium. That this was viewed in Washington as merely necessitarian quickly came to be seen by black activists as beside the point.

2

Wendell and Walter Go to Hollywood

The world's war came home to America on December 7, 1941, years after it had been set alight in Asia and Europe. Typically, Americans responded slowly, even fitfully, to war. Yet the conscience-liberalism that had already begun to tinge popular culture leapt as though from a crouch into a position of almost organic ideological leadership far beyond the modest measures urged by government.

As we have seen, Walter White, by then not only a ranking figure in the NAACP but a syndicated columnist, and a hero among blacks for his reportage of lynching, had begun to regard Hollywood as a target of opportunity. Already he had cultivated the producer Walter Wanger and Wendell Willkie, the defeated Republican presidential candidate in 1940 who had taken on two key posts: special counsel to the NAACP and chairman of the board of 20th Century–Fox. As he told Wanger, he had been "overwhelmed at your not only being willing to give me advice but to give a luncheon for me in Hollywood." They soon began to exchange pamphlets and lists of likeminded friends: Melvyn Douglas, who had taken up the cause of black children, Selznick, Sidney Buchman, who had White to a tea for the Hollywood Anti-Nazi League, Bette Davis, who seemed "very militant," James Cagney, and others who seemed "interested in" the cause or simply had appeared in social problem movies.[1]

For its part, the government inched toward propaganda as a smarmy business that the other side stooped to. At first only humdrum offices took up the duty: Government Reports, Facts and Figures, and, inside the Office of Emergency Management, a Division of Information. They were led by straight-arrow Middle Westerners who at first seemed merely competent—Milton Eisenhower from Agriculture, Elmer Davis, a radio commentator whom *Time* called "clearheaded [and] sensible," and Archibald MacLeish, a poet who promised a "strategy of truth" rather than "ballyhoo methods." Not until summer 1942 would Roosevelt create the Office of War Information.[2]

The task for African Americans was to smooth over internal differences and present a front that White—or someone—could appear to lead. Black opinion needed that sort of organic leadership to give focus to sentiments that ranged from those held by Cayton's friends, for whom the war was "on you white folks," to those of people for whom war was an eternally unrequited opportunity to win full citizenship in return for service. The trick would be for White or another to find some play in the government's propaganda and Hollywood's movies into which blacks might insinuate bargains for promised incremental social gains. Already the roster of black volunteers included most newspaper editors, the NAACP and NUL, the filmmakers William D. Alexander and Oscar Micheaux, and Richard Wright. Far from seeing themselves as dupes of a meretricious white government, they stood as black activists in common cause with conscience-liberals, whose propaganda of national unity might be turned to goals shared with African America.[3]

And of course they had their point. Every black American knew the details of FDR's "black cabinet" appointments, his wife's standing up for Marian Anderson in a gesture that a majority of Americans endorsed, Executive Order 8802 that had created the FEPC, and other favors that for the second time in American history led black parents to name their children "Roosevelt." Already, William Nunn's *Pittsburgh Courier* had begun its Double V campaign with its attendant beauty contests and essay competitions designed to suggest an unbreakable linkage between the national struggle against fascism and the black struggle against racism.[4]

If things went well for blacks, this symbiosis of political futures would grow increasingly public, bringing to an end the traditional black clientage in the Republican party while providing a platform for greater activism within Democratic wartime Washington (and Hollywood). Although at first mainly vague and ceremonial and embedded in high-flown rhetoric such as the Atlantic Charter, the way lay open to convert the ephemeral to the substantive.

The intellectual subflooring for such a new political construction was already in place in the form of a half-century-long popularization of certain anthropological theories that fell under the rubric of "cultural relativism." How this academic pursuit worked to popularize liberal notions of race may be seen in the wartime uses to which the work of the anthropologist Ruth Benedict was put. For years Franz Boas and his students at Columbia had worked out the theory, which holds that culture is learned rather than innate and that therefore cultures (rather than "races") are comparable only with respect to their utility to their group even though they might seem inferior as against Western culture. In the 1920s this new anthropology passed into popular culture when Margaret Mead, a Boas pupil whose windblown likeness to the aviator Amelia Earhart assured her a degree of popular idolatry, wrote an account of childrearing practices in the South Pacific that became a hit among young moderns in search of a guiltfree way to emancipate mothers from ancient ties to *Kinder-Kirche-Küche*.

In 1934 Ruth Benedict wrote a synthesis of the new anthropology in *Patterns of Culture*, which, like Mead's work, became a tabletop success. In 1940, with Boas's encouragement, she brought out *Race: Science and Politics*, an indictment of racism grounded in the idea of cultural relativism. Then came the war, and her book suddenly became the source for a pamphlet circulated among soldiers and civilians alike and then the theme of a widely shown animated movie on "brotherhood." Later, in courses on "tolerance," national committees on racism, and the "social engineering" movement, she offered her work as an antidote to Nazi racism and an assertion that "a nation could be administered without creating victims."[5] Thus the popularized work of anthropologists anticipated a wartime transformation of cultural relativism into a weapon against racism in various popular media.

Thus the incipient alliance of Hollywood, African Americans, and the OWI acted in an environment already made fertile by a popular anthropology rooted in the idea of a multiethnic culture in which everyone had a place. *Newsweek*, for example, noticed Americans finding not only ever more occasions to sing "Ballad for Americans" and thus "wave the flag for tolerance," but even to overflow with such feeling, as they once did in 1939 when Robeson sang the song to a broadcasting studio audience and received a twenty-minute ovation. Educators traded upon it by slipping shards of the mentality into their textbooks, sometimes drawing the wrath of conservatives in fear of change. They formed committees to promote "education through democracy," read magazines like *Common Ground*, and attended symposia on topics such as "Pluralism and Intellectual Democracy." On the eve of war in 1940 the *New York Times* described the trend as a conviction that democracy was "a real, dynamic burning creed worth fighting for." When war came, it was an easy matter to retool the idea into personal testaments such as James B. Conant's *Fighting Faith* (1942) and into U.S. Office of Education tracts on "Education and National Defense." Together they provided a warborne mentality that anticipated the actual advocacy of the still vague conscience-liberalism.[6]

Obviously there was a broadly popular response to the coming of a world war, as well as more specific responses such as Jewish Hollywood's alertness to "these fascist-ridden times." But what of conventional Hollywood genre films, the bread-and-butter of the movielots? How would the war affect, say, typical adventure movies set in the rimlands of "civilization"? Could the "natives" be relocated in the center of the frame and the action with an actual investment in the outcome of the plots? And would each breach of movie formula, each resulting ambiguity, raise contradictions that would challenge surviving conventions and stereotypes, thereby opening up the prospect of fresh formulations grounded in a new politics of race and culture? And could all of this be guided by leaders thrust to the fore from the ranks of minorities themselves?

Some of these intimations of change may be taken up by studying *Sundown* (1941), mainly because documentation of the circumstances of its production survives. Henry Hathaway's African adventure yarn arrived in New York only two weeks after Pearl Harbor, that is, preceded by the ebb and flow of the North African campaign of Field Marshals Montgomery and Rommel. The impact on the movie may be felt in the reception given it by a staff reviewer on the Maryland Censor Board. On his analysis card he wrote that *Sundown* "concerns German inspired uprisings among the native tribes of the Dark Continent and the bearing of such agitations on current world conflicts." In other words, in a single sentence a veteran reviewer's train of thought leapt from mere Hollywood convention—the natives of darkest Africa—to the film's "bearing" on the present.[7]

Indeed, not only had *Sundown,* a prewar purchase as a stock African escapade, been adapted to the war but, in keeping with the Atlantic Charter, it proposed a sketchy successor to colonialism that closely paralleled such a plan proposed by the British Empire Marketing Board. Its release date almost gave it an aura of prescient journalism. Both Hollywood and the *Saturday Evening Post* had bought Barré Lyndon's novel, only to have it rendered moot as the British, Italians, and Germans swept to and fro across the Sahara, struggling for control of the Suez Canal and the oil reserves of the Persian Gulf. It began its run in the *Post* in January 1941 while the fighting stalled, ending a month later as fresh Afrika Korps patrols clashed with forward British units. In this serial form it was no more than a tribute to the bearers of "the white man's burden" in the Horn of Africa during a squabble between tribal enemies and a band of renegade "Shifta." Meanwhile, in Hollywood on February 21, a typist finished Lyndon's first draft script, in which no German yet appeared; a lone Italian was a "residente" on the post rather than a prisoner, and the Shifta were trading gold for weapons, including a machinegun that mischievous Arabs have allowed them to test. Incredibly, Lyndon's blacks were mere "wogs" and their women "spoiled by their splayed nostrils and heavy lips." At last, in April the blue pages reflected events in the war, specifically the British taking of Addis Ababa from the Italians on April 5: The hero asks leave to reconnoiter the tribes now that Abyssinia is "ours."[8]

By then Rommel's armor had thrown the British back into Egypt, save for a besieged force in Tobruk, and settled in for the summer. Then on June 14, as Tobruk repulsed an assault, Walter Wanger, the producer, wrote to his new friend, Walter White, describing the changes in Lyndon's yarn that war had wrought. He began as Harry Levette might have done—by counting the "colored boys" hired to play Lyndon's "wogs"—but ended with a conscience-liberal stress on the respect earned by, and the appreciation of, Negro courage and loyalty that the war had made possible. Next day in the script the Italian was strengthened into a political analyst and pacifist with chunks of expository dialogue to explain the place of Africa in the war. In the last two weeks of June, as the British countered Rommel's thrust, Pallini, the Italian, was given a speech explaining the Germans' geopolitical plot to use Africa as a bridge to Japan. By then the weapons had become Skoda rifles from occupied Czechoslovakia to be used to strike the British rear in the horn of Africa. Finally, Kuypens, a Dutch mineralogist, was rewritten into a German agent. Another character, Zia, an Arab trader with no visible politics, was reshaped into an Anglophile who draws a confession from the German that it is he who runs guns to the renegades.[9]

As the film evolved, Wanger must have recalled that the politics of *Blockade*, his Spanish Civil War film, were slashed by the PCA, for he allowed the script of *Sundown* into their hands for mere hours, delivering it on a Monday and insisting on its return for shooting on the following morning.[10] We cannot know all the details of the transformation that led to this point, but we can know that Wanger took it up with the NAACP's man in Hollywood and that he incorporated a liberal angle into its formerly politically empty plot line. As released it was starkly remote from its origins in the *Post:* It had become colonial without being colonialist; its black soldiers had wives and lived by plausibly authentic customs; its last reel is a half-strangled promise of a new postwar arrangement for Africa. However oblique and muted, Africans had an investment in the outcome of war and movie. Even so, it was all too clear that *Sundown* was not a tract but still a yarn. It received mixed reviews, one focusing on its giving Gene Tierney (Zia) "more important" work, another carping at it as "slick magazine . . . fustian" typical of Wanger's "again trying to mix melodrama with a message."[11]

In any case, *Sundown* opens on a British outpost as it braces for trouble. Its black "Askaris"—soldiers—have already taken casualties, some of whom are buried by their keening widows, who toss clods of earth on their graves. A shadowy German presence threatens a fragile tribal peace. Into the camp comes Zia, the half-caste boss of a network of caravan routes, which in German hands would provide a channel

On its face no more than a conventional African yarn, *Sundown* placed the British army and the Masai tribe of East Africa in alliance against the renegade "Shifta" in a partnership that promised to reach beyond the war years (Bruce Cabot and extras). Copyright United Artists.

through which to arm the tribes and bring the Luftwaffe within range of Suez. At last Zia agrees to side with the British, leading to a chase across the desert, a nighttime assault on the Germans' tribal allies, and a daring rescue of Zia (and thus of British fortunes).

But parallel to this colonialist skeleton outline is another line that not only provides an obligatory romance but also an anti-imperialist sidebar, perhaps a product of the liaison between the Walters, Wanger and White.[12] Thus with America's entry into the war still months away, Hollywood began to adapt its formulas to new conditions. Zia, for example, in Lyndon's novel is no more than an Arab pawn to be won early on, but in the movie she grows into an active force in the outcome of the game. Moreover, in the end she marries a Canadian, evading the PCA proscription against miscegenation by being revealed as merely an *adopted* Arab! B-movie improbabilities aside, beginning with her first meal in camp the old racial rules are overturned. The officers' mess is set as usual, Arabs outside the netting. Besides, says one old hand, she is "chi chi"—a mestiza against whom "even the natives discriminate." But Crawford the Canadian (Bruce Cabot) is having none of it. Not only does he dine with her outside the netting, he explains his motives by invoking the American nonceword *discrimination*, and as though reading from an OWI memorandum he promises that the England that is going to win the war will change much of that sort of "nonsense."

At that moment an incredible union of iconography and audience-memory provides an eerie contrast between Hollywood's old and new versions of Africa. Harry Carey walks into the frame, costumed precisely as he had been in 1931 when he played the title role in *Trader Horn* (shot on location not far from *Sundown*'s purported locale). Looking not a day older, he was an icon expressing Hollywood's shift from the old jungle genre to its wartime mode. Of course there is no record of a spectator noticing; certainly no reviewer recorded it. But the scene must have resonated with some sense of changing political values.

Finally, the new mentality toward Africa is asserted in a last-reel coda. After the British have vanquished the pro-German renegades and restored order to the tribes, the most racist of British officers, as he lies dying from wounds, spills out an odd tale of his father, an Anglican priest who had tried without success to implant in his son a sort of progressive colonialism. Zia and Crawford go to him to be married in his church, which has been ruined by German bombs. With an ethereal light glinting through the splintered roof, they are married as the priest (Cedric Hardwicke) calls for an eventual victory founded upon all churches in alliance. The movie ends with the audience sensing that they will return to an Africa cleansed of colonialism and open to a new day.

If released during the previous year, *Sundown* surely would have earned Wanger a congressional inquiry into his warmongering. But appearing as it did, following Pearl Harbor by two weeks and accompanied by an internationalist slant to its pre-Christmas advertising, *Sundown* took on an authority and voice unwarranted by its own limited merits as melodrama. Bosley Crowther in the *Times* sensed the added weight that the moment had given movies and referred to it in his reviews: *Major Barbara* ("produced in a war-wracked England against odds which only the stiffest courage could lick"); *Sergeant York* ("about the possible involvement of our country in another deadly world war"); *Target for Tonight* ("courage and strength of the British under fire"); and others. Of course, the changing times opened up the movies to a wide range of readings, and *Sundown* was no exception: Crowther may have seen his movies through the prism of war, but a colleague on the *Times* dismissed *Sundown* as no more than "the Boy Scouts in Africa" bent upon saving it "for the British."[13]

Nevertheless, as the war changed random ingredients in the old formulas, it exposed contradictions and forced adaptions to new conditions. Similarly, as even the cheapest Saturday jungle movies introduced their Africans to the center of the frame and the action and gave them a stake in the outcomes of plots, some stereotypes persisted like stains in an old rug, while others faded in the light shed by the war. In Tarzan movies, for example, Sol Lesser quickly adapted the series to the war by replacing the usual ivory poachers with Nazi heavies. In *Tarzan Triumphs* (1943) the Germans force Tarzan to recapitulate the popular notion of the American entry into the war: First they violate his territory; then Zandra, an obligatory white princess of a lost tribe, warns him that if they conquer her land, he is next; and finally, after they fire upon his son, Tarzan boils over—"Now Tarzan make war!" he says. Moreover, Tarzan's "biographer," Gabe Essoe, reported that such incidents followed directly from State Department entreaties to turn the King of the Jungle into a "propaganda weapon."[14]

The introduction of geopolitics into the genre also thrust the painted natives into unfamiliar roles where they grew articulate, prepossessing, and alert to the impact of the war on their domains. As early as 1940, Universal's B-movie *Zanzibar* added a diplomatic crisis to the plot that had been borrowed from an actual clause in the Versailles treaty obliging the Germans to return to the British the skull of a deceased sultan as a talisman of hegemony over East Africa. Thus a mere programmer was made timely by setting it amidst an actual issue: If the heavies succeed in snatching the relic they will destabilize Africa, reopening it to the Germans who had lost it in 1919, whereas if the British hold it there is a *Sundown*-like hint of a postcolonial form of self-determination.[15]

Obviously, portraying Africa as a flashpoint in a global war could lead to scrapping profitable Hollywood formulas, but it also contrasted old with new and raised up creative ambiguities. In *Zanzibar,* for instance, the howling, savage spearbearers are contrasted with Chief Umboga (Everett Brown), who calmly bargains with the British to pacify his people, driven to frenzy by wardrums. The implied paternalism, if anyone noticed, allowed scant inference that he might ever challenge the right of the British to rule his people; nonetheless, the scene played to expectations raised in the era of *Sundown* and the Atlantic Charter.[16]

Of course, a conventional Hollywood solution to unruly, ill-fitting new ideas was to erase them into absentia, or to reshape them into racially neutral, honey-colored exotics. Much as Tarzan stumbled upon the occasional lost white tribe, so in *Drums of the Congo* (1942) the veteran Ernest Whitman was the only black Hollywood regular with a substantive role. Instead there were improbably lightskinned Dorothy Dandridge and Turhan Bey, a Turk who spent a busy decade playing roles that blacks might once have read for. Unfortunately, the actors blamed the resulting black absence not on the wartime drift but rather on a rift in black circles caused by Eastern black activists, whose pressure threatened to erase stock black roles while providing no compensatory bread-and-butter roles.[17]

Clearly, a few not entirely sanguine changes in formula factors did not constitute a revolution. Nevertheless, of the hundred or so movies released in the weeks following Pearl Harbor, a considerable number anticipated changes yet to come. True, *Variety*'s reviewers still spotted survivals of the past, much as astrology coexisted with astronomy: Mantan Moreland's "popeyed porter [who was] fast becoming a fixture in Monogram's pictures," or Louise Beavers's "colored slavey" who seemed "held down." But arrant breaches of etiquette took on a life of their own. Dooley Wilson began the war as Sam the pianist in *Casablanca*, spoke flippantly of a white woman ("if she was black she'd be beautiful") in *Louisiana Purchase*, and joined with white servants in an egalitarian union in *Higher and Higher*.[18] In odd cases, the custom of writing out racial material grew lax. For example, before the war, convention obliged writers to cut scenes such as those involving a creole mistress in the operetta *Naughty Marietta* (1935). But in the 1941 remake of Rex Beach's Klondike gold rush yarn, *The Spoilers* (1906), a whimsical racial scene that had been written out all of previous versions was written back in by Tom Reed and Lawrence Hazard as a neatly turned bit played between John Wayne and Marietta Canty.[19]

Moreover, audiences, or at least the reviewers who wrote for them, took notice. *Time* and *Newsweek*, for example, grumbled at vestiges of plantation movies as a "bad scene" marked by "absurd" black characters. Critics routinely cited black actors as never before, praising Dooley Wilson in *Casablanca*, for example, as "a Negro 'find'" and "the best of the supporting players." A "white" fan magazine even asked Jimmie Lunceford for an essay on the changing times. One black critic hit upon the notion of a structured absence of black roles: In *The Grapes of Wrath*, he reported, "you know they're there by their absence." Even the Hollywood Negroes met to discuss "some sort of check" on "derogatory types." Finally, Walter White began to form a strategy to promote "film[s] about the Negro . . . pictured neither as a buffoon nor as a humble servant," and to complain against specific sequences such as those portraying wild-eyed, manic John Brown in *Santa Fe Trail*. At the same time, a *Times* man thought that even the casual neighborhood moviegoer seemed ready for a break with Hollywood's "all-too-familiar escapist fare."[20]

Could any coherence and direction be given this drift? Walter White, anticipating Nunn's Double V, gave it a try, calling for a dual "fight for liberties here while waging war against dictators abroad."[21] If only he, or someone, could harness this loosely phrased mentality felt singly by Hollywood's anti-Nazi Jews, New Dealers in search of means of recruiting black voters, and African Americans seeking to engage in war, without seeming to be profiteers off its tragedies. And if shared sentiments could be converted into activism, how could short-run national necessity be shaped into a long-run politics of civil rights? That conscience-liberals began to link their goals both to Hollywood's engine of popular culture and to Allied war aims may be seen in White's correspondence. One letterwriter, for instance, praised Metro's B-movie *Dr.*

Kildare's New Assistant (1942) for its multinational cast, "a nice United Nations touch," but also saw a missed chance to insert a bit of the unfolding conscience-liberalism in the form of a black doctor. "Don't they see how they can pioneer a new free world by employing such touches?" she asked rhetorically. And yet she was delighted by the prospect of a crusade against Hollywood "as stirring and promising as any of the principles set forth in the Atlantic Charter."[22]

Less than a week after his column calling for a dual campaign against fascism and racism, White met Lowell Mellett, a Scripps-Howard journalist whom Roosevelt had drafted to take over the motion picture section of OWI. Mellett wished him well and promised to "put in a word" for White in Hollywood, as White began to weigh how to call in debts Hollywood had incurred when he testified on its behalf before the Senate committee investigating its "warmongering." In return White looked to the movielots for help in putting a new African American on the screen. In what amounted to a planted story, the columnist Thornton Delahanty charted a possible course and also hinted at a threat of government intervention: "Washington officials . . . have made it plain to studio executives that the government is definitely interested in having the negro presented properly on the screen," he wrote, and "by slow, and in some cases painful, degrees the film industry is coming around."[23]

Only a fortnight after Pearl Harbor, then, White seemed poised to intrude into the arena described by Delahanty. His friend at court was to be Wendell Willkie, the politician with one foot in the NAACP and the other on the Fox lot.[24] As though heavensent, Willkie's multiple image as Republican liberal, folkish Hoosier, and studio boss, as well as his high tolerance for long lunches with White, suited the task at hand. "I ought to have a tiny bit of influence right now," he told White. "Let's go out to Hollywood and talk with the more intelligent people in the industry to see what can be done." From this opening White began to rough out a year's campaigning that enlisted Willkie for a major address to the NAACP's impending convention in Los Angeles itself, a date in turn made possible by Mellett's helping skirt federal restrictions on needless travel.[25] Meanwhile, White resumed his cultivation of Wanger, Darryl Zanuck, and other moguls, along with leftist actors such as Jean Muir, Melvyn Douglas, and his activist wife, Helen Gahagan. Tied in with Willkie's appearance in the massive sienna-colored Shrine Auditorium, White planned addresses at the city's two major universities and several black churches. Out of all this was to come some shared ideological position toward, as White told Douglas, prodding moviemen "to broaden the roles in which Negroes are pictured."[26] If they won this strange new game, White and his friends would have aligned, however temporarily, African American social goals with the war aims of the nation as expressed in unfocused rhetoric such as Roosevelt's "four freedoms" speech and the Atlantic Charter, echoes of the prewar, left-liberal, antifascist "popular front," and the still-forming mentality of the OWI and its Hollywood branch under Nelson Poynter, yet another newspaperman.[27]

Already those movies in the assembly line or in release unbidden by pressure groups allowed White a good feeling that a genuine movement was marshaling at his back. In fact, he used *In This Our Life* as an opening gun after a friend had touted it as unprecedented because "a Negro is given an opportunity to explain to white folks his ambitions." See it, he urged White, "because it is the type of example you wish to give to movie producers for future pictures." White was a quick study and learned to praise right conduct and to announce his arrival, first by telling Olivia de Havilland of the "spontaneous applause" that had greeted her character's siding with the black student, then by thanking Harry Warner for "the dignified presentation of the young Negro [that] is a refreshing change from the traditional treatment," and finally by (wrongly) attributing it to the "progress" that had ensued after his and Willkie's work.[28]

Actually, at first the campaign met scattered resistance. Within the NAACP were those who sniffed at the Hollywood sojourns as "Walter's thing," an obsessive need to hang about with the famous. Black Hollywood constituted a sort of disloyal opposition bent upon protecting their investment in the status quo and their roles as scamps, savages, and flunkies. On the lots every studio had at least one resident Southerner such as Y. Frank Freeman at Paramount, a "thoroughly unreconstructed Southerner" next to whom White sat at one of Willkie's lunches. And OWI was always of two minds; the official line disavowed any "attempt to solve the problem of Negro-white relations," but its conscience-liberal cell kept "in constant touch" with Hollywood and, as Poynter did, boasted of hectoring Sam Goldwyn "to convert him to our way of thinking." Already, Roy Wilkins had reported that blacks had bluntly turned a meeting on "the morale of the Negro troups" into a vocal demand for "corrective action about the mistreatment of the Negro throughout the whole war effort."[29]

From the beginning White pressed Mellett of OWI to reach beyond the merely necessitarian and even to remain alert to the impact of movies on foreign markets. "I hope you will keep in mind in your new job the necessity of films taking a more enlightened attitude in the picturing of so-called colored people," wrote White as he linked the "constant irritation" of blacks to the "infinite harm in Latin America" caused by moviemade racism. Mellett, for his part, not only promised "to put in a word to the same purpose," but wangled a ticket for Willkie's trip to Hollywood.[30]

Hollywood liberals seemed ready for him. They went to see *Jump for Joy*, a liberal, satiric revue at the Mayan Theatre, where they watched "dicty Negroes" and "ofays"—Harlem patois for snooty blacks and whites—interact. In one skit, Uncle Tom's Cabin has become a "chicken shack" at Hollywood and Vine serving a menu of "social demands as potent as spice." Avanelle Harris, a cast member, recalled that "its message caused a wave of enthusiasm throughout the cast." The angels were themselves Hollywoodians, ranging from moguls like Joe Pasternak to New York lefties such as John Garfield to the new blacks in town, Dorothy Dandridge, Herb Jeffries, and Ellington's singer, Ivie Anderson.[31]

By early 1942, White had arrived on the scene for a schedule of lunches in the commissaries, a meeting at the Academy, a night of tablehopping at the Oscar dinner, speaking dates—six of them in San Francisco—and meetings with "small groups of writers and producers" rendered compliant by, he said, "the terrible pressure upon us" brought "by the war." Ever reminding Willkie of his work on their behalf when the Senate "was trying to lynch the movies," White arrived in February armed with letters of introduction (one from Eleanor Roosevelt), stayed at the lilywhite Roosevelt Hotel, and met with Will Hays, a delegation of local blacks, and moguls who seemed agreeable to "broadening the treatment of the Negro in the moving picture."[32]

If his groundwork lacked thoroughness, it was in its neglect of black Hollywood and his impact on their livelihoods. They hated everything about him: his Eastern roots, his liberal friends, his access to hotels and movielots, his neglect of their stake, even his pinkish pallor and straight hair, with the result that they stiffened against him and thus came across as reactionaries. More than a quarter of a century later Eddie Anderson, a scampish valet to Jack Benny's parsimonious employer, remembered White with unconcealed contempt as "an Eastern phoney trying to be white." White's black counsel responded in kind. "Most of them are ignorant," wrote one man, "[and] can only fit in with the parts they have been playing anyway." Another source dismissed them as "limited in background and appearance" and unable therefore to carry off the roles of ingenues or heroes.[33]

Separating the two factions was an ideological gulf. On the one side stood White's urbane liberalism; on the other a deeply rooted, old-fashioned individualism and its virtues of hard work and earned increments. Many black actors had begun by answering "cattle calls," registering with Charles Butler's segregated version of Central Casting, and hanging out on the corners of Central Avenue, the main drag of "darktown," in the faint hope of being collected by a studio bus in search of extras. By the time of White's arrival many of them enjoyed the security of contracts and regarded themselves as members of a talented guild. Some, like Stepin Fetchit, Bill Robinson, Hattie McDaniel, and Louise Beavers, saw themselves as interracial goodwill ambassadors whose charm contributed materially to good race relations. In no case did

Willie Best (*right*) in the sort of residual bread-and-butter role in *The Kansan* (1943) that earned him a bungalow on South Hobart. Copyright United Artists.

they concur in the low estimates of their work that White's advisers held.

Two typical cases were McDaniel and Willie Best. If Best's bio is to be believed, he was discovered strolling down Central Avenue but bolted fearing arrest by a white man who turned out to be a talent scout. He soon became a "colored star," that is, a featured player with a familiar shtick, a variation of Fetchit's style that earned a six-month contract at $300 per week, a limit on furloughs, and a nice house on South Hobart. McDaniel, a Middle Western veteran of church choirs, temperance union drama contests, vaudeville, and a stretch on the Optimistic Donuts radio show, broke into movies in 1932. She built her career on an accommodating, motherly obesity that helped her win roles. "Everybody loves me," she once said. "When I'm working I mind my own business and do what I am told to do." When White arrived she earned more than $2000 per week.[34]

Of course, Best and McDaniel belonged to an elite. Beneath them was a vast army of the underemployed, including McDaniel's brother Sam, who measured his career in terms of occasional days rather than weeks. Below him were the bit players who worked a for a few dollars a day, a box lunch, and bus fare. In the middle range were those, like Hattie's colleague on *Gone with the Wind,* Butterfly McQueen, whose price during the war reached $600 per week. Their work and its rewards mirrored lives strikingly like those in other crafts: Although a rare black actor earned more than a comparable white, in the main only a few blacks reached the middle range of white actors, and for many there was no floor, no net, beneath their lives on the lowest rung.[35]

But as a group they formed a conservative anchor against White's work, partly because they were not merely actors but solid Los Angelenos who held jobs in the county civil service, appeared in local nightclubs and on radio, and ran storefront acting schools. Moreover, they practiced civic virtue as volunteers in churches, fundraisers, sorority and fraternity officers. Thus for White they seemed no more than rigid, peasant *kulaks* whose prosperous but precarious status warped their politics into a narrow, touchy "false consciousness" that boggled his mind.[36] Therefore, for them he could be no more than a Stalin calling for the destruction of their class. And of course, their fate during the war as adventure yarns migrated from jungles to deserts—being structured out of gigs by Turhan Bey, Frank Lackteen, Abner Biberman, and other whites with a vaguely Asian cast to their features—confirmed them in their worst fears. In domestic dramas the erasure of blacks came as mere wartime realism; Hollywood's notion of the American family tightened down to a servantless nucleus. In musicals, sleek, fair-skinned Easterners got all the gigs—or so it seemed to black Hollywood as they watched Lena Horne, whom they regarded as White's "girl," win a long-term contract. Of course, this slippage in their fortunes had begun in the 1930s, and White therefore became a scapegoat for a trend larger than his campaign. Bill Robinson and Stepin Fetchit had already suffered dropped options and slipped into B-movies. Others hung on as regulars only in cheap programmers: Fred Toones as "Snowflake" in B-westerns, George Reed as a butler in Metro's Kildare series, Mantan Moreland as a bug-eyed driver in Monogram's Charlie Chan series. The women slipped into blessedly invisible radio where they need not compete with younger Easterners. The trend rendered useless Clarence Muse's warning to the young Dorothy Dandridge that "if colored kids get into a scene here, they want them to look black and Negroid."[37]

Their fate seemed maddeningly cruel. Not even their white friends on the lots—and they *had* white friends at the top—could save them. Muse had been Frank Capra's good luck charm in several movies; Eddie Anderson seemed so centered in Jack Benny's act as to seem the *cause* of Benny's success; at Fox Robinson had been the tail of Shirley Temple's comet, so when she burned out, so did he; and on the same lot Fetchit and Will Rogers teamed so closely that friends thought of Rogers as Step's "rabbi," so when Rogers died in a plane crash, Fetchit's career died with him. Trained practitioners like the choiristers Eva Jessye,

Katharine Dunham, Jester Hairston, and Hall Johnson fell back on their music. Canada Lee and a few others could play Broadway when things slumped. And in one instance a studio actually sought out a fabled black performer, Paul Robeson, to break his boycott against Hollywood—which "entirely ignores the many dynamic forces in the world today," he had said—and play in *Tales of Manhattan* (1944).[38] But for most Hollywood Negroes the war grew into a personal and professional disaster.

And yet White's work went badly and provided scant gains to compensate for the suffering of black Hollywood. Not that the moguls stiffed him. Rather, he had not learned his craft of lobbyist, and he and Willkie had miscalculated many of their tactics. White seemed to snub the actors, the local NAACP, and the black press. Willkie forgot the fear generated in the hearts of the moguls by their masters in their New York offices; a few letters from them might have far outweighed letters from Eleanor Roosevelt. Besides, White neglected to learn his way through the maze of Hollywood gatekeepers, agents, and changed addresses, and so squandered hours, even days, mailing notes that came back "not at this add.," leaving his cards in anterooms, scribbling fruitless invitations to meet "any time." At the same time his "thing," his wish to know the famous, led him to cultivate actors, who, as any fan knew, were rendered impotent by their fears of moguls, dropped options, and spiteful gossip columnists.[39]

Moreover, in the early rounds of luncheons White, whose prose often crackled with accusatory imagery, seemed daunted by his elite company. At one lunch at Fox it was Willkie who seemed "hard-hitting and uncompromising," while White merely allayed "fear . . . of any reforms which might cut down box-office returns." Meanwhile, the snubbed local blacks held their own meetings to assert a place for their craft and promote the sort of all-black movies that White found "completely jim-crow"; once one of them even urged seizing the property of Japanese who had been "relocated" in Idaho. And White, now that he had the moguls' ears, received only the dullest of advice, as from Edgar Dale, who urged giving awards to worthy films, making educational films, and planting in features occasional blacks "doing skilled and professional work."[40] Thus in the early moments White flopped for want of a simple, neatly put angle that accommodated past practice while feeling its way toward a new genre that opened movies to the "new Negro."

At his last luncheon on his last day, White sat with the moguls in the Biltmore while the liberals among them picked at their food as though awaiting a sign. He and Willkie intended to return in July, but they needed to be told something—now. "I make one-sixth of the pictures made in Hollywood," said Darryl Zanuck with exaggerated diffidence, "and I never thought of this until you presented the facts." White could hardly lecture them on how to make movies, but they were entitled to some formulation of what the facts meant and how to behave toward them. Waving aside threats, prescriptions, and calls for a token Negro in the Hays office, he asked simply that they show "the Negro as a normal human being and integral part of human life and activity." As he left these powerful men whose company he relished, he felt a clear sense of impending change. As he told a friend on the *Los Angeles News*, when he and Willkie returned they would hold substantive meetings with Wanger, Zanuck, and the rest; then the screenwriters; and, through Cagney and Douglas, perhaps a session with the Screen Actors Guild, at which they would present their plea for "the Negro as a normal human being." Uncannily, he had hit on the *raison d'être* of the old black Lincoln Motion Picture Company in 1915: "to picture the Negro as he is in his every day life." The only difference between them was White's goal of promoting the agenda among powerful white men—and the fact that a world war had helped return the issue to a national scale.[41]

This last event loomed even as the war drove into exile from Frankfurt the cell of Marxist critics who shared the common finding that, as one of them, Theodor Adorno, argued, "the ideas of order [that popular culture] inculcates are always those of the status quo." Even though this was certainly so in the Nazi Germany they were on the run from, White's chore was to hold up as a collective goal the notion that the spontaneity, brashness, and abrasive urbanity of popular cultures would be renewed by war and thereby override the caution and profiteering that drove the business end of show business. The communally shared values that the war stirred might yet induce, as Feibleman suggested, a mood in which blacks might join in defining a new set of terms on which life in America in the future might be based. Thus if the government cried "unity," then conscience-liberals might put their own stamps on it by crying "brotherhood." The increasing frequency with which these noncewords were heard testified to the possibility of a changed mentality of the majority, which might tolerate a challenge to the traditional marginality of blacks. Certainly the Gallup polls that affirmed a general support for the FEPC and other measures attested to the prospect. Surely White thought so, perhaps even feeling that the war had placed the wind at his back.[42] Indeed, his mere presence on the lots was a clear sign of an emergent liberalism. If only he—or the writers—could come up with a genre of war movies that built upon the familiar social problem movies of the Depression years, grant African Americans citizenship in that screen world, put forth a postwar black social agenda, and challenge the pessimism of the Frankfurt analysts, for whom the apparently realistic Depression movies had provided, as Adorno argued, not genuine visions of empowerment but only "solutions [that] would be impossible for them to use . . . in their own lives." Perhaps he could convert the legends of Colin Kelly, Meyer Levin, and Dorie Miller into a formula similar to that already being written for Hawks's *Air Force*.[43]

If only, White wrote, he and Willkie in July could "come back to the coast and finish this job before they cool off or go too far in making all-colored pictures instead of doing the much more important job of decent treatment of the Negro in all pictures." He admitted that in February "they could give me the runaround and get away with it," but this time, with Willkie in tandem, "promises made to Willkie and me jointly would commit them in a fashion they would not dare go back on." In addition he looked to two new weapons. He broadened his circle to include more imposing figures—not only actors but Henry Jaffe, counsel for their guild. Also, OWI had moved into Hollywood and Vine as, he told a friend, "one of the opening guns" in the government's campaign to improve "the status of the Negro in the war."[44]

But what to tell them to produce? He badly needed an angle, some-

World War II, by straining the capacity of public accommodations, as in this Southern bus station, called into question the high cost of maintaining old forms of racial discrimination. OWI-LC.

thing like Roi Ottley's notion of a "New World A'Comin'" coupled with something as substantive as the old Reconstruction cry of "forty acres and a mule." Otherwise, he could offer no lesson plan to accompany the "audiovisual aid" that Hollywood might become. Moreover, within African America his formulation must offer a plausible rebuttal to Cayton's ironic story of the 'cropper who had heard the "Japs declared war on you white folks," indeed must show that the Axis had also declared war on black America and that therefore black Americans would have a stake in the outcome.

A prototype appeared even before White's first journey to the coast. The *Courier*'s Double V campaign ran for weeks through the spring and into the summer, all the while urging black participation in the war against the day of victory when blacks could call in the resulting debt. The kernel of the idea had come from James G. Thompson, a black cafeteria worker at Cessna Aircraft in Wichita. "Like all true Americans," he harbored "a desire for complete victory over the forces of evil which threaten our existence today" even to the point "that we sacrifice every other ambition." But a black patriot could not help but ask: "Should I sacrifice my life to live half American?" Obviously, no. "Victory over our enemies from without" must be linked to, he wrote, "victory over our enemies from within." One of the editors thought that the resulting campaign had already opened up war industries and the officer corps to blacks, resulting in a show of mutual "good faith intentions."[45] It remained only for White and his friends to formulate Thompson's rhetoric into a movie genre.

The first NAACP handout set forth a dichotomy between Axis racism and anticipated American liberalism. "The Axis has utilized Race as a cardinal principle in its arsenal of propaganda," it said of a German "orgy of anti-Semitism" and the Japanese "slogans of Asiatic tribalism." Americans, then, could do nothing less than put aside racial antipathies in the interest of "national unity." For White, then, the role of Hollywood became clear. "If we [say] . . . the American motion picture has rendered disservice to the principles of racial equity," he wrote, "we do so only to identify the mood and temper of the American people today." The modern temper required a repudiation of these old, divisive images: "the Negro as a barbaric dolt, a superstition-ridden ninny . . . a race of intellectual inferiors, cowardly, benighted, different from the superior group." And in their places the nation did not need "a public relations campaign . . . to whitewash us . . . but in the name of those ideas for which all of us are now fighting, we ask that the Negro be given full citizenship in the world of the movie." At the same time, he argued that no studio should erase history by committing "the sin of narrow realism" by picturing poverty and such without reference to the "sad and ugly things that have made them so."[46]

Meanwhile, White prepared for his July return to Hollywood's popping flashbulbs, drinks at the Garden of Allah, chicken soup with the moguls, caucuses with the stars, and stories in *Variety* as the star of "confabs with film execs." He began filing movie reviews into piles of good and bad racial bits: *Sullivan's Travels* and *Blossoms in the Dust*—good, *Belle Starr, Maryland,* and *The March of Time*—bad. He learned to comment on every sort of racial nuance, panning *Young Dr. Kildare* for its stock servant while touting its brownskinned doctor or carping at Metro for its Tarzan series while nagging them for the thin ranks of blacks on the lot. Through Henry Jaffe he caught the ear of Abel Green of *Variety,* who began to play up White's work. So when Hobe Morrison of *Variety* cited a movie in which "one of the sightseer-extras is a Negro, a genuinely realistic touch," White, whose ego was as big as the Ritz, could attribute the bit to his own "fine Italian hand."[47]

At last, in July the NAACP convened under the yellow minarets of the Shrine Auditorium, the Hollywood Negroes all but invisible, the spotlight on Willkie's closing speech. We cannot guess how the studios might have handled the social angles of the war without the NAACP's prodding, but after the cheering died, at the lunch White and Willkie took with seventy moguls, guild members, MPPDA staff, and the Hollywood Victory Committee, Walter Wanger portrayed the movies as "the most valuable means . . . for spreading the American way of life." The difference between this and all previous self-congratulatory patriotism was that African America had been painted into the scene. As White recalled it, he asked the moguls for "a new day" marked by parallel abandonment of stereotypes and a "broadening" of the range of roles. "Delay invites danger," he said. Reporting back to the NAACP, he predicted "a truer picture of the Negro as a normal member of society and an integral part of the civilization of our country and the world."[48]

His brave front aside, White's actual accomplishment remained ambiguous. Apart from the faithful—Wanger and Zanuck—the moguls when not merely balky were at least edgy toward a pushy outsider. Indeed, White found himself in a role analogous to that of Booker T. Washington, a black Republican wirepuller whose power over blacks was a byproduct of his influence over whites, but who could never know the actual limits of white fealty. Some moguls, like Frank Freeman, had predictably declined, but so too had the hoped-for Sam Goldwyn. And of those at table, surely several agreed with Mendel Silberberg, a studio lawyer who doubted that White's "continued presence will be of much value." Hollywood, he said, was "filled with groups and committees trying to put certain thoughts and views into motion pictures," and most of them "soon wear out their welcome."[49] Even Nelson Poynter, OWI's man in Hollywood, despite his willingness "to constantly urge upon the industry the elimination of the negro stereotype" and "the screen's tradition of 'the old Selznick South,'" steered White toward "periodic visits'' rather than some sort of NAACP Hollywood bureau (an idea that, in fact, had occurred to White).[50]

If these forces amounted to no more than low-voltage moral suasion, they must also be seen as signs that the government of the United States, after a hiatus of more than half a century, had begun to take up the black condition as a matter of national interest. For example, one group of OWI monitors reviewed movies not for their impact upon America but rather as eventual exports to allies, usage as armed forces fare, and even for showing to lands regained from the enemy. While carrying no political weight, their judgments revealed a rising expectation of changes in Hollywood's black imagery. ''We are particularly interested in all appearances of dark-skinned races,'' said Edward Barnhart's staff manual. On forms that looked dully like all other such data-gathering forms, the viewers analyzed the quality of ethnic portrayals with uncommon acuity that led to eventual attainments as critics, among them Dorothy B. Jones, Barbara Deming, and Philip T. Hartung (he only weeks away from taking up a column in the liberal Catholic weekly, *Commonweal*).[51]

There is no way of knowing whether White contributed to their sharpened eye for conscience-liberalism, but it certainly colored their

The war provided Sammy Morrison the opportunity to crack the ranks of the East Side Kids, as here in *That Gang of Mine*. Copyright Monogram Pictures.

later work. "Rain, no game," sneered Hartung when *Stormy Weather*, the sort of all-black musical that repelled White, appeared. Deming even grew testy at the slow pace of Hollywood's breaking with "its stakes in the status quo." On the job they overlooked nothing. For instance, in taking up Sam Katzman's *Smart Alecks*, one of a B-movie Dead End Kids series, the viewer took notice of the addendum of a black kid (Sammy Morrison) to the gang, his wearing of his skin as though a jaunty cap rather than a scar, his link to his mother rather than seeming to be a lone black figure in a sea of whites, and his election to say the gang's prayer over a fallen buddy. Another singled out an angry black servant who snapped, "I ain't accustomed to be talked to like trash." And Deming, the sharpest of them, liked the interracial group of sailors who "live [and] pray together" in a coast guard film. Of course, the studio bosses read none of this, but the OWI unit nonetheless reflected a sensibility that was a direct result of the crisis of war and eventually extended to critics in both regional and metropolitan presses. Moreover, whenever the black press learned of it they offered it as a sign of changing times. For example, when the *Richmond News-Leader* said of Ethel Waters in *Cairo* (1942), "There were plenty of times when it seemed the camera hunted her out to the exclusion of the other actors," the *Courier* ran a sidebar on it. At the same time, Southern audiences, led by exhibitors fearing lost sales, theatregoers hungry for liberal drama such as *The Little Foxes*, critics who resented the paternalism, and perhaps the Yankee soldiers on local posts, pressed censors to relax their racial vigilance. For example, when *The Little Foxes* was censored in Memphis, exhibitors on the west bank of the Mississippi played it up as the one "they would not show in Memphis."[52]

Meanwhile, in Hollywood, as movies ground their ways through the system, White waited for those that might show signs of his hand. But as Zanuck had told him in July, "it takes anywhere from three to six months or a year for pictures to get into release." Moreover, Zanuck, who would grow into a genuine ally, insisted that heavyhanded gestures—threats or the appointment of a Negro to the PCA—would be "misunderstood as pertaining to censorship," and therefore White should "leave the whole matter to . . . the individual studios."[53] As for the others, they offered incantation and remembrance of past favors as much as they proposed action. The Warners touted the already released *In This Our Life*. Trem Carr of Monogram, like many others, hollowly promised that "at first opportunity I am going to discuss it with our producers." Others were more vague, promising only to "act in every way possible to further this vital education."[54] Of course there were dissenters. B. G. "Buddy" De Sylva of Paramount lumped White with the advocates of the Double V as war profiteers. "I was a bit riled recently by some of the negro spokesmen who said the negro shouldn't be sent to war unless he could receive equal benefits with the white man," he complained. "I think it is a bad time for the negro to 'try to make a deal.'"[55]

In the face of this resistance White began to press too hard, perhaps beyond where the NAACP might have wished to go. "I consider the matter of the treatment of the Negro in motion pictures of such importance that it takes rank over some other phases of our work," he told Joseph Breen of the PCA. Although his files were thick with expressions of the goodwill of white men, complaints from black fans, memoranda on bits "degrading to Negroes," movie reviews, reports of threatened theatre boycotts, and plans to broaden the coalition, White had not made a single substantive suggestion to the moviemen, had failed to engage the black press, which was beholden to exhibitors for advertising revenue, and had not reached an accommodation with black Hollywood.[56] Other than a few pleas for more bourgeois blacks in crowd scenes, he offered no new angles, no entertaining fusion of politics and art, not even the eventual formulation of introducing a lone Negro into the ranks of a white group; he still knew only what he did *not* want on the screen. The war itself had leapt ahead of him in the way that newspapers played the assimilationist stories of Colin Kelly, Meyer Levin, and Dorie Miller, yet their stories as movie metaphors had so far crossed no Hollywood minds.[57]

This failure of movie politics may be seen in two aborted propaganda movies: Metro's *Liberty Ship* and Warner's *The Launching of the Booker T. Washington*. Both were tributes to the unlovely "liberty ships" that had been cobbled together in haste to meet the shortage of freighters caused by German submarine warfare. Each had stalled, in no small measure as a result of the black characters that had been introduced, perhaps at the behest of White, but had been so garbled as to be unusable. For example, both scripts took up the intricate matter of equitable housing for war workers in such a way as to be divisive.

Both scripts centered on the same nugget of conflict—the black defector in need of moral suasion—and ended on a note of triumph, the launching of a liberty ship as a symbol of interracial achievement. MGM's *Liberty Ship* strayed from its black angle by improbably introducing foreign agents who momentarily win over a black stevedore, as though only duping rather than genuine issues might tempt an African American to turn traitor. In any event, in the last reel he returns to the fold, presumably proving to white people, as the script argued, that blacks embraced the civic virtues of patriotism and loyalty. Out at Warner's lot, Gordon Hollingshead's shorts unit took up *The Launching of the Booker T. Washington*, a story that focused on a Negro who refuses to fight, but ended on the launching, which again confirmed the contribution of African Americans to the war.[58]

Of the two, *Liberty Ship* held out less promise, mainly because its authors failed to deal simultaneously with blacks' rage at the status quo and blacks' faith in their investment in the outcome of the war; that is, they failed to produce a fair fictional replication of the reality of many black warriors. Instead the plot wanders into a longshoreman's buying his mother a house in a white neighborhood, thus supposedly showing the breakdown of old ways as a result of the war, but also leading the storyline off on a cross-purposed tangent. Warner's *Booker T.* took the same line, opening on a squalid alley in the shadow of the capital, an echo of a prewar shot of Dingman's Alley taken by a Farm Security Administration (FSA) photographer. Reinforcing this contradiction between national purpose and national practice, an angry newsy snarls out the day's headline, a story of "Whites Who Refused Occupancy" to a new black tenant. Only a remarkably sophisticated denouement saves the day by balancing two black views of the situation. On the one hand a black soldier acts as mouthpiece for the Double V, refusing to fight for what is bad, he says, but unafraid of fighting for the good to come. Yet as one voice says, the soldier was not advocating mere accommodation: Never learn to accept racism, he says, without raising a fuss. As though unsure of herself the author, Lillian Hellman, added a hyperbolic coda, a socko last-reel tableau with Paul Robeson and the Fisk Jubilee Singers at the Lincoln Memorial on the eightieth anniversary of Emancipation.[59]

Only a thin paper trail survives from the *Liberty Ship* idea, but the Warner Archive allows us a glimpse of the tenuous interaction among OWI, Hollywood, and the NAACP in balancing minority demands for justice and the government's requirements for propaganda. After White's first visit, *Variety* had played the story under a page-one banner, "Better Breaks for Negroes in H'wood," but by May Hellman's script arrived at Warner's and was filed under "Negro Picture." Not until late summer when he called upon Poynter in Washington did White learn of "the Hellman story." We have scant evidence that White had a hand in what followed. All we know is that on October 8 Jack Warner told Hollingshead to get busy on rewriting the Hellman short even if he had to put a writer on overtime, certainly a small sacrifice for his country, Warner said.[60] Perhaps meant only to pad the file with evidence of the studio's patriotism, the memorandum also allowed the inference that Jack Warner had felt pressure from the propwash of White's activities. For whatever reason, by late summer the studio had in hand a script drawn from an actual incident: Marian Anderson's christening of the *Booker T.*, an event that occurred amidst the flurry of black attention to movies. The ceremony, following close upon White's summer visit, had been recorded on newsfilm.

At the same time the black press rushed to cover movies as though at last something big was afoot. If anyone in Hollywood read it, the press must have seemed a warning flare of an impending attack. The *California Eagle* urged its readers to protest to Mellett the release of Metro's *Tennessee Johnson*, a biopic of President Andrew Johnson that nettled black intellectuals because of its crabbed view of Thaddeus Stevens, a hero of black Reconstruction; another protest was directed at Sam Goldwyn's decision to rerelease *The Real Glory* (1939), a colonialist melodrama of American guerrilla war in the Philippines. Goldwyn's decision to reconsider because of the offense given to Filipino allies was taken as "a demonstration of the fact that Hollywood can be whipped into line." In the same week, the *Courier* reported that the pledges given at White's luncheons had been "unanimous." In other reports, episodes featuring a black sailor in Fox's *Crash Dive* were said to be based upon Dorie Miller's big day at Pearl Harbor. On the Warner lot, a black reporter interviewed Bogart, Garfield, and others, drawing from them testimony of their rising liberal mentality. Finally, Jack Warner himself faced pressure. Months earlier in a letter he had pled a paucity of material as an excuse for not filling the screens with black stories—a letter the *Courier* ran on September 26 as though it were exhibit A in a murder trial.[61] Yet another story broke on November 14, too late to affect *Booker T.* but nonetheless part of the rising mood. Apparently Metro had been trying to alter *Liberty Ship* in some way and had fired Caleb Peterson, a young black actor and one of White's most acute informants. A quick note to Howard Dietz at MGM, one of White's most trusted studio men, saved not only Peterson's gig but also another role in a feature film. As Peterson reported to White: "When your information regarding Liberty Ship reached the Coast, they immediately put the colored boy's role back in Bataan Patrol."[62] Taken together, these events suggest that Hollywood had grown accessible to blacks and responded to the conscience-liberal mood that had grown out of the necessitarian aspects of the war.

Whatever its motives, Warner's memorandum went out on a Thursday; on Friday Hollingshead reported that Vincent Sherman was eager to rewrite Hellman's treatment. On Saturday Poynter sent clippings on another black story to goad them on. By Sunday night Sherman and Hollingshead finished their draft and launched *Booker T.*—at the behest of Mellett's OWI. On October 21 they shot locations at Terminal Island, where the ship lay moored while getting rigged for sea, and by November 11 Sherman finished a final draft of the shooting script.[63] It proved a marvel of conscience-liberalism. More than any *completed* movie it took up issues of abiding concern to blacks, hinted at a postwar social agenda, and ended on an integrationist metaphor that echoed Dorie Miller and Colin Kelly—the *Booker T.* setting sail with a "mixed crew."

Along the way to this closure every sequence included what amounted to an official line: as many groups as possible represented in each shot, an improbable black foreman named Ross who reports to the boss that blacks are happy working in the yard and he fears only an emotional overflow on the night of a Joe Louis boxing match, an ironic bit in which a black soldier is refused service at a lunch counter by a white cook who is a fan of Louis's. The rest of the story, told in the dark

Wartime "fair employment practices," at least in some industries, altered the racial etiquette of the workday—as here in the Maryland Shipbuilding and Drydock Company—and formed the backstory of the aborted *The Launching of the Booker T. Washington.* OWI-LC.

streets prowled by the mob overheated by Louis's victory, wins over the soldier to a view of the war broader than merely a white man's war. As the story developed, Hellman's bluntness, such as a flashback to a lynching, was softened while conscience-liberalism was punched up. Sure, lynching happens, but faith in the future, not an urge for revenge, must guide the soldier. Besides, only liberal gestures can save racists from themselves. Fade out on the mixed crew.[64]

At this moment, still remote from a final cut, *Booker T.* may have helped OWI define its mission and move away from Hollywood's usual erasure of the place of blacks in history toward a formulation of a cinematic liberalism. Within OWI a desktop struggle had broken out between competing visions of the war as it affected African Americans. Some men urged a radical black cinema ending with a promised place in postwar America, while others drew the line at "agitating for social equality." Farthest to the left was the notion that an "immediate goal" of wartime America was "to achieve equality of opportunity," an outcome set forth by the creation of the FEPC. As a result of the debate, Sherman's soldier was to become a civilian who is persuaded to enlist, thereby refuting a white opinion that blacks were shirking. OWI's man in Hollywood mediated by asking Hollingshead to "discard" ("rewrite" would have been the verb of choice in polite Hollywood) the script in favor of an angle that equally stressed black dignity and white tolerance with a closure on a harmonious wish for a greater black share in the prosecution of the war effort.[65] At this moment of conscience-liberal epiphany the project stalled and expired. Nonetheless, the debates it had set alight clarified the complex process through which a black genre of war movies would emerge. In fact, in the end both the agency and the studio agreed on a sketch for future scripts that conformed precisely to the outlines put forth in the *Courier*'s Double V campaign. Still open to debate was the matter of how to translate their concept into familiar Hollywood conventions. In a sense *Booker T.* had become a confluence at which the OWI, NAACP, and Hollywood came together to form a civil consensus that had agreed to consider African America as entitled to a share in the stakes of the war. Of course, a cabal of OWI bureaucrats, black lobbyists, and Hollywoodians, should not be expected to produce many films, but they had at least all learned something about how racial propaganda might be put on the screen.

That this complex machinery might actually work may be seen in Metro's *Shoe Shine Boy* (1943), a mere short but one that at least survived to reach the screen. The film historian Lewis Jacobs, then a scriptwriter in the shorts unit, induced the studio to buy Ellick Moll's *Saturday Evening Post* story, assigned Walter Hart to direct, recruited a black kid from the janitorial crew, and egged the actor Sam Levene to work cheap, all in response to a sensed demand for, as Jacobs termed them, "progressive films." In the tightly wound style of half-hour radio shows the story unfolds: A bootblack yearning to be an army bugler buys a pawnshop bugle, begs an audition, and earns a chance to blow for the army. The white habitues of his corner urge him on, and at the climax Levene sends him off with a little speech. You are a true American, he says, blow one in Hitler's eye for us. The kid replies with firm resolve and marches off, in the words of an OWI reviewer, "with troops in action, inspiring them to victory with his trumpet." More to the point, another OWI monitor, ignoring the patrioteering, observed that the kid was a refreshingly "true" sketch of a Negro. Yet by then Jacobs attributed such figures not to White's "hand," but to a war-propelled mood. "It couldn't be done without the war," he said, because "they could not refuse to do this kind of film for fear of appearing slack in 'doing their bit.'"[66] Indeed, by the end of the year the studios were already stirring such bits into their feature-film formulas, much as White, OWI, and the moguls had apparently agreed they would do.

It remained only for moviemakers to take the audience into the arrangement, to make movies that engaged the viewer's sense of the fun of moviegoing rather than, as was reported of showings of the anti-Semitic *Der Ewige Jude* in Germany, all but requiring audiences to remain in their seats during propaganda showings. In this way the alliance that the crisis of war had created would blend good moviemaking with newly phrased unifying ideals, thereby making use of the legitimacy and authority that popularity often confers and thus using popular culture to change ideas rather than to ratify the status quo. Moreover, if the ensuing movies were good enough to endure as classics, they might reach far beyond their merely necessitarian uses and serve a postwar agenda. Such an outcome, of course, rested not upon the merits of the message but rather upon the achievement of making movies good enough to bear the burden of racial politics in a familiar, pleasing style.[67]

In this sense, these three short, aborted, or rarely seen films provided an apprenticeship, a semester of boning up in the relative calm of the shorts units. Feature films were another matter. If Huston and Selznick were already reflecting a national mood in their treatments of *In This Our Life* and *Gone with the Wind*, then only a light hand on the process might be called for. Such a tactic would not be a mere pose; rather, it might appeal to all democracies that were unwilling to stage-manage ideologies yet wished to promote some worthy ideal as a manifestation of national virtue. So the pose of choice for these aliens in Hollywood was that of shy pupil making a suggestion for the class field trip. OWI, for example, despite the conscience-liberal mentality of some of its agents, never officially claimed to wish more than "a representative portrayal of Americans at war" that included "a sprinkling of average looking Negro people." And always they disavowed any intention "to solve the problem of Negro-white relations." Even White liked to ask for only benign goals such as vaguely harmonizing American ideals with practices, hoping that liberal movies would promote "a bond between the races" as "the fundamental thing in the war we are fighting." In any case, the studio bosses did join a wave of ceremonial liberalism—brotherhood weeks and such—by writing checks and chairing committees, as N. Peter Rathvon of RKO and Selznick did for a Victory Through Brotherhood campaign. In private OWI and NAACP played more aggressive roles. "Make them toe the line," demanded one of White's friends. "Mellett Wants to See Scripts," claimed a *Hollywood Reporter* headline that portrayed OWI as a threat to the hegemony of the moguls. And OWI's man on Hollywood and Vine, Nelson Poynter, asserted a duty "to constantly urge" changed black roles, pass on scripts that the NAACP might pitch to the studios, build a network of California blacks "whom we could call upon for advice," keep a weekly log of OWI's pressures on the studios, and keep a running file dedicated to "evaluation" of all movies in release.[68]

Of course, the results were uneven. And some lots such as Paramount, where Frank Freeman ruled, seemed antiquarian in mentality. Their *Dixie* (1943), a biopic of the minstrelman Dan Emmett, was slathered with sentiments established by Technicolor Currier and Ives prints under its main titles as though nothing had happened since 1935, when its director, Edward Sutherland, had made *Mississippi*. But World War II had happened, and as a sign of it *Commonweal* critic Philip T. Hartung, who also reviewed for OWI, panned it for its lack of "social consciousness" and its "Hollywood crooning darkies" that perhaps would have passed unremarked before the war. Yet even Paramount sometimes went along, as in *Star Spangled Rhythm* (1942), which Bing Crosby ended, as though speaking for OWI, by calling for the unity of all the Washingtons—George, Martha, and Booker T.![69]

At the least, however, White, the OWI, and Hollywood, thrust together by the circumstance of war, had drawn the attention of their constituencies to a fresh way of viewing African Americans on the screen and had offered a standard of "progress" that, while hardly contractual, provided a measure of the studios' conduct.[70]

Moreover, White's sense of the politics of art gradually grew from mere connoisseurship toward a broader social vision. Leftist critics of White's work, though, moved by the increasing centrality of movies in their lives, impatiently called for an end to White's "attack via the luncheon table" and the taking up of some sort of "mass action." In fact, he sometimes joined them on special occasions. "The Clarence Muses . . . can spoil nearly everything you and I and the rest of us have been fighting for," he wrote to Fredi Washington, a striking-looking if underused actress whom Adam Clayton Powell had hired for his *People's Voice*. Other blacks tested his pledges by sailing black scripts "over the transom," keeping score in their columns, or playing both sides like Muse, who proclaimed himself as "a force in showlife" in White's camp while holding open the gates to the studios by insisting black actors had "no grievance with the producers."[71] Of course, the black right's refusal to adapt seemed to White's friends a wish "to be injured and insist on being injured" rather than enlist in the cause. But like logotypes on a box of pancake flour or grinning porters in a railway advertisement, they had become anachronisms tossed, as Trotsky had said of the Mensheviks, "into the rubbish-can of history." So in general the center of action was left to the liberals.[72]

White Hollywood, for its part, also enlisted in a liberal, ecumenical left composed of the American Writers Congress, the Hollywood Independent Citizens Committee for the Arts, Sciences, and Professions (HICCASP), and its lineal descendant the Hollywood Democratic Committee (HDC). Moreover, as their black members they solicited not the oldline Hollywoodians but the new crop of Easterners such as Lena Horne and Rex Ingram, and their programs began to reach beyond the culture of the screen toward direct action against local racial discrimination and toward recruiting for the NAACP. Farthest to the left was the Committee for Democratic Culture, which included the presumed Communists Howard Fast and Herman Shumlin and the blacks Fredi Washington and Kenneth Spencer.

Obviously wars breed a patriotic right as well as a left. The Motion Picture Alliance for the Preservation of American Values, for example, routinely linked the NAACP to the "reds." *Variety* itself, perhaps moved by the war's imperatives and stories of CPUSA infiltration of the studios, chided the Hollywood Writers' Congress (HWC), to whom White gave an address, for its attempt "to infiltrate pink and red propaganda into screenplays," prompting a denial from Roy Wilkins. And such alarms had their effects. Zanuck even addressed the HWC, warning them of rushing ahead of the audience's capacity for receiving change. And the writer Salka Viertel remembered she and her worried leftist friends agreed to "respect Hollywood taboos . . . [and] never to consider anything from an ideological . . . point of view."[73]

But taken as a whole, the attacks failed to diminish the significance of the attainment of black seats of power and persuasion in Washington and Hollywood. It remained only for the allies to assert a politics that might disarm the right by using popular culture as a national voice for admitting blacks to the nation's table. They needed only a genre of film that drew nutrients from wartime rhetoric, reduced issues to a human scale, featured stars unafraid to risk their villas on a political movie, and carried traits that might quickly grow familiar enough to earn the generic tag of "war movie." In such a package conscience-liberalism could head off carping from the right, generate a synergy with its audience, take on a life of its own, and offer a vehicle for conveying new racial politics where there had been none.

In this way, movies might create new conditions upon which blacks and whites might agree to fight a war together against external enemies. In place of an externally fixed notion of race relations, the changes brought on by the war might be portrayed as a sort of rolling frontier of shifting relationships that, once tested in genre movies, would seem an unthreatening means of doing what White had asked: granting "citizenship" to black characters in the movies and providing them with an investment in the outcome of the war.

3

The Making of a Genre: The Integration of Colin Kelly, Meyer Levin, and Dorie Miller

As Metro's *Liberty Ship* had been written to persuade white America of the loyalty of black America, so almost every movie that stemmed from White's work spoke to white people as much as to black. It was as though together the OWI-NAACP-Hollywood axis was an organic embodiment of the notion that crisis bred reassertions and enactments of the common core of values that the need for unity had called attention to. At the same time, the actual situation as old segregation barriers cracked under the stress of overcrowding, overburdened public amenities, and crumbling urban transport led to civil strife.

Using the legitimacy that the need for national unity bestowed upon them, conscience-liberal propagandists sought a movie version of Nunn's Double V, an iconic expression that wartime change and peacetime promise could be as one. As the scriptwriter Jesse L. Lasky, Jr., scribbled it on the title page of a script, their duty was a portrayal of a plural American way of life that included White's "normal" blacks.[1]

Black moviegoers not only shared a similar idea but more than ever told the studios their ideas. A black schoolteacher in St. Louis, for example, needled Warner for its lilywhite short *March On, America.* Such prejudiced films made her task doubly hard, she wrote, contrasting the studios' eager response to Roosevelt's Latin American "Good Neighbor Policy." Others sent the moguls' excuses for backsliding to the black press or plugged pet projects such as biographies of this or that African American worthy. That their nagging had an eventual impact was seen in the midst of the Harlem riot of 1943 when Lawrence D. Reddick, curator of the Schomburg Collection of Afro-American Culture, used Hollywood features as well as federal documentaries as magnets to draw Harlem's youth from the troubled streets. Manipulative, yes, but Reddick's tactic also revealed that the newly minted war movies attracted black audiences and provided an ideological alternative to mere rage. Necessitarian or not, the movies held out some sort of promise.[2]

As the scriptwriter Sidney Buchman explained the changed mood to a black reporter, "Hollywood as a whole has recently been made aware of the Negro's true position in America and our responsibility toward the subject." By this he meant not that he had been blind to the African American plight, but that the item had been reinserted in a national agenda and that Walter White had told him so.[3] The impact of this new mentality may be seen in the framing of *The Adventures of Mark Twain* (1942), a flawed biopic that came to White's attention as a result of his asking Arch Reeve of the MPPDA "how many companies are planning pictures in accordance with the pledges." Reeve had little to offer—a couple of deckhands in the *Twain* film—although unknown to him and without guidance from White, out in Burbank the script was already undergoing a wartime retooling. In one draft, Twain is made to seem an abolitionist. As he strolls in Hannibal, Missouri, he encounters a debate between Huck Finn and Tom Sawyer over who has the blackest ears. Nigger Jim is excluded because "niggers" do not count; the law says so. Then someone should change the law, Twain offers.[4] Only a month earlier Breen, whose politics were still locked into making movies merely inoffensive to blacks, had asked Warner to omit "nigger." Thereafter, Jesse Lasky reworked the script, calculatedly striving for a combination of box-office hit and propaganda for the American way. His dual success may be seen in a note from Poynter to Warner in terms so glowing as to seem a regimental citation, praising the studio for giving other nations an idea of "the American way."[5]

Of course, not every movie passed through this process. But the submittal of scripts to outsiders became almost routine, if for no other reason than that it earned the studios' way back into the good graces of a hostile Congress, thus giving them access to supplies of scarce film stock. Transformed from "warmonger" to "essential industry," Hollywood moviemakers became, said an admiring army officer, "a group of wholehearted, willing, patriotic, people trying to do something for the government."[6] Much as Stalin invoked Mother Russia as a goad to patriotism, so Hollywood's conscience-liberalism acquired official cachet. Not that OWI replaced the PCA as arbiter of movie content, but the interaction between the two agencies, along with the NAACP's and the black audience's angles, kept the products from becoming mere patriotic cant. Small deliberate acts—casting more black extras in uniform, for example—placed blacks on a war footing with whites and gave them a visually asserted stake in the outcome of the war. Yet as to an emergent genre of such war movies, by late 1942 there were still only rumors: a Dorie Miller biopic, a black deck officer in *Action in the North Atlantic,* and others. By 1943 Hawks's *Air Force* reminded viewers of the polyethnicity of Kelly's and Levin's adventure, but no Dorie Miller figure had appeared. Make the crew "a cross section of the allies," Hall Wallis had told his writer.[7]

The eventual substance of this still emerging new Negro was held hostage to the inability of conscience-liberals to put forth a figure that worked. If too insistent on a "full share in winning the war," the new man might seem an opportunist. If the OWI liberals themselves seemed too pushy, they risked nettling their congressional masters and even their colleagues who felt racial issues beyond the "responsibilities of an information service" and their duties limited to "better coverage of black beats." Finally, singling out ethnicity as an antidote to Hollywood's portrayal of blacks as "taking no part in the life of the nation" put the liberals in opposition to an official cant that defined America as "a melting pot, a nation of many races and creeds, who have demonstrated that they can live together and progress."[8]

To see how airy sentiment grew into substantive propaganda that pleased and touched its audiences, we must begin with a manageable sample of films: four self-defined "war movies," *Bataan, Sahara, Crash Dive,* and *Lifeboat;* two musicals that revealed the snares in celebrating black life by resorting to all-black milieux, *Cabin in the Sky* and *Stormy Weather; Tennessee Johnson,* a biopic of Andrew Johnson set in a populist fable of the rise of a common man; *Tales of Manhattan,* an anthology starring Paul Robeson in a violation of his promise never to work Hollywood; and *Since You Went Away,* a wistful sketch of the homefront with a sidelong glance at African America. On these movies rode the hopes of the conscience-liberal entente for a propaganda of wartime unity and postwar hope.

For workaday Hollywood the shift in ideology might even seem casual. There, almost any director might be assigned in a single year, as Victor Fleming was, *The Wizard of Oz* and *Gone with the Wind;* routinely contract directors stepped from one chore to another without pause, as Henry King did in *A Yank in the RAF* and *The Song of Bernadette.* Moreover, in the intensely political mood set by the war, personal politics often sharpened. Irving Rapper as dialogue coach on *In This Our Life* barely recalled Anderson's groundbreaking role at the beginning of the war, while at the end he remembered vividly a moment on the set of *The Voice of the Turtle* when Ronald Reagan, with a nod to Anderson (as an elevatorman), predicted a day when America would open up to blacks. George Murphy remembered his own hand in such a story on the set of *This Is the Army* when Michael Curtiz cued a chorus of black dancers by shouting, "Bring on the nigger troops." "Hold everything!" Murphy hollered, as he explained to Curtiz the offense taken by the dancers, who probably preferred "colored troops."[9]

Similar revelations emerged as little flashes of heightened consciousness in the writers' bungalows. John Howard Lawson reveled at his warborne opportunities to work into a string of assignments little flecks of CPUSA "popular front" images: Wanger's *Blockade*, the anti-Nazism of *Four Sons*, the black extras in *Action in the North Atlantic*, and finally *Sahara*, his most pointed essay on racial politics. Sidney Buchman, later fingered as "red" by HUAC, made a longer journey from *The Howards of Virginia* (1940), an anomaly that interwove the American Revolution and the plantation South, to *Talk of the Town* (1942), in which he wrote a solid role for the black actor Rex Ingram that was rooted in his growing sense that the "fundamental thing in this war we are fighting" was that democracy "must be extended and deepened in greater numbers of people among both white and colored." Robert Buckner, a Warner writer, followed a similar course from prewar westerns, among them *Santa Fe Trail*, in which John Brown's madness at Harper's Ferry was made more central than his racial politics, to *Mission to Moscow*, a midwar propaganda movie that included Haile Selassie's protest to the League of Nations against Mussolini's aggression, to *Rogue's Regiment* (1948), an homage to war movies that reaffirmed his wartime conversion. As he told *Ebony*: "I wrote . . . with no preachment, no dialect, none of the usual gags."[10]

Black actors, often from the East, not only played in these movies but, if they failed to give them appropriately modern readings, faced criticism from newly alerted reviewers. Leigh Whipper, the wizened original Crabman of *Porgy*, brought his role of Crooks, the stablehand in Steinbeck's *Of Mice and Men* (1940) from Broadway. But black bread-and-butter was still to be earned in movies like *The Vanishing Virginian* (1941), *Virginia* (1940), and *Robin Hood of the Pecos* (1941), in which he played so slavishly that the *Times* man wrote, "Honestly, we'd never have believed it if we hadn't seen it with our own eyes." At last he scored in the two best roles he would ever have: as Selassie and as Sparks, the preacher and unheeded conscience of a lynch mob in the movie of Walter Van Tilburg Clark's *The Ox-Bow Incident* (1943). But by then there was a rift between Whipper's style and new critical expectations, so the *Amsterdam* played both angles, praising him for using a "rare opportunity" with "dignity" but mourning the "servile" shtick that he brought to it.[11]

But until White and his allies produced a genre that challenged the popularity of Hollywood's South, and until opportunities extended beyond looking to the next bit, walk-on, one-line scene, two-day-with-lunch gig, the blacks had little to show for their work. Until then, success was measured in praise for giving dignity to a stock servant or exploiting some fissure in racial etiquette. As late as July 1943, White was still fobbing off proposed biopics of prim worthies that brought yawns from the movielots. Who would leap at a chance to shoot the Charles C. Spaulding saga of founding North Carolina Mutual Insurance? Who would plunge for a shot at the rights to the story of Félix Eboué, the anti-Vichy, black governor of French West Africa? No? How about an all-black musical? White winced at the idea of the voice of liberalism in the hands of moviemakers bent upon imitating, say, Oscar Micheaux's race movie *Swing*.[12] What, then?

Success for black activists could mean only a genre that caught the spirit the war had already defined as urgent: value-impregnated tales that, like all stuff of genres, ritually spoke to the central values of their audiences, in the process half-forming the mentalities they themselves were half-formed by. As the western endlessly teased the theme of the rugged loner versus society, its hero eternally reborn as towntamer, trailboss, ramrod (but never storekeeper or teacher or other more historically numerous figures), its plots forever drawing taut the play between rough West and effete East, ever worrying the contradiction between savagery and civilization in the American psyche, so conscience-liberals needed to invent a mythic cinema that played upon *their* audience's *Angst*.

Already they sensed their hero should not be too black, too much the loner, and should be, if done well, a black figure set down in a microcosmic company of whites (who would be the better for his having passed their way). Thus it came to pass that the metaphor of the lone Negro set down in a lost patrol, lifeboat, landing party, became the core of a polyethnic genre that would define a black place in American life for the next generation. Its apotheosis was to be reached when Sidney Poitier dropped in on a flock of nuns (rather than soldiers) in *Lilies of the Field* (1963), made them all the better for it, and won an Oscar for his rendering of the role.[13] Not that White's circle drafted a master template for the future. They had already been themselves half-formed by the war and were only half-forming the medium in the image they had begun to choose as the vehicle for conveying their politics.[14]

At last the genre of war movies emerged in late 1942 and early 1943, each one of them following a similar course to completion, screening, and reception. Each began as part of the institutional Hollywood system, grew to maturity in it, and along the way faced up to some sort of guidance or monitoring by the activists, then opened in the theatres, where at least some moviegoers noticed that they were different from the garden variety genre film. Common to them all, then, was not so much machine-tooling by a state apparatus of the sort that guided Fritz Hippler's *Der Ewige Jude* or Riefenstahl's *Triumph des Willens*, but a mentality shared by likeminded persons rendered so by the nature of the war.

Tales of Manhattan slipped through all of them—OWI, Zanuck's office at Fox, White's NAACP—mainly because it had been a "pickup," an independent production that Fox had agreed to distribute. "We were not consulted on this one," said OWI. And yet its makers—Sam Spiegel, a Pole who had represented Universal in Germany; Boris Morros, a Russian émigré; and the French refugee director Julien Duvivier—had concocted it over lunch one day at Chasen's. Together they shared an abiding European contempt for fascism mixed with a folkish image of African America that seemed to its American cameraman no more than "a Sunday shot of a Negro minstrel band." Its own star, Robeson, still being politically formed by the war and acquiring through it his Russian brand of heroic folkishness, would turn on the finished movie.[15] *Tennessee Johnson*, a biopic of President Andrew Johnson in which Congressman Thaddeus Stevens, a "radical" Republican and recently emerging hero of Reconstruction to many serious black readers, had been cast as a heavy, seemed also to slip through OWI checkpoints. Stevens had only just been restored to statesman status by W. E. B. DuBois's *Black Reconstruction* (1935) and James S. Allen's Marxist *Reconstruction: Battle for Democracy* (1937), which refuted the older notion of Reconstruction as a mere orgy of corruption and redefined Stevens as nemesis of the planter class and a source of black political hopes. Like *Tales of Manhattan*, it proved to be a poor choice of ground for a fight. Its blacks had been erased rather than maligned; its hero, though meant to express a populist wisdom, sullied his politics with an offputting peasant's rage at his betters. Then in the midst of production someone drew the attention of David Platt, the *Worker*'s critic, to it; he passed the word to the black press and this brought OWI and White to the Metro lot in Culver City. But even before that, MGM had elided Stevens's black mistress, and OWI had heard "that Negro circles are worried about this picture," a story Mellett hoped "is not justified."[16]

As *Tales of Manhattan* had been an idea of Sam Spiegel's circle, *Tennessee Johnson* also had come from an odd source, a dormant script in Metro's inventory that the conservative writers, Wells Root and John L. Balderston, had revived as a misguided vehicle to promote OWI-style unity. It had begun as *The Man on America's Conscience*, an attempt to rehabilitate Johnson's reputation, which had been sullied by well-known tales of drunkenness, intemperate petty rages, and, worst of all as far as blacks cared, his battles with "Radical" Republicans bent upon insinuating a place for freedmen in the post–Civil War South at the expense of the rulers of the defeated Confederacy. With this as its proposed theme, once White learned that the *Worker* wished to make an issue of it he had no choice but to join in or risk losing credibility. All through the summer the *Worker* had been campaigning for black attention and gratitude by urging racial integration of baseball as an antidote to its wartime decline in both talent and viable franchises, giving more coverage to the Negro leagues than did some black papers. In this setting,

White's work took on an unforeseen urgency and *Tennessee Johnson* an importance as an arena that no one would have freely chosen.[17]

Platt played it masterfully as a potential *The Birth of a Nation*, which he described as part of a pattern that included the rerelease of *The Real Glory*, the rumored cutting of the black scenes from *In This Our Life*, and several reports of recantations of the pledges to White. "Negro Press Attacks Jim Crow Movie, Praises Daily Worker's Campaign," ran one *Worker* headline.[18] Clearly White stood in danger of appearing as a toothless tiger, having elicited empty promises.

At this point, despite warnings from a story editor that both Marxist and black attacks soon would follow because of Stevens's role as a heavy who lived with a black woman, rejoiced at Lincoln's death, and took a hand in Johnson's impeachment, Metro assigned Balderston to rework Root's script. Balderston, who had settled into mere competence after two classic Frankenstein scripts in 1931, even took the trouble to consult the black writer Carlton Moss on how to handle Stevens. With almost all black roles erased anyway, Balderston correctly guessed that Stevens would grow as a point of contention rather than the larger issue of black image.[19] Early in August, Metro received a flurry of letters so tightly bunched and rhetorically alike as to hint of a common origin. In sum, they linked the current war for survival with the disunity that would ensue from a malignant portrayal of one of America's greatest defenders of African American rights. At first OWI and the liberal left waved aside the campaign as the work of radical blacks in league with the CPUSA.[20]

But then Poynter of Hollywood OWI routinely asked Metro for a copy of the script—none of the activists had read it—and for assurances that it would not "militate against . . . national unity," and enclosed a letter from White in which he urged research into DuBois or others who "have not been influenced by the Confederate point of view." White, for his part, intensified his preferred tactics: addressing the moguls in person, in this case Mayer himself and his daughter Irene (Mrs. Selznick), while warning Mellett that Stevens as heavy "would do enormous injury to morale."[21]

By the end of summer they had won their skirmish but lost Mayer's forebearance, if not his allegiance. In August, Mellett and Poynter took an agenda of proposed cuts to Mayer that by November resulted in "much reshooting and cutting." Mayer still treated White politely, reminiscing about a dinner at the Wangers, but to Poynter he played waspish inquisitor, asking if "a minority should dictate what shall be seen on the screen." And inside the walls in Culver City he grew "extremely upset" and railed at the intrusion as "directly a result of the Comunists"—including "the cell in the studio" who must have first leaked the story.[22]

Almost mindlessly an OWI reviewer lost sight of the real goals and treated the new final cut as a victory that it clearly was not. "The Negro question has been sidestepped almost altogether," he wrote of the erasure of African Americans, a line followed by Mellett in thanking Mayer for cutting everything "in it of controversial nature or harmful to anyone of any race, creed, or color." Finally, the OWI men, still counting their censorious achievement as a victory over something, urged both White and the Communists not to crow too publicly over their triumph. To make that "mistake," Poynter told White, might cause Hollywood to stiffen in future encounters. Mellett sent a similar warning to the Communists, asking them to regard *Tennessee Johnson* as "acceptable" and "likely to promote national unity." "To call this a pro-slavery film is preposterous," he angrily wrote. "The Daily Worker by raising this false issue certainly is rendering no service to the American people, least of all to the Negro whose cause it pretends to represent." As though tacking on a coda, Howard Dietz of Metro took a similar tone in warning the CPUSA not to be a pressure group for censorship, a tactic that could not help but invite similar pressure from the "crackers" on the occasion of some future controversial *pro*-Negro film.[23]

On its face the movie as released seemed an advocate of equality, but it was only emptily so in the absence of freedmen. Johnson's love scenes

Conscience-liberals took heart from their campaign against *Tennessee Johnson* (1943), as a result of which Congressman Thaddeus Stevens was softened from a malevolent force to a merely cunning curmudgeon (here Lionel Barrymore as Stevens counts the vote to impeach Andrew Johnson). BFI. Copyright Metro-Goldwyn-Mayer.

with his wife are little gems of populism that testify to his right to fly his own flag, to fish in the stream with everyone else, to rise from mudsill to man of property; indeed, at one point they clinch on the word "equal." Once in office he announces that as Lincoln freed the slaves he will free their masters, as he signs an amnesty. On the other hand, Stevens's "forty acres and a mule" for blacks is seen as no more than cunning revenge on a prostrate South.[24]

In release the Communists picketed, the black sociologist E. Franklin Frazier thought it "hypocrisy," the *Nation* and *PM* panned it. "Negrophiles," sniffed *Time*. Exhibitors, including Al Lichtman, owner of a chain of Washington houses that served blacks, fished for friendly endorsements.[25]

Obviously there was little to celebrate in such reactive attacks on mere targets of opportunity. And yet the gathering of forces against *Tennessee Johnson* anticipated the more affirmative, subtle activism directed against the emerging genre of war movies by the evolving groups of liberal activists in the OWI, NAACP, and Hollywood offices. Together they provided an event that more than any other, save for Randolph's threatened march on Washington, helped test a set of strategies of confrontation that would become a behavioral underpinning of the modern civil rights movement in that it anticipated its eventual growth from local issue to national policy matter. It remained only for the liberals to translate necessitarian propaganda into what Hollywood did best: finding the next hot topic and fluffing it into a cycle of moneymaking movies.[26]

Each of the war movies, as though traced from a template supplied by OWI, used the war to thrust a black figure into a small white circle. Wesley Epps (Kenneth Spencer) in *Bataan* was a preacher in civilian life but thrown by the fortunes of war into a polyethnic platoon; Oliver Cromwell Jones (Ben Carter) in *Crash Dive* combined memories of Dorie Miller with a hep version of the Southern myth of camaraderie across racial lines; in *Sahara* Tamboul (Rex Ingram) spoke for the popular front against fascism; and in *Lifeboat* Joe the Stoker (Canada Lee) is a central figure in wresting control of an open boat from a German. The four movies, appearing in a nine-month span at midwar, simultaneously forecast an enhanced black status as a result of war while showing whites they had nothing to fear from change. Moreover, black volunteerism seemed freely given rather than a ploy from which to exact a postwar payoff. And each revealed the ease with which a few blue pages of change could redefine the politics of the genre of the "lost patrol" movie by typing in "Negro" where it had never before appeared.

Bataan began in the summer of 1942 when Selznick took up the story, then stepped aside and sold it to Metro. Meanwhile, Robert Hardy Andrews, a writer on Dore Schary's Metro lot, tossed in a similar idea about the Corps of Engineers, "the only Army outfit [he said] in which

Negro troops stand equal in every respect with white troops." His first-draft black warrior resonated with both the legend of John Henry and newly minted liberal convention: a "towering Negro" released "from a downriver chaingang" for having helped "stop a flood," but reworked into "an important morale picture . . . with . . . very 'American' characters."[27] Schary imagined Andrews's story as a remake of John Ford's *Lost Patrol* (1934), but slanted to "tell people they were in for a tough fight" while trying "to break the color barrier in American war films." The race angle, of course, obliged Schary to do his best work in Mayer's office, where they all felt stung by the scrap over *Tennessee Johnson.*[28] Fox's *Crash Dive* (1943) seemed even more promising at its start, what with a production team of Zanuck, one of White's circle, as producer; writer Jo Swerling, eventually to advise the War Department on its own propaganda movie, *The Negro Soldier,* and to collaborate with Steinbeck on *Lifeboat;* and director Archie Mayo, a veteran of Warner's social movies of the 1930s. Moreover, in the early going they puffed Carter's role to a scale far beyond his stock stableboy roles, that is, from mere comic relief designed to soften the dangers of submarine service into a substantive role in which he and an old chief, working as a team, make a nighttime amphibious landing at German submarine pens, overpower guards, and withdraw under fire, Jones refusing to leave the chief behind.[29]

Sahara (1943) owed its substance to yet another union of Hollywood system and wartime leftist ideology. John Howard Lawson, the Communist ideologue, borrowed his version of the lost patrol from Mikhail Romm's *The Thirteen* (1937), a tale of Red Army soldiers pursued across the Gobi Desert by the White Army, internationalized it, and changed the unit into a tank crew composed of a sample of the Western alliance, their Italian prisoner, and Tamboul, a Sudanese, as the voice of collective security. In the front office at Columbia, Harry Cohn protected Lawson from rightwing snoops who had hoped to get Lawson fired. "I ain't gonna louse up a picture that's gonna do three million two domestic," said Cohn. At the NAACP White needed only to cheer the "progress" of *Sahara* (and to use it to revive his biopic of Félix Eboué).[30]

Lifeboat (1943) derived from similar sources, albeit left liberal rather than Communist, but suffered most from the continuing problem of how to maintain political coherence in the rough and tumble of movielot operations while struggling against survivals of past practice. Steinbeck, Swerling, and director Alfred Hitchcock intended their lifeboat as an allegory for the Atlantic alliance, having the survivors of a torpedoing join forces to kill a German officer whom they have taken into the boat after their own mortally wounded freighter has rammed his U-boat. But in the script there was a slippage of everything they had agreed upon: A proposed contrast between a coldly charming Bavarian and the argumentative survivors comes off as fascist superiority over democratic squabbling; a bit of tossed-in class conflict seemed beside the point; and the close quarters called attention to the most mannered actors in all of Hollywood—Henry Hull, Tallulah Bankhead, and William Bendix. Worst of all, the black figure was named "Charcoal," of all things (though Swerling dropped this after the first reel in favor of "Joe").[31]

In general, all four movies performed their service as pleasurable propaganda creditably. Perhaps Epps in *Bataan* was a shade too diffident, Tamboul in *Sahara* too much the good soldier, Oliver in *Crash Dive* too much Benny Carter and not enough Zanuck, and the stoker in *Lifeboat* more like a steward than a stoker. But together they set forth on the screen an image that for better or worse defined American interracial life for decades to come: At the end of every day, when the shops close and the machines shut down, black Americans and white have spent their day together and go home to their monochromed neighborhoods. No one in script or in life imagined any other arrangement, at least for now. In any case, they were politically more challenging than any other offering, whether all-black musical, populist fable like *Tales of Manhattan*, or misguided attempt to draw blacks into movies by, as *Tennessee Johnson* had done, casting them out of the story. Unquestionably, war and the expectations it brought had come to matter.

Tales of Manhattan, an anthology held together by the fate of a coat stuffed with money that passes from hand to hand, seemed to be on the right track in its black segment: The coat falls from an airplane into the hands of a black village, and in the end the villagers reject spending their gains on individual blessings—a brindle cow and such—and choose assets they can share, such as new tools so sharp the soil jumps up to meet them. But there was some old-fashioned stuff of which stereotypes were made: A woman falls to her knees in supplication, her eyes bulging in fear; a chorus sings "Amazing Grace"; and Paul Robeson, a leader in their drift toward a shared fate, sings of their joy and thanks in a scene queasily echoing *The Green Pastures*.[32] Out of touch with events, apart from the main Hollywood circles, familiar only with the old rather than the new Negro, *Tales* had simply grafted onto familiar black figures a smidgen of populist egalitarianism. *Bataan*, *Crash Dive*, and *Sahara* were different in that someone with an eye on what was newly possible monitored the making of the movies.

In the first instance, Schary may have shared White's vision of race relations, but nevertheless at some moment near Christmas 1942 White's informant on the lot, Caleb Peterson, heard that the studio was dropping the black soldier from *Bataan*. White carried this news immediately to Howard Dietz, whom he had come to trust, with the result that, as Peterson wrote, "they immediately put the colored boy's role back in Bataan Patrol." By then Andrews's John Henry had become Epps, a soldierly Negro dynamiter and, fortunately for his white pals, a preacher capable of reading prayers over the dead. He, Corporal Jake

The well-meaning populism of the black sequence of *Tales of Manhattan* (1943) clashed with its residual echoes of stock Negro characters who sang either for glory or supplication. BFI. Copyright 20th Century–Fox Film Corporation.

Feinberg, and the others formed a multiethnic band of stragglers who represented American resolve in the face of overwhelming Japanese forces in the southwest Pacific. So pleased were they at Metro, they made a black version of their serial advertisement, "The Lion's Roar," in order to tout its angle of "the spirit of men of all creeds, races, and colors."[33] By then, of course, apart from the actual substance of the movie or its hoped-for reception, through Dietz they knew White was *watching*. As to who watched *Crash Dive* and *Sahara*, in the former case it would be Zanuck, the mogul most open to White's goals, and in the latter Lawson, who served as the eyes of the CPUSA. In the case of *Lifeboat*, it would have been Jo Swerling, by then probably doing double duty on the War Department's own film *The Negro Soldier*.

At any rate, this handful of war movies thrust upon audiences and critics the reception of movies in which was embedded a newly minted, if still emerging, liberal racial ideology. *Tales of Manhattan*, whatever the good intentions of its antifascist makers, had taught them the pitfalls of having all-black material stand for their doctrine. On this the moguls, OWI, the NAACP, and the CPUSA seemed agreed; at least their speeches and slogans said so. "National Unity for Victory over Nazi Enslavement," a clear echo of Nunn's Double V, ran on the *Worker*'s masthead throughout 1942; Robeson's speeches regularly called for "a war to free all peoples"; Poynter, who attended a Robeson speech and applauded it, called for a change in "our domestic . . . attitudes" that would energize the war on "poverty, frustration and fear." The *Worker* covered the event and put its best ecumenical face on the proceedings, reporting that the audience responded "enthusiastically." In such a mood *Tales of Manhattan* could find not a single friendly voice. Robeson himself, back in New York playing Othello, offered to picket his own movie, while on the black right in Hollywood Eddie Anderson called a "secret" meeting to hammer out a complex African American strategy designed simultaneously to protest the stock types in *Tales of Manhattan* and "discourage" the pickets, whose anti-Hollywood tactics he traced directly to the black Communist Charlotta Bass and her *Los Angeles Tribune*.[34] The debate spilled into the white press when Hedda Hopper wished for an old time *Green Pastures* flavor, to which a black soldier replied that "the last of the 'Green Pastures' and 'Uncle Tom's are gone." In the middle between protest and apology stood White and the black press, the former grateful for small favors, the latter for advertising linage, and both finding *Tales of Manhattan* "a mild improvement."[35]

By way of contrast, the war movies seemed heavensent. Everyone "hailed" *Bataan:* MGM's preview cards; the NAACP, which gave it an award as a "needed realistic picture"; OWI reviewers, who said it "deserved all the praise that can be showered upon it"; the black press; the urbane *Times*, which thought Epps "one of the outstanding merits of the picture"; and the *Worker*, which praised not only Epps but the "equal footing" on which he had been placed. Of course, no movie pleased everyone. Fred Allen recalled a couple in front of him who, after two reels of creeping through jungles, departed. "Well, mother, I guess we've seen enough of this picture," the man said. "Yes," replied his wife, "there's too much crawlin' in it."[36]

Crash Dive was less satisfying, burdened as it was by a stock love story and stars in need of friendly camera angles and screen time, but nonetheless Ben Carter played against his old types, joined his mates in their raid on the Germans, and ended the movie in a sequence that moves from a three-shot on the conning tower of his submarine, to his receiving a Navy Cross (remarkably like a news shot of Dorie Miller receiving *his* medal), and finally to an etiquette-breaking handshake with a white officer. "A real step forward," said White; "excellent," said

In *Bataan* (1943), Epps (Kenneth Spencer) was calculatedly centered in the frame, given a military skill, a place in the action, and a civilian calling, all unthinkable attributes before the war that inspired them. BFI. Copyright Metro-Goldwyn-Mayer.

the OWI reviewer, and "something one finds all too rarely in pictures."[37]

Sahara carried the argument still further and in more cinematically rewarding terms. A crippled, straggling tank, low on fuel, clanks aimlessly over the dunes, its crew searching for their unit. Along the way they meet Tamboul, with an Italian prisoner in hand as though liberating Africa in a single stroke. Thereafter, Tamboul often speaks and acts for the Grand Alliance: he defends the Italian's rights as they debate abandoning him in a watersaving triage; his folk wisdom finds water; in a eucharistic trope he clambers down the disused well and catches its trickling water in his cupped hands; as Africa's contribution to the war, he fights to the death against a larger German force bent upon reaching the water.[38] And audiences saw it all. The NAACP linked it to the pledges, praising it as an "outstanding contribution toward the objective stated by Mr. White"; in Harlem, kids stood and cheered Tamboul; the national press caught its drift. Only Lawson lacked faith that conscience-liberalism had grown normative: He guessed it reached the

In *Sahara* (1943) Tamboul (Rex Ingram) was a central figure for it is *his* desert and only he knows how to find water, abandoned forts, and old caravan trails—the lore that Europeans cannot know. BFI. Copyright Columbia Pictures.

screen at all only because "Cohn didn't understand the picture nor what it meant."[39]

Lifeboat, the last movie in the cycle, may have been the least politically satisfying to its liberal viewers. Both its angles—the lifeboat as metaphor for the popular front, and Joe the stoker as a means of integrating blacks into the center of the action—mumbled their lines. Joe is too full of tics and oddments of business. As scripted he is meant to be brave and cool in the situation, but he is too cool, regarding the company with curious eyes, preferring "good" music, refusing to "boogie it up" on his flute. He seems an honest, even pious, sailor, but he has done time for picking pockets, so his bit in the assault on their captured German is to filch his compass and knife. His role in the daily round of life on the boat is that of steward, which he slips into too easily. In the script he agonizes over joining in killing the German because he once saw a mob lynch a Negro, but on the screen his reluctance seems mere tentativeness, and thus a potent black motive for action is erased, as though audiences in 1943 were still unready to arm a Negro even against a common enemy.[40]

No one liked the result. Steinbeck, imagining he had written "a Negro of dignity," asked his agent to remove his name from the credits. At its opening, Bosley Crowther and Dorothy Parker pounced upon its soft center, even arguing that it was pro-Nazi, a charge Bankhead and Hitchcock did their best to deny until she ended the interview by turning on a *PM* reporter and calling his paper a "filthy, rotten, Communist rag." Others in the national press agreed with Crowther and found the stoker a spineless throwback to antebellum times.[41] Billy Rowe's review in the *Courier* not only covered it as a movie in which "Joe stands aside and does nothing" but as a detective yarn in which Rowe discovered signs that Fox had intended to call Joe "Charcoal" throughout and to make more of his criminal past. Abram Hill in the *Amsterdam* reckoned it remote from White's goal of a "vital and realistic interpretation of the Negroes' part in Americana." Finally, Roy Wilkins wrote personally to the studio, labeling Joe a "strikingly nonessential . . . sop" and saying that the "general reaction among Negroes" was one of diminished morale.[42]

The desert island genre adapted to fit the war, *Lifeboat* (1943), portrayed the Allies as "all in the same boat" against a common enemy, although Joe the Stoker (Canada Lee) drew the usual black assignments: steward and pickpocket. BFI. Copyright 20th Century–Fox.

The various pannings of *Lifeboat* notwithstanding, this cycle of war movies at least sharpened and refined the audience's eye so that a wary Hollywood adopted a conscience-liberal stance that extended even into the postwar era of, as the historian James T. Shotwell called it, "the thinking picture." But the relative success of a small body of midwar movies must not be taken as a sign of an ideological consensus. As often as not, good intentions were misread across a gulf between the two cultures—black and white. Put in the starkest of terms, white praise of Stephen Foster's "Old Black Joe" as innocent nostalgia might seem to sensitive blacks an offensive memory of slave times. In more modern terms, to many jazz buffs black music was presumed best when played by blacks, while to White's circle the very idea smacked of the sort of dated Jim Crow mentality against which they fought. The play between these two taste-cultures allowed an insistent minority in Hollywood to call for all-black musicals as fulfillments of the need for a richer African American presence on the screen.

In the middle of the war Hollywood made two such musicals, which brought into play the tension between integration and cultural uniqueness and produced in the minds of black activists no end of anxiety over the implied retreat from integration. Moreover, the two musicals, *Cabin in the Sky* and *Stormy Weather,* went into release during three nasty race riots that simultaneously drew attention to the persistence of racism and seemed to point to movies and other pressures for enhanced black status as *causes* of the riots. And to the dismay of many in White's circle, the musicals revived the matter of the Hollywood Negroes' place in movies in that the large casts placed them in demand again. Additionally, their release coincided with Paramount's release of a couple of biopics of oldtime minstrelmen, each wrapped in a setting of roseate Southern nostalgia at odds with the activists' plans. The clash of ideals may be seen in Metro's casting of Lena Horne in *Cabin in the Sky.* "Your troubles are over," a friendly journalist told White. "I am not sure," he wrote. "I don't think the all-colored picture is the answer." He much preferred her in a drama, perhaps Somerset Maugham's *The Moon and Sixpence,* a project the Hays office objected to, he said, "because of [her] color."[43]

Not that White and his friends had not known of generations of proud African Americans who had boasted of success in comparative terms: Sissieretta Jones was "the black Patti," Lorenzo Tucker "the black Valentino," and so on. But the point was to assert a black identity more fitted to new conditions, and by doing so promote a better metaphor for race relations. Ideally, in this image black and white would be neither as separate as night and day nor as smelted down as in Israel Zangwill's "melting pot," but more like paint speckling an atelier floor or, as Hopper proposed in her column, like black and white piano keys.

At any rate, the musicals went into production while begging the questions of whether or not they merely exhibited blacks as though at a zoo (as Agee would write), or only reflected the segregated facts of real life, or were a retreat from the moguls' pledges, or were a racially collective means of integrating the industry much as *Amos 'n' Andy* would (controversially) do in postwar television.[44]

In fact, the musical had only just begun to mature into a vehicle for taking up racial material. Black versions of white shows—*The Black Mikado* and *Carmen Jones*—had already cracked Broadway. And the musical form itself had grown from light operetta to musical drama, from Victor Herbert's *Red Mill* to Rodgers and Hammerstein's *Oklahoma!* Moreover, *Variety* reported that although "sales departments have always squawked that they have an impossible job in trying to sell them down south . . . interracial leaders contend now that the citizens of Dixie take readily to colored entertainment."[45] At Metro in particular the form promised to regain the popularity of the days of *The Golddiggers of 1933*. Arthur Freed, a songwriter turned producer, had picked up a play by Lynn Riggs that Vernon Duke and John LaTouche (author of "Ballad for Americans") crafted into a Broadway hit, *Cabin in the Sky*. For racial politesse LaTouche consulted the NAACP, and MGM added Marc Connelly, "Yip" Harburg, and Harold Arlen, a writer of old Cotton Club shows reputed to have "a special empathy for blacks." Their director, Vincente Minnelli, also was known for a flair for black material that included a Josephine Baker show and the hard-driving black number "Public Melody No. 1" in *Artists and Models*, which in 1937 Will Hays had thought a "worry" because of its touchy "*racial*" overtones.[46]

For Minnelli the task was to recast the sweetness of *The Green Pastures* into wartime terms or, he said, grind out yet another "naive, childlike stereotype." This balancing act also, of course, obliged him to mediate between urbane Eastern blacks whom he knew and the Hollywood veterans White had snubbed in 1942. As an example, Ethel Waters, who had been in Hollywood since 1929, and Lena Horne, who was widely regarded as White's "guinea pig" to be used to make "a different kind of image for the Negro women," clashed on the set like gladiators, Waters in combat for the status quo, Horne seeming to "start a revolt or steal work."[47]

More than a spat between East and West, old and new, it was also a struggle between two styles of black performance, between those who could "cross over" into white theatres and those who had played out their lives on the "chittlin' circuit." On one side were the baritone Kenneth Spencer, the slick team of Buck and Bubbles, the legendary Louis Armstrong, and the Ziegfeld Follies veteran Ethel Waters, while on the other were the oldtimers whose narrow range and parochial style doomed them to the colored theatre wheels or roles as stooges in prewar movies. Stepin Fetchit, for example, pleaded with Freed for a role in *Cabin in the Sky*, promising to reform his past history of missed gigs and claiming the lead role was all but autobiographical. But Freed's scouts knew what they wanted and that the fossils of Fetchit's era were outworn. "Jazz Lips" Richardson? Not present-day quality. Butterbeans and Susie, two fixtures in the colored circuits? A skinny geezer and his fat partner who seemed not Metro style. And so on. In other words, the men of Freed's unit through a common aesthetic—Metro style—worked toward fresh, racially political goals. The studio also provided an arena in which Minnelli fought its entrenched conservatives, among whom he included Cedric Gibbon's feudal Art Department, for such realistic modes as the genteel black poverty of *In This Our Life* as against Gibbon's wish for a conventional squalor associated with black material.[48]

As released, *Cabin in the Sky* confirmed White's worst fears of all-black material even as it fulfilled the artistic intent of Minnelli. Stagey in design, reminiscent of *The Green Pastures*, a folksy religious fable, the movie portrays the struggle for the soul of Joe, amiable husband of angelic Petunia. They are settled, pious, churched. However, Joe, an elevator operator who describes his job as "the hotel business," is beset by a demonic itch to gamble, to roll his "calamity cubes" in Jim Henry's Paradise, a saloon that reprised the streetscape of sinners in *The Green Pastures*. The struggle for Joe's soul begins when he is wounded in a shooting scrape in the Paradise. The central theme takes over as he clings to life; in his delirium Petunia struggles against Satan's imps and their ultimate weapon, the temptress Sweet Georgia Brown (Horne), against whom gingham-hearted Petunia (Waters) seem to have not a chance. Throughout, there is a sort of yang-and-yin of tone, lighting, costume, and voice, a clash of stark darks and lights, set between which is the gray, earthen world of Petunia, who sings her theme, "Happiness Is a Thing Called Joe." For his part, the struggling Joe (Eddie Anderson) expresses his will to prevail by singing "Life's Full of Consequences." In the end, of course, Petunia wins Joe's soul, thereby placing blacks on the good side of the same sort of ledger Selznick had kept on *Gone with the Wind*.

At the box office all of this worked, for whites perhaps because it exonerated them from complicity in the black plight, while for blacks it may have echoed maternal warnings against the wrong crowd, mean streets, and bad women, particularly the sleekly feral women whose antidote to the half-loaf life had given them was to live off their looks, their wits, and other women's men. But politically it divided critics and put White's pledges to a stress test. Indeed, White's own ambivalence reflected the tangled critical politics. On the one hand, he praised Connelly for "a marvellous job in transforming what was the average white man's notion of Negro religion," while on the other, ever wary of all-black stuff, he could only guess that "MGM thought it was doing a decent job" with sensitive material. Metro, still smarting from *Tennessee Johnson*, trod softly, not only in assembling a race-sensitive unit, but in hiring Billy Rowe as a black flack who praised it as "the nucleus of a new day in Hollywood," an angle played by those black papers that cheered the "long-awaited" movie and its "awe-inspiring" Waters and gleefully reported its above "normal" business in the South.[49]

But the rest of the black press had been made waspishly political by the expectations raised by the war. "An insult masking behind the label of folklore," wrote Ramona Lewis in the *Amsterdam*. She was also saddened by the white people who "seemed to believe this was the normal pattern of Negro life," and who sat through it making "patronizing sounds." "Insulting," said Joe Bostic in the *People's Voice*. "A disservice to race relations," complained White to poor Connelly (who had consulted on the script), particularly because of the "vulgar things" that Horne was made to do, things "they would not think of having a white actress do." But in the main White fretted over audiences and their misreading of the film. "An Azuza [audience] might think it was the berries [that is, terrific]," he warned Connelly.[50]

White maintained a balance between wartime mentality and nostalgic appreciation of oldtime Southern lore. The *Times* delighted in its "bountiful entertainment," while conservative *Time* thought its "Sambo-like entertainers" compromised wartime racial liberalism. *Variety* reviewed it as though an OWI tract rather than a movie and blessed its playing to the "wider interest in the Negro throughout the country," although thinking it "doubtful material in the South." Thus the mainline, urban press had broadened their scope to include the social angle embedded in war movies.[51]

Stormy Weather (1943) was a more prickly subject. Culturally black in its roots, wearing its black patriotism on its sleeve, larded with crossover black performers, it surely promised to be an ornament of conscience-liberalism. It had begun as a Hollywood rarity, an original story, a pet of Hy Kraft, an old lefty who had been tossing it over transoms for months. Yet whatever coherence it might have derived from its leftist sources would seem compromised by the same all-black quality that made black liberals wince. Kraft's working title, *Thanks, Pal,* wore its theme like a bumper sticker: A birthday party for an old hoofer becomes a lead-in to a national voice of gratitude for black participation in past wars, but encased in "the magnificent contribution of the colored race to the entertainment of the world." Indeed, the men in the establishing shots are meant to be James Reese Europe, Noble Sissle, and Eubie Blake; their images are intercut with actual footage of the 15th New York National Guard marching up Fifth Avenue with its Croix de Guerre ribbons flying on its guidons, Hudie Leadbetter, and the Fisk Jubilee Singers, coupled with footage of Harlem, Beale Street in Memphis, the Pekin Theatre in Chicago, and other shrines of African American performing culture.[52]

Its sources on the left notwithstanding, *Stormy Weather* revealed yet another line of last ditches to be fought for. At 20th Century–Fox, as long as Zanuck treated a film as a personal project it stood a chance of responding to pressures from OWI, Walter White, or his house liberals. But in the middle ranks of producers of routine programmers, conscience-liberalism, unlike water, did not trickle downhill. Moreover, they frequently balked at original material that required costly tinkering and delays. Surely this was true in the case of Kraft's treatment. Julian Johnson, a Zanuck man near the top, loved the "historical stuff" and hoped it would stay in, particularly a proposed tragic love story involving Bill Robinson and Florence Mills, a famous black performer who had met an early death in the 1920s. But Johnson also knew that the line producer, William LeBaron, would care little for the project, its historical angle, or its raffish black show business bohemia.[53]

LeBaron's attitude may be found in his playing safe with the most profoundly black element of the movie, its music. At first Fox had taken the unheard-of step of engaging a black composer, William Grant Still, to score the movie. But by early 1943, Still had quarreled with his boss in the music department, who had found the score "too good [because] black musicians didn't play that well." Angrily, Still carried his grievance to the press, hoping for an outcry that might override his boss. As he told Walter White: "It may happen that the big people to whom you talk are perfectly willing and eager to do something constructive, but their efforts are nullified by the . . . heads of departments." The press caught the gist of the argument, knew the movielot politics, and wrote off Still as a hero but nonetheless a "suicide."[54]

But there was more to come. Few actors were left in the pool after Metro's vetting and casting them for *Cabin in the Sky*. The result was two improbable lovers: sleek Lena Horne and old Bojangles, who had not worked in films since 1937. They shot around the awkward pair, amid rumors of a parallel search for a lead whom the "audience would accept as [Horne's] lover." In the end the strain must have affected at least Horne's performance; both she and her director, Andrew L. Stone, recalled her coldness and inability to "display some sort of creditable emotion."[55]

In any case, by the time the movie opened in the summer of 1943, Kraft's tribute to black show business survived only in a cameo of Jim Europe, played by Ernest Whitman, who rose above a lifetime of Negro bits and read the role with precise fidelity to Europe's owl-like, soldierly presence. The rest was a backstage triangle told in flashbacks in which Robinson is a burned-out dancer and Horne a rising star, with Babe Wallace as a youthfully chubby rival to Robinson. The story is told by Robinson to a circle of black kids seated on his porch as he reminisces, each memory serving as cue to introduce a new character or incident from the Jazz Age: Dooley Wilson, a bootblack with a nose for good cigars and an eye for bad women; Fats Waller in his last sly, winking gig before his death; Cab Calloway in white tie and tails doing "Geechee

Joe"; Flournoy Miller and Johnny Lee in their jalopy routine from *Shuffle Along* of 1921; and turns by Zutty Singleton, Ada Brown, and Mae Johnson, the latter singing "I Lost My Sugar in Salt Lake City." The three high moments were Horne looking out on a windblown streetscape singing the title song, Katharine Dunham as a fancy lady strutting with her dancers under the el as they romp through "Diga Diga Doo" from *The Blackbirds of 1929*, and the adolescent Nicholas Brothers in a flashdance that Robinson could no longer do.[56] Only this surfeit of music saved *Stormy Weather* from its actors' limited range, awkward cutting around its two putative stars, an inchworm pace, and a story so devoid of heavies as to lack dramatic conflict. Besides, as did each all-black musical, it risked portraying African America as a happy place with happy problems—just the sort of stuff that White feared played well in Azuza.[57]

The only sanguine outcome was that White used the movie's opening as a gimmick to commend Zanuck and Fox for resisting pressure to withdraw it during the summer riots of 1943, so it became yet another seminar for critics in training to analyze the politics of movies. *Stormy Weather* appeared just as riots broke out in Harlem and Detroit and the "zoot suit" riots hit Los Angeles, which all but scared Fox into pulling the movie. The decision to run it, in fact, earned praise from blacks of all political sectors—from Harry Levette, who feared for its profits following "the depressing effects of the racial outbreak," to Walter White, who congratulated Zanuck for "refusing to permit race riots to change [Fox's] plans." The resulting tension, said White, required "affirmative prevention," which movies might provide, if "getting along together" was ever to come. The national press played its proper part: loved the music, hated the miscast romance. As Hartung wrote in *Commonweal*, Waller's "Ain't Misbehavin'" was a delight, but as to the rest, "Rain, No Game!" *Time* agreed, singling out Dooley Wilson for his "Elizabethan blend of simplicity and skill which today is seldom found outside Harlem's Apollo Theatre." Like almost any wartime movie, it probably made a profit; it had "warm" runs in key cities, reported *Variety*, including two Southern towns. Moreover, it said, as though to conscience-liberals, this hepcat's delight outdrew the pieties of *Cabin in the Sky* by three to one.[58]

These few movies hardly added up to a revolution in movie art, but their half-measures—partly defined by the forces they were trying to redefine, partly an outcome of a test of countervailing if not triumphant forces, partly constrained by the mere coincidence of national and minority goals—nonetheless asserted a place in movie culture where once there had been none. Indeed, the little epiphanies of racial insight they provided were smallish by any subsequent standard: a lone black hero amidst a white circle; or the odd slice of black life; or the occasional breach of armed forces racial policy (long before the forces themselves would change, and therefore speaking with a voice of subtle advocacy);

or the tantalizing coolness of black actors playing their roles as though being set down among these white strangers obliged them to pay out only so much of themselves, as if trolling for fish. However long after the war had ended, the *Amsterdam*'s critic George Norford recalled *Lifeboat* as a unifying metaphor that returning soldiers took as a sign of political change to come. Indeed, the image he called up anticipated precisely the form taken by the most famous Supreme Court cases of the ensuing years, a lawyerish struggle to admit lone little children to all-white circles, much as such lone figures had graced white circles in war movies. Thus the war movies gave visual rhetorical form to postwar conscience-liberalism, drew it toward programmatic action, and perpetuated it artistically in the form as a new stereotype of a lone black person in a white circle. Not that their success opened a sluicegate for similar roles in civilian settings; indeed, late in the war, after OWI budgets were slashed by the Southern-ruled Congress, there arose a distinct sense that the heat was off. In fact, every new role invited the sort of struggle Alvah Bessie and Delmer Daves faced when they lost black female defense plant workers to nameless script doctors' meddling, or the one John Howard Lawson lost when black officers were erased before his *Action in the North Atlantic* reached the screen.[59]

This pull-and-haul between the new and those who feared it can best be seen in Selznick's most self-conscious effort to get civilian life on the screen: *Since You Went Away.* Like so many movies, it grew simultaneously from liberal hopes and the lead weight of Hollywood custom. Like the O'Haras in *Gone with the Wind,* the Hiltons in *Since You Went Away* were blessed with Hattie McDaniel as their servant (Fidelia, now). She and Selznick both tried to modernize her dress, makeup, body english, and even her weight, but in the end a good idea failed to overcome inertial forces that enshrined black performance in a timeless mode. As they crept toward completion in 1944 they seemed unable to engage Fidelia in the war; its impact follows only from the Hiltons' inability to afford her on a sailor's pay, so she works for room and board. Even in the first "page breakdown" of Margaret Applegate Wilder's novel, when Fidelia is feeding two black soldiers they turn out to be deserters. Not that Wilder did not try to reveal ironies brought on by the dislocations of war. In an early script draft Anne, one of the Hilton girls, goes in search of "war work" but flunks a dexterity test while, as the script says, a poorly dressed black girl seated next to her calmly performs the task. Later Anne receives another lesson in wartime populism when her prospective boss turns out to be a black matron with a sort of Lady Bountiful manner toward the underprivileged.[60]

Yet through eighteen revisions in the summer of 1943, a growing team of writers failed to introduce Fidelia to the reality of war. In Wilder's last try, sadly, it was no better. In one comic scene the Hiltons meet her at a railway depot where an attendant requires her to describe items in her lost luggage before she can reclaim it, an occasion for a stream of gratuitous sightgags—a greasy "dreambook" for predicting lottery bets, a large pistol, a bottle of gin, soiled laundry, and a smelly bag of stale clams. F. Hugh Herbert, Selznick's next script doctor, saw the need to cut the scene but insisted on keeping McDaniel's role an old, fat, languid mammy, smelling of lavender.[61] In the movie as released, the train station sequence survives in muted form.

At last, in November Ulric Bell of OWI, by then a sort of federal Hays office, reminded Selznick that there was a war on and that Fidelia should be touched by it. Why not, he said, give her a family whose wartime stresses require her changed circumstances? Perhaps as a result of Bell's "possible retakes," the broadest of Fidelia's comedy is missing from the surviving print. (In an astonishing intrusion into Hollywood custom, another change resulted partly from angry comments by several black Women's Army Corps recruits at a sneak preview in San Bernardino. They complained of a clutch of giggling uniformed black women, and the sequence was replaced by a handsome black soldier saying farewell to his wife and child as he leaves for war.)[62] And Fidelia herself is drafted into the movie's war effort, an event foreshadowed in a prologue that shows the white family as an enduring fortress. A slow pan confirms the idea by scanning the artifacts of family history—car keys, a mounted fish, bronzed baby shoes, snapshots, and finally the gold star in the window signifying the absent father—and thence to the children ineffectually picking up Fidelia's slack by cleaning the house and making breakfast while the mother (Claudette Colbert), slightly at sea, makes do with fractured schedules and balky appliances.

But the true impact of the war upon Fidelia is made manifest not by writing but by McDaniel's retooled performance. Gone is her empty obstreperousness of *Alice Adams* (1933) and *Gone with the Wind*, a brave gesture for an actor who had won an Oscar playing that very trait. Her mien, to both the camera and the family, is a level gaze undiluted by downcast eyes and other servile tricks. As though drawing the viewer's eye to the new McDaniel, a family friend (Joseph Cotten) gives her a charcoal portrait in which he has caught the graying, matronly dignity that the audience is supposed to focus on. McDaniel presses the point when she sits *with* the family during a daughter's graduation; in flowered dress and sensible hat she gives life to the Fidelia that the artist had rendered on paper. She even reads a line that asserts her wartime footing in witty terms when, in response to praise for her cake, she traces its merits not to an ancient recipe but to an "experiment." "I bought it," she says, admitting a guiltless break with the stereotype that defined the kitchen as her only theatre of operations. But McDaniel could push only so much light into the corners of a role intended only for the margin of the frame. It had simply never occurred to Selznick that a movie about the civilian side of the war should include obligatory blacks as the war

Hattie McDaniel infused her Fidelia with a quiet dignity that Selznick reinforced by having a houseguest present her with a penciled sketch (here as Joseph Cotten looks on) in *Since You Went Away* (1944). BFI. Copyright United Artists.

genre had done. His blacks thus take part in the war only as sidebars to white stories or visual flourishes to counterpoint the white center of the action. One of the Hiltons' daughters, for instance, takes her oath as a nurse's aide, promising to minister to the wounded of whatever color or creed, a duty made manifest later when she serves ice cream to a group of amputees that includes a black veteran. Black extras dotted the crowd scenes as staid civilians, crisp soldiers, and families saying appropriately sad farewells—in short, the black bourgeoisie that had been pledged to Walter White in the summer of 1942.

Generally, the studios treated such material gingerly enough to avoid appearing to lay it on with a trowel; nonetheless, an occasional dissenter from the liberal rhetoric complained of its heavyhandedness, as though confirming Goebbels's dictum that "the moment a person is conscious of propaganda [it] becomes ineffective." In the case of *Since You Went Away,* Selznick in fact had laid in gratuitous bits that jarred more than they persuaded. At a party a Jewish officer—"Solomon"—is introduced (and dropped) for no other reason than to trot in a Jewish Navy Cross holder. Another sequence opens not on a person but a *paperweight* on which is inscribed Carl Sandburg's line, "America, thy seeds of fate have borne a fruit of many breeds," a prop from which to tilt up to a diploma of a patriotic Jewish doctor. Finally, Zofia (Alla Nazimova), a welder in Mrs. Hilton's war plant, is so grateful for her life in America that at lunch one day she recites the entire poem inscribed on the pedestal of the Statue of Liberty: "Give me your tired, your poor, your huddled masses yearning to be free . . ."

Certainly a few of the viewers grumbled at the ponderous messages. One of the complainers wished for at least *one* movie that averted its eyes from African America, while another merely snapped at Selznick's Middle Europeans: "Too Jewish." Of course, in a sense the absence of a thick sheaf of such carping allowed the inference that conscience-liberalism was, if not taking hold, at least enjoying the tolerance of the main body of the audience and therefore promised to become the political platform upon which future liberal blacks and whites could campaign.[63]

Yet, as the war wound down, racial material seemed as daunting as ever: hard to work into civilian situations and unpredictable at the box office. A case in point was yet another Selznick movie, RKO's *Till the End of Time* (1946). Both Selznick and RKO leapt at the chance to buy Niven Busch's novella *They Dream of Home*, which was the first popular treatment of the unpredictable social dislocations to be faced by returning soldiers. Weighing heavily in their decision to buy Busch's book was that the principals were *black*. And yet between Allen Rivkin's first treatment in April 1945 and the film's release more than a year later, Busch's black family had become white, perhaps as a result of market forces overriding the liberal racial politics of the OWI and NAACP, which had lost the cachet that the war had once bestowed upon them.

As late as February 1945, Perry Kinchloe and his family had remained black. Perry, huge and powerful but also wounded and wracked by fear of a future in a bed with an exercise bar over it, was at the center of the action. But by April, Tabeshaw, a Pima Indian with a plate in his skull, had become the axis of the race angle, apparently still on the nation's agenda but in need of soft-pedaling. It is the Indian, on trial for car theft, who is the subject of a defense based upon his shock at returning from the Marines, where equality reigned, to civilian life, where it was an empty slogan and where racists prowled the bus stops and saloons stirring veterans against racial minorities. So said the as yet unshot script. By this time Kinchloe was known in the script by his wheelchair rather than his color, a point made final in two drafts in late May in which someone had carefully penciled out every reference to his race. Thus in a few strokes Perry had grown white enough to be portrayed by one of RKO's rising, marketable stars.[64]

In this same spring, the script passed from Selznick to RKO, where Rivkin kept at it under the eye of Dore Schary (producer of *Bataan*). By then, as though Americans were unready to carry the new politics of race into peacetime, the race angle had shrunk to a single incident in a cocktail lounge, while an estimating-script, a casting report, and a January market analysis had erased any reference to blacks. OWI, as though sensing it was on its last legs, praised the sequence—"We applaud the idea of showing that veterans can and will combat bigotry at home"—but also spoke the unthinkable: how easily a couple of sneering racists echoed Nazi beerhall brutes and how pliantly postwar Americans fell in with them. "It will do us more harm than good overseas," wrote Gene Kern of OWI.[65]

Till the End of Time (its release title) also set forth yet another device that became a postwar convention in race-angled movies: that racism always sprang from foreign rather than domestic roots. (Similarly, wartime documentarists, perhaps chary of fragile liberal alliances, had sometimes portrayed racism as a divisive weapon of foreign agents.) Indeed, in an early draft of *Till the End of Time*, in a war plant where a quarter of the workers are black, several white oldtimers grumble over jobs lost to blacks and even set out to drive them away, only later discovering enemy agents sowing dissension. Whatever the reason, Schary and Rivkin reduced their black presence to a single sequence. By September 1945, Kinchloe had been assigned to Bill Williams and Tabeshaw the Pima had been given to Robert Mitchum, the former of a white actor of surpassing cuteness, the latter a sullen, Byronic presence; both had begun to cultivate a teenaged following. Necessarily, the stakes became a matter of postwar readjustment of soldiers to civilian life rather than black soldiers facing the uncharted landscape of postwar racial arrangements. The race angle, then, was reduced to a barroom fight in which a lone black soldier, playing at pinball, hears the taunts of a couple of American War Patriots who are recruiting veterans for a campaign against a cabal of their bugbears: foreign-born labor racketeers, Catholics, Jews, and Negroes. At first the soldier (Caleb Peterson) plays on with cool dignity designed to mask his hurt, then too calmly leaves the frame when the white heroes barge in and fall upon the agitators, a scrap that, says the script, shows that the soldiers will need to fight for "readjustment" (not against racism).[66]

Surely Schary, Rivkin, and their director, Edward Dmytryk, himself a certified lefty, were divided against their own liberalism, wishing for a black angle but tethered to looming postwar hot topics such as conversion to a peacetime footing, as well as to revived concerns for their postwar marketplace. As though an allegory for their plight, all of the veterans of *Till the End of Time* had passed into mufti except the lone black veteran, who, as though clothing race in hopes that ended with the fighting, remained in uniform. The tension between box office and ideals was unmistakable. On the one hand, the studio engaged the American Research Institute and their innovative "want to see" index to confirm the sex appeal of Mitchum and Williams. On the other hand, a little liberalism seemed to go a long way, at least according to their preview cards. Of one survey, almost half the respondents singled out the barroom fight as a scene they liked; 20 percent said they talked about the race angle afterward; and those who bothered to write praised RKO's "tolerance" as it emerged in the black soldier's big scene, where he acted like an average human being. One writer urged still more films that played up interracial "harmony" as a precondition of the postwar growth of democracy. The makers were touched; indeed, Rivkin was "overwhelmed" and years later thought his writing had not been "for nothing." As a sign of their wish to please OWI they held one of their premieres in the Archives of the United States, to the delight of Arch Mercey, who by then had taken over as chief of a films bureau in a new Office of War Mobilization and Conversion.[67]

And yet as released the movie seemed eerily diminished in contrast to the war movies. The pinball scene is a mere sidebar, unforeshadowed, inconclusive. The marines, cleancut, foregivably boisterous, impatient to resume civilian life, are framed in a crowded, happy place when the agitators intrude. The only race angle is the visual one: They barge into a postwar America that *includes* a black soldier, and in contrast to the marines they seem mouthy and clothed in motley. The vets' banter seems as one with jukeboxes and the clatter and ring of pinball. Only the agitators are discordant. Then the movie retreats. Although their racist tirade includes blacks, what riles Tabeshaw is a reference to Jews, and he gives a little speech about a Jewish buddy dead on a Pacific beach. Thus not only does the point at issue slip from race to religion, the black soldier is even denied the right to wade into the fray on his own behalf; he sidles out of the frame, leaving the viewer to infer that racism is in the hands of a few mean men of so little moment that the Negro need only leave the fight to good whites. As though sensing a postwar thermidorean reaction, *Ebony* overpraised the small favor.[68]

Was this scene a sign that conscience-liberalism was going out with a whimper instead of a bang? Perhaps, but these timid ambitions and limited attainments were in fact viewed by millions who not only saw but affirmed their modest goals, thereby perpetuating the genre in a postwar revival. Their misplaced emphases and truncated intentions also revealed the need for a permanent liberal presence in Hollywood, perhaps as a bureau of the NAACP, or even in the form of an emerging cadre of actors such as Sidney Poitier, who after an erratic apprenticeship in army training films, race movies, and black theatre seemed poised to serve as the embodiment of the cool, lone black figure set down among white people much as his forebears in the war movies had been. Certainly the war movies had helped form a liberal expectation of continuity. The receptivity for such a notion—hardly a sign of consensus, but at least a groping toward a different racial future—may be seen in the appearance of race-angled books offered by major university and trade presses. Roi Ottley's *New World A'Comin'* (1943), Gunnar Myrdal's *An*

A turn at pinball by an anonymous black soldier (Caleb Peterson) was the lone survival of a project that had begun as a nearly all-black novel and ended as the all-white star-vehicle, *Till the End of Time* (1946). BFI. Copyright RKO.

American Dilemma (1944), and Rayford Logan's *What the Negro Wants* (1944) spoke for these still formless goals, while only Stuart Omer Landry's *The Cult of Equality* expressed alarm at the corps of government filmmakers that had abetted "Hollywood's racial antagonism" and persisted in grinding out "pure propaganda."[69]

Not only was this sensibility abroad in the land, but liberals promoted it. A *PM* reviewer, for example, although finding the black musicals "zooty" (itself black argot that had penetrated white circles), Jim Crowish exercises, noticed white applause at the Roxy, which, he argued, "makes it clear that the Negro is in the movies, as a top star, to stay [and] there is the promise of better understanding and unsegregated appreciation to come."[70]

This newly civic mentality colored the work of movie monitors, whether OWI, state censors, or PCA. Whereas before the war they had mainly erased blacks from the screen, after 1942 they seemed eager to cheer each new breach with the past. At OWI, for example, Barbara Deming began to formulate a creed as she screened each day's allotment of schlock. Lots of the stuff might get "the stamp of official approval . . . as 'good propaganda,'" she thought. "But a movie is not a handbill. It is the *unfolding drama itself* which speaks with the loudest voice." In other words, she had begun to shape a politics of movie art. Less subtly, Helen C. Tingley at the Maryland State Censor Board, appalled at rumored boycotts in Texas of *Mission to Moscow* as "White House propaganda," urged her board to approve it because it seemed "vitally needed at this time to allay propaganda against our Ally Russia, and to counteract isolationist sentiment which may affect the entire course of the country at the end of the war." And uncharacteristically, Hollywood itself stiffened against Southern censors. As Gradwell Sears of United Artists (UA) said as he readied a suit against Lloyd Binford, the Memphis censor who had cut UA's *The Southerner* (1945), "We are going to fight bias and bigotry in any form when it threatens freedom of the screen," a posture he directly linked to FDR's "four freedoms" speech.[71]

At OWI they built a paper record of Hollywood's changing civility toward African Americans: A black in *Mystery of the Riverboat* seemed uncommonly heroic; a maid in *Cairo* was more "friend" than "servant"; in *Meanest Man in the World* a boss and servant seemed "fraternal"; a black boy joined the East Side Kids in two of their B-movies; a black woman snapped "I ain't accustomed to be talked to like trash" in *Night of Crime*, and so on. Conversely, they recorded survivals of past practice that offended new sensibilities in *The Vanishing Virginian* and others. When they found a genre film adapted to war (such as an African yarn in which the heavy is "an Axis agent," or *Revenge of the Zombies*, in which "a mad doctor of the bayous is making zombies for the Germans"), or when a timely social principle was asserted (as "striking the natives is against the law" was in *Bahama Passage*), they made a point of it in their reviews. As to documentaries, OWI played the role of bean-counters and tallied up the blacks and what they did: none in *March On, America;* two in *Mr. and Mrs. America*, a film about life in Muncie; and in a Coast Guard tribute, *Mississippi Blackout*, with its "quick to learn and deeply religious" crews, fifty-fifty, black and white.[72]

Moreover, as the movies swelled their files they, along with the war itself, produced additional OWI flashes of liberal insight. Deming, for instance, saw in the B-movie *The Great Gildersleeve* a maid (Lillian Randolph) "in the conventional Hollywood-Negro manner" but also detected a subflooring of new meaning. "She manages to maintain in this film more decorum than the other characters," wrote Deming, "because, as an actress, she has found herself a way to connect directly with

. . . Gildersleeve without being swept into the whirlpool of his silliness." Furthermore, the men and women of OWI began to predict negative responses to thoughtless backsliding: The "Jim Crow-ism" of a blackfaced minstrel short thwarted "mobilizing the Negro for the war effort"; if black roles seemed too "likable," racists might read it as perpetuating "the myth of Negro inefficiency and laziness"; while the same role as read by a black viewer "very sensitive to this problem" might end with the viewer "inflamed."[73]

Of course, these flickers of changing racial ideology by themselves do not allow the inference of a mentality shared with audiences. And yet they did anticipate such a sensibility that had leapt ahead of mere government necessity. In the darkened theatres, where psyches tried on new racial ideas and tolerances long before their echoes turned up in Gallup polls, moviegoers in fact went to such movies. True, moviegoers went to see what they liked not for its politics but because they had expectations of pleasure that they hoped would be fulfilled. It was this network of expectations that drew them, not racial politics. But they went. And unbidden by liberals, dozens of movies emitted little organic wisps of new racial meanings. Val Lewton at RKO, for example, produced three neat *film noirs*—*I Walked with a Zombie, Cat People,* and *Curse of the Cat People*—each of which made much of a key black cameo. "Jane Eyre set in the tropics," said Jacques Tourneur of his and Curt Siodmak's *I Walked with a Zombie,* which used a black calypso singer "as a Greek chorus," a bit that did not pass unnoticed at OWI nor, we might presume, among attentive moviegoers. In no less than three pages the OWI man commended its "undertones one could match in no current Hollywood film portraying the Negro" and its "keeping at play . . . ambiguities" that were "over the head of the white characters." In *Cat People,* Gunther Fritsch and Robert Wise's film of DeWitt Bodeen's script, the actor Sir Lancelot (who had played Tourneur's calypso singer) represented a calm center of sanity in a white circle in which nothing was what it seemed to be. And in *Curse of the Cat People* he was a prepossessing houseman originally written as "a middle-aged New England motherly type" who, according to Bodeen, was redirected by Lancelot's reading into it a "colorful, amusing, and different way of presenting expository information."[74]

In the slipstream of any hot trend we might expect a satirist to haze it, and conscience-liberalism was not immune. Preston Sturges in his *Sullivan's Travels* (1942) put some english on the idea in a bit about a filthy, defeated *white* chaingang that is invited to a rural black church for an evening of old movies. The preacher (Jesse Lee Brooks) admonishes his flock with arch irony: "Brethren and sisters, we are goin' to share our pleasure with some neighbors less fortunate than ourselves . . . and when they gets here I'm goin' to ask you once more, neither by word, nor by action . . . to make our guests feel unwelcome . . . nor to draw away from them or get high-tone. For we is all equal in the sight of God."[75]

Musicals boomed and often found a place for a sliver of liberal doctrine, though seldom with Sturges's sly wit. In the most charming (and neglected), *Higher and Higher*, the young cast featured Frank Sinatra, Mel Tormé, the French refugee Michelle Morgan, and Dooley Wilson, the latter on a hot streak that included *Casablanca* and *Stormy Weather*. They spend the movie planning an antic "butlers' ball," an egalitarian affair that was a jiving civilian twist on the war movie genre. Then Hazel Scott, a bundle of intellect, brass, and musicology, was spotted at Café Society by Gregory Ratoff, who made a spot for her in *Something to Shout About* (1943), a musical that also featured Teddy Wilson, a hero among blacks for having integrated Benny Goodman's band in *Hollywood Hotel* (1938), and two black acts not known for crossing over: Chuck and Chuckles and the Speed Kings. Praise be to Ratoff for his "sympathetic treatment," wrote Florine Ross in *PM*, a sentiment echoed by Scott herself. "I hope this trend keeps up," she said in the *Courier*, and called for an end to "hangovers of Jim Crow." The boom in this sort of casting should be seen as more than gestures to please the OWI; every city had its hepcats like the whites who danced in the aisles of the Brooklyn Paramount, and the tradepapers began to take their tastes into account in their movie reviews.[76]

Even when black acts were segregated, their energy and style rattled convention and made the 'cats swing as much as they made Walter White wince. Two of the best, Warners' *Thank Your Lucky Stars* and *This Is the Army*, arrived in 1943, complete with rousing, if Jim Crow, numbers woven into soldiers' "camp shows" put on to raise funds. In the latter, black loyalty is portrayed in a big dance number in a stylized Harlem streetscape that swings its way toward describing "what the well-dressed Harlem man will wear"—zoot suits swapped for army olive-drab. A similar setting—probably the *same* set—showcases the black number in *Thank Your Lucky Stars*. There Willie Best, more or less as himself but in "class A" uniform, comes home to marry "Ice Cold Katie," who is temporizing in her flat while the ensemble, including a svelte Hattie McDaniel, sings out: "Ice Cold Katie, marry the soldier!" Among them are the *doyens* of black Hollywood: Noble Johnson as an Indian, Madam Sul Te Wan as a black Mae West, Jesse Lee Brooks in the clawhammer coat of a stock preacher, all seeming to knowingly parody their bread-and-butter roles. Yet another black gem in a white setting, Paramount's flawed *Star Spangled Rhythm* (1942) gave Katharine Dunham and Eddie Anderson a rollicking spoof of zoot suit style in all its calculated outrageousness. Often these bits passed without a ripple, but *Star Spangled Rhythm* evoked a range of criticism that reflected the evolving aesthetic brought on by the war. A hit, said the *Negro Actors Guild Newsletter* as it counted the black gigs; only an infant's step from

The black production number in *Thank Your Lucky Stars* (1943) revealed the tension between old and new black imagery, as here Jesse Lee Brooks is marrying garish Hattie McDaniel to uniformed Willie Best. Copyright Warner Bros.

convention, said the *Amsterdam* and *Commonweal;* a caricature, said Manny Farber on the left, a sure sign that the studios "have not changed their mind" about African America.[77] And of course, Farber had his point; a trend was not a ukase from a tsar. Notably, Paramount with its minstrelman biopics shied from black specialty acts. And at MGM, apart from *Cabin in the Sky* there was little, perhaps because Horne was seen as Walter White's "weapon to try on the moguls" and therefore too controversial. In any event, she appeared in eight movies in two years, mostly in easily snipped solos, save for *Panama Hattie,* in which she and the Berry Brothers sang of whites "down below the borderline [110th Street, where] they don't kick the gong around." Minnelli remembered *I Dood It,* "a comic potboiler" salvaged from "footage and sets" of a stalled project into which they tossed Hazel Scott and Butterfly McQueen.[78]

Clearly, after half a century of black erasure from life in the movies, a restoration would not be easy. Take as an example *Rhapsody in Blue,* one of a cycle of show-business biopics into which it should have been likely to work black acts. This George Gershwin life provided a neat opening for Hazel Scott, an actual friend of the subject, and Warner Bros. indeed engaged her for a sequence in which she appears in his *Porgy and Bess.* But as production dragged on and the "nut" rose, the bosses went for only the safest of material, thereby shelving its urbanity, its director Reuben Mamoulian (who had done the first *Porgy* on Broadway), its leftist writer Clifford Odets, and gradually all of its black parts. Typically, the Breen office closed off the issue when it fretted over offending colored audiences and spoiling Latin American relations. Finally, as the focus narrowed to Gershwin's private life, the remaining black production numbers seemed too staged to Oscar Levant, a friend of Gershwin who played himself in the movie, and they were cut, thus removing from the center of Gershwin's creative life the African Americans who had inspired much of his work. All that remained were his ache to do a "folk" opera, a glimpse of early triumph as Al Jolson sings "Swanee," and a glitzy ending in which Paul Whiteman pays homage to Gershwin by introducing jazz to a formally dressed crossover audience and promising to "make a lady out of jazz." As to the blacks themselves, only Scott as a classy saloon pianist and Anne Wiggins Brown as tartish dancer to a darkened-down but clearly white male corps de ballet in a sequence from Gershwin's brief opera *Blue Monday Blues*[79] survived the final cut.

The Hollywood career of Katharine Dunham took a similar route. Despite a career on Broadway and on tour in Europe, she spent the war in search of movies that offered more than the odd zootsuiter's moll in *Stormy Weather* or *Star Spangled Rhythm.* She choreographed the short *Carnival in Rhythm* and Abbott and Costello's *Pardon My Sarong,* but near the end of the war her agent was still arranging dinners with producers on whom her potentialities seemed lost and steering the tabletalk toward casting her as Sadie Thompson in Maugham's *Rain,* or perhaps a film of her stage show *Carib Song,* or a bold movie on racial problems, all with dauntingly poor luck.[80]

Nevertheless, black angles continued to turn up in most genres in heretofore unthinkable roles, bits, and dialogue, each speaking its piece for OWI while adding to the slow accretion of a liberal mentality. Even westerns squeezed in a few oddments, no mean achievement in a genre that in antebellum times had all but erased black figures from history. An easy means to segue into a western locale was to open on the Civil War and Reconstruction, from which the hero flees westward, but in such movies before the war—*The Texans, The Last Command, Southward Ho, Belle Starr,* and B-movies like *Robin Hood of the Pecos*—nightriding terrorists were cleansed of their antiblack motives by calculatedly absenting freedmen and thus became mere avengers against greedy railroads or other western conventional heavies. *Santa Fe Trail* (1940), for example, opens on Harper's Ferry amidst the sectional hatreds arising from the debate over slavery, a device for introducing historical figures like the abolitionist John Brown, whom Raymond Massey played with Hitlerian bombast. Driven more by demons than by conviction, Brown surrenders the debate on slavery to Jeb Stuart, an eventual Confederate brigadier who also regarded slavery as a wrong but one that cannot end either as a consequence of Abolitionist pressure or at the price of lost Southern "pride." No matter: the movie moves west and the issue is dropped (leading White to write: "My wife, son and I were inexpressibly shocked"). A similar appeal to Southern pride colored the politics of other westerns: *Dodge City, Virginia City, Ten Gentlemen from West Point,* and *They Died with Their Boots On.* In *Dodge City,* for example, opposing gangs of Civil War veterans brawl in a saloon and vie with each other in singing "Rally 'round the Flag, Boys" and "Dixie," a contest won by the Southerners.[81]

Yet the war affected the western genre in small ways, as in *The Ox Bow Incident,* which its author, Walter Van Tilburg Clark, had intended as an anti-Nazi tract, and its advocates at Fox—Lamar Trotti, Henry Fonda, and William Wellman—each took personal pride in as a voice for conscience-liberalism. The Georgian writer Lamar Trotti in particular felt his liberalism heightened by the war in small ways recorded in his diary. He found himself bristling at racist tabletalk, questioning his own regional ideological baggage, counting the numbers of blacks in parades and in the Senate galleries during debates on polltaxes, feeling their rising presence in crowded depots, and making little gestures such as after reading Lillian Smith's *Strange Fruit* leaving it in a Texas busstop for some other Southerner to pick up and read. By 1944, he found himself arguing at dinner that "Negroes must be permitted to vote" and that "the South will and must face it." And in an encounter thrust upon them by their respective wartime activities, Trotti and Lillian Smith met in Washington where he found that mutually *he* had liked *Strange Fruit* and that *she* had liked *Ox Bow.*[82]

Their western owed much to prewar "problem" movies that often had ended by revealing the good at the core of American life, such as Wellman's own *The Public Enemy* (1931), *Heroes for Sale* (1933), and *Wild Boys of the Road* (1933). But the war clearly had toughened the genre; in *The Ox Bow Incident* no happy ending can head off a triple lynching that two saddleworn, hard-drinking, morally ambivalent heroes (Fonda and Harry Morgan) are powerless to stop. Its only concession to regional pride was Trotti's softening the glare of blame upon the South by making the Confederate officer who leads the party into not only a phoney soldier but a remorseful suicide, unable to face up to a son who had refused to participate.[83]

Despite the nod to Southern sensibility, they did justice to Clark's book, which had been written in the year of the Munich pact as "an allegory of the unscrupulous and brutal Nazi methods, and a warning against temporizing . . . [against] a kind of American Nazism." Even though their movie "fell flat on its face" (Wellman's words), and James

Agee thought its "phonily gnarled" movielot trees portentously stagey, it remained faithful to Clark's goal, a goal, it must be said, which was accomplished in part by Trotti's rounded and toughened black preacher, Sparks (Leigh Whipper) as a man apart from the white mob, refusing to join in, praying over the three men mistakenly hanged as rustlers, and in part by Clark's own two saddletramp heroes, speaking for restraint. The only flaw was in Whipper's own reading of the role, which black critics thought echoed his most unctuous work.[84]

Despite Walter Wanger's prototypical *Sundown*, the genre of jungle movies never fully adopted a war footing, preferring mere erasure as a solution to adapting Africans to the war. The idea of an eventual partnership as a surrogate for colonialism, although adopted as policy by the British after the Atlantic Charter, may have given black Africa an investment in the outcome of the war, but not in the world of the B-movie. Erasure seemed more riskfree than engagement. As Harry Cohn is supposed to have said to a prospective scriptwriter: "No niggers; get me another jungle." Following Cohn's cautious line, every hack arrived at the same solution; Lighten the characters to a neutral brown color, but deny them a specific ethnicity; invest them and their mythical country with a grudge against the Axis; and locate them in a hidden valley or lost city governed by thinly clad Amazons, a dodge that allowed casting offices to recruit from the ranks of reformed ecdysiasts. Two typical factory models were PRC's *Jungle Siren* (1942) and Columbia's *Captive Wild Woman* (1943), the former placing Allied fortunes in the hands of Olympic swimmer Buster Crabbe and the ex-stripper Ann Corio, the latter starring Acquanetta, a coolly beautiful B-movie actor whose mixed ethnicity allowed her to appear as black in the black press and white in the white.

Saturday morning serials followed a similar line, the most ingenious erasure of blacks turning up in Republic's *Nyoka the Jungle Girl* (1942), in which not only was the witchdoctor-heavy played by Frank Lackteen, an actor with a vaguely Arabic face, but the stock savages were rendered obsolete by arming the doctor with a spearthrowing machine! The sequel, *Perils of Nyoka* (1942), exiled Africans by shifting to a desert where Vultura, "the exotic ruler of a band of vicious Arabs," holds sway over her white *dacoits*. Republic's *The Secret Service in Darkest Africa* (1943) played a similar angle, but with a Nazi heavy who improbably kills a local sultan and dons a burnoose so convincingly that the hapless Arabs never spot the ringer in their midst. When they tired of Arabs and Amazons it was an easy matter to relocate to a nameless exotic island, as in *Danger in the Pacific* and Universal's *the Adventures of Smilin' Jack* (1943), where the traitor Kageyama (Turhan Bey) conspires with the evil Fraülein von Teufel (Rose Hobart). And in the odd film like Universal's *Jungle Queen* (1945) for which they trotted out black Hollywood—in this case Clarence Muse, Napoleon Simpson, and Clinton

Rosamond—the writers invented a "mysterious" white queen to rule them.[85]

Once, Warner Bros. tried to serve the cause of war by means of a makeshift recutting of a prewar promo-film for the Belgian colony in the Congo, succeeding only in revealing to themselves how the war had changed their minds and revealed the absurdities embedded in their prewar idea of Africa. As Gordon Hollingshead of the shorts unit told Jack Warner (with no hint of irony), *Congo* showed how the African had progressed from cannibalism to contributing to the war effort! Luckily for the studio, Norman Moray in the New York office quickly saw that their angle might fuel rather than solve the race problem. Necessarily, he predicted, blacks would resent the picture if the "savages" were shown at their worst, while in the South they risked rousing an already rumored reaction to Hollywood liberalism. Thus they faced only two options in treating their misguided purchase: either bury it as a purely "educational" film so dull as to arouse no one, or play up the Belgians. Either way, their dilemma revealed the mindless casualness with which they had once viewed Africans as against their new frame of mind, which at least had thrust upon them the need for new stuff.[86]

Blessedly for audiences, writers found less absurd solutions to the problem of introducing warborne racial material into movies: character and incident that fit both assumptions that audiences were already grafting onto old ideologies and the merely necessitarian needs of the war. At the least, social distance between the races narrowed. In a Dead End Kids movie, for example, a bootblack voices the propaganda line: When a Nazi sympathizer asks for a shine, he replies, "Give you a shine? I'll polish you off quick if you don't get outta that chair." In *Eyes of the Night* (1943), a B-movie detective yarn, a blind private eye and his black valet are more a team than boss-and-flunky. In Samuel Bronston's biopic of Jack London (1943), the hero's link to the proletariat is established when he is fired from a cannery; back home his link to blacks is shown in his familiarity with a family servant. Not only do they share a common fund of knowledge of poverty, but it is she who stakes him to expenses to cover the Russo-Japanese War (where he vainly warns America in 1904 of Japanese expansionism). In two major biopics, *Yankee Doodle Dandy* (1943) and *Wilson* (1943), on George M. Cohan and President Wilson respectively, even the White House servants are given new lines. In the former, stiff as royal courtiers, they fondly recall every president since "Mr. Teddy," and in a production number freedmen file past the looming statue of Lincoln, singing "The Battle Hymn of the Republic" as a voiceover intones the Gettysburg Address. In the latter, Wilson's liberalism is overstated indirectly when one of his daughters decides to do social work among the African Americans in Goat Alley (the capital's slums were well known to Americans).[87]

If the Academy had given Oscars for stretching material to fit OWI needs, *Reunion in France* (1943) would have been a shoo-in. A romantic story of a downed pilot (John Wayne) and a patrician Frenchwoman (Joan Crawford) who seems too cozy with the German occupiers, the film ambles along in search of a way to work in the real war until it becomes a parody that embraces blacks and Allied war aims. At a chic supper club reminiscent of, but too sleek to be taken for, a saloon of the literary Paris of the 1920s, a black jazz combo is improbably playing. As though proving that even a black sideman can strike a blow for freedom, a grinning musician croons to the uncomprehending Germans: "I'll be glad when you're dead, you rascal you—*and Adolph too!*"

We cannot know the precise impact of a cycle of war movies and their resonances in general Hollywood fare, but certainly black activists thought moviemakers had contributed to the ideal of a Double V. Certainly whenever a black soldier praised these gestures a black reporter took heart from it, aired it out in his column, and predicted a lively postwar future of more of the same. And the NAACP gauged its work as so promising that it plotted a postwar Hollywood bureau meant to perpetuate its wartime arrangement, which had grown into a liberal pulpit. And even the OWI liberals proposed some sort of postwar extension of their agency.

If the black gains chronicled here seem not to measure up to lofty hopes, and seem no more than the tics of a culture in crisis, it must be kept in mind: That is part of the point. In cultural crises, new alliances form, new leaders emerge, new fissures open in old structures, new scaffolding rises in place, and in popular culture old genres and formulas take on added weight. Sometimes these shifts in weight and meaning occur in bits so recondite as to seem the sort of lore that only connoisseurs share, not unlike Hitchcock's fans who comb the screen in search of his moment on the screen (in *Lifeboat* he is the "before" shot in a newspaper ad for a dieting regimen), while in other cases they seem to promise such profound change as to seem organic in origin. In this way, their small doses often refer to a shared history and give shared beliefs an entertaining twist, whetting their audience's expectation for more of the same.[88] But what of the hundreds of B-movies and programmers that seemed untouched by the war? It must be remembered that the circumstances of moviegoing must have enhanced credibility. A-movies played in downtown "palaces" accompanied by glossy advertising and were occasions for heavy Saturday night dates, so they took on a cultural importance that warranted attention and receptivity. In other words, if B-movies played matinees and split weeks in "the nabes," accompanied by rude noises made by impudent boys, no one gave them a second thought, but many war movies, playing as they did in picture palaces, took on the cachet of cultural events that *mattered*.

4

The Making of The Negro Soldier

During the New Deal the Roosevelt administration had been as diffident toward producing its own film propaganda as the Congress had been wary of it, at least until Pare Lorentz's famous pair, *The River* and *The Plough That Broke the Plains*, Paul Strand's *The City*, and the Farm Security Administration's photographers revealed how art and message might be combined without the appearance of shameless tubthumping. At a level closer to bedrock, a nation built upon deeply running feelings of the right of the individual to oppose his rulers, to claim "countervailing" powers, the idea of awarding government the right of self-advertisement seemed anathema. Wartime, for a while at least, would perhaps be different, because, as Feibleman's *Theory of Culture* had asserted, wars against external enemies induced a "tendency toward similarity" that invited the government to take a bolder hand in defining its war aims as well as its means of prosecuting the war. In other words, the government felt entitled to assert *Why We Fight*—to borrow the title of its most famous film series. Having shed their coyness toward propaganda, their feeling that only the enemy resorted to it, the government's filmmakers and psychologists rushed to their work with the fervor of converts and with a faith in "social engineering"—the altering of collective belief—that seemed boundless. But what to teach America about racism? Luckily, as one wit said, "Hitler gave racism a bad name"; that is, the nature of the enemy helped modulate a prickly regional issue into a collective, liberalizing mentality.

The struggle to make the army's own documentary, *The Negro Soldier* (1944), a project that was the sum of several antagonistically cooperative interest groups, reveals much about the place of the film of advocacy in a representative democracy. At first the project was restrained by mere necessity. The army wanted only an antidote to the simmering racism in its ranks; Hollywood wished only for a means of earning a medal for its efforts; the social engineers hoped to cultivate their craft in a near-laboratory setting; and the NAACP fished for a way to link its goals to the government's war aims. Meanwhile, conservatives in Congress strove mightily to slash filmmaking budgets while liberals in agencies such as OWI nursed their projects through to the screen in order to enlist the government in their cause.[1]

The army itself was of two minds. The mere presence of an eventual one million black soldiers appalled many of its senior officers, while liberals among the circle of civilians in the War Department faced up to the black presence and imagined that their social engineers might design movies and manuals to create harmony in the ranks across racial lines. How were the two camps to be reconciled? That nettle was left up to the civilians and a group of officers only just drawn from civil life. They were everywhere, from Brigadier Frederick H. Osborn—rich New Yorker, scholar in eugenics, board member of the Social Science Research Council, nephew of Henry Fairfield Osborn (himself a scholar and a major figure in the Museum of Natural History in Manhattan), family friend to Secretary of War Henry L. Stimson and General George C. Marshall, and advocate of film as a medium of education and morale-building—all the way through the ranks to Hollywood civilians like Frank Capra, late of Columbia Pictures.[2]

Of all the army's branches, its Information and Education Division (I&E) most reflected this intrusion of civilian ways. Osborn headed a staff that included such social scientists as Donald Young of the University of Pennsylvania and Samuel Stouffer of the University of Chicago, the latter a senior officer in I&E. Together they put forth an argument not only for the use of film but for systematic measurement of its efficacy. Moreover, their agenda grew beyond short-term goals to include a "strategy of truth" coupled with a trust in "social engineering" that they intended to use to teach liberal reaffirmations of American social beliefs.

The immediate target of their strategy was black disaffection. Judge William Hastie, a War Department assistant for black affairs, kept a clipping file on the incidence of racial strife around army posts, a record confirmed in OWI's own file. Black resentment of Jim Crow bloodbanks, discrimination in industry and housing, the circumscribed role for blacks in the war—all of these and more prodded the black press and a readership that included, said OWI, a "younger and militant Negro clergy" driven by "an anti-war attitude" rooted in the government's slowness to "translate the objectives of the war into realities for Negroes." Necessarily, OWI probed for a means first to convey to blacks a rebuttal to the Japanese portrayal of the conflict as "'a white man's war,'" and second, to mount "an educational campaign" that set forth to African America "a real, legal, and permanent chance for improvement under democracy."[3] Reinforcing this official frame of mind was the army's own manual, which took movies as its point of departure. "When the Negro is portrayed in the movies, or elsewhere, as a lazy, shiftless, no-good, slew-footed, happy-go-lucky, razor-toting, tap-dancing vagrant, a step has been taken in the direction of fixing this mental picture in the minds of whites," it warned.[4]

At first the task seemed paralyzingly hopeless. Opinion samples revealed an "impaired" and "bitter" black army whose disaffection grew with each new Double V sermon preached by their chaplains. Besides, for every black soldier who sneered at the irony of "a discriminatory system at home" contrasted with "the four freedoms overseas," there was a white soldier who nursed a nugget of resentment of blacks bent upon "trying to use the war as a wedge to pry open the doors of social equality." Solutions ranged over mere gimmickry: a proposed "Negro Good Will Caravan," black newsreels, and recruiting makers of race movies.[5]

Much like events in Hollywood, the situation in Washington changed as a result of a coalition of forces: Hastie and then Truman Gibson in the Pentagon; Carlton Moss, a young black veteran of Federal Theatre and radio; and the black press that urged its readers to deluge Lowell Mellett with petitions for some sort of filmed propaganda, and reported the progress of White in Hollywood and every failure of Hollywood newsreels to measure up. Thomas W. Young of the *Norfolk Journal and Guide*, for example, saw two versions of news footage of black engineers, one of them straight reportage, the other intended for whites, "a burlesque and a travesty" of black participation in the war.[6]

If the War Department failed to respond to these entreaties, not only might they drop the problem just where Hastie had found it, but they would leave the field to race-moviemakers for whom black critics had lost all hope. Indeed, early on, Oscar Micheaux, the doyen of race movies, had complained to Elmer Davis in OWI that only a tiny fraction of wartime film "shows the Negro from any standpoint" and offered himself as one who had "learned how and what to do to get [blacks] into the war spirit." A half dozen of these firms, whose profits had been derived from the Jim Crow system that the war was coming to stand against, offered their services, and indeed at first they seemed "an excellent medium for reaching Negroes." Ted Toddy of Atlanta, head of the most enterprising of them, hinted that he had Paul Robeson himself ready to do a movie about the black 99th Pursuit Squadron. And two of them actually made movies: Alfred Sack and his black director and star Spencer Williams made *Marching On*, a grainy, washed-out movie of life on a black post where the troops silence a clandestine Japanese radio station; and the team of Elder Solomon Lightfoot Michaux and Jack Goldberg made a documentary, much of it from the Signal Corps's own footage, *We've Come a Long, Long Way*.[7] Not until the latter film came in, coincident with the completion of *The Negro Soldier*, did the War Department reckon that the ideology of race movies differed from the Pentagon's evolving racial aims of the war—that is, not until Moss's writing forced the army to think through what sort of film they wished to have speak for them to African America.[8]

Why Moss, only just departed from student life at Morgan College and Columbia? Partly it was New York: radio, theatre, the producer John Houseman, and finally a revue he put together for the Apollo, *Salute to the Negro Troops*. But it was also a mood set by the Double V campaign, stragglers from the March on Washington, the black rank and file drawn to the CPUSA by its gestures such as running a black vice-presidential candidate, and the New Dealers who asked "will things be better for us now" that war had come. At first skeptical, as Horace Cayton observed, of the government's "sporadic and unintegrated and insufficient" policies, blacks soon enjoyed the soaring sense of "more attention than [they] had enjoyed since the old Abolitionist days." The feeling extended deep into black circles, including the laborers who had come to Washington to wrestle with the post office entry examinations and win a stable life sorting mail. One such woman, a domestic servant, was transformed by the war when she got a job with the Office of Price Administration and within days found herself in the center of a protest to integrate the OPA's cafeteria, all in a single stroke that would have been unthinkable before the war.[9]

Moss arrived in New York's theatrical bohemia amidst this unfocused energy. His first letter to Archibald MacLeish at the Office of Facts and Figures (OFF, later OWI) read like a leftist version of Micheaux's opener: "Unless we answer the just grievances of the Negro people," it said, enemies "will use them to sow disunity and confusion." Already he had mounted his *Salute* under the auspices of Fight for Freedom, Inc., a coalition of lefties and conservative patriots: Mrs. Calvin Coolidge and Richard Wright, Senator Carter Glass of Virginia and Jack Warner, Lowell Thomas and Paul Robeson. Odd couples all, but a solidly ecumenical résumé entry for Moss. Folded in with Moss's own Council on Negro Culture, it played its *Salute* at both the Apollo and the 3500-seat Mecca Temple in midtown as a fundraiser for recreational programs for the Jim Crow army. On its face an aberrant concoction, the revue nonetheless included as makers, performers, and sponsors an aristocracy of Hollywood: Hazel Scott, Canada Lee, Teddy Wilson, Helen Hayes, Charles MacArthur, Ben Hecht, Ethel Barrymore, Douglas Fairbanks, Spyros Skouras, Wanger, Warner, and others. As a result Moss found himself linked to a winner, and although he could not trace his *Negro*

Soldier gig directly to it, when *Salute* was revived in the spring at the Apollo, with Moss again at its center, he touted it to OWI as a vehicle for admitting past national sins while pointing to a sanguine future.[10]

Luckily for Moss and the army, his homage to black soldiers played while the government's search for filmic tools was at a low ebb. Hollywood movies were slow to start, and its documentaries such as *Liberty Ship* never seemed to make it to the screen; the studios gave as an alibi the wish to avoid "duplicating effort" of the government. When some films—such as Frank Capra's *Why We Fight* series—did appear, they reduced enemies and issues to geeklike comic-book levels that offended reviewers. Moreover, *Salute to the Negro Troops,* or at least its broad-brushed sponsorship, freed the army from the trap of rejecting Moss as too black, too militant, even too "Communist."[11]

In any event, in the summer of 1942 after the Apollo revival, the army (and later OWI) began treating Moss as though he were the black organic intellectual that Walter White had hoped to become, the spokesman through whose veins flowed the sense of the group. Moss, working with Marc Connelly, probably hired as a hedge against disaster, began to make a hymn to black pride, a reason to fight, and a menu of reasons for white soldiers to tolerate black. They toured the posts in search of an angle and a compromise between Connelly's sweetly nostalgic blacks and Moss's *Men of Color to Arms*—the title (borrowed from the abolitionist Frederick Douglass) of a militant first draft. Along the way they picked up two Hollywood script carpenters, Ben Hecht and Jo Swerling, the former a sponsor of Moss's *Salute*. Thus the prospective movie began to take shape in the classic Hollywood manner—assigning script doctors to rework perviously assigned material.[12] In this timeworn Hollywood way the army embarked on a quest mapped out for it by "feather merchants"—the army's slang for meddlesome civilians, in this case Negroes, intellectuals, and Hollywood liberals. The result, God forbid, might convert a besieged army into a social laboratory defined by racial propaganda that few general officers concurred in, addressed to one million black soldiers whom they would as soon do without, and in a newfangled, mistrusted medium.

For the army the most disturbing ingredient of the thing itself was its tone of advocacy. Like any familiar audiovisual aid it combined stock footage (from both Hollywood and the Signal Corps) and talking heads, but it also included reenactments of history. Thus the army's wish for a movie to help smooth over its racial tensions coincided with Moss's hope that under its breath the movie might extend its argument beyond current necessity. Improbably, the army had been implicated by the rush of events in its own eventual racial integration.

The rhetoric of the script embraced what every black activist in Hollywood had been lobbying and sipping lunchtime chicken soup for: a means of enlisting African Americans on the team by showing that they had already been covertly signed up in all of the nation's previous wars, as though making up for generations of structured absences and erasures from newsreels and heroic post-office murals. So rapidly did events carry the idea forward that by war's end the quiet insinuations of *The Negro Soldier* grew insistent in Moss's last project, *Teamwork* (1945). Moreover, blacks *noticed.* As a black show business paper headlined it: "Army Shows Hollywood the Way."[13]

This is not to claim that Moss worked apart as though a Lenin in Zurich. As early as 1928 a thread of conscience-liberalism had appeared in the intellectual quarterlies, providing a growing fund of both theory and data upon which to build a politics of changed racial arrangements. In fact, Donald Young, who in 1928 had edited an "American Negro" issue of *The Annals of the American Academy of Political and Social Science,* spent the war monitoring projects like *The Negro Soldier* and writing manuals such as the army's *Leadership and the Negro Soldier.* He reduced a lifetime of research into convenient "do's and don'ts" that became prescriptions for government moviemaking. No shots of watermelons, no fondness for porkchops, no stock figures from Hollywood lore, no "colored soldiers most Negroid in appearance," no overweening attention to black officers because "the Negro masses" think that "colored men who get commissions tend to look down on the masses." At the same time, with the best of intentions he came dangerously close to Hollywood's practice of absenting and erasing African America. "No Lincoln, no emancipation, or any race leaders, or friends of the Negro," he wrote.[14]

In other words, caution required a middle course that eschewed the extremities of both *ancien régime* and revolutionary vanguard—neither a Bourbon nor a Robespierre be. Sadly, the policy needlessly adopted a timidity that might stifle the message, indeed had already done so in altering Moss's title, and might divide blacks ever after into those with a contempt for half-loaves and those for whom they were too good to be true. Already the government had turned out its share of humdrum films: a one-reeler on the colored section of the National Youth Administration, another on *Negro Colleges in Wartime* and their ROTC units, and *Henry Browne, Farmer,* the only one with a spark of the drama that Moss hoped to attain.

Claude Barnett of the Associated Negro Press (ANP) had been in on a couple of government-sponsored films and felt thwarted by them. Somehow, between idea and result a slippage always occurred. In 1940 he had urged the General Education Board to sponsor a film for the American Negro Exposition in Chicago, but of the resulting *One Tenth of a Nation* could say only that it was "a pretty picture but it did not do what we set out to do." And of *Henry Browne,* an idea he had taken to the Department of Agriculture, he could only report that "my initial idea flew right out the window" to be replaced by "an insipid little story far from our original purpose." At least one black viewer agreed, asking OWI: Is there "only one Negro family in the war and is the only thing they are doing farming?"[15] Actually the film was not all that weak. It was an homage to the bucolic life that Booker Washington had preached in which a black farmer who plants peanuts (for their wartime uses) is seen as one of the "soldiers of production," indeed as part of a continuum between his own kids, who raise a calf and do their chores, and the black warriors in uniform. In fact, Barnett's barbs notwithstanding, not only did the NAACP thank Agriculture for "the admirable farmer and his family" and acknowledge the film's "value both in raising the morale of Negroes themselves and even more in the emphasis to white audiences," but during the Harlem riots, as we have seen, the Schomburg's man played it on his wall.[16]

At any rate, *The Negro Soldier* would be bolder, Moss thought, despite its army sponsors and their Hollywood script doctors. He worked away at it in the Library of Congress, wondering whether the army would accept his script. Meanwhile, back in Hollywood Frank Capra, the nominal producer, chose a director, first William Wyler, who then "got a better offer from the Air Force," and then Stuart Heisler, a journeyman who had weathered racial tensions while shooting *The Biscuit Eater* (1940) on location in Georgia. In turn Heisler, who hoped for a writer who "*really* knows the background of the Negro," met Moss, and they "hit it off like magic" with the result that after a round of fruitless auditions Moss also won the leading role. Within a year they would have a final cut that pleased the army, a black preview audience, and a sampling of reviewers.[17]

Here black leaders picked up gossip about the movie and joined the army in promoting its premiere. For example, when Walter White spoke to the Hollywood Writers Congress on the campus of UCLA in 1943, he told his audience he was "pleased to learn that . . . 'The Negro Soldier' is now being completed [and] . . . is certain to be an outstanding contribution to the morale of Negro troops and civilians, an advance toward better understanding between the races, and a telling blow against Japanese race and color propaganda."[18] Already he was turning over in his mind an expansionary purpose for a movie the army regarded as merely a necessity.

The Negro Soldier as released easily met the army's modest goal, but by placing blacks at the center of an entire movie it also paralleled White's work in Hollywood, thus linking a private black campaign to changes in public policy that blacks had helped force. True, in making its soft plea for black pride while sidestepping the persistence of segregation, it was aimed at the political center. In typical Hollywood fashion it offered the sort of flowing, seamless story, modulated lighting, and smooth optical effects that had made feature films so easily digestible. The difference was that the studio system (it had been shot on the old

That the war altered racial arrangements may be seen on location with *The Negro Soldier* (1944) as Carlton Moss, holding the script, and Stuart Heisler, in captain's bars, shared unaccustomed authority. Courtesy Carlton Moss.

Fox lot on Western Avenue) had been enlisted in a movie that had given African Americans the center of the frame and the action. And following Donald Young's prescription for fresh black iconmaking and the substance of White's pledges, the army had provided a model of a sober black bourgeoisie and its soldier-sons at war against America's enemies. Every performance, every stockshot of blacks in training and combat, every observance of a patriotic ritual signaled the relocation of black visual interest to the center of the movie.

Every image from main titles onward built expectations for the argument to follow. The army's own logotype, an armed eagle, dissolves (unthinkably in any prior year) to the title *The Negro Soldier* "presented by" the Signal Corps. A montage of good, gray black churches carries the viewer into a gothic edifice in which a soldier and a reverent choir are finishing "Since Jesus Came into My Heart." As the hymn fades, a preacher (Moss) puts aside his sermon to introduce the soldiers in the flock, the last of them with a hint of feminism—"Private Parks, First Class," says a female soldier in a closeup, to which Moss replies with pride, "First class indeed." Here he hammers at the army's angle: a reason to fight. He reminisces about Joe Louis's defeat of the German Max Schmeling (in voiceover to news footage) with his "American [not black] fist," a fight that, says Moss, looms as a rematch in a far larger arena. Here Joe Louis is shown leading a training company through an obstacle course while Schmeling goes through his paces as a paratrooper in "the Nazi army." Then, with the shot again favoring Moss, he holds up a copy of *Mein Kampf* and reads its few references to blacks as "born half-apes." But more important, the wide shot of Moss's pulpit resonates with an angle similar to the one the viewer will have glimpsed in *Life* magazine's coverage of the Luftwaffe's bombing of Coventry, the ruined church in *Sundown,* and two other features, *Mrs. Miniver* (1942) and *Sherlock Holmes and the Secret Weapon* (1943), in each of which priests or journalists set forth Allied war aims and the better world that was to come.[19]

From Joe Louis as both tribal and national hero, Moss carries his viewer to a history of African Americans in the nation's wars, a story never before spread to a popular audience. Antique prints and stock-shots (of both newsfilm and Hollywood features such as Griffith's *America* and Victor Fleming's *The Rough Riders*) punctuated by reenactments carry the movie along in unruffled Hollywood style. Only the Civil War, the nation's still divisive *Iliad,* is glossed by tightening down to the Lincoln Memorial and the Gettysburg Address. With the coming of the twentieth century the action shifts to library footage of World War I combat, Croix de Guerres awarded to black soldiers, and parades up Fifth Avenue, with particular attention paid to the 369th New York National Guard. The chronicle then moves to World War II and a *March of Time* sort of reenactment of Dorie Miller at Pearl Harbor, which was at once a central metaphor of the army's wished-for black dedication to the war and a repudiation of Japanese racial propaganda.[20]

Of them all, the most compelling visual trope offering a bluntly racial basis for fighting was a shot of a patently prop-room-constructed stone cairn on which a plaque in English testifies to black heroism in France in the Great War. Then, in a stroke of cutting-room cleverness, the boots of German invaders are supered over it, after which, as Moss explains Nazi cupidity, an explosion shatters the monument. Together with the image of Dorie Miller, it offered blacks a motive to fight. As Moss says of Miller, so much for "Japan [as] the savior of the colored races," so the blasted cairn, purporting to be a testament to French gratitude for the black "hellfighters" of World War I, is shown as a victim of German racism.

Here *The Negro Soldier* shifts to a human scale by taking up the progress of a black soldier from basic training through officers' candidate school and thence to combat. His story is told in voiceover by his mother, a trim, tailored woman in a small stole, the perfect model of Donald Young's black bourgeoisie. She is pleased not only with his soldiering but also with the utopia that surrounds it in which blacks aspire to high rank, meet nice girls at dances, read Langston Hughes in the post library, and go to church on Sunday. The opportunities seem limitless, even including West Point, as though the army really believes it. Returning to Moss's church, the movie ends on a chorus of "Onward Christian Soldiers" and a syncopated "Joshua Fi't the Battle of Jericho" played over a montage of marching men and women in a visual and aural coda of the army's best hopes.

What now? The army wished only that its own troops see it, and even then, gingerly and not as a mandate. But the army's partners saw in OF-51 (its code number) much more. Based upon the social engineers' samples, the movie seemed to demonstrate that belief and ideology were open to persuasion by film, a conclusion gradually shared by OWI, who wished to show it to civilians and the NAACP who saw it as a visual hymn to the Double V. At least it would be better than the tame stuff that Barnett had grumbled about, and it might in the minds of audiences fuse the government's and the blacks' goals into a common cause. Moreover, the timing was right. The riots in Harlem and Detroit during the summer of 1943 had shattered the illusion of interracial harmony, while the army's own data culled from its Research Branch confirmed the bad news in Hastie's clipping file. Still, the army dragged the film through a gauntlet of federal agencies that pored over dailies and rough cuts in search of hidden tinders that might set off riots on its own posts. In fact, when Moss, Heisler, and a civilian consultant ran the film for "a Negro camp outside of San Diego" the commander, certain the film would provoke violence, called out his military police, only to find that the black troops seened prone to violence only if they were *denied* a look at it.[21]

At last, in late 1943 it reached the Pentagon, where Marshall, Stimson, Osborn, General A. D. Surles of Army public relations, and Assistant Secretary John J. McCloy saw it and added suggestions to the growing list. Mainly, they wanted a "toned down" recut that showed "that Negroes did something [in World War I] other than engage in combat" and averted "an erroneous assumption of the overall job of the Army"—presumably not to lead the nation by the hand into racial reform.[22]

Finally, in January 1944 the army decided to use OF-51 in training black recruits while leaving open issues of future uses and editions. However, Research Branch continued to poll the troops and found only sanguine projections of future outcomes. In one sample, 90 percent of black soldiers and 80 percent of whites thought the film should be shown to rookies of both races, seeming proof of the inference that racial attitudes were subject to revision through education. Despite the persistence of army fears of a reaction to its "racial tolerance" angle, the social engineers prevailed. The film went into limited release to training cadres and by spring 1944 had become "mandatory" viewing for *all* troops at continental American replacement centers. Thus for more than a year, until August 1945 when the order was rescinded, almost every soldier who passed through I&E's training programs saw the film. Hence in spite of institutional timidity, the army had joined with black activists and white social engineers in tutoring its troops in an NAACP social goal that had all but become a war aim—"racial tolerance."[23]

Civilian audiences were another matter. Conscience-liberals itched for a civilian movie bedecked with an army eagle above its title, but OWI had already grown leery of budget cuts threatened by conservatives in the Congress. Black expectations had been raised so high by the war as to cause jitters among conservatives, who feared more of the same after the war. They already knew that NAACP membership had risen tenfold during the war and black consciousness had risen with it. White attitudes, even in the South, had also begun to change, if only incrementally. Yet the continuing threat of outbursts of social antipathy deterred OWI from plunging into civilian bookings for fear of the appearance of advocacy and the inference of alliance with an aggrieved minority. Elmer Davis himself saw the agency's precarious position and, caught between the needs of national unity and minority interests, asked for yet another softening cut. As it was, he thought it "perfectly passable in . . . the North" and saw "risks" only in "Atlanta" or other Southern locales.[24]

Of course, in the crisis brought on by the war, African Americans constituted a swing vote between two countervailing white powers and thus might be able to dictate a cultural decision of far greater reach than any white man intended. From the whites' point of view the issue was the extent to which African Americans accepted *The Negro Soldier* as an affirmative sign or as "just 'icing'" on a stale cake. At last they took a collective breath and showed it to two hundred black journalists in the Pentagon; it received a glowing response that indicated a black tolerance for the "strategy of truth" even if it glossed the reality of segregation. Not only the mainline NAACP but even the Marxist National Negro Congress (NNC) praised it as "the best ever done" and called for its release to civilians to which the Army acceded in April.[25]

But it was one thing to release the film and quite another to have it shown. Thereafter the fate of OF-51 relied ever more heavily on black suasion, this time applied to exhibitors, who usually booked films for profit rather than causes. Moss, Truman Gibson (the lawyer who had replaced Hastie in the War Department), and General Benjamin O. Davis, the ranking black officer in the army, personally went to Hollywood to campaign. Luckily for them, even when critics panned its watery liberalism they balanced their opinions by quoting opposing blacks. It "sugar coats," said the *Times* man, and "discretely avoids . . . race problems"; it was "pitifully, painfully mild," wrote James Agee. But Agee also reported that it "means a good deal, I gather, to most of the Negro soldiers who have seen it." *Time* played the same angle, quoting

Carlton Moss receives a civilian award—pinned on by Frank Capra himself—for his work on *The Negro Soldier*. Courtesy Carlton Moss.

Moss himself, who said that the picture would "mean more to Negroes than most white men could imagine."[26]

Drawn together as they were, these critics, the black promoters, and the audiences both commercial and military formed an emerging documentary film culture, which was just beginning to open to the idea of political cinema. Users of such documentaries, such as the United Auto Workers, reported that the film was "raising the morale of the Negro people as well as the white people" while nettling the Memphis censor into banning it.[27] For an acute observer, such films thus anticipated the arrival of a postwar generation of films of advocacy.

Meanwhile, before that day arrived, OF-51 flopped in theatres, victim perhaps of mixed reviews, the dog days of summer, a tiff between the army and the War Activities Council (WAC), a volunteer agency of professionals in the mass media that helped distribute army films to civilian theatres, and finally because theatremen preferred as their "duty" bookings the classier, Technicolored, and apolitical *Memphis Belle, With the Marines at Tarawa*, and *The Fighting Lady*, the latter two of which won Oscars. The hits routinely played twelve thousand houses as against *The Negro Soldier*'s less than two thousand. The only remediable variable was the length of OF-51; its forty-odd minutes either precluded playing it with double features or reduced its number of shows per day. So blacks pressed the army for a shorter version, which increased the playdates up to Moss's reckoning of five thousand houses, perhaps 80 percent of them catering to whites.[28]

Clearly, by the end of 1944 *The Negro Soldier* had become a monster unintended by the army, a black-driven message of "racial tolerance" that conscience-liberals came to regard as a weapon for mounting a postwar assault on American racism. By then African Americans, by welding a solid link between their own goals and the war aims of the Allies, had expanded their prospects for a stake in the outcome of the war, perhaps including a postwar conscience-liberal culture. That the alliance of blacks, their army, and Hollywood saw this prospect became obvious when they joined in a suit to restrain the showing of a rival documentary by a race-moviemaker. *We've Come a Long, Long Way* (1944), by the evangelist Elder Solomon Lightfoot Michaux and Jack Goldberg of Herald Pictures, forced them to ask whether race movies were a black achievement or a regression to Jim Crow. With the same lack of forethought that had guided its racial decisions so far, the army joined blacks in a thicket of intragroup black politics. The actual making of the Goldberg-Michaux movie will be taken up in the next chapter; for present purposes we need only know that it became a *cause célèbre* that forced the army to choose between propaganda that offered a future or one that invoked the past. The army's dilemma arose from its embarrassment at having casually authorized the Signal Corps to supply the filmmakers with stockshots while borrowing footage from Goldberg for use in *The Negro Soldier*. Moreover, Milton Eisenhower, Davis's associate in OWI, had actually abetted Michaux in a meeting arranged through two of his servants who belonged to Michaux's flock. Together the army's assistance and Eisenhower's kindness compelled the Pentagon to choose one vision of postwar racial arrangement over another, Moss's over Michaux and Goldberg's.[29]

The suit ensued from a Goldberg/Michaux injunction against the War Department that restrained them from releasing *The Negro Soldier* to civilians without charge, holding that the policy amounted to unfair competition arising from the army's joining its venture with the NAACP. Their shared goal, as Truman Gibson told a general, should be: "All races play every position on one big team," not segregation. Thus the suit would force the army to testify in open court that indeed they were implicated in marketing a movie that amounted to campaigning for the NAACP.

Not that the army calculated this course; rather, they were caught up in the NAACP's coast-to-coast campaign against the rival film and carried along by its momentum. Roy Wilkins and Gibson assembled a slate of worthies to "assist distribution" of OF-51 that included Nelson

Rockefeller, Mayor Fiorello La Guardia and Francis Cardinal Spellman of New York, Harold Ross of *The New Yorker*, and a West Coast wing. Then–NAACP counsel Thurgood Marshall, Gibson, and WAC filed an *amicus curiae* brief in which they characterized "their" movie as founded "on the premise that racial prejudices which divide our population will have their effect minimized by the dissemination of facts," not only a tenet of social psychologists such as Gordon Allport who thought of prejudice as curable through correct data, but also an anticipation of Marshall's later strategy of introducing sociological data into evidence in Supreme Court cases.[30] Thus the NAACP had enlisted in its cause two federal agencies and a panel of urban conscience-liberals. It remained only to avoid the suggestion of a "Jewish vs. Negro situation." With this in mind Walter White asked Jewish activists to stand with them and made certain that the press releases always contrasted the *movies* and not their *makers*, the one "insulting to Negroes," their own possessed of "enormous potentialities for good in stimulating the morale of American Negroes and in educating white Americans."[31] Anticlimactically, they reached a settlement that allowed *We've Come a Long, Long Way* a few days' "clearance" in which to recover its "nut" unopposed before the release of *The Negro Soldier*.

With the suit behind them, the blacks needed to justify the expense by drumming up an audience, a strategy that included exploiting their new ideological link with the army. With "everything . . . being done that can be done from the Washington end," wrote Edwin R. Embree of the Rosenwald Fund, a benefactor of black causes, it remained only for "many of us . . . to enlist in the cause" with OWI "to help spread the news to commercial theatres." In Hollywood White had already plugged it before the Writers' Congress and both Gibson and Moss spent the summer of 1944 in galas, wringing plugs from moguls ("the greatest War Department picture ever made," said Harry Cohn), prodding the black press and the leftish Hollywood Writers' Mobilization (HWM) into praising their movie as "a real contribution to national unity" and a refutation of "racist lies," while in Washington Philleo Nash in OWI sketched his own strategy.[32] Interracial committees wrote letters, sponsored previews, promoted the shorter version, and roused local allies like Mayor Fletcher Byron's Los Angeles Civic Unity Committee. Meanwhile, Moss escorted General Davis through a round of receptions put on by trade unions, civic groups, and the HWM. The black press joined in, urging the National Council of Negro Women "to rally the public and force the special film, *The Negro Soldier*, to be released in full to audiences of both races."[33]

In this way, only a year from the war's end, African Americans and their allies had breached two redoubts of white privilege, Hollywood and the Pentagon, and turned them to African American purposes. It remained now to set going the heat and pressure necessary to extrude the impact of their victory into peacetime; that is, to expropriate the army's necessitarian movies as vehicles of NAACP goals for years to come. Indeed, as we shall see in chapter 6, OF-51 was first among the films that outlived the war and became a voice in a postwar liberal culture based in schools, trade unions, and, most centrally, audiovisual libraries, the latter an arm of film culture that had barely existed before the war but soon became a presence in national academic life.

Even as war still raged, American teachers and social workers, many of them already devout conscience-liberals, began placing *The Negro Soldier* into civilian programs apart from the army's own usages. Of course, their mentality, under the rubric of "fair play," had always been part of the furniture of American minds, but the war had strengthed the idea by placing it on the agenda of federal agencies. In passing, it should also be pointed out that the movie gave liberals a voice in racial politics that before the war had resided in more narrowly Marxist circles. Now, mainstream activists, through *The Negro Soldier* (with its army eagle over its main titles), possessed their own vehicle to carry wartime mentalities into peacetime. As early as the spring of 1944 they had begun using it to teach "inter-cultural education" and "living together," to cite only two coinages that anticipated a peacetime conscience-liberalism. In one survey of film users, OF-51 ranked third in a lot of seventeen films in effectiveness. Moreover, the high esteem in which it was held reflected a movement among film users themselves toward, as Irving Jacoby, a leader in the postwar audiovisual movement, wrote, "the . . . use of idea films in America." Not only did liberals anticipate this postwar trend, one of their trade papers specifically linked the "great boom in the use of teaching films" to the predicted glut of "government and military films available after the war." Boldly librarians began speaking of the army as a sort of partner in social engineering—"attitude building," they called it—and a hero for its "courage [in] presenting a 'point of view'" on film. Casually they moved from vague hopes for "a better world" toward "a permanent front to act as a corrective democratic force," as one librarians' guild put it.[34]

The Negro Soldier bridged the gap between the army's needs in 1942 and the politics of this emerging film culture. The play in the movie that had allowed both the army and the NAACP to claim it as a success thus led to expectations of "enormous potentialities" once the war had ended. This reckoning of efficacy is, of course, a difficult point to make. As we have seen, early on the Gallup polls revealed a vein of white approval for public gestures and policies such as Eleanor Roosevelt's response to Marian Anderson's contretemps with the DAR or the passage of the FEPC. But apart from this statistical trace evidence, it is possible to discern a seepage of liberal rhetoric into ordinary talk, the way one could spot a liberal because he said "Negro" instead of "colored" or a Marxist because he said "the Negro people." In October 1943, for example, as American bomber crews at an English base received their orders to bomb civilian targets, one pilot recalled cheering a chance to kill "spawners of race hatred and minority oppression," as though reading from a liberal tract.[35]

Whether reflected in polls or not, film librarians presumed an evolving liberal, or as they often put it, "thinking" audience. June Blythe of the American Council on Race Relations, for example, not only believed the army's data on the impact of OF-51 but embellished it, estimating an audience of twenty million already that could expand if, "like any other new market," it was "sought out and educated to the value of film." OWI's files confirmed the impending boom; already their film bookers enjoyed a broad word-of-mouth following that included various urban libraries, the Brooklyn Jewish Community Council, Parent-Teacher Associations, churches, a reformatory in Virginia, and Latin American agencies, all totaling perhaps seven and a half million spectators in 150,000 playdates.[36]

The black and white liberal press provided a backbeat to which the audiovisual librarians marched. "Hats off!" *PM* had cried at the release of *The Negro Soldier*. "It will educate every white American who sees it." At the same time another critic claimed that in "building our democracy [it] is equal to thousands of soldiers, tons of material and volumes of the best anti-fascist speeches." The *Peoples' Voice*, Adam Clayton Powell's paper, called upon women to "rally the public." Another asked that it be turned against "the disgraceful conditions of . . . the War Dept" itself. Moss himself caught the swell; he had begun the film hoping, not to show "what's wrong with the Army," but only to "tell what's right with my people," but he ended the war feeling OF-51 had led white people to ask "what right [we have] to hold back people of that calibre."[37] Clearly, as a result of these forces set loose by the war—a "rising wind," Walter White had called it—the courses of African Americans, social activists, social engineers, and documentary film users intersected. However, even though *The Negro Soldier* took on a life of its own far beyond the army's original narrow intent, it could feed its audience only so long before going stale, and it could hardly speak its piece alone without the ideological support of inventories of similar films. And few titles in the government's stock had ever inspired the outpouring that had greeted OF-51. *The Negro Sailor* allowed ships' companies to believe that the messman's rating awarded to blacks was a permanent condition; *Welcome to Britain* coyly told black soldiers that American racial arrangements were to be observed while resident there; *Westward Is Bataan* caught fleeting images of racial harmony, but only aboard a troop ship from which blacks and whites would disgorge onto separate beaches; the army's cautionary sexual hygiene movies were not only segregated into white and black reels but were almost treasonous in their portrayal of black lasciviousness; and as we have seen, *Henry Browne, Farmer* and *Negro Colleges in*

Wartime were all but shelved for want of a market for their undemanding portrayal of things as they were.[38]

Even the most heartfelt attempts to address black sensibilities in these movies either misfired or were canceled for want of guidance. The worst of them were the sexual cautionary tales that not only nauseated generations of rookies, but also were ruined by some irreducible nugget of racism that the army seemed powerless to dissolve. In *Know for Sure,* for instance, a black squad on a pass follows a white squad to the local black brothel, but back at the post only the blacks have picked up doses of veneral disease, leaving an NAACP correspondent to conclude that "all Negroes have syphilis" and rousing the black troops to "indignation." This touchy subject already nettled black soldiers because the army pretended to have no policy toward prostitution, while in fact practicing a policy that steered white soldiers toward relatively hygienic, safe sex and black soldiers toward the seamiest "red light" districts, with the result that black troops testified to Army investigators that unless they risked VD "we don't have no place to go."[39]

The most blundering of these movies, *Easy to Get,* depicted stereotypes that either White or Breen had long since driven from the commercial screen. It opened on "a whole street duplicating a section of a Negro quarter in a southern town" where it blindly asserted that all strata of black society were broadly painted as the possibly infected population. A black soldier meets a prim maiden in a picture hat whom he squires to a soda fountain, a dance, an evening on a porch swing, as though warning that one might get a touch of something either from a soda straw or a squeaky swing that might have been touched by the black bourgeoisie. Later a "bad girl" is added (Muriel Smith in a lowcut blouse, as though a roadshow *Carmen Jones*), prowling the stags in a seedy saloon, "Blues in the Night" moodily on the soundtrack, cool pimps cruising in and out of the beaded curtains, abandoned dancing on the floor; following is an out-of-focus shot of a pillow, and finally the soldier in bed, alone, spent, dreamy—and having forgotten to use his prophylactic kit. As if this caricature of how one catches VD in black circles were not enough, the denouement left yet another discomfiting message: The fate of a sick black soldier was to be placed in the hands of white-coated, white-skinned medical saviors. The message was clear: The army was really two outfits, the one, black, hedonistic, Dionysian, and *sick,* the other white, Apollonian, and healing. No black worthies in the last reel—Joe Louis, Ralph Metcalf, Jesse Owens, or Paul Robeson—erased the sharp-edged image of a declining black soldier, prematurely old, alone in a darkened room, a victim only of his own appetites.[40]

Then there were the movies that never were. The army air force, following up Truman Gibson's call reminding them of the third anniversary of Tuskegee airbase, started up two films, *Red Tails* and *Wings for This Man,* the former a probable abortion, the latter a bland assertion of what had already been said. "Intended for public release to Negro motion picture theatres," said OWI's daily log. Yet *Wings for This Man* was marked by its calculated, *sotto voce* liberal argument for colorblind integration: It celebrated black fighter pilots without a single reference to their race! The film opened on P-47 Thunderbolts sweeping the skies over Italy, their wing cameras recording the shattered, burning, spinning-out-of-control Messerschidt ME-109s and Heinkel HE-111s downed by their machine-guns. The pilots touch down and cooly recount their exploits with the palms-down gestures that only fliers use to illustrate their maneuvers; the voiceover describes them as just folks, former students and mechanics (cut to classrooms and shops), and well-trained fighters (cut to Tuskegee)—not once calling them black. After all, says the voice—Ronald Reagan—"you can't judge a man by the color of his eyes or the shape of his nose."[41]

And yet, even as liberal rhetoric took the line of effacing blackness, African Americans themselves by midwar reached new levels of in-group awareness. "Who's got the *Courier* and what did it say this week?" the Tuskegee pilots routinely asked, knowing it nettled their white superior officers. "I never see any Col[ored] Service Men in the newsreel," blacks grumbled to OWI.[42] Clearly, the war had put an edge on the presentation of self in black circles. And in its last days, the war offered only a few more chances to imprint this sharpened sensibility on the racial propaganda that blacks would hope to use in the coming peacetime.

For a time every agency seemed to offer an angle. Saul Padover, before the war on the faculty of the New School, proposed to Secretary of the Interior Oscar Chapman an extension of the voice of *The Negro Soldier:* "that Negroes have always been a genuine part of America . . . working to . . . contribute to the total picture of American life." In OWI Philleo Nash touted Moss's new movie, *Teamwork,* which he "hope[d] . . . will be widely seen." As though preparing the way for a politically assertive, war-trained documentary film culture, a new Committee for Mass Education in Race Relations, describing itself as "liberals of social vision," joined with the more leftist American Film Center in October 1944 to announce "a program of educational films" designed to pull the nation through "a time when dangerous racial tensions threaten to disturb profoundly the entire structure of our society."[43] At the same time, Hollywood's documentary units remained fixed on half-measures like Warner's ill-fated pickup of *Congo,* the Belgian film that traced black Africa from canniblism to antifascism in less than an hour.

Although these improvised gestures contributed little to a liberal canon of movies, they vibrated with wishes to do the right thing and revealed a line of argument and an emerging documentary film culture that, taken together, formed the context in which the army was to commission its sequel to *The Negro Soldier.* The title of the project itself was enough to suggest that the army had been all but swept along by the momentum—*Teamwork.*

The Allied invasion of Europe in June 1944 provided the occasion for Moss to take a unit to Normandy and, in the train of the advancing armies, follow a black angle in the persons of the Red Ball Express, a heavily black quartermaster unit that became famous for supplying the rolling front while often under attack. But in the face of a decision to cut back on such films, only the energies of a few influential advocates kept *Teamwork* alive: Gibson; General Lyman Munson, an early defender of *The Negro Soldier;* Anatol Litvak, a Hollywood colonel who had taken a liking to Moss; and Frank Capra, who, Moss guessed, would endorse the film as long as he felt "he is carrying out War Department policy."[44] Even so, it stalled, slowly slipped from Moss's grasp into that of Major Edmund H. North, a Hollywood veteran, and fell victim to quarrels over new guidelines, strictures on raw stock, and fear of celebrating the Express too much. The shifting of its working titles, from *The Soldier in Supply and Maintenance, ETO* to *The Negro Soldier in ETO* and finally to *Teamwork,* testified to its shaky status as the end of the war approached. Not until July did they have a script, probably because it took that long to assemble footage and arrive at an "evergreen" angle that would retain its timeliness no matter which course the war took. It might even have died but for a prodding letter from Roy Wilkins to General Surles urging its completion and distribution. By then, in late summer, as the army's attention turned to occupying a defeated Germany, a task that included selecting films for showing there and in liberated countries, responsibility for such choices began to slip away to the Overseas Branch of OWI, the Library of Congress, the Museum of Modern Art, and Rockefeller's Office of the Coordinator of Inter-American Affairs (CIAA).[45] Saving the film became a challenge as the contact points began to thin out. But even after the German armistice was signed in the spring of 1945, the project survived, albeit contracted out to 20th Century–Fox, and was in the can by November, long after the war that had impelled its making had ended. Eventually *Teamwork* (OF-14), after a last spat over rights to library footage, went into civilian release as a sort of liberal moral victory, since the army no longer had a use for it.

More than any other war documentary, *Teamwork* in every foot of its being—its title, visual rhetoric, imagery, texture, voice of patent advocacy, its singling out a black unit for heroic action—reflected its political origins, and its survival testified to the influence of the conscience-liberal coalition that had brought about its creation down to the last moment of the war. It set a black agenda in that it literally promised African Americans an enhanced status in the postwar world in return for their service during the war.

Every sequence glowed with the message. It opens on a vaulting, polished marble conference chamber, a caricature of the Nazi architectural monumentalism that had become a fixture in Hollywood's anti-Nazi movies. On the soundtrack an almost metallic voice hammers, "as on a broken record," says the script: "Divide and conquer, divide and conquer, divide and conquer." Inside the room a meeting of glossily booted, highranking Nazis is in progress, presided over by a man with an angular face, a sneering mouth that is little more than a slit, and glinting eyes under enameled black hair. The cadenced words are his. The actor is Martin Kosleck, who had earned a steady living during the war playing Nazi heavies who spoke in the clipped accents he had learned in a childhood in Pomerania and an apprenticeship in Max Reinhardt's theatre in Berlin.[46] His speech is a tidy summing up of Hitler's own injunction against "mongrel" races that he had put forth in *Mein Kampf*, but with an American twist intended to divide black from white by "playing on frictions that already exist" and by persuading whites that "the Negro is stupid and irresponsible [and] unfit to handle the tools of modern war." The goal, he says in terms that make clear the uses segregation has for Nazis, is no less than "splitting off the Negroes," thereby reducing the American army by 10 percent. Then an American voice takes over as the image shifts to stock footage (possibly taken from Fritz Hippler's *Westwall* [1939]) of German defenses intercut with shots of Allied convoys

In contrast to Allied racial propaganda, the Germans, as here in *Sieg im Westen*, portrayed Africans as grinning French dacoits. Copyright Transit Films.

steaming toward the D-Day landing in Normandy. As the tiny figures advance across the exposed and smoking beach, the voiceover says with exaggerated irony that they are *truly* a mongrel army composed of "Protestant and Catholic, Jew and Gentile, rich man and poor man, black man and white—they all hit the beach under the same enemy fire. When they are hit, they feel the same pain." That is to say, the voiceover integrated the army before the Pentagon had, in a metaphor that reached beyond the mere necessities of war and in fact pointed toward postwar black social goals. To clinch the point, one of the shots on the beach depicted a bugbear that had nettled many blacks—the early segregation of Red Cross bloodbanks along racial lines. Among the wounded is a black soldier receiving blood—"the same kind of blood flowed from their veins," says the narrator.

As the Germans fall back to the Rhine, a story told in a linear montage of stockshots, blacks are woven ever more deeply into the fabric of the army: Without the Red Ball Express, the movie argues, the advance might have been stalled, giving the Germans time to stiffen. Cutting back to dramatic enactment, white and black drivers of amphibious lighters are seen risking their necks under fire as the voiceover points out that the Germans had predicted that "each second boat would fail [and that] this man [a black driver] was a coward." Later the advance hinges on the drivers again: will this armored tank get its fuel, this rifleman his fresh ammunition clips, and so on. In other words, integration is shrewdly put to the audience not as a favor blacks are asking but as a strategy white America needs for its survival, a metaphorical stroke so unendingly useful that Sidney Poitier, among others, would devote a career to reenacting it in ever higher levels of status and accomplishment. Here the thread of the movie becomes a voiceover list of Nazi predictions of black failures counterpointed by a visual repudiation of each charge. "They said he was shiftless," says the voiceover as the shot tilts up to a black soldier "energetically" (the script says) stringing wire on a pole, a sequence followed by a dozen more accomplishments of black quartermasters and engineers. Midway through the film, the angle shifts more starkly to integration by focusing on *mutually* accomplished tasks—"teamwork." Black and white engineers together lay pipe for fuel lines as the voiceover says "they were busy hating Germans—not each other. . . . Patton's men needed gasoline." Thereafter, blacks and whites operate winches in Cherbourg harbor, unload cargo, and drive the trucks of the Red Ball Express together, a sequence that ends with Eisenhower himself awarding medals to the drivers. Raising yet another cavil—that blacks could not pilot warplanes—the voiceover introduces a squadron of multiengined B-17s protected by pursuit planes of the black 332nd Fighter Group, complete with closeups of a white ("Texan" says the script) bomber pilot and a black fighter pilot ("from Alabama"). Throughout, the integration angle is argued and reargued in both actuality footage and dramatizations of infantrymen, artillerists, armored units, and others.

In an entirely dramatized sequence *Teamwork* reached an integrationist epiphany that is startlingly remote from any message the army may have wished to send its troops; clearly the Pentagon was no longer in control or no longer cared. Up to this moment, the images at least purported to be derived from actual events, but here it is clear that the audience is watching a totemic fiction designed to ram home a point. A German artillery piece is firing leaflets that portray the war as "a rich man's war" and a "poor colored man's fight." First white soldiers, then blacks pick up and read the fliers, then each tentatively looks off camera at the eye level of the other as though the assault will fail because of interracial mistrust. After a suspenseful pause, at last a black soldier picks up his weapon and advances, a cue for the entire line to rise and move out. After this fanciful triumph of Hollywood acting and editing, the film returns to actuality footage of yet another compelling image, that of General Mark Clark, a *bête noir* of blacks left over from when the black 92nd Division had been attached to Clark's 5th Army in Italy, and had been sent to the rear with the quality of its soldiering in question.[47] He is decorating a wounded black soldier in a field hospital, a shot bracketed by others of interracial sacrifices: rows of wounded and a cemetery of serried ranks of grave markers, and finally shots of surrendering Germans and of a swastika atop Nürnberg stadium being blasted to rubble. The inference is clear: Nazism has been defeated by the force of arms of a racially integrated nation. But just to make certain, the coda combines a montage of various units "of Negro troops and white troops of all branches [and] white WAC's and Negro WAC's" with a voiceover that invokes a slogan made famous by Joe Louis: "There's nothing wrong with America that Hitler can fix."

Clearly, conscience-liberals had stolen a march on the army in asserting their ideology as official doctrine. It remained only for them to press their case for immediate release to postwar civilian audiences. Immediately, Walter White, back from a long tour of the fronts where black soldiers had fought, called for a preview for NAACP officers, after which he judged that "as far as it goes, it is a wonderful job, beautifully done and carries a message to be heard by many Americans whose memory is shortlived." Other voices called for its distribution to schools and citizens' groups, a cry heard almost nowhere outside of New York. Nonetheless, Joseph Burstyn, a booker of foreign and other exotic films for the new "art house" market of intimate theatres, picked it up and touted it as "an important screen record of the true role the Negro played in the winning of the war [that] can do much to promote racial unity now and for the future."[48] Coupled with the efforts of the growing ranks of media-conscious—indeed, media-prone—film librarians eager to cultivate new audiences for their programs, which had become features of urban libraries, Burstyn's pickup constituted a liberal step toward a new film-culture drawn to documentary films of persuasion.

Thus even though few theatrical audiences saw *Teamwork*, it formed part of the urban liberal film culture that had won a place as the nation resumed its peacetime footing. *Teamwork* was emblematic of a mood that embraced not only the freshly minted audiovisual movement among librarians but also their version of the social engineers' notion that prejudice could be converted to right thinking by means of education, an idea seconded by the expanding corps of liberal critics who took the trouble to review documentaries. These commentators had already praised *The Negro Soldier* as "a pioneer" in teaching "inter-cultural education" and "living together"; now they saw the postwar ripening of its potential in *Teamwork*. Typical was Roy Wilkins's hope that it would "do much to promote racial unity *now and for the future.*" In fact, even while *Teamwork* was in production a few moguls and their black monitors met to discuss war movies as prospective omens of the future.[49] On the Marxist left, critics joined in, partly to revive old affiliations with black causes. Mildred Fleming in the *Worker*, for example, predicted that films might make "the patched up world hold together," while John T. McManus in *PM* praised *Teamwork* for "the big ingredient" that *The Negro Soldier* had lacked: soldiers "fighting, working, living together in mixed units" that might provide a social metaphor to help the nation through a postwar "developing period of unemployment and economic stress." Moss himself joined in, urging a friend in the NNC to take up films as a propaganda medium. "You ought to have a film program in every Negro center in America," he wrote, predicting that the government's films soon would become available cheaply or even at no cost.[50]

In this way the African American propaganda movement outlasted the ecumenical popular front that had animated the left on the verge of war, and with the defeat of fascism it stood ready to collect its half of the Double V and to use films as a medium through which to clarify and put forth its objectives. And any number of prospective players shared their vision of the late war as a wellspring of their own aims. A historian and board member of the American Film Center, James T. Shotwell, thought the war had seasoned American audiences and prepared them for an age of "the thinking picture." Joseph Foster of the *New Masses* attributed an improved image of blacks in other media to "the impetus of war," a reckoning concurred in by George Norford, critic of the black *Amsterdam News*. And years later, the director Robert Wise remembered the war as a time when "blacks and other minorities [were] involved in the . . . whole thrust to put down the Nazis, and . . . more [interracial] contact . . . undoubtedly had a great influence" on the future.[51] Reinforcing this mentality was a national trend toward wider use of audiovisual teaching devices for advocacy and agenda-setting by activists, and eventually as free or cheap fodder for voracious, product-hungry early television.

Not that the nation marched as one to this tune, even though it had become one of the central distinctions between antebellum and postbellum America. By 1947, conservative congressmen resumed the investigation of Hollywood politics that they had dropped at the onset of war, this time not in search of warmongers but "reds" who had infiltrated the movielots. Moss himself felt their touch as early as 1946, when he was dropped from the *Teamwork* promotion unit as a result of, he guessed, "my un-American past." Elsewhere, a conservative author in New Orleans, Stuart Landry, complained that race relations were going "not so well," which he traced to the "cult of equality" that had mushroomed in federal agencies during the war where its advocates spent their days making "pure propaganda," of which he singled out *The Negro Soldier* as the worst case.[52]

Moreover, in weighing the success or failure of propaganda movies and the prospects for their affecting the future it must be seen that no sweeping transference of hegemony had taken place. Rather, African Americans had simply aligned themselves with a winner, fought well for it, and aimed to collect the reward that they had bargained for and that had been half-promised by more than one federal agency. It was this union of likeminded, countervailing forces brought together by commonly felt aims that survived for its moment in the sun. In more purely political terms, the surface of politics in the short term more resembled a thermidorean reaction carried off by those who hoped for a return to the *status quo ante bellum* rather than a *coup d'état* carried off by conscience-liberals. The reaction notwithstanding, a result of the war was that black ideas in Washington and Hollywood had found their ways into both documentary and commercial movies, thereby holding out hope for the idea advanced by social engineers, that movies mattered in persuasion. That is, *some* change of collective mind had taken place, but not enough to cheer about. As Walter Fisher, a black officer in I&E, recalled: Although *The Negro Soldier* had seemed "one of the finest things that ever happened to America . . . we knew . . . the day of Jubilee had not arrived."[53]

5

Hollywood Wins: The End of "Race Movies"

"Race movies" had not merely risen out of segregation; they had been anointed by it and, after a fashion, prospered from it. At their best as in *The Scar of Shame* (1927), a film by the Colored Players of Philadelphia, they had provided black audiences with a shock of recognition of their plight and put forth a group morale that called upon African Americans to strive for, as one of the character says, "the finer things." At their worst they fed off black misfortune rather than deal with it, parodied bourgeois life rather than set it as a standard, and gave away credibility by setting life in a dark world unsullied by white people and improbably packed with black crooks and cops, judges and doctors, molls and *grandes dames,* so that the subsurface play of the text allowed the inference that blacks had only themselves to blame for the hand they had been dealt. Also running through the worst race movies was a half-hidden wish to be white embedded in the frequent tales of garbled identities, lightskinned casts, and mannered behavior. All of these, to be sure, were the outward signs of the "twoness" of American life about which W. E. B. DuBois had written, but sometimes race movies teased and strummed these feelings rather than take them up as part of the daily round of black life. And sometimes, almost perversely, race-moviemakers drew attention to the unfair comparison of their shoestring work with Hollywood gloss by billing their stars as "the colored Mae West" or "the colored Valentino."[1]

This is not to blame race movies for their lot in life, but rather to anticipate their eventual irrelevance to the black life brought on by the war. In fact, Yiddish filmmakers faced the same critical problem, which stemmed from the appearance of advocating a trait that the film was merely portraying. Like race movies, for every Yiddish film that was hailed as "an heirloom . . . for posterity" or was shot in religiously resonant locations such as Palestine, there was another panned by Jews as pejoratively designed to "injure the reputation of Yiddish theatre."[2]

Before the war, critics reviewed race movies only as artifacts designed to serve a black clientele shut off from the wellsprings of general American culture by a wall of custom, law, and privilege. Tradepapers evolved an ironic voice with which to review them as "made very

Walter White's campaign to end the structured absence of African Americans from movies directly challenged social realities such as the segregated round of life reflected in this New Orleans theatre front. Daniel J. Leab Collection.

Where segregation was not a matter of local law it was defined only slightly less stringently by custom, as in Hazelwood, Pennsylvania. Farm Security Administration—LC.

crudely" but, as in the case of *Harlem Rides the Range*, able to "give colored audiences general satisfaction"; or, critics patronizingly guessed that although blacks would take the films seriously, white kids would enjoy them as "parody." Even censors assumed an arch posture toward them, making allowances for the arcana of black culture. When Joe Breen cut a burlesque-type "bump," some "cooch" dancing, and some black argot from *Double Deal* (1939), the president of the studio, Harwin Dixon, resorted to special pleading. "It must be borne in mind," he argued, "that these lyrics are typical negroid lyrics and certain expressions such as are found in all Negro spirituals and hot numbers."[3]

After the war, as we shall see, the tolerance of critics and censors alike wore thin. The censors cut various oaths, curses, and bared limbs, along with lines like "Hello Eden, how's your hammer hangin'," from Oscar Micheaux's *The Betrayal* (1948), while the critics reported that the Apollo's tough audience openly "laughed at" *Miracle in Harlem* and predicted that "some new departures are necessary if there's to be any respect from Negro audiences for film product with all-Negro casts." The race-moviemen emptily defended their work, claiming only they knew the black "choice in film entertainment" and what they "do not care for," or took extravagant credit for inventing cinematic conventions that blacks delighted in.[4]

World War II, having raised the prospect of a Double V, rendered race movies an anachronism, turned black critics against them, and forced black audiences to opt for joining or not the spirit of the times. After all, how could a segregated movie serve the cause of a war that slowly took on among its aims the self-determination of all peoples and the integration of the blacks into the fabric of American life? The answer to this question soon set race-moviemakers apart from the centers of the prosecution of the war. With some blacks already in the corridors of the Pentagon, dining in the moguls' commissaries in Hollywood, appearing eye-to-eye with the principals in Hollywood war movies, and affecting government propaganda at its source, race-moviemakers had simply lost part of their reason for survival and thus their future place in American movie culture in which the war had begun to redefine a black place.

Not that African Americans elected to snub black institutions; rather, the war had opened up the prospect of redefining DuBois's "two-ness." To take only two instances, the black church would survive because entry to it began at birth and all blacks were nominally included in its client-population, but black baseball—the Negro National League, for example—would die because its pool of talent, and its number of fans, were finite as well as vulnerable to proselytizing by white parallel leagues in search of both black players and fans. Clearly, race movies were more like black baseball than like black churches. Indeed, long before baseball fans turned away from the Negro leagues, black moviegoers all but ceased to support race movies, preferring instead the polish of Hollywood coupled with its freshened uses of black performance. In short, they became "crossovers." And Hollywood soon learned to cater to them by means of advertising, dual openings, and cultivating black critics. The war undeniably had altered an American taste-culture in a way that forced a reconsideration of customary racial arrangements, and in doing so either rebutted the notion of popular culture as mouthpiece of the status quo or spoke for a new status quo in which race movies had no place.

Thereafter, in a curious reversal of roles, Hollywood race-angled movies displayed the wit, spontaneity, and verve that black performing culture had given its audiences, while race movies grew more ploddingly earnest (and white). As to humor, for example, Dooley Wilson in Hollywood movies seemed an earthy, richly "Elizabethan" emissary from the Apollo, while in race movies Stepin Fetchit and Mantan Moreland, the former Hollywood specialists in stereotypical "business," landed starring roles. Of course, in the beginning no one could have anticipated this turnabout, and therefore race movies enjoyed a certain amount of cooperation with the army.

In fact, when early in 1942 race moviemakers began to feel a pinch, it followed not from a policy directed against them but only from a colorblind decision to allocate raw film stock on the basis of prior consumption patterns, which of course favored the major studios. Nonetheless, the effect on race movies was dire, and their exhibitors complained of it to OWI. "I recently noted a restriction . . . on independent negro production," wrote one of them. "And in a democracy such as ours nobody has yet explained how come Metro went ahead and made Cabin in the Sky—and is now making another all negro pix. . . . Meantime the indies whose ideas have always been stolen by the majors were in a position of holding the bag."[5] By then the race-moviemen already teetered on the edge, having survived the Depression, the nagging hostility of black bourgeois parents for whom the movies were trash meant for the riffraff, and the fratricidal competition brought by a prewar boomlet. Besides, the growing dominance of white entrepreneurs who teamed with black performers had clouded their future as providers of specifically black entertainment. In 1941, on the cusp of war, the top of their little world included Harry and Leo Popkin in Los Angeles, the feisty Ted Toddy and his Dixie National Exchange in Atlanta, Bert and Jack Goldberg and their various firms in New York, and the Dallas dealmaker Alfred Sack and his black director Spencer Williams. Occasionally a new firm entered the market, but only one, All-America, a promising underachiever composed of Hollywood veteran Emmanuel Glucksman, ambitious black apprentice William D. Alexander, and the founder of the ANP, Claude Barnett, actually survived the war. Some of them, like Toddy and the Popkins, had begun in "poverty row" in Hollywood; others, like cameraman Don Malkames, had stayed behind when moviemakers moved west from Fort Lee, New Jersey; two of them, Edgar Ulmer and Joseph Seiden, also worked in Yiddish movies; and a few underemployed regional players, such as Hurliman in Florida, clung to life.[6] What they all shared in common was bleak prospects in a war in which they held a diminishing place.

Few of them were known outside their small circle, and all of them lived by their wits between gigs. Alexander had come to Barnett from the office staff of Morgan College. George Randol was a man-of-all-work who had once appeared in *The Green Pastures*, wrote part of an admired Hollywood short, and earned a rave from the trade magazine *International Photographer* for his *Dark Manhattan* (1937) as the equal of "the 'B' class pictures." It had drawn black "crowds . . . throughout the east" perhaps attracted by his Hollywood-style social problem, in this case the numbers racket, woven into a drama that was resolved by a lone hero and starred Harlem favorites like Ralph Cooper (a bandsman and Apollo emcee) and Clarence Brooks (who had played a doctor in John Ford's *Arrowsmith* [1931]).[7] More rarely, Hollywood veterans crossed over into race movies, as B-movie director Harry Fraser and writer Ben Rinaldo did in *Dark Manhattan*.[8]

Obviously race movies, at least the few well crafted among them, had meant something to African Americans, to whom they conveyed a sense of self and group that could be had from no other medium. But even before the onset of war, critics had begun to nag their makers for more sophistication and to bristle at odd accommodations to racism that had marred some of them. Ever more regularly, critics moved away from hollow praise of weak material, sponsoring gestures such as a "Great Negro Movie Month," and inflating black moviegoers into an "insatiable" marketplace. Instead they mourned the slipping away of an opportunity to create an indigenous cinema. From their peak in silent days when Charles Gilpin and Paul Robeson had played in them, race movies had declined so far that in 1937 the Young Communist League picketed Micheaux's *God's Step Children* for its "false splitting of Negroes into light and dark groups" and "holding them up to ridicule," the latter a common complaint of critics who noticed the unintended laughter with which audiences increasingly drawn to Hollywood gloss had greeted race movies. Even when a critic liked one, as when *Variety* judged Cooper and A. W. Hackle's *Am I Guilty?* the peer of "the B output of the major lots," its prospects were weakened by the eternal split of audiences into urbane North and the rustic South that went only for low

On the eve of war, critics thought that "race movies," such as *Harlem Rides the Range* (1940), were still able to "give colored audiences general satisfaction." SCRBC.

comedy.[9] Then there were the white censors, ever wary of gangsters, jitterbugs, and in *God's Step Children* some black homeboy cynicism heard when a crook speaks of the need to split booty with the police. With so many forces at work, a fading genre was doomed during a crisis such as war when the bedrock politics and morale of its audience seemed poised for change.

As race movies worsened, Abram Hill of the *Amsterdam* thought they were so poor that a white conspiracy must be afoot and blacks should "squawk to the high heavens." After 1939, each one seemed more meretricious than its forebear. For each "Negro drama" set in "the poor section" and bent upon rescuing juveniles from delinquency, another, like Fred Myton's *Harlem on the Prairie*, played upon broad dialect comedy of "Jazzbos," a style written in Toddy's *Mr. Washington Goes to Town* by none other than Walter Weems, a gagwriter for the blackfaced vaudevillians the Two Black Crows. The press kit of the latter film proposed a stunt involving "a dusky maiden overcome by laughter." The low point came in a Micheaux film in which the plot took a turn for which he had no insurance shot, a lapse he corrected by placing a parrot on the witness stand in a murder case.[10]

Obviously, if race movies clung to these low grounds as war came, their future would be clouded. In any case, most of their makers felt the loss of momentum and drifted off, Toddy into other entertainment, the Goldbergs into "art films," Sack into foreign films and "skinflicks," the Popkins into B-movies, and Alexander and Glucksman into infant television.[11]

But not at first. Early on, race movies seemed to OWI a cheap access to blacks who were so appalled by lilywhite war movies such as *Sergeant York* as to conclude that "it was a 'white man's war.'" Why not, said an agency report on black morale, make a few "morale-building all-Negro films" and play them off in ghettos and "camp movie houses that served exclusively black soldiers." In this way, said an OWI man, they might exploit "all-Negro" theatres and their midnight shows by engaging "a private company . . . to do films glorifying Negro military heroes, something in the manner of *Sergeant York*" or even "Abbott and Costello" comedies "with an Army background."[12]

For their part, the race-moviemen felt as patriotic as the next American and wished to be "doing something" in the war. Toddy carried to Washington a proposal for a "Negro Newsreel of Victory" and a noncommittal correspondence with Paul Robeson about a movie of the 99th Pursuit Squadron. Oscar Micheaux wrote directly to Elmer Davis, reporting that "we are never shown on the screen in . . . the war effort," which, coupled with lingering stereotypes, left African Americans simmering with resentment. Since his own work "seem[ed] to please my race 100% completely," he could do no less than offer his "little corporation in the interest of the war," failing to point out that he had not worked on a movie in two years and had been peddling his novels door to door.[13]

But as OWI and the Signal Corps drew closer to the NAACP and Hollywood, the race-moviemakers languished, only three of them actually seeing movies into release: Sack and Williams's *Marching On*, Glucksman and Alexander's All-America newsreels, and Goldberg and Michaux's *We've Come a Long, Long Way*. Even then, the grainy, washed-out *Marching On* passed almost unseen, All-America lived almost entirely off the largesse of Signal Corps library footage, and Goldberg and Michaux ran afoul of OWI's decision to release *The Negro Soldier* to civilians, thereby thrusting the two movies into head-to-head competition.

Taken as a group, then, the race-moviemakers lived out the war on the fringes of the action, cooling their heels in Washington corridors, releasing movies to theatres already booked with Hollywood product, facing pickets who increasingly resented movies that "disparaged" blacks, or living off inventory by recutting and retitling it. Oscar Micheaux gave up entirely and lived off hawking his books. Toddy scoffed at demands for "pictures that elevate" and focused on recutting his titles to "give the colored what they want": action, broad comedy, and a wisp of sex. "Titles subject to change without notice," warned his catalogue, in which Lena Horne's (and the Popkins') *The Duke is Tops* became *Bronze Venus* and Cooper's gangland ouevre *Gang Smashers* and *Am I Guilty?* became *Gun Moll* and *Racket Doctor*. In addition he had picked up a run of Eddie Green and Pigmeat Markham's broadly comic two-reelers. Goldberg, except for his and Michaux's documentary, faded from his days when he had done Bill Robinson's *Harlem Is Heaven* (1932); a World War I documentary, *The Unknown Soldier Speaks;* and *Paradise in Harlem* (1940), one of a proposed cycle of "pride in our race" movies that featured a jazz *Othello*. Instead, he spent the war cobbling together shorts from old Soundies (split-reels made for visual jukeboxes), the most interesting of which was *Boogie Woogie Dream* with Horne, Teddy Wilson, and the duo-pianists Albert Ammons and Pete Johnson.[14]

Even the Popkins, who had access to Hollywood casual labor and studios, slumped after a good run through 1941 that included *While Thousands Cheer*, an exposé of fixing football games, complete with newsfilm and UCLA player Kenny Washington; *Reform School*, with maternal Louise Beavers in a drama of "juvenile justice"; *One Dark Night*, which allowed Moreland to get as close as he could to playing straight ("far more entertaining than many Hollywood B's," said *Variety*); and *Four Shall Die*, with Dorothy Dandridge in a reprieve from stock maids. And Sack and Williams, who in 1940 had made the most popular race movie ever produced, *The Blood of Jesus*, lapsed into idleness broken only by *Marching On*.[15]

On the set of a race movie almost all eyes focus on Joseph Seiden, one of the journeyman white directors who had come to dominate the idiom in its latter days.

In its way their *Blood of Jesus* palpably illustrated a wrenching change in black ideology that drew African Americans away from race movies. Before the war, its makers, Sack and his director, Spencer Williams—a black Louisianian, a writer for Christie comedies in the 1920s, and a journeyman actor in both race movies and in Hollywood—thought they knew their audience and constructed *The Blood of Jesus* to suit it. Pious and rural in texture and voice, it "possessed that certain chemistry required by the Negro box office" (said Lester Sack, the firm's accountant). But its primitive salvationism was put forth in a morality play set in "those days . . . almost gone" when a body could relax in the shade, pitted the Tempter and God in a struggle for the soul of a humble countrywoman, and ended with real blood dripping from a Sunday School picture of Jesus hanging above the woman's sickbed—all images that may have played in the prewar black South but earned only loud laughs in the Northern ghettos to which Southern blacks had migrated.[16]

In many ways the war had simply diluted the chemistry of Sack's recipe. The homogenous Southern audience had scattered in search of war work; the Double V had called for an end to old ways; and the war had stirred blacks and their allies as though organic parts of a coherent whole toward the evolving integrationist ideology we have been observing. Thus if race movies had become the OWI weapon of choice, they would have compromised the NAACP's drive for access to centers of white privilege as well as the *Courier*'s notion of a Double V—a black investment in the outcome of the war to be earned by black participation in the prosecution of the war.[17]

Moreover, the one race-moviemaker that OWI had encouraged, All-America, was a flop, and in ways that allowed Washington to take them for a stereotypical smalltime colored business. Even as mainstream newsreels ran their black staples—"Negroes doing rhythmic drills" and tributes to Carver "as a great American as well as a great Negro"—All-America muffed every opportunity. At first OWI had liked their stuff: FDR and the president of Liberia reviewing troops, the impact of rationing on blacks, an antidiscrimination bill in the Missouri legislature, Chandler Owen on his pamphlet *The Negro and the War*, a promo of Negro History Week, the casting of *Porgy and Bess*, and new housing for black warworkers. But toward the end of 1942, OWI began to complain that the firm "did not maintain the high standards during its first months," made poor use of stock footage, lost its "polish," began to settle for "repetitive and undistinguished" potted stories, and suffered from a "creaking" music track. Almost simultaneously, OWI monitors by January 1943 reported that "the Negro received more attention in the major newsreels . . . than for many months previously." In fact, the news footage actually improved in the ways that it located African Americans at the unaccoustomed centers of a few stories and sometimes framed white stories in a circle of the formerly unthinkable black supernumeraries that Walter White had been asking for. When General Mark Clark, for example, received a medal from Eisenhower, a black officer looked on; at a midwar West Point graduation a cameraman picked up shots of black cadets; and in a staple image of Allied harmony, an armed forces boxing tournament, a black fighter knocked out a Royal Navy champion. All of this, coupled with the ever more public awareness that these sequences had resulted from an actual policy of a federal agency, at once atoned somewhat for past erasures from history even as it gave increased weight to the images that black and white audiences saw.[18] Never a preponderance in white newsreels, these images nonetheless reinforced the liberal line that Hollywood had begun to introduce into its features, thereby diminishing the OWI's need for race-moviemakers to the vanishing point. Thus in February 1943, when All-America tried to recover by proposing a documentary on Owens's *The Negro and the War*, the agency had all but turned its back on race movies and their makers.[19]

By the spring of 1943 the race-moviemen, and exhibitors who sometimes played angel to them, had no choice but to pursue independent projects with only routine government assistance. Their concept of the war as of all-black battalions arrayed against foreign enemies left no opening for an African American viewer to imagine a different future. Not that their vision of a once and future segregation was off the mark; self-evidently, as reportage it was far more on-the-nose than the emerging propaganda of conscience-liberalism that OWI and the NAACP had been retailing. Indeed, that was the point. Race movies promised only *stasis,* while Moss's *Teamwork,* for instance, held out the prospect of a Double V. If we may use a bit of historical imagination, a case in point might be a piece of All-America film that an OWI monitor had marked as significant. In it a naval officer says: "Many [Negro] soldiers have already left here and are in the thick of battle. . . . They will leave this conflict far better equipped to take their place in society."[20] Conceivably, he singled out and filed as "interesting" the turn of phrase "place in society" because it referred to a *new* place in society, while in the rhetoric of a race-moviemaker it might have referred to a place unchanged by the destabilizing crisis of war, that is, to African American life as it *had been.*

In this inching away from race movies as propaganda, we may see another sign of the agency's still timid embracing of conscience-liberalism as the basis for its "strategy of truth." The most compelling instance of this was in the War Department's decision to protect its investment in *The Negro Soldier* by standing up to a civil suit filed on behalf of Goldberg and Michaux's *We've Come a Long, Long Way* (1944). The coincident release of the two movies forced the race-moviemakers to seek relief by pleading for the right to an exclusive first run unrivaled by *The Negro Soldier,* on the ground that releasing the army's film to civilian audiences rent-free would constitute an unfair restraint of trade. In the ensuing legal debate over the fine points of marketing, the government necessarily, in spite of itself, hammered out a clearer-cut stance with respect to the politics of racial imagery on the nation's screens. Simultaneously, as it would turn out, the government's lawyers and their black *amicus curiae* would broaden the influence of a newly remade mirror of changing American racial arrangements while extending that influence far into the future beyond the army's original narrow intent and even beyond the era of the war itself.

On one side the army and OWI's film, *The Negro Soldier,* stood as a hotly defended liberal icon of a future integrationism, while on the other Goldberg and Michaux spoke for a world that once had been. As early as 1919 Goldberg had spliced together a few feet of Signal Corps footage into a now lost film, *The Unknown Soldier Speaks,* a chronicle of the black role in World War I that he probably recut into yet another version called *The Negro Marches On* (1936), thereby establishing his credentials as a maven of African American war movies. Michaux's own considerable fame had spread beyond his imposing Florida Avenue church through the medium of his "Happy Am I" chorus, which was heard regularly on a Washington radio station.

When together they asked for access to the stock footage of the Signal Corps, they were treated with the same courtesy any filmmaker might expect. In addition, partly because two members of Michaux's flock were servants to Milton Eisenhower, Davis's colleague in OWI, he interceded on their behalf with the result that the team received the requested footage as well as a trickle of scarce raw stock, consultations on technique, the makings of a music track, and nonexclusive use of Chandler Owens's pamphlet *The Negro and the War*. With as yet no sense of a rivalry between their movie and the army's own OF-51, Eisenhower readily reported to Michaux that "it seems most unlikely that any other organization or film company would undertake a film of the kind you have in mind." But by the end of the year, the parties to the arrangement were brought up short by the shift in the government's posture toward racial matters symbolized by the decision to release *The Negro Soldier* to civilian theatres. In these few months the agency had moved from Eisenhower's easily felt wish to cooperate with filmmakers whose marketplaces had been rooted in antebellum racial arrangements to a point where the army and OWI had agreed to release *The Negro Soldier* to a broad audience with the explicit awareness that the goal was to engineer changed racial ideology. Goldberg and Michaux must have been shocked at the turn of events that shattered the exclusivity with which they anticipated the release of their chronicle of "the advancement and achievements of the Negro race."[21]

Their only hope was to sue the government for its patently unfair competition in hopes of either enjoining the release of *The Negro Soldier* or obtaining some less satisfying means of relief such as a couple of weeks of exclusive "clearance" in which to recover their "nut." Their strategy consisted in demonstrating that their point of view made more civic common sense than did *The Negro Soldier* in the new racial circumstances wrought by the nation's war against foreign enemies whose own propaganda was so patently racist. Whichever film won in the courts stood to affect future portrayals of African Americans on the screen. Either the court would rule that blacks in a setting in which segregation was a settled, normal convention reflected the government's will, or that its propaganda might reasonably point toward a future of a more open, plural society.

The lines were drawn by the films themselves, and *The Negro Soldier* won. Both opened in churches. But Moss's was merely the establishing shot from which to spin out his film; Michaux's was an actual pulpit from which he, dressed in formal wear, droned on in stilted, old-fashioned elocutionary style. Moss's flock were camerawise actors; Michaux's were his own clientele, made wooden by stage fright. Moss hailed a pantheon of black heroes; Michaux prayed over the remains of a single aviator who was "a credit to his race," the cant-phrase that had begun to nettle liberals. Moss portrayed the enemies in the war as of opposing cultures, one democratic, the other fascist; Michaux sketched Hitler as bent upon a narrowly specific assault on African American culture and its "beautiful houses of worship," "thriving enterprises," "famous Negro publications," and a roster of targeted musicians whom he named who would "no longer exist." Moss closed without promises, save those that might have been inferred from the optimistic voice with which *The Negro Soldier* spoke; Michaux baldly, even naively, gave blacks a choice of suffering under "barbarous" Hitler or taking "God's side" and fighting for a "country that has been good to us" ever since 1619! In texture and style Moss's film unwound in classic Hollywood style, all smooth cuts, dissolves, and fades in an uninterrupted narrative paid out in easy doses; Michaux was anything but smooth, fluffing lines, stumbling over the names of the even the most famous black artists, staring vacantly at a single camera setup. *The Negro Soldier* effectively told its viewers that African Americans had arrived in unaccustomed seats of power; *We've Come a Long, Long Way* promised only business as usual.[22]

In view of the aesthetic gulf between the two films, the coalition of OWI, NAACP, and Hollywood liberals had no choice but to defend the right of *The Negro Soldier* to play civilian venues; not to do so opened a vast market to a poor player indeed, and one that not only would revive the most old-fashioned, accommodationist definitions of good race relations but would in its threadbare style confirm the stereotype of the feckless Negro incapable of technical achievement. Black activists had struggled too long to reach the corridors of power that the war had given them access to, only to risk everything by allowing Goldberg and Michaux to speak for them. So they quickly circulated among themselves and their political friends a batch of negative reviews of *We've Come a Long, Long Way*. Accompanied by raves about OF-51. "The [former] picture is lousy," said Wilkins. Michaux himself was its main flaw, reported Julia E. Baxter of the NAACP, because of his rural preacher style. On the other hand, they elicited comment from the MPPDA, WAC, and other agencies on *The Negro Soldier* as a clear voice for "national unity" against "racist lies."[23] Next the NAACP pressed Fredi Washington of the *People's Voice* to denounce Goldberg as a longtime exploiter of black audiences, while Walter White brought the case to the attention of organized Jews in order to head off the appearance of an interethnic spat. Then, in a series of press releases, the NAACP marshaled a national liberal front (even enlisting the government) on behalf of OF-51. In sum, *The Negro Soldier* was portrayed as "a superb document . . . with enormous potentialities for good in stimulating the morale of American Negroes and in educating white Americans," beside which *We've Come a Long, Long Way* seemed "not only faulty in a technical sense, but [it preaches] the theory that Negroes are much better off here than they

The ad-copy for *We've Come a Long, Long Way* (1944) masked its absurd thesis that Hitler's ambitions were aimed directly at Harlem and its finest citizens. NR-LC.

would be under Hitler [and] insults the average Negro theatre-goer" by raising that false dichotomy.[24]

To spread this message among Americans and to "assist distribution" of *The Negro Soldier*, the NAACP built a list of influentials that included Nelson Rockefeller, perhaps as a patron of New York's Museum of Modern Art (MOMA), where *The Negro Soldier* enjoyed one of its best playdates, or for his CIAA and its power over film booking, in Latin America; Francis Cardinal Spellman of New York; Mayor Fiorello H. La Guardia; and *New Yorker* editor Harold Ross. Finally the NAACP filed an *amicus curiae* brief in which they argued that official films provided "the only available medium" for treating the "racial prejudices which divide our population."[25] In effect, the NAACP, using a minor civil suit over two movie shorts, enlisted the army, WAC, and a host of famous liberals on behalf of a propaganda movie that was their medium of choice for engineering changed racial beliefs.

In the end, as we saw in the last chapter, Goldberg and Michaux settled for a few days' clearance that helped them recover their investment. But more important in the long term was the mileage liberals derived from the film and the contest for its exhibition: It rallied their constituency around a substantive issue rather than some ceremonial Brotherhood Week; it contributed another prod to opening up the army to the issue of race; and it served as a model film of advocacy, which social engineers had proclaimed a viable tool.

Thereafter, race movies lost their place in black popular culture, having fallen prey to the changed expectations of audiences who had used the war to break off from the segregated strictures that had generated *Juke Joint, Beale Street Mama,* and the rest. One by one the makers, as we have seen, sank into a slough from which they never again rose, and almost all of them took up other interests. Robert M. Savini, a New York newcomer, scavenged his stock from oddments the majors had passed on, ranging from revival rights to King Vidor's eccentrically socialist *Our Daily Bread* (1933) to pickups of art films, among them Fellini's *La Dolce Vita* (1960). The Sacks bought a list of "skinflicks"; the Popkins went back to B-movies; and so on.

Critics and audiences gave up on them, consuming them as "camp" at the bottoms of double bills, warning their children against their excesses, complaining of them in the press, and always voting with their feet for the Hollywood article. Less and less did journalists hold attendance as a holy obligation of all "good race men." Only the "sure seaters," as *Variety* called the faithful few, persisted in sitting in dark grindhouses, suffering through them. Black audiences had always been responsive to the screen, perhaps as a result of a cultural history that had included call-and-response church services and obligatory handclapping as a group response to music, and other expressions of a community mentality, but as far as movies were concerned, knee-slapping amusement had replaced applauding enthusiasm. "They frequently go into spasms of laughter in the midst of solemn scenes," reported *Variety* at the beginning of the decline. Among the black papers, Dan Burley of the *Amsterdam* left off excusing flawed and cheap work as merely good "colored folks trying to get started" and began insisting that "the lowliest fan in the balcony" was entitled to black cinema that "lifts him out of the commonplace," transports him with a "thrill," and "shows the Negro objectively." *Variety* took Burley's point, excusing an Apollo crowd for its howls of derision at the Popkins' "badly written, badly produced and badly directed" *Gang War* (1940), and charging race-moviemakers with pandering to the riffraff rather than reaching for the black bourgeoisie, first by using "sex bally" in the ad copy, then by settling "for sturdy reaction in theatres such as the Apollo."[26]

The black press had done all it could: plugged each new "major production" that "broke a record" somewhere, each new "inspirational" biopic, and each new release as "the greatest picture yet made with an all-colored cast."[27] The papers had often joined in promotions such as Greater Negro Movie Month and paid tribute to performers for their "roles depicting true phases of Negro life." In a dispute between the Screen Actors Guild (SAG) and a maker of black westerns, for instance, the press took the part of the actors who had resisted the guild's insistence on a union shop. "We never get any jobs to amount to anything in white movies anyway," argued a black actor with the concurrence of the *Afro-American*. "[In] these colored pictures we do have a chance to portray roles that colored America wants to see."[28] But unavoidably, in the war culture *Variety* concluded that their low aspirations rendered them "highly implausible" vehicles for conveying a "positive image," an opinion in which the *Los Angeles Sentinel* joined, reporting that "Negroes are tired of being used as undesirable, lawless thugs." By war's end George Norford in NUL's *Opportunity* took the point. "In terms of social content, race relations or even the advancement of motion pictures as a medium of education and reform," he wrote, they were "negligible."[29]

Contrast, for example, *The Negro Soldier* with Williams's *Marching On*, a surviving race movie of the war period. Before the war, Williams's *The Blood of Jesus* had amounted almost to folk art among his Southern rural clientele; its lack of artifice had seemed a charming flaw rather than a crippling wound. But with the coming of the war movie genre, the racial failings of all movies were revealed to be more clearly embedded in the nature of their production rather than merely in their shoestring budgets. In the Hollywood liberal genre black warriors had come to occupy least some centers of dramatic action and stand eye-to-eye on equal terms with white roles, so that audiences could not help but perceive them as *in* and not merely *of* American society, not merely in the movie but part of its outcome. In contrast with Moss's trotting Joe Louis into *The Negro Soldier* (much as Warner's had done in *This Is the Army*), and watching his "American fist" pummel Max Schmeling, *Marching On* was shot on locations that looked strikingly like Fort Huachuca, a remote desert post that was linked in black minds as a lowly Jim Crow post. In Hollywood movies the contrast was the same: Blacks seemed in as well as of American life, while in *Marching On* they were imprisoned in a crumbling, segregated world.

The plot, an engaging mystery in which soldiers of the 25th Colored Infantry use a tangle of coincidences to expose and apprehend the operators of a clandestine Japanese radio station, had been used dozens of times by B-movie writers, albeit *Marching On* used the radio as its "weenie" rather than secret treasure, a lost mine, or other goal of stock "quest" tales. But its poor quality as against either *The Negro Soldier* or Metro's *Bataan* placed the film in a backwater of wartime filmmaking.[30]

Particularly was this so with respect to the politics of movies. If the Double V had gradually become an unspoken part of official propaganda and the stuff of Hollywood war movies, then what postwar role was left for race movies? Certainly not as bearers of the conscience-liberalism that would grow more programmatic as it anticipated the eventual civil

In contrast to *The Negro Soldier*, Spencer Williams's *Marching On* seemed remote, wrongly costumed, and supportive of the government's panicky "relocation" of Japanese Americans as security risks. University of Illinois Film Archive.

rights movement. All that was left to the race movies was a thin line of rhythm and blues music that crossed over into white adolescents' preserves, much as Ben Frye's mid-1950s "r and b" musicals crossed over into white neighborhoods through hard-driving, raucous acts that had once played only the Apollo. And even this thin sliver of the market dried up when, as each successive wave of black music—Swing, Bop, Cool, Modern—passed into white markets by rechanneling its creative energy into forms and styles that embraced white tastes.

By war's end in 1946, only an occasional race-movieman clung to the prospect of matching the slickness of the mainstream of moviemaking. In that year Savini told Walter White of his wish to resume making movies "in the proper manner," using "only the better class stories . . . and none depicting low standards," and offered them to the NAACP as fundraisers. But the association was having none of it; someone in the office scrawled across the proposal: "come-on ad & agreed not to bother with." Riding the crest of its wartime success, the NAACP bet that the Hollywood majors, along with a still forming documentary film culture, would better serve the aims of the race. Whenever a staff member reviewed a latter-day race movie, someone ruled it a "disgrace" and sent a warning of it to its "branches, particularly those in the South where our members attend theatres where [race movies] ordinarily would be shown."[31] Thus as organized blacks anticipated a continuation of the wartime mentality, they turned away from race movies as a fossil of a segregated time gone by.

With less and less reason for existence, the race-moviemen suffered a slump in both quality and political thrust; or, like Toddy and Sack, lived off retitling and rereleasing their inventories; or turned to the blandly apolitical format of the musical revue, often by assembling the old Soundies that had once been ground out for visual jukeboxes in penny arcades. In a typical splicing job, Alfred Sack atrung five Soundies into *Solid Senders*. William Forrest Crouch, a director of hundreds of Soundies, stirred together a mixture of Mantan Moreland's wide-eyed humor and two crossover acts, Dorothy Dandridge and the Mills Brothers, into a plotless assemblage called *Ebony Parade* (1946), a kind of hour-long, theatrical Soundie. Toddy focused on the broad comedy of his stable consisting of Moreland, Pigmeant Markham, Eddie Green, and John "Rastus" Murray in a cycle of two-reelers led by *Mr. Adam's Bomb* and *Pigmeat's Laugh Hepcats*. The Goldbergs' Herald Pictures took advantage of their New York offices to recruit strong bills of famous performers. Thus they moved from cannibalized films like *1950 Harlem Follies* toward a 1955 crossover cycle of rock 'n' roll revues featuring Count Basie, Cab Calloway, Ellington, Lionel Hampton, Nat Cole, Honi Coles, Nipsey Russell, Dinah Washington, and a leavening of youth-market stars such as the Clovers and Martha Davis.[32] The only overt political linkage the first cycle of crossovers could claim was its coincidence with *Brown vs. Topeka Board of Education*, the judicial overturning of the legal underpinning of segregation.

The confluence of judicial activism and musical crossovers ended up affecting the politics (and economics) of teen culture, but only in a curious way that announced the arrival of a new adolescent politics that was not race-based. In former times adolescent subculture had always been portrayed comically, as though too volatile to be taken seriously. Tom Sawyer, Andy Hardy, the Dead End Kids, and Our Gang all teased and taunted the idea of rebellion against adult authority without overtly joining in the challenge. But after the *Brown* decision refocused national attention on race, the teenagers resumed and made overt an old form of rebellion: seeking solace and friends in some bohemia such as Greenwich Village in cellars where black jazz was played. At the same time, their tastes tempted recording firms to make white "covers" of black music, that is, to record white performers singing music made famous by blacks, a trend that reached its apogee in the career of Elvis Presley, who began his professional life covering black performances and adapting them to white teenaged tastes.

But the mainstream of crossover behavior came in the form of *Rock All Night, Rock Around the Clock,* and *Twist All Night,* three 1957 movies from Sam Katzman's B-unit in which white youths acted out their rebelliousness by taking up the black music of Chuck Berry, Chubby Checker, Fats Domino, and dozens more who were herded like cattle through the thinly plotted revues. The height of their powers actually came with the release of Richard Brooks's *Blackboard Jungle* (1954), which startlingly used Bill Haley's "Rock Around the Clock" as theme music, even flooding the set with it as mood music for the actors. Not only did it provide a sort of cultural/political link between white rebellion and black culture, but it also earned a reputation as a "shocker" that led to an international scandal when an American ambassador set out to have it withdrawn from the Venice Film Festival.[33] In any event, the exploitation of such a narrow taste-culture had been a goal of race-moviemakers before the war; now, as they waned in creative energy their style and substance was "covered" by white B-moviemakers in search of means of teasing the new, raw, black-based, white, teenaged marketplace. Race-moviemen were out of the business for good.

The few attempts of race-moviemen to contain this energy in their own idiom never worked. Savini gave it the best effort, signing the black saxophonist Louis Jordan an accomplished musician with a flair for crossing over and a taste for "nut jazz," or music combined with exaggerated mugging and scatting of lyrics. Into Jordan's brief cycle of musicals were woven social angles such as a plot to keep a black college afloat during a crisis, a touch that moved black charities to use one of them as a fundraiser. But the real star of *Caledonia, Beware, Tall, Tan, and Terrific,* and *Reet, Petite and Gone* was the impish Jordan himself, with his sax and his wide-eyed line of patter that—said one puff—drew "huge crowds." He liked "jivin' around town" in search of "foxy" ladies who did not "talk trash," and songs like "Wham Sam, Dig Them Gams," accompanied by scatted choruses.[34]

Savini's movies showed how to get good mileage out of a then hot musician, but neither he nor his rivals overcame the flaw embedded in the genre: its unfocused blackness that denied spectators the delight of seeing African Americans either in alliance or conflict with white people, a promise held out by the coming cycle of major studio message movies. Instead of the revival of wartime conscience-liberalism embraced by the majors, the race movies filled the emptiness at their centers with vaudeville turns drawn from the colored circuits—Crip Heard, Tondelayo, Deek Watson and His Brown Dots—along with a handful of higher-billed stars from white media, such as Mrs. Joe Louis or Babe Wallace (billed as having "played opposite Lena Horne in 'Stormy Weather'"), and oddly liberal twists of casting, such as white Freddie Bartholomew's cameo role in *Sepia Cinderella*.[35]

There seemed no way out of this thin inventory of dramatic situations: a black college facing a fiscal crisis, a black achiever in danger of being pulled back down into the streets, a black woman who aims too high and forgets her friends, a murder whose solution will save the hero's nightclub (or medical career or business), all of them punctuated by nightclub turns that pad too-thin scripts, form a sort of establishing milieu, and save scenery costs. Bill Alexander's *The Fight Never Ends* (1948) tossed together Ruby Dee's ingenue, woodenly sincere Joe Louis, the Mills Brothers in a musical turn, and a dragged-in story about slums. Norwanda's *No Time for Romance* and *Sun Tan Ranch* were backed by Byron Anderson's Detroit capital and starred William F. Walker, later the first black board member of SAG, but neither received fair distribution. And sometimes terrible material pulled down a solid crossover performer who was working off a favor, as Alexander's *Rhythm in a Riff* and its labored plot dragged Billy Eckstine down with it. The Goldbergs came close with *Miracle in Harlem* (1948), a tale of black economic nationalism in which neighbors save a struggling candy store owner from takeover by a chain; however, the story was lost in a thicket of suspense gimmicks, musical turns, and a cameo by Stepin Fetchit in a role that Fox had fired him from ten years earlier. "I generally falls to pieces around polices," he says. In any case, whether thwarting the heavies in *Miracle in Harlem* or saving Moms Mabley's livelihood in *Boarding House Blues* (1948), race movies had become black sideshows to the center ring in Hollywood, where more blacks worked than ever before.[36]

Worse than that—they *worsened*, perhaps more so than at any time in their history. Actors worked in them because they had to on the way up, as Sidney Poitier did in *Sepia Cinderella*, or on the way down, as Fetchit had done. Or when they were at liberty: Moms Mabley between gigs at the Apollo; Sheila Guyse in *Miracle in Harlem* when a road company of *Memphis Bound* folded and stranded her; Poitier fresh out of the army and sleeping on rooftops; Mantan Moreland because a lifetime in broad comedy had prepared him for nothing else; Bill Greaves as a day job while on Broadway in *Lost in the Stars*, the musical of Alan Paton's South African novel *Cry, the Beloved Country*. "Just a caper, a spoof," recalled Greaves of his movie. "[It] didn't attempt to demean *or* elevate black people." Besides, he recalled, there was nothing in Hollywood until its "sharp left turn" in the coming message movie era. After seeing *Big Timers* Abram Hill of the *Amsterdam* listed the symptoms of the race movies' malaise as though presiding at an autopsy: "amateurish filming, ludicrous situations, lousy sound recording and willful violation of movie techniques." These so warped the movie, he wrote, that it "should have been called LIFE IS A GREAT HUSTLE."[37]

The decline of the genre may be seen in its impact upon the old men of the tribe, Oscar Micheaux and Spencer Williams. For the former the end came swiftly. As usual, his soaring ambition and racial sensibility far outstripped his technical skills and his bank account, not to mention his obliviousness to changes wrought by the war. Nonetheless, inspired by his fans, whose voices he thought he heard asking him "why don't you return to making pictures," in 1948 he reentered the life. As he explained, when audiences complained that "we get *so* tired of *foolishness,*" he replied, "Sounded mighty bad to me—yeah man!"[38] But time and sickness and poverty were already eroding his chutzpah. As his wife reported to her sister, "Dad has arthritis all over his body, but he keeps going." In pain, stiffened, swollen, he plodded on, seeming to live on nervous energy and on the hope that a return to Middle Western roots would restart his engines. "Dad saw that the Book business was going down," his wife wrote, "so he decided that he would try to get back into Pictures. . . . Therefore, he took all his little money and went to Chicago."[39] There, almost home, he took up yet another autobiographical novel, *The Wind from Nowhere,* imposing upon himself burdens that had spoiled every one of his most personal movies. The book was as big as a dictionary, and invincibly resistant to boiling down; inexplicably he lifted his hero's name—Martin Eden—right out of Jack London; only two years beyond a war that had transformed movies, he reached back to one of his familiar dramatic devices, a mistaken racial identity. And he chose for his case an uneven mix of schoolteachers, a radio actor, a dancer, and an understudy in *Anna Lucasta,* thus ensuring that the movie would wear a caste mark peculiar to the genre—an ensemble so varied in talent as to jangle against rather than complement each other's work.[40]

The unpromising project in Chicago called for Micheaux to be at the top of his form, but instead he spread himself thinly, commuting from there to New York with the dailies under his arm, straining his fragile health, and living on the brink of financial ruin. "He is doing it all alone," his wife told her sister. "Isn't that wonderful?" But the stark reality was that the picture was slipping from his grasp. When he drove the rushes to Midway for the flight to New York, he casually left the direction to others. "We were having money problems all the time," recalled a crew member, so "on Sunday we'd go out and sell books" or try to blindbook the unfinished film in Peoria or Joliet. As if the crumbling enterprise were not daunting enough, Micheaux, as was his custom, strained to keep up appearances, squandering money on a limousine and driver to lead the crew to "think he was doing better than he was." Meanwhile, his failing health slowed him to an arthritic "wobbly walk." Toward the end, he spent the winter in New York cutting the film, matching negative, writing ad copy, and raising a last five-

It's on the way. What's on the way?
THE GREATEST NEGRO PHOTOPLAY OF ALL TIMES!
Gala WORLD'S PREMIERE *at a leading* BROADWAY THEATRE Soon!
OSCAR MICHEAUX'S GREAT MOTION PICTURE EPIC
(running time approximately three hours and 15 minutes)

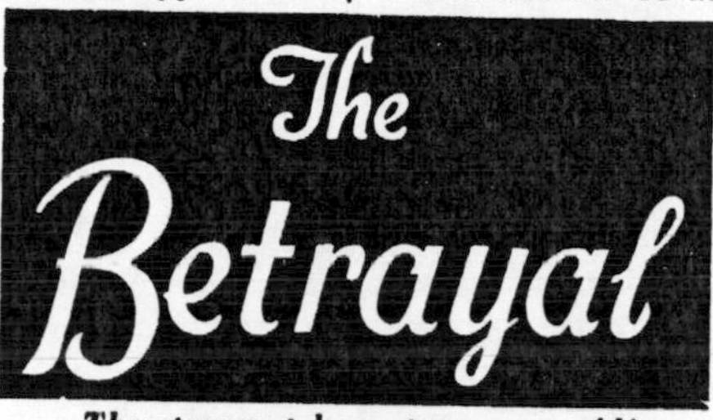

The strangest love story ever told!
Introducing and featuring
LEROY COLLINS, MYRA STANTON, VERLIE COWAN, HARRIS GAINES, YVONNE MACHEN
Based on the immortal novel — "THE WIND FROM NOWHERE"
A Super Collosal Photoplay Available for Exhibition After March 1, 1948
Produced and Distributed by
MICHEAUX PICTURES CORP., 40 Morningside Ave., N. Y. 26

Oscar Micheaux's *The Betrayal* (1948), drawn from his own "immortal" novel *The Wind from Nowhere,* despite its self-proclaimed "greatness" signaled the end of the race movie era. Lorenzo Tucker Collection.

hundred-dollar shot of completion money, all the while aiming for an April opening.[41]

The result was an elephantine flop that the distributor, Savini, premiered before an audience of black and white celebrities and critics who laughed it out of its Broadway theatre. Instead of being the hoped-for hardticket roadshow, it laid an egg that rolled to the bottom of a double bill in Los Angeles. Black critics almost wept and felt "that the film should never have been shown." One of them wished to "sneak away and hide in a corner" rather than face its "acting worse than amateurish, the dialogue ridiculous, the story downright stupid." The whites of course agreed. "Monumental incompetence," one of them wrote, "a preposterous, inept bore . . . less artful than . . . home-movies."[42] Micheaux, sick and in pain, broke and without prospects—but worst of all, guilty of a travesty that had tainted a lifetime of hope and struggle—in the three years he had left never gave it another try.

Williams's fall was no less far; it merely took longer, and it lacked the tragic coloring that Micheaux's hubris lent to almost everything he did. After *The Blood of Jesus* in 1940 his work lost its primitive integrity, partly because his angel, Alfred Sack, linked up with the Goldbergs as though to serve two tastes—North and South—with a pooled inventory. His *Go Down Death* (1946), a pale imitation of *The Blood of Jesus,* attracted attention only for its apparent plagiarism of the poetry of James

Weldon Johnson, the late NAACP leader. Williams's *The Girl in Room 20* and *Dirty Gertie from Harlem USA* were flawed *films noirs* released at the height of a rage for the genre. But compared with the Hollywood article—*Murder, My Sweet* or *The Big Sleep*—Williams's black versions seemed fumbling, poor, ill-lighted counterfeits. *Dirty Gertie* borrowed heavily from Maugham's *Rain* but still could not sustain an audience through an afternoon free of misplaced laughter. He finished his career with *Juke Joint* and *Beale Street Mama,* two witless pastiches of music and slapstick, the latter a bungled story of two "whitewings," or street-sweepers (Williams and Juli Jones), who try to parlay a bundle of found money into a career in the numbers racket. Only an onstage plea from one of the actors saved its Los Angeles debut from closure under pressure from a local Interracial Film and Radio Guild that charged Williams with reviving the "razor cutting, eye bucking, Uncle Tom." Williams, like a clown weeping under his paint, ended his career playing Andy in CBS's TV version of its radio hit *Amos 'n' Andy,* which would also face black protests of its apparent perpetuation of old stereotypes.[43]

By this time critics routinely joined Abram Hill in denouncing the ineptitude of race movies that no longer commanded loyalty "even among a yawning Monday morning audience of thriller fans." The genre had fallen so far short of its former ideals of advocacy, heroism, and cultural nationalism that when distinguished Hollywood veteran Clarence Brooks announced a new film, Jimmy Adamson of the *Sentinel* warned him off. "I hope Clarence will surround himself with sensible people this time," he wrote, "and produce pictures for the general public and not try to satisfy a few simple-minded color-struck Negroes."[44] In other words, Adamson asked his readers to step into postwar life, build on the integrationism put forth during the war, and abandon race movies as an anachronism incapable of engaging a broad audience.

Gradually the middle class and its spokesmen in the press hardened their conviction that race movies belonged to the dead past. *Ebony,* the new glossy magazine that defined and fed the expectations of the new class, struggled to break with the mentality that obliged unquestioned fealty to race movies as black enterprises. On the one hand it reported "hefty grosses" for "all-Negro movies [that] have suddenly blossomed into a million-dollar business," while on the other it dismissed them as "a fly-by-night precarious dream" of exploiters who had "cashed in on segregation." The choice seemed clear: Either race-moviemen would see "Jim Crow slowly fading" and take up "making mixed movies," or they would cling to "crude, corny tales about gangsters and nightclubs" bereft of "Negro uplift."[45]

Ebony's formulation proved prescient; race-moviemen were trapped by the waning of antebellum racial custom. By the early 1950s its erosion had already weakened the monopoly that had allowed Southern bookers to play, as one of Micheaux's cameramen recalled, "race movies good or bad." As black viewers were drawn off to Hollywood's message movies, Lorenzo Tucker, one of Micheaux's veterans, felt that "our people did not support their own." In Toddy's more guiltfree reckoning: "Integration came in then, you know."[46]

For those of them with an eye for omens, *Sepia Cinderella* (1947) should have given them all the bad news they needed. Everything about it signaled its obsolescence in an age when the president of the United States commissioned a study of racism designed to introduce its remedies into public policy and law. Its star was Billy Daniels, who already had scored a crossover success with the recording of his signature song "That Old Black Magic," a moody romantic ballad that would have been unthinkable for a black singer before the war. Its minor players included William Greaves and Sidney Poitier, whose abilities carried them to award-winning success in an integrated future. At its "western premiere" In Los Angeles *Sepia Cinderella* called forth other racial ironies, such as the decision to use its opening as a benefit for Jackie Robinson, who had only just cracked the color barrier to major league baseball. The emcee was Eddie Anderson, who already enjoyed a career in white radio as the foil of the white comedian Jack Benny. The gala was staged at the Lincoln Theatre on formerly prosperous black Central Avenue, a house that soon would fall victim to a black drift toward formerly lilywhite downtown theatres. The stage manager of the event was Wendell Franklin, who soon would become the first black member of the Directors Guild. Finally, the promoters themselves deleted the word "sepia" from the title in their advertising as though papering over the appearance that they were selling a Jim Crow product.[47]

In the ensuing years of an integrated American army in Korea, the overturning of the legal basis of segregation by the Supreme Court, the grudging opening of a few institutions, and the gradual black shift from a strategy of litigation to one of nonviolent direct action, race movies survived only as campish curiosities among such audiences as derisive youth clubs in churches. Other blacks acquired them as fossils of olden times, much as current fans of "black collectibles," such as Aunt Jemima or Uncle Ben advertising memorabilia or *Amos 'n' Andy* videotapes, have taken up their hobbies as a reminder of twice-told tales of former bad times.[48]

Thus, shut out of theatrical markets, their production moribund, race movies survived for another decade on late-night television in Southern markets. Along with Soundies, propaganda films left over from the war, Snader Telescription, and other sources of syndicated fare, they filled the yawning gaps in the daily log of a score of Southern stations struggling through the first years of television broadcasting. In one instance Nate Zelikow, an enterprising young advertising executive in Houston, packaged thirty race movies into his *Ebony Theatre* as a way, he recalled, "to cultivate and capture the lucrative Negro market" and as a means for station managers to show the Federal Communications Commission that they catered to all sectors of their market. By 1955 Zelikow's package included black features, ten years of All-America and Edward W. Lewis newsreels, and odd documentaries such as *One Tenth of a Nation*, and it played Houston, San Antonio, Galveston, Little Rock, and Jackson, among others.[49]

None of this, of course, held out any hope for a revival of the genre. Zelikow turned a dollar on television because he bought titles from Sack at distraint prices. And perhaps he profited because a single night's broadcast might reach an audience far greater than that to be had in weeks of bookings in underused grindhouses, all of it free from the squabbles over percentages and gate-checks that marred dealings between bookers and theatremen. Finally, broadcasting race movies may have expanded the audience to include the black middle class viewers who would have avoided exposing themselves to the indignity of a segregated balcony in a squalid grindhouse. Somehow, watching the movies in a primary social circle of friends of family provided entertainment without the appearance of lending support to the system of segregation. In these private sessions "for members only," race movies survived as a curiosity, like a buttonhook on a knickknack shelf.[50]

African American audiences, made camerawise by the war movies that had relocated blacks more to the center of movie life, knew that race movies had lost their *raison d'être*, so that watching them accompanied a mood of perverse pleasure in calculatedly laughing in all the wrong places—a sort of black nationalist politics of inappropriate behavior. In this sense their laughter was indeed politically purposeful, a way of telling each other that they *knew* not only the absurdity of racism but the absurdity of making movies to accommodate to it. Like the character in Amiri Baraka's one-act farce *Jello*, they had ritually murdered Rochester, Jack Benny's comic valet, a reminder of a racist past, and thereby purged themselves in preparation for whatever peacetime brought.

6

Documentary Film Culture and Postwar Liberal Momentum

No one dared guess the postwar future of American racial custom. Despite the fissures that had opened in the system as a result of the crisis of war, the black penetration into previously inaccessible seats of power, the signs that race had again become a national point at issue, there were conservatives afoot who expected a return to antebellum ways. Parallel to this line of political change, American filmmakers faced an equally uncertain future. On its face, the situation promised only a thermidorean reaction, a return to a familiar equilibrium after the dislocations of war. But at the same time, new conditions also invited a search for means of extending wartime alliances. Such a strategy seemed compelling because formerly stable Hollywood was so unsettled by soaring labor costs, the threat of war-deferred strikes, the buffeting of inflation, a baffling suburban migration by an audience seemingly bent on trying every new leisure-time activity that drew them away from the movie houses they formerly had attended twice each week, and a Supreme Court that threatened to make up for years of wartime judicial peace by inquiring into antitrust violations.

Meanwhile, outside of established Hollywood, and less threatened by these forces, there was a documentary film culture that had been trained and emboldened by the war and, by the summer of 1945, had already begun to set an agenda that far outreached the circumspect goals of their wartime masters in OWI and the Pentagon. Willynilly, it emerged as a political culture composed of filmmakers, film librarians, rental firms, and viewers whom war had taught new respect for and new uses of film. Joining with trade unions and liberal activists, they lobbied to free government films for civilian use even as they began making their own films.

Hollywood eventually would resume its own erratic liberal agenda, but for the moment the studios stood apart, momentum lost, liberal thrust blunted by fears. One of David O. Selznick's advisers expressed one such fear: that a campaign against Southern censors might backfire by stirring sentiment for a widespread ban on race-angled movies. On the movielots themselves, managers felt squeezed between rising costs and raising ticket prices. "A definite trend downward in attendance," Spyros Skouras, president of 20th Century–Fox, told his production chief, Darryl Zanuck. "We must reduce production costs or we will face inevitable ruin."[1] In this mood, the moguls had little choice but to abandon politics to the newly forming film culture of Eastern documentarists.

For a time, then, documentary filmmakers, less fettered by wariness toward box office or stockholders, not only took up racial political issues but renewed their faith in their medium as a tool of the social engineering they had learned during the war. They joined with a circle of like-minded social scientists and growing circles of users of film, many of whose liberal politics had been shaped in the crucible of war. This loose network of advocates felt such a commonality that they soon acted as though in a movement, their efforts held together by their shared faith in the continued efficacy of film as a medium of advocacy.

Almost unnoticed because of the unhyped setting in which independent filmmakers and teachers did their work, documentaries often passed unremarked in the popular press although they may have been seen by thousands of both deeply influenced and deeply influential people. True, *The Negro Soldier* once made it into *Vogue*'s "People Are Talking About" column, and *Daybreak at Udi,* a British quasi-documentary set in colonial Africa, won an Oscar in 1947, but all in all the lack of star quality and publicity was easily taken for lack of impact.

Nonetheless, documentary film grew into a postwar voice of conscience-liberalism that persisted in the face of more famous signs of conservative reaction, and eventually may have provided Hollywood with the mentality tolerant of, and even receptive to, message movies and on the lookout for the incidental politics embedded in feature film. Among intellectuals there seemed not only a rededication to racial reformism, but a redefinition of it drawn from the lore of social science, coupled with a renewed faith in film as an advocate of a remedy for it. Many of their most provocative ideas grew out of Myrdal's *An American Dilemma,* which became a sort of Chilton's parts manual for the machinery of racism; Logan's less famous *What the Negro Wants;* Allport's *The Nature of Prejudice,* which portrayed bigotry as a correctable failure of cognition; and two books rooted in wartime experience, Robert K. Merton's *Mass Persuasion: The Sociology of a War Bond Drive* and Samuel Stouffer's *What the Soldier Thinks*. As August Meier and Elliott Rudwick observed of the historians of the era, "an awareness of both the sufferings of the nation's dispossessed and the enormity of Nazi crimes committed in the name of racial superiority . . . converged with the findings of modern anthropology and environmental psychology to help undermine the prevailing white belief in racial inequality." At the same time, their work began to penetrate scholarly conferences and intellectual quarterlies. This sort of inquiry came strikingly from a group of, as Meier and Rudwick reported, "persons from conventional backgrounds whose outlook shifted considerably to the left in the social and intellectual context of the New Deal and World War II and . . . for whom military experiences during the war provided the crucial turning point."[2]

The early returns on their research not only seeped into politics but enjoyed a degree of approval by the electorate. Although Harry S. Truman sometimes broke the hearts of liberals by joining in anti-red hysteria, in racial politics he commissioned the study of racism that became the eloquent *To Secure These Rights* (1947), which called for nothing less than the abandonment of racist behaviors that had become "burdens on [America's] common conscience . . . and an issue in world politics." Within a year of its appearance it astonishingly graced the Democratic platform calling for an end to segregation and peonage, a peacetime FEPC, federal guarantees of civil rights, and immediate settlement of claims arising from wartime internment of Japanese Americans. Southerners led by Senator Strom Thurmond (D–S.C.) were so certain that, unlike Roosevelt, "Truman means it," they bolted the party and forced Truman to win without them. As though cultivating the "aroused public conscience" that Justice Felix Frankfurter had once called for, the polls revealed a marginal wish to pass the report into law "as a whole," a sense reflected in Truman's mail, which a staff member described as offering "mass support" for FEPC.[3]

A similar mentality leavened the school curriculum, particularly in a widely offered course called "Problems of Democracy" (POD, as pupils called it). A child of the "progressive" education movement, it emphasized "actual" living as against "dead classics," and thus took up "current events" and "social studies" at the expense of history. The trend gave conscience-liberalism a place in the school day, especially among teachers who "wanted to keep alive the boosterism of wartime," and those open to using the "proliferation of audiovisuals" that included surplus films such as *The Negro Soldier*. Typically, such teachers might celebrate Brotherhood Week by showing the film, singing "Ballad for Americans," and hearing reports on black and immigrant worthies. That conservatives noticed may be seen in an American Legion protest of the film *The Brotherhood of Man* and of a "red" bulletin board in New Trier High School. The textbooks bore titles like *Good Will Days,* promised "the promotion of RACIAL GOOD WILL," featured epigrams asserting that "all Americans are brothers," used ethnic poetry such as Langston Hughes's "Weary Blues," and included an account of the old nation when "Americans were a terribly provincial and intolerant people." One book took up a racial incident in Massachusetts that Warner Bros. made into a movie. "It can be done; it is being done," said A. R. Lerner and Herbert Poster's book *The Challenge of Hate* (1946) on ending racism.[4]

Popular culture in all its forms picked up the theme as though ratifying a new status quo in which conscience-liberalism had become the ideology of the moment. In at least two comic strips the changed racial mentality appeared starkly on the lithographed page. Before the war Ken Kling's racetrack strip *Joe and Asbestos* and Will Eisner's Sunday private eye strip *The Spirit* included bug-eyed, liver-lipped comic black dwarves as sidekicks, but by war's end both had become more realistic. Coulton Waugh, who drew a strip for *PM,* spoke for the trend, calling for "using the medium to further the national ideal of tolerance and justice for all people, regardless of race." Comic books took off during the war, rising to a readership of 150 million per month, and on army posts outselling *Time, Life,* and *Reader's Digest* combined. Anxious parents formed the Parents Institute and brought out their own book, *True Comics,* which became yet another organ of liberal rhetoric, featuring such stories as "They Got the Blame" (a series on scapegoating that was reprinted as a pamphlet) and "There Are No Master Races" (yet another version of Gene Weltfish and Ruth Benedict's *The Races of Mankind*). The Writers' War Board brought out *Master Comics,* which Waugh recalled as showing "Negroes working with whites on equal terms." The Congress of Industrial Organizations (CIO), the NUL, and others brought out their own books. There was even an *All-Negro Comics,* which featured a UN troubleshooter, "the American born, college educated, Lion Man," who not only wore the obligatory leotard costume of the comic hero but also scouted for "sharp chicks." The books actually grew so competitive that an NUL officer boasted that "we 'scooped' the other race relations agencies on the comic book," and urged entry into movies.[5]

The trend in sports was more tentative but in the end more celebrated, after the Brooklyn Dodgers signed on Jackie Robinson to play baseball. Although before the war, there were occasional integrated events—such as the annual Penn Relays, which drew so many black athletes that it was known as "the Negro Olympics"—baseball only belatedly caved in to pressure from Sam Lacy of the *Afro* and from the *Worker.*[6]

In 1945 *Variety* played this story of, as one historian described it, the "great assault on white supremacy" in a page-one banner: "GEAR SHOW BIZ VS RACE BIAS." A newly described social type, the "otherdirected" urbanite who derived his or her sensibilities more from immediate peer culture than from tradition, became the core of a cult of the new that helped shape an urban culture in which performers attended symposia "on the status of the Negro in a fighting democracy," impresarios sometimes followed liberal leads in desegregating their theatres, and the rush to smoky cellar clubs and black folksingers seemed so hep that James Agee grumbled at the glut of "self-consciously niggery" singers.[7]

Part of the mood stemmed from teenagers' rebellious fads, which we have already seen in *Don't Knock the Rock.* If their parents were square, they were obliged to be hep; if fathers wore polished brogans, sons wore scuffed loafers; if mothers eschewed smoking, daughters did not; and so on. Unavoidably, then, if parents went to hear the latinate rhythms of Vincent Lopez at the Taft Grille, their children went for the black bands at Roseland. Above all, this politics of warring tastes obliged kids to reach across racial lines, take up the cool patois of the hepcat, dress à la mode in a "zoot suit with a reet pleat." Soon there were intersections of racial culture: Josh White in Village cellars singing "The Free and Equal Blues"; Norman Granz's "Jazz at the Philharmonic"; Duke Ellington playing both Carnegie Hall and the Apollo; whites taking the A train to the Apollo; black kids catching Charlie Barnett and Louis Prima at the Brooklyn Paramount. Moreover, every large city reflected a similar pattern.[8] Optimistically, *Ebony* reported that white youth behaved this way not because "it was the thing to do" but because they had been raised up on a diet of wartime liberalism.

In its activist mode this warborne mentality carried over into the business of show business. By the end of the war the shows of the Hollywood Victory Committee had been integrated. Jack Benny and Stan Kenton played on integrated bills; Ernest Whitman moved from playing the Colored Elks to doing a tuberculosis benefit at the Los Angeles Public Library; Joan Fontaine okayed a date to play a black Women's Army Corps outfit; Lena Horne and Jimmy Durante played the Colosseum in a tribute to two California generals, Patton and Doolittle. Thus it was not only the contrariness of youth but also a changed racial etiquette that in turn promoted a high receptivity for black performing idiom.[9] In the East a similar pattern emerged. Frank Sinatra not only made an antiracism movie but afterward rushed to Gary, Indiana, to help avert a threatened racial rumble. At Lewisohn Stadium in Manhattan, Rex Ingram, Betty Garrett, and Cab Calloway appeared on behalf of a black man blinded in a scrape with Georgia police; the Chicago Human Relations Committee sponsored the concert "Jazz and the Negro People" to promote "tolerance" among adolescents; Ellington and others did fundraisers for the "underprivileged" or against "intolerance." Max Gordon brought the blues singer Chippie Hill out of retirement to play the Village Vanguard; Lionel Hampton played the White House for the first time; Louis Armstrong played the Mardi Gras in

New Orleans; and Josephine Baker broke a barrier at Copa City in Miami.[10]

Theatre, perhaps because it was a medium of words as well as action and because it played cities, also played to the new mood, combining racial politics with showmanship in ways that audiences and critics responded to by praising "social significance" and damning the odd "racial stereotype." The icon of the era was Edith Isaacs's *Theatre Arts* magazine, which brought out a hardbound issue in 1947 dedicated to "The Negro in the American Theatre," a document of such uncommon graphic and editorial quality that it remained a reference for decades afterward. *Othello* became politicized in a way typical of the age: During the war Paul Robeson made the role black for the first time in recent history and thereafter took it on the road on the straw-hat circuit, talked of a USO tour and a British movie of it, and finally brought it back to Broadway in 1948, trotting onstage between the acts to introduce Progressive presidential candidate Henry A. Wallace.[11] Offstage, traveling companies challenged local racial custom by refusing to play Jim Crow houses. Even the musical form took up racial satire: in *Finian's Rainbow* with its burlesque of Southern life and its drawling senator from "Missitucky" who turns black; and *South Pacific* with its cadenced refrain on race hatred—"You've got to be taught, very carefully taught." Topical drama included Richard Wright's *Black Boy*, Lillian Smith's *Strange Fruit* (both taken from popular fiction), and no fewer than three original works about returning black soldiers: Theodore Ward's *Our Lan'*, a tragedy of Reconstruction, which a critic praised for its "contemporary relevance," and two stories of the postwar South, Kermit Bloomgarten's *Deep Are the Roots* and Robert Ardrey's *Jeb*. Opportunists exploited it by ransacking the public domain for black versions of *Pinafore*, *Carmen*, *Faust*, *Lysistrata*, *Pagliacci*, *The Beggar's Opera*, and even *Uncle Tom's Cabin* (with Martha Raye as a white Topsy!).[12] Audiences joined in not only by attending but by becoming inside dopesters too "with it" to accept old racism. *Variety* caught on and warned backers against a revival of *The Green Pastures* partly because "new audiences" in Boston made its tryout "anything but encouraging." And on the left the *Worker* counseled its readers to see only authentic black drama rather than stuff about the impact of racism on whites or on lone black figures with "no roots in the rest of the Negro people."[13]

To take only one of the new dramas, Ardrey's *Jeb* created a tension between Southerners who balked at change and those, black and white, who had been remade by the war. Jeb (Ossie Davis's debut) was a black soldier who had lost a leg in the war. To the old men he was no more than "an old field hand boy," while to younger whites he was "a colored boy who's lost a leg fighting for his country." Both soon learn the army made him an active agent on his own behalf by teaching him "to run an adding machine." "If an ignorant old colored boy like me could learn somethin' fighting in this war," he reckons, "then I got faith and trust white folks they've learned something too." Thus Jeb in his way had taken on the manner of the postwar liberal: magisterial and bent upon carrying the "four freedoms" into churches, schools, and union halls in the form of, as Sacvan Bercovitch put it, an "American jeremiad . . . the public exhortation . . . designed to join social criticism to spiritual renewal."[14]

Hints of this actively tutorial role and the faith in film to convey its substance have already been noted in Saul Padover's proposal to Agriculture for a film about the African American as "an average human being," a project that implied a future liberalism rooted less in a temporary war footing. Less than a fortnight after D-Day in Normandy, even as OWI shrank in wealth and influence, Philleo Nash proposed a project that was aimed pointedly at postwar conditions, perhaps to be steered by some previously unthinkable peacetime equivalent of OWI. Lockheed Aircraft, a bellwether in the California economy, had revealed its own alertness to the prospects for a postwar racial reform when it invited Nash to leave OWI for a project "to determine objectively the results of wartime experience in the utilization of special labor groups; i. e. physically handicapped, minor and the over-age, part-time workers, Negro and Mexican workers." In turning down the offer, Nash looked ahead to a postwar militancy that would carry liberalism "away from the tolerance and good will aspects of minority-group relations toward the management of inter-group relations as an industry and community problem." As we have seen, he was already a liberal mole within the agency, extending its reach beyond the narrow duties prescribed by mission statements, volunteering his services, for example, in composing lists of liberal movies for "citizens" and organizations. It was only a small step for him to regard his war work as of "importance now and to postwar adjustment [that] is so great that I do not feel that I could leave it."[15]

Clearly, Nash and other liberal staff were running a private OWI within the walls of the actual OWI, and they expected their work to continue after the war. Not only had Nash been using the agency's resources to develop filmographies complete with addresses of distributors, a precursor of 16 mm marketing techniques, he was soliciting still more opportunities to reach activists and to develop mailing lists while explaining away favors as deriving from "my friendship for Truman Gibson, not through official channels."[16] Indeed, perhaps through Gibson, black activists learned of Nash's covert activity and sensed that the subtext to the official line ran all the way to the White House. In any case, they asked Truman for a "transition from war to peace" that included "vigorous remedial action" directed at racial problems. Not to do so, Lester Granger of NUL told the president only two weeks after the surrender of Japan in the summer of 1945, was to risk the meretriciousness inherent in standing "before the world as a champion of the oppressed peoples unless we practice as well as preach the principles of democracy." Gradually this link between black fortunes and the role of America as the world's rabbi became a convention of postwar liberal advocacy, thereby providing a reason for the government's movies to enter postwar civilian circuits and provide the nucleus of many inventories of rental film firms.[17]

In addition, as we have seen, *The Negro Soldier* and *Teamwork* became the stakes in a game played out in the agencies over postwar civilian access. Even as the thrust of their politics came to be seen as ever more "painfully, pitifully mild," the press on the left praised one or the other as "a pioneer" in reflecting the pluralism that had been at the bottom of wartime calls for unity, tolerance, and brotherhood. This liberal reading, carrying far beyond the army's original idea, surfaced in the letters of Nash to civilian activists, the NAACP's presentments to the army, and the blurbs of both library and rental catalogues, which touted them as formulas for "living together . . . now and for the future." In a typical case, the CIO urged its members to attend a Milwaukee showing of *The Negro Soldier* for its tribute to "the contributions made by the Negro people throughout our nation's history in establishing the democratic principles for which we are now fighting," a phrasing that preserved a militant edge while *altering* the film's thrust from military to *civil* history.[18]

In the same summer of 1944, Nash all but enlisted as a press agent for the film. When Edwin R. Embree of the Rosenwald Foundation, a well-known angel for black scholars and artists, asked if "there is anything any of us can do to help spread to commercial theatres *The Negro Soldier*," Nash urged an interracial panel to massage pressure points such as Barney Balaban's chain of cavernous Chicago theatres. Meanwhile, OWI agreed to bring forth one hundred and fifty prints.[19] The growing numbers of educational film users rushed to get in line for 16 mm versions. In addition to the OWI's own distribution to PTAs, prisons, MOMA, and the CIAA, totaling perhaps three million viewers, more patently activist groups such as the United Auto Workers (UAW) and the American Council on Race Relations acquired as many as three prints each.[20]

Far from booking the film as a cheap filler or as a dutiful gesture to the army's narrow goals, liberals often presented it as, in a way, *their* film, a herald of their own emerging politics. By thus channeling their members' zest for a ringing message, they effectively italicized OF-51 into a liberal tract that stood on the army's shoulders to proclaim "the contribution that Negroes are making . . . in this People's War for Liberation"—a visual pamphlet that the CIO urged upon its officers and "their families and friends."[21] Not merely a piece about the colored army, said the *CIO News*, it "drives home the point once and for all that Negro or white, our men and women in the armed forces [were] the same" in their desire for "a better world for all of the people." In this way, the army's modest little movie had become liberal labor's weapon in "the battle against bias" with such vigor that the CIO imagined itself in the van of an assault on "commercial movies" that had been "guilty of many acts of intolerance through stereotyped characterizations of racial and nationality groups." "Perhaps," mused the CIO reviewer, "the industry itself can profit" from a look at these films.[22]

Was all of this mere liberal wish-weaving for a postwar moral equivalent of war? Certainly conscience-liberalism had gained legitimacy from the war, if for no other reason than that Hitler had given racism a bad name. But war had also brought substantive wrenching of old ways in the form of, to use the cant phrasing, "cotton movin' west, cattle movin' east, Yankees movin' south, niggers movin' north." Indeed, blacks had moved north, worked for wages (rather than crop shares), sent their children to schools, voted, and returned from the army, like Jeb, with heads spinning with new ideas. Moreover, Southern politicians knew this and regarded it as "grave." Indeed, one of Truman's aides thought that the president "always did feel that there should be a civil rights bill" to attack the "moral dry rot" of racism.[23] True or not, liberals certainly thought so. They lobbied Truman, gave out "unity" awards, made Brotherhood Week a national ritual. Everywhere committees formed against "segregation in the nation's capital" or elsewhere, and editors asked, no longer rhetorically, "Why don't we do something?" Like the media-prone activists the war had made them, they asked for signs and omens. They asked that the navy recommission the *Booker T.* under a black skipper, that a police presence be used to protect black voters and liberal judges, that someone make a movie of *To Secure These Rights*. In a typical letter to Truman, Walter White reported on how liberalism came to football in an interracial game that displayed only "the finest team spirit." And over at Interior someone began reporting on the ease of integration of the National Symphony in the capital's parks as a sign that segregation was far from a "community pattern" that gave theatres the right to exclude blacks.[24]

Meanwhile, documentary filmmakers, audiovisual librarians, and teachers broke with their neutralist past, when they had feared "controversy." Before the war, the American Council on Education (ACE) had limited films to only four bland subjects—voice, grammar, hygiene, and aesthetics—so that even the famous *The Plow That Broke the Plains* seemed useful only for its "mood of rhythmic beauty."[25] In those days, even if a brave teacher pressed on, he or she would have found few catalogues or reviews, scant funds, and most experts calling for restraint rather than boldness in the use of film. "Most documentary films are propaganda films," warned William H. Hartley, a cataloguer of national repute. In a review of *America's Disinherited* (1938) he quoted from a sharecropper—"yesterday we asked for pity, today we demand justice"—but cautioned that "the teacher should also see that the planter's side of the story is told."[26]

In this prewar neutralist mode, racial issues were almost always formulated as between white philanthropists and black mendicants. Hartley, for example, preferred films about "philanthropic efforts on behalf of the Negro." Like Tarzan movies that set Africa in a timeless primitivism, such movies narrowed the range of black action to small folkish measures, as in the Department of Agriculture film *The Negro Farmer* (1938), which linked black progress to home-canning, installing flyscreens, digging privies, and whitewashing, and cited Booker T. Washington's call for putting "brains and skill into the common occupations of life." The resulting avoidance of politics reduced all issues to efficient management and, as a reviewer put it, "constructive . . . steps being taken to improve living conditions." In this setting an African American was "great" only if, like Carver, he could be portrayed "not as an unusual Negro" but one who "is offered many positions but prefers to devote his life to the study of the peanut."[27]

Then came the war and an end to, as Cecile Starr, an activist in the era, put it, "poor fact films that had neither cinematic quality nor ideas." The war, said Irving Jacoby, had "been responsible for the great growth in the . . . use of idea films," rousing an audience, their teachers, and "a generation of film makers."[28] Starr in a recent interview remembered the high energy of the era: the Scots filmmaker John Grierson urging a cinema of advocacy, the Carnegie Foundation giving seed money to the American Library Association (ALA) to promote "films of social content" inspired by the "high idealism" inherited from a war "to make a better world," Iris Barry collecting such films for MOMA, a leftist distributor deciding to "woo" librarians beyond the bounds of his prewar cells of the converted. All of it was bonded to a national "film council movement" in a network of associations: the Educational Film Library Association (EFLA), bookers' guilds, the American Film Center, the International Film Association. "The whole AV field was starting up fresh," recalled Emily S. Jones, one of its leaders. "The people who had founded it . . . were now old-timers, and new people were appearing, many of them out of service in the armed forces." The synergistic alliance gave new life to conscience-liberalism. Even as established politics seemed poised to veer to the right, the ACE predicted a postwar "great boom" in documentaries grounded in the "military films [that] will be available after the war."[29]

From 1945 through 1948, as Hollywood cultivated its first crop of message movies, this new film culture grew not only in agencies and numbers but also in its new sense of mission. What had once been a shared timidity had become a crusading spirit rooted in the social engineers' faith that films of advocacy truly could affect change. Supporting them were the standard works in social psychology, which regarded bigotry as remediable flawed knowledge. It was easy to infer, then, that sweet thoughts about one's fellows could be generated by the flick of a projector switch. The sense of mission was also reinforced by manuals that taught specific strategies on discussing "ways minorities are being treated." By the opening of school in 1946, they began to speak boldly of reaching a "community" beyond the classroom through film forums on "problems of inter-group relations" and films on the "removal" of prejudice.[30] As a predictor of impending success they culled the army's own measurements of success in "attitude building" and its strategies for "presenting a 'point of view,'" and ran the data in their tradepapers. In one story, for example, when soldiers were shown Capra's *The Battle of Britain* most of them got its message that British survival was owed to an unbreakable spirit, but among soldiers who *liked* the film the message came across at a rate 2.67 times higher than among those indifferent to the film. The inference was clear: Whatever the efficacy of army surplus film, continued success obliged them to make new and better films.[31]

Thus, as befitting victors in a war against fascism)—a "double" victory in African American calculus—they moved from mere scavenging of army supplies to manufacturing their own products custom-designed to solve "broader problems" of "education . . . in a democratic society." The idea, said advocate Charles F. Hoban, was to replace "Know Your Enemy" films with "Know Your Neighbor" films. Their rhetoric rang in tones similar to an EFLA resolution to "spearhead drives to broaden the place of film in the present social scene," a sentiment carried to local groups by giving awards for "fostering, in its own community, the effective use of films." Another tactic combined film showings with panels of local worthies, as did a Film Council of America (FCA) meeting in Stamford, Connecticut, in which a lawyer, an FCA delegate, a Pitney Bowes executive, and a member of an interracial commission discussed *The Brotherhood of Man*. By early 1947 *Variety* reported no fewer than fifty such groups linked in "a permanent front to act as a corrective democratic force."[32]

Their tradepapers promised to sharpen the voices of advocacy in film and to reach broader audiences with messages of "better human relations," "religious tolerance," and "brotherhood and equality." June Blythe of the ACE, for example, urged a congress to make more films on "minority-majority group relationships" and to include blacks in a national "plan that will represent . . . all users of the media." "Like any other new market," she argued, "[they] must be sought out and educated to the value of the film." On their own behalf, blacks joined in. *People's Voice*, for example, called on black women to "force" release of OF-51 to civilians; Ann Tanneyhill of NUL urged her agency to take up films as a weapon; and the NAACP remade its fundraising film to include Lena Horne asserting that World War II had been fought "to preserve and strengthen the democratic ideal," which in the coming peacetime must "still be fought for."[33]

Such purposefulness coupled with a rising professionalism promoted a fevered sense of being an organic part of a vanguard that ranged through social engineers, filmmakers, and users of film, unified by a sense that the broad center of American political culture stood in agreement that a Double V had transpired. All that remained, or so it seemed, was for them to speak in concert, define the terms of a liberal hegemony, and grasp the proselytizing opportunity that the new film culture presented. The result would be, they thought, newly elevated standards of film excellence far above those set by old-style "educational" films, and eventually a fresh crop of films capable of delivering "an emotional punch of great intensity."[34]

Take one instance of how these film advocates expected to work. Harry M. Lerner, formerly in I&E, a doctoral student in Teachers' College Columbia University, and a member of the National Jewish Welfare Board, hit upon using "street films" as Reddick had done at the Schomburg during the Harlem riots. Tensions had risen during the summer of 1946 around 161st Street and Broadway as new black residents overflowed into the formerly white neighborhood. Lerner coupled a rally on behalf of extending FEPC with movies thrown on a screen hanging from the third floor of an apartment building. In the resulting multilayered event, both war and postwar movies, an Adam Clayton Powell speech, and a presentation by the League for Fair Play dampened white resentment by pointing out "the parallel of Nazi racial policies" with their own behavior. Powell "leapt to the stand" and "soon multiplied the crowd," who quickly caught the mood of the occasion, which, like so many such rituals, avoided root causes by invoking "the common enemy, Hitlerism, [as] the catalyst for intergroup sympathy and unity," an evasion that disallowed more substantive inquiry into the nettle of racism. Yet the league reminded participants of a parallel to a "Springfield Plan," a wartime Massachusetts curriculum revision designed to rout out racism in pupils before it put down roots, a program so compelling that Jack Warner bought it as the basis for a feature film. A heady mood of victory prevailed, and optimistic reports of the day appeared in *Film Forum Review*, an organ of Columbia's Institute for Adult Education, and other audiovisual tradepapers.[35]

How to channel this fusion of militancy and missionary zeal? An EFLA librarian called for a more aggressive posture by taking control of "the purse strings" by budgeting for film acquisitions rather than relying on handouts from PTAs and Rotary Clubs. For inspiration the New York Film Council asked the *doyen* of documentarists, John Grierson, to address the faithful on "the place of film in the present social scene." And by 1947 Walter White so sensed the self-propelled energy of the times that he called for cannibalizing *The Negro Soldier* for stockshots with which to make a new NAACP promo-film, an idea embraced by their "PR" man Henry Lee Moon who hoped the result might be good enough to serve not only "our branches and friends but something we might be able to put on television." The outcome anticipated by White: a quantum leap from the days of mere "opportunism and the acceptance of second class citizenship toward a new concept which the late war had enormously advanced."[36] In the next few years not only did such rhetoric become part of a generalized "Americanism," but an institutional system of making and distributing its films fell into place.

As the number of titles grew, activists formed agencies such as the Committee for a National Film Cooperative or, like the NAACP, collected brochures of distributors and attended previews of new films. One week it might be *The Sydenham Plan* (1948), a film on the "equal life of health and happiness" in an integrated Harlem hospital, or a rerun of *Land of Liberty*, the old World's Fair film, or *La Montagne est verte*, a biopic of French anticolonialist Victor Schoelcher.[37]

By 1948 their catalogues suggested uses of the films. *The Negro Soldier*, said the NAACP, told how "the services of Negroes during the war reveal to what extent they can and should participate in the civilian professions," and the weak *One Tenth of a Nation* became "a strong plea for a fair place for the Negro in American life." Others evasively traced racism to foreign enemies: the army's *Don't Be a Sucker* told Americans "how Germans destroyed themselves" through racism; the British *Man, One Family* "contrast[ed] fascist and democratic views [as] the lesson learned in World War II"; and *The World We Want to Live In* showed that "while racial hatred was being fostered by the Nazi, freedom of religion was being promoted from all sides in our country." Ringing with active verbs on film's capacity to "foster" liberalism, "combat" racism, "expose" Nazi cant, "work to destroy prejudice," and so on, the brochures boldly set forth a program that linked liberalism to victory. As a blurb for *The Highest Tradition*, a film about black sailors, said: "Their contribution to the war once again shows them equally eligible to fight in building a solid peace."[38] Moreover, the blessings of peace enlarged to include, as an American Jewish Committee (AJC) catalogue urged, "well paid, free and informed teach[ers]" and "better informed young citizens," and a spirit of "international cooperation" inspired by Wendell Willkie's tract on collective security, *One World*. And as in the case of *The Challenge*, a film based upon Truman's *To Secure These Rights*, agencies such as the AJC, UAW, and International Ladies Garment Workers (ILGWU) rushed to rave about each other's offerings.[39]

In 1949 a Twentieth Century Fund study reckoned that the movement sparked by *The Negro Soldier*—one of the "monuments to the power of the educational and documentary screen," it said—signaled an era of film "as an instrument to be used *systematically.*" By then Gloria Waldron, the author, noted striking institutional growth, much of it underwritten by the Carnegie Foundation: OWI's civilian advisers had become the Film Council of America (FCA); EFLA, founded in 1943, entered peacetime at the gallop; the American Film Center (AFC) had merged into the International Film Foundation; Cinema 16 added an artistic dimension; the ALA embraced film. To these signs of institutional growth must be added indicators of booming numbers of conscience-liberals as film users. Waldron cited an exemplary urban library that had acquired 255 titles, booking them for 7000 dates totaling more than 250,000 viewers.[40]

Unfortunately for African Americans, their underrepresentation in these groups during the war was to last long afterward, the activities of Moss, Claude Barnett, and others notwithstanding. As the movement grew, blacks were advisory rather than active, as much a minority on the left as in the nation. The documentaries about them from script to screen were the products of white people. As early as 1944 blacks had attempted to penetrate the system by gathering in New York to formulate an agenda. Horace Mann Bond, president of Fort Valley College in Georgia, and Charles S. Johnson, president of Fisk University, met to discuss a series of historical films of "the romance of old Methodist circuit riding," black life in "old free Charleston," and biopics of Toussaint L'Ouverture, the heroes of the battle of New Orleans, and modern figures such as Duke Ellington and Mary McLeod Bethune. With *The Negro Soldier* and its "high degree of compression" of history as their model, they imagined a cinema that addressed blacks directly. With their unavoidably white filmmaker, Donald Slesinger of AFC, they took "aim at reducing [black] social isolation" by transforming their "speech, dress, and manners" into assimilable patterns. Apart from its accommodationism, Bond and Johnson's "committee of Negro mass education" proposal seemed to Slesinger an opportunity for film to build on "its great and apparently successful use by the armed forces."[41] But sadly, they never arrived at a firm black stance apart from the general run of conscience-liberalism. Either they were scooped by other agencies (as in the case of a film based upon Gene Weltfish and Ruth Benedict's pamphlet *The Races of Mankind*, which had been issued to the wartime army), or they took up problematic material (such as a biopic of James Weldon Johnson or a visual poem of Langston Hughes's *The Negro Speaks of Rivers*) or curiosa (such as Bond's proposal for a history of servants, to be sponsored, they hoped, by Household Finance Corporation). But in the end, the ideas fizzled, their $12,000 stake from Rosenwald ran out, and the project died.[42]

The booming NAACP did no better at making movies, although as clearinghouse at the center of black activism it found its role. Indeed, for more than a year Walter White and his movielot friends contrived a Hollywood bureau of the NAACP as a peacetime extension of his wartime presence, although they eventually gave up "Walter's thing," as

Wilkins called it, for a base in New York documentary. As Wilkins argued in 1947, they should join a cooperative to "figure out an angle where we could get some benefit," a course of action that led them into film use rather than filmmaking.[43] But the lack of focus that he felt never quite zeroed in on substantive projects: They filed clippings from the trades and catalogues, mimeographed their own lists of "visual aids" for "teaching democracy," previewed the current crop, fretted over their own worn and dated promo-film, debated hiring John Grierson to make another, and by 1949 suffered the carping of impatient users of *The Negro Soldier*, which was quickly becoming a chestnut that was, said one user, "not exactly what we are seeking," all the while turning over in their minds improbable projects such as a Negro Educational and Documentary Film Organization, a remake of *Land of Liberty*, White's pet biopic of Félix Eboué, and even an idea entitled *Annie and the Hooded Klan*.[44]

Somehow White had not kept up with the boom in documentary and its break with wartime clientage, perhaps because Hollywood always remained his first love. In a typical instance, he pitched the idea of a movie based upon *To Secure These Rights*, but it became a creature of a coalition of unions and liberal activists. Beginning in the summer of 1948, delegates from textiles, meatcutting, the UAW, the AJC, and the Anti-Defamation League (ADL) hammered out who "must be cut in on" the team that would do the "treatment"—they even knew the lingo. The movie-star Melvyn Douglas was their persuader; he was to wring $6000 from each of them toward an eventual nut of $40,000. By mid-August their producer thought that their documentary was progressing apace and would eventually serve as a rallying cry of American conscience-liberals to support their on-going campaign to broaden civil rights advocacy in their respective communities. By October they had settled on two active Hollywood figures, Maurice and Matthew Rapf, to begin formulating the ideas into a dramatization that simultaneously advocated racially open housing and employment opportunities while, as the minutes of a story conference put it, playing to "the self-interest of the audience." And yet, White could not entirely break free of his addiction to Hollywood. Almost desperately, as though not willing to stake the future on mere sixteen millimeter documentarists, he thrust upon David O. Selznick a similar idea also grounded in the Truman report. He may also have hoped to make a place for black Carlton Moss whom he touted to Selznick as "the brilliant individual who made films for OWI during [the] war." In the end the Eastern group finished the movie.[45]

The NUL was equally tentative, preferring radio or the printed word. Among their unfulfilled projects was Erik Barnouw's *The Story They'll Never Print*, a revision of his award-winning wartime radio script designed to promote "the work of the Urban League in a format that does not have a 'promotional' atmosphere." "Here in a factory, mankind moved forward," Barnouw had written. "Men remembered a war aim and acted to fulfill it." Even such a mild urging to promote hiring highly screened token blacks met resistance, first from CBS, which refused to air it, and then from Armed Forces Radio, which refused to offer it to soldier-listeners. WNEW at last aired the play as performed by the American Negro Theatre, an event that served NUL in two ways: by providing an entertaining dramatization of a "pilot program," and by doing so in NUL's preferred mode, that of avoiding controversy. But it was not until 1960 that NUL set forth its program of vocational training and placement in visual format. Their film, *A Morning for Jimmy*, depicted a black boy's rekindled ambition to be an architect that had been dampened by a "downtown" employer's rebuff.[46]

Despite black distance from the film culture, the movement persisted. From documentary circles came IFF's *Boundary Lines* (a 1947 animated film on "the ugly realities of prejudice and intolerance"), the American Missionary Association's *The Color of Man*, B'nai B'rith's *One People*, and UAW's *The Brotherhood of Man*—almost all of them accessions of the film libraries of the League of Women Voters, the National Conference of Christians and Jews (NCCJ), and others. One of NCCJ's titles, *The World We Want to Live In*, reached an imposing total of twelve hundred prints in circulation. A speaker at a 1947 conference of labor leaders sensed the place of film on the left: an attempt by "the American democratic movement to make adequate use of this greatest of all means of mass communication . . . [which] has been almost completely monopolized by the commercial screen or by reactionary organizations."[47] Certainly it seemed so to the activists who lobbied Hollywood, predicted feature films of Howard Fast's novel of Reconstruction, *Freedom Road*, and Richard Wright's *Native Son*, took note of Gallup polls indicating a tolerance of federal intervention into incidents of racial injustice, and wrote tracts urging new tactics designed to establish new interracial ways of life.[48]

Of all the films, *The Brotherhood of Man* and *The Quiet One* permit us access to both 16 mm and theatrical markets. The former became a staple of classrooms and union halls; the latter was a rare film of advocacy that did well enough to have influenced Hollywood's reentry into the field.

The Brotherhood of Man combined conscience-liberalism, color, and animation so successfully as to shatter the notion of documentary as "educational" film. The film was a creature of UAW and CIO sponsorship (their "contribution to the American people"); of animation artists Stephen Bosustow and John Hubley, whose UPA studio had broken with Disney-style sentimental, anthropomorphic animals in favor of an urbane minimalism; of leftist screenwriter Ring Lardner; and ultimately of Gene Weltfish's pamphlet version of Ruth Benedict's work on racism.

In flat primary colors the movie offered a simple parable against racism, wrapped in Boas's cultural relativism and a thread of Willkie's internationalism. A character a little like Mr. Magoo, one of UPA's commercial triumphs, appears fuddled as a narrator spins out a lesson on "one world," teaching that the earth is shrinking and our remote neighbors will soon be in our backyards—a future that will require our "tolerance." Our hero wakens and, still in pajamas, checks his yard, where, indeed, there *are* igloos and tents where once there had been a lawn. Torn between xenophobia and oneworldism he and his new neighbors stand, appalled at each other's differentness, each with a little gray demon on his shoulder whispering fears that soon will send them at each other's throats. "Wait a minute," says an authoritative radio-style voice, "what about this business of brotherhood?"

Taking this as his own cue, the voiceover tells a child's history of the world's racial groups and their once isolated homes "on the very edges of the world," set apart by the biological "frills" of skin color. "But what about *brains?*" whispers the hero's inner xenophobe. But the hero is having none of it: he defends the cultural relativism at the heart of conscience-liberalism, defining humanity as an organic whole, a family with shared values that include a supreme being, a wish for a stable home, and the tradition of a nuclear family.

Clearly, the moment is at hand for the debate over "nature or nurture"; Herbert Spencer's social Darwinism confronts Boas's cultural relativism. In this movie at least, Boas wins hands down, leaving scant room to argue race as the basis for superiority. In the last moment, right where the clinch would be in a Hollywood movie, the white hero (speaking from *his* porch) wins over his fears and announces, "We can learn each other's ways and live together peacefully." Wild applause from the world's peoples encamped in his yard. "Brotherhood" is the key, he says, along with equal opportunity, education, and jobs for all. Shoulder to shoulder, just before the credit-crawl, they march toward the camera, echoing the ghostly solidarity of *The Sullivans* (1943), a popular war movie.[49]

The childlike images of *The Brotherhood of Man* were an instant hit in their marketplace: the union halls, churches, and schoolrooms where brevity and flashes of color helped sugarcoat Brotherhood Weeks. The UAW's catalogue urged it upon the faithful as a "basic tool" with which to mount a "double barreled promotion" within its locals, and by the end of the year it became "the most widely distributed informational film" in the list and earned enough in rentals that it matched the contributions of ILGWU, AJC, and ADL toward the movie of *To Secure These Rights.*[50] So pleased was the UAW with this success that it planned a live-action prologue in which its chief, Walter Reuther, appears with his "Negro stenographer" in a celebration of the union's own efforts toward a peacetime FEPC for "all religions, races, and backgrounds"; campaigns against both firms and locals that closed doors to blacks; and promises of "aggressive action" to "get PREJUDICES out of people's heads." The left everywhere took to the movie: Moss urged his friends in the NNC to use UAW's filmography in "every Negro center in America"; the American Council on Race Relations called for its showing in "enemy occupied" territory as an antidote to fascism; and even the *Worker* praised it.[51]

Although we lack precise means of measuring the audience of such movies, we can sense their impact from the pitch of conservative reactions to them. The films formed a stiffening front against the right, for not only did this film culture survive postwar reaction by placing its wares in libraries, programs, and curricula, but its success surely anticipated Hollywood's reentry into racial politics in 1949. Conservatives could not let the films pass unchallenged. In Peoria, for example, an American Legion post used its "Americanism Committee" as a club with which to force a library to limit *The Brotherhood of Man* to use only by "bona fide students of propaganda." Throughout the summer of 1948, the decision rent the library's board meetings and led to a report that the ALA had deleted the film from its *Films for Libraries* list, then covered its decision by labeling the film "out of date."[52]

Liberals everywhere rose in protests—the ALA, EFLA, FCA, and others—all affirming first amendment rights of free speech. The black neighborhoods of Peoria joined in, claiming that far from reflecting an alien ideology, the movie spoke for "the American Way of Life." Chastened by the opposition, the Legion wavered, conceding that African Americans had taken a new place in postwar life. This left the Legion only with a spurious defense of its highhandedness: that Lardner's royalties were certain to end up in the hands of the CPUSA. Despite the UAW's entering and thereby nationalizing the debate, the board held to its limiting access to the film, but by then the liberal allies had shown that the Legion's action had been inspired by an alarmist magazine, *Counterattack*, which had described UPA as colored by "Communist leanings and connections."[53]

Eventually UAW won the day, but not before revealing a stress fracture within its own locals. One officer in Peoria Local 974, a library board member, branded *Counterattack*'s charges as "unfounded" and the library's action as "unauthorized," while another union member charged in the local *Journal* that the UAW itself had been infiltrated by reds and that the film had been designed to "create unrest and dissatisfaction" in "the Negro." But by the end of the year, the UAW closed ranks and reaffirmed its wish "to vigorously perpetuate the widespread acceptance of . . . *THE BROTHERHOOD OF MAN*."[54]

In the end, conscience-liberals had fended off a probing sortie from the right and given an important movie national attention among an audience of churched, schooled, and laboring Americans. As a result they had stood up to a postwar thermidorean reaction that sooner or later Hollywood was itself to face. Thus, movies like *The Brotherhood of Man* and the film culture to which they played, coupled with the revival of Hollywood's racial politics in the flurry of message movies in 1949 contributed to defining a peacetime equivalent of the conscience-liberal morale and of the new black place it had urged.

A muted omen of this confluence of parallel film cultures was *The Quiet One,* a sort of urban *Nanook of the North* in its shrewd use of dramatization set in credible, even authentic, locations, all of it held in equilibrium by a cast of actors leavened by acutely intuitive amateurs. More than any other theatrical movie *The Quiet One* (1947) introduced a programmatic scaffolding to the loosely sketched outlines of conscience-liberalism. In this sense, the film was a bridge between the cycle of war movies and the postwar cycle of message movies. Of particular weight was its understated advocacy coupled with the texture of documentary, woven so subtly that its use of playacting seemed organic. Together these traits portrayed a black child-protagonist, a social ruin formed by his squalid surroundings but salvageable through the intervention of a compassionate, yet institutional, liberalism.

The film grew out of a circle of old friends and lefties. James Agee had only just finished writing the text for photographer Walker Evans's pictures of the Depression-ridden South, *Let Us Now Praise Famous Men,* an experience that drew his eye to photographs of Harlem by Helen Levitt, for whose work he wrote an introduction. Together they also shot film of Harlem, which became the one-reel *In the Street,* for which Agee wrote a voiceover. As they worked on this prototype they were joined by Levitt's friend Janice Loeb, a painter with an urge to make a movie about juvenile delinquency. They went to Wiltwyck School in Esopus, New York, with Sidney Meyers, who had spent the Depression shooting and cutting film for two radical groups, the Film and Photo League and Nykino. Predictably, no angels rushed to their doorstep, but with the onset of the postwar film culture at least the prospects for an audience were higher. In this setting they kept at it, added a score by the black composer Ulysses Kay, and began bicycling it around the distributors' offices.

Perhaps its most daunting liability was blunt unwillingness to resort to a Hollywood closure, a last-reel panacea. After revealing the plight of a Harlem boy of the streets from a shattered family who sullenly moves from petty crime to the institutional thicket that juvenile delinquents often were snared in, they had no honest choice but to follow the logic of the situation. Besides, their star was Donald Thompson, a black boy whose own life paralleled that of the juvenile he portrayed. Not only is he allowed to fill the center of the frame as the protagonist, an alienated, dis-integrated victim of a race-based social order, but the central figures among the faculty at Wiltwyck are also black. Therefore, those in command of the situation are not hollowly black as in an old race movie, but firmly so as a result of their authority; yet we cannot know whether they can win the day.

On its face the movie seems to be about a favorite charity of Eleanor Roosevelt's, the Wiltwyck School, but more than an account of an institution, it is also an anatomy of the underclass of African American life and the place of an actual black boy in it. In this "documentary" setting, Thompson's naive response to his world is strikingly revelatory, like a novel of coming of age. He grows and changes with changed conditions, but fitfully, erratically, maddeningly, and without false hope or empty happy ending. The audience is at best left with the prospect that Thompson's heirs might find a place in American life that does not oblige them to steal or kill. In its way *The Quiet One* was a peacetime analog to the cycle of war movies, minus a gratuitous happy ending that promised more than life could deliver.

Obviously the makers were not in pursuit of a prototypal message movie. "The social protest factor was very minor in our thinking," recalled Loeb; rather, with America "in a very sensitive stage of . . . the Negro problem . . . we picked a story common to whites *and* Negroes." In other words, in her way, although she did not compromise the integrity of her material or her vision of it, she embraced the racial sameness angle of the war movie cycle. In a rancor-free setting she integrated her kid into the school (a surrogate of society), thus allowing white liberal audiences to take what they saw as at least a sanguine possibility in a liberal society. But she was not following a formula; as she recalled it, her original focus was vague. She "was interested in Wiltwyck School and touched by the sight of all those kids running around in the country [and] she thought they would be beautiful subjects." Although working in a dramatic mode, in order to avoid too patently formulated incidents they shot "vague" urban locations and "found" situations that were intercut with the stuff of Thompson's encounters with his counselors: meetings that then combined spontaneity with credibility while communicating a liberal hope that change was possible.[55] Moreover, they asked their audience *only* to hope, not to hold out for an improbable transformation of either Thompson or society.

For the first time since Warner Bros.' social problem movies of the 1930s, audiences saw children ruined by their surroundings. Up to a point *The Quiet One* was in that tradition, but only to a point. True, it begins in the kid's rancid, life-deforming neighborhood, but breaks with Hollywood's convention of the last-reel salvation. Unlike *Boys' Town* it ends only with "what they were trying to do at the school," not whether they would succeed in Thompson's case. The viewer knows that the school staff could win by keeping him at school or lose him to his gloomy life in his ratty flat with his defeated, somnolent mother. The heads-or-tails prospects for the kid—the chance for redemption in the

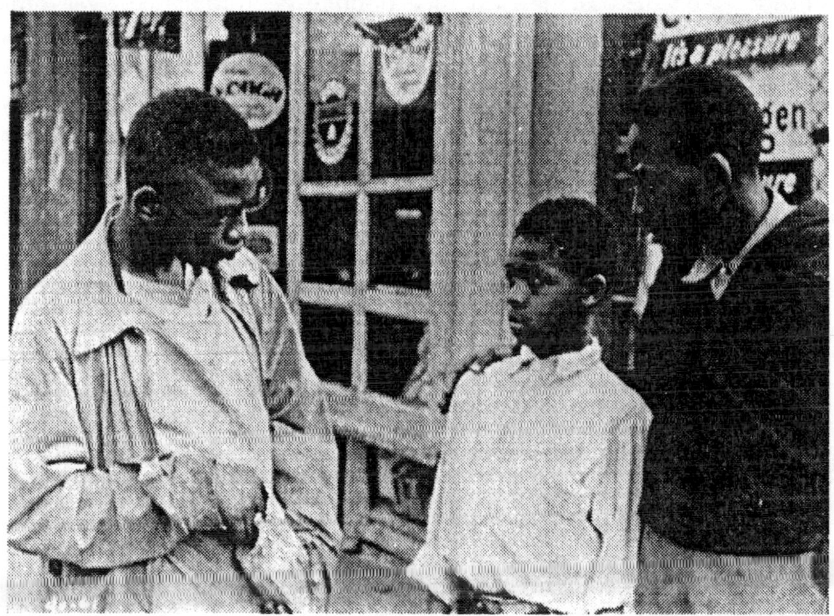

Although a filmed drama, the New York locations and naive actors of *The Quiet One* (1947) gave the film a documentary texture that attracted an audience and may have drawn Hollywood toward a similar realist mode. Copyright Mayer-Burstyn.

therapeutic bucolia of Wiltwyck as against his almost certain swallowing up in the ruined tenements and vandalized stairwells of Harlem—is caught in striking style by two opposing textures of camerawork neatly cut into an either-or story. Underlining the visual tension is the staff at Wiltwyck, daunted by the fragility of their charges and by the endless teetering between small gestures and words whose rightness or wrongness might undo weeks of work. The movie ends, then, not with flags flying but only with a life in the balance between Wiltwyck and the streets, along with a hint of "why they wanted the school supported [and] why the children needed help": a far piece from prewar Hollywood solutions to social dysfunctions, the closures in which the doomed are rescued by kindly judges, probing reporters, honest prosecutors, or wisecracking Irish priests.[56]

More than any other film, *The Quiet One* enjoyed an audience that extended across the gulf between Marxist and liberal, and black and white. The famous such as Eleanor Roosevelt—a patron of Wiltwyck—actress Tallulah Bankhead and radio personality Mary Margaret McBride; academics led by Edgar Dale of Ohio State; and reviewers for magazines ranging from *Redbook* to the *Daily Worker*, from *Vogue* to the

Catholic weeklies: all testified to a popularity unmatched by a dramatized documentary since *Nanook of the North* in 1922.[57] Almost all of them caught the drift expressed by its makers, the wish to place a black kid at the center of the action without making color the central issue; that is, to integrate him and his plight into a setting as a matter of course rather than as a "mcguffin" plunked down for dramatic effect. "The camera, as it explores the streets of Harlem," said one of them, "intensifies our vision, forcing us to take cognizance of an environment to which we might otherwise be blind." Warren Miller, whose novel *The Cool World* would grow into a similar movie fifteen years later, found the heart of its liberalism in the political and aesthetic decision to advocate improvement in the black situation while appearing to treat only a lone boy. "That the boy is a Negro is not invested with special significance; yet in our society," Miller wrote, "the choice of the Negro child as hero has, inevitably, extensions of meaning that go beyond the framework of the film." An entire spectrum of critics, ranging from the connoisseurs who labeled it "brilliant" to the blacks who claimed it as "our film," sang its praises. Bosley Crowther of the *Times* reckoned it "a genuine masterpiece . . . comparable to those stark film dramas we have had from Italy since the war," in fact, no less than the "*Shoeshine* of American life."[58] *Redbook*, which named it "film of the month," the *Daily Worker*, the Catholics ranging from the legates in the Vatican to opinion makers in the American weeklies, even the Soviets, all treated it as "universal." For the CPUSA this represented a retreat from the notion of a separate African American nation, an idea lost in the muddle of a war against racism. Indeed, the *Worker* anticipated the line eventually laid down by the liberal scholar Kenneth M. Stampp—that "Negroes *are*, after all, only white men with black skins." In the *Worker*'s words, viewing *The Quiet One* "could make whites identify themselves with the movie, and show that Negroes are like everybody else." Not that a black critic would go that far: "Universal," yes, said one, but it "could only happen in Harlem."[59]

Clearly, *The Quiet One* spoke to a specific film culture, an audience prepared by conviction to receive it, but it also broadened the prospective viewership to include an unexpected range. "The reaction to *The Quiet One* was astonishing—all kinds of people related to it," recalled Loeb. "Anybody who'd had any kind of sad childhood, including very rich people, would say 'Ah! The story of my life.'" In documentary circles it proved to have remarkable "legs," or staying power; in one urban library as late as 1960, it played thirty-nine dates in a clientele for which thirty constituted a high-normal circulation. In these years the documentary film culture grew from a small circle of leftist advocates who distributed films—UAW, ADL, the liberal churches—to include radical bookers like Thomas Brandon and commercial houses like Teaching Film Custodians and McGraw-Hill, all reviewed in the film guides of EFLA, ALA, and others. By 1953, for example, *The Educational Film Guide: Classified Subject List* recorded more than thirty titles devoted to race relations and a primer on how to link up with the network of distributors, libraries, and reviewers. Periodicals from the new black glossies to *Vogue* covered the formerly arcane world of documentary film. And soon the advocates polished their own lists into highly targeted filmographies like UAW's "Films for UN Day" and the CIO's "Films for Labor." Predictably, social agencies such as the National Probation and Parole Association found the film a useful tool in dealing with their clientele.[60]

Obviously it cannot be argued that *The Quiet One* or, for that matter, *The Brotherhood of Man* singlehandedly transformed American racial ideology, but as part of an emerging, generalized film culture that offered a menu of conscience-liberal films of advocacy, such films were part of an insistent rhetoric directed at an audience for "the thinking picture." In this sense documentaries like *The Quiet One*, if Crowther were prescient in linking it to Italian neo-realism, contributed to a mood that prepared audiences for, perhaps even prodded Hollywood toward, an eventual revival of conscience-liberal theatrical movies.

Already by 1946 Hollywood editorial and story departments were buying properties dense with the stuff and texture of documentaries. Other hints of the drift toward social movies could be found in the rush to shoot features on location in gritty offshoots of *film noir*, itself a genre that criticized society by focusing on a gloomy streetscape in which customary powers and social arrangements are turned on their ends and corrupted. Already a few oddments of social comment had actually reached the commercial screen; in one, the NCCJ trailer *The Drive for Brotherhood* (1948), Gene Kelly uttered the nonceword *togetherness*, and with that term seemed to signal his trust that audiences would know he meant "integration" and, if they were not persuaded by the notion, at least would forgive him for it.[61] Among the short films that began to introduce into studio style some of the traits of East Coast film culture were Dore Schary's *The Next Voice You Hear* (1945); Warners' *It Happened in Springfield* (1945), an account of the aftermath of an actual race riot; *The Burning Cross* (1947), an independently made B-movie; and *Jammin' the Blues* (1946), Warners' one-reel homage to the jazz demimonde by the *Life* photographer Gjon Mili.

As political sensors *The Brotherhood of Man*, *The Quiet One*, and their East Coast successors testified to an emerging mood that Hollywood showed signs of wishing to play to. The documentary medium seemed on the verge of repeating that recent portion of its history when *The Negro Soldier* appeared to "show Hollywood the way." Hollywood filmmakers, perhaps prodded by these two documentaries and the film culture they were part of, appeared ready finally to rejoin the leading edge of a rolling frontier of movies that were both political and profitable.

7

Thermidor

Did Sam Goldwyn actually say, "If you want to send a message, call Western Union?" We cannot know with certainty, but on the other hand, we have his written profession of abiding concern for "social justice" in the NUL organ *Opportunity*, a concern that, he said, came as a result of his reading the charter of the United Nations with its call for international harmony. Of course, neither the epigram nor the essay spoke for the inner values of Hollywood, but their polarity suggested that a wartime tactic—the use of popular culture as a vehicle of political expression—had survived into peacetime and become entangled with the wish to make money, resulting in, as James Agee put it, Hollywood's learning how to have its liberalism land buttered side up.

And yet from 1945 until 1949, the movielots seemed to lapse into an apparent liberal hiatus over which conservative forces exercised a loose hegemony. How to account for this seeming failing of wartime political energy? Certainly the war exhausted intellectual resources, but also the period lends itself to analysis as, rather than a political desert, a seedbed of wartime racial idiom redefined for peacetime consumption. During these years the major studios, along with a few independents, made more than a half dozen self-consciously political films that kept active the essentials of the wartime mentality we have called conscience-liberalism. There were the gemlike one-reelers like *Jammin' the Blues;* animated cartoons like George Pal's *John Henry;* a wartime feature, Warners' *It Happened in Springfield,* which shrank to a short; personal manifestoes like the Oscar-winning short *The House I Live In;* Marxoid allegories like Abraham Polonsky's *Body and Soul;* and genre films like *Cass Timberlane* and *Rogue's Regiment* into which liberal bits—test swatches, really—had been woven. As a Jewish soldier in *Pride of the Marines* (1946) says of liberalism: "Don't tell me we can't make it work in peace like we do in war."

After all, why not? The war had habituated the moguls to standing on the good side of a popular issue, of which racial liberalism still seemed a good example. There was even a postwar equivalent of OWI pressure in the form of the liberal activists who gave them citizenship and brotherhood awards. And of course they knew of the liberal film culture of the documentarists and the boom in imported Italian neorealism and began to play to their markets, albeit circumspectly with an eye on their stockholders.

Of course, they also faced other forces that served as a brake on activist films. They still lacked a generic formula to introduce wartime idiom into peacetime; congressional investigators resumed their inquiry into Hollywood, this time in search of "reds"; stockholders and theatremen pressured them for surefire pap; regional censors, anxious at their failing hold on racial custom, stepped up their work; black actors and activists remained of two minds; the judicially required breakup of the vertically integrated studio system threatened the institution of Hollywood itself; militant craft guilds broke war-imposed silences and drove up labor costs; the audience splintered into volatile taste-groups in search of undefined new forms of movies as well as competing forms of recreation.

Nonetheless, in the apparently quiescent period after 1945 the studios' story departments spent the time in ferment, refining ideas that might work liberal war aims into a postwar ideology. That process and its eventual products coincided with the persistence of black activism that was to carry over from the war into the modern civil rights movement. At the same time, this period of adjustment may be seen as a classic case of thermidor, the cooling of ardor that has followed every era of disquiet from the French Revolution onward, the moment when order seems to matter more than liberty, sameness more than novelty. In this mood it was easy for Hollywood to retreat into familiar ways: cautiously pitching down the middle, living off past successes, reviving the surefire, rewarming its chestnuts.

To date, however, historians have studied only the latter half of this "twoness," the preference for safety first, perhaps because the story of ferment has been inaccessible in studio archives that have only just been opened to view. Their focus, then, has been on a lost moment "between 1946 and 1949 [when] problem pictures were suddenly fashionable [again]," or on a craven sellout to the seekers after "red" moles on the movielots. In his popular *The Liveliest Art,* for example, Arthur Knight wrote that "the hearings of the House Un-American Activities Committee, begun in October of 1947, sent a chill through the studios," an opinion joined in by the next generation of historians, who described an industry "caponized" by fear, "contemptible" in its "unwillingness to stand on principle," and "engulfed" by an "Inquisition." Of course they had their point, as *Variety* did in 1948 when it reported a rush "to drop plans for message pictures like hot coals."[1] But the tradepaper also missed the covert activity in the story departments and at the tables at Lucey's and the Derby where the writers hashed out new angles for new times.

It is this backstory, the story that has already happened before the main titles begin to crawl, that will concern us here, rather than a reprise of the oft-told drama of congressional committee rooms. Yet before taking up this quiet work, we owe some attention to the substances of the thermidorean forces that in fact contributed a dampening inertia to the process of peacetime refocusing.

First there was the changed relationship between Hollywood and its audiences. Unlike their Depression-era forbears, they had wartime savings to spend on new houses with lawns to mow, weekend boats with hulls to be scraped, and other diversions from the movies they had

Postwar changes in the distribution system may have steered Hollywood toward a thermidorean course as, on the one hand, suburbanization thinned the audience . . . Quigley Photographic Archive, Georgetown University.

. . . while on the other hand, new technology such as CinemaScope increased negative costs, leading toward a preference for less risky material that lent itself to outsized treatment. Quigley Photographic Archive.

routinely attended twice a week. Their suburbanization took the bloom off "going downtown" to movies. Higher ticket prices caused second thoughts. If old habits needed another reason to change, the Supreme Court revived its efforts to end blockbooking, blindbooking, and other monopolistic tactics that had defined a familiar formulaic market. Unavoidably, the resulting market would seem fickle, risky, and therefore closed to political new departures. As Philip Dunne wrote in the black press, "The war has taught us that the motion picture is a powerful and persuasive vehicle of propaganda," but also "a very real financial risk" at the mercy of a "boycott by any group . . . [that could] turn a legitimately anticipated profit into a loss."[2] Politics aside, the figures were alarming: declining grosses, rising fixed costs from advertising to rents, a thousand closed theatres since war's end, five theatre chains in the red in a single year, militant guilds driving up labor costs by a third in one fiscal year, while in each year Americans spent a declining portion of income on movies.[3]

Two or three majors barely survived, and then only by selling off their old titles to television. At Fox, as we have seen, Spyros Skouras predicted a "sizeable recession" signaled by an "alarming" decline in Christmas-take coupled with a definite "trend downward in attendance," ending in "almost inevitable ruin" unless they could retrench. The story was the same at RKO, though exacerbated by the changeover to Howard Hughes's ownership, in which seven hundred workers were laid off in a single year (1948).[4]

Everywhere caution reigned, and gambling, Zanuck said, was to be limited to "new stars" rather than new politics. "Give me somethin' I can use and nothin' controversial—like niggers or God," said Harry Cohn at Columbia, a dictum echoed at Universal, where Richard Brooks heard a story conference end with an abrupt "Out! No race problems"; at Metro, where Lewis Milestone recalled "you took orders"; and at Paramount, where the "dyed in the wool conservative" Y. Frank Freeman sank ideas by warning, "It would never go in the South."[5] The mood was infectious, even for Lyman Munson, the reputed "power behind *The Negro Soldier,*" who had retired to Fox. His prescription for Frank Slaughter's *The Dark Garden,* a tale of black and Jewish doctors, for example, was shelving, because it had "a hackneyed . . . 'message' . . . intended to be the brotherhood of man" that not only "would get Joe Breen's axe [but] . . . the South would resent the Jew-baiting label."[6]

Down South, two famous censors, Lloyd Binford in Memphis and Christine Smith in Atlanta, provided their own brand of hedging against liberal politics by stiffening against challenges to their hegemony over local racial etiquette. Binford cut Eddie Anderson from *Brewster's Millions* merely for "a too familiar way about him," Horne from *Words and Music* only because of a personal animus, a couple of kids from Hal Roach's B-movie *Curley* because the South denied "social equality between the races even in children," Cab Calloway from *Sensations of 1945* as "inimical to public welfare," and a number from *A Song Is Born* only because of "a rowdy bunch of musicians of both colors." Nevertheless, change seemed in the air as a result of separate decisions by the NAACP to file *amicus curiae* briefs in censorship cases, the studios to bring to an end their acquiescence to local censorship, and even the Breen office to begin to leave off cooperating with it.[7] Indeed, everyone joined in hooting the censors. Binford, a retired railway worker and salesman who owed his post to the Memphis "boss" Ed Crump, faced hazing from the local press, who thought him "senile," and from showmen who lost revenue to competitors across the Mississippi. In Hollywood, Eric Johnston, the new president of the MPPDA, was joined on the right by Louella Parsons in branding him "Un-American." Studio heads such as Gradwell Sears also stiffened and sought judicial remedies, which he linked to FDR's "four freedoms." And the NAACP, reversing longtime support of censorship, joined in three cases as *amicus curiae,* particularly against vague excuses that a scene might "stir up racial strife." Not to do so, said Thurgood Marshall, will render wartime black gains "completely nullified." In a Richmond case, in which an exploitation film, *The Burning Cross* (1947), had been banned as stirring "animosities," the

NAACP successfully insisted on local release with only "certain deletions" of violence.[8]

Another index of the persistence of a liberal mentality in the face of a thermidorean mood was the willingness of the mossy Academy to hand out Oscars such as that given to *The House I Live In*, the British dramatized documentary *Daybreak at Udi* (1947), and *The Quiet One*, capped by Ethel Waters's nomination for her role in *Pinky* (1949), the first black nomination since Hattie McDaniel's Mammy in *Gone with the Wind*. The liberal drift in this direction was interrupted only by Hedda Hopper's successful campaign for a posthumous special Oscar for James Baskette's Uncle Remus in Walt Disney's backward-looking *Song of the South* (1946).[9]

Another marginally thermidorean influence was in the persons of Hollywood Negroes themselves. Beholden to casting directors, held captive by their trappings of status, celebrated in the new black glossies *Ebony*, *Sepia*, *Our World*, and their town crier the *Los Angeles Sentinel*, they resented the NAACP's "wrong and ill-advised tactics" despite which, they argued, "great strides" had been taken.[10] In the fanzines they were portrayed as soaring over adversity, kept aloft by faith and white friends, relaxing in the Sierra or in black dude ranches or at "dansantes" at the Vernondale Country Club or "debuts" at the March Club, living amidst their white pianos, tiled fireplaces, fake logs, plaster fakirs, Bo-Peep cameos, lace doilies, Orientaloid tapestries, settings of Spode on damask, and photographs of white friends. Only here and there a stress fissure opened, as when McDaniel sold her house for a smaller one and announced a long vacation.[11] Their struggles were treated as examples of civic virtue: McQueen broke an agreement with Jack Benny rather than play an incidental maid; Lillian Randolph and others fought racial covenants in deeds on West Adams; their charities—McDaniel's *Les Femmes Aujourd'hui*, Randolph's Benevolent Variety Artists, and others—held fundraising "soirees" and "affairs" that earned them praise as "clubwom[e]n of distinction." The men promoted their own communal activism such as Muse's radio show on behalf of Bigger and Better Business Week or Nick Stewart's lifelong struggle to keep alive his *Ebony Showcase* theatre.[12] Below them were the scrabblers who met their postwar downturn by teaching acting in storefronts or working in county agencies, and measured out their careers in bits in *Congo Maisie*, *Tarzan*, and *Ramar of the Jungle*. They reached the glossies only in pieces such as "I Tried to Crash the Movies" or "Foot Doctor to the Stars." "We were hardest hit by Hollywood going war conscious," one of them remembered. They avoided the worst indignities of cattle calls, and shapeups on the corner of 12th and Central, where the studio buses cruised in search of extras, only if blessed like Frances Driver, who lived the life of a druggist's wife between gigs in *King Kong* and *The Foxes of*

Harrow. Some were dogged by bad luck: Mantan Moreland lost his steady role in Monogram's Charlie Chan series when the lead, Sidney Toler, died; went on the road only to have his partners die or retire; took up with the feckless Stepin Fetchit; and eventually caught on in Ted Toddy's race movies such as *Mantan Messes Up.*[13]

Gradually the black press turned away from them. Barnett prodded his stringer Harry Levette away from studio boilerplate; the *Sentinel* began an acerbic "Tom of the Week" column; *Ebony,* even as it gave them space to argue that "people want to be entertained, not educated," began to give awards to social movies like *The Boy with the Green Hair.* Nonetheless, they hung on like fossils from an ice age.[14]

After the war, SAG became their last platform upon which to plead for slowing the pace of change, mainly because the guild itself was torn between promoting change and providing for easing the plight of the aggrieved black actors. The result was that through Ronald Reagan's five terms as president from 1947 through 1952, SAG agreed only to encourage an end to stereotypical roles—itself a mild threat to the Hollywood blacks. The fissure widened during a debate over a resolution to place "Negro characters on the screen in the true relation they bear to American life" and to create a standing committee to monitor the goal, with the result that nothing moved beyond the status quo following White's first visit in 1942.[15]

The best of them—Joel Fluellen, William F. Walker, and Ernest Anderson—built careers on trying to humanize the old or by reading for new roles. For the rest, life became a round of cadging bits, entering the invisible medium of radio, and taking out "their hatchets" and attacking Walter White at NAACP dinners and various guild meetings. With undisguised relish Levette, LaMar, and the other reporters wrote of "a whole phalanx of featured players hopping all over Mr. White," branding him a "red" whose campaigns masked his goal of promoting his daughter's career, and calling him "a name conscious . . . Uncle Tom." So instead of White's hoped-for role as a postwar presence, perhaps as boss of a Hollywood NAACP bureau, he heard only an incessant "squawk" from those with, he said, "a vested interest in menial roles."[16]

Indeed, what of the much-desired—at least by White—Hollywood bureau? All of these conservative drags upon activism could be cut free if only there were a black presence exercising hegemony over the scene, a resident liaison with the moguls, a counselor to the aggrieved blacks, a bargainer with the guilds. In 1946 he proposed just such an office—"something like the [Jewish] Anti-Defamative League," as a friend had dubbed it—an idea that simultaneously chilled liberals, who feared the implied censorship, and the blacks who had had enough of "Walter's thing." None of his angels would give him a nickel to support it, not even for an experimental year.[17] Worse, the Marxist NNC planned its own version, perhaps staffed by the historian Herbert Aptheker, Moss, and John Howard Lawson, who would monitor White's proposed branch office "set-up there" while poaching on the same conscience liberals whom White counted among the faithful.[18] So by 1947, White still lacked a base camp in the West.

One last thermidorean force warrants attention: the struggle between HUAC and the CPUSA. The hysteria of which their strident combat was a part shook deeply held convictions of constitutional guarantees of freedom of thought and split moviemakers (and the nation) into partisans of left and right. A neglected side of the story is its impact on African Americans during the volatile time in which they searched for a peacetime equivalent of their old conscience-liberal alliance. First it must be seen that apart from the heavyhandedness of not only HUAC but its opposite number in the California legislature, the Tenney committee, the Communist party was already losing the place that the popular front and the war had given it. Many members drifted from the party, having joined it during the Depression when it seemed the only hope for a "coherent" or "humanist" left through which they might have infected movies with, as Lawson had hoped, "some sort of" social texture in which "good people" struggled and "the hero is the man who fights for society" rather than merely against "bad men."[19]

Far from a disciplined red vanguard on the march, many in the party seemed an intellectual rabble, guiltridden, harried by the party ideologues, and allied only in their contempt for HUAC. Odets felt ruined by Hollywood's "filthy money"; Albert Maltz suffered through a party "trial" for having labeled a tactic "economic nonsense"; Donald Ogden Stewart stood "ready to join hands with the workers" but wondered "how in hell did you meet them" in a daily round of cobbling scripts, catching the Yale-Princeton game on radio, thumbing Trotsky's *The Russian Revolution* over coffee, catching a plane for a trade unionist's speech in San Francisco. European Communists, made testy by this ragged American heresy, all but read them out of the international party.[20] Meanwhile, the Hollywood liberals met at their hangout, Lucey's, to hammer out a non-Marxist "liberalism of the heart," after which they drifted from the groups that had flourished during the popular front.[21]

The moguls, caught in the hysteria without a coherent response, wambled and finally behaved as badly as their worst enemies imagined they might. As the testimony of "friendly" witnesses mounted, revealing a tissue of associations that HUAC wished to seem a conspiracy, the committee shamelessly led witnesses to exaggerate the danger to the republic: "reds" slipped words into scripts as Lawson had used *comrade* once in *Action in the North Atlantic*, they dodged taxes, they consorted with foreign agents, and so on. The studios rushed to make shabby cautionary tales warning of comicbook heavies worming their ways into seats of power. Even the majors joined in these B-movie offerings, Zanuck's own version being George Moore's alarmist *Behind the Iron Curtain.* In New York the paragon of liberals, Dore Schary, succumbed and helped draft the famous "Waldorf statement" in which the moguls appeared to defend freedom of expression while promising to fire Communists on grounds eventually also agreed to by SAG: that their politics rendered their movies "unsaleable."[22] The result was an apparent retreat from politics on the screen—at least until HUAC blew over, the moguls seemed to say.

Oddly, with respect to racial issues there was a certain immunity that protected African American themes from the general carnage, perhaps because when the wartime noncewords *brotherhood* and *tolerance* reentered postwar politics they did so as heartfelt rather than ideological issues. As the director Irving Pichel did in a letter, liberals seemed to speak in slogans. "I have," he wrote of Katharine Dunham, "first hand interest in contributing what I can to the advancement of her race and of understanding between the races."[23]

At the same time, blacks in general had stood apart from the CPUSA, while the party, despite dramatic gestures of alliance with blacks, never fully agreed upon the nature of "the Negro question." The blacklisted writer Dalton Trumbo, for instance, thought the party's wartime posture toward the Negro misguided, even a "great" error, in its decision "not to fight for his employment in pictures, nor honest and decent presentations of him." Moreover, eschewing following a Gramscian line of "class-collaboration," the party left specifically black grievances hanging, and made only gestures: recruiting blacks for its Hollywood Independent Citizens Committee on the Arts, Sciences, and Professions (HICCASP); asking Lancelot to speak on "the political scene"; running David Platt's essays on black movie history in the *Worker;* incorporating race into rhetorical flourishes, as in Fred Rinaldo's linking blacklisting to "a 300 year old blacklist against the Negro people"; and having Trumbo speak at the UCLA conference on "caricatures of African Americans."[24] But in the end the CPUSA lost blacks because none of its formulations of blacks—as separate people, as colony, as oppressed class—galvanized the African America that stood ready to collect the debt owed under the terms of the Double V. As Abe Polonsky recalled of one CPUSA goal: "The idea of a black state was killed by World War II."[25] This break in the tenuous link between black and white left could be seen as early as 1946 when Doxey Wilkerson, a black Communist and professor of education at Howard, lectured white Marxists in their own *Political Affairs* journal by opting for the Double V for blacks whom the war had scattered, urbanized, and opened options for. This while the CPUSA's white ideologues clung to James S. Allen's hope for a black nation on Southern ground.[26]

More than any other figure's, Paul Robeson's fate revealed the widening gulf between African America and the CPUSA. Robeson lingered in a sentimental embrace with the Soviet Union long after the excesses of Stalinism had driven off others, and his uncritical Russophilia soon isolated him and gave the right a neat opportunity to discredit blacks by linking him to the Soviet bugbear. His continued singing of "Soviet land so dear to every toiler" gave the party a recruiter of "the radical youth" that "idolized him" precisely because he was "a figure of greater trust than was a party functionary." But by 1950, HUAC delighted in coaxing black witnesses into repudiating him or confessing to falling prey "to groups fixed up to look like noble causes." The Republican baseball player Jackie Robinson drew congratulations from the black liberal center for his testimony against Robeson, which, one of them said, encouraged blacks to resume a liberal offensive against black Communists who entangled black grievances in Cold War snares.[27] This public spectacle was, of course, the central tragedy of Robeson's life, but it was also a reaffirmation of the black alliance with liberalism.

So far we have seen a considerable burden of thermidorean forces that might have stifled the survivals of wartime liberalism. But it must be borne in mind that even as the drama of HUAC played out, a vigorous documentary film culture had persisted while the reactionary forces crested and even waned. Certainly this was true of Southern censorship, which crumbled under the weight of judicial challenges, the Hollywood Negroes for whom ever fewer roles were available, and even HUAC itself, which, despite the well-documented damage it did both to the Marxist left and to constitutional principles, was short-lived and left a scant legacy, not even a martyr in the person of its eponymous Senator Joseph R. McCarthy. And as Fred Rinaldo had insisted, blacks had suffered relatively little from HUAC because routinely they had been denied steady work anyway.

The way therefore was clear for some resumption of a conscience-liberal cinema, at least with respect to African America. Although at first few films emerged from the story departments, the studios acquired, optioned, or otherwise considered dozens of properties in search of a peacetime genre or formula. As a lot, the few released films attained only a low plateau of advocacy, but *Ebony* and the rest of the black press were grateful for the favors. Moreover, B-movies, famous for their inertial sameness, accommodated to evolving racial sensibilities, their powers derived, it seemed, from the very thoughtlessness with which they were put together, which allowed subtextual images to seep through. As Barbara Deming, an OWI reviewer, described them, they were "the 'quickies' [where] the realities of social antipathy are likely to flare through the fabric of the film [into] antipathies between race and race or class and class."[28] But in this instance, B-movies responded to the residual liberal mood as though leaching through the crust of convention. Despite the best efforts of the studio hacks to contain them in the familiar formulas of race, new elements began to intrude unbidden into the frame.

While, obviously, we can have little access to the mentalities of either B-moviemakers or their audiences, of all Hollywoodians B-movie people were certainly the most distant from political pressures. They were least able, whether through preview cards or box-office returns, to measure the political tolerances of their marketplace, and since their small budgets allowed only minimal risks in reworking the familiar formulas that the habituated audience knew it liked, most changes in B-movies had to be like incremental changes in all forms of popular culture: gradual drifts of wellworn conventions to new forms. Yet each such change not only inched further from the main body of older unquestioned racism, but sharpened the sensibilities of bookers, critics, and spectators.

In small ways, trade, popular press, and movies themselves revealed a sort of normalized attention to racial politics. *Ebony* in a reference to *The Clock* (1945) described black extras as "routine" as though drawing the reader toward the next step. A *Times* man predicted a side-effect of *The Burning Cross:* If movies were cheaply made their backers could "afford the risk of alienating the Southern market." Critics began to sort black roles into "an old-fashioned Sambo performance" or a "very up to date part." On the screen, black players moved toward the center of the frame, sometimes only in the inflection of a pronoun: "Mr. Chan," Moreland says as Birmingham Brown, "there ain't no limit to the cleverness of *us* detectives." Black actors told each other about this trend. "Play yourself," rather than slide into the stock role that Hollywood had once demanded, a black press story urged.[29]

Even antebellum Southern movies and jungle movies, the two genres most addicted to archaic material, gave in to the times: the former simply by suffering almost total erasure from the canon; the latter, evolving by way of World War II mutants such as *Sundown,* by relocating settings to exotic isles and lost tribes of bronzed but ethnically neutral peoples. The B-movie series featuring Jungle Jim, Bomba the Jungle Boy, or Tarzan, along with the waning Saturday morning serials, joined the exodus to a sort of evergreen Micronesia. As early as 1945 *Tarzan and the Amazons* relocated its hero from black Africa to a nameless land ruled by a white tribe led by the *doyenne* of gothic Transylvanian movies, Maria Ouspenskaya. Other strategies included employing surrogate race-angles such as the scientist in *Jungle Captive* (1945) trying to give life to the offspring of an ape and a woman, and casting latinate types in sarongs as the Bomba series did, featuring Laurette Luez in recurring exotic roles.[30] Even so, the reformulations limped so badly as to face hazing from *Variety.* Of *Jungle Goddess* (1948), for instance, it complained of "the same old white goddess among the native tribesmen routine"; and warned exhibitors that "there is no gold buried in this part of Africa."[31]

Of course the black actors took little heart from these survivals of

In the short run, as Hollywood reshaped traditional genres, black roles lapsed into structured absence, as here in *Cannibal Attack* (1954) in which they have given way to ethnically neutral brownskinned peoples on whose behalf no activists spoke. Copyright Columbia Pictures.

wartime trends. One by one those who had lived off the jungle pictures or filled the roles of sidekicks and servants in other series—Charlie Chan, the Great Gildersleeve, or Don "Red" Barry westerns—or provided Hollywood's incidental porters and housemaids, or even played the oiled-up voodoo dancers in zombie movies lost screen time, billing, and roles. The more fortunate passed into radio, the dying days of vaudeville, race movies, or the underemployment that the journalist Leon Hardwick thought the product of a "silent boycott." The apolitical reporters LaMar and Levette, doing their best to soften the fall and to put the best face on things, larded their columns with news of "lucrative contracts" and lists of "sepians" who cadged gigs as extras or roles that "will swell pockets with a nice bit of cash." Or they claimed improbable influence over the moguls, as in reporting "I am very happy to have been again able to convince Hollywood's 'powers that be' that they should" do this or that for black actors.[32]

The musical genre provided considerably more work for African American performers, some of it certain to be cut out in Memphis anyway as subtly subversive to the status quo. Partly, this censoring of performance arose out of a romantic link between ballads and courtship;

that is, even a solo singer of, say, "You're the Top" was singing *to* someone and therefore the number was rendered touchy if done by a black singer. Already, for example, black Billy Daniels had been singing on radio (safely invisible) "That Old Black Magic," but in movies, of course, such casually chosen material became visible and therefore took on an edge. As a case in point, in the B-western *Cowboy Canteen* (1945) the Mills Brothers sang their wartime hit "Paper Doll," a lyric brimming with adolescent yearning for a complaisant lover, "a [paper] doll that other fellas cannot have," a sexual text rendered tolerable to whites by the backbeat created by the nostalgia of thousands of white couples who, who having been parted by the war, tenderly regarded it as "our song" that created a bond between them across space. Unwittingly, and without forethought, then, the war had cast black singers in the role of actors in the romances of white people.

But what of movies that were more forthrightly political? On the lots those that were aborted were the subjects of intense ideological struggle, while those that survived to the screen drew either barbs for the archaic or overpraise for the now normatively liberal. *Song of the South* and *Duel in the Sun* drew protests; George Pal's cartoon *John Henry* was an atonement for his guilt over his misunderstood Jasper series; *Jammin' the Blues*, a moody vignette of jazz cellars, became an icon of hep bohemianism. Together such movies and the audiences' and critics' expectations of and disappointments with them revealed yet another seepage of the racial rhetoric of a new film culture into Hollywood.

In this time of a still emerging black movie politics, sometimes black activists rather than studio timidity blocked a film that had so split blacks into two minds as to scare off studios eager to do the right thing but unsure of what it was. *St. Louis Woman* should have been Metro's splashy, jazzy explosion into postwar black popular culture. Arna Bontemps and Countee Cullen, two alumni of the Harlem Renaissance, had adapted it to the stage from Bontemps's novel *God Sends Sunday* and sold it to MGM as though obeying Abe Hill's goading to get "inside of movie making from the hatching of an idea to the final making." From the spring of 1945 onward, Metro showed its faith in the idea by acting as Broadway angel and by developing it as a star-turn for its contract player Lena Horne.[33]

But here blacks split into two camps, led on the one side by the two writers, and on the other by Walter White and Horne, to whom it seemed no more than a revival of an archetypal colored hussy. Mayer himself came down on the side of doing the film, if only to recover his already considerable investment. The black press quickly warned Horne of her vulnerability: "Lena will regret [her refusal] when it turns out to be the sepian 'Oklahoma' "—without her.[34] Also at stake for Horne was a longshot chance to play Julie the mulatto in Metro's planned remake of *Show Boat* and a more likely chance for a tab-show version of the role in a play-within-a-play in *Till the Clouds Roll By*, their biopic of Jerome Kern.[35]

In any case, the debate subsided after *St. Louis Woman* opened on Broadway in 1946 to mixed reviews that chilled their plans. But it clearly revealed the persistence of the two minds of blacks, the tension between demanding change as against resisting Jim Crow casting. Once again White took the brunt of attacks, this time from the International Film and Radio Guild (IFRG), which depicted the clash of principles as no more than a ploy to land his daughter a role and "to suppress Negro comment." But Horne also felt "caught between two very important forces" and eventually "in dry-dock for a long time because I wouldn't play a gambler's floozy." White did his best to turn it into a political lesson, warning Cullen and Bontemps that "we have a racial stake . . . which can be lost or tragically damaged if we make the wrong movies." Coupled with the white liberals' unwillingness to support White's Hollywood bureau, the incident set back blacks by revealing the extent to which an era of peace obliged them to work out a postwar formula to replace that which the war had induced, a formula in which otherness might be redefined as a normative part of a larger polity.[36]

In 1946, in the propwash of war, African Americans were as ready as they would ever be: ten times their prewar activist strength, with White bent upon a new sortie against Hollywood, the social engineers redoubling their studies of the impact of movies on audiences, and critics growing ever more alert to the politics of movies and of their audiences' capacities to read into movies meanings beyond those intended by their makers. Barbara Deming, for example, had already begun her close readings of actors who by "overstepping the bounds of the script" conveyed "sharply eloquent" layers of meaning unintended by the writers.[37] Moreover, as these changes were reflected on the screen, often only in the most fleeting breaks with convention, each came to matter on a scale greater than its own dimensions. Like each daily victory in a baseball pennant race, the value of each event was weighed partly for itself and partly for its place in a larger accretion, much as, to press the metaphor further, Henry Aaron's seven hundredth homerun derived its value from the six hundred ninety-nine that had preceded it.

African Americans needed only a major movie against which to stake out an ideological position with greater clarity than they had brought to *St. Louis Woman*. Already they had begun to cooperate with the MPPDA against censorship, the last ditch of regional racism; to cultivate East Coast documentarists; to erect a postwar equivalent of White's presence in Hollywood. If only they could define an adversarial position against a major film, they might begin to set forth a group aesthetic that defined themselves within the larger society.

To a great extent, black activists looked to a campaign against Walt Disney's *Song of the South* (1946) as the event that would clarify their goals, mainly because its central "Uncle Remus" character seemed not merely anachronistic but also because he violated canons of bourgeois behavior that White and the NAACP had been promoting ever since the summer of 1942. At the same time, the lines were drawn because the movie presented a soaring opportunity for Disney as well. The studio had been foundering ever since before the war, and its collapse had only just been averted by a timely rescue in the form of wartime contracts with the army and the CIAA. Joel Chandler Harris's stories, purportedly told to him by Uncle Remus, could become part of the scaffolding with which to rebuild the Disney enterprise: The animals that formed the dramatic personae of Remus's stories were to be drawn in the conventional Disney-style sentimental, anthropomorphic cartoons, while the human characters were to be portrayed in a reality mode, an innovative combination that might prove to be a winner.[38] For their part, the blacks needed a major test of whether or not the Double V had survived postwar demobilization, while they also hoped to broaden the terms of new alliances to counteract the dissolution of OWI, the dimunition of the army and its mission, and the passage of Hollywood into new hands, not the least of whom was Hays's successor Eric Johnston, former American Chamber of Commerce head.

Only a month after the invasion of Normandy in 1944, blacks had picked up a rumor of Disney's intentions and sent him a flurry of mail that seemed solicitously helpful but was easily taken by the fieflike studio as alarming and unaccustomed meddling. Herman Hill of the *Courier,* Arch Reeve (newly arrived in Breen's office), Walter White, and even the black Rhodes Scholar Alain Locke of Howard University all weighed in with stern warnings balanced by offers of political and aesthetic solutions. Reeve acted as broker, pointing out that the blacks, although alert to racism, were mostly friendly to Hollywood, a point made in their letters, which were phrased as pleas to avoid lowering black morale through a misbegotten movie or, failing that, risk an enervating campaign of protest. Disney quickly saw the need for bargaining and offered to work with the NAACP in person. Breen, too, wished to avert trouble after three years of wartime good relations between blacks and Hollywood, and urged Disney to counsel with them. Meanwhile, two Hollywood blacks, Caleb Peterson and Leon Hardwick, sent off their own protests, which led Disney to investigate his adversaries and take the measure of their possible Communist affiliations—the *Sentinel* probably was not CPUSA, his advisers said, but the *Eagle* was indeed.[39]

Clearly, the postwar era was different from early Hollywood racial negotiations. The adversaries shared no collective vision that war had helped shape. Rather, the blacks seemed mere complainers at each presumed slight, which nettled Disney who during the war had remained apart from domestic racial politics because of his attention to *The Three Caballeros, Saludos Amigos,* and other CIAA propaganda as well as army training films. Only Locke managed to reach Disney. He had gone to Hollywood to confer with Walter Wanger about steps that the studios might take toward a more contemporary image of the African American. Once having learned of *The Song of the South,* he tried to use it as the occasion for converting Disney. Rather than the stark rhetoric of protest, he praised Disney for a good idea that might, if augmented by enough humane portrayals of black Americans, offset the antebellum stereotype embedded in Uncle Remus. But by summer's end, Locke thought the hour so late that the situation had turned sour enough to leave blacks only with some sort of direct action as their tactic of choice. Disney wavered between the old and the new, first hiring a liberal script doctor in Maurice Rapf, but then blaming the intensifying debate first on a disgruntled black actor who had lost the role of Remus and then on rising of the red menace.[40]

Rapf almost saved the situation from a bad end. With a sentimental, nostalgic treatment by Dalton Raymond—"a professional Southerner," Margaret Mitchell might have dubbed him—in hand, Rapf searched for blacker wellsprings of Southern life by breaking with Harris as his sole source and turning to B. A. Botkin, the editor of the Federal Writers Project, particularly its oral slave narratives from which he culled a book, *Lay My Burden Down: A Folk History of Slavery,* which had only just been published by the University of Chicago. Botkin had turned Remus on his head. Remus's Br'er Rabbit, a cunning trickster perhaps descended from African lore, had been no more than, he wrote, "a politer form, for the entertainment of whites[, of] . . . more caustic tales" of outwitting masters, sardonic jokes, and accounts of "how freedom" came and was lost to "Ku Kluxes." Moreover, Rapf also went about eliding the worst of Raymond's eye-rolling, hysterical blacks, who could have been played only by, as even Disney saw, Butterfly McQueen. If Rapf could accomplish both goals—opening up the readings of black roles and following Botkin's work, which had exposed the "picturesque stereotypes" that had masked "the not so pleasant or picturesque ethics of Jim Crow"—he could create such a solidly built argument that it would undercut both Raymond's nostalgic version and Disney's sentimental recollections of his own childhood readings of Harris's Remus.

But Rapf's is a story of what might have been. Just as Selznick's white-columned Tara overrode Margaret Mitchell's rough-timbered frontier house, Disney's nostalgia overruled Rapf's and Botkin's historical model. So when a minor tiff set Rapf and Raymond at odds it was Rapf who had to go, and with it his antidote to thermidor. By September 1944, the Bank of America put its money on nostalgia.[41]

Even the Southerners in the Breen office felt thwarted by *Song of the South;* the war had taught them to regard black sensibilities as at least on a par with those of the white South. In fact, Breen offered one of them—a native of the "'Deep South' [who] knows the so-called 'negro problems' thoroughly"—to Disney, along with a black consultant as a sop to "our negro friends [who] appear to be a bit critical." Francis Harmon, one of the PCA's Southerners, even offered a way out that rested upon establishing Remus as of a specific "period and place" in the 1870s as a means of "minimizing adverse reactions from certain Negro groups." Furthermore, he even wrote a line to cover Remus's antiquity. "Me and my kind—we's outta date too," says Harmon's Remus. "De parade dun pass us by." But Disney gave little ground, and so Clarence Muse, who probably yearned for the role himself, broke with Disney (or so reported the *Worker*) over the "'Uncle Toms' and handkerchief heads" who had overwhelmed the "dignified" black roles. Disney ended by casting an old black vaudevillian, James Baskette, as Remus, thereby taking his final step toward isolation from both the black activists and black Hollywood circles.[42]

Predictably, no one on the left liked the film, but at the same time blacks were demoralized by its general sweetness and failed to mount a response to it. After all, *their* tribal memory of the old South embraced a common stock of memories shared by the white South; the difference was that the pain of memories of slave times provided lumber for the construction of a modern black identity, while whites held onto the ideologically opposite memory of the happy darkey as an analgesic to mask the pain of the Lost Cause. The movie made only a quarter of a million profit, barely enough to make bank interest, with black moviegoers giving it only a split week in Harlem on a bill with *Mantan Messes Up*. The *Worker* thought it a "slander"; *Ebony* snapped at Baskette for "blocking the road that leads to the advancement of minority groups"; and Crowther in the *Times* spoke for the center in panning "the sweetest most wistful darky slave," an image formed, perhaps, from the antebellum texture of a movie meant to be *post*–Civil War. In any case, he blanched at what he saw. "You've committed a peculiarly gauche offense in putting out such a story in this troubled day and age," he wrote. "One might almost imagine that you figure Abe Lincoln made a mistake. Put down that mint julep, Mr. Disney!" ("Bravo," someone wrote on the clipping in the NAACP's file.)[43]

Indeed, Baskette as Remus *was* the core of the issue. He was so extravagantly "winsome," drawing on all the guile a career on the stage had taught him, that he seemed to overflow with charm, preternatural wisdom, and the unctuousness he drew from the deepest pool of white legend. Centered in the frame where few black actors had ever sat, flanked by two white kids, his woolly head forming a halo as though he were a Tiepolo madonna, his hands gnarled around a crumpled hat, he dominated the scenes in which he taught the children the country ways their urbane parents had thought old-fashioned. He managed to give black viewers a tolerable dignity while playing to whites with a reading so densely packed with ancient props and manners that he transported

Walt Disney's winsome Uncle Remus (James Baskette) split the studio's writers (as well as black critics) with his charming performance that revealed a gaping hole in postwar conscience-liberal aesthetics. BFI. Copyright Walt Disney Studios.

them into a rose-colored past. He lighted his balky pipe with a splinter of kindling, laughed in the sexless falsetto that whites had loved in their blacks, and spun stories from a bottomless memory, many of them about Br'er Rabbit, the harmless version that Harris had learned during the Gilded Age in Fulton County. Each story flowed into an animated sequence that vibrated with life in the briar patch. Between tales he mediated conflict between parent and child, city and country, and even protected his charges from the white trash who live in the hollow. His sprightly theme music was the Oscar-winning "Zip-A-Dee-Doo-Dah (What a Wonderful Day)." How could *anyone*, black or white, resent this happy tale?

For African Americans, here was their main chance to assert a postwar presence by assailing a major, if not booming, movie. But Baskette was too much for them. Despite a few barbs, Baskette's sweet reading of the part dampened hardnosed critics, who waffled and credited Disney with an honest effort to portray the "extremely squalid and servile conditions" in the South, and Baskette with a job that merited "a whole basket full of Oscars." One frustrated critic displaced her rage to the audiences, who, loving Remus *too* much, were "laughing and chuckling" even as, she guessed, they hated "those uppity darkies who just because they got a little more education and went to war, don't know how to stay in their place."[44]

As a result of Baskette's charm, not one group of organized blacks mounted a coherent campaign against Disney's movie. Not only were they staggered by his performance, they were at a loss to define their objections except as a sort of snobbery. June Blythe of the American Council on Race Relations, a shrewd strategist in the use of film propaganda, urged upon the NAACP some sort of response. But even after White wangled a preview from Disney, the black viewers could not agree on what they saw. Gloster Current, a toughminded officer in the NAACP and knowledgeable about show business, seemed taken in by Baskette's "artistic and dynamic" Remus. "My only criticism is," he wrote, "the Negro stereotype of docility . . . interwoven with the motif of satisfaction with slavery." "So artistically beautiful," wrote another, "that is is difficult to be provoked over the cliches."[45] Hope Spingarn of the NAACP traced this mood to Disney's being so "nervous about interracial reaction" that he had left "nothing obviously objectionable about the film [even though] it perpetuates the old clichés." Ann Tanneyhill at NUL sketched a similar dilemma: She raged at the stereotype—"black, fat, greasy, sweaty, laughing, grinning, eyes rolling, white teeth showing predominantly, bowing, scraping hat in hand"—but admitted to falling wistfully under the spell of "quite wonderful" flashes of animation, "a blaze of color," "excellent" music, and, for that matter, "close to a million dollars" in exploitation money. Mary McLeod Bethune of the National Council of Negro Women saw the same "stereotype" and called upon RKO for a broadening of black imagery so as to improve, as social engineers believed possible, "attitudes toward minority groups."[46]

With organized African Americans immobilized, knowing what they hated but unable to propose a new formulation, the movement seemed powerless to regain the momentum that war had once given it under White. In one instance, when White picked a quarrel with Catherine Edwards, editor of *Parents Magazine*, which had given a medal to *Song of the South*, she stood her ground, suggesting on the basis of his clouded recounting of the film that he may not even have seen it, and charged him with crossing over into the camp of the advocates of censorship.[47] But of all the forces that muddled the politics of movies, the worst was yet to come. Conservatives, of course, revelled in Baskette's performance and through Hedda Hopper began pressing the Academy for a special (and eventually posthumous) Oscar. She touted his work in her column and stirred fans to write in, on the occasion of his illness, calling for his Oscar, a campaign that could not help but raise him up in white eyes and diminish the NAACP to a fringe group of cranks.[48]

At least Baskette's Oscar forced the issue by prodding blacks to formulate a more precise account of what was eating away at them and to leave off empty protests such as the *Worker*'s demand "to be stern with Negro artists" who took "degrading" gigs or Muse's nebulous plea that it was "high time that we at home did something about our cultural advancement." The conundrum they faced was in admitting *why* they disliked Baskette's work while letting pass the similar work of McDaniel (who had won an Oscar for it). A partial answer may be found in Ann Tanneyhill's precisely aimed shot at Remus's laughter, the kind, she said, "which we have all learned to abhor . . . loud, long, sustained and vulgar," and most of all, a cackling falsetto that some blacks in olden times had cultivated as a kind of aural metaphor for their powerlessness, as though the shrillness of a Florentine *castrato* persuaded white people that their slaves presented no threat. At the same time, Remus's "vulgar" manner may have uncomfortably reminded the black bourgeoisie of how precariously close to the bottom *any* black, no matter how well off, resided. Black objections to this behavior extended as well to the cartoon figures of Br'er Rabbit and his friends and their raucous voices, liquid body English, slurred accents, and tricksterish cornerboy manner, which the black middle class had spent years trying to train out of its young.[49] In this sense, *Song of the South* clarified movie politics as had no other movie since *Gone with the Wind*.

As *Song of the South* revealed to African Americans a truism of postwar life—that wartime tactics had their limits—so *Duel in the Sun*, King Vidor and David O. Selznick's overdrawn attempt to breathe life into the then fading genre of the western, revealed another. The movies' use of familiar stereotypes sometimes had little to do with calculated wishes to ratify the status quo or to gull witless audiences into the false consciousness of superior/inferior relationships that racism taught. Rather, either because they feared the new or were soothed by the old, Hollywood moviemen preferred safety as against risk. Five months after *Song of the South* went into release, along came *Duel in the Sun* to demonstrate this truism. It had everything: a rousing conflict of railroad baron and cattlemen; a lean, hard hero in Gregory Peck; the most self-conscious vamping since Theda Bara in Jennifer Jones's halfbreed Pearl Chavez; highly saturated Technicolor; a chorus of raw-edged, outsized characters ranging from Lionel Barrymore as the crusty boss of Spanish Bit Ranch through Walter Huston as the jackleg preacher "Sin Killer"—plus Butterfly McQueen as Vashti, the maid, acting as though nothing had happened since 1939, when she played in *Gone with the Wind.*

However much blacks held him in contempt, Remus had held a historical place in *Song of the South,* but Vashti was no more than a signifier of Hollywood's inability to cut free of its racial history. She was there because Selznick insisted on her; she was, as Wendell Green said in the *Sentinel,* an agent of "white chauvinism." Certainly she had no such place in Niven Busch's book. There, she was old and cunning in her dealing with white people, possessed of a lore as timeless as that of Hellman's blacks in *The Little Foxes*—"the old flesh knowledge of the negro," as Busch had written. When she thought of whites at all it was with contempt: "How did white folks get messed up that way?" she thinks while watching Pearl and the satyric Lewt McCanles (Peck) grope at each other. In McQueen's hands, however, she became yet another Prissy, whining, prattling, empty, self-parodying—as Selznick had intended.[50]

An even worse role, from a racial angle, was Pearl. In Busch's book she merely "stood a little way apart not wishing to seem curious or forward." But in the hands of Selznick and Jones she grew seething, feral, instinctive, with lips and eyes that glinted with each change of light and a blouse endlessly slipping so low that it consumed the attention of the PCA. Breen's staff did their best to point out to Selznick the obviousness of Jones's portrayal of sensuality as a racial trait of halfbreeds but only succeeded in joining him in the mire of his own bad writing. At first they complained only that the portrayal of a race with the morals of a lynx was "dangerous" in wartime, particularly in a war in which enemy national policy was rooted in racial theories. (The war was a factor because the movie began during it and would take three years to make.) In any event, the Breen office, with astonishing indifference, let it all pass, claiming that there was no racial prejudice in America against the group in question anyway.[51]

Actually, the "play" in the broadly painted movie allowed the viewer to shim up Pearl's role into a metaphor for the American racial condition. The movie became an homage to the capitalist buccaneering of a sort of rancher-imperialism, a saga of struggle between the colossi of cattlemen and railroaders, the subflooring of almost every western. Then Pearl arrives and the movie turns on its celebrants, snuffs them out one by one, and lets Spanish Bit pass into the hands of the railroad, an epic event given stature by a vast outdoor scene echoing the imagery of the Oklahoma land rush of the 1880s. Thus Pearl seemed a sign that

Butterfly McQueen's shrill Vashti (here with Gregory Peck) in *Duel in the Sun* (1946) revealed the persistence of old roles when in the hands of all but undirectable actors who had an investment in perpetuating them. NSF. Copyright Selznick Releasing.

America's racial heritage doomed its enterprise. But little is made of this trope because Vashti, the Negro, remains a whining cipher, an erasure where Selznick, if he had had the heart for it, might have written a master scene in which Vashti was a black witness to white hubris.

Black critics were having none of it. One of them found Vashti "addlepated" and Pearl "a movie-Mexican touch customary in the middle twenties," and the whites in the national weeklies joined them in the hazing. For its part the NAACP, while noting that in the movie "the colored races are morally and intellectually inferior [and] cannot restrain their violent elemental passions," and perhaps guessing that Selznick himself, knowing he had a turkey on his hands, would saturation-book it, even in New York, and play it off as cheaply and as quickly as possible, opted not to attack it in public. On its face perhaps a mere incremental gain in tactical wisdom, the decision based upon knowing "it has already been judged a bad picture" was indeed a step toward learning a peacetime allocation of resources.[52]

In any event, blacks could claim at least incremental gains: an assertion of a black position against dying Hollywood racial conventions, an alliance with the Motion Picture Association of America (MPAA) in a judicial assault on Southern censorship, a boomlet in short films that

Pearl Chavez (Jennifer Jones), here with Lillian Gish and Walter Huston, seemed a tolerable racial type both because of her vague mestizo heritage and her sexiness, to which only the PCA objected. BFI. Copyright Selznick Releasing.

traced their liberal pedigrees back to the war. Thus the era witnessed a prototypal inquiry into postwar racial opinion and political culture. Moreover, these achievements were not only evidence that a form of conscience-liberalism survived the war in the face of thermidorean forces, but also indicators of an incipient marketplace of liberal ideas that the studios might eventual aim major feature films toward.

At first the evidence of these changes was small indeed and too Hollywoodish by Eastern film-culture standards, rendered bland by timid sales departments, too marked by tractlike OWI rhetoric, and often so inchworm in their gains as to seem hardly worth the bother. Indeed up to 1947 they were all *shorts.*

Moreover, some movies proved unusually resistant to pressure, partly because black activists could not reach a consensus. Cartoons were a particular nettle. During the war the NAACP had built a file on a string of raucous, hard-driving animated cartoons done in a nut-jazz idiom that jarred black sensibilities because they disconcertingly appeared in competition with other cartoons that were patently backward-looking, namely, Hanna-Barbera's and Metro's Tom and Jerry series with its frumpy black housemaid and Columbia's Heckle and Jeckle, two black crows whose eccentric gait owed much to Jim Crow tradition. The jazzy cartoons boggled NAACP viewers because they were cast in a specifically urban style that flaunted a mix of jive-talk, hepcat body english, and flashy zoot suits, in sum an exaggeration of the outrageous behavior of a pioneering urban teen-oriented music culture that already was jamming the Brooklyn Paramount and Roseland to hear its heroes. Four of them had proven particularly nettlesome to the NAACP file-keepers: *Red Hot Riding Hood, Goldilocks and the Jivin' Bears, Coal Black and the Sebben Dwarfs,* and *Uncle Tom's Cabaña,* each because its creators had caught the black idiom that had already crossed over into the imaginations of white adolescents, exaggerated its style, and even celebrated it in ways that rattled blacks ever wary of white humor.

While it was true that a climax of *Uncle Tom's Cabaña,* the opening of Tom's "chicken shack" on Hollywood and Vine, had already been a bit in the liberal revue *Jump for Joy,* blacks fretted over how it would play Azuza (Walter White's pejorative term for squares). Furthermore, what would Main Street or Azuza think of *Red Hot Riding Hood*'s sexy caricature of Lena Horne who has left grandma's house for a job as a riveter at Lockheed and a jitterbugging nightlife? Or what would be the response to *Coal Black,* the parody of Disney's *Snow White,* transfigured into yet another sexy singer who scats her songs and talks jive? *Her* associates were another matter entirely: a black witch who sells apples from a pushcart, seven liver-lipped dwarfs as her court, Prince Chawmin' dressed in a white zoot suit, driving a lowslung purple car, and dealing in black market tires, coffee, and sugar. Ambiguously, the dwarfs enlist to guard America, and the sleeping heroine is kissed awake not by the prince but by a black soldier, whose kiss induces an aura of waving flags in her hair. Clearly, the NAACP was trapped by the ambiguity, complaining of the seven grotesque dwarfs but among themselves, at least, joining in the humor by describing the prince's costume as "a zoot suit with a reet pleat and a reeve sleeve," and raising only a token protest before letting it drop.[53]

But the persistence of rural racial idiom was another matter, and it nettled blacks throughout the war, particularly in the work of a Hungarian immigrant, George Pal, who had perfected a form of animated clay models, or "Puppetoons." Pal, with his European mind uncluttered by American racial furniture, imagined that by creating a puffy-lipped, drawling black child named Jasper, with a mammy who bakes pies that are stolen by a fat, hustling scarecrow in a checked suit, and a wisecracking crow, he was making a kind of "Huckleberry Finn of black folklore." Perhaps in less touchy times black activists might have been amused by his whimsical anachronisms, particularly Jasper, a filiopietistic boy whose invincible rectitude enables him to outwit the two conniving marplots with such regularity that each movie seemed an homage to

Br'er Rabbit. Certainly OWI had sensed the ambivalence, admiring *Jasper's Music Lesson* (1943) for its "lighthearted . . . exciting" treatment of jazz while complaining only of "the assumption that Negro accents are funny in themselves," a waffling induced also by *Hot Lips Jasper* (1944) the soundtrack of which featured the ecstatic trumpet of Rafael Mendez laid over shots of the two black heavies dressed as bebop fans in search of a mess of spareribs and yams.[54]

After the war, however, blacks not only seemed less patient with Pal, but also possessed a national press in which to complain. Indeed, with the war over and blacks seeking a moral equivalent of it, *Ebony*, much to Pal's surprise, took out after Jasper, reporting a rising "protest from Negro groups." Pal, as though responding to *Ebony*, retreated from his misguided dip into folklore and turned to *John Henry and Inky Poo* (1946), a straightforward child's tale of the legendary black gandydancer who challenges and defeats a steamhammer in a spikedriving contest, and a year later produced an endearing tribute to Duke Ellington (1947). Afterward, Pal and *Ebony* indulged in a journalistic lovefeast as a sign of mutual gratitude, Pal's for the tutelage provided by real organic black intellectuals and *Ebony*'s for a sincere public caving in to black hegemony. As Pal said, Rex Ingram (the voice of John Henry) was so affecting that "at the end he was crying . . . [and] everybody was moved." *Ebony* praised Pal's "first," a movie "that deals with Negro folklore, that has a Negro as its hero and . . . has no Negro stereotypes."[55] The result was that not only had Pal learned the lore of his adopted country, but *Ebony* had taught its readers that together they had mattered and had affected movies at their source, a major black social goal ever since 1942.

On another occasion the broker of black culture was the white magazine *Life* along with Norman Granz, a white impresario who for years had been promoting jazz among crossover audiences—Jazz at the Philharmonic, he called his shows. An actuality film rather than an animated one, *Jammin' the Blues* (1946) was a jazz performance recorded on film by *Life* photographer Gjon Mili as though a true jam session. The combination of the stylized, urbane milieu and the music and dance that moodily spun out from it sent a signal to Hollywood that an audience seemed ready for East Coast–style film culture. Never before had jazz been presented in such an unadorned setting undiluted by plot or artifice—other than fresh uses of the smooth suturing of shots into sequences that formed the basis of Hollywood style. In other words, the filmmakers had turned classical Hollywood style in new directions, using it to troll for a hep audience that needed no tutelage in black musical idiom but also had never before seen it in the movies.

The audience was meant to feel it had walked in on a jam session, where it felt welcome and therefore both liberal and hep. Curling cigarette smoke, the cigarette held between the valves of a trumpet; porkpie hats cocked, seemingly forgotten on the backs of heads; open shirts, loosely draped zoot suits; tired musicians, lidded eyes drooping; all in a tight little set broken by geometric shadows—every detail made for a properly cellary scene. The combo drifted into "The Midnight Symphony" on a liquid melodic line backed by softly brushed drums, then into "The Sunny Side of the Street" sung by Marie Bryant while in a languid jitterbug with Archie Savage, and ended on a hard-driving arrangement of the title song. For the liberals there was even an inside joke in the presence of the white guitarist Barney Kessel playing his set in a darkened corner of the frame.

More than any other movie of black culture, *Jammin' the Blues* reached an uncommonly broad audience who registered its approval. It was an artistic piece of "excellent" stature, said Gordon Hollingshead as he sent it out from Warners. Walter Winchell, by then having merged conservative politics with conscience-liberalism in a far from uncommon American mentality, was so taken in by it he thought it had been shot with a hidden camera; *Time* praised it; *Life* named it Movie of the Week; James Agee, despite a contempt for artiness, found it creditable; the *Amsterdam News* claimed so many soldiers—ten million, it said—saw it that all the prints were worn out; and *Ebony* concluded it was "artistic as well as commercial."[56]

Parallel to the release of *Jammin' the Blues*, a string of dramatic shorts appeared, each one an unwitting teaser for its successor, each coyly weaving racial politics into its storyline, each sloughing off its clunking OWI rhetoric in favor of a slicker Hollywood enamel. Together they displayed a coy eagerness to proceed—eagerness because they loaded their plots with indictments of racism, coy because each found a way to blame evil foreign agents for the spread of it.

One of them, *Don't Be a Sucker* (1946), had in fact come directly from the war by way of Paramount, its civilian Signal Corps contractor. Its racism was put in two forms, one Nazi, one American, the latter as a divisive kvetch addressed to crowds by streetcorner orators who rail against "people with foreign accents making all the money" and "negroes holding jobs that belong to me and you." Mike, a casually happy worker, hears some of this "truth" and accepts it until, first, he hears himself, a "freemason," lumped with the "others," and second, he learns from a refugee professor the horrors of Nazi anti-Semitism. "I saw it in Berlin," he says at the cutaway to brutish "Hans" who "pumped up his ego" by bullying Jews. Then vicious *Sturmabteilungtruppen* barge into his classroom and drag him away. Mike's liberalism, of course, remains unsullied in the last reel, earning a place for the film in the catalogues of distributors who overpraised it as "the backbone" of the army's campaign against racism in its ranks.[57] In yet another instance that followed the line of *Teamwork* in laying racism at the feet of Nazis alone, Selznick's *The American Creed* (1947) wore homage to wartime liberalism like a unit shoulder patch. A succession of stars drawn from the studios appears before the camera, each spouting an unremarkable homily, except for, perhaps, Gene Kelly, who in the course of his, introduced the American neologism "*togetherness,*" and James Stewart, who set forth yet another veiled reference to alien sources of racism. He was "sore," he said, at crackpots who were promoting the very ideas the late war had opposed. Such movies, remarkable for their existence rather than their merits, served moviegoers as no more than chasers, but Selznick took his seriously enough to give it a preview, collect response cards, and finally send out his postproduction materials "extra special rush."[58]

The best of these vignettes was the most self-consciously liberal and yet poorly aimed because of its writer's insistence on locating once again the germ of racism in foreign soil. *The House I Live In* (1946) grew out of a huddle of Hollywood's left at a party at Mervyn LeRoy's. More than in the others, politics were embedded in plot, character, and incident rather than "on the nose" rhetoric. LeRoy, whose liberal pedigree extended back to Warner Bros. social movies of the 1930s; Frank Ross, a producer recently arrived from the East; Albert Maltz, soon to be blacklisted; and Frank Sinatra, a youthful but accomplished singer in search of his own liberal politics, together wangled a studio from likeminded Dore Schary at RKO and turned out a little movie that so exemplified the absorption of conscience-liberalism into the mentality of Hollywood's establishment that the Academy eventually gave it an Oscar. But here too the liberals took two steps forward and one back, in that Maltz began by addressing racism as an issue but early on shifted to a generalized plea for tolerance for an unnamed religion. Sinatra as himself takes a break from recording, steps into an alley to smoke, and sees a gang of urchins setting upon a lone victim because, as one of them says, "We don't like his religion, see!" Sinatra cleverly saves the kid from a licking, but once again it is clear that nameless, perhaps foreign, heavies are at work on America's fragile liberalism. "Fellers, listen to me," he says. "Somebody's been making suckers out of you." He restores their sense of ethnic tolerance with a retelling of the legend of Kelly and Levin, complete with a tankshot of the sinking *Haruna,* thence to a peroration on the absurdity of segregating blood plasma, a practice, he says, that might well have cost the lives of the kids' fathers. Like the Lone Ranger riding off after a good deed, Sinatra returns to his gig, but not before breaking into a chorus of the liberal anthem that gave the movie its title.[59]

Driven by the logic of his own role, two weeks after the preview Sinatra rushed to Gary, Indiana, to mediate a racially heated high school strike, then in December received a medal from the Hollywood Women's Press Club: two events which, coupled with the Oscar and quick acceptance by 16 mm distributors, suggested that all that stood between Hollywood and its apparently liberal audiences was a studio with the nerve to plunge in. Indeed, the times seemed ripe for such an adventure, if the fitful output of the half-measures we have seen were indicators.[60]

Of all the foreshadowings before 1949 of an era of "the thinking picture," the only one that commanded the full weight of a major studio commitment was Warners' *It Happened in Springfield* (1946). While not actually a feature, it had begun during the war as an OWI sort of film to be leavened by the production values of a feature, grounded in an actual incident, and produced by a veteran maker of the studio's trademark problem films. Although the end of the war brought an end to the government's investment in such films, the studio decided to carry it to full term, albeit as a two-reeler rather than a feature. In this form *It Happened in Springfield* allows a glimpse at how war's end induced a thermidorean reaction, but one which liberals in a fashion weathered.

The film actually began before the war, when a racial disturbance wracked a Massachusetts town and shook the citizens' image of themselves as a melting pot. In classic liberal fashion they designed a school curriculum to inoculate their children against the virus of racism, a decision that earned them stories in *Women's Home Companion*, the *New York Times*, and two book-length photo-essays, not to mention the pamphlets and mimeographed handouts released by the schools and their consultants, one of whom, Clyde R. Miller of Teachers' College Columbia University, sent a packet to Jack Warner.[61] For Miller, Springfield's dealing with racism as a curricular matter seemed a bold way to face what he called "the growing challenge of nationalistic, religious, and racial disruptions," as well a means to "control prejudice and to strengthen democratic rights" in a decade that may be "the most critical in America's history." Already Miller, a model wartime conscience-liberal, had pressed his own fraternity to open its doors to blacks and had monitored the spread of the Springfield idea to more than two hundred school systems.[62]

Warner liked the idea and in the summer of 1944 assigned it to a likeminded director, Crane Wilbur, who had been raised in integrated public schools, written a prewar script on "tolerance" for the radio series *Big Town*, and apprenticed on Warner Bros. 1930s movies such as *Hell's Kitchen* and *Crime School*. By summer's end Warner's enthusiasm led to a rare decision to shoot on location.[63]

But something was missing. The crisis of war had passed, and with it the moviemakers' stomach for, the nation's urgent need for, and the liberals' peacetime redefinition of their war movie mentality. Even the easily digestible lone black figure that might have passed most readily into a postwar genre was gone. As in a jarring number of race-angled movies, Warner retreated from portraying even a shred of racism as homegrown, insisting instead on placing it only in the mouth of the town's scapegrace, who in turn had culled it from a "Nazi" propaganda leaflet. And circumspectly, not wishing to single out actual victims of racism for fear of arousing it as though a sleeping dog, Warner adopted the same racially neutral casting as Tarzan movies had done, and he insisted the victim should not be shown as a foreigner. Wilbur also sensed the rules of the game, not only as a contract director but from having written *Big Town,* a similarly angled radio show in 1940 in which the victim had no more than the faintest trace of an accent.[64] The resulting coyness, however kindly intended to soften the blow of racism, could not help but blunt the message and deny the audience the experience of implicating itself. From the African American point of view, the moviemakers' indirection, though calculated to mute the animus of racism, not only precluded an assault on racism but served as an erasure of their otherness that galled racists. The subtextual result was yet another warping of the liberal notion of sameness, much as Wilbur recalled his own childhood: "black and white together [and] no making [much of] people because of their color."[65]

Such attitudes, in the absence of an alternative liberal rhetoric, soon diminished the project, rendering moot the writers' wish to avoid the flavor of an OWI tract.[66] After weeks of second thoughts and fears of lost Southern markets, *It Happened in Springfield* lost its nerve. A black pupil's lines were given to a Chinese; a black teacher was erased; a riot at the dramatic core of the movie was stoked not by race but ethnic animosity against—unbelievably—a Swede! And all was stage-managed with a string of remonstrating telephone calls from Hollywood to their location in Massachusetts: Avoid beards, they said, not so hardnosed on the colored angle, and finally, said the cutter's notes, why not make a creampuff version for the theatres that erases the blacks entirely and reserve them for a 16 mm classroom print. At last, as Hollingshead told the New York office, all the highly charged shots were cut, and everything was ready for the release of the most craven two-reeler Warners' had ever put out.[67]

If this seems a case of typical Hollywood evasion, it must be seen in the context of liberal thought of the time, a sort of intellectuals' version of Israel Zangwill's old-fashioned "melting pot." The liberal faith that embraced Wilbur's childhood of uneventful integration in school, Allport's view of racism as a remediable gap in knowledge, and Stampp's ideal of treating blacks as white people with dark skins had already colored half a dozen short movies. In the same spirit, the studio chiefs proudly announced that no expense had been too great to make what they proclaimed as a great movie that was a monument to Warner Bros.' undiminished commitment to social reform.[68] Thus what seemed like corporate shrinking from duty was only a reflection of a collective wish to approach the issue from the angle of consensus rather than confrontation.

This faith in American goodwill at its most pristine may be seen in the curriculum materials generated by the schools of Springfield itself. As early as 1940, social workers had studied "complex problems of [black] social status and economic opportunity," which they hoped to solve through "a constructive program . . . in co-operation" with citizens "in all phases" of urban life. This "Springfield Plan" was a curriculum that placed ethnic harmony at its center by promoting "respect among the children for others" and combating "prejudice" by "making a search for the facts" (much as Allport might have prescribed). By 1946, the year of the movie, the program had achieved national fame, including a page in *Vogue*.[69]

But the movie as released was another story. It paid a high price for its goal of harmony by invoking a classical Hollywood closure on a happy note, while at its core was a distinct lack of faith in its audience and even its own principles. Racism portrayed in such grossly Manichean terms falsely set up a conflict between *alien* heavies and hometown good guys, a formula that precluded showing racism as toxic little cysts harbored by otherwise decent folk. Instead, in their edenic village Wilbur gives the audience a kindly storekeeper with a son in the army, the former played by John Qualen, whose Hollywood career playing Swedes must have undermined the credibility of his being marked off as a victim of racists. One of the heavies—Arthur Hohl, who made a career of wild-eyed manics—enters the store dressed darkly, eyes set in a hard glint, canvassing votes ("if you know what's good for you"). In contrast, Knudsen the storekeeper is an amiable tinkerer, friend to kids, and purveyor of tobacco and a little gossip. In classic Warners style an ensuing crescendo-montage of violent rioting crackles with splintered windows and violated churches, accompanied by a doomsday voiceover. It ends when flinty-faced heavies muttering ad-libs knock Knudsen to the floor and ransack his shop.

"Why him?" asks his son, wounded and still in uniform. Outside the shop, his buddy soberly speaks to two teachers who carry their dismay to a meeting so that we know that good people will not take the outrage in silence. Later one of the teachers leads Knudsen's son through her school full of pupils happily working at polyethnic living. Each child reports on his own subculture even as a voice says they are "all American," and in the end, the set awash in flags, they all sing "America."[70] At this point the formula unavoidably erases African Americans because many anecdotes begin with specifically *Nazi* oppression, which the children have fled, thereby leaving the black kids with the unthinkably disharmonious task of indicting *American* racism. Thus the movie left its audience with a flag-draped ending that denied the audience an encounter with the specific racism that had motivated the school board, the city, and Warners to act. Even then, the studio fretted that the plethora of interracial shots surely would preclude a run in the South.[71]

Few critics reviewed the movie, but those who did deduced the internal skirmishing that had softened its impact. Even OWI in its dying days thought that the film inadvertently made more of a case for the fragility of American liberalism than it did against racism. "Negative content," said their reviewer, and an exaggeration of fascist influence that left audiences in a mood of "smug American self-congratulation." "Unsuitable," she said, for overseas viewing, "particularly in liberated areas" where Nazism once had ruled.[72]

Nonetheless, the trades and African Americans both were grateful for the small favor. "Magnificent," said Hollywood's town crier, the *Reporter*, even as it fretted over how "to combine good citizenship with good picture making." "Bravo," said the PCA of Warners' "helping to increase harmony" that surely "will have a . . . valuable effect." As for the classroom version, a catalogue writer unwittingly revealed the imposing odds against such a valuable effect. "A natural for your school teachers," he wrote of "the neat story which . . . neatly sidesteps a controversial issue." *Ebony*, ever searching for omens of "progress," recounted the history of the Springfield plan but let pass the erasure of a black teacher while cheering the movie as "tip top, [and] not too preachy."[73] In other words, Jack Warner had been prescient in his guess that racism was strong medicine that even liberals willingly averted their eyes from.

Clearly, conscience-liberals were stumped by the problem of making the transition from the role of the nation's partner in a war against fascism to that of a loyal opposition bent upon perpetuating necessitarian war aims into the perpetually advancing liberal future that the documentarists had imagined. That is, from a wartime role as partner in the Double V, when they were cool toward voicing divisive opinions, they needed to move toward a willingness to risk open fights over the pace of change or the form taken by the movies that advocated it. Like the mother in the Jewish gallows-joke commenting on her son's resolve to die killing a German rather than go quietly to the gas chamber, liberals had been admonished: "Don't make trouble." Sooner or later, they would need to follow the lead of *Variety*'s critic, who pointed to the absurdity of a Nordic victim after a world war had raged against anti-Semites and America had been rent by racial strife, a stance also taken by the *Worker*, which found the film provided "no bearing on the Jewish or Negro problem" and therefore let the viewer off scot-free with a "smug . . . attitude."[74]

Yet these bland shorts, designed to ensure that the buttered side of reformism would land uppermost, did breach convention and did test prospects for feature-length films of advocacy. In this context, *It Happened in Springfield* was a cautious gesture founded on a hoped-for symbiosis between idealist makers of films and their consumers, who were already open to new ideas such as location-shooting, psychological sophistication, and "neo-realism."

Take only one instance of their marketplace, Elizabeth Zutt of Evansville, Indiana, a moviegoer and an alumna of Wisconsin, where indigenous progressivism drew her to (once) vote Socialist. In 1945, she studied librarianship at Columbia and as a new Manhattanite embarked on a rich round of moviegoing that included *It Happened in Springfield.* Though moving toward the political center by then, she wrote a fan letter praising the "timely and needed film . . . which our whole country would do well to admire and follow, and [which] is a fine example of what a determined democracy can do."[75] In effect she spoke for a marketplace that the authors of President Truman's *To Secure These Rights* sensed and would play to.

Together with other signs of change—the crumbling Hollywood oligopoly, the erosion of censorship, the persistence of a "liberalism of the heart" among writers, and the buying, if not yet the making, of political movies—these short movies kept open the hope of reaching a film culture that seemed ready for new things. Still, they needed a genre, a formula equivalent to the war movie and its lone black warrior. Selznick once went so far as to use Walter White's column as a classified ad to recruit black men and women story editors (eighty-four applied). Of course, not all moguls behaved this way. As one of White's friends reported: "Since the untimely death of Willkie the movie producers have not been so eager to portray the Negro in his varied and true roles."[76] Or as a tradepaper reporter asked: "Where does show business stand on tolerance?" Nonetheless, despite liberal skepticism there remained in Hollywood story departments, tradepapers, and independent firms a predisposition to keep alive the liberalism that once had been an official line.

During the summer after *It Happened in Springfield,* for example, Sinclair Lewis settled on miscegenation as the core of his novel *Kingsblood Royal,* a fable that linked black and white lives and even included a black family that took up arms in self-defense, an echo of an incident in Detroit in the 1920s. Lewis, hoping to whet Hollywood's appetite, asked Hy Kraft (*Stormy Weather*) to dramatize it even as Jerry Wald at Fox read it and asked Hopper to tout it in her column and *Variety* ran on page one the story of the hot book whose race angle "hasn't dampened the competition among the studios for a first gander." Perhaps displeased with Kraft's work or tepid black responses, Lewis let the idea drop in favor of a movie of his *Cass Timberlane.* In any case, Lewis, not Hollywood, seemed cool to the idea.[77]

But the story departments pressed onward with all sorts of racial material: Lillian Smith's interracial melodrama *Strange Fruit,* Cid Ricketts Sumner's novel *Quality,* William L. White's *Reader's Digest* piece about a "passing" black family, Ralph Ellison's complex anatomy of black life *The Invisible Man,* one of them perhaps the first movie equivalent of the punchy racial stuff of Broadway plays like *South Pacific* and *Finian's Rainbow.*

They were searching, but no one had ever seen the quarry. Was it an acutely sensitive black hero opposed by a gritty cracker? Yet another folksy Remus? A militant advocate of the race? If not a St. Louis fancy lady, then perhaps an earthmother? In Selznick's shop, for instance, nothing seemed "right"; everything snagged between "too hot to handle on film" and merely "interesting." Some proposals almost scored, particularly Ann Petry's *The Street,* a story of "the mixed races and creeds in a Brooklyn street" that seemed "timely and . . . worthy"; or the one about a white teacher in a black school where she learns "of race prejudice [and] . . . pleads for [a] militant fight against color barriers," a story the reader thought "bears watching"; or the "passing for white" story ruled out because of its "passive" Negro who "remains a victim rather than an actor in the tragedy"; or another rejected not so much for "the touchy subject of miscegenation" as its "clumsy handling" of it. Some of course were dogs, such as the one reviewed as "a 20th rate cross between 'Uncle Tom's Cabin' and 'Gone with the Wind,'" or Angela DuMaurier's story of a blind pianist who marries a Eurasian, regains her sight, views the racism around her, and melodramatically restores her innocence by surgically restoring her blindness![78]

Of course, this pursuit of properties rarely emerged into daylight, leaving the impression of a yawning gulf, as Niven Busch recalled it, between "fervent attitudes" and thin "performance"; and between manifestos such as Goldwyn's piece in the NUL's *Opportunity,* in which he claimed conversion to "social justice" as a result of reading the Atlantic Charter, and Hollywood's pitifully few films.[79]

For the moment, then, the vacuum between word and deed left the field to exploitation filmmakers who gauged drift in order to cash in on early returns of incipient fads. One of their products, *The Burning Cross,* appeared late in 1947, and not only may have nudged the majors but drew blacks into its orbit both to overpraise it and to defend it against censorship. Its makers, Walter Colmes and Aubrey Wisberg, patched together on a $10,000 nut a team of underpaid actors, eight days' rental of the old Chaplin studio, a kernel of an idea about a black man who infiltrates the Ku Klux Klan, and "as little story as possible," creating a sensational movie that drew the reluctant NAACP to its defense. "Technically we did not feel the picture was too good," said one officer who felt nonetheless compelled to "support the campaign to have the picture shown." *Ebony,* grateful for a sign, hyperbolically defined it as the antidote to *The Birth of a Nation* that "movie audiences have been waiting 30 years for," and gave the producers a generous puff in which one of them traced its source back to the late war and his polyethnic guncrew who "made me really feel what people could do when united."[80]

Gradually, as the shorts units ground out their testaments to residual conscience-liberalism, the story departments riffled the pages of properties in search of an angle, and the independents adventurously milked the so far untargeted marketplace, the majors returned to their wartime mode by coyly inserting racial bits, all of which liberal critics spotted, called attention to, and overpraised. Typically, in *Mr. Blandings Builds His Dream House* (1948) Gussie (Louise Beavers) wears a uniform so antiseptic, so crisp as to suggest her workplace was a surgery rather than a kitchen. Moreover, she advances the plot when she comes up with the slogan her boss needs at his ad agency: "If it ain't Wham, it ain't ham!" Indeed, all maids seemed more in on the action: In Capra's *It's a Wonderful Life* (1946), she is among the "little people" whose savings are at risk; in *Abie's Irish Rose* (1946), she wishes the celebrants a "mazeltov"; in *Cass Timberlane* she is *Mrs.* Higbe.

What is more, *Ebony* and the press played up the trend as though a continuum or a movement. "Mrs. Higbe" got two pages in which the director George Sidney said, "We didn't want a Mammy or a comedy character." A Southern child's fable, *Banjo*, was praised for its "intelligent, adult, true-to-life Negro servants." And a musical turn in *A Song Is Born* seemed "a long stride forward in bringing Americans of all races together." Moreover, the principals insisted nothing was an accident. Anthony Quinn played an Indian in *Black Gold* not because a gig was a gig but "because it's about time we show that Americans with darker skins are humans"; Rex Ingram boasted that in *Moonrise* his black sage was "the best role ever written for a Negro"; and Robert Buckner, director of *Rogue's Regiment*, said he combined getting "away from the comic domestic roles [with] . . . good, solid, equal part[s] . . . with no preachment." And always the movies seemed, as *Ebony* formulated it, a stride away from the "prewar rut of Dixie-minded presentation" and grounded in "World War II when racism was made unpopular by Hitler." George Norford, writing in *Opportunity*, traced it to firsthand memories of the war when movies like *Lifeboat* had done "wonders for the morale of the Negro GI" while raising the black audience's expectation that "Hollywood would not only continue giving Negroes such roles, but it would go even further in terms of film content."[81]

If this public utterance seems a little highflown, the link between the war and politics colored even the most private thoughts of leftist moviemakers. Carl Foreman, who wrote the first of the impending message movies, always recalled the war as a stage in his "political development"; Abe Polonsky thought of his own circle as itching "to defy the conventions all around us"; Zanuck admitted to Moss that *The Negro Soldier* had helped point his own way toward "postwar change"; Robert Wise remembered that either his friends were "changed considerably by the war" or they seemed "old-fashioned"; and Irving Rapper remembered Ronald Reagan on the set of *The Voice of the Turtle* predicting "the day would come when we'd never use black men as 'help' in movies."[82]

The struggle to bring forth substantive products from this ferment may be seen in the process of making several movies on the eve of the

In *Moonrise* (1948), Rex Ingram repeated his *Sahara* role as giver of water to white men, as though calculatedly bearing wartime images of polyethnic harmony into peacetime. Copyright Republic Pictures.

message movie cycle of 1949: Jules Levey and Herbert Biberman's homage to black music, *New Orleans* (1947); Fox's reworking of the plantation legend from Frank Yerby's book *The Foxes of Harrow* (1947); the pacifist tract *The Boy with the Green Hair* (1947); and *Body and Soul* (1947), Abe Polonsky's boxing yarn as allegory for unrestrained capitalism. Each one of these movies, save for *Body and Soul*, compromised its race angle on its way to the screen, but together they took steps that stoked the liberal audience's hopes for a political cinema.

In this sense they almost constituted a genre called Faint of Heart. *New Orleans*, as an instance, began well enough with a daring black cast of Louis Armstrong, Billie Holliday, and Meade Lux Lewis, and a hidden agenda designed to "break some Hollywood . . . stereotypes," to place "blacks and whites . . . together" in dramatic exchange, and to have a final cut so tightly crafted as to leave "no footage that Dixie can conveniently cut out." Indeed, their opening montage under the main titles was probably the finest piece of black history ever put into a movie, an evocative thread that carried blacks from Africa through the ordeal of "the middle passage" to America, and thence to Storyville and the founding of jazz.[83]

The Foxes of Harrow began with equal ambition, grounded as it was in a "first," a book by the black novelist Frank Yerby to which 20th Century–Fox gave a big budget, massive advertising, and presold word-of-mouth in the form of pickups by three book clubs, sales of a million-two in its first year, and a rousing bidding tourney for its movie rights. *The Boy with the Green Hair* began even more auspiciously, albeit backed by more slender means. Its makers consciously set out to make a pacifist fable in which green hair was to be a simile for brown skin. The RKO film came from no fewer than half a dozen lefties: producers Schary and Adrian Scott, writers Ben Barzman and Alfred Lewis Levitt, director Joseph Losey, and likeminded actors. In their movie a new boy comes to town bearing his stigmata because, as he says, "I am a war orphan"; thus, although he is not specifically black, nonetheless he is an Other capable of serving in two campaigns, against both racism and war. But as though lacking faith in their thrust, the film loses itself in sidebars of xenophobia, conformity, and zealotry, thereby passing up an opportunity much like that in the staging of *It Happened in Springfield*, a neat conflict of ideas, in this case perhaps a sort of children's crusade.[84]

But something happened on the way to the screen. In the case of *New Orleans* the story lapsed into conventional, safer Hollywood romance with marketable whites at its center and blacks shrinking into atmospheric roles. At best its contribution to keeping alive the politics of genre film came in the form of *Ebony*'s obligatory overpraise, which at least contributed to the pitch of audience expectation.[85]

As for *The Foxes of Harrow*, almost from the day the book came to hand Darryl Zanuck saw it for its black angle embedded in conventional plantation legend stuff. And from beginning to end it was in the hands of race-conscious people, from the writer Wanda Tuchock, who had written *Hallelujah!*, John M. Stahl, who had directed *In Old Kentucky* and *Imitation of Life*, and eventually Joe Breen, who remained an imposing arbiter of black material. In the beginning it seemed that they might turn out a real black film. Knowing Yerby and his book, black Los Angeles stood in line at cattle calls or read for the meaty parts of Achille, the rebellious slave, and La Belle Sauvage, who tries to drown her son rather than raise him a slave.

And then Zanuck began to chip away at its substance. In an early story conference in 1946, he brought the staff up short by defining the theme as a struggle for happiness while driving ruthlessly to the top—a hot topic for postwar Americans already reading Sloan Wilson's *The Man in the Gray Flannel Suit*. Thereafter, the black story in its ever-diminishing versions stirred only as though behind this white liberal scrim. Zanuck already knew the PCA would require the cutting of an "octaroon" and her liaison with the rakish hero. And as the white story loomed ever larger, one by one the black parts shrank: Tante Caleen because the PCA proscribed voodoo arcana, the slaves in order to reduce the tension between blacks and whites, a slave insurrection because interracial violence would not pass, and so on, all of it fully three months before Tuchock took up her work.[86]

The Boy with the Green Hair suffered not so much from artistic cold feet as from the takeover of RKO by the conservative Howard Hughes, which brought in its wake the cutting of an already modest budget and a new producer who, Levitt recalled, seemed to hover "around a lot." Even before, the makers lacked faith in their audience. As Paul Hollister of RKO told Scott, their pacifist angle would draw fire from "Mr. Smotcreck Wisenheimer, crying 'propaganda,' 'documentary,' etc." In the end, like the silent soldier playing pinball in *Till the End of Time*, their politics survived only in traces. True, Otherness remained central in that it motivated the heavies, but it surfaced only in the odd throwaway line as when a milkman asks the query that already made liberals wince: Would you want your daughter to marry one?[87]

In the end all of these pressures—formula, marketplace, censors, and simply the boss's taste—reflected the continuing promise of race-angled films if not their imminent arrival. In the big scene in *New Orleans*, what seems like a tidal wave of white denizens of Storyville being banished by the cops is marked only by two black figures. In *The Foxes of Harrow*, Breen had his way and gone were the wisps of anything that might have been a "Negro problem" or cause trouble in the South: not only Caleen's voodoo, but the sexual magnetism between Achille and Belle, and an embrace between a white mistress and a child-slave. And most politically weighty, "Little Inch," a slave who grew into rebellious adulthood in the book, remains a child throughout the movie. Thus Yerby's outsized overturning of the plantation legend became a formula romance whose greatest accomplishment was its one hundred and thirty black extras. Even so, a national weekly, *Time*, praised the surviving bits of "more than ordinary interest in the slaves and their lives," religion, firelight dances, the hawkers and "arabs" of the streets, and the peopling of a vast sugar estate. As for *The Boy with the Green Hair*, *Variety* greeted the remains of its original motif with an arch headline: "Boy with the Green Hair Given Shampoo."[88]

This left *Body and Soul* as the sole survivor of a tentative effort to hold open the door of hope for political film on the cusp of HUAC's return to Hollywood. The movie had everything: a shrewdly crafted script from an active lefty, a black man played with quiet strength, a John Garfield proletarian role set down in the sleazy cosmos of boxing, a *film noir* texture at the peak of its vogue, and a release date that scooped the majors. More than any other movie of its time it played a political angle with a minimum of compromise and, at least for one big scene, with a black figure at its center. It lacked only a denouement in which a black character had an investment. Not only did the movie provide a tragic black man, but unlike many political movies its makers promoted it with bold directness. In fact, Enterprise, the small independent maker,

Politically, *The Foxes of Harrow* (1947)—Frank Yerby's mauve tale of the antebellum South—suffered when Little Inch, the child of Belle and Achille, remained a child on the edge of the frame instead of growing as he did in the novel, into a rebellious adult. Copyright 20th Century–Fox.

seemed itself a sign of a new Hollywood in that in a departure from custom, Bank of America lent money to a politically focused independent. The creative team—Charles Einfeld, formerly a publicity man for the majors, young filmmakers such as Robert Wise and Don Weis, along with the men of the left, writer Polonsky and director Robert Rossen—did not fail them in an age when, as Nora Sayre wrote, soon "the topical would be profitable."[89]

They began with the boxing racket as Polonsky's analog to capitalism, Garfield's memory of life in the streets of New York, and a shared fondness for Odets's *Golden Boy,* in which Garfield had once played and in which Polonsky saw an "original sense" underneath its veneer of "literary" cachet. Yet another perhaps unconscious memory was Garfield's old performance in *Humoresque* (1946), a Warner Bros. mixture of Fannie Hurst's novel and the tailings of Odets's biopic of Gershwin into which he had woven threads of *Golden Boy.*[90]

For Ben Chaplin, the worn, braindamaged black boxer who has become trainer to Charley Davis (Garfield), they chose Canada Lee, who shared both their leftish politics and their New York roots, as well a sense of Stampp's "white men with black skins." As Lee explained, he liked the script because not only did he not need to say "Yessuh, boss," but "nowhere in the entire film is the word 'Negro' used." For Polonsky the Lee role provided an opportunity to use "a black man whose self-esteem is at stake" and a device "to use the black to defy the conventions around us." On the set the mood was one of bright hopes that both Hollywood and the audience were ready for them; as though fine-tuning, Polonsky lingered on the set as a hedge against the residue of Odets's "false notes" and to rein in any urge of Rossen's to tinker should he be carried away by the headiness of the "time of interesting ideas."[91]

As released *Body and Soul* remained true to its bleak urban landscape of prey and predators—boxers and their owners—in which men are used and discarded like implements. Charley Davis is one of the boxers, clawing his way out of the Lower East Side, taking up the values of the bigtimers and their hard women, discarding family and friends on the way up. Only Ben, the black ex-pug, clings to him like a conscience that will not be stilled. Ben's scene, the centerpiece of the movie, comes when Charley's owners arrive at the darkened camp at the end of training, hoping to separate Ben and Charley in order to focus the latter's attention on the fight they plan for him to throw. Ben refuses to leave, but under the stress he cracks and begins fighting a snarling shadow bout with himself and some long-gone opponent, until he sets loose in his brain the embolus that will kill him. At last Charley learns integrity from the dying Ben, his "last tie with decency," and wins rather than throw his last fight, which would have enriched the heavies. The movie ends on the archetypal Garfield line. "What are you gonna do, kill me?" he asks. "Everybody dies." Obviously it was Garfield's movie, but at its moral and dramatic center was the chiaroscuro performance by Canada Lee as Ben, dancing his ballet of death, the clarity of which provided the ethical bridge between the complaisant Charley and the resolute Charley. Without the sacrificial presence of the trainer, *Body and Soul* would have been only another prize ring melodrama. But a black role had made a movie *work*.[92]

What is more, moviegoers *noticed*. The makers, wondering whether the "progressive-minded" mood on the set leached into the movie, giddily heard that HUAC had branded it "subversive." The black press as well as Crowther in the *Times* caught it. "It is Canada Lee who brings to focus the horrible pathos of the cruelly exploited prize fighter," he wrote. "As a Negro ex-champion . . . he shows through great dignity and reticence the full measure of his articulate scorn for the greed of shrewd men who have enslaved him. . . . The inclusion of this portrait is one of the finer things of the film."[93]

Even in a thermidorean age, one thing leads to another. Coincident with the release, RKO bought Joseph Moncure March's *The Set-Up*, and Selznick weighed the purchase of Budd Schulberg's *The Harder They Fall*. Both were stories of boxers who lose crucial matches and title

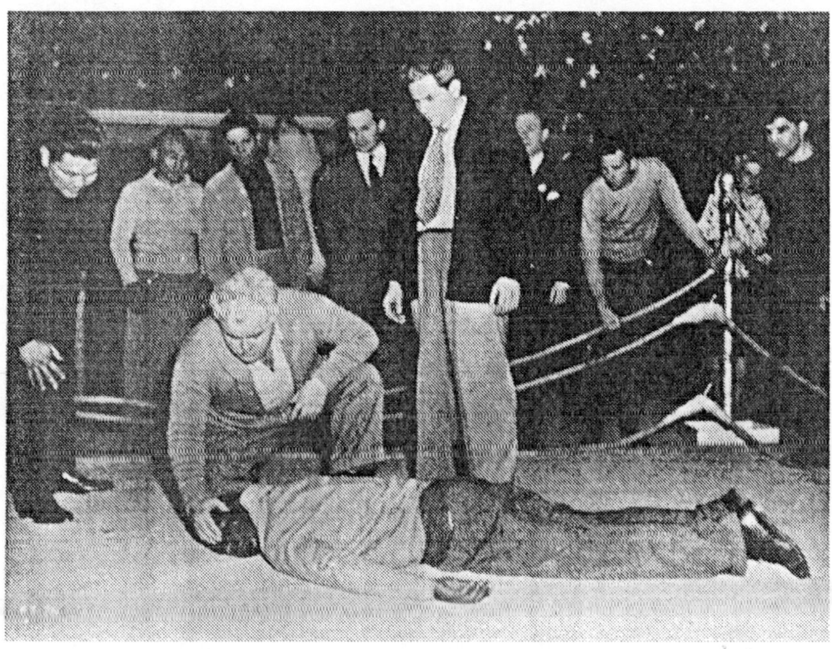

In *Body and Soul* (1948) Abraham Polonsky's script drew an acid parallel between the boxing game and capitalism by using the fallen black Ben (Canada Lee) as its victim. BFI. Copyright United Artists.

shots, the former because of his color, the latter because he is a naive Argentine giant who might well have been better played as black. Particularly in *The Set-Up*, the tension between politics and profit surfaced. At first its makers' goal was a *film noir* that revealed the bigotry visited upon blacks because they were black. As late as the fall of 1948, its intended black star, James Edwards, was portrayed in the press puffs as the star of *Deep Are the Roots* and given top billing.[94]

Then they brushed against the facts of Hollywood life: More than any other studio, RKO polled audiences in search of indicators of star quality. Along came Robert Ryan—Dartmouth alumnus, college boxer, promising actor—who had rotted in B-movies until a streak of good roles in war movies raised his profile. Next to this looming bulk was Edwards, not only unseasoned but known for his restraint rather than magnetism. Unavoidably the director, Robert Wise, saw no "black star with sufficient name value to carry the film" and, turning to Ryan, changed the story into a restrike of *Body and Soul*.[95] What an erasure: As written Edwards might have been in Garfield's role as victim of white heavies, a situation painfully close to reality, and would have tossed off the master line "everybody dies" or something like it!

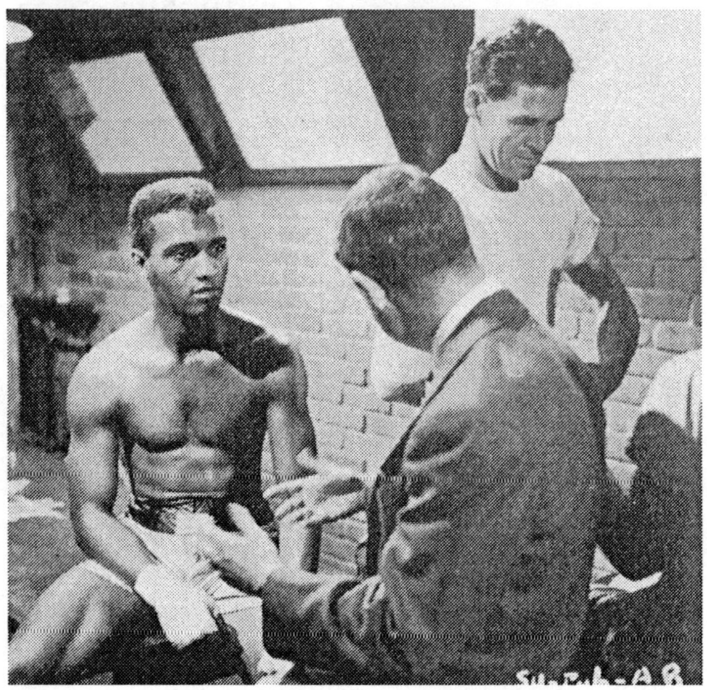

As in *Till the End of Time,* a black literary source of *The Set-Up* (1947)—a Joseph Moncure March poem—gave way to market demands, resulting in a starring role for Robert Ryan (*right*) and a supporting role for James Edwards (*left*), both here being addressed by their director, Robert Wise. Copyright United Artists.

Nevertheless, Polonsky's *Body and Soul* had introduced a black protagonist to the center of the frame, and given him a moral authority to which white people must respond. It remained for others to transform Ben's vignette into the central theme of a genre. As Polonsky recalled, when *Body and Soul* scored a hit it "delivered into our hands . . . that big Hollywood machine"—for a while, anyway.[96] During which time the message movie cycle was about to begin.

8

"A Pot of Message"

We have seen an accretion of black figures intrude into white movies, challenging the thermidorean inertia, keeping open the prospect of a moral equivalent of the war, erratically deconstructing the conventions that had located them on the margin of the movie frame, and providing a basis for the PCA to challenge Southern censors. They lacked only a formula (and perhaps a crisis to propel them), a voice of advocacy, a new calculus of dramatic questing and conflict, and of course a studio willing to take the risks, develop it within the system, and provide heroic options other than happy endings.

The moguls, being what they were—overseers of the stockholders' profits—took to heart the possibilities of *The Quiet One* and *Body and Soul* even as they searched for a riskfree means of dramatizing their political line. The vehicle they chose as a prototype was a cycle of films that attacked anti-Semitism, an unexpected tactic for moguls averse to treating the place of Jews in American life for fear that to assail bigots would only stir them to action. As in their gingerly treating black properties, at first too many story departments followed the line of a reader in Selznick's shop who in 1946 reckoned Hugh Massingham's novel of anti-Semitism *The Harp and the Oak* "a subject much too hot to handle." Yet within a year, as Garson Kanin recalled discussing with Goldwyn the future of Gwethalyn Graham's *Earth and High Heaven*, "anti-Semitism was *in*" and not only "saleable" but "fashionable."[1] In that same summer, *Variety* reported the ambiguity, first praising Schary's *Crossfire* as "a hard-hitting film whose whodunnit aspects are fundamentally incidental to the overall thesis of race bigotry," while noting in passing that RKO had decided to play it off "as whodunnit, sans any anti-Semitic reference."[2]

The moguls had struggled mightily to overcome their customary reticence toward the topic. Even Hitler could not break their silence. Zanuck's *The House of Rothschild* (1933) had succeeded in rendering Nathan Rothschild, the international Jewish banker, as a foxy grandpa, and William Dieterle's *The Life of Emile Zola*, as we have seen, managed to center its dramatic conflict on the anti-Semitism of the French army's scandalous Dreyfus case without once uttering the word *Jew*. Up to 1940, the issue was left entirely to independents such as Charles Chaplin and his parody of Hitler, *The Great Dictator*. What is more, urbane critics such as Crowther of the *Times* caught the lapse as in *The Mortal Storm*, an anti-Nazi film that coyly called Jews "non-Aryans," resulting in, said Crowther, "a lost opportunity" to tell Americans "the light in Germany went out."[3]

Once the war began, of course, the rules changed and anti-Semitism became as much a part of propaganda as had the cultivation of black loyalty. Indeed, coolly fighting beside Epps in *Bataan* was Corporal Feingold; defending the Doolittle raiders in *The Purple Heart* was Lieutenant Wayne Greenbaum; fighting beside Al Schmidt in *Pride of the Marines* was the legendary mortarman Lee Diamond; and in *Till the End of Time* a Marine slugs a bigot on behalf of a dead Jewish buddy. Even after the war they survived, although in maudlin formulas such as Al Jolson's filiopietistic biopic, the assimilationism of the remake of the quarter-century-old *Abie's Irish Rose*, and odd recapitulations of the war such as *A Walk in the Sun* and *Sands of Iwo Jima*.[4]

But underneath the surface pathos the reluctance to corner the rough beast of anti-Semitism remained, along with the fear of stirring it up. *Tomorrow the World* (1944), *The Stranger* (1946), and *The House I Live In* (1946), all wearing their liberalism on their sleeves, all ducked its implications. As we have seen, Sinatra cuts off a kid in his short film before he can say the name of the religion the urchins are persecuting. In *The Stranger* an escaped war criminal comes to a Connecticut village, but not a single citizen can cope with him and he finally dies impaled upon a clockwork condottiere in a clocktower where he has hidden. And in *Tomorrow the World* the Americans are so daunted by a refugee *Hitler Jugend* in their midst, so at a loss to win him over, so at risk of infection by his racism, that one character despairs. "If we cannot solve the problem of one Nazi child now," he says, "heaven help them after the war." The restraint was even agreed to by OWI and the AJC. When Lowell Mellett thought it "unwise from the standpoint of Jews themselves to have a picture dealing solely with Hitler's treatment of their people," the AJC agreed upon a story of Nazi rapacity directed at "all civilian populations" rather than the "particular tragedy visited upon the Jews."[5] And when Jews tried to create a Jewish advisory council in Hollywood, Mendel Silberberg, a veteran studio lawyer, warned that "it would be unfortunate if Hollywood were to place too much emphasis on Jewish issues."[6] Even after the brief cycle of Jewish themes had begun, Lyman Munson of Fox urged a prologue for overseas audiences explaining that anti-Semites were "few" and resisted by "unafraid champions." And in the story departments they routinely asked, "Are audiences ready for it yet?" To which came the routine answer: "I don't think so." Of course, critics noticed, as *Variety* did in finding, for example, *My Girl Tisa* (1947) a "Jewish 'Going My Way.'"[7]

The two most famous of the cycle almost died of institutional reluctance, coupled with the objections of the AJC, which allegedly tried to steer Warner theatres from booking *Crossfire,* and with unpromising audience samplings. Adrian Scott, the producer, and his director, Edward Dymytrk, had engaged John Paxton to adapt Richard Brooks's *The Brick Foxhole* and its homosexual murder victim into a film about a Jewish victim, to be produced at RKO under Schary's domain for a lean budget of $500,000.[8]

Despite their fears, *Crossfire* as released showed that the market would bear a conscience-liberal theme if set in a familiar style, even if, as in this case, the AJC's organ *Commentary* lashed out at its "half-baked 'progressive' catchwords . . . slipped into a routine catchpenny thriller" that surely invited the "boomerang effect" that so many Jews feared. Elliott Cohen's *Commentary* notwithstanding, the movie turned out as a good *film noir* set in a darkling urban scene where morality comes out of a wallet, women have hard edges and soft hearts, snub-nosed pistols are the only life insurance, and the saloon pianoplayer knows more history than Herodotus. A nameless, vaguely Jewish, schnook, perhaps a slacker during the war, has been bumped off. The shrewd cop assigned to the case surmises an acerbic virulence as a motive and engages a slightly cynical, modishly liberal veteran (Robert Mitchum) to trap the killer by baiting him into revealing his hatred of Jews. The result was a neat small victory: Scott and Schary publicly rebutted *Commentary* and the urban press agreed, the *Times* awarding them as "A for effort" despite a wish for a still tougher line of argument.[9] They made some money with a little movie about a social issue, earned mentions in various "best" lists, and signaled to Hollywood that, as *Variety* phrased it, "the idea that pictures on controversial subjects are questionable at the b. o. [box office] has been well beaten over the head," a point extended by Schary and Gregory Peck, star of the next film in the cycle, *Gentleman's Agreement,* in *Negro Digest* pieces in which they invoked the war as the source of the trend and called for specifically black message movies.[10]

Like *Crossfire,* 20th Century–Fox's (and Zanuck's) *Gentleman's*

Agreement began as a toughminded assault on bigotry that eroded in the process of moviemaking and was released as less "hardhitting" than it began. It was an A-movie from the beginning, under the personal supervision of Zanuck, based upon Laura Z. Hobson's Book-of-the-Month selection, with a script by the dramatist Moss Hart, and directed by Elia Kazan, a wunderkind with two hits in two tries—*A Tree Grows in Brooklyn* and *Boomerang*. They went after unusual sophistication, particularly in portraying subtle Jewish mentalities such as covert fears of "the wrong kind . . . the kikey ones who'll give us a bad name," intellectuals for whom Jewishness was no more than a state of mind and perhaps "a matter of pride," and even a character who voiced Hollywood's fear that exposure "will only stir it up again." The only thing missing was Jews; Fox was the "goy studio," and of the entire unit only Hart was Jewish.[11]

Never mind that the anti-Semite came across as so contemptibly oily that, as *Senior Scholastic* had said of *Crossfire*, "most semiconscious anti-Semites will just comfortably set themselves apart from him." The movie as released was slick and star-laden as against *Crossfire*, a mere genre film, and seemed a sign that movies could be "significant" and entertaining.[12] Even *Commentary* liked it for locating anti-Semitism in the minds of ordinary Americans rather than making it a tic of murderous crazies. Moreover, polls revealed that audiences displayed "a significantly more favorable attitude towards Jews," an angle that must have prodded black advocates of message movies. *Everyone* loved it and found it "a credit to the screen": Hedda Hopper, *Variety*, *PM*, *Hollywood Reporter*, Crowther in the *Times*, and the regional press.[13] Awards and honors followed: "ten best" lists, three Oscars, a One World Award, a Unity Award to Peck by Caleb Peterson's integrationist group in Los Angeles.[14]

The impact surely was not lost on blacks, ranging from those at Peterson's affair to those who read a *Variety* reprint in the *Sentinel* warning that "if race hatred grows in America the foundations of our society are weakened." Inside the NAACP flurries of memoranda urged new ideas and alliances with moguls from Zanuck to J. Arthur Rank in London. George Norford summed it up for his *Opportunity* readers: "Having at last mustered the courage to do films on such a controversial issue, it is but another step for Hollywood to talk about prejudice against the Negro."[15]

And Hollywood was watching. Not so much the blacks but the box office. And from the sales departments to the commissaries the studios began to build a frame of mind similar to that which had guided them during the war. Dore Schary phrased it to his salesmen in its mature form in late 1949 after the message movie cycle had moved into its full-ahead mode. As he greeted his conventioneers after taking over production at Metro, he allowed the corporate cheerleading and the parading of

Gentleman's Agreement (1948) provided a sort of shakedown cruise for message movies, even outreaching the eventual race-angled movies in their use of a wider range of Jewish characterization, caught here in several responses to anti-Semitism. BFI. Copyright 20th Century–Fox.

worthies to die down before introducing the new line, included in which was William Faulkner's racial morality tale *Intruder in the Dust*. "Don't be afraid of that term—social background," he warned. "'Crossfire' had social background, and did fine." In other words, he promised them both politics and profits as though in Culver City, at least, one could serve the Lord and get paid for it.[16]

Later that summer, I. H. Prinzmetal, a friend of Schary's in the legal department, summed up the mood in a memorandum to Schary. "Things Are Improving at Metro-Goldwyn-Mayer," he wrote as a preface to retelling a meanspirited event in 1939 when he invited a classmate named Ralph Bunche to lunch at the commissary and was turned away. "What the hell is the idea of inviting a nigger to the Commissary?" asked its manager on the telephone. "How would you like to see the Commissary full of niggers?"[17] Perhaps Prinzmetal's reminiscence was triggered by the news that after five years of postwar tinkering, Hollywood, including his own studio, had entered upon the 1949 message movie cycle. From spring through autumn of 1949 the studios brought forth Stanley Kramer's *Home of the Brave*, Louis DeRochmont's *Lost Boundaries*, Darryl Zanuck's *Pinky*, Clarence Brown's *Intruder in the Dust*, and Joseph Mankiewicz's *No Way Out*. Together they signaled the opening of an era warmed by a sense of urgency arising from not only the money being earned by *Crossfire* or *Gentleman's Agreement* but also a sense that the four years of maturing since the war placed them on the verge of the most important peacetime era of race relations since Reconstruction. Indeed, that these movies grew so quickly to seem corny and dated testified to their arrival early on in the new age.

These films became the cycle that carried the central metaphor of integrationism into the civil rights movement: the lone Negro, or small cell of them being introduced into a larger white group who would be told that they will be better for the experience. Thus the metaphor of lone black warrior thrust among a white platoon, which had been put forth as an icon of a multiethnic war effort, and blossomed into legends such as those of Colin Kelly, Meyer Levin, and Dorie Miller, was revived on the nation's screens in 1949 in a peacetime version.

Although we shall take them up as they appeared, the message movies were in no way part of a timed or planned pattern. Quite the opposite; their releases were coincidental, often rushing, even stumbling, into the theatres. However, as an evolving genre they acted like a collective solution to an aesthetic, commercial, and political problem. Although they learned little from each other, they half-formed the age they were half-formed by. They had in common only a hero who was unobtrusive, unthreatening, much like the lone westerner or *film noir* private eye who is *in* society if not always *of* it, who alters society by compelling its facing up to a character-defining incident, and who leaves them the better for it.

The writers, of course, had their hands full, adapting a formula familiar to generations of moviegoers and dime-novel readers; telling audiences that, much as the Metro commissary sensed itself "ready" for Ralph Bunche in 1947 when in 1939 it had not been so, they too were "ready." And finally, they needed to create a black culture and family into which to wrap the hero who had stood alone in 1944. No more melting pots: tossed salad perhaps, or a paint-spattered floor, or even black and white piano keys playing in harmony, but no crucibles of identity. Yet another matter of public policy—veterans' benefits—had already begun to alter the place of African Americans in the society and to provide heretofore unthinkable openness of opportunity. Even as the movies presented blacks as paragons of heroic virtue, the so-called GI Bill of Rights, through federal housing programs and its provisions for access to education and training, admitted blacks to a meritocracy in much the manner that Ardrey's *Jeb* had dramatized. Thus the movies paralleled actual social change to which Americans would need to adjust even as the movie changes half-formed other social changes yet to come.

Between the spring of 1949 and early 1950, one by one the films enacted shards of this liberal politics. In each the plot unfolded in a cleanlined narrative that took the viewer by the hand through issues, conflicts, and denouements between insistent blacks and their moss-backed white adversaries. At the center were ordinary folk who, like the audiences, were obliged to make up their minds by the last reel. Replacing the platoon or the submarine in this formula was the small town, hospital, or other social circle. Set down in its midst was the black protagonist, often so laden with virtue as to invite carping from critics who thought he tainted the message, yet, as Kramer said, so decent as to oblige the viewer to regard race as the *only* reason for discrimination. In this mode the movies asked audiences to raise their faith only a notch higher to include a black hero who teaches them that he is entitled to intrude on their monopoly of privilege, that he has been harmed by people like themselves, but that no grudge will intrude on their prospects for interracial harmony, and that the whites will be the better for the experience.

Of them all, the first into release most calculatedly drew upon the war movie genre as a basis for its inclusion of African Americans, while carrying it further into the psychic damages of racism and an anticipation of black entry into economic sectors of American life: *Home of the Brave* was its ironic title. The second release, *Lost Boundaries*, extended the formula to embrace an entire black family by setting them down in a sleepy white village. *Pinky*, the third of them, set forth the terms of integration as a Gramscian bargain in which both blacks and whites had a stake. The movie of William Faulkner's race relations fable *Intruder in the Dust* defined black experience as both entwined with white and morally superior to it, so that a conflict in which the attainment of black dignity is at stake could end with white recognition that an inflexibly honorable old Negro becomes "the conscience of us all."

After these films had their brief day, they had helped define the terms of almost every B-movie and programmer that followed, some of which introduced new and interesting complexity. One of the good B-movies, *The Jackie Robinson Story*, traced its hero's intrusion into the lilywhite preserve of major league baseball, "the national pasttime." But it also dug more deeply into black and white fears of change offset by the comforts of holding onto things as they were. A major movie of 1950, *No Way Out*, personalized the issue by hanging the dramatic conflict on the obligation of black and white middle classes to act or risk leaving the field to either white racists or black revanchists. In their ways they proposed a liberal maturing toward a healthy regard for stern consequences rather than sweetly turned endings.

As though reviewing plane geometry before introducing pupils to solid, Stanley Kramer's *Home of the Brave* arrived first and recapitulated the ideology of wartime conscience-liberalism with its central configuration, the white combat platoon into which is dropped the lone Negro who sets in motion the social drama, challenges the whites' complacent racial ideologies, marks their lives by his black presence, and in the last reel brings out, for better or worse, what the whites have within themselves. By means of his fable, Kramer linked the conscience-liberalism of the war with its extension in the age of *To Secure These Rights.* An entrepreneurial, inventive producer of New Deal-ish leaning, Kramer had learned a bit of the business in the Signal Corps and in mailrooms and offices on the movielots, but entered production only through the ranks of the proliferating independents. Joining with Enterprise, the firm that had done *Body and Soul,* he bought a property he hoped to ride in the slipstream of the cycle of anti-Semitism movies.[18]

His company resonated with a leftist sense of mission inherited from the war. The writer, Carl Foreman, spent the war maturing from Dead End Kids B-movies like *Spooks Run Wild* to working on Capra's *Why We Fight,* during which he sometimes "sat around the research department" on Western Avenue with Carlton Moss; later, at Astoria, he would become "good friends" with Kramer.[19] Mark Robson, the director, had come from Val Lewton's unit at RKO to Kramer's first hit, *Champion,* his family's conservative upbringing already leached away by his drift toward Marxism and the NAACP's "concept of fair play." Other leftists included George Glass, who would appear on one of HUAC's lists; Lloyd Bridges, a lapsed Communist; and Jeff Corey, an actor who made the lists of no fewer than three HUAC witnesses. Their financing came from a private investor, Robert Stillman, rather than from conventional Hollywood channels. They would shoot their movie in the slightly outlaw atmosphere that tight budgets demanded and in the secrecy that Kramer required both to scoop the competition and to generate attention at the right moment.[20]

But what of the script, which was, after all, Arthur Laurents's play about anti-Semitism? "Why don't we turn him into a black?" someone asked as they began to adapt Laurents to the screen. "Anti-Semitism's been done." From this perhaps too-good-to-be-true beginning, Robson and Foreman "pretty much did the script without [Kramer]," Foreman playing lefty to Robson's mediator. The script thus negotiated the rapids between the "blatant propaganda" favored by Foreman and Kramer's standing wish for a Hollywood ending—the classic Hollywood hedge against alienating the audience from its wish for the familiar. Foreman contributed a combat-shocked black soldier who spills out a lifetime of repressed rage at the climax of his "cure," while Kramer insisted on using the therapy to semaphore the liberal notion that all men are "the same." Foreman's line anticipated a future of not readily assimilated black militants, while Kramer's wrote in an escape clause through which the black hero could be integrated, a new edition of the liberal line taken during the war—that the black presence, if troublesome, was also susceptible to integration.[21]

With a script in hand, they cast James Edwards, a Knoxville College alumnus, veteran of the 92nd Division in Italy and solid experience in

Deep are the Roots. For two weeks, as planned, they shot in secret, concealing Edwards from view in the guise of a sleep-in janitor, rehearsing at home, viewing army propaganda films, waiting for their moment to expose their plot. Finally a flurry of stories on the impending cycle goaded Kramer into trumpeting their movie with "guts," while racing to beat "Pinky . . . the enemy" and other rumored rivals to the screen.[22]

By March 1949 *Variety* had broken the story of "the year of the problem pic," with *Home of the Brave* in the lead. But Kramer fretted over the final cut. At last he played it "cold" to a preview audience in the academic ghetto of Westwood near UCLA and got a four-minute standing ovation. Foreman had taken Moss as a guest to surprise him with the name of "Mossy" that he had given the hero in his honor, to which Moss responded with a plug in the *California Eagle*. Finally, Kramer thought he had something, created a black press campaign, arranged a Harlem opening at Loew's Victoria (which had bid $100,000 front money against the gross), and set it afloat. Black and white, left and right, praised it, the *Amsterdam* taking it as no less than "a new era for Negroes in Hollywood," a point taken by the "Hollywood Reporter in predicting that "the whole future of the motion picture industry" rode on the "courage and ingenuity that went into the making of *Home of the Brave*."[23]

The reason for the cheers was evident from the first glimpse of the rehabilitated war movie; there at the center of the action was Mossy, the exemplary black intruder who splinters whites into polar opposites of liberals and racists who debate his presence. His passing through their lives at a moment of profound crisis in combat forces them to encounter their racism and choose, or not, a redemptive, progressive outcome. Never mind, for the moment, that it would seem too on-the-nose.

In flashbacks evoked by narcotherapy intended to restore his traumatically paralyzed legs, Mossy's splintered memory dredges up a mapmaking sortie to a Japanese-held island, a tale broken by fragments of an adolescence spent with Finch (Lloyd Bridges), another squad member. On the beach, the stress of combat releases feelings long held in check by Mossy—of otherness, of indignation at offenses, real and imagined—feelings that threaten the unity and success of the mission. The white soldiers represent a spectrum of folkish racial politics: TJ (Steve Brodie), the brittle racist; Finch, a wellmeaning clod; and Mingo (Frank Lovejoy), a voice of liberal optimism.

At a staccato pace they complete their mission on the island, only to leave behind their map case. Mossy and Finch return for it but quarrel, with Mossy preferring to leave without it. Angrily Finch blurts, "Yellow bellied . . ." *nigger*, he means to say, but slurs it to *nitwit*. Finch is shot, captured, tortured, and left for dead as Mossy retreats alone to the beach. Later Finch crawls to the rendezvous and dies in Mossy's arms. As their boat picks them up, Mossy slips into hysterical paralysis and must be carried off the beach.

The rest of the movie is taken up in therapy conducted by a baffled doctor (Jeff Corey) who in desperation taunts him into walking by calling him "dirty nigger," thereby freeing him also to reveal what every liberal sensed: A lifetime of bigotry has made Mossy feel guilty of some nameless sin, which becomes intolerable when combined with Finch's death and the hard little nut of guilt that every soldier feels when he survives and a buddy does not. In the end, in a too neat wrapping, the formula offers up racial integration as an antidote to Mossy's *Angst.* In a value-laden two-shot, Mossy and Mingo walk away from the camera. Mingo by then has lost an arm, and Mossy helps him shoulder his duffle as they walk toward an interracial future in which, together, they will open a diner. Apart from the queasy equation that the imagery invites—a one-armed white man equals one whole Negro—the shot marked the first postwar instance of a visually argued assertion of a social *need* for "integration." Indeed, it anticipated the actual course of American racial arrangements: token blacks in the collegiality of the workplace marked American life long before social distance narrowed in any other setting.

The readership of every black newspaper, in case they missed it in the movie, felt this political angle thrust upon them. The black press ran every puff that George Glass fed them; Walter White called the film "photographed living [that] would find an audience in more enlightened areas"; *Ebony* gave it four pages with stills and praised it for its ploughing "new ground [and] pioneering"; the church paper *Dallas World* broke custom and endorsed it; and writers to the NAACP said it was "four star" and promised to "recommend it highly for its artful gilding of the message in entertaining terms."[24]

On the left, among the ruins of the idea of a black nation, it was easy to sneer at Kramer's eventually famous obviousness, his straight line drawn from first reel to last-reel fulfillment, his commercial sense, and his flawless black token whose rectitude was said to garble the issue and who lacked a single link to, as Marxists said, "the Negro people." V. J. Jerome, the ranking CPUSA cultural critic, for whom integration was mere bourgeois reformism that diverted energy from specific black grievances, thought the movie failed for the precise reason that liberals liked it: Mossy was "no different" from the white soldiers. This even as he enjoyed Mossy's assertiveness, which seemed to erupt organically from "the pressure of the Negro people's movement for equality." In a twist on the same theme the *Worker* ran a letter from Mel Williamson arguing that TJ's uncritical hatred of *everyone* undercut the status of the Negro as a special case. From another leftist angle came the complaint that racial problems seemed solved whenever, as Manny Farber wrote, blacks were tamed by "the rules of the stuffiest white gentility," or, as Warren Miller

In the last reel of *Home of the Brave* (1949), as a sign of recovery, Mossy (James Edwards) joins his white amputee-buddy (Frank Lovejoy) in a partnership, inadvertently inviting a reading that one complete black soldier equaled a damaged white one. BFI. Copyright United Artists.

put it, "once the Negro can be made 'to understand' that the color line is artificial, [and] he can therefore forget its terrible reality." Neither, of course, converted the other, although Glass had solved it in the press kit, at least, by having it both ways. "Mossy," he wrote, "understood the sameness of men, and in understanding the sameness was prepared to fight the artificial barriers." But the left stuck to its point that the "sameness" angle made "it easier for an audience to ignore the special character of the oppression of the Negro people." Of course, this insular debate passed unnoticed in the general press, which tried on for size its new suit of civilian liberalism, as *Life* did in chiding Kramer's "unconvincing" tone but liking his liberal epiphany when "Mossy realizes that despite his color he is no different from other men."[25]

Americans everywhere, North or South, black or white, urbane or folkish, generally liked the movie. Southerners approved because its generically American soldiers allowed viewers to see racism as national rather than Southern in nature. According to the *Defender*, moviegoers from Texas to Richmond in a hundred towns saw it in record numbers, a trend reflected in an *Amsterdam News* story of a wire sent by a Southern booker to UA: "Sensational results in spite of terrific heat wave." And as though ratifying the message, conscience-liberals everywhere from Jewish War Veterans to the Canadian Mental Hygiene Assoication gave

Home of the Brave a shelf full of awards for "outstanding achievement in . . . race relations."[26]

But apart from its independent source and its booming reception, the most important new trait that marked the movie was its classical Hollywood pedigree. All along the line from script to screen it bore the marks of institutional life: the Breen office, the tradepapers, regional censors, preview respondents, distributor feedback, critics. In effect, the entire infrastructure of the industry signaled its readiness to resume the retailing of race-angled material the war had once made necessary. Not that this was the blindly courageous stroke they soon would credit themselves with: They had already made richly promising test-drillings during the cycle of anti-Semitism movies. In other words, though they were on an uncharted course that required new ways of doing business, they knew what they were doing.

Joe Breen himself spoke from the same mentality rather than customary wariness. Cut *jigaboo* and *shine* from the script, he told Glass, not for the simplistic reason of avoiding affront, but to build tension through insult yet "not offend by the quantity of insults." Indeed, the PCA wanted its share of credit for striking a blow for liberalism by persuading Glass to cut from the ad copy a headline that charged Hollywood with having no "Guts." The local censors also went along: in Memphis in a "surprise move," in Atlanta because the movie was a story of universal decency rather than a specific plea to end Southern custom, and in Maryland because the board followed the lead of a panel of advisers drawn from interracial commissions, the rabbinate, the NAACP, and the NUL. Reinforcing the relaxed censorship was a brochure sent out by United Artists with their press agents, who had "special training" in selling the new line. Furthermore, at the top of the MPAA Eric Johnston committed his office with such effect that an early report cited only a single censor in Capetown, South Africa, who balked at playing it. The thin sample of surviving preview responses confirms the timeliness of these departures from past practice: More than half praised the movie, and only one-tenth said "it stinks."[27]

By any measure, then, *Home of the Brave* had become a *beau idéa* of the new Hollywood. It had spoken not only for the liberal center, thereby achieving the goals of its makers, but also for conservatives groping toward adopting their own version of Stampp's hope that "Negroes *are,* after all, only white men with black skins." That is, Kramer's group attained what Hollywood story editors had been tinkering with for four years: a commercial movie laden with racial politics in an entertaining formulaic equivalent to the war movie genre, thereby sidling toward defining the imagery and agenda of the integrationist generation to come.[28]

Not that every formulation of the emerging genre was fated to be an apt one. Louis DeRochemont's *Lost Boundaries* (1949) for example, strayed from the formula adopted by *Home of the Brave*. DeRochemont, already taking up features in the last years of his *March of Time* series, chose an impossibly ambiguous *Reader's Digest* condensed book about a family that had "passed for white," a covert practice that had always raised mixed feelings in both races. Fortunately Walter White, seeking to keep up momentum, praised the script as "one of the finest . . . and certainly the most courageous treatment of the Negro in motion pictures to date."[29]

The idea began just after the war with a chance meeting between DeRochemont and a lightskinned student in the former's hometown in New Hampshire. After the student confessed to only just learning of his Negro ancestry after a lifetime of passing, DeRochemont took the story to *Reader's Digest*, where writer William L. White put it into an inspirational magazine piece and then a thin book. DeRochemont thus provided an ideal link between journalism and Hollywood, where his firm had recently joined with Metro to make modish dramas in the style of neo-realism. He lacked only a liberal amanuensis, since DeRochemont seemed to a close associate "not a crusader but a newsman" whose conscience-liberalism extended mainly to a vague sense of "fair play." At best they might get only an OWI tract done in the mock-journalistic style of a current cycle of location-shot films like *Naked City*.[30]

By May 1948, with their rivals already under way, they had a script that revealed the dramatic enigma at the heart of White's book that militated against good cinema. Passing, after all, was a passive even covert act rather than a heroic gesture, a point strongly taken in an advisory letter from Ralph Ellison whose novel *The Invisible Man* was soon to appear. How could their protagonists act heroically if they lacked the will to assert their own identity, asked Ellison. Things merely happen to them, he pointed out. Only a tougher hero, a doctor who is forthright, energetic, and clearly the master of his milieu, and willing to make the decision to break with passing could save the movie. Only then, wrote Ellison, might the audience feel the ambiguity with which racism tinged all social intercourse. Other correspondents agreed, including one who asked if it were not better to show that whites contributed to black malaise by means of their own racial exclusivity. As the script drafts inched toward a more active voice in order to accommodate to these suggestions, they revealed fissures within the company that the comforting passivity of White's book had masked. Two trusted Southerners in DeRochemont-*Reader's Digest* (LD-RD) revealed the stakes. Johnny Barnwell fretted over a more accusatory script, feeling it would "damage . . . [white] people you will never know," to which Borden Mace, the firm's North Carolinian vice-president, replied that "the 'damage' in my opinion might be beneficial."[31]

In October, Metro turned to Leo Handel's opinion-sampling firm for guidance and, despite hints that city dwellers might accept their film, early in 1949 broke off with LD-RD over, as *Ebony* reported, "the handling of the Negro theme." Coincident with their newfound independence, Walter White pressed upon them his own wish for a movie that would become a "desired yardstick" against which to measure the forthcoming cycle. He even predicted success despite the South's lingering objection to "the Negro in other than menial or comic roles."[32]

Lacking a leftist of Foreman's ideological rigor, they plugged away at it through the spring, struggling over the details of black bourgeois portrayals. The script passed through no less than three writers, each in his turn softening the line of argument at the behest of the various readers. By the time shooting started they had picked as director Alfred Werker, who had once done a neat biopic of Disraeli but who came cheap in 1949 and promised at least a sincerely honest picture. By then they had scraped together a nut of less than $500,000 from their new distributor Film Classic and about $30,000 from LD-RD and other sources.[33] But they had lost benefits such as the cash crop that the connection with the Loew's theatres branch of Metro would have given them—not to mention the fruits of a high-energy Leo the Lion ad-campaign.

Undaunted, by May they managed a rough cut and hoped to mix and score in time for the Cannes Film Festival and a playoff in the heat of August. Then, too late to matter, they showed it to Walter White, who gave them a lesson in racial politics that harked back to his meagre goals of 1942—he asked only for "decent areas and people"—rather than forward to the impending cycle of race-angled movies. Too full of Harlem squalor, he wrote, symbolized by "a zoot-suited, shifty looking character paring his finger nails in front of the boarding house."[34]

As released, *Lost Boundaries* seemed sincere but detached, centering on a lot of white people ennobled by the decent black folk thrust by circumstance into their midst. Coming as it did forty days after *Home of the Brave,* it suffered by comparison, its lilywhite Negroes rendering moot any substantive issue of racial politics, its own cutter still wishing for meatier stuff that would wrench an audience out of complacency. Yet blacks, as White had done, fretted over portraying black and white life as polar opposites—staid, white New Hampshire and sleazy, black Harlem.[35]

Implicitly, *Lost Boundaries* slighted the ideology that White and his circle had cultivated during the war: admission of African Americans to full citizenship by portraying them as rooted in society in a range of roles and entitled to their Double V—a victory over homegrown racism as a *result* of victory in war. Instead, the war propaganda had been turned on its end. White forebearance was asked only toward people as light-skinned as themselves; blacks were mere ciphers with no stake in the game, which they had already won by *acting* white; all the blacks too dark to pass seemed heavies bent upon blocking Dr. Carter (the hero) on his way to lilywhiteness. The scenes that carried these burdens were

Lost Boundaries (1949) managed to be about race relations while placing blacks (William Greaves, here) on the rim of the action—a blocking made possible by focusing on "passing" rather than race. Copyright Film Classics/ Louis De Rochemont.

startling in their usurping the asserted goals of its makers. To account for the Carters' New Hampshire residence, for example, there is the big scene of the doctor's rejection as resident in a Southern *black* hospital because he is too light and Yankeefied. A Harlem sequence designed to depict his son's search for roots is little more than a descent into hell that visually echoes the red-light district in the Army's VD film *Easy to Get*. And finally, in New Hampshire in the last reel the white people are the central figures, founts of Christian virtue who are so warm and well meaning that blacks lost their place at the center of the movie. The resulting reverse spin put on the theme blunted DeRochemont's good intentions: The true protagonists are white people whose virtue is merely tolerating their "white" neighbors upon learning they are "black"; the blacks might as well have been dents in a fender—rendered acceptable when smoothed and repainted; the denouement blinks at the politics of race, leaving the point only that white people are gatekeepers and none but the most stuffily "white" Negroes may pass their admission test. Indeed, the latter notion is the topic of a last-reel sermon as they walk down the aisle of a church in all their whiteness: "Citizenship," the preacher says, is "henceforth extended to all qualified citizens regardless of race or color."

Yet critics hungry for the latest in the message movie cycle cheered loudly, perhaps more than for any other film in the litter. *Life* named it Movie of the Week, setting off a round of raves, brotherhood awards, and hopes by DeRochemont that independents at last would receive recognition for showing how to introduce low budget pictures into the Hollywood system. The Cannes festival, the Los Angeles NUL, seemingly everyone joined in praising, as the Writers Guild said, its "ably dealing with the problems of the American scene." Partly, it must be said, this praise may have arisen from the liberals' sense that they were quietly winning against strident enemies and therefore "prejudice [was] . . . not a subject for harangue."

On the left they were less sure. Crowther in the *Times*, for instance, wrote that "it touches the immediate anxieties of only a limited number of Negroes [and] it may even be regarded by some Negroes with a certain distaste." The Communists pounced upon the same point, José Yglesias grumbling at the "most conventional, the most unreal middle class people" who led audiences to a "sentimental and shallow" empathy that excluded ordinary blacks, a point taken by V. J. Jerome in arguing that the Harlem sequence served only as background against which to contrast the virtue of the fairskinned elite.[36]

Blacks were also uncertain of their critical ground. How could they praise Hollywood for small favors while pointing out the irrelevance of the movie to the general case? Predictably there were raves: ANP found it a "classic"; an *Afro* executive said it "brought tears to my eyes." But *Home of the Brave* had raised hopes for a tougher politics of movies. Lillian Scott in the *Defender*, for example, made sure to praise the "excellent" actors who carried the movie beyond "Hollywood boundaries of mediocrity and fear" but chided DeRochemont for his "less than painfully honest" Southern sequence and his failure to "grapple too strenuously with the issues raised." Even Bob Ellis in the *Eagle*, often a flack for Hollywood, demanded black characters "like everyone else . . . bobbysoxers and young puppy lovers and respectable community members and church-goers." That is, he fell back to White's position of 1942 and asked for inclusion, not for hothouse plants living in isolated splendor at the pleasure of whites. It was left to the actual doctor on whom the original story was based to supply Ellis with the only-then-surfacing missing ingredient: the stuff of black life. "In spite of all that I have accomplished as a white man, I have, more or less, an empty life," he said.[37] On the black left, Fredi Washington, who had interviewed for a role, told her friends to expect nothing from Werker, who seemed uninterested in serious readings, nor from DeRochemont, who seemed disingenuous in claiming he was doing a "documentary." As released the movie merely confirmed for her that Werker had been prejudiced especially for "his handling of the Harlem and Southern Negro hospital scenes."[38]

But the attacks suddenly lost their sting. As though destiny's toy, *Lost Boundaries*, became a point at issue between Southern censors and the odd couple of the MPAA and the NAACP. Thus no matter that its theme split the audiences it had set out to reach; when Southerners attacked it there was little choice but to close ranks and accept it as the prize in a struggle against political censorship. At first, when Borden Mace of LD-RD took it to the PCA in Kramer-like secrecy, Breen had found it a "pleasure" that required not a single cut. Therefore, when Memphis and Atlanta insisted on cuts, LD-RD found itself in the van of the PCA, the ACLU, the NAACP, jurists led by the New Dealer Samuel I. Rosenman, and the Society of Independent Motion Picture Producers. Its movie had become the central issue in a debate over free expression versus the right to suppress in the name of "peace, morals, and good order."[39]

The case dragged on into the 1950s, when *Lost Boundaries* opened in the last of the markets to which it had been denied access and as a result earned a viewership far in excess of its modest pretentions. LD-RD and its allies had aggressively charged the censors with "overstepping their police functions," thereby denying movies "the basic guarantees" of freedom of expression. Never mind that eventually the Supreme Court let stand the decisions of Southern courts that had found in favor of the censors. The notoriety certainly must have boosted sales, raised hopes for punchier racial stuff in the future, and drawn the black press back into a concern for movies. "Despotism," cried one editor. Far from "good order" being the issue, said the *Afro*, it was really Southern fear of "social equality." Thereafter, the press all but made censorship cases a regular beat, reporting on every fissure in the system such as whenever Christine Smith's bosses on the Atlanta Library Board overturned her decisions.[40]

As a result, the fame of *Lost Boundaries* not only persisted but probably enhanced the prospects of its successors in the cycle. Certainly it added to its lists of "bests," its fans who wrote letters commending its "brotherhood of man" argument, and even its fair to good grosses. Even in the South it earned its keep, going five days in Raleigh and six in West Memphis, where Matty Brescia, a Memphis theatreman and member of the Tennessee Civil Rights Committee, played it just out of reach of "this whacky and screwy censor—Binford." Elsewhere in the South they played it off gingerly against "local disapproval" of the "ticklish picture" or, like the manager of the Carolina Theatre in Chapel Hill, played off hoping it was the last of its genre. At LD-RD they bubbled, congratulating themselves on their courageous work that had, as Borden Mace wrote: "helped *condition* people to see injustice."[41] Hyperbole aside, a little movie, partly because of circumstances outside of its not entirely clear text, had made a point of sorts.

Not until *Pinky* (1949) later in the year would the full force of a major studio be applied to the genre. Darryl Zanuck, Fox, and downtown movie palaces all would be marshaled in the trend that so far had the claustrophobic look of B-movies. With *Pinky,* liberalism entered the big time. "Let's give 'em controversy with class," said the boss, Spyros Skouras. "Shock America, Darryl."[42] And so they did, to applause, still more awards and honors, and the first systematically reasoned criticism of the undemanding minimalist changes put forth by message movies.

For the first time a message movie would owe its substance to direct black intervention on the lot, an outcome prayed for by Walter White ever since 1942. The result was the stiffening of a politely liberal novel, Cid Ricketts Sumner's *Quality,* into an intricate fable of integrationist politics. At the center of this tempering process was Walter's own daughter Jane White, an aspiring actress and, as it turned out, a forceful script doctor who with Philip Dunne, a veteran conscience-liberal, shaped a story of Southern race relations into a depiction of a cohesive black community that had not been seen since the war or perhaps even *Hallelujah!* And over Zanuck's resistance Dunne and White injected a fragmentary black position with respect to integration. The scale of their project, its probe into centers of black thought and character, and the risk involved in bungling a lightskinned heroine who might seem a patch of pure white paint spoiled by a drop of black, led to a chain of rewrites beginning in 1948 with Richard G. Hubler's merely faithful draft, other pages by Oscar-winning Dudley Nichols, Zanuck, and White, and finally, in the fall of 1949, Dunne's shooting script.[43]

At first they were yoked to Sumner's characters, each of whom spoke for a point of view: Jake, an older black New Deal-ish sort; Arch, a radical journalist from the North who drives a car, wears a beret, and has a well-modulated voice, light skin, and a writing style that sets alight black political demands; Miss Em, a dying white matriarch with a maternal respect for "colored people" and an old woman's sense of the rightness of old ways; Pinky, a lightskinned nurse who feels trapped among them but who may opt out of the debate by marrying white and moving north; Dicey, her dark grandmother who knows ancient things; and various black doctors and white judges, and townspeople who lend variety and spice to the politics. Of course Arch and Miss Em are the polar opposites, and in the early drafts Pinky brings them face to face in a master scene intended to focus *their* debate and sharpen *her* politics.

In the original and in the early drafts the rightwingers have all the good lines. Jake swaggers about, boasting of the coming jobs and integration, and of an end to servile manners. But when Pinky asks how, he lamely replies that he and his friends up North were working on it. Then under her withering gaze he admits he is merely running his mouth to no purpose. Later he is shown to be even more of a scapegrace when he is tried for bilking Pinky out of money, and plays a shameless "Tom" to a white judge who lectures him on the need for black leaders who are able to cooperate with white people. Arch, at least before he slowly evaporates in the ensuing drafts, speaks out for federal agencies sent to protect the civil rights that he had fought for in the late war, but in the end he is as impotent as Jake. On the right, both Dicey and Miss Em stand up for the old ways. For Dicey, dependence on the New Deal was only a return to slavery, while for Miss Em the antidote to the plight sketched by Arch is a Booker Washington solution to raise up blacks chained by ignorance and poverty. As Miss Em says, Pinky is trained to do something useful for a future black society, when blacks will have their own school boards, police, and hospitals. In the end, she delivers her theory in the form of a legacy with which Pinky is expected to create "Miss Em's Hospital and Nursing Home for colored people"—an institution changed in the final draft to a clinic and nursery, complete with black staff.[44]

How could Zanuck save this creaking property, particularly after having hired Nichols, a frequent collaborator with the Catholic conservative, John Ford, whom he had engaged as director? They seemed baffled by the problem of adapting Sumner to the racial politics of 1949. Their best idea was a courtroom scene in which Pinky contends for her legacy, which is challenged by Miss Em's family; in this way the trial becomes a test of Southern justice and its impact on skeptical blacks. If she wins, she has the means to work within the system; if she loses, she joins Arch's radical party.[45] Good, clearcut case and a solid center of dramatic conflict. But by June 1948 they were still snared in Sumner's Jeffersonian liberalism that required from the black characters more forebearance than choice. Moreover, Zanuck and his trusted stenographer Marilyn Mandeville still saw two lines of converging conflict: the struggle over Pinky's inheritance as well as a fraternal black debate between Arch and Pinky, not to mention a sidebar argument between Arch and the fading Miss Em. If for no other reason, Zanuck liked Arch as Pinky's agent provocateur without whom she lacked a debating partner. In fact by July he hoped to toughen Arch's line because Miss Em was winning their encounters. In the ensuing draft they actually part as respectful adversaries, he claiming he would rather die than submit to humiliation, she insisting that he demanded everything too fast.

Unfortunately, this promising electric exchange was dropped and its substance remained as no more than a throwaway line, because Pinky wins in court not only without Arch's intervention but solely as a vindication of Southern white justice. By September Nichols and Zanuck, having no more use for Arch's radical black nationalism, gave some of his lines to Pinky so as to sharpen the conflict between her and the white litigants seeking to recover Em's legacy. In this way, they focused

Pinky's politics on a real issue and gave her a nugget of inner rage without reference to Arch the outsider. She is even made witness to a near-lynching complete with baying hounds and vigilantes breaking in her door as a source of a keener black consciousness. Her line expressing her rising social vision is uttered as she slumps on Miss Em's now empty bed, pleading with her memory for help—help, she asks, in how to use this house for "my" people, for "all" people.[46] In the release print, the line is even better used by making it the clincher in the debate with her suitor who has asked her to do as he has done: run from racism to Denver where no one will know and "there will be no Pinky Johnson."

As though at the end of his tether, Zanuck sent this draft off to New York to be read by Jane and Walter White, the NAACP staff, and Walter White's fiancée, the journalist Poppy Cannon. White quickly gave political perspective to this gesture in a note to Zanuck: "It begins to look as though what you and Wendell and I have been working for all these years is beginning to show results."[47] At first they lit into the script, White hoping to steer them toward a recognition of the war as a source of change, indeed an "important revolution in the thinking of Southern white people, particularly students and veterans." But Roy Wilkins and the others, less aware of changes already made, bristled at its "female Uncle Tom" and the "underlying theme that agitation is wrong . . . [that] good-will will eventually correct matters, and—most dangerous of all—[that] segregation should be accepted." Only ruthless rewriting, Wilkins insisted, could stiffen Pinky's "lack of militance."[48] Of course, he had missed previous drafts that had puffed Pinky's rising racial social conscience, but so too would an audience.

In any case, Zanuck was at a loss, angry, and torn among the script, the NAACP's "militant propagandist attitude," and the stockholders and theatremen who held the real influence and power. He lashed out at his New York polemicists in ten densely packed pages in which he snapped at their "poisonous" rhetoric and "impatient and scornful" barbs, but left open a faint hope that Jane White's "experience in the theatre" would restore their balance and form the basis for "constructive criticism" that would sharpen Pinky's urge for "militant action" as against Miss Em's stand "for 'slow reform,'" thereby shortening the odds that their picture might be completed and "prove beneficial to the cause of the American Negro."[49]

Zanuck persisted, reminding them that the conscience-liberalism that had risen during the war had been an organically white-angled phenomenon and that whites were the target of his *Pinky*. Success would come only if the movie made "the white majority of the United States experience emotionally the humiliation and hurt and evil of segregation and discrimination . . . [and] carry away a sense of shame [so] . . . their feeling and thinking will be changed." To accomplish this when they resumed work in the fall of 1948, Zanuck dropped

Nichols and took on Dunne and Jane White as script carpenters.[50] Working separately, Jane mainly on weekends, they saved Nichols's best stuff: his Southern texture; his drawling, untidy, querulous folk; the peeling wallpaper, shabby coaches, and dirt roads that contrasted with glimpses of a clean, well-lighted North. As for Pinky, they at once brought her into sharper relief while enfolding her in a wider black circle (minus Arch). She is given a line of development. At first not allowed to feel anything for the old black woman, Dicey, she soon draws closer, a visual image sharpened by her encounter with two black kids on the road to darktown to whom she forthrightly identifies herself as colored. And later, like Saul on the road to Tarsus, she cries out her conversation to Miss Em: at last she has begun thinking black![51]

By New Year's 1949, Dunne had tried two drafts, which pleased neither Zanuck nor the blacks, who had been shaken by the "Dixiecrat" movement and Truman's near-defeat in November. Indeed, the industry itself fretted over Truman's increasing racial activism. Two Breen office men early on discussed the script on the telephone and whether "some might accuse the industry of lining up with" the sentiments expressed in *To Secure These Rights*, resulting in an anti-Hollywood "agitation [that] might endure for several years" and implicate the industry, and invite Southern reprisals in the form of renewed censorship and even Ku Klux Klan activism. Petrified at the thought of giving comfort to censors, they considered advising Fox to avoid "trouble spots" in booking the South as a hedge against "the danger of censorship," an important tactic to weigh in their view because they guessed (erroneously) that women's clubs that had provided word-of-mouth for *Gentleman's Agreement* had no counterpart in black circles or (even more erroneously) in any urban, liberal or Jewish networks.[52] On the Fox lot itself, unknown to either the blacks or the PCA, they were equally petrified. First, there was the conservative Ford and what might become of Pinky's black sensibility in his hands. In this political setting Dunne readily saw Jane White's arrival as "valuable insurance," and apparently so did the studio if its whirl of welcoming delights—a shopping tour, a liveried driver, and a room at the Sunset Towers—was meant as a sign. For their part, the Whites regarded the invitation to Jane as a vindication of Walter's decade of campaigning against an array of ideological enemies. In a whimsical letter to Poppy Cannon, Walter teasingly hoped Hollywood glamour would not taint Jane's judgment, but in a more somber voice feared a script that might displease everyone: the Hollywood Negroes, the CPUSA, and the African American press.[53]

On paper, at least, the collaboration went swimmingly. As Jane White and Dunne worked their way through the pages, anonymous marginalia testified to their little victories. "Good point—shall be covered," someone, perhaps Dunne, would say. "Thank you," said the scrawl. "Changed . . . Guilty as charged," and so on down the margins. And not merely on bits of local color, but substantive points such as the tension between Pinky's blackness and her Southernness. The points grew even finer: "No matter how *educated* she is, she is still *colored.*" "Exactly," conceded the voice in the margins, as they pressed to finish by February in time for Ford's scheduled start of shooting. By then Jane White had done all she could and wished only that she might have saved some "dark-skinned Southern negro characters" to manifest the forthright militance that Arch had once brought to the script.[54]

Even so, inertial forces chivvied the work. Back east, the Dixiecrat movement had not healed, and Truman, as yet unsworn, barely survived the election. In the Breen office, they still pressed for accommodation wherever the film might be "unacceptable" to the South. And on the lot there was Ford, who already sized up Pinky's role as "an aristo in a tumbril" going to her doom and her Aunt Dicey as an "Aunt Jemima" ever ready to burst into song. He was a "shock treatment," recalled Waters, and so cruel "I almost had a stroke."[55]

Zanuck, protecting his investment in the work White and Dunne had achieved, decided to replace Ford before *his* politics colored the ideas of the others. Allowing the famous, almost sacred, veteran to plead illness, Zanuck turned to Elia Kazan, a product of the radical Group Theatre and Frontier Films, and a tyro who had to his credit four solid movies in four attempts: including Zanuck's own *Gentleman's Agreement.* Kazan's only—at the moment, inconsequential—liability was that Jack Warner in 1947 had told HUAC that he was a "subversive." With respect to *Pinky* he was pragmatic, at best hoping only to avoid "taking a subject which has got dynamite in it and castrating it," but also feeling he had inherited "crap" and a star who seemed not only white but *too* white—"white in her heart" even.[56]

Despite Kazan's worst fears *Pinky* turned out as a passably good commercial expression of the conscience-liberal formula, an ideological heir to the war movie genre, and an extension of it deeper into black circles. In fact, long before the NAACP's *Brown vs. Topeka Board* case called attention to the courtroom as civil rights arena, Pinky spoke for her black community by carrying its interests into the dramatic setting of a Southern courthouse. Moreover, she did so without trotting out the gothic stereotypes that passed for white Southerners in most movies. And though they did not shoot on location as Kazan, for one, wished, they neatly caught a Southern mood in everything from dress extras to local color sets.

More than anything, *Pinky* offered a plot in which something *black* was at stake: the core-conflict in which Pinky struggles to bring a black clinic into being. This dramatic center is given deeper meaning by having Pinky return to the South, undecided about remaining, indeed undecided about marrying into the white world, and so untutored in Southern racial arrangements that she is at a loss as to who she is and where

Of all the message movies, *Pinky* (1949) came closest to facing up to the gulf between the races and black strategies for dealing with it: the options represented here by Ethel Waters, Jeanne Crain, and William Lundigan—images of tradition, black consciousness, and "passing." Copyright 20th Century-Fox.

she fits in. It is here that her white suitor (William Lundigan) pleads for flight to the West where "there will be no more Pinky Johnson," to which she counters in a closeup, "You can't live without pride." Old Aunt Dicey wishes her to nurse the dying Miss Em (Ethel Barrymore) in her big house in an almost ritual farewell to the patrician South, to which Pinky agrees after establishing a coolly professional rather than servile association. From her black connections—old, handkerchief-headed Dicey, the unctuous petit bourgeois Jake (Frederick O'Neal), the knife-toting, wenchy Rozelia (Nina Mae McKinney), the cerebral Dr. Canady (Kenny Washington)—she learns the variety and shrewdness of black tactics for dealing with the daily grind of racism and chooses the courthouse path that the NAACP had come to prefer as a strategy.

As she studies her options, Pinky nurses Miss Em to the dignified death that earns her a place in the old woman's will: the inheritance of the big house that she will transform into "Miss Em's Clinic and Nursery School." First, however, she must win the house in court against the challenge of Miss Em's greedy relations, a drama often read as the assertion of white paternalism rather than black resistance. In any case, Pinky understands that even if Miss Em's legacy echoed a white *noblesse oblige* it *also* allowed her to create what will become a black *and* Southern institution under the tutelage and control of black Dr. Canady and nurse Pinky Johnson. A last reel, sweeping crane-shot pulling away from the house, its identifying sign, and its happy children affirms this essentially black solution on Southern ground.

This reading of the film takes a black nationalist line, an angle not always seen by critics, even those who had been made sharply attentive to black politics as the message movie cycle matured. The more popular centrist reading of the film as a plea for racial harmony, coupled with its being a big, plump major movie by the most major of the oldline studios and its rapid obsolescence as a result of the pace of the impending civil rights movement, should not be allowed to blur the accomplishment of *Pinky*'s makers. They had taken up the abrasive issue of racism, and given it a dramatic conflict with real black stakes in its outcome, set in real courtrooms, centered on a character who engaged the loyalties of both blacks and whites who together acted out plausible futures of race relations without rubbing the noses of the losers in their defeat.

Given this complex fabric, almost all critics missed something, particularly those whose antennae locked onto signals of Hollywood's traditional cupidity. Crowther, ever in search of a flash of liberalism, liked "all its virtues" but winced at the "passion for paternalism" and the "'old mammy'" that it "extolled" under its breath. Other liberal voices found it affirmed Southern resistance to change, a South African paper judging it an "endorsement of apartheid." The black press took the same course, finding it, as the *Defender* did, "'meaty' entertainment" but mounted on "shock absorbers," or as had the *Eagle*, a "false picture which had good scenes in it." Thus for every viewer who regarded it as a sign of Hollywood's "growing up," another such as Cab Calloway thought it so opaque that "all too few white people will realize its purpose . . . or sympathize with it." *Ebony*, taking into account such misgivings, reckoned that on balance "the key to the Pinky role is the growth of racial awareness" during the film.[57] Although white critics were friendlier, like Crowther even as they praised it as "socially significant" they damned it where it "shirks the true colour problem." As Elspeth Grant archly put it in the *London Graphic*, "Having taken [racism] up, Mr. Zanuck seems to put it down again exactly where he found it."[58] Apart from needling an industry "that doesn't employ Negroes," even the Marxist left followed the same line, V. J. Jerome, for example, admiring the ominous Southern ambience as "the sharpest of its kind" in the genre, and delighting in "a great, overpowering moment of film realism" when two cops learn that Pinky is colored and reprogram their etiquette accordingly. But Miss Em and the fairminded judge seemed figments of "the good white fairy of Hollywood." *Variety* liked the way its "Americanism" fought racism without resort to "the slimy tactics of

Communists," most certainly an incantation to ward off the fear that HUAC would try to link all reformism to the cunning of the CPUSA.[59]

The uneven critical response aside, *Pinky* more than any other message movie had taken on a mantle of dignity derived from both its source in a major studio and its playing off in the picture palaces, an aura that may have benefited the liberal cause that had faced a bit of a scare in Truman's narrow victory on a platform that had included the substance of *To Secure These Rights*. Even the censors treated *Pinky* with circumspection; the PCA simply let drop a suggestion by its house Southerner, Francis Harmon, that Pinky be related to a known white man as though conforming to old Southern etiquette obliging decent treatment of colored offspring of miscegenist unions. Parallel to its release, the MPAA had already decided to challenge in court any cuts by state censors based upon race. And as to the PCA's own code, studios began arguing that its own miscegenation clauses were unenforceable. And in New York, Walter White offered the NAACP as yet another *amicus curiae* in the many cases making their ways to the Supreme Court. For her part, Christine Smith in Atlanta caught the trend and even joined it. "I know this picture is going to be very painful to a great many Southerners," she said, "but at the same time it will make them realize how unlovely their attitudes are." Even in Memphis it suffered the loss of only a few moments of impending violence. Thus cuts were made in only a few places where, said the *Defender*, "illiteracy rules" and even these were overturned by courts that upheld the right to show films "which are in aid of better race relations"—as the NAACP described a Marshall, Texas, decision.[60]

Pinky and its cohorts may even have, like all movies, half-formed the social behavior they were half-formed by. In Atlanta, for example, exhibitors weighed higher grosses over racial etiquette in declaring formerly white-only seats "open to Negroes." Indeed, in the South and in the nation *Pinky* boomed, earning four million dollars by year's end, much of which came from blacks who had broken family rules against sitting in Jim Crow houses. Some theatremen reported that black audiences grew more truculent and even vandalistic after seeing message movies. "Since playing *Pinky* and *Home of the Brave* we have noticed an increase in belligerence of our colored trade," complained a California exhibitor of a trend on the heels of the cycle. More politically focused, Atlanta's black leaders predicted a different, if not entirely unrelated, mood: "The picture will inspire Negroes to do bigger things than they have in the past because of the effort Pinky made for her race."[61] As for the white South, Zanuck expected to "break down taboos and get our picture booked in practically every city below the Mason-Dixon line," which, he thought, "every citizen should cheer about." And if the film seemed so soft as to allow conservatives to "gloat," Zanuck reminded White, as though taking over leadership of their warborne alliance, that in the midst of rising expectations "sometimes the aim is more important than hitting the bull's eye."[62]

Less than two months after this, in late November, Metro contributed its own movie to the cycle, adding still more prestige by drawing upon a distinguished novel by William Faulkner, who soon would be awarded a Nobel Prize. Thus in yet another case, literary source and wartime Hollywood mentality imparted a high gloss to the ideology of integration. Much as Zanuck had steered *Gentleman's Agreement* and *Pinky,* Dore Schary assembled a group led by Ben Maddow, a radical shaped by the Depression, and director Clarence Brown, a Tennesseean and maker of MGM's most prestigious films who had never forgotten witnessing the Atlanta race riots as a child. Together they might override the conservatism of Faulkner's regionalism as well as persuade Mayer that the film's "prestige" should outweigh his misgivings toward the liberal work of his son-in-law Schary.[63] The idea for the movie came to Brown after reading Faulkner's *Intruder in the Dust* in galleys. But the book that to him seemed "as little as I could do to make up for Atlanta" and the property with which to be "the first of its kind," to Metro was a sleeping dog better left undisturbed. "Mayer thought I was crazy," Brown recalled years later, and he overheard someone sneer: "We don't want to make *that* goddam thing." But with Schary's arrival from RKO (where he had done *Crossfire*), Brown gained a friend at court when Schary chose the book as a contractually guaranteed personal production. Even then, Brown recalled that "instead of helping you they do everything in Christ's world to hinder you."[64]

At first glance it seemed too Southern, what with Brown's roots in Atlanta and Tennessee, his decision to break MGM custom and shoot on location (in Faulkner's Oxford, Mississippi), and his rapport with the mayor and townspeople. Indeed, the editor of the local paper imagined the film as "the most eloquent statement of the true Southern viewpoint of racial relations . . . ever sent out over the nation." Faulkner himself, ensconced in his nearby house, offered asides on casting and locations. Ben Maddow set aside his Yankee radicalism and, with scant interference from the others, finished a draft by Christmas 1948 that froze Faulkner's region in time, caught its ancient guilt over miscegenation, yet inched toward some fairmindedness toward African Americans. Still without altering the social order, he reordered some of Faulkner's indirection, opened up the action, and cut several regional apologia and racial epithets.[65]

By then, with rumors flying about soon-to-surface message movies, Schary broke the parochial Southern spell and submitted Maddow's work to the NAACP, which gave it a black imprimatur, perhaps in exchange for a sermonic coda tacked on to hammer home its message. Henry Lee Moon, the NAACP's public relations man, judged it "an excellent script, on the whole, the kind of film we can endorse," and urged Walter White "to give Hollywood the 'Go' sign." Despite an internal split—Jane White tolerated "nigger" for credibility's sake while Walter predicted its setting off resentment—Moon predicted a movie "more satisfying than any of its forerunners," partly because its "suspense and action" would make the "message acceptable to the masses of moviegoers."[66] Clearly, Hollywood and the NAACP still clung to their wartime union and hoped that its magic would still bring in both converts and cash.

Meanwhile, in Oxford through the spring of 1949, they shot their movie, so careful not to violate racial etiquette that the locals gave them a farewell fishfry. The harmony cracked only once, when Brown asked the black juvenile Elzy Emmanuel to play a cemetery scene with such oldtime eye-popping fear that Maddow was amazed. Emmanuel at first refused, although "finally," said *Ebony*, he was "forced to do the stereotype." Of course, the point here is not Brown's lapse into shooting a black figure whom he recalled from Southern lore. Rather it was the shift in cultural politics that the war had brought and that had prodded Maddow, *Ebony*, and for another instance, Bob Ellis in the *Eagle* to angrily respond to what was "cruel of producer Brown to jockey the young Negro player . . . into a Willie-Best-Eye-Rolling comedy part."[67]

Nonetheless, unified in their cause, Brown's team turned out a movie of striking acuity, though like the other message movies, it had parts that eventually wore their age awkwardly. Like the others, too, it used a lone Negro in a white setting as a dramatic device through which to enmesh blacks and whites in a mutual fate. However, Maddow extended the idea through Faulkner's metaphor for the collective guilt with which the novelist seemed possessed: black Lucas Beauchamp (Juano Hernandez), owlish, cold, with a deathly pallor who, in the establishing shots, is led by police through a rough, sullen, almost porcine mob, to jail, where he will be indicted for the murder of Vincent Gowrie, scion of a clan of poor whites. "Tell your uncle I wants to see him," he says to young Chick Malleson (Claude Jarman, Jr.), thus tying his lawyer-father and the Malleson family to the fate of a Negro. At first, almost flippantly, Chick says of the proud, aloof Lucas that they were "going to make a nigger out of him once in his life," but soon remembers the old story of Lucas's kinship to his grandfather, a lineage through which Lucas acquired the farm that sets him apart from most blacks. The meaning of the story sharpens as Chick recalls falling into a stream, drying out before Lucas's fire, and eating a meal for which he rudely tried to pay as though avoiding the role of guest and its implied equality. The memory is the first of several through which Chick begins to learn that one could be "sad, or proud, or even lonely, inside a black skin, too."

Lucas is in jail as accused murderer because of his own antipathy

Lucas Beauchamp (Juano Hernandez) in *Intruder in the Dust* (1949) called forth white resentment by *not* "playing the nigger." Here he walks into the general store—in his elegant attire: hat, morning coat, cravat, and with a gold toothpick, iconically "white." BFI. Copyright Metro-Goldwyn-Mayer.

toward Gowrie, who resented his wearing of white caste marks: a widebrimmed slouch hat, a big .41-calibre revolver, and a gold toothpick. To save the old man, Chick and two cohorts, black friend Alec (Elzy Emmanuel) and the oldest white woman in town, Miss Habersham (Elizabeth Patterson), set out to exhume Gowrie's corpse to compare bullets (Lucas's pistol being a rare .41). Miss Habersham, as though sharing Chick's link to Lucas, guards the jailhouse door against a mob until the kids return with their evidence. Here Maddow, more than any other writer of the genre, implicates his audience by making his mob not salivating geeks nor, as he wrote, a cruel or ugly crowd but rather a group remarkably like the audience. It is Chick's uncle who hammers the point: The killer, he says, easily should have been able to pin the crime on Lucas because of the two hundred years of racial history that welded the plain people of the mob (and the audience) into one in its hatred of Lucas. But when Chick and Alec bring in their bullet and expose the killer (another Gowrie), the lawyer sets forth Schary's liberal coda: *We* were in trouble, *not* Lucas, he says, looking down on the quietened town square. But it will be all right, he muses, if only a few refuse to run from history. Lucas is himself to the end, unchanged, wearing his arrogant badges—toothpick, watchfob, hat, string tie, and pistol—as he pays his two-dollar fee to the lawyer and waits for a receipt. It is the whites who have been changed by his presence in their lives. As Malleson says, watching Lucas cross the square, there passes the keeper of his conscience; then, turning as the script directs, into the camera as if toward the audience, he takes a beat and says: "our conscience."[68]

No vehicle could have done greater justice to the emerging notion of a common conscience across racial lines. From the first glimpse of Lucas from a high angle, followed by fleeting takes of his face through the mob, then in the half-light of his cell, thence to his rising to full height in the square, the whites are not free to ignore him or set him apart. He became what the war movie genre and its "unity" propaganda had begun to assert, the center of a conscience-liberal consensus.

Not that liberals considered this metaphor of common conscience powerful enough to solve all their problems. Its acceptance in theatres was never taken to mean that white people would break off from their racial history. Rather, except for a few who thought *Intruder in the Dust* too on-the-nose in its rhetoric, they almost unanimously read it as its makers intended: as an assertion of the thrust of liberalism in a particular time, and on a human scale that avoided the purely political and therefore offered change as a prospect rather than a program. For example, the *Oxford Eagle* and the *California Eagle*, the former white and rural, the latter black and urban, agreed on the movie, the former for its "groping for fair play and tolerance" while avoiding mere "indictment," the latter calling it "a smashing weapon against intolerance." Together they constituted a striking consensus of black and white agreement on newly defined terms of postwar racial arrangements rooted neither in empty nostalgia nor interventionism, but rather in the shared nonceword *tolerance*, which both must have learned during the war. Other papers were less rhapsodic but at least cheered: ranging from the *Times*'s claim that "here, at last, is a picture that slashes right down to the core," to the *Memphis Press-Scimitar*'s reckoning that "because it is entertaining, its argument will be heard—understood—perhaps heeded." Even the Communist V. J. Jerome, though skeptical of reformism, thought Lucas "towers easily over all" and saw "poetic justice" as one of the results. Dissenters nagged only at particulars, as José Yglesias did in finding it "curiously neutral" in the way it hinged on two kids and a geezer.[69]

Intellectuals placed it at the top of the genre. One of them, Judge J. Waties Waring, was a liberal scion of an old Charleston family in whose court the NAACP in 1947 won a landmark case involving black voting, a decision of which he said, "It is time for South Carolina to rejoin the union." He praised Schary for "all the beauty and intangible essence we have missed in so many Hollywood productions." Even Ralph Ellison, no friend of the genre, reported that in Harlem at least they did not laugh it off the screen and thought it promised ensuing changes. In the industry, Eric Johnston spoke of threatened censorship as "a perversion of the educational process," and Schary tried to boost Brown's spirits following the film's slow start. "I know how depressed you are about the lack of business," he wrote, "but don't let that destroy the fact that you've made a great document. . . . While we are in a profit business, we occasionally must be prepared for a commercial loss as long as we know we have gained in dignity and stature."[70]

Slow business notwithstanding, by the end of 1949 the genre promised enough on the whole that the B-moviemaker Eagle-Lion signed Jackie Robinson to do a biopic about his 1947 entry into white baseball, an event that itself had conformed to the plots of the war movie genre and anticipated the theme of the peacetime message movies.[71] Robinson played himself with winsome sincerity as a dutiful child of a genteel family. Despite its comicbook style and familiar devices (like its calendar-leaf montage of time passing), it outreached the majors in its showing the tension of integration as well as the ambivalence of some blacks. But its adversarial core made it work. On one side Robinson's preacher prods him "for the whole colored people," while on the other stands farm team manager Clay Hopper (Richard Lane), who is made to ask of Branch Rickey, boss of the Brooklyn Dodgers, "Do you really think he is a human being?" In the balance is acceptance by the fans and players, an outcome signified by a trope of Moss's *Teamwork,* black and white hands in closeup, and by Hopper who in the end says, "He's a gentleman." Too pat? In actuality, either the Dodgers learned to behave like Hopper, or Rickey traded them away and the fans readily were converted. In fact, actual audiences at ballgames are used so that, as in no other message movie, moviegoers can watch people like themselves do the right thing, a device that increases the political weight of a thin B-movie. Like most B-movies it pleased its fans more than its critics, who either patronized it as "sincere" or carped at its "overtactful" and "corny" story that was inlaid with "half truths." "Just a second feature, not too well made," said *Variety,* and with a "quicky flavor."[72] But more important than connoisseurship was the blunt introduction of racial politics into B-movies, perhaps helping turn popular taste away from the surviving black flunky roles in B-westerns and thrillers. Ensuing from, if not caused by, *The Jackie Robinson Story,* a genre of B-movies celebrated folk heroes, some of them drawn from sports and some of them including African Americans, a sort of tale of unbridled success that later became a staple of movies-made-for-TV. Indeed, such message movies reached into the reputedly staid Eisenhower Republican years and kept open at least a storybook movie politics as well as meatier fare.

One of the best of the continuing cycle, both on its merits and in its influence on the times, was Joseph Mankiewicz's (and Zanuck's) *No Way Out* (1950). It pressed its point the hardest, literally threatening the viewer with the prospect of race riots if America remained racially inert, and introducing a foreboding future in which the muted rage at the core of many social transactions between blacks and whites breaks like a festering sore and threatens to infect a larger sector of the community. What is more, early on Zanuck knew he wanted a tabloid style: He replaced his black lead, James Edwards, with Sidney Poitier, an ambitious newcomer whose barely controlled style seemed right for the film. It was to be, Zanuck hoped, as real as blood and guts in its raw race-baiting, without a trace of treacly Negrophilia. As though smelling a hit, all of the Fox producers known for topical movies volunteered to make it, save for two holdouts who warned of its hysteria and its sure defeat at the hands of Southern censors and box offices.[73]

As early as Christmas 1948, long before the cycle had begun, Zanuck, along with Philip Yordan, author of a black version of a Polish-American melodrama, *Anna Lucasta*, began a script from a treatment by Lesser Samuels about a black intern who must treat a virulent racist who has been wounded in a gunfight with police. At first, before the cycle became a trend, they were snared in liberal cant, unable to have their white doctor play martinet to Poitier, unable to see an ending that did not include the death of the black intern at the hands of a crazy racist, and chained to the notion that contact with liberals should teach the heavy "something."[74]

But by spring 1949, as they saw how good or bad message movies could be, they relented and began to create their own liberal cliché and the kernel of Poitier's lifelong role: the restrained black who withholds himself from whites until they accept him on his merits, who commands the frame by standing apart, who demands neither hero worship nor condescension, nor even to enter the white world, but only the civility due any professional. Yordan also went for the complexity of black life: there is Dr. Luther Brooks (Poitier), struggling achiever; the accommodationist Negro who refuses treatment by any but a white doctor; Brooks's sociologically plausible family and his wife, a sensible woman but wracked by deeply rooted fears of white peoples' capacity for mischief; and his extended family who hold him in awe as the one that broke the barrier to medical school.[75]

The final ingredient was cool, brown Poitier himself, fresh from *Lost in the Stars* on Broadway, thence to tests, interviews with Mankiewicz, a berth on the 20th Century, an apartment in white Westwood, a soaring boost in income, and a career in the movies. He would play the simmering healer against Richard Widmark's cornered, hurt racist, Ray. Together they provided an adversarial resonance that carried the movie into combativeness that put at risk the genre, its box office, the rearming of retreating censors, and the audiences and critics who so far had found it easy to march with them along this rolling frontier of melodramatic portrayals of racial integration. The complexities grew exponentially.

For example, Brooks will determine not only to treat the racist but that in the coming racial clash he will join the defenders of the ghetto; that is, he will act out DuBois's "twoness" and have both blackness and entry into white circles. Crowther saw this as a neat challenge: "'No Way Out' poses the problem and says in effect 'What are you going to do about it?'"[76]

That this angle—blacks as a combative collectivity against rabid racism and quiescent white tolerance of it—marked a coming of age may be seen in the debate it provided censors already in retreat under judicial pressure. In fact, the studio called upon Walter White to plant a piece in the *Times* in which he granted the stridency of the movie but came down on the side of freedom of the screen. It would help the picture off to a good run, they said, and encourage Hollywood to keep at it. White did his duty and sent circulars to his NAACP branches urging local resistance to censors "to achieve maximum success."[77]

What White and the studio feared, of course, was timid black leaders who, like Jewish opponents of *Gentleman's Agreement,* feared that by exposing virulent racism they risked poking a stick at a dozing beast. Signs that they were correct in their reckoning ranged from the PCA to local boards. But when Breen argued that its "inflammatory flavor" particularly its "race riot," might bring on carping from "special pleaders," the studio countered with a copy of a fan letter that angrily took issue with the movie as the latest in a long line of the "nigger lover" studio's work that spoke with the voice of a too liberal government propaganda movie. In the face of such a blunt challenge to the entire movement, which had begun within a setting of government intervention, Jason S. Joy, speaking for Fox, insisted on a fight against the racism that clearly existed and a public revival of the old alliance with White. Indeed, for his part White leapt to the renewal of the fight, urged the branches to take action, and personally took up individual cases. As he told a critic, the Hollywood cycle plus *The Quiet One* "mark a great step forward in the motion picture industry," adding that "the ever increasing nationwide concern about human rights is in part due to the new type of pictures which Hollywood is making about the Negro."[78] To take only one outcome, in Baltimore Carl Murphy, publisher of the *Afro-American* and a familiar figure on interracial commissions, broke with White in demanding cuts of references to riots, but the censor board chair, as though recognizing White's standing in the matter, reported directly to him of the decision to side with Murphy rather than the NAACP. Clearly, even if picking a course through the intricacies of race and censorship was difficult, blacks had become an imposing presence in the lobbies and boardrooms of state houses.[79]

Finally *No Way Out* lost to censorship only a few references to "niggers" and revenge, but Mankiewicz's glossy, brittle style survived. A polished, soundstage variant on *The Naked City* genre, it opened on a

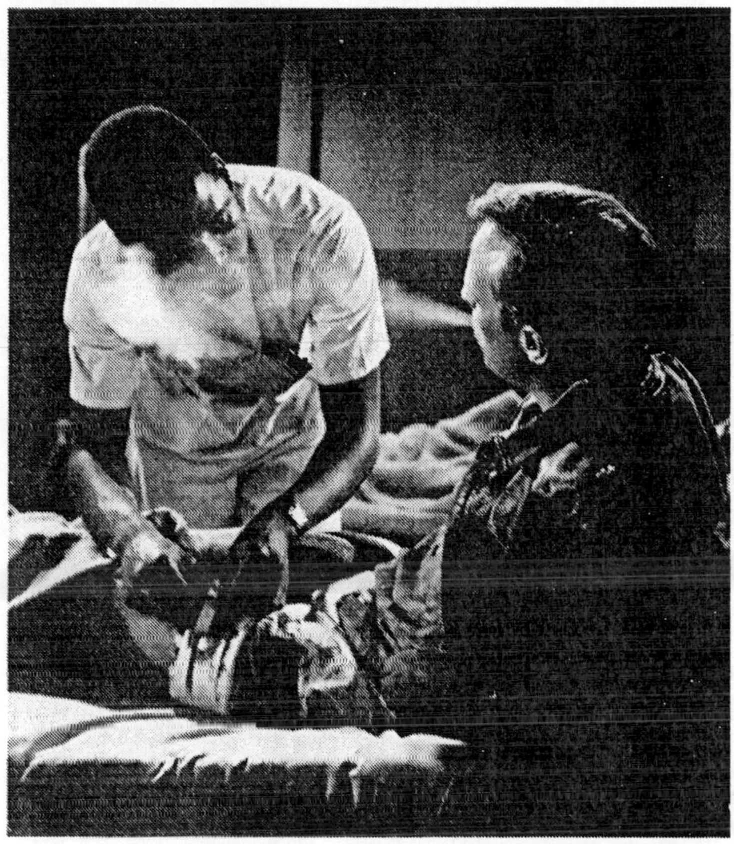

No Way Out (1950) did its best to "shock America" epitomizing racism in the person of a lone psychotic criminal (Richard Widmark) who taunts a dutiful black doctor (Sidney Poitier), thereby freeing the "average" American from such feelings. Copyright 20th Century–Fox.

routine change of shift in an urban hospital. The daily round is shattered when two thieves, each with a gunshot wound, are brought into Emergency where Dr. Brooks, a black intern, is on duty. Under a torrent of racial abuse he not only examines their wounds but routinely checks for other symptoms, among which he spots signs of a tumor in one man. In testing for it he takes a spinal tap, following which his patient dies, setting loose another round of racist rage and threats of revenge upon not only Brooks but also Beaver Canal, the black ghetto. Brooks calls for an autopsy, which would confirm his diagnosis as well as head off the threat of violence, but the family members refuse: the most vengeful among them specifically because he wishes to stoke the passions in the streets. Signs of the street fighting mount—anguished families, ter-

Although rabid white racism seemed a tolerable theme in *No Way Out,* the black organized resistance demanded by this exhorter (Dots Johnson) discomfitted state censor boards. BFI. Copyright 20th Century–Fox.

rorstricken bystanders—and the wounded drift in, including a woman who spits out her venom at Brooks. The only remedy looms clear: Brooks must surrender himself as the "murderer" of his patient, thereby forcing an autopsy that would confirm his finding, discredit the surviving racist, and place a lid on the rioting.

The film was striking in its resistance to a happy closure that was a reprise of *The House I Live In.* Ray, the racist, goes unrepentant to the end. But there is also a credible slack in the racism of his slatternly sister (Linda Darnell), who is less willing to have her racism serve as the motive for a pointless riot. Her wambling opens the way to the autopsy that vindicates Brooks and heads off violence. Here the first round of message movies would have ended—in the restoration of harmony. But Mankiewicz had pressed forward as though in a van. His blacks were seen as prepared to act communally, almost militarily, on their own behalf without a Lincoln figure with which Yordan had begun. The "Lincoln"—the chief resident—merely backs Brooks's play. Moreover, black Beaver Canal debates its options within realistic family circles and other social settings absent from the first of the genre.

Despite its touchy violence, the metropolitan press, black critics, and many donors of awards praised *No Way Out* and refused to flinch from its harshness. They seemed to accept its veiled liberal faith in the correctability of racism and in the eventual overriding of divisive and destructive forces in the society. Witnesses reported everything from stunned silence to frequent applause at its compelling bluntness. White preferred it even to his daughter's movie, *Pinky*, and following his lead critics bubbled at "Hollywood's most powerful anti-hate film," touting it as "the greatest step forward in the fight against prejudice since the nickelodeon." As to its forward thrust, the sister of a featured player, Dots Johnson, loved it because it signaled "that the colored race is fighting back." Years later, Ruby Dee recalled it as "a step forward, revolutionary, really," compared with its forebears, which had seemed a collective "liberal compromise with truth."[80]

Unavoidably, of course, the play in the movie allowed less sanguine readings. Anticipating the thrust of Poitier's career, Gavin Lambert spoke for those who found "an unblemished Negro and a vicious white neurotic is an extreme and rather narrow dramatization of the general problem." This "unbridled smacking of the lips" in a "supertabloid geeklike style," according to some, merely invited audiences to "sit back, relax, and feel that their conscience is now clear." Indeed, two social scientists, Martha Wolfenstein and Nathan Leites, probing "a deeper level" found a "boomerang effect" rooted in the image of a competent Negro doctor surrounded by signifiers of his tentativeness and perhaps malevolence. Others found a backbeat in offcamera riot, a throb of an older bugbear: anguished "'white womanhood' assaulted by the 'bestial Negroes.'" And to still others, a bargain seemed to have been struck that said "a white corpse must be 'violated'" in order to admit blacks to their circle, a dilemma from which there seemed "no way out."[81]

Whatever their obvious flaws, these message movies effectively set before popular audiences a racial agenda that had followed from national goals that had taken form in during the war and had struggled through a thermidorean peacetime period marked as much by *To Secure These Rights* as by conservative HUAC. While it cannot be shown that the mentality of the age of integration that followed derived directly from the movies that ran from *Bataan* through *The Quiet One* and beyond to *No Way Out*, we do know that those who saw the movies and wrote down their responses had internalized a racial ideology that not only clashed with antebellum racial practice but in the next generation became a part of a "Second Reconstruction." In fact, measured by box office success in the South, the myth of an intractably conservative Southern mind itself had come to an end. Much as George Norford had seen *Lifeboat* as a harbinger of postwar liberalism, so Lillie M. Jackson of Baltimore NAACP saw a similar link with the past in *No Way Out*, which she likened to a war movie climaxed by a "victorious battle . . . by our boys."[82]

9

Settling In, Settling For

The movies through which a liberalism of conscience was retailed to a broad audience have suffered at the hands of historians who have been unimpressed by their apparent low voltage, their message that had grown quickly old hat, their limiting of racial discourse to the admission of a single iconic black into a white circle (platoon, courtroom, surgery, and of course, on televised news after 1954, *school*). But their formula had been uncannily prescient in anticipating, even half-forming, the shape that racial integration would actually take. That is, as surely as one black figure entered the circles in *Sahara* and *No Way Out,* so in actuality the Supreme Court obliged voting registrars and school boards to give blacks access to the ballot box and the classrooms, formerly white preserves of privilege, a pattern followed by American business circles in engaging what came to be known as token Negroes. Certainly the mainline civil rights activists adopted such strategies as their own, and almost as certainly, white Americans who tolerated or even welcomed the change did so according to the formula that movies had provided—taking an initiatory black figure into a professional or institutional circle, a bank or school—while fudging the issue as it applied to primary groups such as church, neighborhood, and family circle.

In addition to this limit on collective social imagination, movies as a medium for anticipating change faltered for their own internal reasons: Success of movies, even message movies, obliged Hollywood to repeat itself simply as a matter of knowing which side its bread was to be buttered on. As we have seen, only the crisis of war and the dislocations that followed it shook the social equilibrium enough to take even the minimal risks that war movies and message movies had represented. This built-in thermidor that in the absence of crises guided Hollywood may be followed in the careers of two fine actors, Sidney Poitier and Harry Belafonte, the former circumspect, overcontrolled, the latter the product of bohemian cellars where folksongs were sung to leftish audiences. In the decade of the 1950s, as we shall see, Hollywood chose Poitier and elected to exclude Belafonte, to repeat itself rather than break new ground—at least until the crisis of the civil rights movement provided it with the occasion to restart its stilled engines.

We began by taking up movies as ritual that codified values and also happened to maximize studio profits and win Oscars. In seeking these badges of approval, moviemakers created the stuff of value-impregnated myths, often at their most ritualistic in the replicated formulas of B-movies and genre movies. Thus in dealing with racial issues before the war they often preferred erasing blacks or at the very least treating them as the different Other, in keeping with their actual social status. But the war had brought decent, self-effacing blacks into the circle, and their place in it was enlarged in the message movie cycle. Enter Poitier, whose performance persona lent itself to a gentle politics of the center; exit Belafonte, whose edgy intensity did not commend itself to conscience-liberals in search of riskfree formulaic reprises of battles already fought.

Poitier's perennial hero we might liken to Gawain in the medieval legend: At first he knows nothing of the nature of his quest, but only that he must make it; only later does he come to understand that his object is the Holy Grail. And with Poitier as with Gawain, it turns out that the stakes in the search are as much political as individual. Gawain learns that his behavior forms some vital link with the healing of the mythical Fisher King, and that, in turn, both the quest and the restoration of the king to health and potency have a bearing on, as Jessie L. Weston had it in *From Ritual to Romance*, healing "the misfortunes of the land." Poitier, the latter-day Gawain, will always be met on the screen facing tests and trials that have such universalizing consequences. Like Lucas Beauchamp in *Intruder in the Dust*, he is "the conscience of us all."

Belafonte's fewer heroes, on the other hand, are more clearly Byronic, doomed outlaws. Whether in *Carmen Jones* or in his own *Odds Against Tomorrow*, they seem hellbent for outlawry and thence to their deaths. In brief, Poitier's character worked the centers of the American ethos; Belafonte's played its rimlands. If this seems to reassert a determinism at the core of popular culture that dooms it to promote the status quo, it must also be seen that the racial status quo, or its ideology at least, had been transformed by war. But more than that, chance and accident *also* matter in the unfolding of history, and by chance Poitier was technically readier for his role than was Belafonte for his, the latter not yet having used his loosely worn singing style to free his tense acting style. So it was Poitier who dominated the racial politics of the ensuing quarter of a century of black movies, and in doing so doomed himself to a career of brilliantly acted ritual repetitions of *Bataan*.

The resulting genre of liberal movies was full of obligatory closures in which the heavies—whether flinty bankers or sneering crackers—came to a bad end brought on by the resolve of the hero, who wished only for fair play. Life, of course, was different: full of ambiguities and snares—and no dissolves. Moreover, in life an accomplished goal only exposed the next goal to be striven for, while in movies it might end only with exhibitors calling for more of the same, much as *King Kong* was followed by *Son of Kong*. As a result, for many years, until the national crisis over civil rights in the 1960s intervened, American racial politics easily outran the movies' feeble attempts to keep up. Without war and crisis to provide thrust, Hollywood was left with only its sense of the marketplace as a guide to conduct.

The era began with John Garfield's urge to remake Hemingway's *To Have and Have Not*, this time with a black character as chum to Harry Morgan rather than the elfin rummy who had replaced him in Howard Hawks's version in 1944. The result was *The Breaking Point* (1951), a bold stride toward a humane portrayal of interracial comradeship. The era was to end, however, with Jules Dassin's *Up Tight* (1967), a restrike of Liam O'Flaherty's novel of the Irish rising in Dublin, *The Informer*, which John Ford had made into a movie in 1935. This time it was about a black insurrection in Cleveland in which white liberals were placed on the margin of the action, prattling, overdressed, irrelevant, as a guerrilla war raged about them.

Between these two movies was the age of Sidney Poitier, which reached apogee in 1963 when he won an Oscar in Ralph Nelson's *Lilies of the Field* for his lone black protagonist, this time dropped amidst a klatsch of nuns rather than a squad of ragged soldiers. It was an age in search of a liberal energy that the war had once provided, a sense of adventure that rivaled the customary reliance on the proven and the normative. The result was a rising pitch of criticism directed at Poitier and the keepers of his image, as though blaming Poitier for the cooling down of the passing era of liberalism.

In much the same way, historians have settled upon rabid anti-Communism as the nutrient of the era, which seemed adrift to the political right, but the era was more profoundly marked by its preference for the virtues of consensus and restraint than its preference for right-wing extremists. Not that critics of Senator McCarthy were not entitled to their rage. The urge for consensus that was accompanied by, and perhaps was in part caused by, a sense of having missed out on the benefits of a victorious wartime alliance that quickly broke apart into a "cold war" led to a mood of meanly seeking out and blaming those who had covertly sold off the fruits of victory to their Communist masters in Moscow. In such a mood McCarthy was no more than a symptomatic pimple rather than a lethal cancer. Thus, although his committee in the Senate, HUAC, and the FBI recklessly injured innocent persons and violated their rights to privacy and freedom of expression, the diminished drive of liberal politics derived more from broader shifts in generational style. This cooler political idiom was driven less by fear of reactionaries and more by the diminution of the, as Siegfried Kracauer wrote, "progressive attitude which undoubtedly owes much to wartime experiences." Nonetheless, visible causes attract more attention than less sweeping, less focused circumstances, so that a cooled leftist political ardor was readily attributed to "a blacklisting of ideas" arising from reactionary hysteria. Thus for every observer who, with Arthur Knight, thought "groundless" the fear that "Un-American trials [*sic*] would drive all progressive thinking off the screen," there were Hollywood liberals who overvalued "this Red Menace" that Hedda Hopper, for one, thought would destroy America, and who therefore signed "the Waldorf Statement" and other devices for denying employment to known Communists. Other Hollywoodians of the center and right attended lectures on "Hollywood commissars," snooped for HUAC, combed scripts for red cant, paid for so-called "clearances" of suspected red performers, and began to sound like secret agents: "Destroy these wires when you have finished," wrote Lyman Munson to a colleague after discussing a movie about the FBI.[1]

The short-term effect in Hollywood drove the moguls much as any market force would have done. Leftists found everything from assignments to golf matches canceled; even "friendly" witnesses who testified before HUAC as atonement for their "un-American" pasts felt hobbled and severed links to anything political; and everyone knew a story of aborted projects, recut films, or a "terrified" studio.[2]

In the blacks' case, victimization was less obvious because so few of them worked anyway. HUAC's boldest target, Paul Robeson, served poorly as a sign of the stifling of movies because he had long since foresworn Hollywood. As for the Hollywood Negroes, they either took out tradepaper ads testifying to their Americanism and urging blacks "not to be deceived by Communist doubletalk"; or, like Harry Levette, warned against "so-called liberal interracial groups"; or on the left admitted to being "duped"; or, like Canada Lee, confessed that opposition to lynching drove them into the arms of the CPUSA. Of course one never *knew* why things happened. Claude Barnett's proposal to the United States Information Agency (USIA) in 1952, *The Negro in America*, appeared to die of the agency's fear of the hold Southern congressmen exercised over their budget, but unknown to Barnett may also have suffered from his cultivating Reed Harris, a civil servant who once had been cruelly grilled by McCarthy.[3] But in this white man's squabble, blacks seemed no more than pigeons in a confidence game, much as they were portrayed in an anti-red quickie, *I Was a Communist for the FBI* in which Reds speak of tremendous profits drawn from "niggers" as a result of the party's defense of accused rapists in the Scottsboro case in the 1920s.[4]

But a look at the movies themselves reveals not so much a waning of politics as a change in style to accommodate to what the comedian Bob Newhart referred to as a "buttoned-down," circumspect, gray-suited taste-culture. True, the Fund for the Republic's *Report on Blacklisting* (1956), drawing on MPAA data, concluded that "problem" pictures had slipped from a quarter to a tenth of output; Allen Rivkin noticed a waning "populist spirit"; and John Stone, a watchdog of Jewish roles, foresaw an avoidance of movies "dealing with racial and religious relations." But these observers may have merely noted a fading of the "geeklike" tabloid style of message movies in favor of a genre of "serious" films with social themes that ranged from Broadway adaptations like *Come Back, Little Sheba* to westerns like *High Noon*. So routinely did blacks begin to appear in normative roles in these movies that the older style of message movie would have seemed strident. They were cops and judges in *None Shall Escape* (1944), *Trial* (1955), and *Detective Story* (1951), a fisherman in *The Breaking Point* (1951), a wounded veteran in *Bright Victory* (1951), and others. Indians also received liberal attention in a cycle of movies such as Hall Bartlett's Oscar-nominee, *Navajo*, and Delmer Daves's *Broken Arrow*. Thus American society at large seemed either a "prosperous, stable, bland, religious, moral, patriotic, conservative, domestic, buttoned-down" happy nation, or a "bleak and disillusioned age" that sharply assailed itself in books like David Riesman's *The Lonely Crowd* that gave their names to the period.[5]

It was this setting for which Poitier and Eisenhower, each in his field, became eponyms who conveyed—not invented—the spirit of the times. The complex president played political naif: shrewdly bumbling, calculatedly garbled in public, hard as flint within his circle, capable of seeing "either" *and* "or," impatient with black "second-class citizenship" but put off by "social mingling." Even when "justly aroused" he seemed to prefer "working like yeast, quietly."[6] Poitier's autobiography, *This Life*, revealed a similar circumspection. Encountering friction in a strange town: avoid trouble by using "my 'cool'"; facing down a critic: "cool out on him"; and so on. Even in analysis he felt "uptight, silent, and sullen" with "my psychological guard . . . up," and in fear of a meltdown that "I might not be able to control." Indeed, his career rested on it: "If ever I can control that 'control,' *then* I will be an actor."[7] Of course, the president and the actor were not alone. In similar style Mel Tormé sang, Lauren Bacall acted, the Modern Jazz Quartet played. At the end of the era in 1960, even the Greensboro students in the first "sit-in" behaved à la mode in neat shirts and ties, cool masks, and cryptic rather than expansive oratory. This is not to reduce politics to shtick, but rather to see that political limits were defined by a self-imposed taste for the cool and an avoidance of declamation.

Yet behind this cool facade, a certain amount of racial ferment persisted. Urban and educated whites tolerated the idea of an integrated society. And teenaged children—black and white—grew into a distinctive "crossover" taste-culture that was loud, truculent, clannish, as they "hooted and scoffed" at square culture. Soon they became a target audience with a taste for *Rock Around the Clock* and other movie-rituals of rebellion, which often included black acts in their casts. Blacks weighed as a market factor not only because of rising incomes but because of the portions of it—half again greater than whites'—spent on immediate gratifications rather than on powertools and lawnmowers. By 1950 their numbers alone pressed against customary barriers of segregation that began to give way, aided by a combination of direct social action and judicial remedy. Meanwhile, as suburbanization thinned the pool of moviegoers, exhibitors built, as *Variety* put it, "modern nabe houses." Coupled with art houses, these neighborhood theatres served newly selective audiences rather than habitual ones.[8]

New conditions required new practices such as granting black neighborhoods first-run movies, exploiting the "unusually high" impact of black press previews, advertising in the black press, consulting with black ad-men, and other means of taking into account the black audience. All of this eased the threat of, said *Variety*, a "classy suburbs vs. 'Rundown' Rialto" pattern and inspired a rash of both redecorating downtown houses and shutting Jim Crow theatres, which taken together nurtured an urbane audience ready for new things.[9] In one Baltimore instance, the Fulton, the Bridge, and the Met were, respectively, a grindhouse, a "nabe," and a former Loew's first-run house, all struggling to survive a black migration into their market. The Fulton became a supermarket; the Bridge revived *Cabin in the Sky*, doubling it with a race movie, *Boarding House Blues;* and the Met played first-run black product like *The Jackie Robinson Story*. Older black theatres quickly responded, the Harlem reviving *Imitation of Life*, the Royal (the last vaudeville house) countering with a Carver biopic, *The Peanut Man*, while the marginal houses along the main black drag withered and died, resulting in a net gain of two refurbished black houses and an enhanced image for the old black Rialto.[10]

Soon the trades reported "Negro clientele is an important factor" and "Negro-theme Pix Return to Vigor," although sobering their readers with stories of bafflement at black preferences for *King of Kings* but not for *The Intruder* (about a racist rabblerouser), and of "wariness of southern theatremen" faced with a rise in vandalism and violence. Black fan mail expressing "great pride" in new war movies like the story of black quartermasters, *Red Ball Express*, a story of the all-Nisei 442nd Regimen-

Local 181 (Baltimore) of the projectionists' union at the Fulton, a white "nabe" that quickly became black and then a supermarket in the postwar rush to break out of old ghettos—a migration that, coupled with the Paramount case, altered the socioecomonic basis of movie distribution. Collection of Dr. Robert B. Headley.

tal Combat Team, *Go for Broke*, and others, was sent to the press, the studios, and even the Breen office.[11]

A lively corps of critics attentive to the audience lectured the moguls. As their dean, Lester Walton, wrote in 1949, he "hoped big box office business and favorable reviews have fully convinced the producers that the progressive step was worthwhile, and . . . like 'Ole Man River,' will keep on rolling along." They peppered their stories with gossip of impending "realistic" race-angled material, a Scottsboro exposé, and other projects of benefit to "Sepia Artists," hectored *Lydia Bailey* for leaching out the black element of the Haitian revolution and *Battleground* for its lilywhite treatment of the Battle of the Bulge, goaded black writers into "channeling" their anger into scripts, and hailed each new casting twist such as black Frank Silvera's General Huerta in *Viva Zapata*.[12] Among the white serials, the *Reporter* predicted "the whole future of the motion picture industry is dependent on the kind of imagination, courage, and ingenuity that went into the making of *Home of the*

Brave," or like *Variety,* linked liberalism to the box office in reports on "great" business here and "spotty" business there, or like Crowther in the *Times,* praised the "educational impact" of message movies. Even V. J. Jerome of the CPUSA joined in, despite ideological fears that reformism could only "retard" genuine political consciousness. In Hollywood itself in 1951, Ralph Bunche, who once had been denied entry to the Metro commissary but by then was a Nobel laureate, presented Oscars to Zanuck and Mankiewicz. By the end of the 1940s, *Variety* thought race-angled movies had reached the top of genre films, just as Poitier began to think them "repetitive."[13]

Meanwhile, the fading censors contributed to the persistence of the liberal ideology by consulting blacks and by sharing each other's decisions among the state boards, thereby keeping in touch with national trends.[14] At first the black consultants mainly took up jungle movies—"goona goona" epics, in *Variety* patois—the grindhouse staples assembled from barebreasted anthropological footage, intercuts of burlesque queens, stockshots of rainforests, and fake horny gorilla surrogates for the black brutes of American folk lore. In Maryland, for example, Carl Murphy of the *Afro* was called in to advise on *I Married a Savage, The Bride of the Gorilla,* and others, in the process establishing a black stake in issues other than the use of "nigger" in the dialogue. In addition, the local boards subscribed to the trades, whose reports of the "word-of-mouth" that might "build" *Bright Victory* or the "ready-made audience" for *The Jackie Robinson Story* kept the boards aware of their own parochialism.[15]

Taken together, these institutional forces were a "cultural system," which formed a sort of "intellectual framework" that Americans had inherited from the war years and that persisted in halfway defining both life and the movies. And yet without the war as driving engine, Hollywood struggled to keep pace with the schoolbook Americanism, the Gallup polls that credited all but the most uneducated Southerners with liberal thoughts, and the increasingly activist and liberating court decisions that marked the era, all of them, it must be recalled, arising from a culture for whom buttoned-down coolness was the preferred mode.[16] The struggles of individual movies to prevail against the national wish for a deadpan exterior reveal both the persistence of liberal politics and its circumspection.

The best of them was *The Breaking Point* (1950), Warner's neglected remake of Howard Hawks's *To Have and Have Not* (1944). From the beginning it was John Garfield's project, the latest in a career marked by conscience-liberal gestures that included *Pride of the Marines,* in which he played opposite a Jewish veteran, and *Body and Soul,* in which he played opposite Canada Lee's tragic black boxer (he later wrote about the experience for NUL's *Opportunity*). He wished to merge two of Hemingway's characters: Eddy the white rummy who, with Hawks's inter-

Two versions of Hemingway's *To Have and Have Not* provided the hero, Harry Morgan, with two variations on the sidekick role: here as feckless white rummy (Walter Brennan with Humphrey Bogart and Lauren Bacall) in Howard Hawks's 1944 film . . . BFI. Copyright Warner Bros.

cession in 1944, had been played with impish charm by Walter Brennan, and Wesley, a black deckhand who is bolder and more reliable in a shooting scrape, but missing from the 1944 movie. Oddly, William Faulkner, who wrote Hawks's script, might have made much of him, perhaps another Lucas Beauchamp. In any case, Garfield in 1951 insisted that he should be "kicked up" (his argot for "accented"), made black, and brought closer without being too maudlin. The result was an interracial, egalitarian refinement of the classical Hollywood sidekick role, a relationship in which even their families are drawn together. Moreover, not only did Garfield's idea prevail, but it heightened the tension between the two men and the circle of cops, loansharks, and smugglers who threatened them. And viewers, at least on the left, caught its sense. "We are especially grateful [for] the relationship between these two men," wrote Seymour Peck, even as Juano Hernandez as the deckhand won a place in the press blitz as "Hollywood's Hottest Negro" actor.[17]

As to the rest, they were gems of conscience-liberalism enameled over with the racial ideology and agenda that had been set by *To Secure*

These Rights. *Young Man with a Horn* (1951) was the first of them to wear its garbled liberalism on its sleeve. It had begun as Dorothy Baker's homage-novel to the trumpeter Bix Beiderbecke, thence to a script that in Walter White's mind would make up for canceling *St. Louis Woman*, and finally into a vehicle for a hot new star (Kirk Douglas) in an erotic triangle that diminished Baker's black parts. Surviving was one good role, that of Art Hazzard (Hernandez), a fatherly tutor to the white hero in search of "a note nobody ever heard before," but a sidebar to the main storyline. *Ebony*, like much of the black press overplayed it as a once "too hot to handle" sign of "substantial progress for Hollywood."[18]

Kenneth Roberts's *Lydia Bailey* (1952) suffered a similar fate as Zanuck shifted its center from Toussaint L'Ouverture's Haitian revolution to romantic white story. The black politics should only be a background for the personally scaled story, Zanuck told his writers, who, he said, should not for a moment follow the intricacies of a "cause." The

. . . and in Michael Curtiz's *The Breaking Point* (1951) as Hemingway intended, as a black man who is an active agent in the plot, a role insisted upon by John Garfield, a leftist bent upon a postwar conscience-liberal agenda. BFI. Copyright Warner Bros.

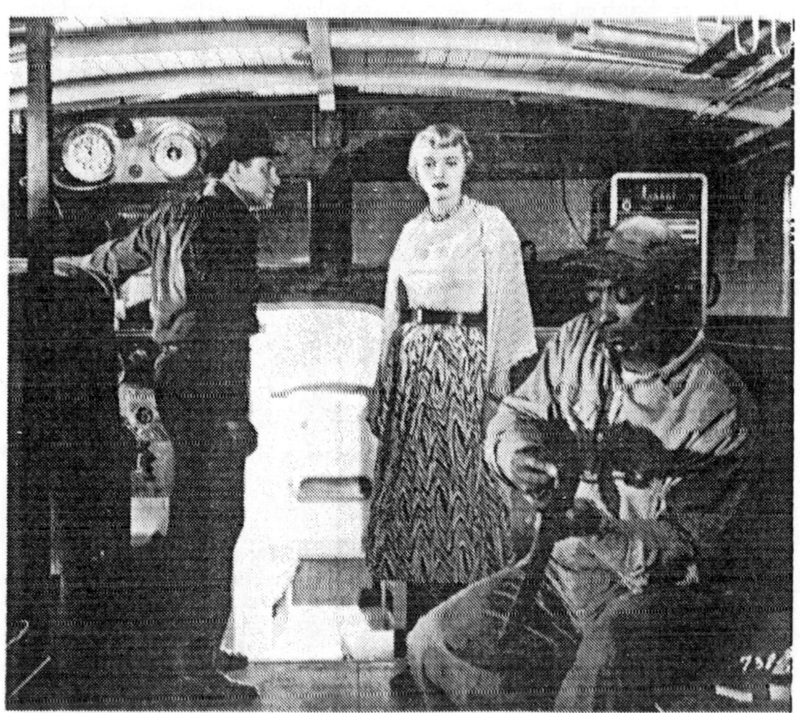

Darryl Zanuck's film of Kenneth Roberts's *Lydia Bailey* (1952) retained its high adventure but shed its Haitian politics, transforming King Dick (William Marshall in white) from a revolutionary into a mere rogue. Copyright 20th Century–Fox.

only black survivors were in a shadowy backstory in the hills above Port-au-Prince and in the person of King Dick (William Marshall), a white-suited giant who knows all, has a string of "talented" mistresses, and carries a cocomacaque—more as a scepter than a club. Again, *Ebony* had no choice but to overpraise Dick and portray the Haitian angle as "glorified," while on the left they sneered at Zanuck's willful retreat to the safety of romance.[19]

In Zanuck's and other cases, such backsliding can be followed in the paper trail in the archives, but sometimes the softness of racial politics was owed more pointedly to the intercession of cautious censors and their guarded black counselors, as though the censors were more mistrustful of the audience than of Hollywood. In the case of *The Well* (1951), the Popkins' reentry into the Hollywood system, the blacks feared "me-too" violence that might follow a B-movie about an impending race riot. *The Well* was a minor hit shot on location with a low nut, enhanced by a distribution deal with UA, and a spate of tabloid ads that teased: "Maybe you haven't found him because he's a WHITE man,

Sheriff!" It was about a black girl who has fallen into a disused well, setting off rumors of kidnapping by whites; a crescendo of tension leads up to her rescue by a white drifter (and backhoe operator) who dredges her from the well in a circus of television coverage that might have cued a riot. Fortunately for its backers, many critics saw it as a fable about harmony, but in the censor boards cautious blacks fought every one of its dramatic sequences.[20] In another instance of retreat from obvious implications, Arch Oboler's *Five* (1951) teased around the sexual center of prejudice in a cautionary tale set in a post-thermonuclear holocaust in which the pointlessness of racism is tossed aside by killing off the lone black survivor of the disaster (a timidity echoed in 1959 in *The World, the Flesh, and the Devil*), which seemed to critics "monumentally silly" in its picking at the pimple of racism while the earth slowly became a barren rock.[21]

And yet if retreat from lofty goals and restraint in style characterized movies with a self-consciously racial thrust, almost any genre film preserved residues of oldtime OWI tracts such as the lone black figure who lends dignity and color to the proceedings. The result was a steady flow of films but frozen as though sequels to *Home of the Brave*. No longer a structured absence nor an erasure from history, nor for the most part an exotic Other, the blacks in them, however, seemed doomed to be the eternal subjects of a tale of an already attained goal—one black figure per group. And there was no war or crisis as yet to create the disequilibrium and loosened bonds of custom that would allow blacks to reopen negotiations begun during the war.

The list of releases seemed at once admirable for its scope and damnable for its reluctance to press beyond what the supercool postwar era would tolerate. Each jungle movie had its Oxonian doctor or sage, each adventure its obligatory blacks. Joe Walcott's trainer in *The Harder They Fall* (1956); Don Blackman, who helps Alan Ladd "free Cuba" in *Santiago* (1956); Edric Connor as Daggoo in *Moby Dick* (1956); James Edwards's supernumerary in each new war movie, and his luckless parking lot attendant in *The Killing* (1956); Frank Silvera's "chameleon-like" (said *Ebony*) cop in *Crime and Punishment* (1959); Geofrrey Holder's "erudite leader" in *Dr. Doolittle* (1968); the temple dancers of Carmen DeLavallade and Isabel Cooley in *The Egyptian* (1954) and *Cleopatra* (1963); Woody Strode's roles in John Ford's westerns; Poitier's Simon the Cyrenian in *The Greatest Story Ever Told* (1965); Coley Wallace as Joe Louis in yet another biopic (1953); Lena Horne as Julie the mulatto in *Show Boat* performed as a play-within-a-play in the Jerome Kern biopic *Till the Clouds Roll By* (1952); and the familiar blacks in modern classics such as Ethel Waters's Berenice in *Member of the Wedding* ("earthy and warm-hearted and wise cook," said *Ebony* dutifully).[22]

For the moment, on the edge of the acceleration of the civil rights movement from local issues in Montgomery, Alabama, in 1955 and

Greensboro, North Carolina, in 1960, into nationally focused campaigns that enjoyed daily exposure to a television audience, it seemed that the only missing ingredient was the domestic crisis that might redirect some attention to Hollywood. Indeed, that would come to pass, but not until 1963 when Herbert Hill, labor secretary of the NAACP, went to Hollywood to resume Walter White's campaign (White had died in 1955), this time in the aggressive style of a labor negotiator. But that is another story that led to outcomes in the 1970s and after. Into this hiatus of leftist pressure came studio chiefs bent upon promoting new conventions of racial drama. The icons chosen to serve this era were Harry Belafonte and Sidney Poitier, the former a sort of Dionysian figure ever on the edge of throwing over the traces, the latter more in control, more the Apollonian Negro whose inner resources assure his survival.

The problem for Belafonte's work was that Hollywood's way of taming unfamiliar and outlaw material was to treat it "warmly" or lay it into reverently treated classics, or, once made, to play it off quietly as a "prestige" picture. Belafonte suffered all three. He began with *Bright Road* (1953), a product Charles Schnee's B-unit at Metro drew from Elizaberth Vroman's story of a black teacher (Dorothy Dandridge) in a rural school who struggles to reach a new and alienated pupil (Philip Hepburn). His coming-of-age scene and his acceptance by the class come after he saves them from a swarm of bees by cleverly finding the queen and using her to lead them away. Poor Belafonte had little to do but render his approval. Critics yawned and nobody went to see it. Both blacks and Metro were at a loss, the former trapped into too loudly praising it, the latter burying it. Metro sales, fearing both its nonmagnetic low-key mode and the prospect of a hostile southern greeting, "brushed" it off in alloting exploitation budgets, and played it off as a "warm and tender" Christopher Award winner that disdained "racial . . . propaganda." The Urban League tried to save it by urging members to promote it and heap awards upon it. At the same time they disagreed with MGM, sensing its greatest appeal would be in the South, a judgment shared by Vroman herself, who tried to arrange an integrated premiere on federal ground at Maxwell Air Force Base in Alabama. But nothing could save it. "We could not get anyone in to see [it]," said Schary; "commendable" anyway, said the *Defender*.[23]

A year later Belafonte appeared in *Carmen Jones* (1954), a film of Mike Todd's prewar all-black version of Bizet's opera *Carmen*. Once a freakish hit, by the 1950s it seemed merely a projection of Spanish stereotypes onto blacks and therefore an easy target for critics in search of backsliding. Its earthy raffishness, saturated color, and humorless literalness "whipped relentlessly [said Robert Hatch in the *Nation*] into a Hollywood pattern," invited critical zingers like James Baldwin's report that it looked life "straight in de eye." Simultaneously it scared the trades into fretting over "the reaction of the South" and rankled blacks, even though Fox had promised Breen to cut its "vampy" aspects. The result was a creaking anachronism that earned dutiful praise as "another great step forward" and faint hopes by its director Otto Preminger that a strong European box office might save it.[24]

Thus by mid-decade Belafonte had violated two taboos: making a "warm" little picture and making a revered classic. Either he had twice blundered in his choice of material, or the racial politics of the nation's cities had simply outrun the movies' capacity for change. That Hollywood may not have been up to handling the rising pitch of racial politics may be seen in Belafonte's next movie, *Island in the Sun* (1957). Its author, Alec Waugh, intended it as a Caribbean metaphor for American racial tensions, and 20th Century–Fox had purchased it in the same spirit—as much a crusade as a moneymaker. Indeed, Zanuck had such faith in its political impact that he sat out the publishing season of 1955 (the year of Martin Luther King's Montgomery bus boycott), hoping for a hot book that would override resistance in the South and for time to disarm the PCA's wish to soften an interracial love story, perhaps by having a mulatto woman learn that after all she was, a PCA memorandum said, a pure white girl.[25] Also at issue were three of the book's voices of change, two black, one white. There was Grainger Morris, a black lawyer much admired, even loved, by Mavis (Joan Fontaine), a highly placed, liberal white woman. "Grainger was wonderful," she thought. "He wasn't mild and meek. . . . It was only with the . . . underprivileged that he was . . . infinitely tolerant." Then there was the Belafonte role: David Boyeur, the rabblerousing, cynical, cricket-playing trade union boss.[26]

At last it seemed that a studio would let slip Belafonte's tether, which had rendered him wooden and wasted in *Bright Road* and *Carmen Jones*. Zanuck seemed delighted to be again tweaking Southern white sensibilities, and Robert Rossen, the director, appeared excited by the prospect of returning to issues he had first encountered in *Body and Soul*. Then the texture softened. At the height of tension in Montgomery, Zanuck emerged from his first story conference still certain that his theme was social change *but* in good order, he said, and with civility. For example, in one of Belafonte's big moments Boyeur snaps at a white adversary that "color" is at the political center of every event on their island of "Santa Marta"; Zanuck insisted that they play the scene ever so lightly.[27]

Worse than playing Belafonte's Boyeur lightly, as though an echo of Harry the smoky-cellar folksinger, was the decision to cut the militant lawyer Grainger entirely and to give his softer lines to Boyeur. Truman Gibson, once the ranking black in the Pentagon and by 1957 consulting for the PCA, was puzzled by the erasure. Nothing *wrong*, he thought, but by cutting a role he "identified with . . . some of the basic reasons why [West Indians were] . . . pushing toward dominion status" were lost.

All that remained was a movie bathed in color and filled with stars, each entitled to a big scene through which they swirled as though in a Restoration comedy. On cue, conservatives in mustaches harrumphed their speeches, Boyeur twitted Government House, and politics remained where Zanuck had dropped them in *Pinky*. "We had to fight to say the word *love*," recalled Dorothy Dandridge as a shopgirl in love with a British lad with whom she chastely elopes offcamera to London. Mavis and Boyeur end a cool love affair with a parting played as though carved in stone. "He was black and I was yellow," Fontaine told her friends.[28]

What went wrong with this grand, near-operatic epic? Surely the makers were made skittish by the baleful eye of the PCA; and as surely Gibson was no Walter White; besides, there was no war whose slogans might have guided them. Certainly *Ebony* thought that "the Hollywood censors had made their pressure felt." Indeed, it gave Zanuck credit for the "seething mass of black people straining against the domination of these few whites" that had been his goal, and even credited Breen with a

In *Island in the Sun* (1957) Zanuck saw a revival of conscience-liberalism but gave in to pressure to lower the pitch of both politics and passion, including this scene between Harry Belafonte and Joan Fontaine, which did not survive the final cut. Copyright 20th Century–Fox.

A more politically tinged cut was that of a radical lawyer whose softened lines were given to Boyeur (Belafonte), a rakish labor boss, thereby diffusing Alec Waugh's already thin book. BFI. Copyright 20th Century–Fox.

wish to avoid "an unfair portrayal [that] . . . could inflame Negro people."[29]

In any case, perhaps for the last time, censors neutered a political film, albeit so brassily that it escaped no critic's barbed wit. Belafonte and Fontaine agreed that it had become a "terrible" case of "what might have been." Nunnally Johnson reported that in the preview "every time the story came to a big dramatic climax, the house roared with laughter."[30] "I am black," wrote Philip Roth of the film, "but o my soul is Technicolor." The rest of the weeklies agreed, tweaking Zanuck for his "camouflage for [a] hot issue" that made it "the worst of the summer's 'adult' films." As *Variety* said, it was only "enough to offend the South and disappoint . . . [the] North." However, their fan mail reflected the depths of racial antipathy that the PCA had urged them to dampen. For every letter that praised it as a means to promote "brotherhood," there were a dozen that spat against it as "propaganda" on behalf of an eventual "mongrel" nation. Oddly, audiences must have loved it for its tropical setting; it earned 20th's biggest profit since *The Robe*.[31]

Belafonte did not work in Hollywood for months, and only then in two movies, one of which was his own: Metro's *The World, the Flesh and the Devil* (1959), a *film noir* of the post-Mayer era, and *Odds Against Tomorrow* (1959), a creature of his own Harbel. The contrast was startling. The former film was a preposterously paltering retreat from racial issues that any TV viewer had come to see as urgent. Echoing the forced harmony of wartime movies, the interracial platoon of 1943 had become three survivors of a holocaust that empties Manhattan. At first, writer/director Ranald MacDougall teased around the edges of the black survivor's entry into a white world. Emptily, Belafonte plays with their toy trains, eats and drinks their provender, lives their life (without *them*), at last discovering one of their women (Inger Stevens) with whom he carries on a witty telephone flirtation which ends in a *menage à deux* fully as chaste as that in *Island in the Sun*—until the last white man on earth (as far as they know) turns up! Then the men dance on the cusp of taking direct action against each other (as though the woman had no investment in the outcome). Creepily, while the planet has become a vacant mote in the galaxy they act out a racial etiquette invented as a social control over nineteenth century slaves. For Belafonte it was "one of the worst experiences in my life." At first "an incredible opportunity," its soft ending "upset" him enough that he felt "stilted and very stiff," but too fearful of Hollywood's "sealing" its doors to future black material if he walked away from it.

Five months later, Belafonte's own firm, in association with Max Youngstein, a young producer at United Artists with a yen for backing politically challenging independent films, released its own revision of the war movie, this time with an edge on it: a theme of integration—or else. All seemed copacetic. Youngstein liked Belafonte's activism—"a real *schtarker* and he paid for it," he recalled of his black partner whose career had already, he guessed, been blighted by his politics. Belafonte had come to United Artists with William McGivern's novel, which he pitched as a cautionary tale about the racism that might "rip apart" our "destiny together." They took their book to Abe Polonsky who ever since *Body and Soul*, had been blacklisted, and to Robert Wise for whom it provided a return to the little RKO-style movies such as *The Curse of the Cat People* with which he had begun.

By the end of 1958, Polonsky gave them a draft made problematic only by a "coda" (Polonsky's term) that perhaps compromised Belafonte's sense that "racism kills in the end" everyone it touches. And yet, they saw themselves as a likeminded circle united by, as Belafonte recently put it, "a great sense of community" capable of "a lot of discussion" without rancor, and in the end secure in their faith that UA would offer "absolutely no interference." By then they needed only some one to "front" for Polonsky and turned to the black novelist, John Oliver Killens, who proved a trebled asset in that he provided a mask for the ostracized Polonsky, a black logotype for Belafonte's Harbel company, and a loyal friend who, for the rest of his life remained resolute in claiming authorship "unless," as Belafonte recently put it, "he was released from his oath."[32]

Thereafter, they shot exteriors in rural New York and then in the streets of Manhattan, and then cut and mixed in time for a release in the fall of 1959. In one of those rare marvels of a confluence of complementary ambitions, everyone received a payoff of sorts. Youngstein and UA broke even in the short run and made an eventual profit, not to mention an enrichment of their reputations for blending politics and quality; Polonsky grasped an opportunity to do work he could feel good about; Killens by fronting earned a welcome screenplay credit and added to his reputation as a politically aggressive black writer; Wise reasserted his reputation for turning out small gems of genre film; and Belafonte by hanging out "the shingle of producer," the only African American to do so at the time, successfully circumvented the Hollywood politesse that had hobbled earlier black material, including his own few films. Indeed, decades later, Belafonte still thought of *Odds Against Tomorrow* as one of a growing canon of realistic genre films meant to win back audiences by offering them socially significant movies as against bland television; "it changed the face of Hollywood forever," he proudly remembered it.[33]

Odds Against Tomorrow came at its viewers from a half-toned, graying screen as at first no more than a conventional "caper" movie such as *The Asphalt Jungle.* But it was also a criminal's version of a medieval quest. Belafonte's character is a musician struggling to keep his family together while scrounging to pay off gambling debts owed to a group of coolly ominous creditors. At this vulnerable moment he is recruited by a team of bankrobbers, a disgruntled and dishonorably discharged cop and a weathered, inwardly raging, perhaps impotent Southern racist. In this wartime platoon movie stood on its end, its characters drawn to each other by the commonality of bitterness and failure rather than the holiness of their cause, the thrust is more urgent, more insistent on a bad end unless they can live in enough harmony to pull their job. In bleak *film noir* style, the sun never shines and a heavy casually bursts a kid's balloon with his lighted cigarette. Perhaps there is a neat, sane life somewhere, but Ingram (Belafonte's character) cannot have it. Indeed, he is hostile to it, a loner, and suspicious of, as he tells his wife, "your ofay friends who are going to save the world." His only code is that of the horseplayer: If you lay five hundred on a horse and lose, you always pay, never welsh. He lives at night rather than in sunlight where bad things happen, buildings are angular and threatening, policemen feckless, crooks threatening. With evil prowling the sunny streets, plots are made only in seedy, dark rooms over whiskey in jelly-glasses.

The trio knocks over a small rural bank, but nothing goes well, and as their plan unravels, the racism at the core of their group eats away at their cohesion. As their botched job tightens the suspense, they crack; the racism takes over their plan and eventually kills them as they strug-

Harry Belafonte's own *Odds Against Tomorrow* (1959) reopened racism as an issue by reinventing the platoon movie, this time as a team of bank robbers whose job is spoiled by racial antipathy. Copyright United Artists.

gle atop an oil tank that explodes, charring them to ashes—moving a cop to remark dryly, and too on-the-nose for Polonsky's taste, that you can no longer tell the black corpse from the white.

Here someone at UA wambled. In the ads the racial was played down, a sign that they had decided to play it off without the political urgency with which they had begun. Not only did they play it off as part of a double bill, they saturation-booked it in major cities like Los Angeles and headlined the ad copy merely "This is real . . . this is raw" without specifying what "this"—the racism—was. Nonetheless, critics and audiences behaved well toward the movie and caught the importance Belafonte had wished it to convey. Generally, dissenting critics balanced their cavils with friendly copy as well. In *Variety*'s view, for example, its "allegory about racism" and its uncommonly good focus on a "normal, middle-class Negro home" were balanced by its too-pat ending, while to the *Saturday Review* its commendable theme was "hardly a breathtaking idea these days." Even among black critics, bifurcation ruled: Almena Lomax, for example, loved its "foreign" mood, but Belafonte's radical "nappy look . . . we don't dig."[34] Thus even when the circumstances of production were in the hands of a certified lefty, marketing and reception might still scare off future investors, particularly at that moment in 1959 less than a year away from the nationally arresting Greensboro sit-ins.

In the meantime, Hollywood faced the same thermidorean pressures that had always dampened its ardor for risk and guided it toward circumspection. Not that the studios casually elected to repeat a tamely liberal cinema; rather, the internal crises of the impact of television, the breakup of the vertically integrated system, the threat of takeover by conglomerates, and the evolution of segmented and fickle markets drove them toward, as *Variety* reported in 1953, "fewer and bigger pictures," selling off disused realty, dumping film archives to TV stations, and taking austerity measures such as making "runaway" films abroad. The resulting mood of caution edged the moguls toward a compromise between leading "a revolution in the imagination and behavior of Americans," as Martin Dworkin put it, and merely retreating into what Ring Lardner, Jr., called the "'Caine Mutiny Effect,'" the proffering of a liberal goal in reel one only to later invoke "reality" as a barrier to its attainment.[35]

The cautionary ending of *Odds Against Tomorrow* promised only conflict and tragedy unless Americans faced up to domestic racism (the thieves: Belafonte, Ed Begley, and Robert Ryan). Copyright United Artists.

The resulting movies marked the decade and in effect fed straightlines to a generation of waggish critics. As early as 1951 in *Bright Victory*, the theme of the message movies seemed safe only in a gimmicky plot in which a veteran must be blind in order to learn that all men are equal. In the same year, an anti-KKK tract, *Storm Warning*, could play only if its locale, Vicksburg, and its black victims were both erased, and a coda provided in which the hero sees that the evils of the South can be rooted out only by Southerners. The most warped instance of such indirection was John Ford's *Sergeant Rutledge* (1960). In this courtroom drama, a black soldier on the frontier is exonerated by a jury of good white people, but the evidence against him is so stacked and his innocence so trickily proved that, in this decade in which Eldridge Cleaver described rape as a political act, the stereotyped black brute reasserted itself in white memory.[36]

In another case, a sweet, well-received movie of Fannie Hurst's *Imitation of Life* (1934), a story of life on the edge of passing, was remade by Ross Hunter and Douglas Sirk into flashily Technicolored melodrama. In the original film, black and white mothers are partners in a pancake flour business and their daughters are friends—at least until Peola (Fredi Washington), the black girl, decides to pass and becomes an obligatory tragic mulatto who watches her own mother's funeral as a weeping outsider, but signifies her coming to terms with her ethnicity by attending a "colored" college in the South. But in 1959, the two women are merely mistress and servant and the black daughter (Susan Kohner) is played as a Tondelayo sitting at the end of the bar, fractured by the angular light that Sirk gave her. The melodramatic conventions that often awarded little dramatic victories to powerless women did little for the blacks, save to falsely place hope in the person of gospel singer Mahalia Jackson, who sang at the last-reel funeral.[37]

Almost any movie might be grace-noted with faint echoes of old liberal victories: In *The Young Don't Cry* (1957) a black woman takes pity on a white delinquent; in *Wild River* (1960) a white New Dealer defends black workers on a TVA dam; in *Your Cheatin' Heart* (1964) singer Hank Williams had a wizened black tutor; *The Eddie Duchin Story* (1955), said the *Sentinel*, had a "number of atmosphere players"; in *God's Little Acre* (1958), said *Variety*, a black farmer was "the only sensible human being of the lot"; in *Spartacus* (1961) Woody Strode played a black gladiator; in *The Last Angry Man* (1959) an angelic Jewish doctor takes a black street kid under his wing; and in dozens of movies black *fonctionnaires* speckled the squadrooms, hospital wards, and social agencies.[38]

Southern genre film, good and bad, bore the same trait of indirection. In Kazan's *Baby Doll* (1956), it was well used in the form of "scornful," wizened blacks who acted like a Greek chorus in commenting on a decadent, gothic South under whose "onionskin thin surface" was, said Kazan, "a titanic violence." *Ebony* trained itself to praise such slivers of meaning as Dilsey, the servant in Faulkner's *The Sound and the Fury* (1959) who seemed a bedrock of "strength and skill . . . supporting the troubled, decaying [white] clan."[39]

In the years following the war, American urban audiences also received a stream of foreign movies, mainly neo-realistic, mainly in art houses, and therefore meant to be taken as art. And yet, with respect to racial ideology they were as beset by indirection as American films, perhaps more so, as though Western intellectuals awaited some sign from blacks pointing the way to the next goal. In fact, in the 1940s, they were startlingly like their American cohorts in their insistence that all people were one under their multicolored skins. In the French case, the blacks were either fortunate colonials fighting side-by-side with their "old friend" the French army or beholden to French abolitionism, as in Duvivier's *The Imposter* (1944) and *La Montagne est verte* (1950), the latter a biopic of Victor Schoelcher, a French abolitionist who helped end slavery in 1848. When they took up American racism, as Sartre did in *The Respectful Prostitute* (1947), they were so off the mark that bookers played them off as "sexational" pornography rather than polemics.[40]

The Italians came out of the war politically leftist but ambivalent toward African Americans. On the one hand, as Raymond Borde and André Bouissy wrote, "the Left discovered in the war a kind of anti-Fascist golden age," while on the other, Cesare Zavattini wrote: "I defend the Negroes but I would never give them my daughter." At their best the resulting movies admitted blacks into Marxist theoretical system; at their worst they killed them off for trifling with Italian women. In the first instance, Roberto Rossellini's *Paisan* (1946), a black soldier in Naples has a drunken reverie while seated on a pile of rubble in the company of a waif to whom he describes, increasingly hollowly, the extravagant welcome home that soon will be his. Coming to his senses, he breaks off and describes the "shack" he actually lives in and the slim likelihood of any sort of welcome for a black soldier. Later, the waif, who has been stealing and supplying the black market with American military materiél, is caught by the soldier, who in a shattering scene is struck dumb by the poverty of the defeated Italians who live in caves. As reported in *Masses & Mainstream,* the scene indicated that "as an American Negro he understands only too well the plight of the Italians," or, in other words, in the Marxist formulation, the black soldier is as one with the white masses of the world.[41]

The other neo-realist films, at least those that reached America, played the same angle, albeit less well. Luigi Zampa's *Vivere in Pace* (*To Live in Peace*) used a black soldier in a drunken circle of allies and former enemies who convey the absurdity of war. "The only pure presentation of a man of his race," said James Agee, "that I have ever seen in a movie." We cannot know precisely what Agee meant, but because the role was the first since Stepin Fetchit to use clownishness to undercut the

Italian Marxist films linked racial issues to the class struggle as in *Paisan* (1946), where Dots Johnson catches a *scuggnizzo* who has stolen his boots but comes to regard himself and the boy as proletarian victims. NSF. Copyright OFL/Capitoni Film.

stolid rigidity of white dominance, he may have found in Zampa's movie a small instance of a leftist use of clowning to challenge the survival of antebellum racism in postwar movie culture. More in keeping with the American gangster formula, Alberto Lattuada's *Senza Pieta* (*Without Pity*) offered another raffish Negro, this time one who has taken up with Italian black marketeers. In a last-reel chase, MPs, Italian police, and gangsters pursue him and his woman through a ruined Livorno streetscape until at last their Jeep crashes and overturns on a beach where, with the upturned wheels still spinning, the theme music that had accompanied their scenes in search of freedom from these snares changes to "All God's Chillun Got Wings." Corny, but the point is the same. In death they are only people, no longer separated as in life by the biological trivia of race.

Not only did these Italian movies follow precisely the same course and derive the same political sensibility from the war as had the Americans', Italian movies of the 1950s regressed into the same sort of stasis as American films had done. At most they reinforced the PCA's and the NAACP's challenges to state censorship, on one occasion being attacked by the PCA for their unrelenting portrayal of "American Negroes as simple children of nature." Blacks were particularly nettled by *Angelo* (1951), a movie about "a little Italian waif whose father was a Negro GI." The ads for it asked "could their love overcome this barrier," to which the movie replied with a thumping "no": The mother dies in tragic childbirth. Thereafter, Italian movies forgot the war entirely and returned to staple black exotics and entertainers. In *Anna's Sin* (1954) and *Mambo* (1954), Katharine Dunham was the *doyenne* of an exotic dance troupe who appeared in the latticework between white plot incidents; in Fellini's *La Dolce Vita* (imported in 1960 by the old race movie firm, Astor) blacks were only fey props symbolizing decadent modernism; and in the Maciste series (1960s) white bodybuilders stood in for the erased legendary Carthaginian.[42]

Leftist internationalism also embraced African Americans in Italian movies, as in *Vivere in Pace* (1946) in which John Kitzmiller joins in a pacifist spree with a Wehrmacht soldier. Copyright Lux Pao Film.

Of all the European moviemakers, the British, struggling as they were both to overcome the dominance of Hollywood imports and live down the conservative films made by the Empire Marketing Board and the Post Office film unit, offered African Americans the least. At best they struggled to shift the British mentality from paternalism toward "our African colonies" to the sort of "partnership" sketched in W. H. Auden's *God's Chillun.*[43] Of course, few such films played American dates, not even *My Song Goes Forth,* a celebration of the Jubilee of Johannesburg featuring Paul Robeson's talking head. As to the features, they were torn between Harry Watt's 1950s movies that pitted pristine Africa against European despoilers and poachers, and others that formulated a theme of modernism versus primitivism personified by colonial commissioners and halfcaste Tondelayos who drive men to "go native." Among the best were Michael Powell and Emeric Pressburger's *The End of the River* (1948), in which Sabu opts for a "simple life" far from "a civilization he cannot understand," and Carol Reed's film of Joseph Conrad's *Outcast of the Islands* (1952), in which a godlike white trader (Ralph Richardson) fails to save his protégé, a petty criminal (Trevor Howard), from following a brown girl (Kerima) up an opaque Malayan river to his fate. In one film the "natives" are timeless, in the other they are a threat, much as they would have been in *Trader Horn* in 1931.[44]

No British movie, even those that made some mark in America, entirely broke with its colonial sources. In 1947, *Daybreak at Udi,* an Oscar-winning product of the Crown Film Unit done in a *March of Time* style, was about Ibos in the upper Niger who, said the voiceover, yearn for "community development, public hygiene, and literacy" through which they "are starting to bridge the centuries dividing their way of life and ours." Colonial commissioners are seen as mediators in a debate between "a higher standard of living" as against "traditional ways," a conflict paternally resolved when the British modify a tribal dance so that it ends with village males helping found a midwives' clinic. Despite its Oscar, exhibitors played it off in midtown, if at all, on bills with anthropological films and away from black audiences. As though fearful of black audiences, exhibitors gave similar treatment to Donald Swanson's South African film, *Jim Comes to Jo'burg,* perhaps because it resembled an oldtime race movie, stringing together acts such as the African Ink Spots and the Jazz Maniacs into a sort of quest movie. "Impishly wistful little story," said Crowther in the *Times.*[45]

Even when the *mise-en-scène* so resembled that of an American movie, the imports lacked an edge. *Variety* presumed that *Pool of London* (1950) had been made "with an obvious eye on the American market" made hot by message movies. A good little *film noir* that, as many Ealing films had done, embraced London and its folk, *Pool* seemed so "tastefully done"—not to say bland—that *Variety,* the Maryland censor, and the Breen office agreed on its suitability for Americans: this despite

Colonial officers and tribesmen, often as themselves, including here Ibo elder Oso Anibbebe in *Daybreak at Udi* (1947)—a dramatized documentary of the tension between the modern and the traditional—taught postwar audiences to reexamine colonialism. BFI. Copyright Empire Marketing Board.

Maryland's fear that it might "insite [*sic*] to racial riot," and the PCA's fretting over its physical intimacies. Its Jamaican sailor, Johnny (Earl Cameron), has a brush with the law over casually smuggling cigarettes as a favor to a pal, passes into the East End underworld while on the run, and meets a white movie cashier (Susan Shaw) with whom he has latenight coffee, a dance date, and a predawn walk in the rain past the usual sights (salvaged from a stalled documentary) to his ship, where his hasty sailing mercifully (for the censors) breaks off the liaison.[46]

Of them all, Thorold Dickinson's *Man of Two Worlds* (1946) drew

Earl Cameron and Susan Shaw in *Pool of London* (1951), playing with a restraint that anticipated censors' fears of "racial riots." BFI. Copyright Ealing Studios.

the best analogy between a dying colonialism and the shifting American racial scene—so much so that the NAACP briefly considered a tie-in. Despite a scarcity of color film cameras and stock made worse by allocations to *Henry V,* it had begun in 1944 when the Colonial Office pulled Dickinson off an Army film to work on an expression of hope for a postwar successor to colonialism.[47] The "man" of the title is Kisenga (Robert Adams) tribesman, physician, and concert pianist, who breaks off a concert tour to return to Africa to take up the struggle against the tsetse fly—and against Magole, the tribal elder (Orlando Martins) who resists modernity because it places his ancient powers at risk. "We don't like a white man with black skin," he tells Kisenga. Following a climax in which a colorful ritual all but subdues Kisenga and his sciences, the villagers harry Magole from their midst and permit the British to haul them to safety in the highlands.

No other movie so clearly set forth the notion of postwar partnership, and thus offered an analogue to the American drive for racial change. And yet the response of blacks to it revealed a gap between war-heightened expectations and the buttoned-down politics of the postwar era. What seemed to Dickinson "all the Negro students in Britain" rose and attacked the film in forums and in the *Times*, while in America black activists debated, then rejected, it. At first Walter White saw it as a useful parallel to the American case, but poet Langston Hughes reckoned it Magole's, not Kisenga's, movie because in black terms he was "really the hero, and the only one who seems to understand what the British colonial system is all about." In the end the NAACP came down on Hughes's side, either because of the presumption of a "savage-under-the-skin" who will revert at the first drumbeat, or because "the fate of Imperialism throughout the world is being decided" on terms that were already outreaching the modest proposals of *Man of Two Worlds* (and *Daybreak at Udi*). In any case, reviewers in America yawned and gauged it "watery propaganda" and at best "honest [and] dull."[48] Most bookers let it pass as though sensing a broad compass of liberals shared some sentiment akin to Hughes's.

At issue here, of course, was not the fate of a few movies, but how a postwar African American and liberal film culture perceived them. Heightened expectations stiffened resistance to all sorts of films that might have been praised before the war. Even *Ebony*, which was friendly

In Thorold Dickinson's *Man of Two Worlds* (1946) the struggle between modernism and tribalism is in the hands of Kisenga (Robert Adams), a black Albert Schweitzer, and Magole (Orlando Martins, *right*), the heavy whose traditional authority is at stake. Copyright Two Cities.

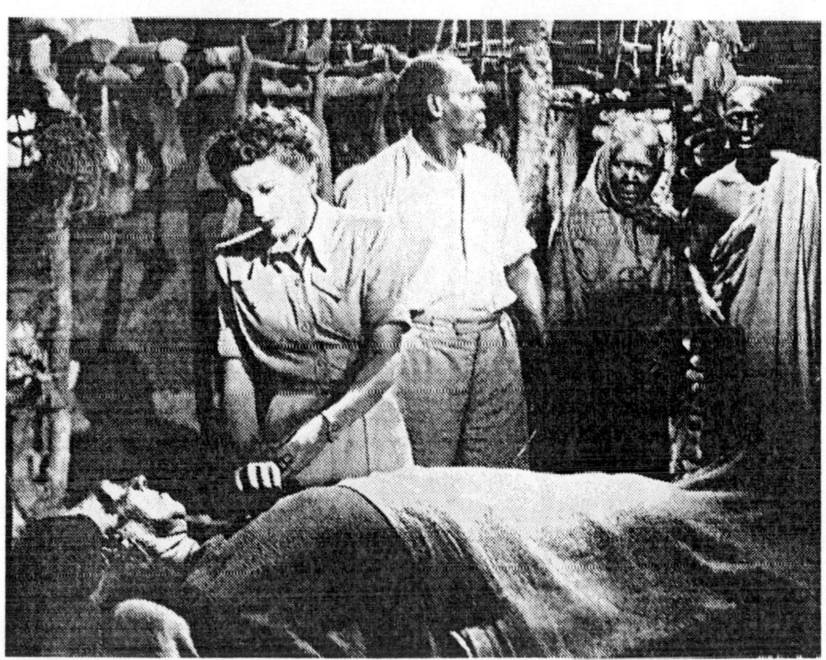

to almost any apparently sincere cinematic effort, thought *Pool of London* "dodges the implications of the situation it has created." And by 1950, the NAACP revealed its growing coolness toward movies from abroad, first by conferring with Hughes before using a film as a fundraiser, and second by the staff's reluctance to attend previews: More than half of them sent regrets in reply to an invitation to screen *Pool of London.*[49]

This gulf between past and present mentalities may be seen in the reception accorded Richard Wright's *Native Son* (1951), a famed prewar novel, a Broadway play produced by John Houseman and Orson Welles, and a postwar movie produced by Jaime Prades of Buenos Aires, directed by a leftist French director, Pierre Chenal, and written and acted by Wright himself. "Movies were his dish," a friend once said, and Wright's life confirmed it: He was an addicted moviegoer, interrogated Welles for inside dope, followed Steinbeck and Herbert Klein to Mexico to shoot *The Forgotten Village,* offered himself to OWI, and pitched black ideas to the National Film Board of Canada, Columbia, and anyone else who listened. By 1947, *Native Son* was in process despite being ten years old in a world changed by war. Undaunted, its makers sailed from France for New York, then Chicago, cutting a long script as they went. Unhappy with their locations, they departed and recreated a South Side slum in a Buenos Aires suburb, coaxed black English from a partly Hispanic cast, and lost touch with Wright's roots. The result was a strident, off-the-mark script in which street blacks are made to say "hot diggity dog" and "you blokes," women have "scantily clad bosom[s]" and dresses "pulled taut," and a voiceover is to speak in ponderous travelogue tones. By the end of 1949 with a full cast signed on, they were still rewriting and reshooting; by spring 1950, they wrapped final shooting $200,000 over budget, with editing yet to be done, and quarrels over style still clouding the final cut. In the end Wright, as his friend Welles sometimes did, left the cutting to others and let the film slip into the hands of a small distributor that assured its burial. "Stands little chance in the US," said *Variety* of a movie meant to please both postwar America and Marxist Europe by coupling racism and class conflict, a link few African Americans would have wished to make. Censors added their own resistance, particularly out of fear of "racial misunderstanding" and "friction" arising from its shrill ad copy such as: "A dead white girl—a nigger runs—what do you think happened?"[50]

As released the movie hammered home its points like a tract, and the actors declaimed their lines as though they were stump speeches. It also revealed the extent to which a foreign political voice, might sound off-key for having missed the shifting racial mentality of black and white Americans. Instead of incisive cinema, then it strove for obviousness. How shall we portray a white woman whose social convictions extended to racial issues? Easy. Put her in bright colors, dangle a cigarette from her wanton red mouth, give her tastes that run toward sweaty prizefights, jazz, and negligées—all codified in Hollywood lexicon as signs of deviance. Her mother's liberalism rises from the same metaphor that ran through *Bright Victory* whose blind veteran is able to see racial equality as sighted persons never will; her blindness accounts for "her deep interest in colored people." In contrast, her father has his sight but is capable only of "doing missionary work." After Bigger Thomas (Wright himself), the hero, inadvertently in a panic kills his liberal benefactor Mary Dalton, he is left with only one *real* friend, Jan, a radical lawyer who drinks Cuba Libres and, like the other lefties, tries too hard much as Mary had done: They hear a black singer and "all colored people are so gifted"; they hire Bigger as chauffeur, then ride up front and urge him to join a union; and *always* they insist "I'm on your side." The movie comes to life only after they are offscreen and Bigger is on the run from a crime he had not committed and a world he never made, hiding in ruined slums as the police ransack his haunts, and as the streets throb with the rhythm of the chase. In contrast, the trial that should have been the climax of a crackling story slips through Wright's fingers and trails off into Marxist cant spilled by Jan, the lawyer.[51]

"It was the damnedest thing you've ever seen," recalled Wright's friend Horace Cayton of the movie, which arrived on the heels of the message movie era that had helped sharpen black moviegoing. Bookers and ad-men were confounded, eventually playing it off as an apolitical "Dynamite Loaded Story of a Negro and a White Girl." Reviewers, the few who saw it, labeled it "awkwardly amateurish" or impolitely said, "I think it stinks." The NAACP, ever in search of a fundraiser or a sign of progress, pleaded "disgust" at its "sordid details" that might serve as "propaganda to continue race prejudice" and "damage our cause." In a national mood in which Walter White's new book was titled *A Rising Wind*, the NAACP took credit for driving *Amos 'n' Andy* from network television, and Poitier had finished *No Way Out* and signed for Zoltan Korda's *Cry, the Beloved Country* to be shot in the heart of apartheid in South Africa, *Native Son* could not help but seem an anachronistic, shoestring race movie.[52]

For the rest of the decade not a single European import deviated from the pattern of shrill rhetorical promise in the establishing shots from which the last reel retreated. *Simba* (1955), a lone British attempt to treat Kenyan nationalism, dug no more deeply than the daily press's reportage of Maumau terrorism. Ten years after *Pool of London*, Janet Green's police-procedural *Sapphire* (1959) wandered through the same London underworld, this time in Technicolor, and this time bolder in depicting the racism of thugs and cops alike, perhaps, said *Variety*, "inspired by" recent race riots in Notting Hill Gate. But Green thought its race angle "watered down" from her original scripts, and indeed race seems no more than a quirk of taste much like Mary Dalton's through which Scotland Yard infers that a murder victim is black from her red underwear! In turn, they are led to the murderer, an owlish, gray sort who, like the killer in *Crossfire*, kills to sate an inner racist demon.[53] *The Woman for Joe* (1955) was a carney melodrama with Earl Cameron in a small role that, said *Variety*, "breaks little new ground." *Sea Wyf* (*Wife* in the United States, 1957) featured Cy Grant as "Number 4," the black member of a shipwrecked party who has no more to do than had Canada Lee in *Lifeboat* a dozen years earlier. *Calypso* (1959), with Grant again, a folkish tale set in Trinidad, teased around a mulatto family's search for a white husband to enhance their daughter's social standing. Others offered no more than walk-ons: Paul Danquah's sailor in Shelagh Delaney's *A Taste of Honey* (1962); Johnny Sekka's cynically wise servant in *The Woman of Straw* (1964); boxer Hogan Bassey's appearance as "himself" in *The Heart of a Man* (1959).[54]

Even at their best these movies ran up false colors. In *Flame in the Streets* (1959), for instance, Roy Baker's idea had been to test glib liberal politics inside a family circle, the conflict here issuing from a liberal union leader (John Mills) facing his daughter's marriage to a black man (Sekka). But the point is lost not in kitchen table debate but in a wild, overblown Guy Fawkes Day riot and in red herrings in the form of a black slumlord in a big car with its seats covered in leopardskin and carrying his pregnant white wife. At home, Mills's wife (Brenda DeBanzie) is waspish, tautly fearing for her daughter, and spitting out her anger at an African mask. By tossing aside the genuine debate to which Mill and DeBanzie were entitled and closing on upbeat music the movie ended as, *Variety* said, a "not highly original peck at the color problem."[55]

Why should such retreats characterize so many movies? Brock Peters, who had played a fey West Indian in a *ménage à trois* in *The L-Shaped Room* (1962), traced it not so much to overt racism but to a need for "palatable" black characters who avoided "too much of a virile black image." Even when British movies led with a known American, as in *The Hill* (1964) with Ossie Davis as a colonial soldier jailed in a disciplinary camp, the point was sometimes so preciously drawn as to be lost on Americans. Davis's form of striking a blow for equality, for example, is to demand equal punishment, in this case in the form of a man-made hill in the desert that the prisoners, like Sisyphus, are obliged to climb over and over to exhaustion. "Permission . . . [to] run over the hill with the white men," he asks as though integrating a lunch counter. Few other national cinemas took up the slack. Marcel Camus's *Orfeo Negro* (1959) was startling in its rich color, carnival setting in Rio, hard-driving Samba beat, blackening of the myth of Orpheus and Eurydice, and the decision of Lopert to break out of the art house circuit, but unfortunately had so little impact that its American star, the singer Marpessa Dawn, could not use it to hype her career in either singing or film.[56]

In an age of indirection, to what did audiences turn for meatier politics? One classic periphrastic ploy was to elect a stand-in for African Americans, mainly Indians. The decade opened with *Broken Arrow* and closed with *Flaming Star*, both of which meant something to black moviegoers, the latter film so much that one critic reported it had "an underground reputation in black urban high schools."[57] Not that this was so new. Ever since Griffith's *Broken Doll* (1909), filmmakers had sentimentalized Indians, so much so that Zanuck once cautioned a writer against "the old familiar theme of the poor, downtrodden Indian." In a typical wartime expression, *Buffalo Bill* (1944), the scout and showman William F. Cody, morosely surveying the carnage after a battle, answers an officer's query, "They were all my friends." And in generations of westerns, mutual respect between cavalry and Indians was preserved by finding cupidity in white renegades in Indian mufti or in crooked Indian agents rather than in the policies of the government or the army.[58]

Broken Arrow possessed more impressive credentials: in Elliott Arnold's novel *Blood Brothers*, which had appeared in the same year as *Gentleman's Agreement*, and a director, Delmer Daves, who in conversation revealed "a special interest in the American Indian since childhood" and spoke of summers spent in Hopi "holy weeks." Their wish for authenticity extended to casting only one recognized star (James Stewart). And, seeing an obvious parallel in black and Indian plights, they played in the press and the ads Walter White's blurb: "It packs a terrific wallop against prejudice."[59] The hero Jeffords, a classic liberal, is caught between revanchist whites and Indians. He is even a stereotyped sacrificial liberal in that the death of his Indian wife is the occasion for peace and a conciliatory speech by the Apache chief, Cochise. "As I bear the murder of my people," he says, "so you will bear the murder of your wife." Of course, another reading might be that all of the dead in the movie are Indians, as though a warning that entering white circles can only result in death.[60]

The success of *Broken Arrow* stirred a cycle with racism at its center. Typically, as Selznick told Schary in weighing a biopic of the athlete Jim Thorpe: "I like the potential for making a picture that would take a roundhouse swing at prejudice." And in the same vein, in considering a remake of the old chestnut *Ramona*, Zanuck asked his writer to "eliminate most of the old fashioned stuff." *Variety* routinely reviewed the products as to their success at "tak[ing] the redskins' side" or teaching "a salutary lesson in tolerance."[61] Toward the end of the decade the tendrils of culture, clan, and tribe grew so intricate, even tortured, in their view of race relations that they seemed mannerist. The *Spectator*, for example, thought John Huston's *The Unforgiven* (1960) so "odd-looking and odd-feeling" that it could only speculate that it was nettled by some nameless "bee in [its] bonnet."[62] But so hot was the topic that all the networks started Indian series. As Sam Marx said with unintended oxymoron after a poll taken by the ad agency Young and Rubicam, "The public loves the Indian stuff [so] . . . we intend to portray the Indian as a human being, despite his being a savage."[63]

Of them all, *Flaming Star* may have meant the most to African Americans. Like *Broken Arrow*, it set out to use the western idiom to deal with racial politics, but unlike most of its peers it eschewed obliqueness and laid into a melodrama a story of ethnic tension. It began at Fox in 1958 with a draft by Nunnally Johnson and was pitched to the New York office as a universal essay on racial tolerance. But from top to bottom, no producer picked it up, at least until 1960. Then David Weisbart, who liked it as a social document, was assigned to produce just as the studio cast Elvis Presley in the role of Pacer, a mixed-race cowboy who lived with his white father (John McIntyre) and Indian mother (Dolores Del Rio). They engaged a western writer then on a hot streak, Clair Huffaker, to give bulk to Pacer's part without diminishing the brotherhood angle. Late in 1960, they chose an action-director, Don Siegel, which, coupled with a decision to lay in songs to take advantage of Presley's shtick, seemed to promise a contradictory goal: a movie in the tradition of *Pinky* and *Broken Arrow* but with music.[64]

The result was a movie that succeeded in ways none of them had expected, certainly far more than anything that Belafonte had been allowed to do and more than the common run of interesting sequences in movies. Black youths took to it, perhaps because Pacer's mixed identity replicated their own tensions between goals and ghettoes, or perhaps because of the voice of Presley's own identity as poor white who brought black musical idiom to a white audience. From reel one, the intergroup tensions tighten as Kiowas raid a farm, forcing white neighbors to demand of Pacer's mixed family a declaration of racial loyalty. At first his father insists on the right to choose peace rather than sides, but his wife's death at the hands of bushwhackers renders the issue moot and drives Pacer into the arms of the Kiowa side of his pedigree, where his half-brother Buffalo Horn (Rodolfo Acosta) again demands tribal fealty. Each ensuing incident becomes a matter of blood that demands choices that Pacer refuses until at last, mortally wounded and incapable of fighting, he leads one of his white half-brothers to the safety of the ranch but returns to the Kiowas to die as an Indian. The forked path of the plot ended as a neat and surely unintended analogue for the black sense of the "twoness" of American life. By avoiding a falsely easy solution, Siegel had signaled an important break with Hollywood formula in a popular movie of this sort. Thus *Flaming Star* capped off the decade by reaching beyond the static frontier left by the message movie era and probing the prickly matter of ethnic pluralism. No other genre could say as much throughout the calm before the Greensboro sit-ins of 1960.[65]

As we have seen, the era of conscience-liberalism from war through the message movie cycle was followed by, if not a political ice age, at least a politics of cool, buttoned-down style. But it is important to note that parallel to this apparent calm, a range of critical voices persisted in expressing a wish for a break through the cooled crust to the still-warm film culture beneath it; the popularity of *Flaming Star* itself testified to the young audience's willingness to watch for it. Doc Young and other black critics grumbled at the practice of casting famous blacks such as Archie Moore and Althea Gibson from the sporting world "in degrading roles [as] part of a plot to maintain the old racial status." The trades joined in, complaining of residual "familiar bwana monkeyshines."[66] But no liberal consensus emerged to define the goals that had seemed so clear when guided by war aims. On the one hand, as seen in a 1953 report by Edward Madden of NBC "to the Negro community," the network boasted of a new policy to cast roles according to "integration without [racial] identification," as though legislating the notion that under the skin all Americans were alike. On the other hand, fear of the new gripped everyone: Blacks feared movies focused on "miscegenation" rather than racial politics; the studios still fretted over the Dixiecrat movement and its impact on Hollywood. As the producer Albert Zugsmith recalled, Hollywood was faithful to "equality and all that" but paradoxically "scared shitless to try a really black picture."[67]

The tension between coolness and ardor may be seen in four failed movies of 1958–1959, the eve of the "freedom rider" summer and a year from Greensboro. *The Night of the Quarter Moon, St. Louis Blues, Anna Lucasta,* and *Take a Giant Step* each revealed the problems in dealing with the interiors of African American life. *St. Louis Blues* suffered from a fear of depicting black conflict as though a biopic of the composer W. C. Handy foreclosed writing in black heavies. Moreover, casting musical figures—Nat Cole and Eartha Kitt—led to the storyline being reduced to a string of vaudeville turns. And rather than seeking universal themes *in* black culture, its makers enameled on a coat of "common, human problems." A twenty-two-day shooting schedule, coupled with the obligation they felt to ensure a crossover audience by squeezing in twenty-six of Cole's recording-hits, required juggling the stars' nightclub gigs. The strain ruined the movie and, according to its director, Allen Reisner, led them to quickly "get the picture out and [not] worry too much about the concept." *Variety* found the result so "genteel" that "you might wonder why" blacks bothered to sing Handy's blues.[68]

Down in Culver City at Metro, Zugsmith set about making an exploitation movie that teased around the sensational aspects of race relations while at the same time tweaking the studio's reputation as "a bastille [sic] of conservatism." But the weak script, unfounded in any core of actual black life, doomed the eventual film, *Night of the Quarter Moon,* to the exploitation grind houses. Throughout its hasty shooting schedule, the actors tinkered with it, director Hugo Haas tossed into it his familiar women placed in degrading jeopardy, and the studio played it off in a shrill style. Its defining scene was a courtroom sequence in which a judge requires a woman to disrobe as proof of her racial identity. The result was a lost opportunity to play honestly to an increasingly apparent attention being paid by Americans to the national racial crisis in their midst.[69]

Even prospective movies that were pedigreed dramas such as Louis Peterson's *Take a Giant Step* (1959), Philip Yordan's *Anna Lucasta* (1959), and Lorraine Hansberry's *Raisin in the Sun* (1961), faced the problem of Hollywood timidity and the resulting wish to launder the more strident aspects of black culture as a device for assuring broader appeal to whites. All three black movies (Yordan's was actually a veneered-over, ten-year-old melodrama about Polish immigrant life) seemed torn between plunging into the incipient market and altering themselves to fit outmoded racial ideas, between reaching for values that television could not handle and adapting themselves to TV's bland tastes. All were cluttered, naturalistic, busily detailed looks at the husk of black life, but each of the independent movies—*Giant Step* and *Lucasta*—were only superficially so, having "perversely," said one critic, chewed on more than they had bitten off.[70] Only *Raisin in the Sun,* by a major studio with a major star and supporting cast, dared to portray a genuine core of black culture (albeit minus a few shards of black politics). In the end then they pleased no one—whites, black nationalists, or black assimilationists.

Through this prim era floated Sidney Poitier, a bland antidote to racial tension. Beginning with his restrained intern in *No Way Out* he adapted his controlled persona to his craft much as Eisenhower had done to his. Next he was a South African priest in Alan Paton's *Cry the Beloved Country,* a sentimentally hopeful treatment of apartheid in which teeming black Jo'burg was more of a heavy than was the Boer racial system. In the gossip that flowed back from Africa, Canada Lee complained of "degrading" treatment, while, in keeping with his emerging film persona, Poitier was quoted as accepting indentured servitude to Zoltan Korda as a means of entry into the country, sloughing it off as a case of taking "a punch in order to land a harder one." In a movie more about racial amity across barriers than about the barriers, Poitier played a priest caught between the cultures, the role that would become his property in the ensuing decades. A black critic pronounced it "a fresh wind," liberals agreed, and the NUL used it as a fundraiser.[71]

Thereafter, almost all of his roles bore the same burden of restraint in the service of harmony, with himself as the honest broker torn between polar loyalties. *Red Ball Express* (1952) combined barrackroom rivalry with a tribute to the black role in the invasion of Europe. "A little step forward," said the *Eagle,* and done with "dignity and a good amount of equal treatment." A year later he was in not a platoon but a black basketball team led to victories by its white founder. "Okay," said *Variety*, with a minimum of "soapboxing." In William Wellman's Disney-like dog-movie *Goodbye, My Lady* (1956) he had the Remus role in *Song of the South*, retooled into self-possessed, educated farmer "from across the river" who becomes a force in the coming of age of a white boy. In a bigger, better message movie in the grand style of the genre, Richard Brooks's film of Robert Ruark's *Something of Value* (1957), Poitier was again caught between cultures in the struggle, as Brooks said, to get whites "to relinquish the role of masters and become allies" in Kenya. Everyone suffers, of course, for the point is that racism hurts. But it is Poitier's wife and eventually himself who die as his friend, a white farmer (Rock Hudson), swoops up his son, his stake in a better future, and saves him from death. Brooks himself saw the irony in this revival of the "white man's burden" and in spite of himself found it a "laughable" foreshadowing of the chain that literally bound Poitier to Tony Curtis in *The Defiant Ones* (1959). Four years later Poitier repeated the role and the message in a Presbyterian tract, *The Mark of the Hawk*, in which he steers African nationalism away from "the desire to destroy" and to a happy end. Sometimes, as in *Band of Angels* (1957), a misfired film of Robert Penn Warren's book, Poitier's maturing craft almost saved a movie from itself (and, in this case, a fading Clark Gable and a "bored" director). But in the end, although Poitier emerged unscathed, Archer Winsten in the *Post* thought the movie had done little "to elevate itself above soap opera," and *Ebony* reckoned it only an also-ran in the "race relations derby." As each succeeding movie aimed ever more predictably down the middle, Poitier's hopes for a breakthrough *this time* would be, as in *Paris Blues* (1961), dashed by a case of studio cold feet. That movie, about two jazzmen who meet two schoolteachers on vacation in Paris, begins as a bohemian story of interracial flirting, but by the second reel the four merge unremarked into color-coded pairs (Poitier and Diahann Carroll, Paul Newman and Joanne Woodward). Three years later, he appeared in a costume melodrama of Vikings versus Moors, *The Long Ships*. *Variety* reported Southern pressure to trim Poitier's harem of its white odalisques, but the script saved them the trouble by having him, blessedly for the censors' sake, take an oath of chastity for the whole movie. In 1960, the keepers of his image cast Poitier in a retread of the World War II genre, *All the Young Men*, this time set in Korea and intended "to present the Negro in a position of leadership," as if the army had not already done so.[72]

This unfair chronicle of a career was not meant to blame a fine, disciplined actor for an exhausted age that had run dry of ideas even as the civil rights movement began to heat up in Montgomery, Tuscaloosa, Greensboro, Little Rock, and elsewhere. Rather, events provided Eisenhower with an opening to act boldly in using federal powers to hold open the schools of Little Rock, far earlier than they provided

At first blush Poitier saw *Paris Blues* (1961) as a chance to give movie politics another spin, but a case of studio cold feet resulted in the conventional one black pair and one white pair, as acceptable in Paducah as in Paris. BFI. Copyright United Artists.

Hollywood with a crisis it could understand well enough to formulate into politically engaging or even informative movies. Nonetheless, in three good movies that spanned the decade Poitier used his emerging screen presence to at least make a few attempts.

As in the past, such material owed its being to liberals whose reformist politics made them prone to respond to crises in ways that drew them to Poitier as their instrument. Such a moment came in 1954 with Evan Hunter's *The Blackboard Jungle,* its audience readymade by teenagers raised up on rock 'n' roll and rebellion, adults made tense by crumbling cities, disaffected youth, *Brown vs. Topeka Board,* and serialization in the *Ladies' Home Journal.* The story of redemption in a slum school was also an event in a struggle in Culver City among Mayer, who once ran Metro as a fief, Schary, the no longer young Turk, and Richard Brooks's tabloid mind. To the oldtimers, Schary and Brooks seemed "a little red," obsessed with "dirty fingerprints" in their projects, and in this case, hellbent on placing an "arrogant [black] smart ass" at the center of their movie.[73]

These forces easily inspired the dismay of Eric Johnston in the

MPAA, Senator Estes Kefauver, who used it as the pretext to "probe" Hollywood again, Mayer's cronies on the lot, and Ambassador Claire Booth Luce, who would squelch its showing at Venice. The slum classroom was like the war movie platoon in its polyethnicity, but far from being soldiers, the students were castoffs of demoralized society represented by the beleaguered, cynical, burned-out teachers. In the central trope a young teacher is reduced to tears when he offers to play for his class his collection of jazz masters, which they greet with a spree of giggling, howling vandalism while the soundtrack overrides the jazz with Bill Haley's "Rock Around the Clock"—which Brooks had played on the set as a mood piece.[74] At stake was the liberal hope: whether society could marshal its best values in time to save its less fortunate from the worst of the system.

The drama centers on Dadier (Glenn Ford), a teacher not yet worn down by the system, and Artie (Vic Morrow), a snarling, hateful kid bent on leading the class to a bad end. Between them is Miller (Poitier), who may yet be won over to civility. In their key scene, Dadier must disarm knife-wielding Artie, forcing Miller to choose. Miller's opting for the teacher, for the good of the group, and for liberalism's faith in redemption was not so cheap a trick as to end on a happy closure, but its makers did intend a reaffirmed American faith in the worth of the individual in a possibly hospitable society. Left unsaid, of course, were the fates of real-life, ordinary boys left in undiminished poverty and untouched by the good intentions of a movie. Yet audiences loved its proffer of hope. From its first previews in Encino to its turn as *Life*'s Movie of the Week, its title became a nonceword for urban despair and prodded educators to take up remedies for their own "jungles." In Encino they liked it, 260–13, thought it excellent, even magnificent (save for a dissenter put off by a black lead), and it went on to earn the ten-million profit that Schary had predicted for MGM. Its spectacular success promised a booming return to self-consciously social films: It made Luce look like a vulgar, kneejerk anti-red at Venice, stiffened the MPAA's resolve against her and other censors, and confirmed Poitier as a moviestar icon of a seamless, waxy-smooth liberal politics. In each new movie he learned to play to the edge of his control, as though simmering beneath a surface of repressed stammers and catches in the throat that functioned like volcanic fissures through which hidden powers seeped.[75]

Three years later, Poitier's next vehicle, *Edge of the City* (1957) carried the genre—for by then Poitier's movies had become a genre—into the family circle itself, the last bastion of racial exclusivity. It too seemed bold and timely following both Eisenhower's uncharacteristic decision to send troops to Little Rock to reinforce a judicial finding that racial integration of schools was required by the Constitution, and the film's having enjoyed a TV viewership of millions in its original format on Philco Playhouse as *A Man Is Ten Feet Tall.* Almost as conspirators,

Edge of the City (1957) was startling in its insistence on defining racial issues as complex, perhaps implacable, and embedded in ordinary folk as well as in the crazies of *No Way Out*—and for carrying the drama into the quiet corners of ordinary life. Copyright Metro-Goldwyn-Mayer.

writer Robert Alan Aurthur, Poitier's agent Martin Baum, and NBC's Fred Coe struggled to bring Poitier to the small screen despite an apparent blacklist on which his name had appeared.[76] As he improved in his role as ambassador between the races, he and these artificers of his image effectively half-formed the next decade's racial history.

Poitier was Tommy, a stevedore easily the superior of any other man in his gang, particularly Axel (John Cassavetes), a neurotic deserter, and Charlie Malik (Jack Warden), a sadistic boss who cannot bear the black intruder into his circle. Tommy invites Axel to dinner, into his innermost circle where few whites have ever intruded and where Axel sees the happy contrast with his own moody, haunted life as a deserter. "Tommy, of course, *is* the way Axel *should* be," said David Susskind at the beginning of production. Yet obviously, Tommy has replaced Charlie at the center of Axel's dock life, resulting in a daily round of baiting and harrying until they fight with baling hooks and Tommy dies—Poitier's finest scene in the way he allowed the crust of his control to crack and reveal the magma underneath. Axel, overcome with remorse at the silence extorted from him by Tommy's killer, finally informs on him, and subsequently makes peace with both his family and the army. At last Axel was ready to face himself, said Metro's synopsis, and to straighten out what remained of his life, leaving the audience, of course, to conclude as in other cases that white well-being hinges on black sacrifice, a point not lost on black critics, who began to carp at Poitier's work. Indeed, director Martin Ritt recalled that Tommy's death stirred "a goddamned riot in the theatre."[77]

Nonetheless, as a message movie it was a roaring success. Overwhelming, gripping, and other raves, said the preview cards as they praised the use of race as a fact rather than an angle (but for one disserter against this sort of "thing"). The black press liked its "mixed"-cast story in which, as *Ebony* wrote, race was "completely ignored," thus contending, much as Stampp's formulation of liberal goals had assumed, that Negroes were "innately" "white men with black skins." The trades and the national press joined in. "Provocative, courageous," said *Variety;* "startlingly good," said *The New Yorker.* They had narrowed the focus of the issue to a small arena on terms challenging to audiences, much as the old war movie genre had wished to do.[78]

At the same time, it must be said that the age remained resolutely as cool as ever. Circumspection still governed the presentation of self, and ethics and politics, as Riesman had pointed out in *The Lonely Crowd,* seemed "otherdirected" and drawn from peers rather than from inner absolutes and traditional adages. Thus Poitier's work teetered on the edge of change, even half-leading it, but always in a cooled-down mode increasingly defined by the keepers of his image, whose fiscal duties included husbanding a star too valuable to risk on flights of radical daring. Thus from 1959, the year of *The Defiant Ones,* through 1963, the year of his Oscar for *Lilies of the Field,* he became more star than actor, a fact recognized by a growing pool of black and white fans, critics, and, it must be said, bankers, as well as those charged with "finding stories for Sidney" that advanced the edge of change without risking the star.[79]

Much as Eisenhower had defined the national politics of the era, so Poitier was able to define the last years of the genre of combat movies, each with its lone black hero, that had begun with Walter White's visits to Hollywood in the 1940s. But the exhaustion by 1968 of the genre and the ennui of its audience, both becoming apparent as new social conditions thrust up new cinematic formulations, coincided with the exhaustion of Poitier's own genre. The sweet, well-meaning ambience and performances of *Lilies of the Field* (1963), *To Sir with Love* (1967), in which he played the lone black teacher in a slum school (not unlike Dadier in *Blackboard Jungle*) in the East End of London, and *Guess Who's Coming to Dinner* (1968), in which he was promoted from the intern in *No Way Out* to internationally famous physician to the United Nations, formed the apogee of a career that would soon start its slide toward nadir. By 1968, the nation had experienced three major assassinations,

Homer Smith (Sidney Poitier) in *Lilies of the Field* (1963) tutored a group of nuns in the nuances of spirituals, a movie version of Poitier's real life mission as an icon of a "crossover" sensibility. Copyright United Artists.

including that of Martin Luther King, a failure of oldline black leadership, a loss of collective black focus on shared goals, a retreat into black nationalism, and a waning attention to poverty in the cities on the part of national white politicians.

Thus Poitier, who should have enjoyed a career as ever-expanding as that of Bette Davis or Spencer Tracy, found himself charged as an accomplice in a plot to diminish national attention to racial issues. His black (and white) critics grew in numbers, in the blunt cruelty of their attacks, and in their eagerness to erase the memory of his having attained professional heights never before reached by an African American performer. His era had begun with Hollywood's preference for his work over that of Belafonte (and all other black performers, male and female, save for the song-and-dance work of Sammy Davis, Jr.). It ended in a slough of racial self-recrimination brought on by African American critics too young to remember Hollywood before Poitier had helped change it. In classic liberal fashion he assumed blame for events and felt trapped by them. "The closest Hollywood came" to good black portrayals, he recalled, was "the one-dimensional, middle-class imagery I had embodied." Therefore, he concluded, he felt a "unique relationship to both sides of the problem." As Stepin Fetchit had become an eponym for uncle tomming, so Poitier had done for cinematic obsolescence. A piece about a football player turned action-actor was thoughtlessly headlined, "Don't compare me with Sidney, his pictures don't make money anymore." Through it all, Poitier remained at home, feeling each "cheap-shot," but declining to answer in public such essays as Clifford Mason's acerbic *Times* piece, "Why Do White Folks Love Sidney Poitier So?"[80]

He simply had lasted long enough to become old hat. Times and goals had changed. Much as the catchphrase "a credit to his race" had been proudly attached to Joe Louis only to turn sour during the war, so Poitier's paragons, which had been part of new postwar racial arrangements to which blacks were able to consent, gradually passed into self-parody. After the political murders of major figures of the 1960s, the old bargain not only seem violated, but newly violent urban conditions forced a reopening of negotiations for fresh terms that were far more African American nationalist in their texture. The presentation of self in all its aspects—dress, music, body language—defined the African American on the screen. In the crisis in which politicians foresaw a nation of two cultures, one black and poor, the other white and comfortable, in which each graphic television report of urban violence helped redefine blacks as violent, volatile, and unrestrained by white law or convention, conscience-liberal movies came to an end, along with the careers of actors such as Sidney Poitier who had given their professional lives to them.

Contrasts were everywhere: between buttoning down and "letting it all hang out," forthright John F. Kennedy and sweatily meretricious Richard M. Nixon, the cool blacks of Greensboro and the particolored robes of Ron Karenga's cultural nationalists, the self-effacing athletes before TV coverage and the hotdogging later athletes for whom style mattered as much as substance, the old litiginous strategy of the NAACP and the "Maumauing" of post liberal activists, and so on.

The engine of change was television. To the extent to which it claimed to report news while also meeting the wishes of the viewer, it became like movies had been in half-forming the forces it was half-formed by. A given program reached millions of viewers in a commonly shared, though physically isolated, moment that contributed to a sense of belonging to, as Benjamin Singer called it, an "electronic community." The masses of blacks and whites in marches on Selma and Washington, and the eventual riots at the cores of great American cities, eventually stretched from news footage to primetime melodramas that desperately sought a "relevance" that no producer would have cared about in former times. For hours on end, television began to offer, as Clarence Mitchell of the NAACP reported, "a profoundly constructive effect" on racial politics, or as Nicholas Katzenbach of the Department of Justice phrased it, "a central means of making a private moral conviction public"; still more pointedly, as Bill Monroe of NBC formulated it, television became "the chosen instrument of the black revolution."[81]

Meanwhile, Hollywood's sense of itself, at least with respect to the treatment of African America, slowly lost its clarity of purpose. By 1969, *Newsweek* portrayed the studios as victims of "cultural changes they [could not] comprehend," as they not only stammered in expressing a politics of newly volatile race relations, but also lost their place in the front rank of popular arts. And as they slumped, contempt for movies among blacks grew apace. Poitier himself felt that in the movielots the feeling was that "we don't have race movies, we have Sidney Poitier films." And among the audiences, for every critic who cautiously thought that "too much authenticity in this area can be uncomfortable," there were legions of fans like those who, as the Poitier character in *The Defiant Ones* had leaned over from his perch on a moving train to help the white convict to whom he had been chained, shouted, "Get back on the train, you fool!" Indeed, when a sample of high school students was polled after seeing *Up Tight* (1967), the black version of O'Flaherty's tale of the Irish rising, they vastly preferred the rebellious antihero as against the figures who, though no less "black" in their politics, counseled restraint.[82]

On the left, African Americans began to seek political advantage among the opportunities presented by the breakup of the classical studio system and the intervention of the federal Equal Employment Opportunity Commission (EEOC). Following visits to Hollywood in the mid-1960s by Herbert Hill, labor secretary of the NAACP, during which he threatened to seek to "disfranchise" studio guilds that had been denying blacks access to employment through grandfather clauses, the studios began to grudgingly (and without federal monitoring) admit black apprentices to the guilds, thus opening the movielots to new ideas. Meanwhile, independent filmmakers, much as Levitt, Loeb, and others once had done, began to find an audience. LeRoi Jones, a poet who by 1967 had become Amiri Baraka, spoke of the film of his drama *Dutchman* as "the beginning of new movies . . . [of] revolutionary revelation." And H. Rap Brown, who had succeeded to the leadership of the Student Non-Violent Coordinating Committee, touted *Up Tight* as "well done" except that it "should have been for the Negro what 'The Battle of Algiers' should have been" for its oppressed constituency in French North Africa.[83]

The studios themselves felt the heat, not only from declining ticket sales, but from critics such as Crowther of the *Times*, who diffidently proposed that "it would seem good business . . . if more films on so-called dangerous subjects, such as the Negro problem, were made at limited costs." And from blacks came attacks on specific films such as a

Stanley Kramer's *The Defiant Ones* (1958) seemed too "on the nose" for some political tastes, but nonetheless good (in its tabloid fashion) in its use of a chain, first as a shackle of two enemies (Tony Curtis and Poitier), then as the metaphorical bond between them. BFI. Copyright United Artists.

lilywhite version of William Styron's controversial novel *The Confessions of Nat Turner*, in this case so barbed as to induce dropping the idea, a decision that led the *Sentinel* to proclaim blacks had made "Hollywood aware of this tide of black power." In this mood, quasi-independent filmmakers such as Melvin Van Peebles made startlingly violent, truculent celebrations of black outlawry such as *Sweet Sweetback's Baadasssss Song* (1971) that lashed out at Hollywood classical conventions while drawing an urban, youthful black and crossover audience that for a decade prowled neighborhood theatres in search of sequels that challenged the mannered style of, say, *To Sir with Love*.[84]

Amidst this clangor, Poitier made the last movie of his liberal period, a film that emerged from his own creative centers and even his own firm. *Brother John* (1971) revealed the nature of the changed times and Poitier's distance from them. The movie was a deistic fantasy about "an observer from another world who walks the earth . . . [to] determine whether mankind is worthy of salvation"—an unintended parody of Poitier's slowly evolving actual role in Hollywood and his preference for cool detachment. In an era when a typical bumpersticker slogan snarled out, "If you are not part of the solution then you are part of the problem," detachment amounted to treason. And critics were having none of it. "Deadpan holier-than-thou immobility," said one of them of a movie that seemed aimed toward Poitier's "own canonization."[85]

The era of conscience-liberal movies ended as though awaiting its own moral equivalent of OWI and Walter White: a fresh response to new conditions created by the civil rights movement. The movies that had defined the terms of an age of integration would themselves be succeeded by the movies they had foreshadowed. The new movies so avidly sought an African American audience that *Variety* called them "blaxploitation" movies and a weekly news magazine warned America to "prepare to meet thy boom." But that is another story.

Abbreviations

AA	*Afro-American* (Baltimore)
ACE	American Council on Education
ACG-CU	Alexander C. Gumby Collection, Columbia University
AFC	American Film Center
AFI/CAFS	American Film Institute Center for Advanced Film Studies
AFRA	American Federation of Radio Artists
AHC-WY	American Heritage Center, Laramie, Wyoming
AJC	American Jewish Committee
AMPAS	Academy of Motion Picture Arts and Sciences
AN	*Amsterdam News* (New York)
ANP	Associated Negro Press
AVNA-DC	Audiovisual Section, National Archives, Washington, D.C.
BFI	British Film Institute
CB-UT	Clarence Brown Papers, University of Tennessee
CB-CHS	Claude A. Barnett Papers, Chicago Historical Society
CCNP	Coordinating Council of Negro Performers
CD	*Chicago Defender*
CE	*California Eagle* (Los Angeles)
CIAA	Coordinator of Inter-American Affairs
CIO	Congress of Industrial Organizations
CPUSA	Communist Party of the United States of America

DGA	Directors Guild of America
DOS-TX	David O. Selznick Papers, Humanities Research Center, University of Texas at Austin
DS-SHSW	Dore Schary Papers, State Historical Society of Wisconsin
DW	*Daily Worker* (New York)
EFLA	Educational Film Library Association
EPFL	Enoch Pratt Free Library (Baltimore)
FD	*Film Daily*
FDR	Franklin D. Roosevelt Presidential Library
FEPC	Fair Employment Practices Commission
GEH	George Eastman House Museum of Photography, Rochester, New York
GPJ-UCLA	George P. Johnson Collection, University of California at Los Angeles
HDC	Hollywood Democratic Committee
HH-AMPAS	Hedda Hopper Papers, Academy of Motion Picture Arts and Sciences
HICCASP	Hollywood Independent Citizens Committee for the Arts, Sciences and Professions
HR	*Hollywood Reporter*
HRC-TX	Humanities Research Center, University of Texas at Austin
HST	Harry S. Truman Presidential Library
HUAC	Committee on Un-American Activities, House of Representatives
HWM	Hollywood Writers' Mobilization
ICCASP	Independent Citizens Committee for the Arts, Sciences and Professions
IFRG	Interracial Film and Radio Guild
ILGWU	International Ladies' Garment Workers Union
ITC-DC	Irving Thalberg Collection, Dartmouth College
JBC	John Baker Collection
JWJ	James Weldon Johnson Collection, Beineke Library, Yale
LAS	*Los Angeles Sentinel*
LAT	*Los Angeles Times*
LA-WSU	Labor Archives, Wayne State University, Detroit, Michigan
LC	Library of Congress
LD	Louis DeRochemont Papers
LD-RD	Louis DeRochemont–*Reader's Digest,* Inc.
LH-JWJ	Langston Hughes Papers, Johnson Collection, Yale
LM-AHC	Lyman Munson Papers, American Heritage Center, Laramie, Wyoming

LM-FDR	Lowell Mellett Papers, Franklin D. Roosevelt Presidential Library
MGM-LD	Metro-Goldwyn-Mayer Legal Department
ML-BU	Mugar Library, Boston University
MM-UG	Margaret Mitchell Papers, University of Georgia
MMR	Modern Military Records
MOMA	Museum of Modern Art, New York
MPAA	Motion Picture Association of America
MPD	*Motion Picture Daily*
MPH	*Motion Picture Herald*
MPPDA	Motion Picture Producers and Directors of America (later, MPPA)
MSCB	Maryland State Censor Board
NAACP	National Association for the Advancement of Colored People
NA-DC	National Archives, Washington, D.C.
NA-MD	National Archives, Suitland, Maryland
NCNW	National Council of Negro Women
NJ&G	*Norfolk Journal and Guilde*
NJFA	National Jewish Film Archive, Brandeis University
NNC	National Negro Congress Records
NR	*New Republic*
NR-LC	National Association for the Advancement of Colored People, Manuscript Division, Library of Congress
NUL	National Urban League
NYA	*New York Age*
NYT, NYTM	*New York Times, New York Times Magazine*
OCP-HST	Oscar Chapman Papers, Harry S. Truman Presidential Library
OF-HST	Office File, Harry S. Truman Presidential Library
OFF	Office of Facts and Figures
OWI-LC	Office of War Information, Library of Congress
OWI-NA-MD	Office of War Information, National Archives, Suitland, Md.
PA-NYPL	Performing Arts Branch, New York Public Library
PC	*Pittsburgh Courier*
PCA	Production Code Administration
PD-USC	Philip Dunne Papers, University of Southern California
PFA	Pacific Film Archive
PN	Philleo Nash Papers
PR	Paramount Pictures Records
PV	*People's Voice*
QRFS	*Quarterly Review of Film Studies*

RKO	Radio-Keith–Orpheum
SAG	Screen Actors Guild
SDB	*Story Department Bulletin*, DOS-TX
SHSW	State Historical Society of Wisconsin
SJS	Stephen J. Spingarn Papers
SCRBC	Schomburg Center for Research in Black Culture
SRL	*Saturday Review of Literature*
SIU	Southern Illinois University
TB	Thomas Brandon Papers
TCFA	20th Century–Fox Film Archive
TI&E	Troop Information and Education
UA	United Artists
UAW	United Auto Workers
UCB	University of California at Berkeley
UCLA	University of California at Los Angeles
USC	University of Southern California
USO	United Service Organizations
Var.	*Variety*
WAC	War Activities Council
WBA	Warner Bros. Archive
WDA	Walt Disney Archive, Burbank, California
WGA-W	Writers Guild of America—West
WSU	Wayne State University, Detroit, Michigan
WW-JWJ	Walter White Papers, James Weldon Johnson Collection, Yale
WW-SHSW	Walter Wanger Papers, State Historical Society of Wisconsin

Notes

Preface

1. See Thomas Cripps, "Making Movies Black," in Jannette L. Dates and William Barlow, eds., *Split Image: African Americans in the Mass Media* (Washington, D.C., 1990), 125–31.

2. Runciman quoted in David Plante, "Profiles: Historian," *New Yorker*, Nov. 3, 1986, pp. 63, 80.

3. Peggy Harper, "Dance in a Changing Society," *African Arts/Arts Afrique* 1 (Autumn 1967): 10.

4. John Kenneth Galbraith, *American Capitalism: The Concept of Countervailing Power* (Boston, 1972); and for two critical surveys of recent criticism, Norman F. Cantor, *Twentieth Century Culture: From Modernism to Deconstruction* (New York, 1988), and Noel Carroll, *Mystifying Movies: Fads and Fallacies in Contemporary Film Theory* (New York, 1988).

5. Stuart Hall, "Signification, Representation, Ideology: Althusser and Post-structuralist Debates," *Critical Studies in Communication* 2 (June 1985); 92, 100 ("pluricentered" and "theatre"); Jeffrey Morton Paine, *The Simplification of American Life: Hollywood Films of the 1930s* (New York, 1988), 8 (quoted); see also Hall's "Gramsci's Relevance for the Study of Race and Ethnicity," *Journal of Communication Inquiry* 10 (Summer 1986): 5–27.

6. On the black actor Stepin Fetchit as a sort of "auteur," see Thomas Cripps, "Stepin Fetchit and the Politics of Performance," 35–48, in Paul Loukidas and Linda K. Fuller, eds., *Beyond the Stars: Stock Characters in American Popular Film* (Bowling Green, Ohio, 1990).

7. James A. Snead, "Recoding Blackness: The Visual Rhetoric of Black

Independent Film," *Whitney Museum of American Art: The New American Filmmakers Series,* program no. 23, p. 102.

8. James K. Feibleman, *The Theory of Culture* (New York, 1946, 1968), 7, 43, 96.

9. I adapt this term for a liberalism of the heart from the secession movement of 1860 when border state Whigs, anxious over a Civil War in which their states might become battlefields, fell silent on the issue of slavery while Northern Whigs who continued to speak against slavery became known as "conscience-Whigs."

10. On necessitarianism see Richard Dalfiume, "The 'Forgotten Years' of the Negro Revolution," *Journal of American History* 55 (June 1968): 90–126, and revisions in his "Commentary on 'The Effects of World War II on American Society,'" given April 2, 1981, Organization of American Historians, Detroit.

Chapter 1
Antebellum Hollywood

1. Malcolm X (with Alex Haley), *The Autobiography of Malcolm X* (New York, 1964), p. 32.

2. David O. Selznick to Sidney Howard, Jan. 6, 1937, in Rudy Behlmer, ed., *Memo from David O. Selznick* (New York, 1972), 151.

3. On universalism as a vehicle for ideology see John Tulloch, *Australian Cinema: Industry, Narrative and Meaning* (Sydney, 1982), 32, 111.

4. Anderson to Russell Holman, Sept. 19, 1934, in Laurence G. Avery, ed., *Dramatist in America: Letters of Maxwell Anderson 1912–1958* (Chapel Hill, 1977), 50–53; Stark Young, *So Red the Rose* (New York, 1934); Joseph Breen to John Hammel (Paramount), May 28, 1935, PCA-AMPAS, on "nigger"; and on New Deal critics, Barton J. Bernstein, "The Conservative Achievements of Liberal Reform," in Bernstein, ed., *Towards a New Past: Dissenting Essays in American History* (New York, 1969), 263–88.

5. Nick Roddick, *A New Deal in Entertainment: Warner Bros. in the 1930s* (London, 1983), 133–43.

6. Roddick, *A New Deal in Entertainment,* 138–39; see also *Angels with Dirty Faces* file, PCA-AMPAS.

7. Frank Capra, *The Name Above the Title: An Autobiography* (New York, 1971), 148. "The miracle works," wrote Capra of a typical closure in *Lady for a Day.* "Apple Annie's daughter marries nobility . . . [and] the 'conspirators,' from governor to panhandlers, grow an inch or two in tolerance."

8. Thomas Cripps, *Slow Fade to Black: The Negro in American Film, 1900–1940* (New York, 1977), chaps. 2, 7, 12, on race movies and politics; Thomas Cripps, "The *Birth of a Race* Company: An Early Stride Toward a Black Cinema," *Journal of Negro History* 59 (Jan. 1974): 28–37; a print of this film is in LC.

9. Cripps, *Slow Fade to Black,* chap. 10.

10. F. L. Herron, memo, Aug. 22, 1929; Jason S. Joy to George Kann, MGM, Feb. 22, 1929; Lamar Trotti to M. McKenzie, memo, Oct. 19, 1928, in *Hallelujah!* file, PCA-AMPAS.

11. Jason S. Joy to Julia Kelly, June 21, 1930; Daniel Lord to Kelly, copy, June 12, 1930; JK[elly] to Joy, enclosing Lord's letter, June 17, 1930, PCA-AMPAS; "A Letter from Walter White," *Close Up,* Aug. 1929, pp. 105–6; and

Floyd C. Covington, "The Negro Invades Hollywood," *Close Up*, April 1929, pp. 113–14.

12. Henry Blanke to Hal Wallis, Dec. 23, 1935, in *The Green Pastures* file, WBA-USC; Marc Connelly, *Voices Off-Stage: A Book of Memoirs* (New York, 1968), chap. 4; interview, Connelly and Cripps, New York, April 15, 1978; interview, Connelly and A. Weiner, April 9, 1965, Madison, Wisconsin, in SHSW; and Thomas Cripps, "A Monument to Lost Innocence," introduction to Connelly, *The Green Pastures* (Madison, Wisc., 1979), 11–39.

13. *Green Pastures* budget, Jan. 3, 1936; Hal Wallis to William Keighley, copy, Jan. 17, 1936; on cuts, Wallis to Blanke, memo copy, Jan. 21, 1936, *Green Pastures* file, WBA-USC; Connelly on the budget, Connelly-Cripps interview.

14. Cripps, "Monument to Lost Innocence," 35–39; *Var.*, Aug. 18, 1937, p. 1.

15. Selznick–Kay Brown correspondence, May 28, 1937–June 16, 1937, box 10, *Nothing Sacred* file, DOS-TX; *The Wet Parade* (1932), notes on wardrobe, production 604, pamphlet file, "Afro-Americans in Motion Pictures," UCLA; Hal Wallis to Henry Blanke, copy, Jan. 20, 1936, *Green Pastures* file, WBA-USC, for instances of casual racial references.

16. For examples that passed unremarked, *Revival Days*, Nov. 22, 1929, and *Goat Alley*, Nov. 15, 1929, WBA-USC.

17. Joseph Breen to J. R. McDonough, Sept. 14, 1938; Ned DePinet to McDonough, cable, Oct. 5, 1938; McDonough to Pandro S. Berman, cable, Oct. 5, 1938, in *The Story of Vernon and Irene Castle* file, RKO-UCLA. For revisionist view of the impact of the Southern box office see Thomas Cripps, "The Myth of the Southern Box Office: A Factor in Racial Stereotyping in American Movies, 1920–1940," in Lewis L. Gould and James L. Curtis, eds., *The Black Experience in America: Selected Essays* (Austin, 1970), 116–44.

18. Jason S. Joy to D. F. Zanuck, Feb. 26, 1932; Joy to Will Hays, carbon, March 25, 1932 (*Chain Gang*); Breen to Maurice McKenzie, carbon, March 26, 1934; I. Aust to Breen, March 13, 1934 (*Birth of a Nation*); Harry Zehner to Breen, Jan. 24, 1935 (on *Imitation of Life* grosses); Dolph Frantz, *Shreveport Journal*, carbon, to Breen, Aug. 25, 1937 (*Artists and Models*); Breen to F. L. Herron, carbon, Sept. 13, 1937 (*Daughter of Shanghai*), in PCA-AMPAS.

19. Lewton to Selznick, May–June 1937, box 10, *Nothing Sacred;* Kay Brown to Selznick, March 15, 1936, on PCA and race angle of *Wingless Victory*, box 6, 1937–1939, "Brown" file, both DOS-TX; interview, Milestone and Cripps, June 1970; review of *One Third of a Nation*, Paul S. Nathan, PR-AMPAS.

20. N. Dora Stecker to William H. Short, March 24, 1929, in Motion Picture Research Council records, Hoover Institution on War, Revolution, and Peace, Stanford, Calif.; and Val Lewton to Davis Orr, memo, carbon, May 4, 1939, box 6, "Brown" file, 1937–1939, DOS-TX.

21. Barnett to Jackson, Oct. 16, Sept. 25, Dec. 18, 1933; March 7, 1934; Jackson to Barnett, June 16, 1934; Barnett to Jackson, Sept. 10 [1935]; Jackson to Barnett, Jan. 15, 1936, in CB-CHS; see also *New York Post*, April 7, 1937, clipping, TB-MOMA.

22. On black Hollywood see Cripps, *Slow Fade to Black*, chaps. 4 and 11.

23. Interviews, Martin Wilkins and Lawrence Lamar and Cripps, Dunbar Hotel, Los Angeles, Calif., June 1970.

24. *Wonderbar* anticipated a genre of black musicals extending from *Stormy Weather* to *The Wiz.*

25. both the PCA and Virginia censors passed *One Mile from Heaven,* PCA-AMPAS.

26. *The Birth of the Blues* script, March 17, 1941, pp. A-3, B-1, 5, in ITC-DC; a print is in LC.

27. *St. Louis Blues,* script by Moffitt and Malcolm Stuart Boylan, adaptation by Frederick Hazlitt Brennan; scripts dated Dec. 26, Aug. 8, 1937, and July 22, 27, 1938; see also NYT, Feb. 9, 1939. John C. "Jack" Moffitt and Duke Atterbury to "Jeff" [Lazarus, the producer], July 22, 1938, in PR-AMPAS.

28. Hedda Hopper to N. Peter Rathvon, RKO, copy, Nov. 7, 1947, enclosing a list of eighty-four Communists whose work might have been stopped before the war if only the moguls had heeded her in HH—AMPAS; NYT, Oct. 13, 1940; Felix Walter, "Hollywood Goes Slightly Pink," *Canadian Forum* May 1933, pp. 300–301; George Eels, *Hedda and Louella: A Dual Biography of Hedda Hopper and Louella Parsons* (New York, 1972), for a recent biography.

29. Robert Sklar, *Movie-Made America: A Social History of American Movies* (New York, 1975), chap. 15; and Larry Ceplair and Steven Englund, *Inquisition in Hollywood: Politics in the Film Community, 1930–1960* (Garden City, N.Y., 1980), chaps. 4–6; NYT, Aug. 9, 1934, April 30, June 4, 1939, Feb. 3, 1940, June 1, 1941; and Ella Winter, "Hollywood Wakes Up," NR, Jan. 12, 1938, pp. 276–78.

30. *Beast of Berlin* script in ITC-DC with, laid in, LAT, Nov. 19, 1939; NYT, Nov. 20, 1939; on *Confessions of a Nazi Spy,* Hal Wallis and Charles Higham, *Starmaker: The Autobiography of Hal Wallis* (New York, 1980), 70–71; and on lobbying by a consul, Breen-Gyssling correspondence, 1937–1938, *The Great Dictator* file, PCA-AMPAS.

31. K. R. M. Short, "Hollywood Fights Anti-Semitism, 1940–1945," in Short, ed., *Film and Radio Propaganda in World War II* (London, 1983), 148–49; Lester D. Friedman, *Hollywood's Image of the Jew* (New York, 1982), 78–79; Patricia Erens, *The Jew in American Cinema* (Bloomington, 1984), 148–56.

32. "Henry" [F. Pringle] to John L. Balderston, July 1, 1942; Balderston to Pringle, July 7, 1942, in box 1, Balderston Papers, LC.

33. See William Alexander, *Film on the Left: American Documentary Film from 1931 to 1942* (Princeton, 1981), chap. 6, on *Native Land,* and pp. 28–34, 60–61.

34. Walter Niebuhr to Walter White, Jan. 24, 1932; A. E. Spingarn to White, memo, n.d.; White to Joel Spingarn, memo, n.d., with Spingarn's holograph reply, in NR-LC; Alain Locke–Mary Beattie Brady correspondence, 1931–1932, in box 1, Harmon Foundation records, LC; for other ephemera sent by filmmakers, see series 7, box 32, NUL-LC; see Erik Barnouw, *Documentary: A History of the Non-Fiction Film* (New York, 1974), 85, to contrast black indifference to film with John Grierson's reckoning of "cinema as a pulpit."

35. Michael and Jill Klein, "*Native Land:* An Interview with Leo Hurwitz," *Cineaste* 6 (1974): 3–7; Leo Hurwitz, "One Man's Voyage: Ideas and Films in the 1930s," *Cinema Journal* 15 (Fall 1935): 1–15; *Var.,* May 13, 1942, p. 8; NYT, May 3, 12, 1942; *Time,* June 8, 1942, pp. 51–52; *Native Land* print in MOMA; DW quoted in Russell Campbell, "Radical Cinema in the United States, 1930–1947: The Work of the Film and Photo League, NyKino, and Frontier Films"

(Ph.D., Northwestern, 1978), 364–79, 405; Leo Hurwitz–Cripps telephone conversation.

36. Raymond Fielding, *The March of Time, 1935–1951* (New York, 1978), chap. 11; a print of *Land of Liberty* is in LC. Its credits say MPPDA itself "presents."

37. Dale to Walter White, Feb. 14, 1942; J. R. Jones to Frank Schiffman, Apollo, copy, March 24, 1941; White to Eugene Martin, copy, Sept. 23, 1940; Jones to White, Sept. 20, 23, 1940; White to staff, Sept. 13, 17, 1940; Robert Huebsch, Twin-Coast Co., to White, May 22, 1940; Jones to White, July 4, 1941, in NR-LC; *Crisis* 44 (Oct. 1937): 294–96, 316; and *Var.*, June 21, 1939, p. 11.

38. Gwendolyn Bennett, for the committee, to "Friend," May 30, 1939; see also Emmett May to George Murphy, Jr., NAACP, Oct. 10, 1939; George Miller to Catherine Freedland, July 4, 1941, in NR-LC.

39. American Council on Education Studies, series 2, no. 1 (April 1937), *The Motion Picture in Education: Its Status and Its Needs,* p. 21.

40. Allied Non-Theatrical Film Association, *ANFA Yearbook 1946* (New York, 1947), title page; William H. Hartley, *Selected Films for American History and Problems* (New York, 1940), 40–41, 136–37, 168–69, 208–9.

41. Hartley, *Selected Films for American History,* as above; and [Charles Hoban], Committee on Motion Pictures in Education, *Selected Educational Motion Pictures: A Descriptive Encyclopedia* (Washington, 1942), 171, 205, 286; fragment of *Let My People Live* in GEH; *Educational Film Catalogue* (New York, 1939), 159. *Let My People Live* director Edgar G. Ulmer made race movies, Yiddish films, and Hollywood B-movies. Memorandum of agreement, Sept. 15, 1937, in *Carver* file S-2513, MGM-LD.

42. Other subjects listed in Cripps, *Slow Fade to Black,* chaps. 13 and 11 in notes, and p. 298; Fielding, *March of Time,* 330–39, for volumes and numbers; viewing copies of many issues in both AVNA-DC and BFI.

43. Garth Jowett, *Film: The Democratic Art* (Boston, 1976), pp. 288–89, 310, 316; and Roger Dooley, *From Scarface to Scarlett: American Films in the 1930s* (New York, 1981), 611.

44. Finis Farr, *Margaret Mitchell of Atlanta* (New York, 1965, 1974), 26–30, 39–44, 50, 76, 90–93; Mitchell to Katharine Brown, March 8, 1937, in MM-UG.

45. Mitchell to Commager, July 10, 1936; Mitchell to Herschel Brickell, July 7, 1936; Mitchell to Dixon, Aug. 15, 1936; Mitchell to Paul Jordan-Smith, May 27, 1936; Mitchell to Ruth Tallman, July 30, 1937, in Richard Harwell, ed., *Margaret Mitchell's Gone with the Wind Letters, 1936–1949* (New York, 1976), 7, 38–39, 19–21, 52, 144, 162; Farr, *Mitchell,* 157.

46. Sidney Howard To Selznick, n.d., box 7, "Writers" file, DOS-TX; Selznick to Howard, Jan. 6, 1937, in Behlmer, *Memo,* 151.

47. Roy Wilkins to A. B. Spingarn, July 25, 1938; Wilkins to Selznick, July 25, 1938; Wilkins to Charles H. Wesley, July 25, 1938, in A. B. Spingarn papers, LC; Wesley to Wilkins, July 30, 1938, in NR-LC; Jacqueline Anne Goggins, "Carter G. Woodson and the Movement to Promote Black History" (Ph.D., University of Rochester, 1983), 213; interview, Walter Fisher and Wesley, summer 1985, during which Wesley recalled no specific inquiries put by Selznick.

48. On scripts: Howard to Mitchell, Nov. 18, 1936; Wilbur Kurtz to Stacey

et al., memo, copies, Jan. 14, 1939, Nov. 15, Dec. 21, 1938, Jan. 3, 14, 1939, in MM-UG; Selznick to Howard, Jan. 6, 1937, in Howard papers, UCB.

On Kurtz and Myrick: Kay Brown to Mitchell, Oct. 1, 13, Nov. 16, 20, 1936; Mitchell to Brown, copies, Oct. 6, 1936, Feb. 14, 1937, July 7, 1938; Mitchell to Selznick, Oct. 19, 1936; Mitchell to Russell Birdwell, Nov.–Dec. 5, 1936; Kurtz memos, Dec. 21, 1938 and n.d.; Kurtz to Miss Dabney, copy, Dec. 22, 1938; Kurtz to Myrick, Dec. 27, 1938; Kurtz to Beverly M. DuBose, copy, Dec. 28, 1938; Mitchell to Brown, copy, Feb. 14, 1937 (black opinion); Myrick to "Dear John," n.d.; Myrick to Mitchell, Jan. 11, 15, Feb. 12, 14, March 12, April 17, 1939, in MM-UG; Kurtz to Howard, Feb. 8, 1938; Selznick to Howard, Nov. 13, 1936, in Howard papers, UCB.

There are also four feet of Kurtz papers, a batch of *Gone with the Wind* ephemera, and a "personality file" in Atlanta Historical Society.

On Kurtz: Selznick to Kay Brown, wire, box 6, "Wires" file, DOS-TX.

49. Mitchell to Brown, April 17, 1939, MM-UG.

50. See note 2. On the erasure of lynching and thus of an outrage that legitimized black political goals, see Sidney Howard refusing "to indulge in anything which makes the lynching of a Negro in any sense sympathetic," quoted in Ron Haver, *David O. Selznick's Hollywood* (New York, 1980), 140; and Leonard J. Leff, "David Selznick's *Gone with the Wind:* 'The Negro Problem,'" *Georgia Review* 38 (Spring 1984): 146–64.

51. Walter White to Selznick, June 18, 1939, and White to Howard, July 13, 1938, in Howard papers, UCB; Kay Brown (on White) to Marcella Rabwin, Jan. 18, 1939, *Gone with the Wind* file, box 58, DOS-TX; Myrick to Mitchell (on Johnson), April 17, 1939, MM-UG; and Roy Wilkins on White in conversation with the author.

52. Susan Myrick, *White Columns in Hollywood,* ed. Richard B. Harwell (Macon, Ga., 1983), 159 (on "exclusive" interview); Mitchell to Kay Brown, Aug. 13, 1947 (on Lizzie McDuffie, ER's maid), in MM-UG; *Crisis* 46 (Dec. 1939): 381; Mitchell to Selznick (on watchdogs), Jan. 30, 1939; memo, n.d., from Society for Correct Civil War Information, both in MM-UG. No evidence survives of Selznick's consulting revisionist history such as W. E. B. DuBois's *Black Reconstruction in America, 1860–1880* (New York, 1935); Edgar G. Brown to Selznick (on ER), wire, copy, Jan. 5, 1938, "Wires" file, box 6, DOS-TX; Cripps, *Slow Fade to Black,* 359–62; Roland Flamini, *Scarlett, Rhett, and a Cast of Thousands: The Filming of Gone with the Wind* (New York, 1975), 184, 216, 288; Myrick to Mitchell (on McQueen), Feb. 12, 1939, in MM-UG; and Victor Shapiro, "Diary of Gone with the Wind," mss in Special Collections, UCLA; and on Polk, Myrick, *White Columns* 202.

53. Sample in Peter Noble, *The Negro in Films* (London, [1948]), 75–79; W. L. Patterson quoted in John D. Stevens, "The Black Reaction to *Gone with the Wind,*" *Journal of Popular Culture* 2 (Fall 1973): 366–71; Cripps, *Slow Fade to Black,* 363–64, for CPUSA response; David Platt to Cripps, n.d.

54. Leff, "Selznick's *Gone with the Wind,*" 157; on the black journalist Earl Morris, Carlton Jackson, *Hattie: The Life of Hattie McDaniel* (Lanham, Md., 1989), 41–43; Goodwin reported in "n——" deleted "from no higher authority than George Cukor, director of the opus," quoted in Harwell, *Gone with the Wind Letters,* 273; see also LAS, Feb. 9, 1939, and PC, Feb. 18, 1939; Val Lewton to Selznick, June 7, 1937, copy, "1939–1940" file, box 14, DOS-TX, on Polk and

McDaniel agreeing to say "nigger" referring to "no 'count" blacks; Lewton to Selznick, June 9, 1939; Selznick to Lewton, same day, *GWTW* file, DOS-TX.

55. The film is in general video release; a print is in AVNA-DC.

56. James Agee, *Agee on Film: Reviews and Comments* (New York, 1958), 107; Pare Lorentz, *Lorentz on Film: Movies 1927 to 1941* (New York, 1975), 180–83.

57. Noble, *Negro in Films*, 75–79; Platt to Cripps, n.d.; many talks between Moss and the author, 1969–1990; Jackson, *Hattie*, 49–50, on DW; NYT, Dec. 22, 24, 1939, and DW, Jan. 9, 1940.

58. *Crisis* 48 (Jan. 1940): 17; Cripps, *Slow Fade to Black*, 364.

59. Cripps, "Winds of Change: *Gone with the Wind* and Racism as a National Issue," in Darden Asbury Pyron, ed., *Recasting: Gone with the Wind in American Culture* (Miami, 1983), 137–72, samples AA, NJ&G, PC, AN and *Gary American*.

60. AN, March 16, 23, 1940; AA, March 30, 1940; NJ&G, May 16, 1940; *Gary American*, March 15, 1940; AA, March 9, 1940.

61. AA, March 23, 30, 1940; NJ&G, March 23, 1940; AA (Washington), March 23, May 18, 1940; AA, March 9, 1940; PC, March 9, 1940; *Opportunity* 18 (April 1940): 100; *Crisis* 42 (April 1940): 103; George E. Haynes to Walter White, March 28, 1940; White to Walter Winchell, copy, May 20, 1940; Thurgood Marshall to NAACP committee, memo, March 4, 1940; "NAACP Hits Revival of 'Birth of a Nation,'" press release, March 22, 1940, in NR-LC; McDaniel's speech in *Hollywood Outtakes/Manhattan Movietime*, Johns Hopkins University showing, Oct. 23, 1983.

62. Fidler cited in Cripps, *Slow Fade to Black*, 364; Jackson, *Hattie*, passim; Selznick to L. V. Calvert, March 25, 1940; Selznick to William S. Paley, Jan. 3, 1940; Mitchell Rawson to Selznick and Daniel Shea, copy, Jan. 19, 1944 (on Southern angle), all in McDaniel file; Gladys Louise Branch to Selznick, Oct. 18, 1940, "People," B–C file, box 12, DOS-TX.

63. Muse's Letterhead/résumé in author's possession; on Hughes's Soviet film, Cripps, *Slow Fade to Black*, chap. 6.

64. Story written for Bobby Breen [anon.], n.d. (on types); Breen story "dictated by Mr. Lesser" for Hughes, carbon, Jan. 13, 1939; Hughes and Muse drafts, Jan. 26, 1939, and March 1939; Lesser's comments in *Way Down South*, Feb. 15, 1939, revised from first draft by Michael Simmons, Feb. 8, 1939, LH-JWJ.

65. Main work of Hughes and Muse in drafts Jan. 22, 1939, through March 1939, and anonymous marginalia; see also discarded scenes from Simmons's draft, Feb. 6, 1939; and "Dialogue & Music for Way Down South," n.d., by Hughes and Muse in LH-JWJ.

66. *Way Down South*, Lesser's notes, March 28, 1939; memo for Hughes and Muse, "A Résumé of Life in America, 1846"; more on their duties in Lesser's revisions of Simmons's draft, Feb. 15, 1939, in LH-JWJ. Film viewed through courtesy of Irwin Markisch, Warner Bros., N.Y.; AN, July 29, Feb. 18, 1939.

67. Owen Dodson and Arna Bontemps to Hughes, Sept. 1944, on *The Negro Speaks of Rivers* by American Film Center perhaps; David Wolper and Richard Kollmar to "Langston," May 27, 1946, in Hughes papers, Fisk University, Nashville, Tenn.; draft, *Sailor from Harlem* or *The Chocolate Sailor* draft, Hughes papers; draft translation, *L'Amitie Noir;* "Story Bases for Paul Robeson

Screenplay"; "Exodusters" treatment, in Hughes papers; *I Wish You'd Let Me Love You*, treatment, Oct. 26, 1957, on interracial friends in the recent South, and others in LH-JWJ.

68. Lenore Coffey to Walter Wanger, Aug. 20, 1941, in *Mississippi Belle* file, no. 2494, WBA-USC.

69. Breen–George Gyssling (German consul) correspondence, in *The Great Dictator* file, PCA-AMPAS.

70. The photograph is in C. L. Sulzberger, ed., *The American Heritage Picture History of World War II* (New York, 1966), 95.

71. Walter Wanger to Selznick, Nov. 11, 1941, "Misc. People" file, W-2, DOS-TX.

72. Thomas C. Cochran, *The Great Depression and World War II, 1929–1945* (Glenview, Ill., 1968), 103.

73. See Cochran, *Great Depression and World War II*, 76, 91–92, 103–6, 111–15, 124, 175, 181, 185; Paul K. Conkin, *The New Deal* (New York, 1967), 71–75; Richard Polenberg, *War and Society: The United States, 1941–1945* (Philadelphia, 1972), 2, 29, 243, 208–9, 194–96; Richard Kirkendall, *The United States, 1929–1945* (New York, 1968), 171–79, 206, 214; John M. Blum, *V Was for Victory* (New York, 1976), 38–39, chap. 6; Keith Nelson, ed., *The Impact of War on American Life: The Twentieth Century Experience* (New York, 1971); August Meier and Elliott Rudwick, "How CORE Began," *Social Science Quarterly* 49 (June 1969): 789–99; Harvard Sitkoff, "Racial Militancy and Interracial Violence in the Second World War," *Journal of American History* 58 (Dec. 1971): 661–81; Richard Dalfiume, "The 'Forgotten Years' of the Negro Revolution," *Journal of American History* 55 (June 1968): 90–106; and his *The Desegregation of the United States Armed Forces: Fighting on Two Fronts, 1939–1953* (Columbia, Mo., 1969), chap. 6.

74. Lee Finkel, *Forum for Protest: The Black Press during World War II* (Rutherford, N.J., 1975), 108–25; Harvard Sitkoff, *A New Deal for Blacks* (New York, 1978), 313–15; Patrick S. Washburn, *A Question of Sedition: The Federal Government's Investigation of the Black Press During World War II* (New York, 1986), 53–55, 100–102; John B. Kirby, *Black Americans in the Roosevelt Era: Liberalism and Race* (Knoxville, 1980), 53; Helen Gahagan Douglas, *A Full Life* (Garden City, 1982), 134, 184–91, 226–28.

75. Finkle, *Forum for Protest*, 108–25; Kirby, *Black Americans*, 225.

76. Carlton Moss, Council on Negro Culture, to Archibald MacLeish, [Feb. 30, 1942]; Moss to Philip Wylie, March 21, 1942, in folder 002.1, director's decimal file, entry 5, box 3, OWI, RG 208, NA-MD.

77. Richard Wright to Archibald MacLeish (OFF), Dec. 21, 1941, OFF, alpha. file, "Negro" folder, entry 5, box 40, RG 208, NA-MD.

78. Blum, *V was for Victory*, chap. 6.

79. George H. Gallup, *The Gallup Poll: Public Opinion, 1935–1971* (New York, 1972, 3 vols.), 1:142, 209; American Research Institute, microfilm reel 2, "Hollywood," Sept. 10, 1940; OWI, *American Attitudes: World War II*, Vol. X, "The Negro and the War" (Washington [1943]), passim.

80. Morton Sosna, *In Search of the Silent South: Southern Liberals and the Race Issue* (New York, 1977), 95–97, 143 (SCHW); 186 (Smith); 118–19; 109–10 (Raleigh).

81. Horace Cayton, "Negro Morale," *Opportunity*, Dec. 1941, p. 371; OFF,

Bureau of Intelligence, "Negroes in a Democracy at War," box 22, PN-HST (survey offered only a choice between victory or democracy; a case for black dissent is argued in Clayton R. Koppes and Gregory D. Black, "Blacks, Loyalty, and Motion Picture Propaganda in World War II," *Journal of American History* 73 (Sept. 1986): 383–406, and in their *Hollywood Goes to War: How Politics, Profits, & Propaganda Shaped World War II Movies* (New York, 1987), chaps. 4 and 6.

82. Account derived from a survey of *Var.*, 1942–1944, including forty-eight specific racial events that broke with prewar etiquette. See also, Joe Glaser to Bob Shaw, Sept. 15, 1941, Dec. 9, 1941, Jan. 9, 1943; Bob Kerr to Shaw, Jan. 28, 1943, on refusals, grosses, and gigs, in Gus Sun Theatrical Agency records, Ohio State Historical Society, Columbus.

83. *Var.*, March 31, 1942, p. 43; Nov. 3, 1943, p. 42; July 5, 1944, pp. 35, 38; Sept. 6, 1944, pp. 36–38; Dec. 13, 1944, p. 44; Sept. 13, 1944, p. 1.

84. *Var.*, Nov. 20, 1940, p. 2; Aug. 19, 1942, p. 3; July 29, 1942, p. 7; May 20, 1942, p. 36; Robeson in Spain is seen in the film *The Tallest Tree in the Forest* (1977); for his film career, Thomas Cripps, "Paul Robeson and Black Identity in American Movies," *Massachusetts Review* 11 (Summer 1970): 468–85; for the definitive biography see Martin Bauml Duberman, *Paul Robeson* (New York, 1988).

85. *Var.*, March 31, 1943, p. 43; Aug. 12, 1942, p. 4; June 10, 1942, p. 46; July 19, 1944, p. 1; July 5, 1944, p. 36; Aug. 5, 1942, p. 1.

86. J. Fred McDonald, "Stride Toward Freedom: Blacks in Radio Programming," unpublished paper, courtesy the author, 22–24. James Agee, "Pseudo-Folk," *Partisan Review*, Spring 1944, rpt. in *Agee on Film*, 406, kvetched at "Ballad for Americans" for its overexposure. *Var.*, surveyed from 1942 through 1944. See also MacDonald, *Blacks and White TV: Afro-Americans in Television since 1948* (Chicago, 1983), 1–8; *A Testimonial Program for Canada Lee* (WOR, June 9, 1941), in LC. *Var.*, March 22, 1944, p. 3.

87. On Dorie Miller, John Toland, *But Not in Shame: The Six Months after Pearl Harbor* (New York, 1961), 86–88. Integrationist myths also appeared in British (*In Which We Serve*), German (*Triumph des Willens*), and Soviet (*Alexander Nevsky*) films. Miller-like tales were in *Teamwork* (1945) and *Crash Dive* (1944). A photograph of Miller receiving his Navy Cross is in Bernard C. Nalty, *Strength for the Fight: A History of Black Americans in the Military* (New York, 1986, 1989).

88. Frame enlargement from *The Maltese Falcon* is in Richard J. Anobile, ed., *The Maltese Falcon* (London, 1974), 173. For a casting dilemma over which sort of black actor to play Sam the pianist in *Casablanca* see Steve Trilling–Hal Wallis correspondence, Feb.–April 1942, file 1882, WBA-USC.

89. Davis quoted in Whitney Stine, *Mother Goddam: The Story of the Career of Bette Davis* (New York, 1974), 154, 161; for blue pages see *In This Our Life* file 1998 in WBA-USC. One dated Nov. 10, 1941, 123–25 was probably to be shot on Nov. 27, stamped with "Irving Rapper," voice coach who remembered little of this angle in Rapper to Cripps, n.d. See also Trilling to T. C. Wright, copy, Dec. 1, 1941, in file 698, WBA-USC.

90. Interview, Ernest Anderson and the author, June 1970.

91. *In This Our Life* script, Nov. 10, 1941, pp. 123–26, 51, annotated for reshooting, and other drafts in file 1998, WBA-USC.

92. Ed Scofield press release, file 698, WBA-USC.

93. Thomasina W. Johnson, Alpha Kappa Alpha, to Warner Bros., Sept. 30, 1942; P. L. Prattis, PC, to Warner Bros., June 6, 1942; Darius Johnson, "college man," to Warner Bros., June 1942; W. A. Johnson, educator, to Bette Davis, copy, Sept. 4, 1942; John S. Holley, Washington, to Warner Bros., Aug. 9, 1942; G. M. Shurlock, MPPDA, to Jack Warner, Jan. 6, 1942, agreeing to cuts of "savage abandon," with blue pages enclosed, Nov. 1942; Charles D. Wherry to Jack Warner, Sept. 15, 1942, all in *In This Our Life* file, WBA-USC. See also Walter White's form letters sent to each principal in NR-LC.

94. *Daily Var.*, April 7, 1942; *Var.*, April 8, 1942; HR, April 7, 1942; MPD, April 7, 1942; Mrs. Alonzo Richardson, Atlanta Board of Review, to Joseph Breen, June 6, 1942, in *In This Our Life* file, PCA-AMPAS.

Chapter 2
Wendell and Walter Go to Hollywood

1. Wanger-White correspondence in WW-SHSW; see also White to Lowell Mellett, July 8, 1942, in LM-FDR; White to Melvyn Douglas, Dec. 7, 1940; White to Laura Veiller, copy, Oct. 24, 1947, in NR-LC.

2. Allan M. Winkler, *The Politics of Propaganda: The Office of War Information, 1942–1945* (New Haven, 1978), 23–33.

3. Winkler, *Politics of Propaganda*, 31; "play" here as in the play of a steering wheel, derived in part from the reader response criticism of, for example, Umberto Eco, *The Role of the Reader* (Bloomington, 1979).

4. For the black break with the Republican party, see Nancy J. Weiss, *Farewell to the Party of Lincoln: Black Politics in the Age of FDR* (Princeton, 1983), 257–66; NYA, Oct. 20, 1945; Marian Anderson, *My Lord, What a Morning: An Autobiography* (New York, 1956), chap. 17; and PC, from Jan. through April 1942.

5. Judith Schachter Modell, *Ruth Benedict: Patterns of a Life* (Philadelphia, 1983), 248–49, 254, 265–67, quoted; Ruth Benedict, *Race: Science and Politics* (New York, 1940), 259–66, on scientists vs. racism, and 206–8, on Hitler.

6. Philip Gleason, "World War II and the Development of American Studies," *American Quarterly* 36 (biblio. issue 1984): 343–58, quoted; NYT, Feb. 23, Aug. 2, 1941, on Clyde R. Miller's (Teachers College, Columbia) advocacy of liberal textbooks and a defense of colleagues against Gov. Herman Talmadge (Ga.).

7. *Sundown* analysis card, box 21, MSCB.

8. Barré Lyndon, *Sundown* (New York, 1941); *Saturday Evening Post*, Jan. 18, 1941, pp. 9–10, 84–88, and weekly thereafter until Feb. 22, 1941, pp. 31–33, 108–13; and his *Sundown: A Play in Three Acts*, typescript; *Sundown*, first continuity, Feb. 21, 1941; *Sundown* treatment, typescript, n.d., 180 pp., all in Barré Lyndon Collection, AMPAS. Campaign chronology from James Lucas, *The War in the Desert: The Eighth Army at El Alamein* (London, 1982), 267–68. Hathaway's copy of the script, AFI Collection, Louis B. Mayer Library, Hollywood, Calif., has no political marginalia, and in a brief telephone talk in 1980 he recalled the film only as the adventure yarn that Barré had intended.

9. Wanger to White, copy, June 14, 1941; White to [Rosemary] Foley, July 17, 1941; *Sundown* revisions, June 15, 1941, p. 22, box 93, WW-SHSW; Bill

Tinsman to Dan Keefe, June 11, 1941; Keefe to John Murphy, wire, May 7, 1941, seeking Army assistance because of "importance at this time," box 1, *Sundown* file, RG II, UA-SHSW. Changes, blue and yellow pages, June 15, 17, July 15, 19, 1941, WW-SHSW.

10. Joseph Breen to Wanger, carbon, Feb. 25, 1941; Rosemary Foley to Geoffrey Shurlock, Aug. 18, 1941; certification form, Sept. 16, 1941, in PCA-AMPAS.

11. MPD, n.d., thought it "suffers" from changes; HR, n.d., thought it merely "a swell piece of entertainment" that would help Tierney; NYT, n.d., thought it "fustian," all in PCA-AMPAS.

12. White's visits began at least as early as fall 1940. See Wanger to Selznick, wire, copy, Nov. 11, 1941, "Misc. People" file, W-2, DOS-TX; and Wanger to White, copy, June 14, 1941, on *Sundown*, in WW-SHSW.

13. Crowther's reviews, *New York Times Directory of Film* (New York, 1971), 74–79; NYT, Dec. 26, 1941.

14. *Tarzan Triumphs* (1943) and *Tarzan's Desert Mystery* (1943), reported in Gabe Essoe, *Tarzan of the Movies* (Secaucus, N.J., 1973), 115.

15. *Zanzibar* screenplay, Nov. 15, 1939, and *King of the Zombies* screenplay, March 17, 1941, in ITC-DC, and laid in, LAT, April 1, 1941; and Charles I. Bevans, comp., *Treaties and Other Agreements of the United States of America, 1776–1949* (Washington, D.C., 1939), vol. 2, p. 158.

16. *Zanzibar* screenplay, ITC-DC.

17. In addition to *Drums of the Congo* (1942) and *Nyoka the Jungle Girl* (1941), see Cripps, *Slow Fade to Black*, chap. 2; and *Var.*, May 28, 1941, p. 19; July 22, 1942, p. 8; Jan. 10, 1940, p. 14; Dec. 3, 1941, p. 18; April 16, 1941, p. 18; April 8, 1942, p. 8; see also AN, March 11, 1939; March 14, 1941; May 31, 1941; and poll in *Var.*, March 31, 1943, p. 44.

18. Reviews cited in Cripps, *Slow Fade to Black*, chap. 13, notes 11–39.

19. Rex Beach, *The Spoilers* (New York, 1906), 114; and *The Spoilers* (1942), print in LC.

20. AN, Feb. 3, 1940; Cripps, *Slow Fade to Black*, chap. 13; Walter White to Warner Bros., Feb. 4, 1941, in WBA-USC.

21. NYA, Dec. 20, 1941.

22. Lola Kovner to Walter White, Nov. 28, 1942, in NR-LC.

23. Lowell Mellett to White, Dec. 26, 1941, copy, box 18, LM-FDR; *Herald-Tribune* (New York), Jan. 21, 1942; and White to "Dorothy" [Parker], Feb. 2, 1942, in NR-LC.

24. Carlo Curti, *Skouras: King of Fox Studios* (Los Angeles, 1967), pp. 75–76; Glendon Allvine, *The Greatest Fox of Them All* (New York, 1969), p. 178.

25. Walter White, *A Man Called White* (Bloomington, 1948, 1970), pp. 198–200; *Var.*, April 15, 1942, p. 5, and May 6, 1942, p. 5; White to Lowell Mellett, July 8, 1942, in gratitude for "arranging plane reservations for Mr. Willkie," which will have a "very helpful effect on Negro morale," in box 18, LM-FDR.

26. White to Melvyn Douglas, Dec. 7, 1940, through Jan. 1941, in NR-LC.

27. Clayton R. Koppes and Gregory D. Black, "What to Show the World: The Office of War Information and Hollywood, 1942–1945," *Journal of American History* 64 (June 1977): 87–105. The "popular front," by urging prosecution

of the war, deemphasized the "Double V": see Mark Naison, *Communists in Harlem during the Depression* (Urbana, Il., 1983), 312–13.

28. Frederic Morrow to White, memo, May 20, 1942; White to DeHavilland, copy, May 25, 1942; White to Harry M. Warner, copy, May 25, 1942, in NR-LC.

29. White to Laura Veiller, copy, Oct. 24, 1947, in NR-LC; interview between Roy Wilkins and the author, New York, Aug. 1976.

30. "RECOMMENDATIONS," on which had been penciled "do not print in the report," specifically limited "responsibilities," in PN-HST. On Poynter's work, see "Weekly Log," May 29, 1942, entry 566, box 3510, RG 208; and Lowell Mellett to Jack Warner, copy, Oct. 14, 1942, entry 264, box 1443, RG 208, OWI, NA-MD; Wilkins to White, memo on "conference called by Office of Facts and Figures in Washington, March 20, 1942," March 23, 1942, in box 42, folder "Internal Security—Treas—NAACP," SJS-HST; White to Mellett, Dec. 24, 1941; Mellett to White, copy, Dec. 26, 1941; White to Mellett, July 1, 8, 1942, in LM-FDR.

31. Edward Kennedy Ellington, *Music Is My Mistress* (New York, 1973), 175 ff.

32. White to Mrs. Beatrice Buchman, copy, Jan. 14, 1942, a circular setting forth his agenda; White to Frances Inglis, copy, Jan. 21, 1942; Selznick to White, Jan. 23, 1942; Sidney Wallach, American Jewish Committee (AJC), to Leon Lewis, copy, Nov. 7, 1940; Mrs. Wilkic Mahoney to White, copy, undated; White to Will Hays, copy, Feb. 4, 1942; Eleanor Roosevelt to "To Whom It May Concern," copy, Feb. 17, 1942, in NR-LC. Wilkins suggested blacks not accept as progress any all-Negro films, preferring reflections of integration into American life: Wilkins to White, Feb. 10, 1942, in NR-LC.

33. Norman O. Houston, Golden State Mutual, Los Angeles, to White, Sept. 16, 1943, in NR-LC; telephone interview between Eddie Anderson and the author, Los Angeles, June 1970.

34. Best file, and others, in GPJ-UCLA; Jackson, *Hattie*, 81–110, on impact of White's work; Best's and McDaniel's contracts in, respectively, *Pillar to Post* file 633 and *Affectionately Yours* file 349, WBA-USC; McDaniel's federal Employment for Specific Assignment form reported 1944 income peak at $1750 per week on *Be It Ever so Humble*, in "SSU—Special Assignments—1945" file, WBA-USC.

35. Compare two distinguished Europeans, Vladimir Sokoloff and Victor Francen, who might earn $750 to $2000 respectively, while equally accomplished Americans' incomes ranged from that of a former leading man, Ralph Bellamy, at $3333.33 per week (three weeks guaranteed) to that of Ann Harding who began the war at $1000 (or only $150 above McDaniel) but on *Mission to Moscow* got $4166 per week for six weeks. A B-movie star, Veda Ann Borg, never earned more than $750 per week, a far lower figure than McDaniel's. But at the low end of the scale, Hattie's brother Sam got only $250, and Leigh Whipper got only $500 for a week's work as Haile Selassie on *Mission to Moscow*. See *Mission to Moscow* file 428, and "SSU—Special Assignments—1945" file, WBA-USC.

36. Offscreen black life may be found in LAS, CE, and PC, in the columns of Billy Rowe, Harry Levette, Lawrence LaMar, Ruby Berkeley Goodwin, and others, in the society pages, and in the advertisements for local radio stations and nightclubs. In GPJ-UCLA biographical files many of these sources are gathered

as clippings. "False consciousness," of course, was a Marxist neologism for the mentality induced by a state cultural apparatus that diverted workers from their true class interests.

37. For career data by name, see GPJ-UCLA. Robinson and Fetchit were idle after 1936 save for a B-movie for each, *One Mile from Heaven* and *Charlie Chan in Egypt;* Toones's billing as "Snowflake" in *Mexicali Rose* (1939), and other films; Ernest Morrison in Dead End Kids movies, *Smart Alecks* (1942) and *Mr. Wise Guy* (1942); Moreland's reviews, *Var.*, April 8, 1942, p. 8, and Oct. 25, 1942, p. 12; Muse's warning in Earl Conrad, *Everything and Nothing: The Dorothy Dandridge Tragedy* (New York, 1970), 33; see *Var.*, March 4, 1942, p. 8; Feb. 3, 1943, p. 21; Sept. 9, 1942, p. 14; March 11, 1942, p. 20.

38. GPJ-UCLA bio-files; see too Jessye to King Vidor, April 25, 1942; Vidor to Frank Capra, copy, July 7, 1942, in Vidor papers, HRC-TX; on Lee, *Var.*, March 8, 1944, p. 2.

39. "Walter White—Work Sheet, Feb. 17–26, 1942"; Eleanor Roosevelt to "To Whom It May Concern," copy, Feb. 17, 1942, in NR-LC.

40. Edgar Dale to White, Feb. 14, 1942; [White] holograph memo, n.d., in NR-LC; *Crisis* 44 (Oct. 1937): pp. 294–96, 315; White, *A Man Called White*, 200–201; Lowell Mellett to White, April 21, 1942, refers to Dale's work, in NR-LC. On the black mood, conversations in June 1970 with Muse, Ernest Anderson, Eddie Anderson, Carlton Moss, and William F. Walker; "Minutes of Special Meeting," Feb. 16, 1942, in NR-LC; Jackson, *Hattie*, pp. 100–103, for Aug. 1942 meeting called by McDaniel.

41. White to Sara Boynoff, *News*, March 12, 16, 1942, in NR-LC; CE, July 31, 1915, quoted in Cripps, *Slow Fade to Black*, p. 76.

42. Adorno quoted in Judith W. Hess, "Genre Films and the Status Quo," *Jump Cut* 1 (May–June 1974): 16–18; see too Louis F. Helbig, "The Myth of the 'Other' America in East German Popular Consciousness," *Journal of Popular Culture* 10 (Spring 1977): 797–807, quoting Russel Nye, *Notes on a Rationale for Popular Culture* (Bowling Green, n.d.), 6, on "the experience of the majority."

43. Hess, "Genre Films," 18, quoting Adorno.

44. White to Sara Boynoff, April 1, 13, 1942, in NR-LC.

45. PC, Feb. 7, 1942 (Thompson's letter); July 4, 1942, for "Double V Girl of the week"; Washburn, *A Question of Sedition*, 54–55.

46. Minutes of Feb. 16, 1942, meeting; reminders for White in California, July 8, 1942; press release, "Race—A Basic Issue in This War"; memo, n.d., "Films: Portrayal of Negroes In," in NR-LC. White's recollection of the pledges was that he asked for a 10 : 1 ratio of white to black in crowd scenes, and received 15 : 1.

47. *Var.*, June 17, 1942, p. 5; White to Lola Kovner, May 1, 1942, in NR-LC.

48. White's welcome speech, p. 14; press release, Arch Reeve, MPPDA, July 18, 1942; White to Sara Boynoff, July 6, 1942; undated roster, "Los Angeles Branch Officers," June 22, 1942, in NR-LC. Black Hollywood was represented by Levette, LaMar, Almena Davis, Hall Johnson, A. C. Bilbrew, Muse, Clinton Rosamond, and Fay M. Jackson, whom White would recruit for his postwar Hollywood bureau.

49. Mendel B. Silberberg to White, Aug. 28, 1942; a day on which Poynter urged White to keep his distance, in NR-LC.

50. Poynter to White, Aug. 29, 1942, in NR-LC.

51. Barnhart's guidelines and review of *Shoe Shine Boy* in Office for Emergency Management records, NA-MD, lent by Professor K. R. M. Short, University of Houston. Reviewers' names on "Evaluation Sheets" in OWI-LC. See Barbara Deming, *Running Away from Myself: A Dream Portrait of America Drawn from the Films of the Forties* (New York, 1969), 2.

52. *Smart Alecks, Night for Crime,* and *Mississippi Blackout,* analysis forms in OWI-LC; Darryl F. Zanuck to "Sam" [Goldwyn], July 21, 1943 [sic], in NR-LC.

Saenger Theatre Chain clipping books, HRC-TX; on movies for troops, Lt. John S. Arthur to E. V. Richards, April 22, 1942; Brig. Gen. George Hunter to Richards, April 24, 1942; and A. W. Dent, Dillard University, to Richards, April 24, 1942, in Richards papers, HRC-TX. In Saenger books see particularly *States* (New Orleans), Feb. 16, May 7, June 1, 8, 15, July 6, 27, Aug. 19, Sept. 2, 14, 1942; Ted Luizza's reviews in *Item* (New Orleans); *Times-Picayune* (New Orleans), Oct. 28–30, 1942, in which no fewer than three stories on *Tales of Manhattan* ran. PC, Oct. 3, 1942, on *News-Leader; Var.*, Jan. 14, 1942, p. 6; Feb. 4, 1942, p. 7; Feb. 18, 1942, pp. 2, 18, on *The Little Foxes* and censorship.

53. Darryl F. Zanuck to "Sam" [Goldwyn], copy, July 21, 1943 [*sic*], in NR-LC.

54. Harry and Jack Warner; Alfred L. Wright, attorney; Fred W. Beetson, exec. vice president, MPPDA; Sidney Buchman, WGA-W; Trem Carr, Monogram; Cliff Work, Universal; Sol Lesser, copies of all, dated July 24, 1942, in NR-LC; Zanuck to Eric Knight, copy, July 22, 1942, in Knight papers, Macungie, Pa., lent by Professor David Culbert, Louisiana State University.

55. B. G. DeSylva to Zanuck, copy, July 27, 1942, in NR-LC.

56. White to Breen, copy, Aug. 21, 1942, with which compare press releases, "Film Executives Pledge to Give Negroes Better Movie Roles" and "Film Executives Pledge Better Roles for Negroes at Conferences with NAACP Secretary," July 31, 1942, in NR-LC. Sample of correspondence: "Miss Crump" to White, memo, Aug. 13, 1942; John S. Holley to White, Aug. 20, 1942; Sam Bischoff to Holley, Dec. 8, 1942; White to Harry Warner, copy, Aug. 24, 1942; George B. Murphy, Jr., National Negro Congress (NNC), to White, Aug. 31, 1942; Crump to staff, Aug. 7, 1942, and *PM* clipping, undated, in NR-LC.

57. Miller's story made NYT only by March 13, 20, 1942, and sporadically thereafter on May 11–13, 28, 1942, June 10, 1942, Dec. 15, 29, 1942, while Kelly's played for more than a year beginning with his death in action, Dec. 13, 1941, and ending with the christening of a Liberty Ship in his honor, Dec. 14, 1942; PC for link of Miller with *Crash Dive,* Sept. 12, 19, 1942; on Navy Cross, May 9, June 6, 1942; see navy's film *December 7* for a dramatization of Miller's feat and for Navy Cross award.

58. CE, Sept. 24, 1942, on christening; Lillian Hellman, *Negro Picture,* treatment, 14 pp., May 7, 1942, in Hastie file, RG 208, NA-DC.

59. *Liberty Ship* treatment, MGM-LD.

60. *Var.*, March 25, 1942, p. 1; and PC, April 4, 1942, in which Oscar dinner conversations were to result in "better roles for colored actors." Hellman's treatment, May 7, 1942; Poynter to White, Aug. 29, 1942, in NR-LC; Warner to "Holly," Oct. 9, 1942; Hollingshead to Steve Trilling, Oct. 12, 1942, WBA-USC, said they were acting at the request of Lowell Mellett.

61. CE, Sept. 3, 1942, on *The Real Glory* and *Tennessee Johnson;* PC, Aug.

29, 1942, on unanimity; Sept. 12, 1942, on *Crash Dive*, interviews; Sept. 26, 1942, on Warner's interviews.

62. Caleb Peterson to White, Oct. 22, 1942; White to Peterson, copy, Nov. 2, 1942; White to Howard Dietz, copy, Nov. 11, 1942; Dietz to White, Nov. 5, 1942; and Peterson to White, Jan. 7, 1943, relating the story to ensuing gigs, in NR-LC.

63. Lola [Kovner] to White, Oct. 22, 1942, and *Var.* clipping [Oct. 21, 1942], in NR-LC; Hollingshead to Steve Trilling, Oct. 12, 1942; Mellett to Jack Warner, Oct. 14, 1942, thanking him for resuming work; Hollingshead to Warner, Oct. 13, 1942, on Sherman's quick work; Frank to Anthony, wire, Nov. 5, 1942, seeking stock shots of Joe Louis in action, presumably to use in *Booker T.*, in WBA-USC.

64. Hellman treatment, passim.

65. Nelson Poynter to Gordon Hollingshead, Dec. 12, 1942; anonymous memo, Nov. 9, 1942, in Hellman file, WBA-USC, both of which rang with liberal conviction, Poynter calling for an end to "subservient" business.

66. *Shoe Shine Boy* print in LC; telephone interview between Lewis Jacobs and the author, July 21, 1977; Ellick Moll, "You'll Never Get Rich," *Saturday Evening Post*, Nov. 21, 1942, pp. 18, 112–13, ended with the kid in Africa playing "a blue note which had been born on that Dark Continent, and been torn away long ago, and [now] to sing for the freedom his great-grandpappy had been robbed of."

67. On the idea of propaganda as forecast for future social agendas—without forethought sometimes—I am indebted to Professor Wilhelm Van Kampen, of *Die Landesbildstelle*, Berlin, for patient conversations; on overdrawn, too on-the nose propaganda that flopped, specifically *Der ewige Jude*, see Stig Hornshøj-Møller and David Culbert, "'Der ewige Jude' (1940): Joseph Goebbels' Unequaled Monument to Anti-Semitism," *Historical Journal of Film, Radio and Television*, 12 (1992), 41–68.

68. Poynter to White, Aug. 29, 1942, in NR-LC; HR, Dec. 18, 1942, in box 89, "Kay Brown, 1938–1942" file, DOS-TX; Weekly Log, May 29, 1942, approving a *Tarzan* movie, not for its race angle but treatment of "the rubber problem in Germany," entry 566, box 3510, RG 208, NA-MD; "toe the line" in Lola to White, Oct. 22, 1942, cited in note 63. Movies that evidenced backsliding led Poynter to confess "we were not consulted on this picture," in Poynter to White, above.

69. White to Laura Veiller, Oct. 10, 1947, on Freeman, NR-LC; Jay Leyda, ed., *Voices of Film Experience: 1894 to the Present* (New York, 1977), p. 450; Hartung in *Commonweal*, July 9, 1943, p. 302.

70. Arch Reeve, MPPDA, "for immediate release," July 18, 1942, in NR-LC.

71. White's clipping file *was* in temporary box 277, NR-LC; PC, Nov. 7, 1942, Isadora Smith said movies could "mold" ideals; PC, Oct. 24, 1942, Alice Key made early use of "integration" as new coinage; *Washington Gaily* [sic] *News*, Aug. 1, 1942, praised the "great dinner in Hollywood" while running boilerplate on *Tarzan's New York Adventure* in which he is knocked "in an attack by savages"; PV, Sept. 12, 1942; White to Fredi Washington, copy, Sept. 21, 1942, on Muse, in NR-LC; PC, Oct. 10, 1942, on Earl Dancer's sailing a biopic of Crispus Attucks over the transom; *Var.*, June 17, 1942, p. 5, quoted John

Gassner, Yale, on the coming "mature films in America after the war"; *Var.*, April 15, 1942, p. 5; White to "Irene and David" [Selznick], copy, July 28, 1942, on White's failure to seat a black man on Nelson Rockefeller's Committee on Inter-American Affairs; Peter Noble, *The Negro in Films* (London, 1947), 217; Carey McWilliams, *Brothers Under the Skin* (New York, 1951), 46–47; PC, Sept. 12, 1942, on Muse's column; AN, Aug. 14, 1943.

72. Norman O. Houston to White, Sept. 16, 1943, in NR-LC; Leon Washington in LAS, n.d., in NR-LC, for needling White's "attack via the luncheon table."

73. *Var.*, March 15, 1944, p. 3; July 12, 1944, p. 1; Dec. 1, 1943, p. 2; Nov. 17, 1943, p. 1; HDC minutes, June 1, July 7, Aug. 4, Oct. 13, 1943; HDC roster, Aug. 1944; HDC membership list, Aug. 1944, all in HDC records, SHSW; on Hollywood Anti-Nazi League, see its pamphlet, *Heil Hitler* (n.d.) in Pamphlet Collection, Special Collections, UCLA; AN, July 1943, in GPJ-UCLA; Dana Burnett to Michael Blankfort, Dec. 23, 1944, box 9, Blankfort papers, ML-BU; HDC Executive Board minutes, Nov. 27, 1944; Helen Gahagan Douglas to George Pepper, June 12, 1944; Revels Cayton, Minorities Director, California CIO Council, to Pepper, July 20, 1944; Pepper, HDC, to Hollywood Roosevelt Hotel, Dec. 21, 1944, in HDC-SHSW. Telephone interview between Howard Koch and the author, July 12, 1977, on absence of orthodoxy ("you just came in and joined"). For the moment CPUSA membership mattered less than profit as when Garson Kanin, *Hollywood* (New York, 1974), pp. 215–17, reported on Harry Cohn's refusal to fire John Howard Lawson from *Sahara*. *Var.*, Feb. 9, 1944, p. 8; Roy Wilkins to Thomas Griffith, Feb. 29, 1944, in NR-LC; Dalton Trumbo, "Blackface Hollywood Style," *Crisis* 52 (Dec. 1943): 365–67, 378; *Writers' Congress: The Proceedings of the Conference Held in October 1943 under the Sponsorship of the Hollywood Writers' Mobilization and the University of California* (Berkeley, 1944), 14–18, 27, 32, 495–501, 629, for speeches by White, Zanuck, and William Grant Still; Robert Vaughn, *Only Victims* (New York, 1972), appendix, with which compare conference members for a profile of Hollywood left; Bruce Cook, *Dalton Trumbo* (New York, 1977), 147–47; Ceplair and Englund, *The Inquisition in Hollywood*, chap. 6; for personal anecdotes see Maurice Zolotow, *Shooting Star: A Biography of John Wayne* (New York, 1974), chap. 19; George Eels, *Ginger, Loretta and Irene Who?* (New York, 1976), 58–59; Kay Gable, *Clark Gable: A Personal Portrait* (Englewood Cliffs, 1961), 25, 68; Lee Israel, *Miss Tallulah Bankhead* (New York, 1972), 252; Max Wilk, *The Wit and Wisdom of Hollywood* (New York, 1971), 135; *Var.*, Feb. 9, 1944, p. 8. The catechismic testiness of the era has been told to me in interviews with Lewis Milestone (June 1970), John Cromwell, HICCASP officer (Dec. 24, 1976), and Dore Schary (in several telephone talks). Salka Viertel, *The Kindness of Strangers* (New York, 1969), 211–15.

Chapter 3
The Making of a Genre

1. Lasky's holograph note on *The Adventures of Mark Twain* script, file 2703, in WBA-USC; Arch Reeve to White, July 24, 1942, in NR-LC, on the pledge; see also Breen to Jack Warner, June 17, 1942, file 2703, in WBA-USC.

2. Blanche L. Patterson, Sumner School, St. Louis, to Gordon Hollingshead, Aug. 28, 1942, in "Hellman Picture" file, WBA-USC.

3. For a sample, Jason S. Joy to John S. Holley, copy, Sept. 2, 1942, in NR-LC, and a sample of Wherry's later letters through 1971, lent by Carlton Moss; Lawrence D. Reddick, "Movies in Harlem: An Experiment," *Library Journal* 68 (Dec. 1943): 981–82; PC, Sept. 26, 1942, for Ernest Johnson letter to Warner Bros., June 12, 1942; Warner Bros. to Johnson, ibid.; Breen to Warner, June 17, 1942, file 2703, WBA-USC; and Sidney Buchman replying to Booker Brown, PC, Oct. 31, 1942.

4. Arch Reeve, MPDDA, to White, July 24, 1942, in NR-LC; and Lasky's annotated *Twain* script, WBA-USC.

5. Poynter to "Dear Jack" [Warner], Jan. 21, 1942, file 2703, WBA-USC.

6. Letter quoted in Sklar, *Movie-Made America*, chap. 15; see also Garth Jowett, *Film, the Democratic Art: A Social History of American Film* (Boston, 1976), chap. 12.

7. PC, Sept. 24, 1942, on *Action in the North Atlantic;* Hal Wallis and Charles Higham, *Starmaker: The Autobiography of Hal Wallis* (New York, 1980), 80–81.

8. OWI alpha. file, "Minorities—Negro—Negro Opinion Study," Oct. 1942–Jan. 1943, 16 pp., in PN-HST; for a social scientist on "prejudice" as a form of correctable ignorance, Gordon W. Allport, *The Nature of Prejudice* (New York, 1953), 6; on the two-mindedness of OWI, Recommendations (n.d.), and holograph note: "do not print with report," in PN-HST; OWI quoted in Harry Albert Sauberli, "Hollywood and World War II: A Survey of Themes of Hollywood Films about the War, 1940–1945" (M.A. [Cinema], University of Southern California, 1967), appendix; Walter White, "Statement to the Negro Public, Particularly in Los Angeles," Sept. 19, 1942, holograph draft; and Arch Reeve, MPPDA press release, in NR-LC.

9. Telephone interview between Irving Rapper and the author, Aug. 1977; Victor Lasky and George Murphy, *Say . . . Didn't You Used to Be George Murphy* (n.p., 1970), 257. True or not, moviestar yarns are intended to convey a recalled mood. Curtiz got it wrong anyway; his amended cue was "bring on the *colored* nigger troops."

10. *Gung Ho* (1943) contained no less than three speeches arguing that a crack unit of amphibious Marines could not succeed without "harmony" in the name of "democracy, freedom, and equality," and defined as "no prejudice—racial [or] religious." PC, Sept. 19, 1942, touted *Talk of the Town*, and on Oct. 31, 1942, ran Buchman's letter to Booker Brown, Interstate United Newspapers; "Rogue's Regiment," *Ebony* 3 (Sept. 1948): 31–33.

11. NYT, Jan. 29, 1941; AN, May 8, 15, 1943.

12. White to Jason S. Joy of Fox, Roy Wilkins, and Judge William Hastie, July 22, 1943, in NR-LC, on Spaulding; White to Lowell Mellett, Feb. 25, 1943; Mellett to White, copy, March 1, 1943, "White" folder, box 18, LM-FDR, on Eboué.

13. On the anatomy of a black genre, Thomas Cripps, *Black Film as Genre* (Bloomington, 1979), chap. 1.

14. Manuel Quezon to Lowell Mellett, Aug. 17, 1942, et seq., in boxes 1439–40, entry 264, OWI Domestic Operations Branch, Bureau of Motion Pictures, Office of the Chief, RG 208, in NA-MD; OWI Manual cited in Koppes and

Black, "The Office of War Information and Hollywood," 87 ff.; see also Sauberli, "Hollywood and World War II," pp. 321, 51; and Dorothy B. Jones, *The Portrayal of China and India on the American Screen, 1896–1955* (Cambridge, Mass., 1955). In another rerelease dispute, that of *Gunga Din,* OWI objected to a stridently played nationalistic cult leader (Edouardo Ciannelli), perhaps because he was a voice of anticolonialism. See Film Analysis Section, entry 587, box 3522, RG 208, in NA-LC. On other cases, mainly B-movies, see files on *Little Tokio* [sic] *USA, White Cargo,* and *White Savage,* in box 3520, entry 567, OWI, RG 208, in NA-MD.

15. Nelson Poynter to White, Aug. 29, 1942, NR-LC, on OWI's nonrole; Cripps, "Robeson and Black Identity," 468–85; Paul Robeson, *Here I Stand* (New York, 1958), 39; Georges Sadoul, *Dictionnaire des Cineastes* (Paris, 1965), 76–77, found Duvivier merely "un bon directeur d'acteurs, ayant le sens de l'atmosphere [et] realisme poetique"; on the one hand the French chose it as their first postliberation movie, NYT, Oct. 6, 1944, while *Daily News* (New York), Oct. 13, 1942, thought his negativism mere Communist dogma; on the cameraman, Charles Higham, *Hollywood Cameramen: Sources of Light* (Bloomington, 1970), 154.

16. I. H. Prinzmetal to D. O. Decker, May 1942, no. 1257, MGM-LD, reported eliminating Stevens's black mistress; Arch Mercey to Nelson Poynter, June 22, 24, 1942, on "circles"; Mellett to Poynter, Aug. 4, 1942, entry 566, box 3510, OWI, RG 208, NA-MD, on hoped-for "unjustified" story of black "resentment."

17. A run of DW in LC; I. H. Prinzmetal to D. O. Decker, May 1942, no. 1257, MGM-LD.

18. After Platt's story appeared, Mellett admitted to Poynter his hope that "it is not justified in its assertion that the picture is calculated to arouse widespread resentment among Negroes," Aug. 4, 1942, in entry 566, box 3510, OWI, EG 208, in NA-MD; see also DW through its summer campaign; and Platt to White, Aug. 8, 1942, with enclosure, in NR-LC.

19. R. B. Wills to Kenneth MacKenna, memo, "confidential," June 20, 1939, on Marxists; early treatments by Alvin T. Meyer and Lowell Brodaux, June 23, 27, 1939, after which they were hired, Nov. 1, 1939; and carbon memo, April 26, 1944; and on subsequent treatments, Sloan Nibley to I. H. Prinzmetal, May 16, 1940; undated treatment by Lloyd Paul Stryker; see also D. O. Decker to J. Robert Rubin, March 8, 1945, all in file 6408, MGM-LD. John L. Balderston, "Andrew Johnson: The Man on America's Conscience," May 20, 1942; Balderston to William Dieterle, Sept. 3, 1942, in Dieterle papers, USC; "Fifty Filmographies," *Film Comment* 6 (Winter 1970–71): 101; Andrew Sarris, *The American Cinema: Directors and Directions, 1929–1968* (New York, 1968), 255; Stanley Hochman, ed., *A Library of Film Criticism: American Film Directors* (New York, 1974), 89–97; telephone interview between Carlton Moss and the author, July 6, 1977. See also Balderston to Mayer, et al., Aug. 31, 1942, on rewriting to please "the Reds and the Blacks," in Balderston Papers, PA-NYPL.

20. Poynter to Mellett, Aug. 25, 1942; Mellett to Poynter, Aug. 28, 27, 1942, in entry 264, box 1438, OWI Domestic Operations Branch, Bureau of Motion Pictures, Office of the Chief, RG 49, NR-MD; Robert Lippins, William D. Kaplan, and Amelia Kristol, all of Newark, all to Metro, Aug. 9, 1942; Vivian Johnson, Brooklyn, to MGM, Aug. 10, 1942; W. L. Modlin, Aug. 11, 1942; Mrs.

F. J. Burke, Aug. 29, 1942; and Nena Beth Shaw, Oklahoma City, Aug. 12, 1942, all in MGM-LD. On the film, Dorothy B. Jones to Poynter, copy, Aug. 6, 1942; Poynter to Mellett, Aug. 6, 1942; Mellett to Maurice Revnes, MGM, Aug. 18, 1942; White to Mellett, Aug. 17, 1942, in entry 566, box 3510, Film Analysis Section, Office, RG 208, NR-MD.

21. White to Poynter, Aug. 26, 1942; White to Mayer, n.d.; Mayer to White, Aug. 19, 1942; Mellett to Mayer, Nov. 25, 1942; Poynter to Edward J. Mannix, Sept. 2, 1942, entry 566, box 3510, LA Office, OWI, Office of the Chief, RG 208, NR-MD.

22. Poynter to Mellett, Aug. 25, 1942; Mellett to Poynter, Aug. 27, 1942, entry 566, box 3510, OWI, RG 208, NR-MD; White to Mrs. Charles E. Russell, copy, Aug. 20, 1942; Lucy Stewart to White, copy, Aug. 24, 1942, on a Johnson biographer, T. F. Woodley; White to Mayer, Aug. 3, 1942; White to "Dear Irene" [Mayer Selznick], copy, Aug. 4, 1942; Mayer to White, Aug. 19, 1942, inviting him to see a rough cut, NA-LC, the last also in file 1253, MGM-LD.

23. Poynter to Eddie Mannix, Sept. 2, 1942, seeking a print; Howard Dietz to Poynter, Feb. 3, 1942, with Dec. 7, 1942, enclosure, leftist press release, in entry 566, box 3510, OWI, NA-MD; White to Mellett, copy, Aug. 17, 1942; Poynter to White, Aug. 28, 1942; Dietz to White, Sept. 16, Nov. 5, 1942; Poynter to White, Nov. 3, 1942; White to Judge Hastie, wire, Nov. 20, 1942; White to Dietz, copy, Nov. 27, 1942; Hastie, "Memorandum Concerning 'Tennessee Johnson'" [Nov. 27, 1942], with a scene of black officer candidates; George B. Murphy, NNC, to White, Dec. 11, 1942; Dietz to White, Dec. 2, 1942, quoting Mellett; MGM press release, n.d., NR-LC. Holograph production notes, n.d., Dieterle papers, USC; I. H. Prinzmetal to J. Robert Rubin, Loew's N.Y., Sept. 1, 1942, reporting OWI request for "certain changes"; D. O. Decker to Prinzmetal, Sept. 18, 1942; Dietz to J. K. McGuinness, Sept. 4, 1942, latter two on retakes and lunch with White, respectively, in file 1257, MGM-LD; White to Mellett, Nov. 27, 1942, objecting to Johnson's amnesty policy; and Mellett to Platt, copy, Jan. 9, 1943, in LM-FDR.

24. Screened at Films, Inc., Atlanta, courtesy Doug Lemza and Lee Tsiantis.

25. Frazier to Lichtman Theatres, copy, Feb. 22, 1943, in NR-LC; *Time*, Jan. 11, 1943, p. 88; *PM*, Jan. 13, 1942; L. D. Reddick to Mellett, Jan. 6, 18, 1942, protesting OWI's lack of "action"; Reddick to Howard Dietz, Dec. 15, 1943, citing NNC protests; Mellett to Platt, copy, Jan. 9, 1943, all in entry 566, box 3510, OWI, RG 208, in NA-MD; Jon tuska et al., eds., *Close Up: The Hollywood Director* (Metuchen, N.J., 1978), 126, in which Dieterle recalled retakes only for neatness; H. G. Barbes, Lichtman chain, to White, Feb. 23, 1943, in NR-LC; Ernest Johnson, "Fight on Film 'Tennessee Johnson' to Be Waged," n.d., CB-CHS; *Var.*, Dec. 30, 1942; AN, Dec. 10, 1942.

26. By then "integration" had become a neologism; see Alice Key, PC, Oct. 24, 1942, on "full screen integration." R. W. Burchfield, *A Supplement to the Oxford English Dictionary* (Oxford, 1976), 324–25, records earliest use as Aug. 5, 1948, in *Richmond Times-Dispatch*, and NYT, June 1, 1955.

27. Memo for file, ending as sold to MGM; and Peter Viertel to Selznick, June 24, 1942, in "Bataan Story" folder, box 8, DOS-TX; Andrews to Cliff Reid, carbon, July 20, 1942; *Big Town* treatment (n.d.), 8 pp.; and New Orleans treatment, in which Andrews and Crane Wilbur are shown to have taken up

radio themes such as "American virtue" and openness to others, all in Andrews papers, ML-BU.

28. Dore Schary, *Heyday: An Autobiography* (Boston, 1979), p. 127, on assuming credit having "cast one of the soldiers as a black [and] Andrews was never told which character it was to be." See Andrews to "Harrison," carbon, June 11, 1943, Andrews papers, ML-BU. Telephone interviews between Tay Garnett and Dore Schary and the author, Aug. and March 1977 respectively, in the former of which Garnett admitted he "never considered [him]self very political." See also Fredda Dudley Balling, *Light Up Your Torches and Pull Up Your Tights* (New Rochelle, 1973), 248; and Lawrence Suid, *Guts and Glory: Great American War Movies* (Reading, Pa., 1978), 45–47.

29. Mel Gussow, *Don't Say Yes Until I Finish Talking: A Biography of Darryl F. Zanuck* (Garden City, 1971), 105; W. R. Burnett, *Crash Dive* story outline, April 21, 1942; Julian Johnson to Zanuck, April 22, 1942; Zanuck to Milton Sperling, 7-page carbon, April 23, 1942; Jo Swerling, synopsis of "final script," July 18, 23, 1942; notes on conference with Zanuck and revised temporary script, July 6, 1942, in TCFA-UCLA.

30. John Howard Lawson, *Film: The Creative Process* (New York, 1964), 40–42; Kanin, *Hollywood* (New York, 1974), 216; and Bob Thomas, *King Cohn: The Life and Times of Harry Cohn* (New York, 1967), 299.

31. Scripts in UCLA script collection and in file 2212, TCFA-UCLA, particularly Steinbeck's *Lifeboat*, 244, in which stoker is a "nigger" and other drafts; thence to Swerling's stoker who speaks against lynching, as contrasted with dialogue taken from the screen in which the stoker is a compromise.

32. *Time*, Sept. 21, 1942, p. 69, had reported the sentimentalist John Ford was to direct; see scripts 2155.1 through 2155.8, the latter labeled "dialogue taken from the screen," particularly 2155.6, *Tales of Manhattan*, seq. F, Nov. 26, 1941, in TCFA-UCLA.

33. *Bataan* scripts, file 1280, MGM-LD; Caleb Peterson to White, Jan. 7, 1943, in NR-LC; AN, June 12, 1943; I. H. Prinzmetal to Carter Barron, copy, April 19, 1943; Barron to Harry Rapf, April 6, [1943]; Rapf to Dietz, copy, May 13, 1943, in file 1280, MGM-LD, all of which reflect OWI and Pentagon interest.

34. *Worker* sample, summer 1942; by then Robeson had become a black cultural nationalist and pan-Africanist as the CPUSA began to emphasize OWI-like "unity" rather than demand redress of grievances, so in a way it was he who seemed the odd man out. On black Hollywood, ANP boilerplate, Aug. [1942], in CB-CHS; Ethel Waters with Charles Samuels, *His Eye Is on the Sparrow* (New York, 1951), 257, disagreed with the pickets; Almena Davis, "How 'bout This?" *Los Angeles Tribune*, May 24, 1942; and Davis to White, May 5 and Sept. 14, 1942; and Tom O'Connor *PM* clipping, in NR-LC.

35. Sam Spiegel to White, Sept. 1942; ——— to Hopper, copy, undated, sent by S. P. Eagle [pseud., Spiegel] to White; White to Tom O'Connor, copy, Sept. 23, 1942, in NR-LC; and for example, AN, Aug. 15, Oct. 10, Nov. 28, 1942; see also, Manny Farber, "Black Tails and White Lies," NR, Oct. 26, 1942, p. 467; and *Var.*, June 3, 1942, p. 2, for Walter Winchell's opinion.

36. AN, June 12, 1943; Howard Strickling to Howard Dietz, April 3, 1943, on Glendale preview; and Harry Rapf to Dietz, copy, May 13, 1943, in file 1280, MGM-LD; OWI Log, June 30, 1942, entry 567, box 3520, OWI, NA-MD, missed Epps but praised *Bataan* for its inclusion of Filipino allies. NYT, n.d., and DW,

June 9, 1943, in Andrews papers, ML-BU; CD, March 7, 1943; AN, March 13, Dec. 26, 1943; NYT, June 4, 20, 1943; *Var.*, March 31, 1943, p. 38. Fred Allen to Arnold Auerbach, June 30, 1943, in Joe McCarthy, ed., *Fred Allen's Letters* (Garden City, 1965), 34.

37. Gussow, *Don't Say Yes*, 105; various scripts and Zanuck's conference notes in file 2191, TCFA-UCLA; White to Walter Wanger, April 20, 1943, in NR-LC; *Crash Dive* sheet, OWI analysis sheets, OWI-LC; and for a national magazine, Philip T. Hartung, *Commonweal* 38 (May 14, 1943): 100

38. Lawson, *Film: The Creative Process*, 40–42.

39. White to Walter Wanger, April 23, 1943; Roy Wilkins to M. Spingold, copy, Feb. 16, 1944; press release, "Columbia Pictures Praised for Ingram Role in 'Sahara,'" Feb. 17, 1942, in NR-LC; Sue Lawson to Cripps, Dec. 3, 1977; Thomas, *Cohn*, 299; *Commonweal* 39 (Nov. 12, 1943): 96–97; *Var.*, Oct. 13, 1943, p. 2; *Los Angeles Daily News*, June 11, 1943; NYT, Nov. 12, 1943; AN, Feb. 5, 1943; *PM*, April 15, 1943, which also reported on Ingram's segregation on Brawley, Colorado, locations.

40. John Steinbeck, *Lifeboat*, 244, on Joe's "look"; Jo Swerling's revision, April 30, 1943 (no. 2212.3), has Joe speak against lynching; and no. 2212.3, a compromise that puts the lynching speech into another's lines, in file 2212, TCFA-UCLA.

41. Steinbeck to 20th Century–Fox, Jan. 10, 1944; Steinbeck to Annie Laurie Williams, Feb. 19, 1944, in Elaine Steinbeck and Robert Wallsten, eds., *Steinbeck: A Life and Letters* (New York, 1975), 266; Lee Israel, *Miss Tallulah Bankhead* (New York, 1972), 235–36; NYT, Jan. 23, 1944.

42. PC, Jan. 29, 1944; Madison Jones, NAACP, to Roy Wilkins, copy, Jan 20 [*sic*]; Wilkins to William Goetz, copy, Feb. 17, 29, 1944; Goetz to Wilkins, Feb. 23, 1944, in NR-LC; AN, Jan. 29, 1944; *Var.*, March 31, 1943, p. 39.

43. Kyle Crichton, *Look* editor, reputed CPUSA member, workname Robert Forsythe, to White, April 9, 1942; White to "Kyle," copy, April 13, 1942; White to Lena Horne, copy, March 17, 1942, in NR-LC.

44. See Thomas Cripps, "*Amos 'n' Andy* and the Debate over American Racial Integration," in John E. O'Connor, ed., *American History/American Television: Interpreting the Video Past* (New York, 1983), 33–54, on the debate over whether all-black shows were omens of integration or residues of segregation.

45. *Var.*, June 10, 1942, p. 3; Aug. 12, 1942, p. 3; April 8, 1942, p. 22; March 31, 1943, p. 39; May 26, 1943, p. 2; June 9, 1943, p. 1, for a sample of the times.

46. Drafts of the play in Lynn Riggs papers, box 1, AHC-WY; see also file 1267, MGM-LD; and Marc Connelly to Walter White, Nov. 17, 1942, in NR-LC.

47. Vincente Minnelli and Hector Arce, *I Remember It Well* ([London], 1974), 54–55, 68, 78, 97, 121–23; for "Vince" as apprentice see Arthur Freed Oral History, Columbia Oral History Project, no. 1614 (Dec. 1958); Will Hays to Joseph Breen, Sept. 27, 1937, in PCA-AMPAS; Lena Horne and Richard Schickel, *Lena* (New York, 1965), 134–37, 153–54; Waters and Samuels, *His Eye Is on the Sparrow*, 258–61; telephone interview between Minnelli and the author, Aug. 4, 1977, in which he found Waters "difficult" but likeable; James Haskins and Kathleen Benson, *Lena: A Personal and Professional Biography of Lena Horne* (New York, 1984) 74–79.

48. Stepin Fetchit to Lew Brown, wire, July 16, 1942; Mayer to Arthur

Freed, wire, July 14, 1942; Marvin Schenk to Al Lewis, copy, July 21, 1942; Schenk to Freed, wire, Aug. 12, 1942; Billy Grey to Schenk, Aug. 15, 1942, in file 1267, MGM-LD; Minnelli and Arce, *I Remember It Well,* chap. 9.

49. Marc Connelly to Walter White, Nov. 17, 1942; White to Connelly, Nov. 20, 1942; Lola Kovner to White, March 25, 1942, "nice going," in NR-LC; Charlie Sands, "Motion Picture Study Club," Washington, D.C., to Freed, Feb. 12, 1942, calling for George Washington Carver biopic as useful as overseas propaganda, in Freed papers, SHSW; AN, Nov. 7, 14, 1942; *Negro Actors Guild Newsletter,* April 1942, p. 1, Jan. 1943, p. 1; AN, March 6, 1943; *Var.*, Feb. 10, 1943; March 10, 1943, p. 2; April 8, 1943, p. 3; AN, June 19, 1943, April 17, 1943, May 8, 1943; AA, April 3, 1943; *Time,* April 12, 1943, p. 96; *Post* (New York), quoted in Donald Bogle, *Toms, Coons, Mulattoes, Mammies & Bucks* (New York, 1973), 131; *Var.*, April 8, 1942, predicting "Metro's 'Cabin in the Sky' Buy May Pave the Way for More Negro Films," while also pointing out the rivalry between daring production and conservative sales departments; on Billy Rowe, Rowe to Freed, n.d., and on fissure among black critics, Earl Dancer to *Courier,* copy to Freed, in Freed papers, SHSW; on PCA intervention, see Geoffrey Shurlock's marginalia on the script in ITC-DC; and on submittal to NAACP, Joseph Schrank to NYT, Jan. 22, 1983.

50. AN, June 13, 1943, and PV, Feb. 27, 1943, in "S" folder, box 1440, entry 264, OWI, RG 208, in NA-MD; White to Connelly, copy, Nov. 21, 1942; and White to Edwin Embree, copy, Feb. 13, 1942, in NR-LC.

51. *Time,* April 12, 1943, p. 96, and other journalistic citations in note 49; *Var.*, April 8, 1943, p. 3; NYT, May 28, 1943.

52. *Herald-Tribune* (New York), Nov. 29, 1942; Hy Kraft, *On My Way to the Theatre* (New York, 1971), 102; *Thanks, Pal* script draft in ITC-DC.

53. Gussow, *Don't Say Yes,* 104–14; Kraft, *On My Way,* 102; E. C. Lavigne to William Goetz et al., Sept. 11, 1942, on buying; Julian Johnson to Goetz, Jan. 11, 1942; Johnson to William LeBaron, and synopsis of *Thanks, Pal,* Oct. 2, 1942; Kraft, "Thanks Pal Screenplay," Nov. 21, 1942; Frederick Jackson and Ted Koehler, "Stormy Weather," 1943, in *Stormy Weather* file, TCFA-UCLA.

54. *Los Angeles Tribune,* Feb. 15, 1943; William Grant Still to White, June 2, 1943; Ethel Johnson, Delta Sigma Theta, and Alice Webb, to White, March 31, 1943, backing Still; Johnson and Webb to Irving Mills, Fox, copy, March 11, 1943; Still to White, on cuts, including a "ballet," March 30, 1943; Still to White, April 27, 1943, in NR-LC; and Still, "The Negro and His Music in Films," *Proceedings of the Writers Congress . . .* (Berkeley, 1944), 277–79.

55. Horne and Schickel, *Lena,* 164; AN, Feb. 13, 20, 27, 1942, and Jan. 16, 1943; *PM,* March 22, 1943, in GPJ-UCLA; CD, April 17, 1942, on Robinson's firing after a fistfight on the lot; AN, Jan. 16, 1943: not even Shirley Temple "could restore him to the good graces of the movie moguls until . . . the current wave of interest in Negro professionals."

56. Flournoy Miller to White, copy, Jan. 11, 1938; Charles Correll and Freeman Gosden [Amos 'n' Andy] to Miller, Oct. 14, 1941; Miller's contract with Fox, Feb. 5, 1942, at $750 per week; *Shuffle Along* contract, March 18, 1949; *Amos 'n' Andy* contract with CBS, Sept. 1, 1949–Aug. 31, 1950, all photocopies, in Miller papers, AMPAS, as a typical black career course.

57. Haskins and Benson, *Lena,* p. 88, quote NYT on *Stormy Weather* as a case of "the desires of Washington . . . for increased employment of Negro

citizens in certain heretofore restricted fields of industry," confirming White's fear of all-black films.

58. Manny Farber, "The Great White Way," NR, July 5, 1943, p. 20; *Var.*, March 10, 1943, p. 34; June 2, 1943, p. 8; *Daily Var.*, May 27, 1943; HR, May 27, 1943; *Var.*, Aug. 4, 1943, p. 9; Aug. 11, 1943, p. 15; *Time*, July 12, 1943, pp. 94–96; Philip T. Hartung, "Rain, No Game!" *Commmonweal*, July 23, 1943, pp. 344–45; *Var.*, July 12, 1944, p. 1; NYT, July 2, 20, Feb. 7, June 6, 1943; *Post* (New York), Oct. 27, 1943; AA, July 31, 1943; PC, July 31, 1943; CD, July 31, 1943; AN, July 31, 1944; White to Zanuck, wire, July 2, 1943; Jason S. Joy, Fox, to Roy Wilkins, March 31, 1944, in NR-LC.

59. Draft script, *The Very Thought of You*, with marginalia by Jerry Wald, in Daves papers, Stanford University; and Alvah Bessie, *Inquisition in Eden* (New York, 1965), 74–75.

60. "Page breakdown," *Since You Went Away*, pp. 24–25, box 7; synopsis 1, in box 31; Wilder's first rough draft, May 1, 1943, pp. 29–34, in box 24, *Since You Went Away* (SYWA), in all DOS-TX; Jackson, *Hattie*, 85–86.

61. Draft dated June 29, 1943, pp. 59–63; and F. Hugh Herbert to Selznick, July 23, 1943, in SYWA box 24, DOS-TX.

62. Retakes suggested by Ulric Bell, penciled holograph, Nov. 30, 1943, SYWA, box 24; Marie E. Hicks, Lucile Gaskin, et al. to Selznick; and preview cards, in box 26, all in DOS-TX.

63. *Goebbels Tagebuch*, March 1, 1942, quoted in David Welch, *Propaganda and the German Cinema, 1939–1945* (New York, 1983), preview cards, SYWA box 26, DOS-TX.

64. *Till the End of Time*, Feb. 17, 1945, Kinchloe is black; but Jan. 17, 1945, 22, color gave way to a sketch of his bed; drafts April 27, May 28, 1945, in "Treatments, Synopses, Scripts," boxes 154–55, in DOS-TX. Filed with May 28, 1945, draft is a carbon sheet by Rivkin entitled "Theme," which is asserted as postwar readjustment rather than race, in above group, box 121.1, DOS-TX.

65. Rivkin's first script under the new arrangement dated March 6, then 28, with Schary as producer; estimating script, July 12, 1945; market analysis, Jan. 29, 1945; and Ben Piazza to William Dozier, Sept. 27, 1945, casting report, all in file 521, RKO-UCLA. Penciling-out in May 28 draft. Gene Kern, OWI Overseas Bureau, to William Gordon, July 24, 1945, also in file 521, RKO-UCLA.

66. Rivkin's "final script," Aug. 31, 1945; "as shot" script, Sept. 28, 1945; cutting continuity, May 16, 1945; and various blue pages, through summer, all in file 521, RKO-UCLA, had dropped the race angle save for the pinball sequence.

67. Preview Analysis by ARI jury system, Aug. 14, 1946; for premiere at RKO Hill Street, see Jim Wilkerson to N. Peter Rathvon, April 15, 1946; for its getting the values they had hoped for, George M. Dorsey to Paul Hollister, RKO, July 16, 1946 (following showing at National Archives through Arch Mercey, chief of the New Motion Picture Division of War Mobilization and Conversion); and Mercey's correspondence with N. Peter Rathvon, RKO, July 1946, in file 521, RKO-UCLA; transcript of Sheila Graham's Sunday radio show, MBS, March 12, 1950, and inscription of his copy of the script, both in Rivkin papers, box 34, AHC-WY.

68. *Ebony*, Aug. 1946, p. 33.

69. Stuart Omer Landry, *The Cult of Equality: A Study of the Race Problem* (New Orleans, 1945), pp. 14, 291–93.

70. *PM*, Feb. 26, 1943, clipping in SCRBC.

71. Deming on *Underground Agent* (1942), OWI-LC; Tingley, referring to *Var.*, July 7, 1943, on analysis card, alpha. file, MSCB; PM, Aug. 22, 1945, on Sears.

72. Alpha. file, OWI-LC.

73. Alpha. file, OWI-LC; Lillian Berquist, "Short Review: Minstrel Days," Oct. 22, 1942, in entry 567, box 3522, OWI, RG 208, NA-MD.

74. Telephone interviews with Gunther Fritsch and the author, Aug. 1976; Robert Wise, Aug. 1978 and Aug. 1980; and DeWitt Bodeen, Oct. 1976; and Bodeen to Cripps, Aug. 13, 1976. Lancelot does not appear in early drafts: see file 435, *Curse of the Cat People*, and file 386, *Cat People*, in RKO-UCLA; Charles Higham and Joel Greenberg, eds., *The Celluloid Muse: Hollywood Directors Speak* (London, 1969), 209, 218–19; and Joel Siegel, *Val Lewton: The Reality of Terror* (New York, 1973), passim; *Var.*, March 17, 1943, p. 23; *I Walked with a Zombie* evaluation in OWI-LC, and in box 3522, entry 567, "Film Analysis Section," OWI, RG 208, in NA-MD; and on *Revenge of the Zombies*, *Var.*, Aug. 26, 1943, clipping and analysis card in MSCB.

75. *Sullivan's Travels* (1942); a copy of the script, Sturges papers, UCLA; Joel McCrea, the star, recalled the unit thought it important to get the flavor of the scene "right," telephone interview between McCrea and the author, Dec. 1976.

76. NYT, Jan. 22, 1944; Joshua Logan, *My Up and Down, In and Out Life* (New York, 1976), 74; OWI analysis sheet, box 3522, entry 567, OWI, RG 208, in NA-MD; PC, Aug. 22, 1942, quotes Scott and *PM; Var.*, April 23, 1943, clipping in MSCB.

77. Reviews of *Star Spangled Rhythm* and *Thank Your Lucky Stars* in *NAG Newsletter*, Oct. 1943; AN, Aug. 26 and Oct. 7, 1943; *Commonweal* Oct. 8, 1943, p. 612, and Aug. 1943, p. 466.

78. Minnelli and Arce, *I Remember It Well*, 127–29; Minnelli-Cripps interview; Charles Higham and Joel Greenberg, *Hollywood in the Forties* (London, 1968), 173; PM, Nov. 11, 1943; NYT, Nov. 11, 1943; Cripps, *Slow Fade to Black*, 355.

79. *New York Daily News*, Nov. 11, 1942; *Var.*, Jan. 20, 1043, p. 3; telephone interviews between the author and Irving Rapper, Aug. 1976, and Howard Koch, Jan. 1981; memoranda of agreement: Anne Brown, Aug. 24, 1943; Hazel Scott, July 31, 1943, in file 610; Walter MacEwen to Jack Warner, copy to Wallis, May 29, 1941, on hiring Gershwin's friends and Mamoulian; Warner to Odets, copy, April 14, 1942, et seq.; Breen to Warner, July 6, 1943; Warner to Jesse Lasky, copy, Aug. 6, 1943, and others on Rapper's slow pace and ensuing costs; "Charlie" to "Jack," Nov. 13, 1944, on Levant; memo for file, Feb. 14, 1944, on cuts, all in file 2197, WBA-USC; see also David Ewen, *George Gershwin: The Journey to Greatness* (Englewood Cliffs, 1971), 305–6; and Higham and Greenberg, *Hollywood in the Forties*, pp. 180–81.

80. Dunham interview for Rediffusion, London, June 18, 1957, box 22, Dunham papers, SIU.

81. Walter White to Warner Bros., Feb. 4, 1941, in NR-LC; Cripps, *Slow Fade to Black*, 359, 375.

82. Walter Van Tilburg Clark, *The Ox-Bow Incident* (New York, 1940), 99–

104, in which Sparks is merely "a queer, slow, careful nigger" who is the butt of humor, while in the movie he is taken to be a preacher; on adaptation, George Bluestone, *Novels into Film: The Metamorphosis of Fiction into Cinema* (Berkeley, 1957), chap. 6; Julian Johnson to Zanuck, May 7, 1942; Johnson to William Goetz, May 23, 1942; script 2188.2, p. 17; Johnson to Jason S. Joy, May 7, 1942, in file 2188, TCFA-UCLA. On principals: James Brough, *The Fabulous Fondas: An Inside Look at America's First Theatrical Family* (New York, 1973), 97–98; William Wellman, *A Short Time for Insanity: An Autobiography* (New York, 1974), 28–29; Dana Andrews, Columbia University Oral History Project, vol. 322, p. 1438.

83. "Final" script, June 3, 11, 1942, blue page 106, Sparks reports Tetley's death while a voice reports on his pose as Southerner, a line given to Gil, one of the protagonists in the movie, in file 2188, TCFA-UCLA.

84. Walter Prescott Webb, afterword to Signet Classic edition (1961) of Clark, *The Ox Bow Incident*, 223–24, quoted; Wellman, *A Short Time*, 28–29, on the flop; NR, May 17, 1943, pp. 669–70; AN, Dec. 22, 1943; *Spectator*, Aug. 6, 1943, p. 127; AN, May 13, 1943; *Agee on Film*, vol. 1, p. 44; Walter White to Walter Wanger, April 23, 1943, NR-LC.

85. Alpha. file, OWI-LC.

86. Hollingshead-Moray correspondence in *Congo* file, WBA-USC.

87. Alpha. file, OWI LC.

88. For a literature on the matter of what movies communicate and with what effect, particularly with respect to African American material, see Cripps, "Making Movies Black," in Dates and Barlow, *Split Image:* and John G. Cawelti, *Adventure, Mystery, and Romance: Formula Stories as Art and Popular Culture* (Chicago, 1976), 35–37, on "cultural images, myths, and themes in archetypal story forms" that "affirm existing interests," "resolve tensions and ambiguities," "explore . . . the permitted and the forbidden," and "assist . . . assimilating changes"; Jeanine Basinger, *The World War II Combat Film: Anatomy of a Genre* (New York, 1986), 61–62, on *Bataan* as accretion of traits that viewers see over time as the genre creates a following whose appreciation is built upon imaginative reworking of the familiar.

Chapter 4
The Making of The Negro Soldier

1. The theme of this chapter owes much to Thomas Cripps and David Culbert, "*The Negro Soldier* (1944): Film Propaganda in Black and White," *American Quarterly* 31 (Winter 1979): 616–40, including documents researched and lent by Culbert.

2. Capra, *Name Above the Title*, chap. 3, "The Great Struggle"; Osborn's obituary, NYT, Jan. 7, 1918; Osborn, *Preface to Eugenics* (New York, 1940); Cripps and Culbert, "*Negro Soldier,*" 620, particularly Culbert's interviews with Osborn and Paul Horgan.

3. Cripps and Culbert, "*Negro Soldier,*" 620–21, citing Culbert's interview with Donald Young as well as Young to Culbert, Dec. 27, 1976; Samuel Stouffer, *What the Soldier Thinks*, in RG 330, Modern Military Records, NA-MD, and *Studies in Social Psychology in World War II* (Princeton, 1949–1950, 3 vols.); Young edited *Annals of the American Academy of Political and Social Science* 223

(1942), "Minority Peoples in a Nation at War; Paul F. Lazarsfeld and Robert K. Merton, "The Psychological Analysis of Propaganda," in *Writers' Congress*, 362–80; OWI, *American Attitudes: World War II*, Vol. X "The Negro and the War," passim.

4. [Donald Young], *Leadership and the Negro Soldier*, Manual M5 (Washington, 1944), 4.

5. Major Bell I. Wiley, *The Training of Negro Troops*, study no. 36 ([Washington], 1946), for oral testimony of black soldiers. "Report on Negro Morale," sampling survey and suggestions, in entry E-5, box 6, alpha. subject file, 1939–1942, OFF, RG 208, NA-MD; five-city survey of blacks and antidotes to plight in PN-HST; T. M. Berry, Group Morale, to George Barnes, March 18, 1942, entry 3, box 65, Bureau of Intelligence, OFF, "Negro" folder, RG 208, NA-MD; anon. memo for [Ulric] Bell, copy to [Henry] Pringle, n.d., lists suggestions for "basic governmental action that will encourage negro morale"; Bell to Carlton Duffus, Treasury, June 2, 1942, on "Caravan"; Berry, "Blue Print Program for Strengthening Negro Morale in War Effort," March 15, 1942, all in entry 5, box 40, OFF, RG 208, in NA-MD; Roy Wilkins to Walter White, March 23, 1942, on "conference" in OFF, March 20, 1942, in box 42, folder "Internal Security Treas—NAACP," in SJS-HST; PC, spring 1942 and Sept. 5, 1942, in which Double V clubs are urged to monitor FEPC. The most informative handling of these sources is Clayton R. Koppes and Gregory D. Black, "Blacks, Loyalty, and Motion Picture Propaganda in World War II," *Journal of American History* 83 (Sept. 1986): 383–406; and their *Hollywood Goes to War: How Politics, Profits & Propaganda Shaped World War II Movies* (New York, 1987), albeit with conclusions different from those in this book.

6. CE, Sept. 3, 1942, on Mellett; PC, Aug. 29, 1942, on "unanimous" pledges, and Sept. 12, 26, Oct. 31, 1942, on whites; Thomas Young, NJ&G, to Clark Davis, Lichtman Theatres, copy, Oct. 24, 1942, entry 566, box 3510, OWI, RG 208, in NA-MD.

7. Oscar Micheaux to Elmer Davis, Oct. 22, 1942, entry 264, box 1433d, OWI Domestic Operations, Bureau of Motion Pictures, Office of Chief, RG 208, NA-MD; PC, Sept. 19 and Oct. 3, 1942 on Toddy; *Marching On* in University of Illinois, Film Archives, courtesy Prof. Robert Carringer; Arch Mercey, OWI, to George Barnes, Feb. 29 [*sic*], 1943, OWI alpha. file, "Minorities—Negro—'Negro Cavalcade,'" discusses Emmanuel Glucksman's All-America Films, Hurliman Films; Nash, OWI, to Dave Frederick, Aug. 22, 1944, and Frederick to Nash, Feb. 24, 1944, in PN-HST. Michaux and Goldberg will be taken up in chap. 5.

8. The mood is caught in Ellen Tarry, *The Third Door: The Autobiography of an American Negro Woman* (New York, 1955), chaps. 12–14; and by Arline Neal and other informants in *Wartime Washington* (WETA-TV, 1985).

9. Arline Neal in *Wartime Washington;* Cayton in Harvard Sitkoff, "Racial Militancy and Interracial Violence in the Second World War," *Journal of American History* 58 (Dec. 1972): 661–81, echoing Feibleman in his feeling that "the greater the outside danger . . . the more abundant the gains for Negroes"; Cayton, "Fighting for White Folks?" *Nation*, Sept. 26, 1942, pp. 267–70.

10. Carlton Moss to Archibald MacLeish, Feb. 1942; Moss to Philip Wiley, March 21, 1942, in folder 002.1, entry 5, box 3, OWI, RG 208, in NA-MD; letterhead roster, Dec. 27, 1941, heralding *Salute to Negro Troops*, color litho.,

lent by Moss; program for the revue; and telephone interview between Moss and the author, Jan. 1986.

11. Nelson Poynter to Lowell Mellett, Oct. 13, 1942, in LM-FDR; on another film see William J. Blakefield, "A War Within: The Making of *Know Your Enemy—Japan,*" *Sight and Sound* 52 (Spring 1983): 128–33; on NAACP as "under direct Communist influence," Gen. A. D. Surles to McGeorge Bundy, "confidential," Feb. 2, 1942, in entry 5, box 40, OFF, RG 208, NA-MD.

12. Moss in conversations since 1969; interview between Marc Connelly and the author, New York, April 14, 1978, recalled the trip but only notes taken; Frank Capra to Gen. Osborn, Aug. 26, 1942, in SPSP 413.56 (8-26-42) cited in Ulysses Lee, *The Employment of Negro Troops: Special Studies* (Washington, 1966), 387.

13. *Negro*, Sept. [1944?], pp. 94–95, in JWJ.

14. "Suggested Motion Picture of the Negro in the US Army," enclosure in Donald Young to David Culbert, Dec. 27, 1976; Lee, *Employment of Negro Troops*, 387; manual cited in Cripps and Culbert, "*Negro Soldier.*"

15. Claude A. Barnett, ANP, to Victor Roudin, copy, March 26, 1952, in CB-CHS; and William Ashby, NUL, to Elmer Davis, entry 264, box 1431, OWI, RG 208, NA-MD.

16. Print in AV section, NA-DC; and stills in box 1569, entry 302, OWI, RG 208, NA-MD; Walter White to Claude Wickard, Nov. 3, 1944; White to "Executives," Oct. 30, 1942, in NR-LC; Seymour L. White, "American Films in Britain," *Film News* [EFLA organ] 5 (April 1944): 6, on *Henry Browne*'s two-thousand-plus British playdates; Lawrence D. Reddick, "Free Movies in Harlem: An Experiment," *Library Journal* 68 (Dec. 1943): 981–82.

17. Nelson Poynter to Lowell Mellett, Oct. 13, 1942, pleased with Hecht, Swerling, and Moss; Osborn to Capra, Sept. 2, 1942, in Lee, *Employment of Negro Troops*, 387, in which he is "doubtful" about "glorification" of blacks; see also Moss to Donald Young, Aug. 26, 1942, box 224, Records of Civilian Aide to Secretary of War (Hastie file), RG 107, MMR, NA-DC; interviews between Moss and the author, Aug. 1977 and May 1984; interview between Capra and the author, La Quinta, Calif., Dec. 31, 1976; telephone interview between Stuart Heisler and the author, Feb. 17, 1977; Cripps and Culbert, "*Negro Soldier,*" 624–25; Axel Madsen, *William Wyler: An Authorized Biography* (New York, 1973), 224–25; shooting script and early draft, May 31, 1943, Sept. 17, 1942, in proj. 6022, box 12, A52-248, RG 208, NA-MD.

18. *Writers' Congress: Proceedings*, 14–18.

19. The hymn was a staple of evangels; lyrics by R. H. McDaniel, music by Charles H. Gabriel, copyright 1912 by Homer Rodeheaver. The shot of Coventry is in Sulzberger, *American Heritage Picture History of World War II*, 116.

20. As released the film combined dramatization, "glass shots" (enactments against a background painted on glass in miniature), and stockshots from features. Budget in 333.9 IG, box 1160, Records of the Inspector General, RG 159, NA-MD; script, May 31, 1943, p. 12; a glass shot intended "to work in two or three Negro soldiers with white soldiers"; Gen. Lyman Munson to Anatol Litvak, Nov. 1, 1943, box 304, RG 107, MMR, NA-DC, on "censorship [which] prohibits . . . Negro soldiers poses of intimacy with white [nurses]."

21. *Leadership and the Negro Soldier*, pp. iv, 64, on suggested training uses; Heisler-Cripps interview, Feb. 17, 1977; *National Film Board of Canada Newslet-*

ter, Feb. 4, 1944, p. 2, reported on the coven of agencies, copy in entry 269, box 1486, OWI, RG 208, NA-MD; Munson to Litvak, Nov. 1, 1943, in 062.2, box 304, RG 319, MMR, NA-DC.

22. Karl Marks to John Hubbell, Jan. 12, 1944, "OF-51" file, 062.2, box 14, in RG 111, AV section, NA-DC; "reaction of Negro and White Soldiers to the Film 'The Negro Soldier,'" April 17, 1944 (439 black, 520 white, Camp Pickett, Va., 91% of blacks liked it "very much"; 67% white thought it "very good); and F. Douglas Williams to Richard Hull, Sept. 11, 1943, on survey design "of a film for Negro soldiers which plays up the part of the Negro," both in 061.2, box 303, RG 319, MMR, NA-DC; but Lee, *Employment of Negro Troops,* 387, found a Hondo airbase sample in which it seemed to do "more harm than good" and "was resented by many."

23. War Dept. circular 208, May 25, 1944, 413.56 AG, box 3241, RG 407; circular 283, Sept. 19, 1945, 413.53, AG, box 3237, RG 407; Brig. Gen. C. T. Lanham, Director, I&E, to Karl Korter, June 6, 1946, 062.2, box 374, RG 319, MMR, NA-DC.

24. Paul Horgan to Lyman Munson, Nov. 6, 1943, 062.2, box 304, RG 319, MMR, NA-DC.

25. Capra, *Name Above the Title,* 358–62; Mabel R. Staupers, NAACP, to Maj. Gen. A. D. Surles, Feb. 25, 1944; NNC to Surles, wire, Feb. 19, 1944, RG 107, MMR, NA-DC.

26. NYT, April 22, 1944; *Nation,* March 11, 1944, p. 316; *Time,* March 27, 1944, pp. 94, 96; *Negro,* Sept. 1944, p. 94, and other clippings in GPJ-UCLA.

27. NJ&G, July 7, 1945; Truman Gibson to Negro press, memo, Feb. 26, 1944, announcing release, in Civilian Aide file, box 250, RG 107, NA-DC, as well as other ephemera such as Tony Marinovich press release, June 28, 1944.

28. Mimeo. analysis of bookings by War Manpower Commission (n.d. [July 1944]), in Taylor Mills to Francis Harmon, July 22, 1944, entry 269, box 1488, RG 208; and Mills to Truman Gibson, May 1, 1944, entry 268, box 1484, RG 208, NA-MD; WAC, *Movies at War* (New York, 1945), 42, with Francis Harmon to David Culbert, Jan. 26, 1977; booking data for thirty-one exchanges in entry 269, box 1485, RG 208, NA-MD; Noble, *Negro in Film* 99–100, lists black theatres by state; Lehman Katz to Lyman Munson, wire, [June 19, 1944], in proj. 6024, 062.2, box 12, A52-248, NA-MD; WAC publicity, July 21, 1944, box 1, Albert Dean papers, MOMA; Weekly Report . . . ," Lehman Katz to Paul Horgan, May 3, 1944, 319.1, box 370, RG 319; Gibson to Litvak, April 14, 1944, on marketing, in proj. 6024, 062.2, box 12, A52-248, NA-MD; Moss-Cripps interview, Dec. 1976; Gibson to Benny Hamilton, Aug. 18, 1944, box 224, RG 107, NA-DC, on more than three thousand white theatres that played the film.

29. Jack Goldberg to Francis Harmon, Feb. 28, 1944, in entry 269, box 1488, OWI, RG 208, NA-MD; affidavits of John J. McCloy and Truman Gibson, Taylor Mills to Harmon, July 22, 1944, ibid.; on WAC meeting, Robert S. Benjamin to Gen. Lyman Munson, April 1, 1944, 062.2, box 224, RG 107, NA-DC; telephone interview between Milton Eisenhower and the author, Oct. 1976.

30. Gibson to Munson, July 7, 1944, cited above; Manual Darrin et al. to Stimson, petition, June 19, 1944, in box 224, RG 107, NA-DC, in which OF-51 was offered as an antidote to "disgraceful" racism in the "War Dept."

Wilkins to Gibson, Jan. 3, 14, 15, Feb. 1, 3, 1944; Wilkins to Maj. Homer B.

Roberts, Feb. 9, 1944; U.S. Dist. Court, S. Dist., N.Y., *Negro Marches On v. War Activities Committee*, copy, n.d.; Gibson, *amicus curiae* brief, 2 pp., n.d.; Thurgood Marshall to Pauline Lauber, HWM, May 2, 1944; Robert Rossen to Frank Capra, March 30, 1944, in NR-LC; on censors, alpha. file, analysis cards, box 22, Feb. 13, 1945, in MSCB (on Pennsylvania censor).

31. Jack Goldberg to Rep. Andrew J. May, April 1, 1944; Goldberg to White, May 25, 1944; Ralph Cooper to White, June 8, 1944; Julia E. Baxter to Wilkins, Nov. 4, 1944; press release, April 27, 1944; White to Thurgood Marshall, May 4, 1944, NR-LC.

32. Edwin R. Embree to "Dear Philleo" [Nash], June 29, 1944; Nash to Embree, July 3, 1944, box 1, PN-HST, supplying data as "the most popular single film we now have"; Cohn quoted in Gibson to Litvak, April 14, 1944, in proj. 6024, 062.2, box 12, A52-248, NA-MD.

33. Clippings, programs, correspondence in Moss papers (lent by Moss), and Stuart Heisler papers, UCLA; AA, April 7, 1945, reported a poll of GIs who favored better movie roles for blacks, citing OF-51 as a model.

34. PV, April 2, 1944; Leonard Bloom, CE, March 16, 1944, and Esther Berg, "Films to Better Human Relations," reprinted from *High Points* (Brooklyn Jewish Community Center), all in Moss papers, used the nonce words "living together," etc.; Hartley, *Selected Films for American History and Problems*, 40–41, 136–37, 168–69, 208–9, quoted; Jacoby in Cecile Starr, *Ideas on Film: A Handbook for the 16 mm User* (New York, 1951), xiv–xv; telephone interview between Starr and the author, June 1990; Commission on Motion Pictures in Education, *Motion Pictures for Postwar Education*, American Council on Education Series 1, no. 21, vol. 8 (Washington, 1944), 3; *Var.*, Feb. 19, 1947, clipping in NR-LC, the "front." See chap. 6 for additional citations of library tradepapers.

35. Among the growing canon that uses Umberto Eco's (and others') idea of the "openness" of texts, see Ellen Elizabeth Seiter, "The Promise of Melodrama: Recent Women's Film and Soap Operas" (Ph.D., Northwestern, 1981); Ian Hawkins, *Münster: The Way It Was* (Anaheim, 1984), 92, citing the pilot.

36. Blythe in Elizabeth H. Florey, ed., *Films for International Understanding* (New York, [1947]), 71–72. On bookings: Curtis Mitchell to Stanton Griffis, April 12, 1944, box 1484, entry 268; Taylor Mills to Edgar Baker, June 8, 1944, box 1486, entry 269; C. R. Reagan to Louis Ludlow, June 10, 1944, box 1581, entry 305, Non-Theatrical Div., Motion Picture Branch, OWI, RG 208; *Army Pictorial Service Annual Report* (July 1944–June 1945), 42, on July Pentagon showing, in 319 APS, box 271, A45-196, all in NA-MD; Film Council of America, *Sixty Years of 16 mm Film, 1923–1983: A Symposium* (Evanston, 1984), 148–59; Iris Barry, MOMA, to Rudolph Montgelas [Aug. 1944], War Dept. folder, central files, MOMA: 3250 persons saw OF-51, July 24–30, 1944; Walter Brooks, *Film News* 5 (April 1944): 9–10, urged plants to buy prints; Catherine Preston to Joseph Brechsteen, Sept. 13, 1944, entry 268, box 1483, NA-MD (Lorton Reformatory); "16 mm Films—Latin American Program—Summary by Title," box 218, central file 3, records of CIAA, RG 229, NA-MD, reported 43,025 Haitian viewers, sixty-nine dates; C. R. Reagan to Truman Gibson, Jan. 4, 1945, box 224, RG 107, MMR, NA-DC, reckoned June 1944–Jan. 1945 audience at 3,220,000; Dorothy E. Cook and Eva Rahbek-Smith, *Educational Film Guide* (New York, 1945), 152.

37. PV, April 2, 1944; PM, April 22, 28, 19, 1944, and other clippings in

NR-LC, Moss papers, and Heisler papers; on "War Dept.," Manuel Darrin et al. to Henry L. Stimson, petition, June 19, 1944, box 224, RG 107, MMR, NA-DC.

38. Collier Young to Philleo Nash, Sept. 5, 1944, PN-HST, on the official touchiness that affected cutting of *The Negro Sailor;* stills, *Negro Colleges in Wartime,* entry 302, box 1571, RG 208, OWI, NA-MD; script in box 1569, analyses of it, entry 271, box 1490, RG 208, OWI, NA-MD; distribution record in entry 268, box 1483, RG 208, OWI, NA-MD; *Negro Colleges in Wartime* played at least one library: Fern Long, Cleveland Public, to White, Dec. 14, 1942, NR-LC.

39. [First name illegible] Dudley to Roy Wilkins, memo, copy, Jan. 21, 1944, in NR-LC; Capt. Marcellus Goff, VD officer, Ft. Devens, memo, Aug. 20, 1943, on "no place," and other correspondence, in box 254, RG 107, Hastie file, NA-DC; Wiley, *Training of Negro Troops,* chap. 6, and Report MTO-70, box 1030, RG 330, NA-MD.

40. Print in AV section, NA-DC; the instructor's manual, TF-1423 WD, quoted an observer on Joe Louis's defeat of Max Schmeling: "a timely allegory of the Negro's role in crushing Nazism."

41. Daily Activity Report, April 25, 1945, in frame 925, SFP 151, 122.07; and Oct. 11, 1944, in Army Air Force Archives, NA-DC.

42. "Stan," speaking from audience, 99th Pursuit reunion, National Air and Space Museum, spring 1988, on *Courier;* Hazel Gross, Stamford, Conn. to the president, Sept. 26, 1944; and to Philleo Nash, Oct. 16, 1944; and Nash to Gross, Oct. 6, 1944, in box 1, PN-HST.

43. Saul K. Padover to Secretary of Agriculture, memo, Aug. 17, 1943, in box 38, "Committee on Race Relations" folder, OCP-HST; and Nash correspondence above; Charles S. Johnson, chair, Committee on Mass Education in Race Relations, and Donald Slesinger, American Film Center, to Walter White, Oct. 21, 1944; White to Johnson, copy, Oct. 23, 1944, delegating a person, both in NR-LC.

44. "Carlton" to "Truman," Friday, n.d., box 224, RG 107, Hastie file, NA-DC.

45. Wilkins to Gen. A. D. Surles, copy, Aug. 22, 1945, in NR-LC; on the MOMA, OWI, CIAA project, records in LC.

46. Print of OR-14 in AV section, NA-DC; script and production file in proj. 11,015, 062.2, box 19, A52-248, NA-MD; on Kosleck, Richard Gertner, *International Motion Picture Almanac* (New York, 1975), 123.

47. A. Russell Buchanan, *Black Americans in World War II* (Santa Barbara, 1977), 96–97, wherein is cited *Crisis* 25 (April 1945): 97; NAACP Board of Directors' Minutes, May 14, 1945, 6, in NR-LC, discussing Clark's invitation to Truman Gibson to visit the Italian front to inquire into the reasons for poor combat performance by the black 92nd Division, which led to a press conference in Rome in which Gibson admitted derelictions, which in turn polarized black opinion.

48. Walter White to Robert Patterson, April 8 and May 9, 1946; White to Thurgood Marshall, Roy Wilkins, and Ollie Harrington, April 24, 1946; Patterson to White, April 17, 1946; Jeannette Samuelson (Mayer-Burstyn Theatres) to "Friend," July 11, 1946, in NR-LC; Maurie Odenker to Public Relations, War Dept., May 28, 1946; James Ray to Chief, Army Pictorial Service, May 13, 1946, clearing for civilian use; Ray to June Blythe, May 16, 1946, clearing for commer-

cial use; Revels Cayton to Gibson, April 29, 1946, for NNC use; Ray to Moss, May 3, 1946, RG 107, Hastie file, NA-DC.

49. *Var.*, Sept. 28, 1944, clipping, AMPAS; Wilkins to Surles, Aug. 22, 1945, NR-LC.

50. Fleming, DW, Jan. 5, 1945; *PM*, n.d., "Black Films" file, MOMA; Crowther, NYT, to Walter White, June 20, 1946, urging attendance at *Teamwork* preview, in NR-LC; Moss to Revels Cayton, n.d.; Cayton to Moss, April 29, 1946, in NNC-SCRBC.

51. Joseph Foster, "Hollywood and the Negro," *New Masses*, Oct. 24, 1944, p. 28; NAACP press release, Oct. 6, 1945, in NNC-SCRBC; Wise interview with Cheryl Ashton, March 3, 1976, cited in Ashton, "Black Image in Film," 56, 58.

52. Moss to Revels Cayton, box 72, reel 34, NNC-SCRBC. Inferences of Moss's leftist links were never covert: He wrote the rebuttal to Rushmore's *Gone with the Wind* review for DW; his *Salute to Negro Troops* letterheads listed a spectrum of left through right activists; he was friendly with NNC members; he was active in HICCASP; he taught in the California Institute for Labor Education and the World Peace Conference. So any dutiful HUAC detective could have followed the trail. Indeed, he was fingered by "friendly witnesses" albeit with "Carleton" blessedly misspelled, thus confusing him with another writer. See Moss to James Evans, civilian aide, War Dept., April 9, 1946, box 224, RG 107, Hastie file, NA-DC. On "cult," see Landry, *Cult of Equality*, 8, 14.

53. Interview between Walter Fisher and David Culbert and the author, Washington, July 1977, the informant a captain in I&E.

Chapter 5
Hollywood Wins

1. Several conversations with Lorenzo Tucker through 1970s.

2. Commodore Hotel meeting, Grand Street Boys Assn., Jan. 1, 1922, screening of Seiden's Lower East Side film; "Jewish Films in Own Tongue," *Var.*, clipping; *Jewish Ledger* (Hartford), July 23, 1930, Seiden papers, NJFA.

3. FD, June 20, 1939; unident. clipping, June 6, 1939; HR, Nov. 11, 1937, in *Harlem Rides the Range* file; Harwin Dixon, Argus Pictures, to Breen, Oct. 20, 1939; MPH, Dec. 16, 1939, in *Double Deal* file, PCA-AMPAS.

4. *The Betrayal* file, MPD, June 30, 1948; on Apollo, see clipping, *Miracle in Harlem* file, in PCA-AMPAS; MPH, April 12, 1947, quoted in Norman Kagan, "Black American Cinema: A Primer," *Cinema*, Fall 1970, p.3; interview between Ted Toddy and the author, Atlanta, June 1977.

5. Charlie Rossi, Strand Theatre, Schroon Lake, N.Y., to Lowell Mellett, n.d. [Dec. 3, 1942], entry 268, box 1440, RG 208, NA-MD.

6. Firms may be traced through *Film Daily Yearbook* entries; Cripps, *Slow Fade to Black*, chaps. 7, 12; ephemera in Seiden papers, NJFA; Peter Bogdanovich, "Edgar G. Ulmer [interview]," *Film Culture*, nos. 58–60 (1974): 189–238. Telephone interview between the author and: Malkames Aug. 1974; Popkin, June 1970; Toddy, Aug. 1975 and June 1977; and Lester J. Sack, accountant, Sackamuse, Dallas, June 1970.

7. James Asendio, "History of Negro Motion Pictures," *International Photographer* 2 (Jan. 1940): 16–17; Randol's short was *Deep South*, which won an

Oscar nomination: Robert Osborne, *Academy Awards: Years with Oscar* (Los Angeles, 1978); on a Randol revue, NYA, Jan. 13, 1940.

8. Interview between Virginia Kiah, daughter of Kiefer Jackson, and the author, Lillie Carroll Jackson Museum, Baltimore, Md.; conversations between Pat and Harriet Aveney Harrison and the author, 1970s, LC (where one of Eloyce Gist's films in deteriorated state reposes); Seiden ephemera, NJFA: He also shot Palestine films for Jewish consumption, through his firm, Judea Films.

9. Cripps, *Slow Fade to Black,* chap. 12; Malkames interview, June 1974.

10. Cripps, *Slow Fade to Black,* 347; alpha. file, *Gang War, God's Step Children,* and *Double Deal,* in PCA-AMPAS; scripts: *Am I Guilty?, Reform School, Harlem on the Prairie, Mr. Washington Goes to Town,* and *One Dark Night,* ITC-DC, particularly marginalia.

11. Toddy interview, June 1976, and Lester Sack interview, June 1970.

12. *"REPORT ON NEGRO MORALE,"* n.d., marked "confidential," entry 3, box 65, "Negro" folder, Bureau of Intelligence, OFF, RG 208, NA-MD.

13. Toddy covered in black press: NYA, Dec. 13, 20, 1941; *Atlanta World,* Jan. 1, 2, 1942; DW, Aug. 22, 1942; PC, Oct. 10, 24, Sept. 19, Oct. 3, 1942; *Var.,* June 18, 1942; PC, March 7, 1942; on Popkins, AA, Sept. 14, 21, 1940; Oscar Micheaux to Elmer Davis, OWI, Oct. 22, 1942, in entry 264, box 1443d, OWI Domestic Branch, Bureau of Motion Pictures, Mellett folder, RG 208, NA-MD; John P. Nugent, *Black Eagle* (New York, 1971), 111–14.

14. On *Lucky Ghost* particularly see *Var.,* April 7, 1943, p. 6; PC, June 13, 1942; AN, Sept. 7, June 8, 1940; titles (and changes) in Toddy catalogue, courtesy of Toddy; Toddy interview, June 1976; Popkin interview, June 1970; Ben Rinaldo interview, June 1970; alpha. file, résumés, GPJ-UCLA. On Goldberg, Robinson, Soundies: AN, Aug. 14, Sept. 25, 1929, ACG-CU; *Var.,* Aug. 22, 1928, p. 37; AN, Aug. 25, 1926; *Var.,* March 15, 1932, p.6; May 31, 1932, p. 29; AN, June 1, 8, May 25, 1932; *Harlem is Heaven* in JBC-UKC; on Goldbergs' later career, *Var.,* July 23, 1940, p. 10; *Boogie Woogie Dream,* courtesy Sammy Gertner, Baltimore.

15. On Popkins's films: AN, Aug. 24, 1940; AN, June 17, 1939, praising Beavers's "deeply sympathetic" reading; *Var.,* May 3, 1939, p. 16, judging it "surefire"; Harry L. Fraser, *I Went That-A-Way,* unpublished autobiography, courtesy Audrey B. Fraser. On Sack and Williams: Thomas Cripps, "The Films of Spencer Williams," *Black American Literature Forum* 12 (Winter 1978): 128–34; Adrienne Seward, *Spencer Williams,* "Whitney Museum of American Art: The New American Filmmakers Series," no. 24, pp. 1–2; Edward T. Clayton, "The Tragedy of Amos 'n' Andy," *Ebony,* Oct. 1961, pp. 66–73; fugitive bits in AN, Dec. 5, 1928; May 29, March 6, 1929; *Post* (New York), Aug. 29, clipping in PA-NYPL; *Var.,* June 26, 1929, p. 11; Dec. 12, 1928, p. 17; PC, Nov. 12, 1927; March 17, Aug. 18, 25, Oct. 27, 1928; CD, Dec. 20, 27, 1930; alpha. file, GPJ-UCLA; Williams's scripts, *The Lady Fare* and *The Framing of the Shrew,* in LC copyright file; his *Brown Gravy* in Robert Stendahl Coll., Gary, Ind.; *Var.,* Feb. 9, 1938, p. 14; AN, Feb. 25, April 15, 1939; Sack to Nate Zelikow, Aug. 11, 1955, Zelikow Productions records, Houston, Texas.

16. Lester Sack interview, June 1970; Lester Sack to Cripps, Oct. 2, 1970; and Alfred Sack to Cripps, Jan. 12, 1968; AN, Sept. 30, 1939, on black New York preferring "sex and glamour rather than social realism or religious allegories."

17. Walter White to Lowell Mellett, Feb. 25, 1943; Mellett to White, copy, March 1, 1943, in box 18, LM-FDR, touting his own script idea, a biopic of Felix Eboué, a black colonial governor appointed to the French pantheon; White to Jason Joy, Fox, July 22, 1943, and White to Roy Wilkins and Judge Hastie, memo, copy, July 22, 1943, pressing for a biopic of Asa Spaulding, founder of North Carolina Mutual Insurance Company, a treatment of which was enclosed, NR-LC.

18. "Newsreels and OWI Campaigns and Programs: Jan. 1943," Report no. 7 (Feb. 3, 1943), marked "restricted," pp. 10, 13; and Report no. 8, p. 10, Bureau of Intelligence, Media Division, OWI, RG 208, NR-MD, on "standards," and on OWI reviewer's complaint about *March of Time* segment "The Navy and the Nation," with black "grinning, toothy" train porter.

19. Arch Mercey, Bureau of Motion Pictures, to George Barnes, Assistant to Director, Feb. 29 [*sic*], 1943, in alpha. file, "Minorities—Negro—'Negro Cavalcade,'" and also see Dave Frederick to Philleo Nash, Aug. 24, 1944, not entirely giving up on Glucksman's "potentialities," in PN-HST.

20. "Newsreels and OWI Campaigns," Report no. 7, p. 13, cited in note 18.

21. Telephone interview between Milton Eisenhower and the author, summer 1977; Michaux to Eisenhower, Feb. 3, 1943; Eisenhower to Michaux, copy, Feb. 3, 1943; Jack Goldberg press release, n.d.; George A. Barnes to Goldberg, copy, March 2, 1943, in box 224, RG 107, Hastie file, MMR, NA-DC, lent by David Culbert; reproduction of a poster in Cripps and Culbert, "Propaganda in Black and White."

22. Videotape of the film loaned courtesy MacDonald Associates, Chicago, Ill.

23. Roy Wilkins to Truman Gibson, Jan. 3, 14, 15, Feb. 1, 3, 1944; Wilkins to Maj. Homer B. Roberts, Feb. 9, 1944; Julia E. Baxter to Wilkins, Nov. 4, 1944, in NR-LC; Gibson to Judge Hastie, March 29, 1944, in box 224, Hastie file, MMR, RG 107, NA-DC.

24. Goldberg to White, May 25, 1944; Ralph Cooper to White, June 8, 1944; press release, April 27, 1944; White to Thurgood Marshall, May 4, 1944; Marshall to editor, PV, copy, May 9, 1944; PV, May 13, 1944; press release, "NAACP Deplores Legal Action Against Film 'The Negro Soldier,'" April 27, 1944; on Jews see White to Milton R. Konvitz, May 5, 1944; Konvitz to Rabbi Lewis Finkelstein, copy, May 17, 1944; Marshall to White, memo, May 4, 1944; Konvitz to White and Wilkins, April 24, 1944; White to Joseph Proskauer of American Jewish Committee, Finkelstein of Jewish Theological Seminary, Rabbi Stephen S. Wise, and Joseph Willens, wires, all May 1, 1944, in NR-LC.

25. U.S. Dist. Court, S. Dist., N.Y., *Negro Marches On v. War Activities Committee*, copy, n.d.; Gibson et al., *amicus curiae* brief, n.d., 2 pp.; Thurgood Marshall to Pauline Lauber, exec. sec., HWM, May 2, 1944; Robert Rossen to Frank Capra, March 30, 1944; White to Marshall, May 4, 1944, in NR-LC.

26. *Var.*, Dec. 6, 1940, p. 16; April 3, 1940, p. 16; Oct. 2, 1940; June 18, 1940, p. 18; AN, Sept. 30, 1939; Oct. 12, 1940; and Aug. 19, 1939, Burley quoted.

27. AN, Dec. 13, 1941, on *Four Shall Die* as "the greatest"; Jan. 8, May 14, 21, April 9, 1938; June 16, Oct. 21, 1939; Aug. 20, Sept. 3, 1939.

28. AA, Oct. 22, 1938, on SAG, see also similar case in *Var.*, June 10, 1942, p. 27.

29. LAS, Dec. 30, 1940; George Norford, "On Stage," *Opportunity*, Summer 1947, pp. 74–75.

30. *Marching On* (1943), University of Illinois Film Archive, viewed through courtesy of Professor Robert Carringer.

31. James Asendio to "Friend," [Dec. 4, 1943]; Flournoy Miller to Walter White, Nov. 11, 1938; race moviemakers' ephemera; and Gloster Current memos, in NR-LC.

32. *Ebony*, Aug. 1946, p. 21; AN, Sept. 10, 1949, on Fritz Pollard and Sun Tan and Soundies; "How Movies Are Made," *Ebony*, March 1947, pp. 40–43, on Crouch; *Ebony Parade*, JBC-KC; *Solid Senders* and *You Must Have Been a Beautiful Baby*, Ernie Smith Collection, New York City; AN, March 19, 1949, on *Harlem Follies; Var.*, Jan. 1, 1947, p. 16; LAS, Feb. 12, March 24, 1948; CE, Sept. 30, Jan. 20, 1948; AN, March 17, Dec. 1, 15, 29, 1945; Jan. 5, 19, July 6, 27, Aug 31, 1946; Feb. 21, 28, April 3, 1948; CD, April 30, 1949; Toddy brochure retitlings; AN, March 19, 1949.

33. Interview between Richard Brooks and the author, Hollywood, July 1977.

34. CE, Aug. 19, 26, 1948; LAS, Sept. 30, Oct. 14, Aug. 19, 1948; CD, Aug. 21, 1948; *Var.*, Sept. 1, 1948, p. 7.

35. *Var.*, Nov. 29, 1944, p. 38; AN, June 1, Oct. 12, 19, Dec. 7, 1946; Jan. 4, 1947, on box office; CE, Feb. 10, 1949; *Var.*, June 19, 1946, like *Beware* for "wise direction [and] music"; Nov. 28, 1945, p. 47, noted Jordan's popularity in B-movies by title; AN, Sept. 13, 1947, on Goldbergs; LAS, Sept. 5, 12, 1946, *Boy What a Girl; Var.*, July 30, 1947, p. 20, on *Sepia Cinderella* in which Gene Krupa sat in with Sid Catlett's band.

36. CE, Aug. 19, 26, 1948; LAS, Sept. 30, Oct. 14, Aug. 19, 1948; CD, Aug. 21, 1948; *Var.*, Sept. 1, 1948, p. 7; interview between William F. Walker and the author, Aug. 1977, on Norwanda; interview between Ruby Dee and the author, Lebanon, Pa., Jan. 26, 1970, and AN, Feb. 28, 1948, on *The Fight Never Ends;* NYT, Oct. 24, 1949; CD, Nov. 5, 1949, on *Miracle in Harlem;* FD, Aug. 11, 1948, p. 5; "A Star Fizzles," *Ebony*, Nov. 1945, p. 38; Henry T. Sampson, *Blacks in Black and White: A Source Book on Black Films* (Metuchen, N.J., 1977), see title index for a genre inventory.

37. "A Star Fizzles," *Ebony*, Nov. 5, 1949, p. 38, on Sheila Guyse stranded; Sidney Poitier, *This Life* (New York, 1980), 124; telephone interview between William Greaves and the author, July 1977; Cripps, *Slow Fade to Black*, 348, on Hill.

38. Micheaux herald in research files, *Post-Newsweek TV* (WTOP-TV, Washington); LAS, Nov. 24, 1949; AN, March 19, 1949; interview between Norman Burford and the author, Washington, D.C., Aug. 1977; interview between Carlton Moss and the author, Iowa City, June 1973; NYA, June 26, 1948.

39. "Alice" [B. Russell Micheaux] to her sister Ethel, Jan. 7, 1948, in Richard Grupenhoff, *The Black Valentino: The Stage and Screen Career of Lorenzo Tucker* (Metuchen, N.J., 1988), 141.

40. Interview between Burford and the author; credits in Sampson, *Blacks in Black and White*, 182.

41. Alice to Ethel, Jan. 7, 1948; and interview between Burford and the author.

42. CD, July 17, 1948; NYA, June 26, 1948; James Hoberman, "A Black

Pioneer: The Case of Oscar Micheaux," *No Rose*, Fall 1976, pp. 23–31, cites white press; on censorship see alpha. file, PCA-AMPAS and MSCB.

43. LAS, Jan. 23, 1947; Cripps, "Films of Spencer Williams," pp. 128–34; Clayton, "Tragedy of Amos'n' Andy," pp. 66–73; and Thomas Cripps, "Amos 'n' Andy and the Debate over Racial Integration," in John E. O'Connor, *American History/American Television* (New York, 1983), pp. 33–54.

44. AN, Nov. 17, Dec. 18, 1945; LAS, Oct. 7, 1948, on Adamson; *Var.*, April 17, 1946, p. 7, for statistics such as houses up 10 percent, twenty-five pictures in production, average nut at $20,000, grosses running $40,000–60,000, and so on.

45. "Negro Movies Hit Paydirt," *Ebony*, Sept. 1946, pp. 32–45; *Tall, Tan and Terrific* ad copy, *Ebony*, Nov. 1946, p. 2; CD, April 30, 1949, also ambiguous in praising Eddie Green for lack of smut while avoiding comment on broad style.

46. Interview, taped, between Don Malkames and Lorenzo Tucker and Stephan Henriques, Aug. 1974, WTOP-TV, Washington; Cornelius Johnson, "Baltimore and the Black Star in a Black Movie," interview with Nikki O'Daniel, unpublished paper, Morgan State University, 1971; interview, Toddy and the author, June 1977; and Alex Albright film *Boogie Woogie in Black and White* (1988), an account of the making of *Pitch a Boogie* (1947).

47. LAS, Oct. 7, 1948. *Sepia* and *tan* were euphemisms for *black*.

48. In Pleasanton, S.C., for example, part of a school day would be used to show *Bronze Buckaroo* or another race movie: conversations with Professor George Sinkler, Baltimore. On collectibles: catalogues of Barr Harris, auctioneer, Baltimore, and George Theofiles, *Miscellaneous Man* (New Freedom, Pa., 1980s). On popularity of *Amos 'n' Andy:* interviews between Florence Connors and Carolyn Houck and the author, EPFL reported demand of the films.

49. Nathan A. Zelikow to E. M. Glucksman, Sept. 30, 1953; Glucksman to Zelikow, Oct. 2, 1953, Aug. 23, 1954; Zelikow to Joseph Plunkett, Nov. 9, 1954, in Nate Zelikow Productions records, Houston.

50. Conversations between Nate Zelikow and the author, beginning June 1970.

Chapter 6
Documentary Film Culture and Postwar Liberal Momentum

1. Barbara Keon to Selznick, April 21, 1945, box 6, Story Dept., DOS-TX; Spyros Skouras to Zanuck, copy, Jan. 13, 1947; Zanuck to Joseph Schenck, Jan. 22, 1957, in Lyman Munson papers, AHC-WY.

2. August Meier and Elliot Rudwick, *Black History and the Historical Profession, 1915–1980* (Urbana, Ill. 1986), 73–74, 109 (on Stampp), 113–15 (Myrdal), 137–51.

3. President's Committee on Civil Rights, *To Secure These Rights* (Washington, 1947), 141; Polenberg, *One Nation Indivisible*, chap. 4; Richard Dalfiume, *Desegregation and the U.S. Armed Forces*, chap. 7; James R. Fuchs, "Oral History Interview with Andrew J. Biemiller [Wisc. legislator, UAW official]," (Washington, 1977), pp. 49–50, HST; Thurmond quoted in Alfred Sternberg, *The Man from Missouri: The Life and Times of Harry S. Truman* (New York, 1962), 315; Frankfurter quoted in review by Marshall Fishwick, *Journal of Popular Culture*

11 (Fall 1977): 363; sample polls in George H. Gallup, *The Gallup Poll: Public Opinion, 1935–1970* (New York, 1972, 3 vols.), 1: 142, 396, 528, 658, 722, 748, 782, 810; holograph note on Gallup, 1944, NR-LC.

Dudley G. Roe to Truman, June 6, 1945; Truman to Roe, copy, June 6, 1945, "Analysis of the President's Mail on FEPC," holograph report, Oct. 20, 1945, 4 pp., reports "mass support" outside the South; Jerry Voorhis, copy, "Proposed Fair Employment Practices Bill," holograph, July 14, 1945, in OF misc. file, box 210 (1945), OF-HST, HST, all evidences of Truman's investment in a liberal racial policy.

4. CE, Sept. 3, Jan. 1, 22, 1948, on Loren Miller and N. Peter Rathvon, RKO, as Brotherhood Week planners; *ALA Bulletin*, July–Aug. 1948; "Facts on *The Brotherhood of Man*," Film Div., UAW-CIO, n.d., both in UAW-WSU; Robert Hampel, *The Last Little Citadel: American High Schools Since 1940* (Boston, 1986), p. 45, on "boosterism," and pp. 48–49, on "proliferation"; for "POD" sourcebook, A. R. Lerner et al., *The Challenge of Hate*, no. 1 in a series (New York, 1946), pp. 34–37; Hilah Paumier and Robert Haven Schauffler, *Good Will Days* (New York, 1947, 1956), forepages.

5. Coulton Waugh, *The Comics* (New York, 1947), 344–46; *All-Negro Comics*, June 1947; Maggie Thompson, "Blue Suit, Blue Mask, Blue Gloves—And No Socks," in Don Thompson and Dick Lupoff, eds., *The Comic-Book Book* (New Rochelle, 1973), 118–43; Ann Tanneyhill to Guichard Parris, March 10, 1947, series 7, box 5, NUL-LC.

6. *Afro* and *Worker*, summers 1940s; Jules Tygiel, *Baseball's Great Experiment: Jackie Robinson and His Legacy* (New York, 1984).

7. *Var.*, Jan. 10, 1945, p. 1; Claude H. Nolen, *The Negro's Image in the South: The Anatomy of White Supremacy* (Lexington, Ky., 1967), 204, 207, quoted; David W. Riesman, *The Lonely Crowd: A Study of the Changing American Character* (New York, 1950); *Var.*, Nov. 6, 1946, pp. 57–58, and March 10, 1948, p. 24, on Clark Forman, theatreman, as "noted exponent of racial equality"; Agee, *Agee on Film* vol. 1, p. 235 (rpt. from *Nation*, Dec. 28, 1946), and pp. 404–10 ("Folk Art," rpt. from *Partisan Review*, Spring 1944).

8. David J. Rothman, "Documents in Search of a Historian: Toward a History of Childhood and Youth in America," in Theodore K. Rabb and Robert I. Rotberg, eds., *The Family in History: Interdisciplinary Essays* (New York, 1971), p. 187, for Capt. Marryat's witnessing a disobedient American boy whom his father explained away as a particularly "sturdy republican"; and on youth subculture, Paula S. Fass, *The Damned and the Beautiful: American Youth in the 1920s* (New York, 1977); James B. Gilbert, *Cycle of Outrage: Juvenile Delinquency and the Mass Media* (New York, 1986); and Mark Thomas McGee and R. J. Robertson, *The J. D. Films: Juvenile Delinquency in the Movies* (Jefferson, N.C., 1982); as well as personal recollections reinforced by a sampling of *Ebony*, 1946–50.

9. Hollywood Victory Committee bookings in "Miscellaneous Correspondence, 1940s," box 278, DOS-TX.

10. Survey of *Var.* and *Ebony* after 1945, almost every issue of which reported breaches of racial etiquette among performers: *Var.*, Sept. 10, 1947, p. 54, on Hill; Jan. 17, 1951, p. 50, on Baker; LAS, Sept. 5, 1946, on Horne; *Ebony*, Nov. 1949, pp. 45–46, on "swinging" folksongs.

11. Edith J. R. Isaacs, *The Negro in the Theatre* (New York, 1947), passim; Thyra Samter Winslow, "The Negro Entertainer," *Stage Pictorial* (1946): 16–19, 55–56; Jose Ferrer, "The Negro in the American Theatre," *Var.*, Jan. 9, 1946, p. 300; and almost any issue of *Var.*, 1940s.

12. *Var.*, Jan. 15, 1947, p. 52; Nov. 12, 1947, p. 8; June 16, 1948, p. 49; April 12, 1947, p. 71; April 19, 1950, p. 1; June 13, 1945, p. 57; April 18, 1945, p. 1; Oct. 3, 1945, p. 1; Sept. 25, 1946, pp. 18, 36, 57; Sept. 18, 1946, p. 52; July 28, 1948, p. 100; May 14, 1947, p. 1; May 30, 1945, p. 52; March 10, 1945, p. 54; July 4, 1945, pp. 1, 27; Sept. 19, 1945, p. 1; Sept 12, 1945, p. 54; Dec. 19, 1945, p. 1; June 19, 1946, p. 51; Jan. 1, 1947, p. 42; June 5, 1946, p. 68; May 22, 1946, p. 57. LAS, Aug. 22, 1946. *Var.*, Oct. 23, 1946, p. 118; Nov. 6, 1946, p. 57; Oct. 16, 1946, p. 59; Aug. 28, 1946, p. 1; *Ebony*, May 1947, p. 38 ff. *Var.*, April 23, 1947, p. 52; March 11, 1947, p. 63; April 2, 1947, p. 1; Nov. 26, 1947, p. 1.

13. DW, Oct. 16, 28, 1945; *Var.*, Feb. 14, 1951, p. 50.

14. Robert Ardrey, *Jeb*, third draft, Dec. 31, 1945, Ardrey papers, ML-BU; DW, Feb. 25, 1946, and Jan. 21, 1945, in which Ann Seymour found Robert Earl Jones in *Strange Fruit* deriving "inspiration from his people"; *Story Department Bulletin*, March 16, 1946, p. 8, in DOS-TX; Sacvan Bercovitch, *The American Jeremiad* (Madison, 1978), xi, quoted in David Brion Davis piece, *New York Review*, Feb. 13, 1986, p. 7.

15. Saul K. Padover, Interior, to Sec. Oscar L. Chapman, memo, "On Negroes," Aug. 17, 1943, in "Committee on Race Relations" folder, box 38, OCP-HST; Dwight L. Palmer, Lockheed, to Philleo Nash, June 17, 1944; Nash to Palmer, June 19, 1944, "Correspondence 1943–1944, H–Q" folder, box 41, PN-HST.

16. Nash to Myra Blakesley, N.J. Goodwill Commission, copy, Dec. 13, 1943; Nash to Marshall Field, % *Chicago Sun*, copy, May 19, 1944, "Correspondence 1943–1944" folder, box 1, PN-HST. Contrast Nash with Elmer Davis's official line: OWI not to be used "as a means of guiding American opinion," thus "our interest in minorities is limited to . . . countering enemy propaganda." Quoted in statements sent by Nash to J. G. Weir, copy, Nov. 11, 1944, "Correspondence, 1943–1944" folder, PN-HST.

17. Lester Granger to Harry S. Truman, Aug. 27, 1945, in OF-91B, April-May 1945, box 437, OF-HST.

18. PM, July 22, 1943; *CIO News* (Milwaukee), June 5, 1944, CIO records, LA-WSU, lent courtesy of August Meier and Elliott Rudwick.

19. Embree to Nash, June 29, 1944; Nash to Embree, copy, July 3, 1944, in "Correspondence, 1943–1944"; Nash to A. A. Liveright, copy, May 14, 1945, "Correspondence 1945," both in box 1, PN-HST.

20. Booking action as cited in chap. 4, note 37.

21. *CIO News*, Feb. 21, 1944, and June 19, 1944.

22. *CIO News*, July 7, 1944, and June 26, 1944, quoted; and June 5, 1944, for its focused liberal rhetoric: OF-51 showed "what the Negro race has done to earn its place in American life."

23. The idea of propaganda as an unbidden agenda-setter owes much to talks with Professor Wilhelm van Kampen, Berlin; Robert A. Garson, *The Democratic Party and the Politics of Sectionalism, 1941–1948* (Baton Rouge, 1974),

chap. 6; Jerry N. Hess, "Oral History Interview with Joseph G. Feeney" [HST assistant, 1952–1953], 28–29, HST; and President's Committee on Civil Rights, *To Secure These Rights*, p. 173.

24. Leon Hardwick, "What Is IFRG?" in NR-LC, on Unity Awards; White to Truman, Oct. 3, 1945, in OF-92B (1945), box 437, April-May folder, HST-HST, on football as "affirmative action"; Irving C. Root, Watergate Concerts, to Oscar Chapman, Interior, copy, Oct. 31, 1946, "Racial Minority Groups" folder, box 38, OCP-HST, on concerts; Ida Fox, Committee for Racial Democracy in the Nation's Capital, to Chapman, Nov. 11, 1946, OCP-HST, on "pattern"; Lt. Cmmdr. Philip E. Valdez to Truman, Oct. 22, 1948; OF misc. file (1950), cross-ref. sheet; Joseph A. Dombrowski, Southern Conf. Educational Fund, New Orleans, Oct. 24, 1950, cross-ref. sheet, on protecting Judge J. Waties Waring; Jerry Voorhis, "Proposed FEPC Bill," William L. Patterson, Civil Rights Cong., to Truman, Oct. 27, 1948, cross-ref. sheet as above; Philip A. Vaughan, "The City in the American Creed: A Liberal Awakening During the Early Truman Period, 1946–1948," *Phylon* 34 (March 1973): 51–62; Homer C. Hawkins, "Trends in Black Migration from 1863 to 1960," *Phylon* 34 (June 1973): 140–52, citing Luther Gulick in *American City*, on "why."

25. ACE Studies, series 2, vol. 1, no. 1 (April 1937), *The Motion Picture in Education: Its Status and Needs*, p. 21.

26. William H. Hartley, *Selected Films for American History and Problems* (New York, 1940), pp. 40–41, 136–37, 168–69, 208–9.

27. Hartley, *Selected Films*, as in note 26; Charles Hoban, Committee on Motion Pictures in Education, *Selected Educational Motion Pictures* (Washington, 1942), pp. 171, 205, 286.

28. Starr, *Ideas on Film: A Handbook for the 16 mm User*, pp. xiv–xv.

29. Emily S. Jones, "Remembering EFLA 1945–1958," *Sightlines*, Fall/Winter 1983/84, pp. 6–7; telephone interview between Cecile Starr and the author, June 13, 1990; ACE Comm. on Motion Pictures in Education, series 1, vol. 8, no. 21 (Oct. 1944), *Motion Pictures for Postwar Education*, p. 3; Harcourt Brace et al., *A Report to Educators on Teaching Films Survey* ([New York, 1948]), 36–37; Elizabeth Florey, ed., *Films for International Understanding* (New York, 1947), 50; C. R. Reagan to White, Jan. 4, 1944, NR-LC, reporting 25,000 projectors to "enrich" programs.

30. Patricia O. Blair, ed., *Making Films Work for Your Community* (New York, 1946), 330, on army films; Charles F. Hoban, Jr., *Movies That Teach* (New York, 1946), 79, 25; Walter Arno Wittich and John G. Fowlkes, *Audio-Visual Paths to Learning* (New York [1946?]); *Var.*, May 21, 1947, p. 1, on urging LC to get army film; Feb. 19, 1957, in "Hollywood Bureau" file, NR-LC; John R. Miles and Charles R. Spain, *Audio-Visual Aids in the Armed Forces: Implications for American Education* (Washington, 1947), 62–63, 88–89, 92–93, excerpts from *What the Soldier Thinks*, on impact of films; Orville Goldner, "Film in the Armed Services," symposium in Godfrey M. Elliott, ed., *Film in Education* (New York, 1948), 403–4, on army's "courage"; *School Review* 53 (Dec. 1945): 571, on universities and army film; EFLA minutes (1947), lent by Helen Cyr, EPFL; *The Film Counselor* 1 (Oct. 1950), ephemera in TB-MOMA, on community.

31. Miles and Spain, *Audio-Visual Aids in the Armed Forces*, 62–63, 88–89, 92–93, on *The Battle of Britain* impact.

32. Hoban, *Movies that Teach*, 58–61; EFLA minutes (1947); *Var.*, Feb. 19, 1947; and on awards and community, *Film Counselor* Oct. 1950, n.p.

33. Esther L. Berg, "Films to Better Human Relations," in *High Points* (n.d.) in Moss papers; Berg and Dina M. Bleich, "Classroom Utilization of Films for International Understanding," in Florey, *Films for International Understanding*, 53; June Blythe, quoted, in Helen Seaton Preston, ACE, ed., *Use of Audio-Visual Materials for International Understanding . . . June 14–15, 1946*, ACE Studies, series 1, no. 25 (Washington, 1946), 93, 110; Gloria Waldron, *The Information Film: A Report of the Public Library Inquiry* (New York, 1949), 281, a lone warning against manipulating the screen for "their own ideologies."

34. Undated treatment; Oliver Harrington to White et al., copy, Dec. 31, 1946, and replies; file on "screen media" consultants, in NR-CL; *Film Forum Review*, Winter 1946–1947, pp. 29–31; Fall 1947, pp. 23–33, for reviews, lent by Cecile Starr.

34. Miles and Spain, *Audio-Visual Aids in the Armed Services*, 96–98; Hoban, *Movies that Teach*, 85–61; Goldner, "Film in the Armed Services," in *Film in Education*, 403–4, on "attitude building"; Alfred McClung Lee, *Race Riots Aren't Necessary*, Public Affairs Bulletin no. 107 (Washington, [July 1945]), 3, quoted.

35. *EFLA Bulletin* 1 (May 29, 1945): 5; *EFLA Service Supplement*, no. 46.1 (Feb. 1946): 1–2; Harry M. Lerner, "Street Films for Unity," *Film Forum Review*, Fall 1947, pp. 2–5, on "the street," lent by Cecile Starr.

36. W. A. Wittach, "It's Time the Baby Walks Alone," in *EFLA Bulletin* 1 (May 29, 1945): 5 on Grierson; undated treatment; Oliver Harrington to White et al., copy, Dec. 31, 1946, and replies; "Plan for Movie Trailer Membership Campaign," PR Dept., [NAACP], March 3, 1947; White to Harrington, Feb. 4, 1947; Harrington to White et al., Jan. 27, 1947; Moon to White, July 16, 1954; DeRochemont to White, July 16, 1954, et seq., in NR-LC.

37. Film brochure file, in which find Committee for a National Film Cooperative, mimeo., Sept. 10, 1947; Oscar Canstein, Negro Educational and Documentary Film Association, to White, April 27, 1947; Sherman Price to "Friend," Jan. 6, [1949], on Sydenham; Carnegie Endowment and Federation of Women's Clubs MOMA show of *Land of Liberty* [June 1, 1949]; AJC to Moon, Jan. 4, 1952; various in-house proposals, NR-LC.

38. *News from NAACP* [1948], on "Teaching Democracy . . . Audio-Visual Aids," 2 pp., annotating two dozen items from the old *Carver* biopic to *To Secure These Rights*.

39. Nanette Atlas, ed., *Selected List of Human Relations Films* (New York, n.d.), AJC pamphlet included *Film Tactics* (1947), *Assignment Tomorrow* (1945), *One World or None*. On *The Challenge*, Maury J. Glaubman to White and Wilkins, Feb. 2, 1950, in NR-LC.

40. Waldron, *Information Film*, 7, 16, 41, 121 (quoted), 135–47, 205, on *American Dilemma* as possible film, and p. 175 on "Library C" and resources.

41. Bond to Johnson, copy, March 26, 1944, Bond papers, Amherst College, lent by Prof. August Meier. Bond saw documentary as a way around black actors who "found difficulty stepping out of their accustomed roles." See also Film Committee meeting, ca. April 1944; Johnson to Bond, April 27, 1944, on joining AFC; Slesinger, "A Map of Forces," *Film News* 5 (April 1944): 4–5, touting *The Negro Soldier*, in Bond papers.

42. Minutes, second meeting, Mass Education Committee, May 13, 1944; Donald Slesinger to Bond, Aug. 8, 1944; Bond's resignation, Sept. 9, 1944; manifesto, "The Committee for Mass Education in Race Relations" for "liberals with vision"; and treatment, *Outline Form for Film Scenario Ideas,* in Bond papers, Amherst College.

43. Wilkins to White, Sept. 12, 1947; Jeannette Samuelson to NAACP, telephone memo, June 19, 1946, on Crowther as ICCASP member, in NR-LC.

44. NAACP release, n.d.; Albert Baker Lewis to Madison Jones, Jr., Nov. 6, 1947; Marion Wynn Perry, memo, Jan. 24, 1947, on promo; R. C. Bolton to NAACP, Dec. 28, 1949; IFF [Julien Bryan] to NAACP, Jan. 30, 1951; in addition to Canstein, Price, AJC, and other proposals in note 37, all in NR-LC.

45. Herbert B. Jackman, UAW, to Douglas, Sept. 16, 1948; minutes, "civil rights committee," Oct. 15, 1948; "cut in" in Paul Sifton, UAW, to Douglas, July 22, 1948; Victor Reuther to Douglas, n.d., on Douglas's role; T. C. Robinson, Nassour Studio, to Douglas, Aug. 12, 1948, with "outline"; minutes, Oct. 15, 1948, on Rapfs; minutes, Sept. 8, 1948, in box 4, Douglas papers, SHSW. The result: *The Challenge,* 30-min. film. White to Selznick, wire (copy) and reply, both Nov. 10, 1947, on Moss, in NR-LC.

46. Ann Tanneyhill to Guichard Parris, March 10, 1947, box 5; and other Tanneyhill correspondence, box 11; Barnouw to Parris, Dec. 6, 1949, with copy of film proposal, box 1, all in series 7; *A Morning for Jimmy* file, box 4, series 5; and "Dynamics Films" file, box 8, series 3, all NUL-LC; Erik Barnouw to author, Aug. 28, 1991, and telephone conversation, Aug. 27, 1991; and Barnouw, *The Golden Web,* 197.

47. Barnouw, *Documentary,* 185; Fielding, *March of Time,* 288–89, 301; Waldron, *Film Library,* 84, 135–40, 147, on funding sources; and on films, 44, 52–54, 75, 119–23, 160–62, an optimistic report, though dismayed at dependence on donors, 230. Black press: LAS, Feb. 12, 1948, on Contemporary Films' list; AA, June 15, 1946, on *Don't Be a Sucker* on foreign racism; LAS, June 6, 1946, on the same in *Teamwork; Var.,* Feb. 19, 1947, p. 1.

48. Jarvis Couillard to Oliver Harrington, Oct. 11, 1947, and to White, Oct. 30, 1946; Archer Winston clipping on AMA film; White to Moon and Wilkins, July 12, 1948, on *On Guard,* their old promo-film; digest of minutes, Feb. 26, 1947, meeting of UAW, ILGWU, and American Labor Education Service, all in NR-LC; Gallup poll data as cited in note 79 to chap. 1, above; on Marxist left see HICCASP film committee minutes, Sept. 17, 1945; George Pepper to Helen Gahagan Douglas, wire, copy, Aug. 30, 1945; Clayton Russell to HICCASP, Sept. 11, 1945, in HICCASP-SHSW, on various projects including a Jack Chertok, Michael Blankfort, Abraham Polonsky proposal to teach police sensitivity to blacks.

49. Prints in EPFL and LC.

50. H. B. Jackson, UAW Film Div., "Report on Activities of UAW-CIO Film Division since January 1, 1948," in UAW-WSU.

51. "UAW-CIO Presents an Introduction to 'The Brotherhood of Man,'" Sept. 13, 1946, a treatment , on "Prejudices"; Moss to Revels Cayton, n.d., reel 34, box 72, NCC-SCRBC; and Cayton to Army Services Forces, copy, March 1946; Mary Jane Grunfeld, mimeo., March 20, 1947, in NR-LC; and DW, Feb. 27, April 6, 1947.

52. "To Officers and Members of the International Executive Board—

UAW-CIO: Recommendations Regarding UAW-CIO Film—*Brotherhood of Man,*" n.d., 13 pp., UAW-WSU.

53. Ibid., especially letter no. 173, Sept. 15.

54. Bernard McGuire to *Peoria Journal,* Oct. 25, 1950, copy in "To Officers and Members" (cited in note 52), p. 11; *Library Bill of Rights,* adopted, ALA, Atlantic City, June 18, 1948, reprinted in *ALA Bulletin,* July–Aug. 1948; H. B. Jackson, UAW Film Div., to Xenophon Smith, Peoria Library, copy, Nov. 14, 1950; resolution, UAW Board, Dec. 13, 1950; Film Div., UAW-CIO, *Facts on Brotherhood of Man,* n.d., 13 pp. UAW-WSU, and a few facsimiles in TB-MOMA.

55. *Nation,* Dec. 28, 1946, quoted in Agee, *Agee on Film,* vol.1, p. 235; "Folk Art," *Partisan Review,* Spring 1944, rpt. in ibid., pp. 404–9; on Meyers, Walter Rosenblum, "*The Quiet One:* A Milestone," *Photo-Notes,* Spring 1949, in Lewis Jacobs, *The Documentary Tradition: From Nanook to Woodstock* (New York, 1971), p. 246; Laurence Bergreen, *James Agee: A Life* (New York, 1984), 292–94, 328.

56. Bari Lynn Billiard and Helen Levitt, "*The Quiet One:* A Conversation," *Film Culture* 63–64 (1976): 127–39; print in EPFL; cast included an actual counselor, Clarence Cooper, and underemployed actor Estelle Evans.

57. Citations in *Members Film Series, 1966–1967,* Baltimore Museum of Art, 1967; brochures in NR-LC, MOMA, and PFA, where also see ad mattes and typescript "Background Information" sheet, 2 pp., and tradepaper raves, HR, April 1948; AN, Feb. 5, 12, 1949; Richard Meram Barsam, *Nonfiction Film: A Critical History* (New York, 1973), 218–19, reckoned its success, along with *Louisiana Story,* "promised new hope" for commercial distribution of political film.

58. Miller cited in Jacobs, *Documentary Tradition,* 247–50, from *Masses and Mainstream,* March 1949; see also Rosenblum in Jacobs, 246, on "a weapon of decency," and Crowther cited in Bergreen, *Agee,* 328.

59. CD, May 14, Jan. 22, March 5, April 23, 1949, from debut to awards; for CPUSA, Gilliard and Levitt, "*The Quiet One,*" 137–39, balancing Jose Yglesias's praise as against Platt's reservations; AN, Feb. 5, 12, 1949; LAS, May 26, 1949, on "Harlem"; see also *Films in Review,* Feb. 1950, pp. 32–33, on *The Roosevelt Story* and Canada Lee.

60. Gilliard and Levitt, "*The Quiet One,*" 137–39; circulation file, 1961, bookings for Baltimore, EPFL, lent by Helen Cyr; *Education Film Guide* (New York, 1953), alpha. listing; *Var.,* June 19, 1946, p. 1, on Steinbeck's *The Forgotten Village* as tradepaper item; Oct. 2, 1946, p. 1, on reviving *Native Land;* July 2, 1947, p. 13, on *The Roosevelt Story; Members Film Series,* on serials; Film Div., UAW, *Films for UN Day—1949* (Washington, 1949), and CIO FILM Div., *Summer 1949 Supplement: Films for Labor* (n.d.), both in UAW-WSU; NYT, March 21, 1949, on social workers' using it.

61. Gloster Current to White et al., Feb. 21, 1947, proposing Selznick, maker of the trailer, as producer of an NAACP trailer, enclosing *Herald-Tribune* (New York), Feb. 21, 1947; Selznick to Mr. Scanlon, Feb. 28, 1947, et seq., "Miscellaneous Correspondence," box B, in DOS-TX, and script drafts of *The American Creed.*

Chapter 7
Thermidor

1. Arthur Knight, *The Liveliest Art: A Panoramic History of the Movies* (New York, 1957), p. 267; Jowett, *Film: The Democratic Art*, p. 337, on "capon"; Sklar, *Movie-Made America*, p. 167, on "contemptible" Hollywood; Ceplair and Englund, *Inquisition in Hollywood*, p. 340, on *Var.*; Daniel J. Leab, *From Sambo to Super Spade: The Black Experience in Motion Pictures* (Boston, 1975), p. 135; Higham and Greenberg, *Hollywood in the Forties*, p. 68.

2. Dunne's bylined piece, AA, July 9, 1949.

3. Michael Conant, *Antitrust in the Motion Picture Industry* (New York, 1978), 170–71, income and costs; 147, theatres; 142, 139, 120, 11.

4. Spyros Skouras to Zanuck, Jan. 13, 1947, copy, in LM-AHC-WY; Steve Trilling to Vincent Sherman, Nov. 19, 1948, in Rudy Behlmer, ed., *Inside Warner Bros., 1935–1951* (New York, 1985), 308–9, on avoiding a "gamble"; Ron Haver, "The RKO Years," *American Film*, Dec. 1978, p. 82 ff.

5. "Confidential Notes for Conference," Jan. 3, 1947; Zanuck to Fred Metzger et al., May 12, 1947; Zanuck to Joseph Schenck, Jan. 22, 1948; Lyman Munson to Zanuck, Feb. 6, 1948, LM-AHC-WY; interview, Milestone and the author, June 1970; telephone interview between Nunnally Johnson and the author, Aug. 1977, on Freeman; Kanin, *Hollywood*, 213–14; Paul Mayersberg, *Hollywood, the Haunted House* (London, 1967), 122–23, on Cohn; and Richard Brooks, "Interview," *Movie* 12 (Spring 1965): 2–9.

6. Munson to Julian Johnson, copy, Sept. 11, 1946, quoted; Martha Geiger to Munson, April 30, 1947, on "power," in LM-AHC-WY.

7. David Lamont Sims, "Movie Censorship in Memphis, Tennessee, 1879–1973" (University of Tennessee, unpublished, 1975), 56, 65, 71; *amicus curiae* papers in UA-SHSW.

8. Sims, "Movie Censorship in Memphis," Chap. 4; *Var.*, Jan. 5, 1949; Barbara McKeon to Selznick, copy, April 21, 1945, in box 6, Story Dept. file, DOS-TX; on Sears see PM, Aug. 22, 1945; *Var.*, May 2, 1945, clippings in box 21, "analysis cards," *The Southerner* card, in MSCB; AA, Sept. 27, Oct. 25, 18, Nov. 8, 15, 1947.

9. Cobbett Steinberg, *Reel Facts: The Movie Book of Records* (New York, 1978), pp. 25, 42, 47, 52; Hedda Hopper–James Baskette correspondence, HH-AMPAS.

10. Charlotte Ruby Ashton, "The Changing Images of Blacks in American Film" (Ph. D., Princeton, 1981), 33–34; AA, June 6, 1942; Leab, *From Sambo to Super Spade*, 125; LAT, Feb. 20, 1944; AA, Jan. 9, 1944; Nov. 19, 1949, on White's impact.

11. Bioclippings in alpha. file, GPJ-UCLA, including *Silhouette* on McDaniel; and typical stories in LAS, April 3, May 8, June 19, 26, July 3, 10, 1947; "Rochester," *Ebony*, Nov. 1945, p. 13 ff; "My Life with Hazel Scott," Jan. 1949, pp. 42–50; Feb. 1949, pp. 19–23; on Eddie Anderson, p. 27 ff., on Nat Cole's house; "Homes in Hollywood," April 1948, pp. 49–51; "California Vacation," May 1948, pp. 19–24; "Film Formula for Glamour," June 1948, pp. 30–33; "Toni Harper," June 1948, pp. 60–65; AN, May 11, 27, 1950, on a McDaniel party and plight; CE, Jan. 26, May 4, 1950, on Randolph; March 24, 31, 1949, on Carmen DeLavallade's debut and Jessie Mae Beavers's wedding; June 16,

1949, on McDaniel's wedding and shopping; Nov. 24, 1949, on Vernondale; LAS, May 16, 1946, on *Les Femmes* link to Delta Sigma Theta; Jackson, *Hattie*, chap. 6.

12. *Var.*, Oct. 3, 1949, p. 36, on McQueen; *Ebony*, Jan. 1947, p. 14; "Sammy Davis," Dec. 1950, pp. 45–48; LAS, Sept. 12, 1949, on Randolph's house; May 16, 1946, on *Les Femmes* and Muse; Oct. 3, 1946, on Horne advocating FEPC; June 20, 1946, on Nick Stewart; Miriam Geiger to Lyman Munson, April 30, 1947, in LM-AHC-WY, on a white angel, plugging Bill Walker, later first black board member of SAG.

13. "I Tried to Crash the Movies," *Ebony*, Aug. 1946, cover; "Foot Doctor to the Stars," Sept. 1948, pp. 16–20; "Rochester," Nov. 1945, p. 14 ff., on "club" women; interview between Francois Andre and the author, Hollywood, June 1970; LAS, Aug. 1, 1946; interview among Martin Wilkins, Lawrence LaMar, and the author, Los Angeles, June 1970; telephone interview between Eddie Anderson and the author, June 1970; telephone interview between the author Carolynne Snowden, Los Angeles, June 1970; LAS, June 12, 1947, on Driver; AN, Feb. 22 and March 15, 1947; and Toddy interview, Atlanta, June 1976.

14. LAS, Jan. 6, 1949, on Levette charge of Hollywood's "almost deliberate intention" to avoid black material; Barnett to Levette, copy, March 8, 1949; Levette to Barnett, March 14, 1949, CB-CHS; LAS, Feb. 20, 1947, on "Tom"; *Ebony*, March 1949, p. 34; Julia E. Baxter to Roy Wilkins, April 10, 1944, on new trend: Juano Hernandez as judge in *None Shall Escape*, NR-LC; *Los Angeles Tribune*, Feb. 24, 1944.

15. Stephen Vaughan, "Sambo and Black Dignity," pp. 1–32, paper read at OAH, March 1990, grounded in SAG board minutes, SAG archives, Hollywood: Aug. 20, 1942, p. 2131; Sept. 14, 1942, p. 2147; March 1, 1943; pp. 2286–87; May 24, 1943, pp. 2355–56; Sept. 29, 1947, p. 3362 (resolution); Sept. 15, 1946, p. 3081; Oct. 20, 1947, p. 3372; Nov. 4, 1947 (resolution); Nov. 24, 1947, pp. 3399, 3401, John Dales to Eric Johnston, Oct. 1, 1947.

16. Resolution 4, Oct. 11, 1946, in SAG archives, cited in Vaughan, "Sambo and Black Dignity," 11; telephone interviews between William F. Walker, Ernest Anderson, Joel Fluellen, and the author, from 1969 onward; LAS, Sept. 19, 1946; Dec. 12, 1947, on SAG and "boycott"; interview with Fluellan cited in Jackson, *Hattie*, 110, suggests his resolution before SAG was a means of creating a third force between White and the Hollywood blacks; White to Roy Wilkins, Jan. 28, 1946, in NR-LC; for the Hollywood black point of view, Jackson, *Hattie*, 108–11; AA, Feb. 9, 1946, Levette on "phalanx"; White to Numa Adams, copy, Sept. 25, 1947, on "vested interest"; White to "Dear Dutch" [Sterling Brown], Feb. 20, 1946; see also White to George Heller, AFRA, wire, Aug. 15, 1947; Franklin H. Williams to White, memo, Aug. 5, 1947, on McDaniel, in NR-LC; and PC, Feb. 2, 1946; and Lisa Mitchell, "'Mammy" McDaniel as the Definitive Matriarch," LAT, Nov. 7, 1976.

17. Edgar Dale to White, Feb. 14, 1942, on "League"; White to E. R. Embree, Oct. 10, 1942, on Selznick's alleged suggestion that Bontemps or other Negro sit in Hays office; black soldiers' correspondence, summer 1945; Julia E. Baxter to White, memo, n.d., flop of a bureau fundraiser at Commodore; Elmer A. Carter to White, Sept. 25, 1945, on a black in MPAA; White to Embree, Dec. 11, 1945, predicted fear of "pressure," in NR-LC; inter-

view between Roy Wilkins and the author, New York, summer 1976, on "Walter's thing."

18. Revels Cayton to Lawson, copy, June 10, 1946, on Aptheker; Jan. 28, 1946, on White; Cayton to Moss, copy, April 24, 1946; Moss to Cayton, April 22, 1946, reel 34, box 72, NNC-SCRBC; telephone interview between Aptheker and the author, summer 1990.

19. Guy Endore, "Reflections on Guy Endore: Oral History Project" (UCLA, 1964); outline lecture notes in box 41, Lawson papers, SIU, on CP rhetoric; Edward L. Barrett, Jr., *The Tenney Committee: Legislative Investigation of Subversive Activities in California* (Ithaca, 1951), 64–65, 137–38, 150–51, 199–201, 215, 168, 270, 479; George Murphy with Victor Lasky, *Say . . . Didn't You Used to Be George Murphy?* (n.p., 1970), 257; Ronald Reagan, *Where's the Rest of Me? The Autobiography of Ronald Reagan* (New York, 1965), 166–68; Axel Madsen, *John Huston: A Biography* (Garden City, 1978), p. 94, on HR finding *We Were Strangers* "shameful" Marxism.

20. Donald Ogden Stewart, *By a Stroke of Luck! An Autobiography* (New York, 1975), 233–34; "Why the League Was Formed," Hollywood Anti-Nazi League pamphlet, n.d.; HDC "Report of Campaign Activities . . . as of October 27, 1944," in HDC papers, UCLA; HICCASP minutes, April 30, 1946, in SHSW; Abraham Polonsky, "How the Blacklist Was Formed," *Film Culture* 50–51 (Fall/Winter 1970): 41–48; Ashton, "Blacks in American Film," 133; *Var.*, June 11, 1947, p. 21; Ceplair and Englund, *Inquisition in Hollywood,* 232–33, on Maltz and the "DuClos letter" on the apostasy of the CPUSA.

21. Ceplair and Englund, *Inquisition in Hollywood,* 218–25, and on pedigrees of HDC, HWM, and HICCASP; William F. Nolan, *John Huston: King Rebel* (Los Angeles, 1965), 73, on Lucey's restaurant as liberal haven.

22. HDC, "Report on Campaign Activities . . . ," listed Rex Ingram, Calvin Jackson, and the Nicholas Brothers, and tactics such as "special [radio] spots for Spanish and Negro voters"; and other HWM, HICCASP uses of blacks, in SHSW; On Waldorf, Ceplair and Englund, *Inquisition in Hollywood,* 328–31; Schary, *Heyday,* 164–66; Dalton Trumbo to Paul Jarrico, July 28, 1953, box 5, Trumbo papers, SHSW, on Schary as equivocator, lent by Professor John Wiseman.

23. Irving Pichel to [William?] Durant, n.d., Dunham papers, SIU.

24. Trumbo to "Jack" [Lawson], Dec. 6, 1953, box 5, Trumbo papers, SHSW, quoted in debating "progressive content" of war movie cycle; HICCASP minutes, Jan. 28, 1947, SHSW, on Lancelot; black citations in note 20 for other activities; Rinaldo to "member," April 26, 1952, box 40, Lawson papers, SIU; David Platt, "The Hollywood Witchhunt of 1947," *Jewish Currents,* Dec. 1977, pp. 24–30, on early HUAC impact.

25. Interview with Polonsky, Beverly Hills, July 20, 1977; Bartley Crum to White, Nov. 10 [1947]; White to Melvyn Douglas, Feb. 3, 1941; press release on Trumbo and Ring Lardner, testifying to a willingness to draw closer to the Marxist left, praising Lardner for *Brotherhood of Man* and Trumbo for his UCLA speech, NR-LC.

26. Doxey Wilkerson, "The Negro and the American Nation," *Political Affairs* 25 (July 1946): 852 ff.; James S. Allen, "The Negro Question," *Political Affairs* 25 (Nov. 1946): 1046–1132, in reel 2, series 118, NNC-AAS; Nora Sayre, *Running Time: The Films of the Cold War* (New York, 1982), 32–33.

27. Navasky, *Naming Names*, 186 ff.; Starobin, *American Communism in Crisis*, pp. 9–11, 78–79, 101, on Charlotta Bass as CP; NYT, July 15, 1949, on Robeson as putative "black Stalin," clipping book, NUL-LC; *Var.*, June 6, 1950, p. 2, on Josh White on "noble causes"; *Var.*, Feb. 25, 1952, p. 57, Robeson on tour; *Var.*, Feb. 25, 1948; CE, Feb. 19, 1948, on Robinson's wellwishers; William G. Nunn to Lester Granger, July 25, 1949; Granger to Robinson, copy, July 19, 1949, quoted; and clippings, in series 1, box 155, HUAC file, NUL-LC; DuBois–Herbert Biberman correspondence in Herbert Aptheker, *The Correspondence of W. E. B. DuBois* (Amherst, MA, 1978), vol. 3, p. 175.

28. Barbara Deming, "The Library of Congress Film Project: Exposition of a Method," *Quarterly Journal of the Library of Congress* 2 (Nov. 1944): 10–11.

29. *Ebony*, Feb. 1948, p. 34; NYT, June 1, Nov. 27, 1947, on Willie Best, who might be "left out"; CE, March 31, 1948, on "up to date" Randolph role; NR, March 7, 1949, on Robert Davis losing role to Bogart, *Knock on Any Door;* vertical file, SCRBC; LAS, June 10, 1948, on how to play; LAS, June 24, 1948, on a "sympathetic" role; George Norford, "On Stage," *Opportunity*, Summer 1947, pp. 164–65; LAS, July 22, 1948; Jan. 1, 1948, on "little progress" because HUAC "scared them."

30. NYT, April 13, 1945, on Ouspenskaya; *Commonweal* 46 (April 18, 1947): pp. 16–17, on *Tarzan and the Huntress;* titles in alpha. file, GPJ-UCLA.

31. *Var.*, Nov. 3, 1948, p. 14; for contrasting opinions of Leigh Whipper in *Undercurrent*, *Var.*, Oct. 2, 1946, p. 8, and *Ebony*, Oct. 1946, p. 18.

32. LAS, Aug. 28, 1948, Dec. 11, 1947, July 31, Aug. 14, 1947, for example.

33. AN, March 31, 1945; Walter Winchell's column, Oct. 3, 1945, sent with White to Horne, copy, Sept. 19, 1945; Mayer to White, wire, Aug. 21, [1945]; White to Mayer, copy, Sept. 4, 1945; White to Cullen exchange, Sept. 1945, setting a reading; Leon Hardwick to Wilkins, Aug. 25, 1945; Wilkins to Hardwick, copy, Sept. 12, 1945; White to Mayer, Oct. 4 and 6, 1945, in NR-LC.

34. Mayer-White correspondence, note 33; *Herald-Tribune* (New York), April 1, 1946; *Daily News* (New York), April 1, 1946; *Post* (New York), May 12, 1946, all in NR-LC; AN, July 6, 1946.

35. Haskins and Benson, *Lena*, 126, on *Show Boat;* Horne and Schickel, *Lena*, 187–92; Herbert S. Nusbaum, MGM, to Cripps, Dec. 18, 1980, record reveals no plans to produce the film.

36. Clippings in White papers, JWJ-Yale; PC, Sept. 8, 15, 1945; AN, Sept. 22, 1945; *Var.*, Sept. 15, 1945; LAS, Aug. 30, 1945; Horne and Schickel, *Lena*, 188; Haskins and Benson, *Lena*, 104; "Meet the Real Lena Horne," *Ebony*, Nov. 1947, pp. 9–14, for "drydock" story; LAS, June 27, 1947; White to "Countee," n.d., and other correspondence, Aug. 1945, in NR-LC.

37. Deming, "Library of Congress Film Project," 10–11; Lyman Munson to Zanuck, Feb. 6, 1948, LM-AHC-WY, on "progress"; John Howard Lawson to Jane Merchant, April 1, 1971, copy, in box 78, Lawson papers, SIU, on giving "a much more 'modern' treatment of Al Jolson's blackface routines" in The Jolson Story, muting its "racist" roots and focusing on "its meaning" to Jolson.

38. David Culbert, "Walt Disney's Private Snafu: The Use of Humor in World War II Army Film," in Jack Salzman, ed., *Prospects: An Annual Journal of American Cultural Studies* 1 (Dec. 1975): 80–96; *Var.*, Nov. 6, 1946; Richard Schickel, *The Disney Version: The Life, Times, Art, and Commerce of Walt Disney*

(New York, 1968), 159, 276–77; Bob Thomas, *Walt Disney: An American Original* (New York, 1976), 201; and Leonard Mosley, *Disney's World: A Biography* (New York, 1985), 206; Roy Disney and John Rose to Walt Disney, May 3, 1946, on negotiations with Lucien Harris, in WDA.

39 Herman Hill to Disney, Aug. 19, 1944; Arch Reeve to Hays and Breen, Aug. 18, 1944; White to Disney, July 20, 1944, on reading Hopper; Disney to White, carbon, July 25, 1944; White to Disney, Aug. 1, 1944; Breen to Disney, Aug. 1, 1944; Peterson and Hardwick to Disney, Aug. 22, 1944; Terry Harper to Disney, memo, Aug. 14, 1944, in WDA.

40. Alain Locke to Disney, Aug. 8, 1944, in WDA; telephone interview between Maurice Rapf and the author, March 1990.

41. Maurice Rapf, untitled, bound, 6-page memo; Jonathan Bell Lovelace, Bank of America, to Disney, Sept. 18, 1944, both in WDA; B. A. Botkin, *Lay My Burden Down: A Folk History of Slavery* (Chicago, 1945), 2, 137.

42. PM, Dec. 24, 1946, vertical file, SCRBC; *Var.*, Aug. 10, 1944, in AMPAS; Breen to Disney, carbon, Aug. 1, 1944, touting Harmon; Harmon to Breen, carbon, July 31, 1944, with rewrites; Disney to Breen, Dec. 11, 1944; Breen to Disney, Dec. 13, 1944, all in PCA-AMPAS; *Var.*, Nov. 6, 1944, on "idealized" Southern movie "in progress"; and DW, Jan. 18, 1945, quoting Muse, and Jan. 8, 1945, Muse on costuming.

43. NYT, Dec. 8, 1945, in NR-LC; DW, March 2, 12, Feb. 24, 1947; *Var.*, Nov. 6, 1945, focused on apolitical animation as did Disney's ad copy; on nostalgia defined as "memory without pain," Fred Davis, *Yearning for Yesterday: A Sociology of Nostalgia* (New York, 1979), 51, cited in Paul Monaco, *Ribbons in Time: Movies and Society since 1945* (Bloomington, [1987]), p. 100.

44. LAS, Jan. 16, 1947; AN, March 15, 1947; *Ebony*, May 1947, p. 3; Edward D. C. Campbell, *The Celluloid South: Hollywood and the Southern Myth* (Knoxville, 1981), 151–52, on South's reading it as a "golden film of the Old South's glory" and "one of the best"; LAT, Jan. 31, 1947, on protest.

45. June Blythe to White, Sept. 5, 1946; Current to White et al., memo, copy, Nov. 22, 1946; Richard Condon to White, Aug. 13, 1946, in NR-LC.

46. Hope Spingarn to White, Nov. 1946; Noma Jensen, undated review report, NR-LC; Bethune to Charles Levy, RKO, copy, Dec. 16, 1946, in Bethune papers, NCNW, lent by Bettye Collier-Thomas; Tanneyhill to Guichard Parris, memo, Nov. 21, 1946, in NUL-LC; NYT, Nov. 28 and Dec. 14, 1946, cited in Campbell, *Celluloid South*, 152; Erik Barnouw, to Cripps, Aug. 28, 1991; and interview between Barnouw and the author.

47. Press release, "Parents Magazine Rapped by NAACP," Jan. 10, 1947; Catherine Edwards to White, Jan. 14, 1947; White to Arthur Spingarn et al., memo, Jan. 18, 1947, asking for rebuttals to Edwards. Leab, *From Sambo to Super Shade*, 137, reports it was "picketed more heavily" than any film, citing *Ebony*, Feb. 1947, p. 36; see also Jackson, *Hattie*, 115.

48. Baskette to Hopper, Oct. 1, 1946, and June 23, 1947; C. W. Hill to Hopper, March 26, 1948; Charles E. Butler [director, black central casting] to Hopper, Feb. 20, 1948, in Baskette file, HH-AMPAS.

49. DW, Jan. 18, 8, 1945; Bogle, *Toms*, 136, argues that the film "glaringly signaled the demise of the Negro as fanciful entertainer"; Tanneyhill to Guichard Parris, memo, Nov. 21, 1946, in NUL-LC.

50. LAS, Feb. 27, 1947; Niven Busch, *Duel in the Sun* (New York, 1944),

97; telephone interview between Busch and the author, Dec. 9, 1980, thought changes followed from Selznick's being "crazy to get recognition as a writer." McQueen's anachronistic work in this era remains an anomaly; see Jack Warner to Jerry Wald, copy, Dec. 28, 1944, file 2086, *Mildred Pierce*, WBA-USC, discussing her unbilled bit in which she kept her job as though protected despite its requiring retakes, looping, and recording lines as wild sound to be laid in later.

51. Contrast Pearl in three versions: the film; Busch, *Duel in the Sun*, 35; and Luigi Luraschi to William Dozier, copy, Jan. 22, 1944, in DOS-TX.

52. LAS, Feb. 27, 1947; Julia E. Baxter to Roy Wilkins, May 12, 1947; White to Selznick, copy, May 21, 1947, in NR-LC; see also NR, May 19, 1947, p. 33; and Philip T. Hartung [ex-OWI], *Commonweal*, May 23, 1947, p. 143.

53. White to Harry Warner, copy, April 28, 1943; Odette Harper to Mr. Skolsky, copy, May 1, 1943; Julia E. Baxter to Harper, April 16, [?]; Madison S. Jones, NAACP, to MGM, copy, Nov. 14, 1949; Miss Kirin to Jones, memo, copy, Oct. 31, 1949, complaining of the maid in *Tom and Jerry* who carries dice and a razor; Jones, memo for file, Nov. 4, 1948; E. L. McEvoy to Jones, Oct. 20, 1948, finding NAACP "over-sensitive"; Edna Kirin to Henry Lee Moon, copy, Oct. 11, 1948; Baxter to Moon, copy, Oct. 20, 1948; *Los Angeles Tribune*, Nov. 20, 1948; Jones to T. L. Griffith, Dec. 7, 1948; White to Jones, Feb. 18, 1949; press release, Feb. 3, 1949, in NR-LC.

54. OWI report by Dorothy B. Jones, Peggy Fenwick, and J. E. Johnston, April 20, 1943, and July 31, 1945, in entry 576, box 320, RG 208, NA-MD: *Music Lesson* and *Jasper and the Beanstalk* (1943), they said, used "stereotypes" but provided no "problems"; Liane Richter, July 1943, reviews *Music Lesson* twice; Philip T. Hartung, Feb. 16, 1944, on *Jungle Jive;* five more Jasper cartoons reviewed, 1943, in OWI-LC.

55. F. S. Harmon to A. S. Howson, Warner Bros., Sept. 10, 1937, in *A Race Riot* file, WBA-USC, on proposed film of Ken Kling's *Joe and Asbestos; Var.*, Feb. 4, 1942, p. 8; Dec. 2, 1948, p. 8; Carl Kinsey, "Hollywood's New Screen Productions," *Musician* 47 (April 1942): 58; DW, Feb. 22, 1950, clipping in SCRBC took issue with them; "Little Jasper Series Draws Protest from Negro Groups," *Ebony*, Jan. 1947, pp. 30–31.

56. David Meeker, *Jazz in the Movies: A Guide to Jazz Musicians 1917–1977* (London, 1977), no. 955, thought it "phoney"; James Agee, *Nation*, Dec. 16, 1944, p. 753, thought it "too full" of jazz mood; *Time*, Dec. 25, 1944, p. 50; *Life*, Jan. 22, 1945, pp. 6–8; *Theatre Arts* 28 (Dec. 1944): p. 725; AN, Feb. 5, 12, 1949; Gordon Hollingshead to Norman Moray, telephone memo, file 1469, WBA-USC; *Var.*, March 21, 1945, p. 45; Leab, *From Sambo to Super Spade*, p. 174, on *Ebony*.

57. Script in PAR-AMPAS, titled "Release Dialogue Script," May 1, 1946, no. 1613.

58. *The American Creed* scripts, "Scripts, B-C" file, box 24; Selznick to Mr. Scanlon, Feb. 28, 1947; Spyros Skouras to Selznick; correspondence through Feb. 1947; in "Misc. Correspondence," box B; "Final" of Feb. 16, 1946, noted that preview cards collected; last draft, Jan. 22, 1947, "pink-tabbed," marked "extra special rush, please," in DOS-TX.

59. Maltz's notes and drafts, in Maltz papers, ML-BU, and Maltz papers, SHSW; LeRoy, *Take One*, 129, 155; *Var.*, Dec. 6, 1944, p. 1; DW, June 3, 1945, clipping in SCRBC, along with *The House I Live In* pamphlet.

60. *Var.*, Oct. 31, 1945, p. 1; Dec. 5, 1945, p. 2; Kitty Kelley, *His Way: The Unauthorized Biography of Frank Sinatra* (Toronto, 1986), 488.

61. Clarence I. Chatto and Alice L. Halligan, *The Story of the Springfield Plan* (New York, 1945); James W. Wise, *The Springfield Plan* (New York, 1945); Crane Wilbur to "Dear Holly," and enclosure, Sept. 16, 1944, citing Helena Hunt Smith, "Your Town Could Do It Too," *Woman's Home Companion* clipping; Ray Graham, "Report of Progress of Americans All–Immigrants All, 1943–1944" (mimeo.); "Facts About the Springfield Plan," all in file 1469, *It Happened in Springfield*, in WBA-USC.

62. Syllabus, Springfield College, inscribed by Miller to Warner; Miller to Crane Wilbur, Aug. 8, 1945; Hollingshead to Ray Obringer, copy, Aug. 23, 1944, in file 1469, WBA-USC.

63. Wilbur to Hollingshead, Sept. 16, 1944, pleased with Warner's enthusiasm but fearing New York, which, he thought, had an aversion to social movies, in file 1469, WBA-USC; *Big Town* script, undated, 8 pp., and Robert Hardy Andrews to Wilbur, carbon, Sept. 9, 1940, in Andrews papers, ML-BU.

64. Warner to Hollingshead, Sept. 1, 1944; and memo, n.d.; Charles Einfeld to Hollingshead, Sept. 12, 1944, in file 1469, WBA-USC; and *Big-Town* script, Andrews papers, ML-BU, in which the "accent" line appears.

65. Telephone interview between Mrs. Crane Wilbur and the author, July 14, 1977.

66. Dialogue transcript, *It Happened in Springfield;* Col. Curtis Mitchell, Pictorial Branch, to Warner Bros., copy, Nov. 30, 1944, having no objection to the film; Breen to Warner, Oct. 10, 1944; "Holly" to Ray Obringer, Sept. 22, 1944, file 1469, WBA-USC.

67. Hollingshead-Wilbur telephone transcript; *Sweet Land of Liberty* [working title], cutter's notes, Nov. 20, 1944; Hollingshead to Warner, Dec. 16, 1944, on OWI; Hollingshead to Norman Moray, Dec. 16, 1944; "Crane" to "Holly," wire, on replacing the black teacher, in file 1469, WBA-USC.

68. Breen to Jack Warner, Oct. 10, 1944, file 1469, WBA-USC.

69. Springfield Council of Social Agencies, A. Abbott Kaplan, chair, *Social Needs of Negroes in Springfield, Massachusetts* (Springfield, ca. 1940), 3, cited; *Springfield Republican*, March 7, 1956, obituary of John E. Granrud in which the "plan" was listed first among achievements; "Springfield—History" folder, Springfield Public Library; *Springfield Republican*, April 25, 1945, premiere; *It Happened in Springfield*, undated Warners' pamphlet; Nancy Flagg, "A City Takes the Cure," *Vogue*, Feb. 1, 1946, p. 169 ff.; [Springfield Public Schools], *Democratic Procedures, Grade 9, The Contributions of Nationalities . . .* ; Springfield Public Schools, *Public Opinion and How It is Influenced* (Springfield, n.d.), 33, on prejudice.

70. Reference videotape in LC; see also dialogue transcript, file 1469, WBA-USC.

71. Norman Moray to "Holly," Dec. 14, 1944; Hollingshead to "Colonel" Warner, Dec. 16, 1944; Hollingshead to Moray, copy, Dec. 16, 1944, in file 1469, WBA-USC.

72. Eleanor Berneis [?] review, Feb. 10, 1945; W. S. Cunningham, Feb. 10, 1945, in OWI-LC.

73. *Showman's Trade Review*, April 7, 1945; HR, April 4, 1945, in file 1469, WBA-USC; *Ebony*, Nov. 1945, p. 38 ff.; *Educational Film Catalogue*, 159.

74. *Var.*, June 13, 1945, p. 2; July 19, 1944, p. 18; Mildred Fleming in DW, n.d., in file 1469, WBA-USC.

75. Elizabeth Zutt to "Gentlemen," May 12, [1945], and other mail in file 1469, WBA-USC; and telephone interview between Zutt and the author, May 21, 1986, in which she graciously tried to recall her frame of mind but did not recall her letter.

76. White to Selznick, April 5, 1946, in "Christians and Jews—NAACP" file, box 89, DOS-TX; "Elaine" to "Walter," Oct. 14, 1948, WW-JWJ; and LAS, Jan. 9, 1947.

77. Kraft, *On My Way*, 122–32; Mark Schorer, *Sinclair Lewis: An American Life* (New York, 1961), 743–57; *Var.*, Feb. 2, 1947, p. 1, quoted, and Nov. 26, 1947, p. 1; Wald to Hopper, "Friday," in HH-AMPAS.

78. "People—S" file, box 2, on a "goodwill among mankind" project; SDB, March 11, 1946, p. 15, on Brooklyn story; galleys submitted by Ruth Smith for the teacher; SDB, Feb. 16, 1946, p. 33; SDB, March 16, 1946, pp. 12, 14, on passive Negro; SDB, Feb. 16, 1946, p. 13, on Massingham's *The Harp and Oak* as "too hot"; SDB, Feb. 16, 1946, p. 33, on *The Street* as "too controversial"; SDB, Jan. 19, 1946, on *Home of the Brave* as "not commercial at this time"; SDB, Jan. 19, 1946, pp. 12, 14, on DuMaurier, in "Misc. Story Dept. Correspondence," in DOS-TX; Ann Petry to the author, Dec. 1990, recalled no offer from *any* studio for *The Street*.

79. Interview between Niven Busch and the author, Dec. 9, 1980; Samuel Goldwyn, "How I Became Interested in Social Justice," *Opportunity* 24 (Summer 1948): 100–101.

80. AA, Aug. 9, Sept. 27, Oct. 4, 18, 25, Nov. 8, 15, 1947, on censors; telephone interviews between Joel Fluellen, June 1970, and Walter Colmes, Aug. 1977, and the author; Dr. J. M. Tinsley to White, Oct. 3, 1947; R. E. Hughes to White, Nov. 19, 1947; Madison S. Jones, Jr., to Hughes, copy, Dec. 9, 1947, in NR-LC; *Ebony*, Sept. 1947, pp. 36–47.

81. "Hollywood Calls Negro Maid 'Mrs.' for First Time," *Ebony*, Nov. 1947, pp. 23–24; "Rogue's Regiment," *Ebony*, Sept. 1948, pp. 31–33; "A Song is Born," *Ebony*, May 1948, pp. 41–43; *NYT Directory of Film*, 382; "Black Gold," *Ebony*, Oct. 1947, pp. 39–41; "Moonrise," *Ebony*, July 1948, p. 51; "MGM Studio Has Three Other Films with Good Negro Parts," *Ebony*, May 1949, pp. 24–26; "Movie Maids," *Ebony*, Aug. 1948, pp. 56–59; other tradepaper ephemera in Richard Fleischer papers, USC; *Var.*, May 17, 1950, p. 7. *Ebony's* regular column "Film Parade" broadened the analysis of Hollywood beyond mere personal achievement. George Norford, "On Stage," *Opportunity* 25 (Summer 1947): 74–75, 167.

82. Telephone interviews between Carl Foreman, Aug. 1977, Carlton Moss, July 1977, and Abraham Polonsky, July 1977, and the author; *Var.*, May 17, 1950, p. 7, on Dore Schary's promise to do social drama; Irving Rapper to Cripps, Feb. 5, 1977; Ashton, "Blacks in Film," 56, quoting Wise.

83. "New Orleans," *Ebony*, Feb. 1947, pp. 26–30; LAS, Sept. 12, 1946; AN, Jan. 23, 1947.

84. Alice Payne Hackett and James Henry Burke, *80 Years of Best Sellers, 1895–1975* (New York, 1977), 142–45; Schary, *Heyday*, 168, 170, recalls only an amiable struggle with Hughes; Foster Hirsch, *Joseph Losey* (Boston, 1980), 31–39; telephone interview with Levitt, Jan 1992.

85. "New Orleans," *Ebony*, Feb. 1947, pp. 26–30.

86. Telephone interview between Frank Yerby and the author, 1976, noncommittal but reporting his preferred distance from the film; telephone interview between Wanda Tuchock and the author, July 14, 1977; Rex Harrison, *Rex: An Autobiography* (New York, 1975), 95, 99, 101, on Zanuck; Phyllis Klotman, "A Harrowing Experience: Frank Yerby's First Novel into Film," *CLA Journal* 31 (Dec. 1987): 210–22; Zanuck story conference, July 18, 1946, on Jerome Cady et al. synopsis of July 19, 1946, in file 2315, lent by Professor John Wiseman, Frostburg, Md.; *The Foxes of Harrow*, "final" script, March 14, 1947, marginalia, pp. 59, 88, 137, warned of problems, in ITC-DC; Breen to Jason S. Joy, carbon, April 22, and March 25, 1947, in PCA-AMPAS, fretted over how sexuality would be construed by African Americans; *The Foxes of Harrow* data sheet, GPJ-UCLA, for names of black actors; LAS, Aug. 8, April 3, 1947.

87. Breen to Harold Melniker, RKO, Aug. 27, 1947; "Proposed Cuts in Budget," n.d.; Adrian Scott to Schary, memo, copy, Sept. 12, 1947; Paul Hollister to "Ade" [Scott], Sept. 3, 1947, in Scott papers, AHC-WY; "final" script, ITC-DC; telephone interview between Regis Toomey and the author, June 1970; telephone interview between Alfred Lewis Levitt and the author, Jan. 1992.

88. Campbell, *Celluloid South*, 162–63, surveyed the national press; *Time*, Oct. 13, 1947, p. 105; *Var.*, June 13, 1948, p. 10, on *Tap Roots*; *Var.*, Nov. 17, 1948, p. 13, Sept. 8, 1948, p. 3; Philip T. Hartung, "Mind Your Psyche," *Commonweal*, Jan. 21, 1949, pp. 377–78.

89. Bernard Eisenschitz, "Abraham par lui meme," *Positif* 84 (May 1967): 7–17, on personnel; Guiles, *Hanging On in Paradise*, 242–43, 245, on stars and budget; Sayre, *Running Time*, 32–33.

90. William Pechter, "Abraham Polonsky and *Force of Evil*," *Film Quarterly* 15 (Spring 1962): 52, on sources; telephone interview between Polonsky and the author, July 1977, on Odets's "sense"; Larry Swindell, *Body and Soul: The Story of John Garfield* (New York, 1975), 228–29; John Garfield, "Our Part in 'Body and Soul,'" *Opportunity*, Winter 1948, p. 20.

91. Canada Lee, "Our Part in 'Body and Soul,'" *Opportunity*, Winter 1948, p. 21; Polonsky interview, cited in note 90; see also Michel Delahaye, "Entretien avec Abraham Polonsky," *Cahiers du Cinema* 215 (Sept. 1969): 31–38; "Canada Lee Back in the Ring," *Ebony*, Aug. 1947, pp. 16–17; Eric Sherman and Martin Rubin, eds., *The Director's Event: Interviews with Five American Filmmakers* (New York, 1970), p. 10, on "interesting" time; Richard Koszarski, *Hollywood Directors, 1941–1976* (New York, 1977), 47–53, on Rossen's conservative family and radical politics and his guess that "after the war" audiences required a more thoughtful "reality."

92. The *film noir* texture derived from well-cast character actors: Joseph Pevney, William Conrad, Hazel Brooks, Art Smith, Anne Revere, and Lloyd Gough, some of them lefties with a feel for the material. On action in ring, Charles Higham, ed., *Hollywood Cameramen: Sources of Light* (Bloomington, 1970), 82, 89.

93. LAS, March 1947, GPJ-UCLA; NYT cited, Leab, *Sambo to Super Spade*, 138–39; Bogle, *Toms*, 139–40.

94. Quinn Martin to Harold Melniker, March 25, 1947, and press kit, Oct. 15, 1948, in file 652, RKO-UCLA; on original black angle, Bob Ellis in CE,

June 9, 1949; see also Eileen Bowser, *Film Notes* [MOMA] (New York, 1969), 116–17.

95. Wise seminar transcript, no. 569, April 7, 1979, p. 2, AFI/CAFS; NYT, March 30, 1949, on Ryan's career.

96. Pechter, "Polonsky," 52, quoted.

Chapter 8
"A Pot of Message"

1. SDB, Feb. 16, 1946, p. 13, in DOS-TX; Kanin, *Hollywood*, 247–49.

2. *Var.*, June 25, 1947, p. 8.

3. *Var.*, June 18, 1947, p. 3; on HUAC's impact on *Crossfire*, see "Adrian Scott" file, box 127, Schary papers, SHSW; on German pressure against *The Great Dictator*, see Breen and George Gyssling correspondence in title file, PCA-AMPAS; K. R. M. Short, "Hollywood Fights Anti-Semitism, 1945–1947," in Short, ed., *Feature Films as History* (London, 1981), 162–63, 167, Crowther quoted, 158. The standard histories are Lester D. Friedman, *Hollywood's Image of the Jew* (New York, 1982), particularly chap. 3; and Patricia D. Erens, *The Jew in American Cinema* (Bloomington, 1984), chap. 5.

4. Short, "Hollywood Fights Anti-Semitism," 157–89; for a boomerang effect in Germany see Thomas Cripps, "Der Ewige Jude," in Christopher Lyons, ed., *Encyclopedia of Film* (Chicago, 1985), 149; see too *Sword in the Desert* (1948), a first Hollywood recognition of the state of Israel; and for criticism of the moguls' timidity toward Jewishness, Capt. Greer Williams, USAAF, to Albert Maltz, Sept. 7, 1945, box 5, Maltz papers, SHSW, objecting to "the name Diamond as being insufficiently Jewish to hammer home the point."

5. Correspondence between Mellett and AJC, Feb. 5, 13, 1943, in entry 264, box 1440, RG 208, NA-MD.

6. Silberberg quoted in Erens, *Jew in American Cinema*, 187–88, 170, citing Mayer: "If you bring out a Jew in a film—you're in trouble." The council was eventually called the Motion Picture Project.

7. Lyman Munson to Zanuck, copy, Feb. 6, 1948; Julian Johnson to Zanuck, copy, May 3, 1948, and Munson to Johnson, copy, Dec. 2, 1946, in LM-AHC-WY, quoted on "audiences"; *Daily Var.*, clipping, in file 2701, TCFA-UCLA, quoted; Dermay Tilleau, "Jewish Stereotypes in American Movies," *Film Sense*, Jan.–Dec. 1952, pp. 5–6, referred to Hollywood as "an Anglo-Saxon screen"; LAS, Nov. 14, 1946, on maudlin *Abie's Irish Rose* as "a hate film"; on Jewish intergroup harmony strategies see Lance J. Sussman, "'Toward Better Understanding'; The Rise of the Interfaith Movement in America and the Role of Rabbi Isaac Landman," *American Jewish Archive* 34 (April 1982): 35–51; and on fraternal debate, transcript of a dialogue between Oscar Cohen, ADL, and Dore Schary, lent by K. R. M. Short.

8. Schary, *Heyday*, 156–57, 160; Erens, *Jew in American Cinema*, 175; Ron Haver, "The RKO Years," *American Film*, Dec.–Jan. 1978, p. 28 ff.; Eric Goldman, "The Fight to Bring the Subject of Anti-Semitism to the Screen," *Davka* 5 (Fall 1975): 24, cited in Erens, chap. 5; Dymytrk, *It's a Hell of a Life*, 92, on 14 percent decline in anti-Semitism in a sample of moviegoers.

9. *Crossfire* took on a certain weight as a result of its place in a popular film noir cycle that included *Boomerang*, *The Naked City*, and *Call Northside 777*, as

well as its bold use of nonpejorative typecasting: Sam Levene as the Jew, Robert Ryan as flinty heavy, and so on. Elliott E. Cohen, "Letter to the Movie-Makers," *Commentary* 4 (Aug. 1947): 110–18; Dore Schary, "Letter from a Movie-Maker," *Commentary* 4 (Oct. 1947): 344–49; NYT, July 23, 1947; see also *Time*, Aug. 4, 1947, p. 76, finding hatred so "extravagant" as to allow casual anti-Semites to "identify out" of self-implication; James Agee, *Nation*, Aug. 2, 1947, rpt. in *Agee on Film*, vol. 1, pp. 269–70; *Life*, June 30, 1947, p. 71 ff.; *Var.*, Nov. 12, 1948, p. 8, said it was "a credit to the screen"; *Var.*, Aug. 27, 1947, p. 31, reported the army thought it acceptable for domestic posts only and the navy rejected it as "not suitable."

10. *Var.*, July 7, 1948, p. 1, reckoned that together *Crossfire* and *Gentleman's Agreement* earned $5,000,000 over their nut; Steinberg, *Reel Facts*, 45–46, on Oscars, and 145, 313, 429 on "bests"; *Negro Digest* stories excerpted in AN, Jan. 24, 1948, and LAS, June 24, 1948; see LAS, July 22, Jan. 1, 1948, on black ambivalence, praising "straight" roles unmarred by any "effort made toward pleasing any special section of the country," while sensing that HUAC had "scared them."

11. Hartung in *Commonweal*, Aug. 1, 1947, p. 386.

12. *Senior Scholastic*, Sept. 27, 1947, p. 31; see also *Var.*, May 12, 1948, p. 5; *Time*, April 12, 1948, p. 100, reporting that Paul Lazarsfeld minimized the impact on opinion of any film by contrasting liberal message with conservative fan magazines; see also Howard Dietz, "Must Movies Be Significant?" NYTM, Jan. 27, 1948, pp. 18, 44; Thomas F. Brady, "Hollywood Tackles the Facts of Life," NYT, March 16, 1947; and on the "play" in the film, Moss Hart reported a grip who said the film taught him "to be good to Jewish people because you never can tell when they will turn out to be gentiles," reported in John Mason Brown, "Seeing Things," SRL, Dec. 6, 1947, p. 71, cited in Erens, *Jew in American Cinema*, 179–80. I have twice heard another version in which caution is dictated by the possibility that you may be talking to a Jew. All may be apocryphal: Brown's grip improbably says "henceforth"! *Canadian Forum*, May 1948, pp. 39–40, thought the "charade" structure an inadvertent confirmation of suspicions of Jewish guile; and John McCarten, *New Yorker*, Nov. 5, 1947, pp. 97–98, concurring with *Time* and others in presuming no anti-Semite would recognize himself in the movie, which thus was a mere "slap on the wrist,"

13. Elliott E. Cohen, "Mr. Zanuck's Gentleman's Agreement," *Commentary* 5 (Jan. 1948): 51–56; Irwin C. Rosen, "The Effect of the Motion Picture *Gentleman's Agreement* on Attitudes toward Jews," *Journal of Psychology* 3 (Oct. 1948): 525–36; Russell Middleton, "Ethnic Prejudice and Susceptibility to Persuasion," *American Sociological Review* 15 (Oct. 1960): pp. 679–86. AN, Jan. 24, 1948, cited Schary as feeling movies *worked* by replacing misinformation, much as Allport argued in *The Nature of Prejudice*. NYT, Feb. 29, 1948; *Var.*, Nov. 12, 1947, p. 8; PM, Nov. 12, 1947; HR, Nov. 10, 1947; NYT, in *NYT Directory*, 94; on Crowther on "the Bilbos and the Rankins," Erens, *Jew in American Cinema*, 194.

14. Steinberg, *Reel Facts*, 45–46, 144, 313; *Time*, April 12, 1948, p. 100; CE, Jan. 22, 1948, on Peck; Feb. 5, 26, 1948; *Time*, Dec. 20, 1948, pp. 44–52; and Nov. 17, 1947, p. 105; *Var.*, Jan. 28, 1948, p. 7; March 24, 1948, p. 24; April 7, 1948, p. 6; Anne Strick, "Peck on Prejudice," *Negro Digest*, July 1948, pp. 17–20.

15. LAS, Nov. 14, 1946, on *Var.*; White to Poppy Cannon, Aug. 26, 1947;

White to Oliver Harrington et al., memo, Nov. 5, 1946, in WW-JWJ on new alliances; CE, June 3, 1948, *Crossfire* unit doing a film on black housing; George Norford, "The Future in Films," *Opportunity*, Summer 1948, pp. 108–9. See also Russell Campbell, "The Ideology of a Social Consciousness Movie," *Quarterly Review of Film Studies*, Winter 1978, pp. 49–71, for comment on incrementalism, which to Marcusians may seem only "repressive tolerance," and for incrementalism as compared in art and baseball, specifically E. H. Gombrich's idea that a painting "collects its meaning from what has gone before and what may come next," so "the batter swings freely, the way the painter paints, but the swing itself is bound by the ghosts of every other swing," as Adam Gopnik wrote in "Quattrocentro Baseball," *New Yorker*, May 19, 1986, pp. 89–92.

16. "Dore Schary—Sales Meeting," Feb. 8, 1949, in box 107, DS-SHSW.

17. I. H. Prinzmetal to Schary, July 21, 1949, box 108, DS-SHSW.

18. The message movies, save for *Lost Boundaries*, played variations upon the familiar lone hero of the western; see Will Wright, *Six Guns and Society* (Berkeley, 1975); John T. Lenihan, *Showdown: Confronting Modern America in the Western Film* (Urbana, 1980); and Robert B. Ray, *A Certain Tendency of the Hollywood Cinema, 1930–1980* (Princeton, 1985), chap. 2; *Var.*, May 29, 1946, p. 1; telephone interview between Kramer and the author, July 13, 1977; Kramer to Cripps, Sept. 15, 1976; CD, April 30, 1949, specifically claiming the soldier became black as a result of *Crossfire*'s release.

19. Telephone interview between Foreman and the author, July 15, 1977, and conversations with Carlton Moss from 1969 onward.

20. Telephone interview between Mark Robson and the author, July 28, 1977, and with Moss and Foreman, cited in note 19; Vaughan, *Only Victims*, appendix 1, on Glass, Corey, and Bridges; telephone interview between Kramer and the author, March 30, 1972, Kramer recalled Stillman's investment as $350,000, but *Var.*, March 2, 1949, p. 3, placed it at $600,000, and contract, UA-SHSW, had it as $385,000 along with $600,000 for two other films.

21. *Var.*, March 2, 1949, p. 3; AN, April 9, 23, May 7, 1949; CD, April 2, 1949; AA, April 30, 1949; CD, May 14, 1949; *Var.*, June 11, 1947, p. 9; *Agee on Film*, vol. 1, pp. 269–70; *Var.*, Nov. 10, 1948, p. 24; NYT, May 23, 1949; Foreman interview, July 13, 1977; and telephone interview between Arthur Laurents and the author, July 13, 1977.

22. LAS, March 10, 1948, on Edwards; telephone interview between Jeff Corey and the author, Aug. 9, 1977, along with those previously cited.

23. Robson, Corey, Moss, Kramer, Foreman interviews; CD, May 14, 1949, on Westwood; *Var.*, March 2, 1949; AN, April 9, 23, May 7, 1949; CD, April 2, 1949; AA, April 30, 1949; CD, May 14, 1949; HR cited in Donald Spoto, *Stanley Kramer: Filmmaker* (New York, 1978), 53.

24. "Home of the Brave," *Ebony*, June 1949, pp. 59–62; Chaudhuri, "Negro in Motion Pictures," 41, 47–50, 143, quoting Moss; CE, June 30, 1949; *Post* (New York), May 13, 1949, thought it Pollyanna-ish; AA, July 16, Aug. 6, 27, 1949, quoted *Memphis Commercial-Appeal* on racism as national in scope; HR, April 29, 1949; *Good Housekeeping*, July 1949, p. 201; Mayersberg, *Hollywood*, 196–97; *Dallas World* cited in CD, July 30, 1949.

25. Jerome, *Negro in Hollywood*, 42; DW, July 25, 1949; Warren Miller, "Films: Home of the Brave," *Masses & Mainstream*, July 1949, pp. 79–82; *New Leader* clipping, in Robert Delson and Albert Hemsing to Roy Wilkins, April 8,

1949, in NR-LC; Manny Farber, *Movies* (New York, 1971), 69, reprint of *Nation* piece, regarding it as "well played and punchy" but lacking "bite" because of Edwards's "passive" reading while tormented by his enemy; press kit synopsis in NR-LC; *Life*, May 23, 1949, p. 143; AA, April 23, 1949, on Glass.

26. CD, July 30, 1949; AA, Aug. 6, 27, Nov. 5, Oct. 15, April 23, 1949, April 2, 1949; LAS, July 28, 1949; CE, April 21, Sept. 29, 1949; LAS, April 14, May 5, Aug. 13, June 2, 16, 1949; *Herald-Tribune* (New York), on White's approval, clipping in NR-LC; "Movie debut," *Ebony*, April 1949, p. 25; AA, Aug. 27, 1949, on Memphis press; *Var.*, May 4, 1949; HR, April 29, 1949; *Daily Var.*, April 29, 1949; MPD, April 29, 1949, in PCA-AMPAS.

27. Breen to Glass, carbon, Feb. 16, 1949, on "insults"; Glass to Milton Hodenfield, MPAA, carbon, Feb. 18, 1949, agreeing to changes; Gordon S. White, MPAA, N.Y., to Roger Lewis, carbon, May 17, 1949, on "guts," to which Glass agreed; CD, Oct. 15, 1949, on Atlanta; NJ & G, Aug. 6, 1949, on Memphis; NYT, July 30, 1949; Aug. 27, 1949, on Johnston vs. censors; three meetings of MSCB with NAACP and NUL, in box 18, MSCB; *Var.*, May 11, 1949, clipping in MSCB, on UA's brochure; Ashton, "Blacks in Film," 67, for *Daily News* sample.

28. CD, July 30, 1949; AA, Nov. 5, Oct. 15, Aug. 6, April 2, 1949; Mr. Offutt to Roy Wilkins, memo, April 20, 1949; Neil Scott to White, wire, May 5, 1949, in NR-LC, on NAACP; "Home of the Brave," *Ebony*, June 1949, pp. 59–62; Robson interview, July 1977, thought the film "had contributed so much to the advancement of colored people"; Deming, *Running Away from Myself*, 9, was so taken with it that she grafted it onto her memory of *Guadalcanal Diary* (1943); William L. Burke, "The Presentation of the Negro in Hollywood Films, 1946–1961" (Ph.D., Northwestern, 1965), 191–96, saw Mossy's narcotherapeutic "cure" as a ritual conversion from paganism to Christianity, part of a thesis in which blacks are icons in a symbolic struggle between savagery and civilization.

29. Telephone interview between Louis DeRochemont and the author, July 11, 1977; interview between Borden Mace and the author, Research Triangle Park, N.C., Dec. 1, 1980; and Lothar Wolf and the author, Florence, Italy, Dec. 5, 1979; W. L. White, *Lost Boundaries* (New York, 1947, 1948); CD, June 5, 1948; Walter White to "Dear Louis," Feb. 25, 1949, closing "you are at liberty to use this letter"; and May 23, 1949, in NR-LC.

30. W. L. White's name on a book jacket enjoyed popular credibility, having led to two movies, *Journey for Margaret* and *They Were Expendable;* DeRochemont and Mace interviews, in the latter of which he seemed a "crusader."

31. Paul [Palmer], *Reader's Digest*, to "Louis," May 18, 1948; Frank Taylor to Kenneth MacKenna, with Ellison's "Lost Boundaries 8-23-48," 8 pp.; Jack Haeseler to DeRochemont, Feb. 23, 1949; EHS to [PP], Aug. 27, 1948; "Lost Boundaries—Criticism"; "Johnny" [Barnwell] to DeRochemont, Jan. 15, 1949; "Borden" Mace to DeRochemont, Jan. 25, 1949, all in LD-AHC-WY.

32. Motion Picture Research Bureau [Handel], "*Lost Boundaries* Pre-Production Test"; Dallas, the only Southern market, registered a 55 percent wish to see it; DeRochemont interview, 1977, indicated a nut of $500,000 drawn from personal funds, First Division Pictures, and Warners, but table in papers with postproduction costs reached almost $1 million. Black pay: Lee got $750 per day, Whipper $55, in LD-AHC-WY; *Var.*, Feb. 18, 1948, p. 6; "Lost Bound-

aries," *Ebony*, May 1948, pp. 45–49, and June 1949, pp. 51–53; White to DeRochemont, May 23, 1994, in NR-LC.

33. Gene Ling to "Louis," Dec. 6, 1948; DeRochemont to Ling, wire, Dec. 15, 1948; Ling to "Louis," Dec. 22, 1948; Lothar Wolf to DeRochemont, Jan. 25, 1949, was shocked by Barnwell (note 31) and disagreed, as did Mace, Jan. 25, 1948; Kenneth Payson Kempton to DeRochemont, Feb. 27, 1948 [*sic*]; anon. undated note; and "Thoughts on Script dated Feb. 21, 1949 from Alfred Werker"; Mace to Ling, wire, May 18, 1949, on scoring; negative cost inferred from estimated gross, Aug. 25, 1949; two projected budgets, June 1, 1949; and Mace to DeRochemont, May 31, 1949, in LD-AHC-WY. MGM's proposed budget before breach was $1,140,000 of which $300,000 was overhead.

34. Mace to Ling, wire, May 18, 1949, LD-AHC-WY; White to DeRochemont, copy, May 23, 1949, in NR-LC; Lothar Wolf interview described location shooting in Harlem.

35. Frank Jotterand, "The White Negro," trans. of hostile review at Cannes; "Notes for Louis after Sat.," in LD-AHC-WY.

36. CD, Jan. 14, 1950, on awards; AA, Sept. 24, 1949, on Lee; *Life*, July 4, 1949, pp. 64–66; Chaudhuri, "Negro in Film," 114, 50, citing *Newsweek;* DeRochemont to Ling, copy, Jan. 18, 1950, on recognition; and April 28, 1950 in LD-AHC-WY; Crowther, *NYT Directory of Film*, 103; Manny Farber, *Nation*, July 30, 1949, pp. 114–15, on blacks as stoics; Jerome, *Negro in Hollywood Film*, 29–33; DW, July 1, 31, 1949, in SCRBC; NR, July 4, 1949, p. 22.

37. AN, May 7, 1949; ANP in AA, July 23, 1949; AA, Aug. 6, 13, Oct. 29, 1949; AN, July 9, 1949; NJ & G, Aug. 8, 1949; CE, Aug. 11, 18, May 7, 1949, on Ellis; CD, Aug. 27, 1949; AA, Sept. 24, 1949, a sampling of a large outpouring.

38. Fredi Washington to Darr Smith, carbon, Aug. 2, 1949; and Washington to Carlton Moss, in Washington papers, Amistad Center, New Orleans, La.; and AN, Aug. 6, 1949, on a "Committee for the Negro in the Arts" that complained Werker had slighted blacks.

39. Mace to Breen, wire, June 18, 1949; Breen to Mace, carbon, June 22, 1949, in *Lost Boundaries* file, PCA-AMPAS; *Var.*, March 8, 1950, p. 4; NYT, Feb. 5, 1950; Nov. 18, 1949, on Memphis; Aug. 21, 1949, on Smith; AA, June 10, 1950, on ACLU; AN, Nov. 28, 1949, on Supreme Court; Lester Velie, "*You Can't* [*sic*] See That Movie: Censorship in Action," *Collier's*, May 6, 1950, p. 10 ff.; Patrick Murphy Malin to DeRochemont, May 15, 1951, on ACLU vs. Censors; Mace to Malin, May 21, 1951, on Atlanta; DeRochemont to Eric Johnston, copy to Ellis Arnall, exec. director, Independent Producers Association, Aug. 29, 1949; Matty Brescia to DeRochemont, wire, Oct. 30, 1949, et seq., on Binford; Chauncey W. Lever to DeRochemont, Aug. 20, 1949, on censorship as factor in Georgia politics, all in LD-AHC-WY.

40. AN, Nov. 28, 1949, on Supreme Court; AA, Sept. 3, 1949, on "police functions;" NJ&G, Sept. 3, 1949, "despotism"; AA, April 29, 1950, "good order"; AA, April 1, 1950, on Smith and "equality"; and alpha. file, PCA-AMPAS and MSCB.

41. Some fan letters from Indiana, all dated Nov. 2, 1949, reeked of campaigning; Brescia to DeRochemont, Oct.–Nov. 1949, on liberal Southern opinion; E. C. Smith, Carolina Theatre, to Mace, Dec. 3, 1949, in LD-AHC-WY; and Mace interview.

42. Curti, *Skouras*, 77–78, plausible and appropriate but unsubstantiated.

43. Poppy Cannon to White, copy, Nov. 10, 1947; White to Cannon, Aug. 26, 1947; White to Oliver Harrington et al., mimeo., Nov. 5, 1946, in WW-JWJ; and Philip Dunne to Zanuck, April 19, 1948, in PD-USC; twenty drafts in file 2391, TCFA-USC; beginning with Hubler's, March 21, 1948, retitle of *Quality* to *Crossover*.

44. Untitled draft, anon., May 25, 1948, pp. 34, 49, 56–57, 66–71, 108–9, 118–21, 155–56, in file 2391, TCFA-USC.

45. "*Pinky*," story conference, May 25, 1948 (date in holograph), Zanuck, Nichols, Mandeville attending; and "Untitled Script to be Produced by D.F.Z.," file 2391, TCFA-USC.

46. "*Pinky*," conference on second draft of June 11, 1949, same conferees as in note 45, June 18, 1948, pp. 4, 14, 15, 22, after which summer frequency lessened; conference on screenplay of July 7, 1948, met Sept. 30, 1948, pp. 1–8, in file 2391, TCFA-UCLA. In this draft, Jake gets some of Arch's lines, to be read "parrot-like."

47. White to Zanuck, copy, July 7, 1948, in NR-LC; Dunne to Zanuck, copy, Oct. 25, 1948, in PD-USC; and Dunne, "*Pinky*," revised, Jan. 12, 1949, in file 2391, USC.

48. White to Zanuck, July 7, 1948; Wilkins to White, 1948, on unconscious white prejudice toward activism in tandem with Dicey's approval of white superiority as in her raising Pinky as a white child, in file 2391, TCFA-UCLA.

49. Zanuck to White, copies to Jane White, Wilkins, Poppy Cannon, and Arthur Spingarn, 10 pp., Sept. 21, 1948, in NR-LC.

50. Zanuck to White, Sept. 21, 1948, in NR-LC; and Zanuck to "Dear Dudley," copy, Nov. 1, 1948, in PD-USC.

51. Nichols draft, Oct. 6, 1948, folder 2, Nichols papers, USC; compare with Dunne and Nichols "revised final script," March 5, 1949, in PD-USC.

52. Telephone memo, [Stephen] Jackson and Francis Harmon, March 31, 1948, 4 pp., in *Pinky* file, PCA-AMPAS.

53. Walter White to Poppy Cannon, Jan. 2, 19, [1949], in WW-JWJ, in which he also wrote, "The script of 'Quality' has been completely rewritten to meet our objections."

54. Jane White, "Suggested Changes and Additions to January 12, 1949, Screenplay of '*Pinky*,'" in file 2391, TCFA-UCLA and PD-USC; Zanuck to Dunne, Jan. 17, 1949; Dunne to Zanuck, Jan. 18, 1949; Zanuck to Jane White, Feb. 1, 1949; Dunne to Zanuck, Feb. 2, 1949, on "our little pals the Communists" opposing the film; "Recapitulations of Major Points Made 1/26/49 [*sic*] to Mr. Zanuck"; Dunne to Zanuck, Feb. 3, 1949, on "talky and confusing" *Lost Boundaries*, in PD-USC; *Var.*, Jan. 26, 1949, p. 26; and Feb. 16, 1949, p. 9.

55. Breen to Jason S. Joy, carbon, Feb. 28, 1949; Joy to Breen, March 2, 1949, in *Pinky* file, PCA-AMPAS; Dunne to Zanuck, Feb. 11, 1949, on Dunne's reservations toward Ford, in PD-USC; telephone interviews between Dunne and the author, Aug. 17, 1977, and Kazan, Oct. 29, 1976; Gussow, *Zanuck*, 179, Zanuck on Ford as case of "great" in one genre, "helpless in another"; Waters, *His Eye Is on the Sparrow*, 270–72.

56. Kazan's recall varies. See Kazan, *A Life* (New York, 1988), 374–76, for a biting appraisal of film and cast; in Kantor, Blacker, Kramer, *Directors at Work*,

147, he refers to Frontier; in Koszarski, *Hollywood Directors*, 258–68, he cites no eastern film life; in Ciment, *Kazan on Kazan*, 59–60, he is harsher; but see Robin Wood, "Elia Kazan Interview," *Movie* 19: 1–31; in interview between Kazan and the author, Middletown, Conn., summer 1985, he took a middle course while working on his autobiography; Thomas H. Pauly, *An American Odyssey: Elia Kazan and American Culture* (Philadelphia, 1983), 107–12, finding Hollywood slick; see also AA, April 23, 1949; LAS, Oct. 20, 1949; Bogdanovich, *Ford*, 84–85; telephone interview between Jeanne Crain and the author, July 1985, she thought *Pinky* a challenging opportunity and seemed to feel untapped as a source of the film's history.

57. PCA hoped to soften its bold angle by giving her a white relative; see Francis Harmon, memo, n.d., *Pinky* file, PCA-AMPAS; in ad copy, "She passed for white appeared in smaller type than the more conventional poignant story of a girl who fell hopelessly, desperately in love": see LAS, Dec. 8, 1949. *NYT Directory of the Film*, 104; *Sun* (South Africa), quoted, LAS, Nov. 30, 1950; CD, Nov. 26, 19, 5, 1949, Nov. 5 on "growing up"; Oct. 8, 1949; CE, Oct. 20, 27, 1949; NJ&G, Oct. 11, 1949; AA, Oct. 8, Sept. 24, 1949, for David Bethea and James Hicks praise; AN, Sept. 17, 1949; AA, April 23, June 11, 1949, for Levette; *Ebony*, Sept. 1949, pp. 23–25.

58. *Daily Graphic*, Nov. 25, 1949; NYT, Sept. 30, 1949, Crowther; *Mirror* (New York), Sept. 30, 1949; *Post* (New York), Sept. 30, 1949, Archer Winsten's "socially significant" phrase; *World-Telegram* (New York), Sept. 30, 1949, for Leo Mishkin's dismay over casting Crain; *Time*, Oct. 30, 1949; *Newsweek*, Oct. 30, 1949; and Dunne's signed piece on race and movies, clippings in *Pinky* file, PCA-AMPAS.

59. Jerome, *Negro in Film*, 23, 29, quoting Bob Ellis, CE; NR, Oct. 3, 1949, p. 23; *Daily Var.*, Sept. 30, 1949; Seymour Peck, *Daily Compass*, Sept. 30, 1949; *Var.*, Sept. 30, 1949; FD, May 6, 1949, in PD-USC; see also Theodore, "Negro in Hollywood," 87–88; in a rare critical recognition of *Pinky's* meaning see Russell Campbell, "The Ideology of the Social Consciousness Movie: Three Films of Darryl F. Zanuck," *QRFS* 3 (Winter 1978): 49–71, particularly: "The American capitalist system is flexible enough to absorb the rightful anger of its temporarily disadvantaged minorities without cracking apart at the seams"; Christopher John Jones, "Image and Ideology in Kazan's *Pinky*," *Literature/Film Quarterly* 9 (Summer 1981): 110–20, an appreciation of the moral dimension of casting Crain, who as Pinky could have chosen against being black. See also Kazan interview, Oct. 8, 1975, AFL/CAFS, on *Baby Doll*.

60. AA, Nov. 12, 1949, on Smith; Nov. 26, 1949; Harmon and Stephen Jackson, memo, n.d., on pending *Curley* case and politics; Jason Joy to Breen, March 2, 1949, reporting that Fox prepared for rejection in South, *Pinky* file, PCA-AMPAS; CD, Nov. 19, 26, June 21, July 22, 1949; Allen Rivkin to Walter White, March 24, 1952; White to Eric Johnston, Feb. 8, 1952; Robert Carter to White, July 8, 1952, in NR-LC.

61. Review of *Pinky* by "EBK," n.d.; Board of Directors minutes, Nov. 15, 1950; Panero Theatre Co., Delano, Calif., to Alex Harrison, Fox, Oct. 17, 1950, cc White; Harry G. Ballance, Atlanta, to Zanuck, Nov. 18, 1949, in NR-LC; Harry Levette to Harry Brand, Fox PR, copy, Feb. 11, 1950, in CB-CHS; Jones, "Ideology of the Social Consciousness Movie," 49–71, citing *Var.*, on balcony of Atlanta Roxy opening to blacks.

62. White to Zanuck, Nov. 5, 1949; Zanuck to White, Dec. 7, 1949, cited; and White in NYA, Nov. 1, 1949, in WW-JWJ.

63. Walter to Jane White, Jan. 29, 1949, JWJ-Yale, asking her to carry marked script to Zanuck: interview between Clarence Brown and the author, Palm Desert, Calif., Dec. 1976; telephone interview between Ben Maddow and the author, June 1970; Maddow to Pauline E. Degenfelder, March 27, 1972, lent by Maddow; Regina K. Fadiman, *Faulkner's Intruder in the Dust: Novel into Film* (Knoxville, 1978), 27–28.

64. Brown interview, Dec. 1976; and Schary, *Heyday*, 213, recalling "Brown buttonholed me and I was able to persuade Mayer . . . We bought the book."

65. *Oxford Eagle* clippings, CB—UT; Fadiman, *Intruder*, 32–33; Bruce Kawin, *Faulkner on Film* (New York, 1977), 40; and Brown and Maddow interviews, cited in note 63.

66. Moon to White, copy, Dec. 28, 1948; White to Schary, wire, Jan. 10, 1949; Schary to White, Jan. 12, 1949; Moon to William Wang, MGM, Nov. 25, 1949; White to Schary, copy, Feb. 24, 1949; Schary to White, Feb. 21, 1949, after speaking with Jane White, in NR-LC; Joseph L. Blotner, *Faulkner: A Biography* (New York, 1974), vol. 2, pp. 1157, 1277–78, 1284, on Faulkner's sale of rights for $40,000 (Kawin, *Faulkner*, p. 40, says $50,000) and agreement to work on script though never invited.

67. Clippings in CB-UT; Fadiman, *Intruder*, 32–36, 86; Maddow interview: Elzy's take never "in a written way"; Maddow to Degenfelder; Ellis quoted, Fadiman, *Intruder*, p. 36 and note 18.

68. Scripts in CB-UT.

69. *Oxford Eagle*, Oct. 20, 1949; CE, Nov. 17, 1949; *NYT Directory of Film*, 103; Jerome, *Negro in Hollywood Films*, 36–41; *Memphis Press-Scimitar*, Oct. 12, 1949; *Commercial Appeal* (Memphis), Oct. 12, 1949; *Nashville Banner*, Oct. 13, 1949; *Atlanta Journal*, Oct. 16, 1949; *Dallas News*, Oct. 12, 1949; *New Orleans Item*, Nov. 4, 1949; *Washington Daily News*, Jan. 26, 1950; *Washington Post*, Jan. 28, 1950; *Los Angeles Herald and Express*, *Cleveland Press*, Dec. 2, 1949; *Kansas City Star*, Jan. 18, 1949; *Columbus Dispatch*, Jan. 12, 1950; *Toledo Blade*, Dec. 16, 1949; *Rochester Times-Union*, April 8, 1949, etc., in CB-UT; and DW, Nov. 23, 1949.

70. Waring to Schary, copy, March 21, 1950; Schary to Brown, Nov. 29, 1949, in CB-UT, and in Fadiman, *Intruder*, 41; Ralph Ellison, *Shadow and Act* (New York, 1964), 264 ff.; CD, Nov. 12, 1949, on censors; March 18, April 8, 1950; serial ephemera in CB-UT; for black opinion, CD, March 18, 1950; Nov. 26, 1949; Feb. 25, 1950, for Lillian Scott and A. S. Young interview with Schary; AA, Nov. [?], 1949, on LaMar; Feb. 4, Jan. 29, 1950; *Ebony*, Dec. 1949, p. 7, on ad copy; *Herald-Tribune*, Nov. 13, 1949, on White as "weak, limp, nerve-frayed and exultant"; Moon to William Wang, Nov. 1949; Bobby Branch to Wilkins, undated; and Wilkins to Ludlow Werner, copy, Dec. 6, 1949 (after *Ebony*), in NR-LC.

71. On Robinson, Jules Tygiel, *Baseball's Great Experiment: Jackie Robinson and His Legacy* (New York, 1983); *Var.*, Jan. 25, 1950, pp. 6, 34, on his radio show; AN, Feb. 18, 1948, on preproduction; *Var.*, April 5, 1950, ad copy. In the movie, art imitates life as it ends with Robinson testifying on Americanism before Congress.

72. *Var.*, April 5, 1905, p. 23; *Christian Century*, April 21, 1950, p. 175; NYT, May 17, 1950; AN, Sept. 2, 1950; *Commonweal*, June 2, 1950, p. 198; *Time*, June 5, 1950, pp. 86–87; NR, June 12, 1950, pp. 16–17; *Compass* and DW, May 1950, in SCRBC.

73. Geist, *Pictures Will Talk*, 152 ff; Julian Johnson to Zanuck, Jan. 3 and Dec. 28, 1949, on producers and South; Michael Abel to Zanuck, Dec. 31, 1948, in file 2420, TCFA-UCLA; AA, Oct. 22, 1949; and CD, March 18, 1950.

74. *No Way Out* treatment, 112 pp., by Lesser Samuels; Yordan to Zanuck, and Zanuck to Yordan, March 22, 1949, in file 2420, TCFA-UCLA; Zanuck to Samuels, Feb. 1, 1949; Zanuck to Yordan, April 27, 1949, "confidential"; F. D. Langton to Zanuck, Feb. 9, 1949, on concept; Zanuck to "Pink" [Langton], Feb. 9, 1949; Langton to Zanuck, Feb. 26, 1949, on Kazan; Yordan, "First Draft continuity," April 15, 1949; draft 2420.4 after conference with Zanuck, April 18, 1949; dialogue taken from screen, July 26, 1950, all in file 2420, TCFA—UCLA.

75. Yordan-Zanuck correspondence, cited in note 74.

76. Sidney Poitier, *This Life* (New York, 1980), 126–33; CD, Aug. 13, 1949, on tests flown to Europe; AA, Oct. 22, 1949; CE, Oct. 6, 1949; Hoffman, *Poitier*, 15–83; *Var.*, April 28, 1958, p. 60; Ewers, *Poitier*, 65; NYT, Aug. 17, 1950.

77. Malcolm Ross, Fox, to White, July 31, 1950; release to branches, copy, Sept. 21, 1950, on "success"; Skouras to White, Sept. 5, 1950, thanks, in NR-LC.

78. Breen to Joy, Fox, carbon, Oct. 6, 1959; Joy to Breen, Nov. 3, 1950, enclosing Roger C. Foxx, Minneapolis, 20th Century–Fox, Sept. 12, 1950, but holding that hundreds of letters ran 99–1 in favor, all in PCA-AMPAS; White to Sidney Lopez, copy, Aug. 31, 1950, NR-LC, also seeing 1942 through *No Way Out* as a political continuum..

79. Carl Murphy to Eric Johnston, carbon, Oct. 20, 1950; Sydney R. Traub, MSCB, to White, Oct. 30, 1950, in NR-LC.

80. NYT, Aug. 17, July 30, 1950, in which Frederick O'Neal said "it reflected the conscience of the American people"; Arthur Knight, "The Negro in Films Today," *Films in Review* 1 (Feb. 1950): 14–19; sample of the trades in *No Way Out* file, PCA-AMPAS: HR, Aug. 2, 1950; *Daily Var.*, Aug. 2, 1950; *Var.*, Aug. 2, 1950; MPD, Aug. 2, 1950. On White, White to Elizabeth and Waties [Waring], July 21, 1950; Zanuck to White, July 31, 1950; White memo, n.d. [1950], in NR-LC. See also *Var.*, Aug. 9, 1950, clipping in GPJ-UCLA, praising Zanuck's attack on "troglodyte racists"; White to Zanuck, wire, quoted in AN, Aug. 12, 1950, on the film as sign of "maturation of the moving picture industry." Awards: PC, Oct. 7, 1950, CORE; CD, Aug. 26, 1950, Foreign Press Association; AN, Sept. 21, 1950, American Negro Theatre, and more. Interview between Ruby Dee and the author, Lebanon, Pa., Dec. 1969. For general black approval: AA, Sept. 9, Aug. 12, Oct. 14, 21, Aug. 26, 1950, quoting *NAG Newsletter;* CE, Aug. 25, 1950; PC, Aug. 12, 19, 26, Sept. 2, 23, July 22, 1950; CD, July 29, Aug. 26, 1950; LAS, Oct. 12, 1950; NJ&G, Sept. 2, 1950; NYT, Aug. 24, 1950.

81. Warren Miller in *Jewish Life*, undated clipping in SCRBC and in minutes, Oct. 18, 1950, box 11, MSCB, in which he argues for retitling as *Don't Hit Back* "for the out is clearly shown to be the way of servility, the way of competing with whites on the white man's terms"; see also AA, Sept. 23, 1950, for Mankiewicz's open letter in which he argues for liberals there can be no "happy ending" in movies; Jerome, *Negro in Hollywood Films*, 20, thought it a means "to

continue the pattern"; Manny Farber in NR, cited in *Negative Space*, 60, for "geeklike"; *Var.*, Aug. 2, 1950, p. 16, thought it "a long, wordy film with spotty prospects"; CE, Feb. 23, 1950; NYT, Aug. 20, 1950, in which Thomas Pryor thought they had "squandered" their punch; *New Statesman*, Sept. 30, 1950, pp. 322–23, for Gavin Lambert; *National Parent-Teacher Magazine*, Oct. 1950, p. 38; *Rotarian*, Dec. 1950, p. 38, which objected to its "psychopathic" treatment of racism; Wolfenstein and Leites, "Two Social Scientists View *No Way Out:* The Unconscious Versus the 'Message' in the Anti-Bias film," *Commentary*, Oct. 1950, pp. 388–89; and see also their *The Movies: A Psychological Study* (Glencoe, Ill., 1950); and Burke, "The Negro in Hollywood Films," 212 ff., in which he offers a variation on the theme of Dionysian vs. Apollonian, black vs. white, societies, in which Brooks is seen as Christian convert rather than pagan because of his dual ethical code, at once black and integrated.

82. AA, Aug. 12, 26, Sept. 9, Oct. 14, 21, 1950.

Chapter 9
Settling In, Settling For

1. Knight, *Liveliest Art*, 267; Jowett, *Film: The Democratic Art*, 337; Sklar, *Movie-Made America*, 267; Ceplair and Englund, *Inquisition in Hollywood*, 340; Leab, *From Sambo to Super Spade*, 135, on tension between moviemen and black activists; Higham and Greenberg, *Hollywood in the Forties*, 68; Pells, *Liberal Mind in a Conservative Age*, 307, on studios' timidity; Bogdanovich, *Fritz Lang in America*, 83–84, on Lang's "trouble"; *Var.*, Nov. 15, 1951, p. 2, on "clearances"; March 21, 1951, p. 2, on HUAC; Munson to Engel, copy, April 18, 1947, in LM-AHC-WY; Eels, *Ginger and Loretta*, 58–59, on Lela Rogers's scanning scripts for "red" propaganda; LeRoy, *Take One*, 157, "deplored the excesses" as well as the propaganda; *Var.*, March 12, 1951, p. 1, on WGA and Waldorf statement; *Vigil*, March 1949, copy in HH-AMPAS; in which also see Hopper to N. Peter Rathvon, RKO, Nov. 28, 1947, on "menace"; Siegfried Kracauer, "National Types as Hollywood Presents Them," *Public Opinion Quarterly* 13 (Spring 1949): 56–57.

2. Pechter, "Polonsky," 47–54; Zanuck to Lyman Munson, copy, Jan. 20, 1948, in LM-AHC-WY; Platt, "Hollywood Witchhunt," 24–30; Guy Endore, "Reflections," on being cut off from friends; Fidelifax, Inc., brochure [a detective agency], May 9, 1946; and Robert Donner to Hedda Hopper, April 9, 1951, alleging that Howard Duff belonged to "front" groups, both in HH-AMPAS.

3. Navasky, *Naming Names*, 192–94, on a black "clearing" process and William Marshall's report that Lena Horne worked but "little" before or after HUAC's days; Ashton, "Blacks in Film," 133, citing *Hollywood Citizen-News*, June 13, 1952; Fred Rinaldo, circular to members, box 40, Lawson papers, SIU; AA, May 5, 1951, in which Levette blamed Caleb Peterson for steering Horne into politics; AA, Aug. 26, 1951, on "infiltration of Reds into the script departments"; Louise Beavers's pleas to Hopper for relief from blacklisting, in HH-AMPAS; LAS, July 14, 1949, on Lee; CE, July 21, 1950, on Horne and HUAC; *Var.*, June 4, 1952, p. 35, on ACLU decision to represent Hazel Scott, allegedly blacklisted by Dumont network; on Reed Harris, Victor Roudin to Claude A. Barnett, March 24, 1952, in CB-CHS.

4. *I Posed as a Communist for the FBI*, script, working title, Oct. 1, 1950, p.

72; revised "final," Dec. 3, 1950, pp. 59, 62, and clipping in WBA-USC; see also Maurice and Matthew Rapf and Charles Palmer correspondence, 1950, in *Civil Rights Story* file, MGM-LD; and telephone interview between Maurice Rapf and the author, Dec. 1987, in which an intended film about peonage and lynching cases based upon Department of Justice files in which the agency cooperated came to an end only when the FBI denied further cooperation, not on the grounds of overt politics but simply because J. Edgar Hoover's staff were "not exactly friends of Dore Schary."

5. John Cogley, *Report on Blacklisting* [New York 1956], vol. 1, "The Movies," 282, 284; Erens, *Jew in American Cinema*, 197–98, cites Rivkin and *John Stone Report*, no. 25 (Jan. 30, 1951). For bleak or contemptuous sketches: Michael Wood, *America in the Movies* (New York, 1975); Peter Biskind, *Seeing Is Believing . . . the Fifties* (New York, 1983); Andrew Dowdy, *The Films of the Fifties: The American State of Mind* (New York, 1973); Gordon Gow, *Hollywood in the Fifties* (New York, 1971). On film and society: Paul Jensen, "The Return of Dr. Caligari: Paranoia in Hollywood," *Film Comment* 7 (Winter 1971–72): 36–45; Lawrence L. Murray, "Monsters, Spies, and Subversives: The Film Industry Responds to the Cold War," *Jump Cut* 9 (Oct.–Dec. 1975): 14–17; see also *Vigil, Firing Line*, and other rightwing ephemera and correspondence including that of "Operative 888," who reported on "pinkoes" back to the silent era, in HH-AMPAS. On analytical literature: William H. Whyte, Jr., *The Organization Man* (Garden City, 1956); Riesman et al., *The Lonely Crowd: A Study of the Changing American Character* (Garden City, 1950); A. C. Spectorsky, *The Exurbanites* (New York, 1955); Vance Packard, *The Status Seekers* (New York, 1959); and Sloan Wilson's novel, *The Man in the Gray Flannel Suit* (New York, 1956).

6. Robert F. Burk, *The Eisenhower Administration and Black Civil Rights* (Knoxville, 1984), 16–20, 23, 25, 90–91, 134. Said Eisenhower to his attorney general: "Aren't we better off staying out of it?"

7. Poitier, *This Life*, 336, 310, 272, 10, 16, 76–79, 125, 166.

8. NYT, Nov. 18, 1949, on Atlanta; AA, Dec. 30, 1950; *Var.*, Jan. 14, 1951, on Wilmington; Sept. 19, 1956, p. 2, on rock music "hooliganism" in UK; William A. Rossi, "The Booming Negro Market in Men's Shoes," *Boot and Shoe Recorder*, Sept. 1, 1961, pp. 36–39, on blacks' tastes and budgets; Barbara Jordan and Shelby Fearon, *Barbara Jordan: A Self-Portrait* (Garden City, 1979), 53, on crossover taste; James Gilbert, *A Cycle of Outrage: America's Reaction to the Juvenile Delinquent in the 1950s* (New York, 1986), chap. 11; *Var.*, May 26, 1954, p. 18, and May 5, 1954, p. 25, on black markets and WLIB commercials; *Var.*, Dec. 27, 1961, p. 6, on volatile "twist" audiences.

9. *Var.*, Dec. 15, 1954, p. 26, on "Rialto"; Aug. 12, 1953, p. 7, on art houses and black moviegoing habits.

10. Sherry H. Olson, *Baltimore: The Building of an American City* (Baltimore, 1980), 364–74; AA, Feb. 4, 1950, on *Cabin in the Sky;* April 1, 1950, on *Peanut Man;* May 20, June 10, 1950, on *Jackie Robinson Story;* Sept. 2, 1950, on *Boarding House Blues;* also DW, Aug. 18, 1949; and personal recollection of racial succession, 1950.

11. Walter White to Clem C. Ransome, Sept. 17, 1951, in NR-LC; Yoshi Tamaki to Mildred Martin, *Philadelphia Inquirer*, May 23, 1951, in Lektrafile, MOMA; Robert Davis piece, n.d., GPJ-UCLA; CE, Nov. 29, 1951, Poitier and segregated *Red Ball* locations; *Var.*, Oct. 7, 1964, p. 1, "vigor" of black boom;

July 13, 1960, p. 1, on sit-ins and bookers' wariness; May 16, 1962, p. 70, on "clientele"; Dec. 19, 1962, p. 5, on *Intruder;* John H. Moore to Cripps, Feb. 3, 1968, on "colored theatre," Rock Hill, S.C., billing *God's Little Acre* as "see how white folks live."

12. NYT, Nov. 25, 1949; *Sunday Compass*, July 30, 1950, on Walton, VF-SCRBC; "Films on Race Problems Rated Among Best Bets . . . ," *NAG Newsletter*, Dec. 1949, p. 2; AA, Jan. 28, 1950, on *Scottsboro* project; Dec. 16, 1950, "sepia artists"; etc.

13. "Ralph Bunche Goes to Hollywood," *Ebony*, July 1951, pp. 71–72; *CCNP Newsletter*, 1954–55, in CCNP-SCRBC, Charles Shorter to Roy Wilkins, May 3, 1955, NR-LC; *Var.*, Feb. 27, 1957, on NUL; LAS, Oct. 25, 1956, on CCNP; *Reporter* quoted in Spoto, *Stanley Kramer*, 53; *Var.*, Aug. 23, 1950, p. 20; NYT, March 15, Nov. 25, 1949, Crowther; CD, Oct. 23, 1949; AA, June 9, 1951, and Sept. 27, 1952.

14. CD, Oct. 23, 1952, Supreme Court overturns Marshall, Tex., *Pinky* case; *White Cargo* file, box 22, MSCB; Geoffrey Shurlock telephone memo, July 24, 1950, *Well* file, PCA-AMPAS, warning of "serious censorship difficulties" unless epithets cut; Sydney R. Traub, MSCB, to White, Nov. 14, 1951, citing AA, Nov. 10, 1951, in NR-LC, on black split over *The Well* in Maryland; *Var.*, July 25, 1951.

15. Joseph Breen to William Gordon, carbon, May 15, 1950, in *Bright Victory* file, PCA-AMPAS, indicating censor cognizance of "word-of-mouth"; MPD, May 15, 1950, *Jackie Robinson Story* file, PCA-AMPAS; and in same file, on Jersey City Italians' charge of an anti-Italian Hollywood "conspiracy," Breen to Eric Johnston, carbon, Nov. 2, 1950.

16. Woodruff D. Smith, *The Ideological Origins of Nazi Imperialism* (New York, 1986), chap. 1, argues that societies have "intellectual frameworks they inherit," a sort of "political sphere," an idea adapted from Clifford Geertz's idea of a "cultural system"; cited, pp. 10, 16, 17. See Gallup, *Gallup Polls*, vol. 3, pp. 1250–51, 1402, 1507, 1563–68, 1940–41, on various race-angled opinion samples, particularly on *Brown vs. Topeka Board of Education*.

17. Garfield to Curtiz, Jan. 16, 1950; Curtiz to Ranald MacDougall, carbon, memo, Feb. 10, 1950, complaining of new revisions that would confuse the movie; Jerry Wald to MacDougall, carbon, memo, April 5, 1950, asking more humor among the kids; and clipping, *Compass*, Oct. 8, 1950, on Peck, in file 2306, WBA-USC; and Ernest Hemingway, *To Have and Have Not* (New York, 1987) 10, 26, 38, 39, 68, 69, 76–77, 87, 105.

18. White to Poppy Cannon, Dec. 3, 1945, on Richard Condon's wish to talk over the Hollywood situation with White and Milton Sperling, a Warner in-law; Condon to White, copy, undated, on Sperling's kidding fears of the loss of Southern market, in WW-JWJ and NR-LC; "Young Man with a Horn," *Ebony*, Dec. 1949, pp. 51–55.

19. Milton Krims, *Lydia Bailey* treatment, April 9, 1947, on political backstory; conference notes on, April 17, 1947; Charles O'Neal, outline, June 24, 1950, laying backstory over establishing shots as song of a balladeer; and other notes on local color in file 2481, TCFA-UCLA; Jean Negulesco to Michael Blankfort, March 1, 1951, urging love story angle because lovers, he said, do not discuss love in terms of politics; see also Negulesco to Jules Schermer, Jan. 11, 1951, complaining of expository dialogue, in Blankfort papers, ML-BU; CE,

June 21, 1951, Ruby Berkeley Goodwin reported Dale Robertson got the lead when Tyrone Power felt upstaged by the original black story. "Lydia Bailey," *Ebony*, Jan. 1952, pp. 39–44; DW, Aug. 1, 1952; July 17, 1952; *Var.*, May 28, 1952, p. 6; and ephemera in GPJ-UCLA; AA, June 21, 1952, for White's failed bid to invite Paul Magloire of Haiti to Baltimore premiere. DW, July 17, 1952 for CPUSA split, Ben Levine liking Ken Renard's "wise" Toussaint; Platt chiding it for Blankfort, HUAC "fingerman," and its flawed slavery sequences; and Jerome admiring it to some degree as "a new tactical concession from the enemy . . . the racist ruling class."

20. Anderson interview, June 1970; AA, Jan. 3, 1953, for ad; *Var.*, Sept. 5, 1951; CD, Aug. 25, 1951; *Var.*, May 30, 1951, p. 4, on UA; for black division, CE, June 21, 1951; AA, Nov. 10, 1951; MSCB analysis card; minutes, Aug. 20, 1952, and Nov. 1951 board meetings, listing black attendance; Sydney R. Traub to White, Nov. 14, 1951, refusing to cut "inflammatory" words; White to Traub, Nov. 12, 1951, dismissing black "hypersensitivity" to "important" film, in NR-LC; "Deep is the Well," *Ebony*, Feb. 1951, pp. 38–42.

21. DW, April 3, 1951; *Var.*, April 25, 1951, p. 6; Ashton, "Blacks in Film," 172–74.

22. From 1950 through the 1960s *Ebony* each month and *Variety* almost weekly gave space to small changes in portrayal and importance of black roles that added up to a swelling of numbers as well as incremental variations. See for example: "Frank Silvera," *Ebony*, March 1952, pp. 51–52, for his subsequent roles as Asians, Mexicans, Spaniards, and so on. "The Egyptian," *Ebony*, Aug. 1954, p. 83 ff.; *Var.*, Oct. 10, 1956, p. 5, on *Ten Commandments* and on *The Joe Louis Story* use of Schmeling as heavy whose victory made "trouble" in Harlem; April 7, 1954, p. 5, on "passive resistance" of Southern bookers to black biopics; Dec. 24, 1952, p. 6, on Muriel Smith as Aicha in *Moulin Rouge;* Jan. 6, 1954, p. 52, on blacks as "themselves" in *The Glenn Miller Story;* May 25, 1956, p. 6, for Isabel Randolph cast as maid called "Mrs."; LAS, March 5, 1959, on Duke Ellington scoring *Anatomy of a Murder; Var.*, June 11, 1952, p. 18, on B-movie biopic of Stephen Foster with Louise Beavers as, perhaps, the last "Mammy"; on *Show Boat* tabloid, Haskins, *Lena*, 100–01; *Ebony*, June 1958, p. 76 ff., on *South Pacific* and its liberal hymn "You've Got to Be Carefully Taught"; "The Member of the Wedding," *Ebony*, Dec. 1952, pp. 47–51; Fred Zinnemann to Cripps, Dec. 24, 1970; Louis G. Giannetti, "The Member of the Wedding," *Literature/Film Quarterly* 4 (Winter 1976): 28–38, judged it "one of the neglected minor masterpieces."

23. LAS, July 17, 1952, on MGM's "building Harry"; corroborated by telephone, Schary to Cripps, Feb. 7, 1979; Schary, *Heyday*, 258; Sol [Baer Fielding?] to Schnee, wire, April 23, 1953, good reviews save for *Post;* Howard Strickling to Howard Dietz, wire, April 23, 1953, on NUL award; Dietz to Strickling, April 21, 1953, on Christopher medal; Velma Allen to Metro, March 26, 1953, on black society; Vroman to S. B. Fielding, March 25, 1953, on Maxwell AFB, in file 1600, *See How They Run*, MGM-LD; Wesley B. Brazier to Lester Granger, May 5, 1953, on film that had to be sold to activist groups"; Brazier to "Guich" Parris, June 16, 1953, on Los Angeles NUL sending 5000 invitations; "Guich" to Brazier, copy, May 19, 1953, on Southern "appeal," in "Los Angeles 1948–1961" file, box 42, series 5, NUL-LC; Mittinell Wheeler to Parris, n.d., on donating a white Atlanta theatre for an integrated premiere, in *Bright Road* file,

PCA-AMPAS. Reception: CD, May 16, March 21, 1953, preview; *Var.*, April 8, 1953, p. 6, quoted; "See How They Run," *Ebony*, April 1953, pp. 43–48; AA, May 9, 16, 1953, on "warm" story; *Catholic World*, May 1953, p. 145, good white review; tape roll 1, P451/408, Belafonte British interview lent by Frank Holland, Aston Clinton, Bucks: and telephone interview, July 7, 1992, between Harry Belafonte and the author.

24. "Dorothy Dandridge's Greatest Triumph [*Carmen Jones*]," *Ebony*, July 1955, p. 37 ff.; Hatch quoted in Ashton, "Blacks in Film" 157–58; James Baldwin, "*Carmen Jones:* The Dark Is Light Enough," in *Notes of a Native Son* (Boston, 1965), 46–54; and "Life Straight in de Eye," *Commentary*, Jan. 1955, pp. 74–75; *Hue*, July 28, 1954, pp. 22–26; *Var.*, Feb. 23, 1955, p. 3, on Southern "reaction"; Oct. 20, 1954, pp. 12–13, on black and European prospects; Oct. 13, 1954, p. 7, on three-city premiere; "Do Negroes Have a Future in Hollywood?" *Ebony*, Dec. 1955, p. 24, in light of *Jones*'s glamor; CD, July 16, 1955, on *Pravda* regarding as "trash"; passed MSCB after three viewings; script drafts in file 2591, TCFA-UCLA.

25. Bertram Bloch to David Brown, April 25, 1955, on Zanuck's motives; Zanuck to Eric Ambler, June 6, 1955, on South; Frank McCarthy to Zanuck, [April 19, 1955]; Ambler to Zanuck, May 17, 1955, on compromise, in file 3006, TCFA-UCLA.

26. Alec Waugh, *Island in the Sun: A Story of the 1950s Set in the West Indies* (New York, 1955), was laden with such unfilmable expository dialogue.

27. Moseley, *Zanuck*, 288–91, sees Zanuck as bold and the studio as cautious.

28. Zanuck to Al [?], Nov. 29, 1955, 6 pp., on politics; Zanuck and Rossen, memo, dictated Paris, Aug. 11, 1956, on color, feelings over theory; Zanuck and Alfred Hayes, story conference, June 1, 1956, on premature racial film, in file 3006, TCFA-UCLA; Gibson to Col. Frank McCarthy, July 19, 1956, *Island* file, PCA-AMPAS; Fontaine, *No Bed of Roses*, 245; *Var.*, July 10, 1957, p. 1, Bogle, *Toms*, 172; Nunnally Johnson to Robert Goldstein, June 24, 1957, in Dorris Johnson and Ellen Leventhal, eds., *The Letters of Nunnally Johnson* (New York, 1981), 151.

29. *Var.*, July 10, 1957, p. 1; "Island in the Sun," *Ebony*, July 1957, 33–37.

30. Johnson, *Letters*, 151; *Var.*, July 10, 1957, p. 1; Fontaine, *No Bed of Roses*, 245.

31. "Island in the Sun," *Ebony*, July 1957, pp. 33–37; Roth in NR, July 29, 1957, p. 21; Geoffrey Shurlock to J. J. Cohn, carbon, May 13, 1955, *Island* file, PCA-AMPAS; fan letters in MSCB; *Var.*, July 10, 1957, 1, for Belafonte's opinion.

32. Interview between Max Youngstein and the author, Bel Air, Calif., Aug. 1980; Belafonte interview, roll 1, P451/408 tape; Polonsky interview, Aug. 1977, on McGivern's book as "an exciting premise"; Belafonte-Cripps telephone interview, July 7, 1992.

33. Polonsky, Aug. 1977, said "John Oliver Killens had nothing to do with *Odds Against Tomorrow*" except lending his name; confirmed by Youngstein, Aug. 1980; Killens in conversation, Nov. 15, 1978, claimed authorship of the draft Belafonte pitched to UA; in article by Almena Lomax, *Los Angeles Tribune*, in GPJ-UCLA, Killens apologizes for changes made by others, a story retold to Morgan State University students, Nov. 15, 1978; telephone interview between

Belafonte and the author, July 7, 1992; in Killens's papers, ML-BU, there is no file on *Odds Against Tomorrow;* Polonsky's diary, vol. 41, Jan. 17, 1958, "making progress each day"; vol. 48, Nov. 14, 1959, "except for Wise's [end], mine"; "Movie Maker Belafonte," *Ebony,* July 1959, p. 94 ff.; Gabe Sumner to James Gould, UA, copy, July 22, 1959, in Wise papers, box 14, USC, makes no mention of Killens; Youngstein affidavit, March 29, 1979, notarized, Vincenza S. Bartolotta, notary, attesting she paid Polonsky $35,000 "for writing" and for "changes" in *Odds Against Tomorrow,* author's possession.

34. Wise to Forrest Johnson, copy, Dec. 13, 1958, calling for "new end," in Wise papers box 14, USL, perhaps prodded by Geoffrey Shurlock to Philip Stein, Feb. 18, 1959, objecting to "nigger" and to Southerner's suicide, in PCA-AMPAS; Almena Lomax clipping, cited in note 33; Hollis Alpert, "D for Effort," SRL, Oct. 3, 1959, p. 29; *Var.,* Oct. 7, 1959; "Movie Maker Belafonte," *Ebony,* July 1959, p. 94, and trades, in *Odds* file, PCA-AMPAS.

35. *Var.,* April 29, 1953, p. 7; July 22, 1953, p. 5; Sept. 22, 1954, p. 5, quoted; Nov. 10, 1954, p. 3, on TV; April 29, 1959, p. 4, on selling off realty; March 12, 1958, p. 5, on "runaways"; Gilbert Seldes, *The Public Arts* (New York, 1956), 193, quoting Lardner; Martin S. Dworkin, "The New Negro on the Screen," *Progressive,* Oct. 1960, pp. 39–41, and issues through Feb. 1961.

36. For racial sameness in action see *Detective Story* script, Feb. 3, 1951, cast list, no race prescribed; Feb. 19, 1951, yellow page 26, prescribed "a Negro policeman," in William Wyler papers, file 4, box 31, UCLA; *Bright Victory* script, 1950, pp. 50, 62, 120–21, in Mark Robson papers, UCLA; Jerry Wald to Jack Warner, Feb. 1, 1949, on *Storm Warning,* in file 8246, WBA-USC; character sketch of Burt Rainey, Heisler papers, UCLA; interview between John Ford and the author, Beverly Hills, Calif., June 1970, regarded *Rutledge* as a tribute to blacks, a point uncritically taken in Andrew Sinclair, *John Ford* (New York, 1979), 190–92.

37. Charles Affron, "Performing Performing: Irony and Effect," *Cinema Journal* 20 (Fall 1980): 42–52, sees Peola as violator of racial etiquette, an outlaw, while other blacks are "acceptable," belying the contradictions she represented; Jon Halliday, *Sirk on Sirk* (New York, 1972), 132, finds Sirk "embraced melodrama," while in conversation, Sept. 3, 1972, London, he spoke to me of using it merely to circumvent Universal studio practices.

38. These bits and dozens more could be quite small though nonetheless jarring. In *Tender Is the Night,* Dick Diver in a Paris saloon, unable to compose, watches helplessly as Earl Grant insouciantly, glibly improvises on the house piano, thus establishing wordlessly the waning of Diver's powers.

39. Kazan interview, AFL/CAFS, Oct. 8, 1975, pp. 66–67, on "scornful" blacks like "the fools of Shakespeare"; *Post* (New York), Dec. 23, 1956, liked the "retainers," while Hazel LaMarr, LAS, Jan. 17, 1957, thought them vulgar; "The sound and the Fury," *Ebony,* May 1959, p. 127 ff.

40. *The Imposter,* print in BFI; "The Mountain is Green," *UNESCO Courier,* Sept. 1950, p. 10, AAS; *Aventure Malgache* (1943), print in BFI; see also *Service Cinematographique de l'Armee,* footage of Josephine Baker entertaining French troops in Africa, print in BFI; see also Truffaut, *Hitchcock,* 249; *Var.,* Nov. 26, 1947, p. 11, and Jan. 15, 1947, p. 18; *La Putain respecteuse* file, and *Var.* clip judging it "way off" and giving mere "lip service" to liberalism, in MSCB; NYT, July 11, 1957, "age had withered" it.

41. Pierre Laprohon, *The Italian Cinema* (New York, 1972), 87–92, 187, quotes Borde, Bouissy; Cesare Zavattini, *Zavattini: Sequences from a Cinematic Life*, trans. William Weaver (Englewood Cliffs, 1959), 133, 235–36, 248; *Paisan* in BFI and Cineteca d'Italia, Torino; see also Jose Luis Guarner, *Roberto Rossellini*, trans. Elizabeth Cameron (London, 1970), 20; Joseph Foster, "Italian Story," *Masses & Mainstream*, May 1948, p. 85.

42. Michael Silverman, "Italian Film and American Capital, 1947–1951," in Patricia Mellencamp and Philip Rosen, eds., *Cinema Histories, Cinema Practices*, vol. 4 in "American Film Institute Monograph series" (Frederick, Md., 1984), 35–43, traces the growing conservatism of Italian film to the influx of American money though based on a single interview. *Vivere in Pace* (1947) and *Senza Pieta* (1948), both in Cineteca d'Italia; *Agee on Film*, vol. 1, pp. 283–84; Herb Tank, DW, Nov. 25, 1947, disagreed; CD, March 25, 1950; *Senza Pieta* analysis card and minutes, Oct. 11, 1950, on low "tone," MSCB; "Black Star of Italian Movies," *Ebony*, Nov. 1951, pp. 71–73; "Senza Pieta," *Ebony*, Nov. 1948, pp. 62–65; CD, Aug. 27, 1950; "Paisan," *Ebony*, April 1958, p. 19; AN, Jan. 8, 1949; *Var.*, Feb. 11, 1948, p. 14; Feb. 16, 1949, p. 3; see also Mayer, *Merely Colossal*, 218, 221, 233; on *Angelo:* AA, Jan. 13, 19, 1952; Aug. 18, 1951, quoted; on *Toxi:* "Shirley Temple of Germany," *Ebony*, Jan. 1953, p. 67 ff.; *Var.*, Sept. 17, 1952, p. 6; and "Was ist eigentlich mit Taxi geworden?" *Gong* 7:15 ff. On Dunham, Giovannella Zannoni, *Catalogue of Existing Film of and by Katherine Dunham* (Carbondale, Ill., 1973); see also CD, Sept. 1, 1951; "Anna's Sin," *Ebony*, March 1954, pp. 33–37; "Mambo," *Ebony*, Dec. 1954, pp. 83–85; "Miss Dunham Trains Dancers for New Film" *Ebony*, Sept. 1958, p. 121 ff. For sample of *Maciste* and *Ercole* titles see Lo Duca, *L'Eroticisme du cinema* (Paris, 1962), vol. 1, p. 62, and vol. 3, p. 79; Leprohon, *Italian Cinema*, 175–76; Lo Duca, vol. 1, p. 124, holds that colonialist films like *Les Conquerants solitaires* (1952) featured "le blanc deshabille" as well as the naked black women of American convention.

43. Mark Koenigil, *Movies and Society: Sex, Crime, and Censorship* (New York, 1962), 95–96, on colonial view of African filmgoers. *Colonial Cinema* 6 (Dec. 1948): 90 ff.; "Colonial Film Unit . . . in the West Indies," *Colonial Cinema* 9: (June 1951): 40 ff.; "Demonstration Teams in Uganda," *Colonial Cinema* 8 (March 1950): 3 ff.; Norman Spurr, "The Use of Disney's Hookworm Film [in] . . . Uganda," *Colonial Cinema* 8 (Dec. 1950): 28 ff.; and other issues. *God's Chillun* and other colonial titles in National Film Archive, *Catalogue of Viewing Copies* (London, 1951).

44. Walter Reade-Sterling program notes; Lovell and Hillier, *Studies in Documentary*, 60–61; *Var.*, Jan. 23, 1952, p. 6, on *Outcast of the Islands* and censor; *My Song Goes Forth* print in BFI.

45. *Daybreak at Udi* and *Drums for a Holiday* in BFI; clippings, VF-SCRBC; NYT, June 2, 1950; DW, June 2, 1950; NR, June 12, 1950, pp. 16–17; NYT, Feb. 6, 1952; Oct. 2, 1949; *Ebony*, Oct. 1951, pp. 59–61; and Walter White to staff, July 24, 1951, in NR-LC.

46. Charles Barr, *Ealing Studios* (London, 1977), 117; George Perry, *Forever Ealing: A Celebration . . .* (London, 1981), 150; *Var.*, Feb. 28, 1951, p. 18; minutes, June 9, 1951; Sydney R. Traub to H. S. Taylor, carbon, Dec. 6, 1951, in MSCB; clippings: *Today's Cinema*, Feb. 15, 1951; HR, Aug. 7, 1951; *Var.*, Feb. 28, 1951; Kenneth Bates to Breen, carbon, Aug. 25, 1951; agreed to

cuts in Breen to George M. Thornton, July 25, 1951, all in PCA-AMPAS. E. H. Rea in AA, Feb. 23, 1952, a sample of UK film.

47. Telephone interview between Dickinson and the author, Aston Clinton, Bucks, June 1979.

48. Print in BFI; "Film Parade," *Ebony*, Oct. 1946, P. 18; Dickinson-Cripps interview; Hughes to White, July 27, 1946; A. B. Spingarn to White, July 25, 1946; Poppy Cannon to White, July 25, 1946; Louis Martin to White, July 25, 1946; Eleanor Roosevelt to White, July 25, 1946; Lewis Gannett to White, July 25, 1946; White to Cannon, copy, July 30, 1946, poll results to be given to J. Arthur Rank, in NR-LC. *Var.*, Dec. 4, 1946, p. 1, on poll; July 24, 1946, p. 14; *Spectator*, July 26, 1946, p. 87; AA touted it in rerelease, July 24, 1952.

49. DW, June 2, 1950; "Pool of London," *Ebony*, Oct. 1951, 59–61; *Var.*, Feb. 28, 1951; Walter White to staff, memo., July 24, 1951, in NR-LC.

50. Thomas Cripps, "*Native Son* in the Movies," in David Ray and Robert M. Farnsworth, eds., *Richard Wright: Impressions and Perspectives* (Ann Arbor, 1973), 101–16; NYT, May 21, 1950; Michel Fabre, *The Unfinished Quest of Richard Wright*, trans. Isabel Barzun (New York, 1973), 212, 261–62, 272; Francis Harmon to Robert Hakim, carbon, June 16, 1941, in Hakim file, PCA—AMPAS, on "serious difficulties . . . of political censorship" fearing to "fan the fires of race prejudice" and to spread communism; *Var.*, Aug. 13, 1951; MPD, Aug. 20, 1951. "Dick" Wright to Houseman, April 28, 1941, on profits, Houseman papers, UCLA; *Var.*, March 26, 1941, p. 52, praise for "grim" play; Feb. 19, 1941, p. 49; Oct. 8, 1941, p. 51; Aug. 20, 1941, p. 43, on profit; Wright on film cited from Harry Birdoff in Constance Webb, *Richard Wright: A Biography* (New York, 1968), 293, 186–89. Log of state censor actions, PCA-AMPAS: Ohio, Pennsylvania, New York cut it. See also CD, July 21, 1951; Feb. 2, 9, 1952.

51. Print in LC; *Var.*, April 25, 1951, p. 14, "underhand stab at the U.S."

52. AN, June 23, 1951; ad mattes, Cripps, "Native Son in the Movies"; LAS, Aug. 16, 1951; NYT, June 18, 1951; *Commonweal*, June 29, 1951, p. 286; CE, Aug. 16, 1951; LAS, Dec. 14, 1951, citing Wright; CD, Oct. 1, 1949, casting; CD, Sept. 2, 1950, Chicago locations; "Native Son Filmed in Argentina," *Ebony*, Jan. 1951, pp. 82–86. *Daily Compass*, June 18, 1951; NYT, June 24, 1951; DW, June 21, 1951, SCRBC; many NAACP responses; see, for example, Franklin H. Williams to White, Oct. 8, 1951, in NR-LC. Revival review: *Berkeley Barb*, Dec. 7–13, 1973, "honesty and sensitivity."

53. Telephone interview between the author and Janet Green (June 1979) and Yvonne Mitchell (London, June 1979). Mitchell liked working in it because of its antibigotry stance. Green had written "on spec" and thought it hard to sell without masking its "social problem" aspect; though mixed in reception, she thought it had done well in U.S. *Ebony*, Dec. 1959, p. 51; LAS, Aug. 23, 1959; *Commonweal*, Oct. 16, 1959, p. 76.

54. *Var.*, Aug. 7, 1957, p. 1; Sept. 7, 1955, p. 6, on *The Woman for Joe:* May 8, 1957, p. 6, on *Sea Wyf;* June 18, 1958, p. 6, on *The Wind Cannot Read;* May 27, 1959, p. 6, and June 11, 1958, p. 11, on *Calypso;* June 17, 1959, p. 6, on *The Heart of a Man*.

55. *Var.*, Jan. 27, 1961, p. 13.

56. Roger Ebert, LAT, Nov. 30, 1969, quoting Peters; interview between Peters and the author, Hollywood, June 1970, in which he hoped *The McMasters* would introduce a virile male; *Breaking Point*, a play source for *The Hill*, Jan. 3,

1953; and script draft, Feb. 1964, pp. 52, 59, in file 1780, WBA-USC; *NYT Film Directory*, 150; *Var.*, Jan. 27, 1960, p. 13, on Cannes and "clicks" in Paris for *Orfeo Negro*.

57. Richard Thompson, "Thunder Road: Maudit—'The Devil Got Him First' (1969)," in Todd McCarthy and Charles Flynn, eds., *Kings of the B's: Working within the Hollywood System* (New York, 1975), 207.

58. Zanuck to Philip Dunne, June 26, 1952, in PD-USC; Jensen, *Fritz Lang*, 133–34, Lang exonerated Indians of marauding by revealing attackers as Confederate renegades in mufti.

59. Daves to Cripps, March 2, 1971; "Broken Arrow," *Ebony*, Sept. 1950, p. 3; CD, July 15, 1950, interview with Alfred A. Duckett; White to Zanuck, copy, June 8, 1950, and June 14, 1950, in NR-LC.

60. The best study of *Broken Arrow* is Angela Aleiss, "Hollywood's Idea of Postwar Assimilation: Indian/White Attitudes in *Broken Arrow*" (M.A., Columbia, 1985); see also John E. O'Connor, *The Hollywood Indian: Stereotypes of Native Americans in Films* (Trenton, 1980), the first scholarly effort to study studio records as a source for the subject.

61. Schary *Heyday*, 147–48, on Selznick; Zanuck to Philip Dunne, June 26, 1952, in PD-USC, on *Ramona;* see *Sunburst* outline in James Warner Bellah papers, ML-BU; O'Connor, *Hollywood Indian*, p. 47, on *Devil's Doorway; Var.*, Jan. 20, 1954, p. 6, on *Taza;* April 3, 1957, p. 6, on "honorable" Indian of *War Drums;* Feb. 5, 1958, p. 20, on *Fort Bowie* and *Gun Fever; Drumbeat* file, WBA-USC; *Var.*, May 19, 1954, p. 6, on *Yellow Tomahawk* and *Drums across the River;* Oct. 12, 1955, p. 22, on *Apache Woman;* June 30, 1954, p. 6, on *Apache;* Nov. 11, 23, 1955, p. 6, on *Vanishing American* remake; April 30, 1958, p. 6, on *The Light in the Forest.*

62. Alan LeMay to Agnes L. Tucker, copy, May 8, 1957, LeMay papers, UCLA; Madsen, *Huston*, p. 180; Nolan, *Huston*, 176; *Var.*, March 30, 1960, p. 6; *Spectator*, June 17, 1960, p. 884; Peter Wollen, "The Auteur Theory," in Bill Nichols, ed., *Movies and Methods: An Anthology* (Berkeley, 1976), 537–39, on *The Searchers;* Patrick Ford to Bernard Smith, copy, Jan. 21, 1963, in Ford papers, Lilly Library, Indiana University, on wishing to remain true to his father's vision of *Cheyenne Autumn;* V. F. Perkins, "Cheyenne Autumn," *Movie* 12 (Spring 1965): 36–37, on recut that made it one the "great ruins"; *Var.*, April 25, 1962, p. 6, on *Geronimo* and its "literate" Indians.

63. *Var.*, Oct. 31, 1956, p. 31, on Marx's TV *Broken Arrow;* Oct. 5, 1955, p. 31, on *Brave Eagle*, CBS "sustaining" show with "reverse english" Indian hero; Nov. 1, 1961, p. 56, on *The Dispossessed*, Westinghouse "special" on Indian plight "parallel to some contemporary social problems."

64. "Dad" [Zanuck] to Richard Zanuck, wire, March 25, 1958, on *Broken Lance* [*sic*] as personal project; Philip Dunne to Buddy Adler, March 14, 1958, moved by; Arthur Kramer to Adler, Feb. 27, 1958, with producers' report; Julian Johnson to Arthur, Feb. 24, 1958, on timeliness; Arthur Kramer to Ted Strauss, Feb. 21, 1958; Herbert Bayard Swope to Arthur Kramer, wire, March 3, 1958; Kramer to Adler, producers' report, Feb. 27, 1958, citing Weisbart; Weisbart to Adler, June 2, 1960, on adding songs; Wentzle Ruml III to Richard Brown, May 19, 1960, on postponing Pacer's death and building pitch; Charles Einfeld to Weisbart, Nov. 7, 1960; Don Siegel to Harry Brand, copy, Oct. 13, 1960, in TCFA-UCLA; "Working within the System: Interview with Don Siegel," *Movie*

15: 1–2, 9; Alan Lovell, *Don Siegel: American Cinema* (London, 1975), 56; Stuart M. Kaminsky, *Don Siegel: Director* (New York, 1974), 148–49, asserting Johnson had written it for Brando; Johnson to Cecil Johnson, June 24, 1960, in Johnson and Leventhal, *Letters*, 185, seeming distant, referring to Huffaker as "the fellow who is arranging the script"; *Var.*, Dec. 21, 1960, p. 6.

65. Lovell, *Siegel*, 56; revised *Flaming Lance*, Aug. 8, 1960, p. 41, in TCFA-UCLA; Thompson, "Thunder Road," on its following corroborated in Baltimore bookings.

66. Doc Young, "The Queen of Slave Roles," LAS, Aug. 27, 1957; Oct. 15, 1959, on need for "upbeat" black roles; Oct. 22, 1959; *Var.*, March 3, 1965, p. 6; Sept. 14, 1960, pp. 18, 20.

67. *Var.*, March 18, 1953, p. 34, and June 12, 1968, quoting respectively Edward Madden (NBC) and Brock Peters; telephone interviews between Albert Zugsmith and the author, June 1970 and Feb. 1988.

68. *Los Angeles Tribune*, March 28, 1958, on Cole, working to end "old stereotype . . . without making controversial or message pictures"; "St. Louis Blues," *Ebony*, May 1958, p. 27, judged "one of the top," but missed Handy; *Var.*, April 9, 1958, p. 6; on production, telephone interview between Allen Reisner and the author, Feb. 21, 1988.

69. Zugsmith interviews, 1970, 1988, also guessed MGM made its nut despite burying.

70. DW, Aug. 27, 1945, on stage *Anna; Var.*, April 11, 1956, p. 64, revival; Nov. 19, 1959, p. 10, on Kitt's "superficial" reading; April 15, 1959, p. 10, quoting Will Jones; Yordan interview, June 1970, regarded it as gritty naturalism; *Var.*, Sept. 9, 1953, p. 71, *Giant* tryout, Philadelphia; Jan. 31, 1957, West Coast company; "Take a Giant Step," *Ebony*, Sept. 1959, p. 48; Philip T. Hartung, *Commonweal*, Oct. 16, 1959, p. 76; *Var.*, Dec. 9, 1959, two reviews; April 27, 1960, p. 15, UA's sloughing it off; Alyce Key clipping, GPJ—UCLA, on internal friction; Mark A. Reid, "The U. S. Black Family Film," *Jumpcut*, #36 [May 1991], 81–88, a well researched piece on this subject.

71. AA, Aug. 5, 1950; Sept. 9, 1950, on indenture; *Ebony*, July 1951, p. 57; CD, Oct. 28, 1950, on Lee; May 5, 1951, for denials of treatment; Poiter, *This Life*, chap. 9; *Var.*, June 21, 1950, p. 8, on signing; Lawson, undated memo for file, asserting authorship for "friend"; and George [Wilburn?] to Lawson, March 18, 1949, box 40, Lawson papers, SIU; Barbara Duffin, "Sidney Poitier," Morgan seminar paper, pp. 1, 10, on "punch"; Walter Reade-Sterling press kit for critical sample; NYT, Jan. 24, 1952; CE, June 23, 1952, Bob Ellis column; AA, Feb. 2, 1952, James Hicks's praise; March 7, 1953, benefit; Guichard Parris to NUL staff, Oct. 31, 1952, in box 1, series 5, NUL-LC; telephone interview between Poitier and the author, March 1981.

72. "Red Ball Express," *Ebony*, June 1952, pp. 51–53; CD, April 12, 1952; CE, Nov. 1, 1951; AA, May 24, 1952; *Var.*, Jan. 20, 1954, p. 18, on "soapboxing." *Var.*, April 11, 1956, p. 7, and Wellman, *A Short Time for Insanity*, 97, on *Goodbye My Lady;* Poitier, *This Life*, 174–75, on roles' "significance." Paul Meyersberg, "Richard Brooks," *Movie* 12 (Spring 1965): 10–12; NR, Oct. 21, 1957, pp. 21–22, on *Something of Value*. "Mark of the Hawk," *Ebony*, April 1958, p. 91 ff.; *Var.*, Feb. 12, 1958, p. 6, on "spotty" prospects; June 12, 1957, p. 4, on writing off "Dixie": Poitier interview on his lagging fees. LAS, March 13, 1958, star bio; Feb. 26, 1959, Doc Young; Lerone Bennett, "Hollywood's First

Negro Movie Star: Sidney Poitier," *Ebony*, May 1959, 100–108, on Ruby Dee's assertion that "the world is now ready"; *Var.*, May 1, 1957, p. 3, Poitier sidebar; Poitier cited, transcript of Pandro S. Berman conversation, n.d., file 1837, MGM-LD; LAS, Sept. 28, 1961, *Paris Blues;* LAS, Sept. 1, 1960, and "All the Young Men," *Ebony*, Aug. 1960, p. 83 ff., on producer; Beverly Linet, *Ladd: The Life . . .* (New York, 1979), 236–37, on tension between Ladd and Poitier; *Var.*, June 17, 1964, on *The Long Ships;* "Band of Angels," *Ebony*, Sept. 1957, p. 58 ff; Kenneth Cox to W. L. Guthrie, Feb. 18, 1957, on segregation; Charles "Chick" Williams to Jack Warner, July 11, 1957, on black consultant; Geoffrey Shurlock, PCA, to Warner, Feb. 8, 1957, on unacceptable sex between master and slave, in file 835, WBA-USC; *Var.*, July 10, 1957, p. 5, on "Dixie."

73. Schary, *Heyday*, 278–86; interview between Millard Kaufman and the author, Hollywood, June 1970; "Scott" [Meredith] to "Evan" [pseud. of Sal Lobino], Feb. 25, 1954, on *Journal;* Hunter to "Scott," May 10, 1954, seven days before *Brown* decision, arguing for cuts of black skin in "unfavorable light," Evan Hunter papers, ML-BU; Brooks AFI/CAFS seminar, May 25, 1977, on Eddie Mannix, who thought it "red," and $380,000 nut; Poitier, *This Life*, 171–75; Brooks-Cripps interview, June 1970.

74. Schary, *Heyday*, 285–86; Brooks-Cripps interview, Dec. 1976, on Italy, MPPA.

75. Schary, *Heyday*, p. 286, on earnings; "Blackboard Jungle," *Ebony*, May 1955, pp. 87–93, on black reception; praise sample, in PCA-AMPAS; preview cards in MGM-LD; HR, Feb. 2, 1955, in particular for conservative Jack Moffitt review. *Var.*, July 13, 1955, p. 7, on censors in Atlanta; Aug. 31, 1955, p. 2, on Venice; Pandro Berman to "Red" [Maurice Silverman], MGM, copy, May 5, 1965, on Luce as "useful," in file 1837, MGM-LD; Robinson McLilvaine, State Dept., to Arthur Loew, Sept. 19, 1955, in *State Department Bulletin* 33 (Oct. 3, 1955): 537, denying Luce had acted on behalf of State; Luce to Hedda Hopper, Nov. 21, 1955, claiming hundreds supported her; Luce to Mrs. Ralph K. Merriam, Oct. 24, 1955, admitted action taken as "official," though had acted alone against "Communists" and that MPAA had acted "voluntarily," in HH-AMPAS.

76. Martin Ritt, seminar, AFI/CAFS, May 4, 1970, on own blacklisting; Harold H. Stern to David Susskind, Jan. 19, 1956, affidavit testifying to Ritt's denial of CPUSA affiliation, to accompany contract, Ritt file, box 37, Susskind papers, SHSW; Poitier-Cripps, interview, crediting Martin Baum with steering through politics of casting; telephone interview between Robert Alan Aurthur and the author, July 1977, recalling the tearful meeting at NBC.

77. Susskind's "rough" draft for trailer, quoted, "A Man Is Ten Feet Tall" file, Susskind papers, SHSW; final synopsis, mimeo, Dec. 10, 1956, in C-602, MGM-LD,; Ritt, AFI/CAFS seminar, quoted.

78. Preview cards, *Edge of the City* file, box 17, NBC records, SHSW; clipping on prospects, file C-602, MGM-LD; "Edge of the City," *Ebony*, May 1957, p. 75 ff., proudly liberal, thought Poitier "could have been white"; LAS, Feb. 7, 1957, on CCNP calling it "a revolution;" DW, Feb. 14, 1957, in SCRBC, said "power-packed . . . realism," though with no unions; *Var.*, Jan. 2, 1957, p. 6, praised as "never preachy" social document; LAS, March 22, 1956, on Sylvania Award for NBC; LAS, March 28, 1957; black press sample in Ashton, "Blacks in Film," pp. 160–61, including Albert Johnson on black audiences wanting to know why Poitier had to die. See *Film Quarterly* 13 (Fall 1959): p. 39.

79. Bennett, "Poitier," *Ebony*, May 1959, pp. 100–8; Poitier, *This Life*, pp. 335–40.

80. Poitier, *This Life*, pp. 335–40; NYT, Sept. 10, 1967; see also Aug. 9, 1970; *Time*, March 7, 1969, p. 71.

81. William Small, *To Kill a Messenger: Television News and the Real World* (New York, 1970), pp. 43, 45, 50, quotes Mitchell, Monroe, and Katzenbach; Benjamin D. Singer, "Mass Media and Communications Processes in the Detroit Riot of 1967," in Alan Wells, ed., *Mass Media and Society* (Palo Alto, 1972), pp. 140–50.

82. *Newsweek*, June 30, 1969, pp. 82, 86; Poitier-Cripps interview, Nov. 1980; James Baldwin quoted in Ashton, "Blacks in Film," 169–70, on "fool"; Barbara A. Greadington, "The Effect of Black Films on the Self-Esteem of Black Adolescents" (Ph.D. University of Miami, 1977), 79–84, 155.

83. Interviews between Herbert Hill and the author, beginning in Nov. 1983, Washington, D.C.; Baraka quoted in Leacock-Pennebaker press release, n.d., in author's possession; see also *Vogue*, April 1, 1967, p. 95, praising the technique of *Dutchman* despite being put off by its "queasy polemic"; NYT, March 3, 1967; *Var.*, Dec. 18, 1968, p. 7, quoting H. Rap Brown; a story corroborated by interview between Julian Mayfield, who appeared in *Up Tight*, and the author, July 1976, College Park, Md.

84. NYT, May 26, 1964; LAS, March 21, 1968; and on *Sweetback*, Thomas Cripps, "*Sweet Sweetback's Baadasssss Song* and the Changing Politics of Genre Film," 238–61, in Peter Lehman, ed., *Close Viewings: An Anthology of New Film Criticism* (Tallahassee, 1990).

85. Poitier, *This Life*, 327, quoted; telephone interview between Ernest Kinoy and the author, Aug. 1977; Poitier-Cripps interview, Nov. 1980; Ernest Kinoy and Ron Milner screenplay in Kinoy papers, SHSW, sampling of press in Marill, *Films of Sidney Poitier*, 186–88.

Index